Volume One

A Survey of
Presbyterian Mission History in Africa

Historic Beginnings (c.1790s to c.1930s)

edited by J. C. Whytock

BARNABAS
ACADEMIC PUBLISHERS

BARNABAS
ACADEMIC PUBLISHERS

**A Survey of Presbyterian Mission History in Africa:
Historic Beginnings (c.1790s to c.1930s) – Volume One**

© J. C. Whytock
Barnabas Academic Publishers (an imprint of CLF)
19 Oude Pont Street
Wellington Business Park
Wellington, Western Cape, South Africa
www.clf.co.za

All rights reserved. No part of this publication may be reproduced, stored in a retrieval system, or transmitted, in any form or by any means, electronic, mechanical, photocopying, recording or otherwise, without any prior written permission of the publisher.

Design and layout by: Anna-Marie Brink
Cover design by: Anna-Marie Brink
Cover page: Baobab near bank of the Lue, a tributary of the Zambezi River. Tree observed by Thomas Baines (1820–1875) while accompanying Dr David Livingstone on his Zambezi Expedition. Painted in 1858. With license obtained from KEW Images, https://images.kew.org/botanical-art/landscapes/baobab-near-bank-lue-adansonia-digitata-654507.html
Printed and bound: Print on Demand (Pty) Ltd

First edition: 2023

ISBN: 978-1-86804-540-2

Dedicated to the Memory of

Nelson Pilile Mpayipeli

Paul D. Chinchin

William John Paul (Paul) Bailie

†

*Then those who feared the LORD spoke with one another.
The LORD paid attention and heard them,
and a book of remembrance was written before him
of those who feared the LORD and esteemed his name.*
Malachi 3:16 ESV

†

Contents

Foreword – *Ronald Munyithya* 9

Acknowledgements 11

Abbreviations List 14

Charts, Timelines, Lists, and Maps for Volume One 22

Illustrations for Volume One 24

List of Contributers for Volume One 30

Introduction – *J. C. Whytock* 35

Volume One
Historic Beginnings and Developments
Part One:
Western & Southern Africa: **Historic Beginnings & Developments**

1. Beginnings, Part One: West Africa c.1790s, First Efforts
   J. C. Whytock 50

2. Beginnings, Part Two: The Cape, c.1800–c.1840s, Taking Root
   J. C. Whytock 61

3. Presbyterian Missions and a New Nation: Liberia, 1833–1894
   Steve Curtis 83

4. Survey of Presbyterian Churches of Southern Africa, 1841–2000: With a focus on the tributary streams of the UPCSA
   Douglas K. Bower 102

5. Sound the Trumpet: The Life and Ministry of Tiyo Soga, 1829–1871
   John S. Ross 126

6. Daniel Lindley, the American Board of Commissioners and South Africa
   Dale W. Johnson 146

7. Alexander Dewar, The Free Church in South Africa, and its Resuscitation post-1900
   Nelson Pilile Mpayipeli 167

8 "The Lovedale Method," Context, Development, & Transmission
   J. C. Whytock 181

9 The Presbyterian Story in Nigeria, c.1846 to Independence
   Todd Statham 205

   Bio Inset: Mary Slessor, 1848–1915
   Todd Statham 227

10 Equatorial West Africa and American Presbyterian Missions: Gaboon, Corisco
   J. C. Whytock 231

   Bio Inset: Robert Hamill Nassau, 1835–1921
   J. C. Whytock 244

11 Ibia J'Ikenge: The First Ordinand in the Corisco Presbytery
   Mary Cloutier 248

12 The History of Presbyterian Missionary Work in Ghana & Togo before WW2 (In Two Parts)
   Hans Blix Duodu 270

   Inset: "The Mother of our Schools" – Akropong Seminary, est. 1848
   J. C. Whytock 317

13 Beginnings of Presbyterian Work in German Kamerun, c.1879–c.1940
   Mary Cloutier 323

   Bio Inset: Lydia Walker Good: Native American Missionary to Gabon & Cameroon
   Mary Cloutier 346

Part Two:
Eastern & Central Africa: Historic Beginnings & Developments

14 The Livingstonia Mission and Synod
   Humphreys F. Zgambo 354

15 The Blantyre Mission and Synod
   Humphreys F. Zgambo 379

16 The Nkhoma Mission and Synod
   David Kawanga 403

17 Presbyterian Mission through Education of Indigenous Clergy, including a Case Study of Blantyre Mission's Harry Kambwiri Matecheta
   Thoko M. Chilembwe 428

18   Mauritius: Two Missions and an Historic Joining and Receiving, c.1810–c.1900
     J. C. Whytock 439

19   The American Presbyterian Congo Mission (APCM) c.1890–c.1945
     J. C. Whytock 453

     Bio Inset: William Henry Sheppard, 1865–1927
     Barry Waugh 471

     Bio Inset: Joseph E. Phipps – Missionary to the Belgian Congo 1895–1908
     Mary Cloutier 476

20   Part One: The Roots of The Presbyterian Church of East Africa: The East Africa Scottish Mission 1889–1901
     Watson A. O. Omulokoli 481

     Part Two: Presbyterian Developments in Kenya, c.1901 to 1946
     J. C. Whytock 490

     Bio Inset: Minnie Cumming Watson
     Nancy J. Whytock 511

21   Foundations of the Free Presbyterian Mission in Zimbabwe
     J. Cameron Fraser 517

22   History of Presbyterians in Rwanda
     Ezra E. Kwizera 538

Part Three:
The Nile Corridor: Historic Beginnings & Developments

23   The American United Presbyterian Church and its Mission in Egypt: Pioneering Efforts
     Milton Lipa 552

     Bio Inset: Tadros Yusif: The First Ordained Egyptian Presbyterian Pastor
     Sherif A. Fahim 571

     Bio Inset: Mary Galloway Giffen, 1842–1881: The First Missionary of the ARP Synod of the South
     Alex Pettett 575

     Inset: The Resignation of Hope Waddell Hogg
     Sherif A. Fahim 577

24   The History of Early Presbyterianism in Sudan, c.1890s to c.1950 (Part One)
     Andrew Okuch Ojullo 582

25 Ethiopia and the United Presbyterian Mission c.1918–c.1950s
   J. C. Whytock 604

   Bio Inset: Thomas A. Lambie: Missionary-Entrepreneur
   E. Paul Balisky 614

   Bio Inset: Gidada Solan, 1899–1977
   E. Paul Balisky 620

Part Four: *Themes*

26 Scots Presbyterians and the NGK/DRC of South Africa
   Retief Müller 624

27 African Presbyterian Sung Praise – Principles, Early Psalters and Hymnals
   Nancy J. Whytock 638

   Bio Inset: John Knox Bokwe, 1855–1922
   Nancy J Whytock 663

   Bio Inset: Ephraim Amu, 1899–1995
   Nancy J Whytock 667

28 Presbyterian Ethiopianism in South Africa and Malawi
   Rhodian Munyenyembe 672

29 Old Princeton Seminary & the Missionary Imperative
   James Garretson 690

   Inset: Princeton Theological Seminary Alumni who served in Africa, 1812– c.1930
   J. C. Whytock 705

30 Jewish and Muslim Missions in Northern Africa
   J. C. Whytock 714

   Inset: The Scotch Church, Algiers c.1880s to 1935
   J. C. Whytock 734

31 The Legacies of the African American Missionaries at the American Presbyterian Congo Mission
   Kimberly D. Hill 736

32 Revival and Exile: The Madeirans, A Story of Influence on the Fringe
   Nancy J. Whytock 751

An Epilogue on Historic Beginnings and Developments
J. C. Whytock 765

Index 772

Foreword

Ronald Munyithya

In his small book *How Africa Shaped the Christian Mind*, Thomas C. Oden, a Methodist theologian, describes Africa as the seedbed of Western Christianity. Historically speaking Africa is probably the earliest home not only to Christianity but Christ himself. Egypt was a haven to baby Jesus when Herod the Great wanted to kill Him. If tradition is anything to go by, Simon the Cyrenian must have, in person or otherwise, taken the amazing gospel story back to his African home after witnessing the crucifixion and resurrection of Christ even before the spiritual ink of the Great Commission dried on the pages of history and his cross bruises on his back healed. The same is true of Evangelist John Mark, whom history puts on the pioneer platform of early church missions to Africa. Since then, the gospel highways have continued to witness the rich back-and-forth traffic of the gospel between Africa and the West and within Africa. No wonder Dr Whytock has initiated this timely book project.

When the gospel flames of African early Christianity were turned to embers by the tenth-century, long medieval spiritual depression and corruption, coupled by Islamic invasion from the 11th–12th century, dimmed the Christian witness in the African continent and it went underground, but was never extinct. For almost nine long centuries, Africa seemingly became a "Dark Continent." Ironically, the underground rivers of the gospel power, like volcanic blood veins, were neither congealed nor dried. They relentlessly pulsated with gospel life. In the 16th century, the Holy Spirit rekindled the embers into flames of Reformation, first in Europe and subsequently in North America. The result was great spiritual awakenings hitherto unwitnessed except in the apostolic age. Out of these awakenings, with Reformation as their bedrock, emerged a vigorous missionary enterprise that targeted Asia, the Orient, and back to Africa, its seedbed.

This magnificent work, edited by Dr J. C. Whytock, is the retelling of how the old yet new Christian faith, fired by Reformation of the 16th century, made a vigorous homecoming to the African continent in Presbyterian mission tributaries. The story is a piece of artistic beauty whose underlying theme is geographical gospel expansion and spiritual impact undergirded by Reformation forte.

Volume One maps out a four-pronged continental penetration strategically from four cardinal points of the compass: from the West, the South, the East and lastly from the North along what Dr Whytock calls the 'Nile Corridor' forming, as it were, a redemptive sign of the cross. These prongs made an explosive gospel convergence at the heart of the continent. The picture so painted is truly a testimony of Historic Beginnings and effects. The dark continent was steadily becoming a lighted city on a hill as it had been earlier.

At the end of *Volume One*, readers are ready for the changes afoot and we thus anticipate *Volume Two: Modern Beginnings*. This takes us to the era where the tilting of the demographics of church growth from the Northern Hemisphere to the Southern has occurred and will continue to light the continent with gospel life.

Dr Whytock, et al have done the African church proud by walking her current and future Christian generations down the roadmap of her Christian heritage. The wide authorial spectrum representing both the majority and minority worlds coupled by scholarship depth turn the work into one of the historical treasures not only of the twenty-first century but of many centuries to come.

Judged on its own merit, *A Survey of Presbyterian Mission History in Africa* is not a mere historical narration of Western Christian missions to Africa but a ground-breaking catalyst seeking to revitalize the African Church back to her unfinished work once witnessed between the second and third centuries of the Christian Era.

It is my prayer that this book will not only inform but educate; not only stimulate but inspire; not only encourage but invigorate the African church to recapture her former zeal for biblical truth and missions even as we pray in John Knox's spirit "God give us Africa or we die." Yes, in the words of the popular African chorus:

If you believe and I believe
And together Pray,
The Holy Spirit must come down
And Africa shall be saved.

And Africa shall be saved;
And Africa shall be saved;
The Holy Spirit must come down
And Africa shall be saved.

Ronald Munyithya
Kenya

Acknowledgements

Throughout the years of this project, I have incurred many debts. I first extend a word of appreciation to all the writers who have laboured so diligently. Thank you for your part in this survey of mission history. You have been a delight to work with. I feel that I have gained many new friends and have truly been enriched.

A debt is also owed to the eleven theological institutions in Africa where I have lectured over the last twenty years. These, together with various speaking engagements in many African communities have brought many contacts, stories, and side trips to graves, old churches, and former mission stations. The students and colleagues at these institutions have been so helpful to collegially build-up an understanding beyond books and archives and I have truly benefited. You are all part of the story of this work.

I want to acknowledge appreciation for the way in which the late David B. Calhoun, Covenant Theological Seminary, St. Louis gave consultation concerning Princeton Seminary and Presbyterian missions in Africa and direction to materials. He was a true encourager. To Sam Logan, World Reformed Fellowship, and to Richard Ball, the web manager for Haddington House, I am appreciative of your help in promoting an initial news release (about what was then a proposed project) to specifically inform and recruit potential writers several years ago.

I offer sincere appreciation to Haddington House Trust, Charlottetown, Prince Edward Island for their resources to help with not only being a centre to make this project become a reality but also for providing resources through many Trust donors to fund this project. Thank you immensely.

I recognise the very long list of people all around the world that I have communicated with in the search to find writers and locate a piece of information or an illustration: the late In-Whan Kim, Patrick Diniso, Felix Konotey-Ahulu, Colin Mbawa, Robert Norris, Davi Gomes, Don Fortson III, Greg Steward, Donald Fairbairn, John Muether, Donald Duff, Dave Eby, Victor Nakah, Kenneth Stewart, Larry Brown, Michael Jaatinen, Don Codling, Norman Reid, Dan Wilton, Greg Livingstone, Patrick Daly, Allan Harman, Sid Garland, Gareth Burke, Kevin McDonald, Dean Weaver, Ric Cannada, Solano Portela, Andrew McGowan, Nick Needham, Wilbert Chipenyu, Jeff Haschick, and Ikho Magodla, not to mention also all the contributing writers themselves. Thanks to John N. Akers for a beautiful prayer about this project and the inspirational words he gave us as we pressed on with it. My apologies to any whom I have failed to mention who over the last four years of this project have guided me in this way.

Thank you to those who helped with providing information and direction to key source materials: Elsie McKee, emeritus professor Princetown Theological Seminary; Vince Ward, missions for the RPCNA; Wayne Sparkman, The Historical Center of the Presbyterian Church in America, St. Louis, Missouri; the Presbyterian Heritage Center, Montreat; and the Presbyterian Historical Society, Philadelphia.

For those who read over MS and added facts, checked spelling, provided direction, or answered questions related to this project and the task of editing, a sincere thank you: Ronald Munyithya, Elsen Portugal, John Grotenhuis, D. Douglas Gebbie, Frank Sindler, Joster Jumbe, Duncan Graham, Cameron Fraser, and Nigel Anderson. I am grateful to Ian Hazlett for allowing me to ask some initial questions about editing such an undertaking as this project and am grateful for the wisdom that he offered. The shortcomings are mine. Also, appreciation is expressed for the two conferences of the Presbyterian Scholars' Conference I was able to participate in, organised by Jeff McDonald and held at Harbor House on the campus of Wheaton College, Illinois. Discussions and exchanges which emerged from these were most valuable.

For the libraries which individual contributors used for their writing and the many people whom they have consulted we owe a great debt. Often these names are noted in various chapters by the contributors. Despite the many challenges of Covid-19 for entrance to depositories and libraries, creative ways were found in several instances. In particular, to the following institutions and staff who helped in the verification process of checking for bibliographical materials and kind assistance with aiding the research for this volume I mention: Cory Library, Rhodes University, Grahamstown, SA and Louisa Verwey; International Library of African Music (ILAM) at Rhodes University; The Theological Library at the University of Stellenbosch; The DR Church Archives, Stellenbosch and senior archivists Karen Minnaar and Amy Rommelspacher who helped so much with the search for illustrations; Caven Library, Knox College and Kelly Library, St Michael's College, University of Toronto; Westminster College Library and also the Archives of the United Reformed History Society, Cambridge and particularly to Helen Weller; SOAS Archives and Special Collections, London; Buswell Archives and Special Collections, Wheaton College; Gamble Library, Union Theological College, Belfast; the British Library, London; University College, London; the Cambridge Centre for Christianity Worldwide; New College Library, Edinburgh; the National Library of Scotland; the University of Edinburgh Library; and the Centre for the Study of World Christianity Library, Edinburgh.

Acknowledgements

In the preparation of volumes one and two, three contributors passed away in 2022 before submission of manuscripts: Nelson Pilile Mpayipeli (March 2022), Paul Chinchen (July 2022), and Paul Bailie (November 2022). We honour them on our dedicatory page. Nelson Mpayipeli's chapter was compiled posthumously from his post-grad thesis; Paul Chinchin's chapter was taken up by his twin brother Palmer Chinchen; and Paul Bailie's chapter was done at a late date before publication through the generous support of Watson Omulokoli and the research efforts to make deadlines by the Whytocks.

On a personal note, during this project, we had an extended period of time helping care for my father who died in 2022. Our days during that time developed a routine of care, visiting and editing. Each day we would be greeted – "How goes the book?" That daily question kept us persevering, accountable and also is part of our story of the line of those who have aided this project.

As *Volume One* neared its final manuscript stage, we were afforded wonderful hospitality through a ministry opportunity in Campbeltown, Scotland for six weeks at the local Free Church. The dear folks there no doubt heard many things about the history of missions in Africa and were warm encouragers.

As general editor I must express gratitude to my wife, Nancy, who has been the administrator of this project. She has corresponded literally around the globe to keep our records as straight as possible with the large team of writers involved with this project, and she has spent hours corresponding with archival depositories and making arrangements with numerous special collections. She has studied the text, read it, poured over it, and has been a tremendous support to keep this project rolling along.

I express sincere appreciation to Christian Literature Fund, with its imprint Barnabas Academic, Wellington, South Africa and its staff and editor Gideon van der Watt who were visionary to make this work take flight across Africa and beyond.

At the end of the day, as general editor I accept the reality that there will be limitations and areas that will need improvement. The work continued to grow as we proceeded and as more mission stories kept emerging. Some of these we had to make difficult decisions about as to what to leave out but often to only draw pointers for further engagement. Also, I recognise that many writers faced tremendous difficulties accessing archival and library material during the Covid-19 pandemic which fell during the timeline allotted to this first volume which was to emerge prior to the 200th anniversary of the constituting of the first presbytery in Africa, 1 January 1824. I invite correspondence with readers to help us see where there are areas needing attention.

J. C. Whytock

Abbreviations List

      ABC African Bible Colleges

  ABCFM American Board of Commissioners for Foreign Missions

      ABU African Bible University (Uganda)

      ACS American Colonization Society

    AEPC Africa Evangelical Presbyterian Church

     AFM Abyssinia Frontiers Mission

   AFPCZ African Free Presbyterian Church of Zimbabwe

      AIC African Initiated/Independent Churches

     AIM Africa Inland Mission

     ALC African Lakes Company/Corporation

  Annals *Annals of the Free Church of Scotland 1843–1900*, 2 volumes, ed. William Ewing

   APCM American Presbyterian Congo Mission

   APBC African Presbyterian Bafolisi Church

   APMT Presbyterian Cross-Cultural Missions Agency (of the Presbyterian Church of Brazil) [IPB]

   ARPC African Reformed Presbyterian Church

     ARP Associate Reformed Presbyterian Church

   ARTS Africa Reformation Theological Seminary

     ATR African Traditional Religion(s)

   AUPM American United Presbyterian Mission

     BCA British Central Africa

BCEA(KE) Bible College of East Africa, Kenya

BCEA(RW)	Bible College of East Africa, Rwanda
BCEA(TZ)	Bible College of East Africa, Tanzania
BDCM	*Biographical Dictionary of Christian Missions.* Ed. Gerald Anderson.
BEA	British East Africa
BFBS	British & Foreign Bible Society
BFM	Board of Foreign Missions
BM	Bethel Mission
BPC	a) Bantu Presbyterian Church of South Africa b) Bible Presbyterian Church [Uganda]
BPCIA	Bible Presbyterian Church in Africa
BWM	Board of World Missions [PCUS]
CAP	Church of Africa Presbyterian
COPC	Cameroon Orthodox Presbyterian Church
CCC	Church of Christ in Congo/Église du Christ Au Congo
CCK	Christian Council of Kenya
CCAP	Church of Central Africa Presbyterian
CFM	Committee for Foreign Missions
CECE	Coptic Evangelical Church of Egypt
CMS	Church Missionary Society
CSM	Church of Scotland Mission
CoE	Church of England
CoS	Church of Scotland
CPA	Comprehensive Peace Agreement
CPC	a) Communauté Presbytérienne au Congo/Presbyterian Community in Congo b) Cumberland Presbyterian Church
CPK	Communauté Presbytérienne de Kinshasa/Presbyterian Community of Kinshasa

CPKI   Communauté Presbytérienne au Kivu/Kivu Presbyterian Church, KPC(DRC)

DACB   *Dictionary of African Christian Biography* [electronic]

DMS   Danish Mission Society

DRC
- a) Democratic Republic of Congo
- b) Dutch Reformed Church [of South Africa]/NGK Nederduitse Gereformeerde Kerk [van Suid-Afrika]

DRCM   Dutch Reformed Church Mission

DSCHT   *Dictionary of Scottish Church History and Theology.* Edited by Nigel de S. Cameron et al.

EARF   East Africa Revival Fellowship

EARM
- a) East Africa Reformed Mission
- b) East Africa Revival Movement [see also EARF]

EASM   East Africa Scottish Mission

ECB   Evangelical Churches Bethel

ECC   Église du Christ au Congo/Church of Christ in the Congo

ECO   A Covenant Order of Evangelical Presbyterians

EE   Evangelism Explosion

EEG   Église Évangélique du Gabon/Evangelical Church of Gabon

EFZ   Evangelical Fellowship of Zimbabwe

EMDOA   Evangelical Mission Society for German East Africa

EMS   Edinburgh Missionary Society

EOC   Ethiopian Orthodox Church

EPC
- a) Église Presbytérienne Camerounaise
- b) Église Presbytérienne au Congo/Presbyterian Church in Congo [1966–1970]
- c) Evangelical Presbyterian Church [America]
- d) Evangelical Presbyterian Church [Ireland]

EPCG   Evangelical Presbyterian Church, Ghana

EPCM   Evangelical Presbyterian Church of Malawi and Mozambique

EPCO Église Presbytérienne Camerounaise Orthodoxe/Orthodox Presbyterian Church of Cameroon [or Cameroon Orthodox Presbyterian Church]

EPCS Evangelical Presbyterian Church of Sudan

EPCSA Evangelical Presbyterian Church in South Africa [formerly Tsonga Presbyterian Church]

EPCSL Evangelical Presbyterian Church in Sierra Leone

EPCSS Evangelical Presbyterian Church of South Sudan

EPCT Evangelical Presbyterian Church of Togo

EPR Église Presbyteriénne au Rwanda/Presbyterian Church in Rwanda

ERPC Ethiopian Reformed Presbyterian Church

Fasti *Fasti Ecclesiae Scoticanae. The Succession of Ministers in the Church of Scotland from the Reformation. Comp.* Hew Scott et. al.

FCS Free Church of Scotland

FCSA Free Church in Southern Africa/Free Church in South Africa

FGM Female genital mutilation

FMC a) Federated Mission Council
     b) Foreign Mission Committee

FPCS Free Presbyterian Church of Scotland

FPCU Free Presbyterian Church of Ulster

GAC General Administrative Committee

GEC Global Evangelical Church

GMC General Mission Committee

GMS a) Glasgow Missionary Society
     b) Gospel Missionary Society

HBCUs Historically black colleges and universities [in the USA]

HHK Hersteld Hervormde Kerk/ Restored Reformed Church

HMCs Historic Mission churches

HWTI Hope Waddell Training Institute

IBEAC Imperial British East Africa Company

IBMR	*International Bulletin of Missionary Research*
IBPFM	Independent Board for Presbyterian Foreign Missions
ICRC	International Conference of Reformed Churches
INPC	Independent Native Presbyterian Church (Open for Reunion)
IPB	Igreja Presbiteriana do Brasil/Presbyterian Church of Brazil
IPC	Independent Presbyterian Church (Kenya)
IRPGE	Reformed Presbyterian Church of Equatorial Guinea/Iglesia Reformada Presbiteriana de Guinea Ecuatorial
KCA	Kikuyu Central Association
KPC	Kivu Presbyterian Church (DRC)/Communauté Presbytérienne au Kivu (CPKI)
KST	Knox School of Theology
LM	Lausanne Movement
LMS	London Missionary Society
MCS	Maryland Colonization Society
MMU	Ministers' Mission Union/Predikante Sendingvereniging
MT3	Mobile Theological Training Team [2003–2023, renamed SEED]
MTW	Mission to the World [of the PCA (America)]
MYEPC	Mehrete Yesus Evangelical Presbyterian Church in Eritrea
NAPARC	North American Presbyterian and Reformed Council
NBSS	National Bible Society of Scotland
NGK	Nederduitse Gereformeerde Kerk [van Suid-Afrika]/DRC Dutch Reformed Church [of South Africa]
NSTA	Nkhoma Synod Teachers' Association
NYCS	New York Colonization Society
OPC	Orthodox Presbyterian Church [North America]
PBFM	Presbyterian Board of Foreign Missions [PCUSA]

PEMS Paris Evangelical Missionary Society/SMEP Societé des Missions Évangélique de Paris

PCA a) Presbyterian Church of Africa
     b) Presbyterian Church in America
     c) Presbyterian Church of Australia

PCB Presbyterian Church of Brazil/Igreja Presbiteriana do Brasil

PCC a) Presbyterian Church in Cameroon
     b) Presbyterian Church of Cameroon/Eglise Presbytérienne Camerounaise
     c) Presbyterian Church in Canada

PCCs Pentecostal/Charismatic churches

PCE Presbyterian Church of England

PCEA a) Presbyterian Church of East Africa
      b) Presbyterian Church of Eastern Australia [formerly Free Presbyterian Church]

PCG Presbyterian Church of Ghana

PCI Presbyterian Church in Ireland

PCL Presbyterian Church of Liberia

PCM Presbyterian Church in Mauritius/Église Presbytérienne de Maurice

PCN Presbyterian Church of Nigeria

PCOS Presbyterian Church of Sudan

PCOSS Presbyterian Church of South Sudan

PCSA a) Presbyterian Church of South Africa [1897–1958]
      b) Presbyterian Church of Southern Africa [1958–1999]

PCSL Presbyterian Convention of Sierra Leone

PCU Presbyterian Church in Uganda

PCUS Presbyterian Church in the United States

PCUSA Presbyterian Church in the United States of America

PC(USA) Presbyterian Church in the United States of America [post-union 1983]

PHSA Presbyterian Historical Society Archives [Philadelphia]

RCEA	Reformation Church in East Africa
REC	Reformed Ecumenical Council
RPC	Reformed Presbyterian Church [Sudan, now SRC]
RPCES	Reformed Presbyterian Church, Evangelical Synod
RPCI	Reformed Presbyterian Church of Ireland
RPCM	Reformed Presbyterian Church of Malawi
RPCNA	Reformed Presbyterian Church of North America
RPCS	Reformed Presbyterian Church of Scotland
RPCSA	Reformed Presbyterian Church of Southern Africa
RPCU	Reformed Presbyterian Church in Uganda
RSCHS	*Records of the Scottish Church History Society*
RTS	Reformed Theological Seminary [USA]
RUF	Reformed University Fellowship
SARM	Southern African Reformed Mission
SEED	Serve to Educate, Equip and Disciple
SMEP	Societé des Missions Évangélique de Paris/Paris Evangelical Missionary Society
SMS	Scottish Missionary Society
SOAS	School of Oriental and African Studies
SIM	a) Sudan Interior Mission b) Serving In Mission International [originally Sudan Interior Mission]
SPEC	Sudan Presbyterian Evangelical Church
SRC	Sudanese Reformed Church
SSPEC	South Sudan Presbyterian Evangelical Church
TEE	Theological Education by Extension
TPC	Trinity Presbyterian Church [Sudan]
UBI	Uganda Bible Institute

UCZ	United Church of Zambia
UDACZ	Union of the Development of Apostolic Churches in Zimbabwe
UFCS	United Free Church of Scotland
UMCA	Universities Mission Central Africa
UP	Uganda Presbytery of the RCEA
UPCC	United Presbyterian Church Congo
UPCNA	United Presbyterian Church of North America
UPCS	United Presbyterian Church of Scotland
UPCSA	Uniting Presbyterian Church of Southern Africa
UPCUSA	United Presbyterian Church in the United States of America
WARC	World Alliance of Reformed Churches (1970–2010)
WARM	West African Reformed Mission
WCC	World Council of Churches
WCIU	Westminster Christian Institute Uganda
WCRC	World Communion of Reformed Churches (2010–)
WFMS	Western Foreign Missionary Society
WPM	World Presbyterian Missions
WRF	World Reformed Fellowship
WTC	Westminster Theological College
WTSU	Westminster Theological Seminary Uganda
WW	World Witness [of the ARP]
ZCC	Zimbabwe Council of Churches
ZHOCD	Zimbabwe Heads of Christian Denominations

Charts, Timelines, Lists, and Maps for Volume One

Map of Africa 1806	*38*
Map of Africa 1914	*39*

Part One: Western & Southern Africa map portion — *49*

Map of Eastward Extension of Cape Colony	*73*
Timeline showing notable events in Southern Africa and in the Presbyterian Churches	*104–105*
Map of Natal Colony	*161*
Chart of the Principals of Lovedale Institution	*189*
Map of Equatorial West Africa	*237*
Map of select Mission Stations of Basel & Bremen Societies in Gold Coast and British Togoland, c.1919	*276*
List of Early Scottish Missionaries, Gold Coast	*312*
Chart of the Principals of Akropong Seminary	*321*
List of early Long-term PCUSA Missionaries to Cameroon	*340*

Part Two: Eastern & Central Africa map portion — *353*

Map of Livingstonia Mission	*365*
Map of Nkhoma Mission	*409*
List of Nkhoma Mission Stations in the Historic Period to c.1939	*422*
Timeline for the Livingstonia, Blantyre, and Nkhoma Missions	*426–427*
List of Early Publications of which the CSM (BEA) was involved	*497*
Map of Kikuyu Mission	*507*
List of Elders ordained at Thogoto & Tumutumu 1920	*510*
Map of Rwanda	*546*

Charts, Timelines, Lists, and Maps for Volume One

Part Three: **The Nile Corridor map portion**	*551*
List of American UP Missionaries in Egypt 1898	*567*
List of American UP Mission Stations along the Nile Corridor	*568*
Map of Egyptian Sudan showing Nile River transport route for missionaries	*582*
Map of South Sudan showing three regions	*586*
Timeline of the UP Mission in Egyptian Sudan	*598–599*
The Egyptian Sudan UPCNA Missionaries 1919	*599*
Statistical List for UP mission in Egyptian Sudan 1917	*600*
Part Four: **Themes**	*623*
Chart of CoS & FCS ministers, licentiates, and students who served in the DRCSA	*633-636*
Chart of Some Early Psalters and Hymnals associated with Presbyterian Missions in Africa	*653–659*
Chart of Princeton Theological Seminary Alumni who served in Africa, 1812–c.1930	*705–713*
Map of North Atlantic showing the route of the Madeiran refugees	*759*
List of First Ordinations of Ministers in the Historic Period	*769–770*
List of the First Historic Presbyteries in Africa c.1790s to c.1940	*770–771*

Illustrations for Volume One

Map of Africa 1806 (with permission of Cory Library)	38
Map of Africa 1914	39
Western & Southern Africa Part One title page	49
Historic Engraving of Freetown	52
Governor Zachary Macaulay	53
Susa Grammar title page, 1802, first Scottish Presbyterian contribution published for an African language	56
George Thom	62
(St. Andrew's) Scottish Church, Cape Town	65
Thomas Pringle	70
Map of Eastward Extension of Cape Colony	73
John Bennie	75
Burns Hill Missionary Station, painting by Thomas Bowler	76
John B. Pinney	87
John L. Wilson	88
James M. Priest	92
Edward W. Blyden	95
James J. R. Jolobe	115
Tiyo & Janet (née Burnside) Soga	133
Mgwali Church (photo N. Whytock)	137
Pilgrim's Progress title page and dedication page	138
Daniel Lindley	147
The Daniel Lindley family	158
Map of Natal Colony	161
Alexander Dewar when Moderator of the FCS GA	170
Ox wagon crossing Keiskamma River	175

Illustrations for Volume One

Lovedale stamp	*181*
William Govan	*184*
James Stewart	*186*
Cecilia Makiwane stamp	*187*
Class photo, c.1890s	*189*
Oromo girls	*194*
Lovedale printing class	*197*
Boarders, residents and staff, early 1890s	*201*
Hope M. Waddell	*209*
Essien Essien Ukpabio	*213*
Rev. Essien Essien Ukpabio with family, c.1900-1910	*213*
Hope Waddell Training Institution, founded 1895, photo of one of the buildings, c.1951	*223*
Bank note of Mary Slessor	*227*
Mary Slessor (centre – seated) with Arthur Wilkie (right). Wilkie conducted her funeral.	*229*
Stamp of Gaboon Mission Church	*233*
Miss Isabella Nassau	*235*
Map of Equatorial West Africa	*237*
Fetichism in West Africa book cover	*244*
Left: Anyentyuwe (governess) and her daughter, Right: Nassau and his daughter (Mary)	*246*
Ibia J'Ikenge	*248*
Rev. Ibia J'Ikenge with presbyters	*263*
Andreas Riis	*272*
J. G. Christaller	*273*
Mr & Mrs J. Zimmermann	*273*
Alexander Worthy Clerk	*275*
Map of select Mission Stations of Basel and Bremen Societies in Gold Coast and British Togoland, c.1919	*276*
Crest of The Presbyterian Church of Ghana	*277*
Christiansborg Fort	*282*
David Asante	*285*

Synod of Gold Coast after Scottish Mission involvement	307
Dr Arthur W. Wilkie	313
Missionaries, c.1893	325
Lydia Good, c.1910	349
Lydia at Baraka Women's Meeting, 1909	349
Eastern & Central Africa Part 2 title page	353
Two stamps in honour of Livingstone	359
Robert Laws	360
Xhosa Missionaries from Lovedale to Livingstonia	362
Advert for published works by Dr & Mrs Robert Laws	363
Map of Livingstonia Mission	365
Ilala, first steamship on Lake Nyasa, Livingstonia Mission 1875	367
Loudon Church c.1910 (with permission of the National Library, Scotland)	368
Emmeline Dewar Book Title Pages	369
St. Michael's and All Angels' Church	388
First church of the Blantyre Mission	388
Dictionary of the Nyanja Language	390
Drs. Hetherwick and Laws	390
Mvera Church (with permission of the DRC Archives)	404
Rev. Andrew Charles Murray (with permission of the DRC Archives)	405
Rev. Theunis Botha Vlok (with permission of the DRC Archives)	405
Evangelists of Nkhoma Mission, 1928 (with permission of the DRC Archives)	408
Albert Namalambe, an Evangelist (with permission of the DRC Archives)	408
Map of Nkhoma Mission (with permission of the DRC Archives)	409
Union Bible title page	417
"An Outschool"	430
Harry Kambwiri Matecheta	435
Rev. Jean LeBrun	440

Illustrations for Volume One

Port Louis Harbour, Mauritius, 1889	442
Hymnal prepared and printed on Mauritius in 1838	443
Evangelical Protestant Chapel, Port Louis	445
Lapsley Steamer	461
APCM missionaries, 1909	462
Mission printing press at Luebo Station	466
Lapsley Memorial Church	469
William and Lucy Sheppard and family	473
Joseph Phipps	477
Sir William Mackinnon monument (photo N. Whytock)	482
Original Expedition at Mombasa, September 1891	483
Thomas Watson	487
David Clement Ruffelle Scott	491
Henry E. Scott	493
Watson-Scott Memorial Church, Kikuyu	498
First eight ordinands in the CMS, BEA mission (with permission of the National Library, Scotland)	503
William & Myrtle Knapp	505
Kikuyu Mission Map	507
Minnie Watson and her nursery school	513
Minnie Watson leaving Kikuyu on retirement, 1931, pictured here with two of her first female students	515
John B. Radasi	518
FPCS, South African Mission Ingwenya, Letter 27 January, 1930 from John Tallach to Principal Henderson, Lovedale	520
John Tallach	521
James Fraser & members of class at Ingwenya, 1939	526
Petros Mzamo	529
David Ndlovu and Dr James Tallach at Mbuma Mission Hospital	532
Map of Rwanda	546
The Nile Corridor Africa Part 3 title page	546
Pioneer missionaries 1854-1864 (two composites)	564

Jubilee Anniversary of the American Mission, missionaries and national workers	*566*
Tadros Yusif	*574*
Mary Galloway Giffen	*575*
Map of Sudan showing Nile River that provided transport from Khartoum to Doleib Hill for the missionaries	*582*
Map of South Sudan showing the three regions	*586*
Book Cover on *The Shilluk People*	*587*
Lambie as a young man	*614*
Book Cover of Lambie's *A Doctor without a Country*	*617*
Rev. & Mrs Gidada Solan	*621*
Themes Part 4, Dr Robert Kerr	*623*
Andrew Murray, senior	*626*
Andrew Murray, junior	*627*
Bambo Isake Mchochma Mlaliki, one of the early evangelists in the Nkhoma Mission – he took the name Andrew Murray (with permission of the DRC Archives)	*631*
1867 Complete Arabic Psalter with hymns and spiritual songs	*646*
1920 Tune Book for Arabic Psalter	*646*
The 1922 Xhosa Psalter	*648*
Benga hymnal	*649*
Bemba hymnal	*660*
Title page of Tiyo Soga's copy of the 1849 *Incwadi Yamaculo*	*661*
John Knox Bokwe	*663*
Amaculo ase Lovedale, 5th edition	*664*
Ephraim Amu	*668*
Pambani J. Mzimba	*677*
Princeton Theological Seminary, Alexander Hall	*691*
Archibald Alexander	*696*
Clarence W. Duff (Photo courtesy of Donald Duff)	*702*
Robert H. Nassau	*702*
Mission Institute, Wellington, South Africa	*713*

Letter of Robert Kerr on PCE Jewish Mission Letterhead	721
Gateway to Rabat, Morocco	722
Dr Kerr setting out to Sallee on visitation when it was all barricaded, and all other Europeans afraid to go in for fear of their lives	725
The Scotch Church/Église Écossaise, Mustapha/Algiers	734
William Sheppard with Congolese men (used by permission, PHSA, William H. Sheppard Papers. RG 457, Box 4, 835.03.20a)	741
Hampton Institute	742
Alonzo & Althea Edmiston with their eldest son, Sheman Kueta Edmiston (used by permission, PHSA)	745
Robert Kalley	753
W. H. Hewitson	754
Harbour, Funchal, Madeira, 1840	758
Map of the North Atlantic Ocean showing the route of the Madeiran refugees	759
First Presbyterian, Portuguese, Springfield	762

The images used are from sources now judged to be in public domain, unless otherwise stated.

List of Contributors

Volume One

E. Paul Balisky is a retired SIM missionary having served in Ethiopia in church planting, supervising development projects, teaching in Bible Schools, and also at the Ethiopian Graduate School of Theology in Addis Ababa. His PhD, from the University of Aberdeen, was published as *Wolaitta Evangelists: A Study of Religious Innovation in Southern Ethiopia, 1937–1995* and he authored *Thomas A. Lambie: Missionary Doctor and Entrepreneur*. He lives in Grande Prairie, Alberta.

Douglas Kinsman Bower is the minister at Trinity Presbyterian Church (UPCSA) in Meadowridge, Cape Town, South Africa. He completed his Hons BA thesis at the University of Pretoria on Presbyterian history in SA, and his undergraduate studies were at George Whitefield College, Muizenberg for the NWU degree. He formerly pastored in Pretoria at St. Columba Church.

Thokozani Malitoni Chilembwe is the school chaplain at Henry Henderson Institute of the Church of Central Africa Presbyterian, Synod of Blantyre and associate pastor at Michiru CCAP, Malawi. He has his BScE from Mzuzu University and BD from the University of Malawi and was a co-editor to prepare a new edition of *Blantyre Mission: stories of its beginning* (Mzuzu: Luviri, 2020).

Mary Carol Cloutier is associate professor of intercultural studies at Moody Bible Institute, Chicago. She served as a missionary with the Christian & Missionary Alliance, training church leaders, at Institut Biblique de Bethel, Libreville, Gabon and is the author of *Bridging the Gap, Breaching the Barriers: The Presence and Contribution of (Foreign) Persons of African Descent to the Gaboon and Corisco Mission in Nineteenth Century Equatorial West Africa*. Her PhD is in intercultural studies from Trinity Evangelical Divinity School.

Steve Curtis is the founder and international director for Timothy Two Project, International. He is an extraordinary researcher in missiology with the faculty of theology at North-West University (NWU), Potchefstroom, SA and is active in the World Reformed Fellowship (WRF), serving as convenor of its missions and evangelism commission. He is a ruling elder with the Evangelical Presbyterian Church. His PhD is from NWU in missiology, and he is the author of *Reach and Teach* (Wipf & Stock).

List of Contributors

Hans Blix Duodu obtained his Diploma in Pastoral Studies at London Reformed Baptist Seminary, has a keen interest in church history and is a fellow of the Association of Accounting Technicians (AAT) UK. He teaches accounting with Activate Learning at Banbury and Bicester College, Oxfordshire and is a Financial Accountant for the NHS. He is from southern Ghana, commenced his university studies at the University of Cape Coast, then Birkbeck College (University of London), obtaining his BSc (Hons). He is a masters candidate at Durham University. His research interests are in Biblical & Historical Theology.

Sherif A. Fahim is a lecturer and administrator at Alexandria School of Theology, Egypt. He is a graduate of Alexandria University, Alexandria School of Theology, Moore Theological College, and the PhD in Biblical Studies from Puritan Reformed Theological Seminary, Grand Rapids, Michigan. He is the general director of El-Soora Ministries and an elder in the Presbyterian Church in Egypt.

J. Cameron Fraser is a minister of the Christian Reformed Church. He was born in Zimbabwe (Southern Rhodesia), grew up in Scotland, and pastored in Western Canada for over thirty years. He studied theology and missions (ThM) at Westminster Seminary (Philadelphia) and has a DMin in pastoral care from Trinity Evangelical Divinity School. He has been an active writer and editor and lives in Lethbridge, Alberta. He is the author of *Thandabantu: The Man Who Loved the People*.

James M. Garretson is an ordained minister in the Presbyterian Church in America (PCA). He has pastored congregations in the OPC and the PCA and taught at Knox Theological Seminary, Fort Lauderdale, Florida. He has authored and edited six books related to Old Princeton, including *Princeton and Preaching*, *Pastor-Teachers of Old Princeton*, and *A Scribe Well-Trained*. He is a graduate of Covenant College, Regent College, and Westminster Seminary, California (DMin). He was also the ministry director of the Christian Union's campus outreach at Harvard Law School.

Kimberly D. Hill is assistant professor of U.S. and African American history at the University of Texas at Dallas. Her PhD is from the University of North Carolina at Chapel Hill with a thesis on the work of three women from the American South who became missionaries in the 19th century. She has contributed to *Faith and Slavery in the Presbyterian Diaspora*, edited by William Harrison Taylor and Peter C Messer, and is the author of *A Higher Mission: The Careers of Alonzo and Althea Brown Edmiston in Central Africa* (University of Kentucky, 2020).

Dale W. Johnson is the distinguished professor of church history at Erskine Theological Seminary in Due West, South Carolina and a ruling elder in the Presbyterian Church in America. He has a PhD from Georgia State University and concentrates on Reformation and modern church history. He is the co-author of *John Knox: An Introduction to His Life and Works*.

David Chiguzeni Kawanga is lecturer in theology and church history at Zomba Theological College, Malawi and registrar for the Board for Theological Studies of the University of Malawi. He has served as a lecturer at other colleges in Malawi and South Africa. He has a master's from Stellenbosch University – thesis: "The Priesthood of All Believers – The Theological Understanding Within The Nkhoma Synod of The Relationship Between Members and Office-bearers." He is a minister of the CCAP and a PhD candidate at the University of Aberdeen.

Ezra Eugene Kwizera is the campus director for Reformed University Fellowship (RUF) at Makerere University and former librarian at Africa Reformation Theological Seminary (ARTS), Kampala, Uganda. He is from Rwanda and has a BSc Hons from the University of Rwanda, College of Science & Technology, Butare/Huye campus, where he studied electronics and telecommunication engineering before doing the MDiv at ARTS.

Milton Lipa is minister of the Entebbe Presbyterian Church (PCU), Uganda; serves as the Uganda board chair for the Trinity Center for World Missions; and is an adjunct lecturer for their programme through the Westminster Christian Institute, Uganda. He did his MDiv at Africa Reformation Theological Seminary and also serves with the Shalom Health Church Network.

Retief Müller is associate professor of Mission and World Christianity at VID Specialized University, Stavanger, Norway; former director of the Nagel Institute for the Study of World Christianity at Calvin University, MI; former associate professor of church history at Stellenbosch University; and assistant professor of Christian Studies at Keimyung University, South Korea. He is a graduate of the University of Pretoria, Columbia Theological Seminary, and Princeton Theological Seminary (PhD); authored *The Scots Afrikaners* (Edinburgh, 2021); and was ordained by the DRC in SA.

Rhodian Munyenyembe is senior lecturer and head, Department of Theology and Religious Studies, Mzuzu University, Malawi and has a PhD (Ecclesiology) from the University of the Free State, SA. He is the author of *Pursuing an Elusive Unity: A History of the Church of Central Africa Presbyterian as a Federative Denomination (1924–2018)*, Langham, 2019. He is an elder in the CCAP.

List of Contributors

Andrew Okuch Ojullo is academic dean and lecturer at Knox School of Theology in Mbale, eastern Uganda and is originally from Pochalla, South Sudan. He completed his MDiv at Africa Reformation Theological Seminary, Kampala, Uganda; previously studied at Westminster Christian Institute, Kampala and at Zetech College, Nairobi; and is a ThM candidate at Puritan Theological Seminary.

Watson A. O. Omulokoli is the chancellor of Africa International University, Nairobi, Kenya; associate professor at Kenyatta University, Nairobi; patron of Bible Translation & Literacy (E.A.); and adjunct professor at Akrofi-Christaller Institute, Accra, Ghana. He did his PhD in church history at the University of Aberdeen, his MA at Wheaton Graduate School, and the BTh & BA at Warner Pacific College, Portland, Oregon. He is the author of *Christianity in Africa: Select Pillars From Kenya* (Nairobi, 2017).

Alex Pettett is the executive director of World Witness, the board of foreign missions of the Associate Reformed Presbyterian Church in Greenville, South Carolina. He has served in Israel, Turkey, and the USA. He has an MA in Judaic Studies from Hebrew University in Jerusalem.

Nelson Pilile Mpayipeli was a minister of the Free Church in South Africa and was ordained in 1983 and began ministry in the Burnshill District, then in Somerset East District, and finally the Ngcingwane and Centane District. He studied at Evangeli Xhosa Bible School, Kentani, Transkei; Decoligny Theological College, Umtata, Transkei; and did the post-graduate diploma at the Free Church College, Edinburgh. He had also served with Radio Xhosa, assisted at Dumisani Bible School, and was active in the church courts of the Free Church in South Africa. He died in March 2022.

John S. Ross has over forty-five years' experience in pastoral ministry and mission: a missionary in Nigeria, he became CEO of Christian Witness to Israel, taught at Dumisani Theological Institute, SA and in between pastored four congregations. He holds a PhD (University of Wales) in mission history and authored, *The Power and the Glory: John Ross and the Evangelisation of Manchuria and Korea* (Christian Focus, 2022).

Todd Statham is the Christian Reformed campus minister at the Okanagan campus of the University of British Columbia, Kelowna, BC and a former lecturer at Zomba Theological College, Malawi, ministering alongside the Blantyre Synod of the Church of Central Africa Presbyterian (CCAP). His PhD is from McGill University, Montreal.

Barry G. Waugh is an independent scholar and a congregational member in the PCA. His PhD is from Westminster Theological Seminary, Philadelphia and he has written for the *Westminster Theological Journal*, *The Confessional Presbyterian*, and online venues including his own site, *Presbyterians of the Past*, as well as the Alliance of Confessing Evangelicals' blog, Reformation 21, and Reformed Forum. He was a contributor to *B. B. Warfield: Essays on His Life and Thought* and edited *Letters from the Front: J. Gresham Machen's Correspondence from World War I*.

J. C. Whytock, editor for the Africa Survey Textbook Project, is lecturer at ARTS, Kampala; director and editor for Haddington House Trust, Prince Edward Island; and a fellow of the Royal Historical Society. He has served as a pastor, church planter, and theological missionary and is the former acting principal of Dumisani Theological Institute & Bible School, Eastern Cape, SA. His PhD is from the University of Wales, published as *"An Educated Clergy"* (Paternoster/Wipf & Stock); and was a contributor to *A Companion to the Reformation in Scotland* (Brill, 2022).

Nancy J. Whytock, administrator for the Africa Survey Textbook Project, and former librarian and academic skills tutor at Dumisani Theological Institute, Eastern Cape, SA. She is production editor for the *Haddington House Journal*. She has served at various African colleges as a tutor and librarian and as a facilitator for North-West University, SA. She has a BA in music and history, holds an MA in Applied Linguistics from Lincoln Christian University, Illinois, and is a graduate in Biblical studies of Ontario Theological Seminary (Tyndale University).

Humphreys F. Zgambo is lecturer in church history and theology, Faculty of Theology, University of Blantyre Synod, Malawi; extraordinary researcher in the Unit for Reformational Theology and Development of the South African Society, North-West University, SA; and moderator of the Blantyre City Presbytery, CCAP Blantyre Synod. He holds a PhD from NWU – thesis title: "Ethnicity in the Church and Church Structures: an assessment of the CCAP Livingstonia and Nkhoma Synods in Malawi." He has served various congregations of the CCAP.

Introduction

J. C. Whytock

This is a longer-than-normal preface and has morphed into a full introductory chapter as this project has developed. We hope that it will help to explain some basics about these two volumes, set out some key ideas from which we have been working, and provide readers with some operating principles as to how to use these volumes. We begin with the challenges of such a work.

Challenges

Mission history is a complex field and can be overwhelming. Such is the case with Africa and mission history. Having taught on this subject now for several years, I have consistently found it fraught with several challenges in attempting to organise such a vast scope of research materials:

- Even finding a starting point can be difficult. For example, there are various periods of mission historiography at play when it comes to Africa: the colonial or imperial period, the nationalist period or post-colonial/de-colonial, and the adaptationist period – to name the major divides. Or should we start at the beginning and return to the Ancient Church or even the Biblical records of Africa, or are the later periods more relevant to students today? Just figuring out where to start is a challenge, coupled with the task of finding a workable organisational system.

- A close challenge to this is also the temptation to rush through a particular narrative and fail to appreciate the stories surrounding the missions and their personnel, contexts, agendas, achievements, failures, indigenous leaders, developing structures, and rituals.

- Another challenge here concerns the interpretative schools of historiography which can become overbearing, and the result can be that exceptions are ignored or compressed as there are many contradictions that just do not always fit neatly into historiographical categories.

- The challenge to do analysis, which of course must be done, is enormous as that analysis must start first with a knowledge base of the story and that in itself imposes all kinds of questions for the historian. It is not an easy task to gather information and knowledge to aid our understanding and interpretation of the story.

- A further challenge in mission history is that interpretation can very easily become hagiography or perfectionism as a caricature type in writing. Often such a caricature occurs when context is ignored or there is a failure to observe key elements and take an obtuse selective approach.

- The opposite can equally be a challenge. That is, one discovers, one aspect that just does not fit one's perception and therefore all is dismissed.

- There is also the challenge of writing for the academy *and* for a broader readership of a variety levels of training programmes *and* for the community at large. To find the balance here for informing, helping with understanding, edifying, and awakening interest is no easy task. It is a balancing act in many ways and presents much challenge so that the writing does not just become the preserve of the solitary monograph for the academic but will be used much wider in teaching and personal reading.[1]

- The final challenge I will mention, is the problem of not being able to find much of the mission history that I wanted to teach (particularly on Presbyterian missions) readily available in one or two books. What I found myself searching for was lost in old books, or in archives that were usually inaccessible. This despite the internet age, and unfortunately much was being lost or forgotten. This present work grew out of this last challenge as well. For some, especially in *Volume Two*, the chapters or sections have never appeared in accessible print form, so hopefully this will help us to remember and bring forth the challenge to write more. There are no doubt other complexities – there are so many tributaries of different Presbyterians, that in itself is a challenge! – which could be mentioned concerning writing mission history, but the point has been made: it is not always an easy road and is fraught with many challenges in compiling a mission history.

---

1 See, "Introduction: Towards a history of evangelical histories," in *Making Evangelical History: Faith, Scholarship and the Evangelical Past*, eds. Andrew Atherstone and David Ceri Jones. Routledge Studies in Evangelicalism (London/New York: Routledge, 2019), 1–21. On broader challenges one can find such in the popular work by Margaret MacMillan which is aimed at a different audience, yet the principles remain, *The Uses and Abuses of History* (Toronto: Penguin, 2008). Writing history and mission history is a challenging task. Also, Carl R. Trueman, *Histories and Fallacies: Problems Faced in the Writing of History* (Wheaton, IL: Crossway, 2010).

It is hoped that the book before you will provide that base from which to start to surmount some of the above challenges. The stories have been collected and organised from the various tributaries to present the larger picture, at least as much as possible. They aim to provide ample factual chronological inclusion, to lift out key persons, themes, places etc., and to interweave appropriate background. It is sincerely hoped that from this work further critical reflection and understanding will arise. Some chapters of this book may hint at that next stage of critical analysis, but that is not their chief focus. Given the foundational, gathering and organising nature of this work, the first matter to be established is that of the parameters which have been used for this two-volume survey. Below we now set forth the working parameters/definitions for this book.

Africa

We begin by making the point that this work is about the continent of Africa – a wide sweep of immense geography literally from the great cities which define its northern and southern reaches and have had historic links symbolically to Presbyterian missions – *from Cairo to Cape Town* – to islands east and west with historic connections to Presbyterian missions – *from the Banana Islands to Mauritius*. What an incredibly diverse geographic continent and today a geo-political entity:

- 55 to 61 countries (depending upon how these are classified geographically and politically)!
- over 2,000 mother-tongue languages, plus dialects, depending again upon classification systems,
- over 3,000 indigenous tribes, and
- those who settled in Africa throughout its more recent history – Arab, Jew, Portuguese, Malay, Dutch, British, German, Chinese, Italian, Indian, Pakistani. The list could go on and on, and the discussion and debate will turn to who is indigenous, but we will leave that for now.

The point is clear – this is a work dealing with Africa and will range across this vast continent geographically and politically and will intersect literally with so many people groups, it is at times an encyclopaedic challenge to writer and reader.

A Survey of Presbyterian Mission History in Africa

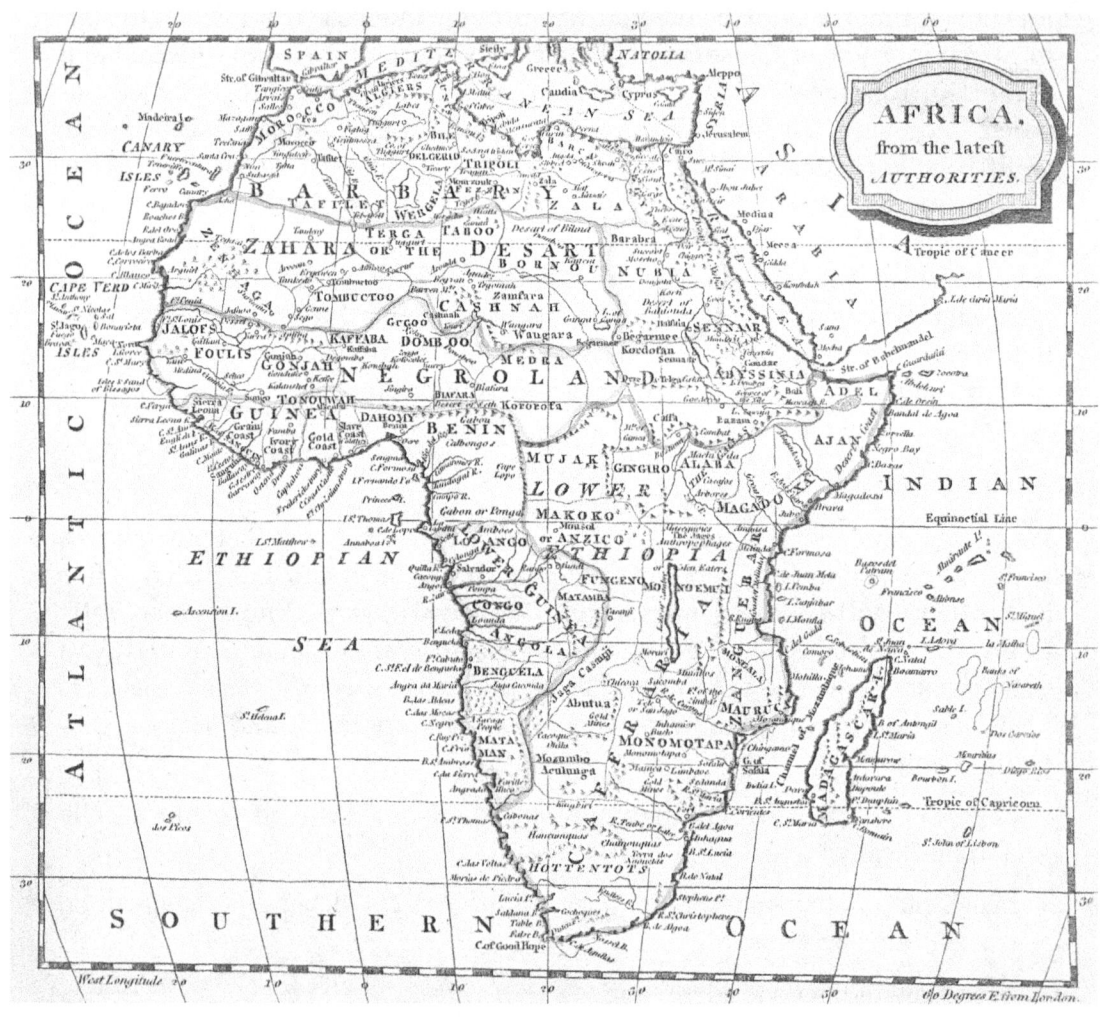

Map of Africa 1806 (with permission of Cory Library)

Introduction

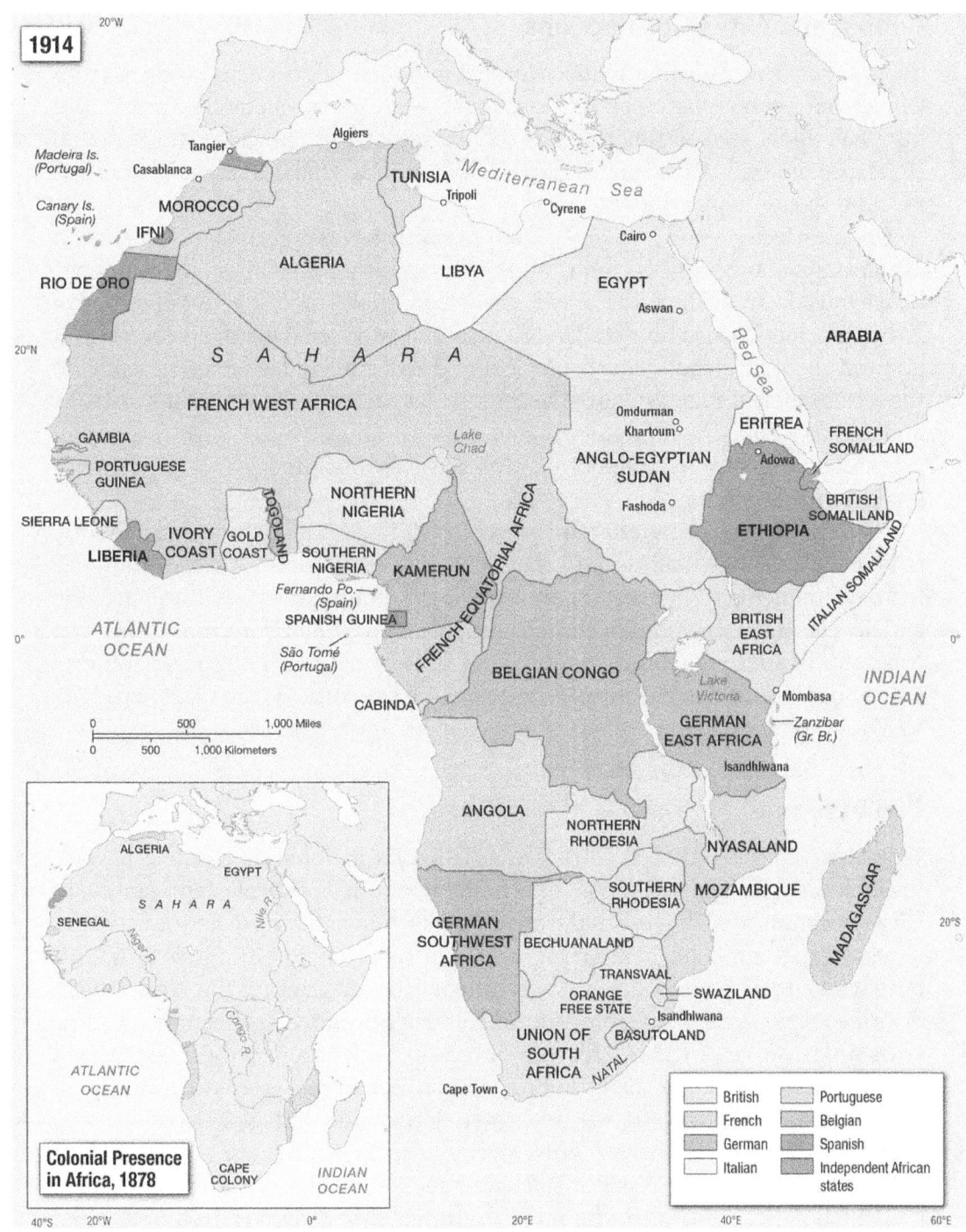

▲ Map of Africa 1914

Global and Inter-Connections

Yet in saying this we will also discover that missionaries, agencies, and churches came from a whole range of locations external to Africa, so as the canvas will also include the global dimension as context must be established. This is not an isolated work only about one continent, Africa; it is global in context, and this must be always kept in view.

Donald Macleod said it well, "… Presbyterianism was not, and is not, insular. It is a global phenomenon, as vibrant and durable as any other Christian tradition."[2] So we must keep the focus balanced as we read: this is a book about missions in Africa, but it must also be global in orientation as stories relate to theological and cultural thought globally, to theological and cultural controversies globally, to the ecclesiological expressions of the church and parachurch in missions globally, and also as well to the migratory theme globally. Thus, the diasporic theme will surface as necessary in different ways in these two volumes concerning Africa and external to Africa.

As a survey of Presbyterian mission history in Africa, historic and modern, readers will also see that the stories bisect the wider world of African studies as the developments of linguistics, anthropology, ethnography, political struggle and development, relations of church and state, and Christianity and culture and tribe, etc. all are somewhere contained in each story. Thus, though our volumes may appear focused in nature and limited as mission history, they will hopefully be a door to many wider areas of study connecting disciplines of study.

Presbyterian

This is also a work that is Christian *and* denominational as a study, namely Presbyterian, or focused upon one branch within the protestant family of Christian churches. That raises the opening question of trying to define this term "Presbyterian" and how to use it for this historical study. Put in simple terms, we have worked from the model of some form of connectedness to the Westminster documents, whether the Confession of Faith or Shorter Catechism, or in some cases a derivative of these. This can be traced back through the Presbyterian Church of Scotland and also the English and Irish Presbyterian Churches (of the same or close time frame) and their derivatives and global connections stemming from within this family of churches that all share a genealogical connectedness to these Westminster documents in some way. This does mean a distinction has been made from the Continental and related grouping, often

---

2   Macleod, *Therefore the Truth I Speak: Scottish Theology 1500–1700* (Fearn, Ross-shire: Mentor, 2020), 11.

referred to as Reformed, yet genealogically rooted back through a different documentary confessional and catechetical stream, related closely, and even parallel, yet a different genealogy. That means at times the two "traditions" of churches, *Presbyterian* and *Reformed*, may be very close yet nevertheless they are rooted genealogically in their own families. All who develop such books, as this one and similar type works, face working through the basic matter of definition and how to set forth the parameters. This book operates on the same working schema that Gary Neal Hanson stated:

> PRESBYTERIANISM is the portion of the Reformed branch of Protestantism that originated in the Church of Scotland and the seventeenth-century English separatists who were attempting to make the Church of England more thoroughly Reformed through the work of the Westminster Assembly (1643–1653); and it came to include the churches they fostered through colonialism and missionary endeavors. The name refers to a central issue of polity: their churches are governed by "presbyters," a transliteration of the Greek word for "elders." Presbyterian Churches are close kin to the continental denominations that took the name "Reformed," the term for their shared theological heritage, which is often, albeit imprecisely, referred to as "Calvinism."[3]

Yes, Reformed churches are *'close kin'* to Presbyterians, but they share a different genealogical documentary path from the Presbyterian churches. An older work such as Richard Clark Reed's 1905 *History of the Presbyterian Churches of the World* was inclusive as to what was Presbyterian and included both genealogical traditions even though the title may not have suggested such at first glance.[4] This book you are reading today takes the more specific genealogical family of those which emerged in the Westminster tradition howbeit, Scottish, English, Irish and their global extensions. So, it shares more with the working parameters of the new *Oxford Handbook of Presbyterianism* and also the new book, *Reformed & Evangelical across Four Centuries: The Presbyterian Story in America*.[5] Now, that relationship to this documentary tradition of Westminster – as mediated via its

---

3   Gary Neal Hanson, "Sixteenth-Century Origins," in *The Oxford Handbook of Presbyterianism* (Oxford/New York: Oxford University Press, 2019), 10.
4   This 1905 work was revised and updated and given a new title in 2013: James McGoldrick with Richard C. Reed and Thomas Hugh Spence, Jr., *Presbyterian and Reformed Churches: A Global History*. Original 1905 (Grand Rapids: Reformation Heritage, 2013).
5   Nathan P. Feldmeth, S. Donald Fortson III, Garth M. Rosell and Kenneth J. Stewart, *Reformed & Evangelical across Four centuries: The Presbyterian Story in America* (Grand Rapids: Eerdmans, 2021), 1.

Scottish, English and Irish churches and related societies[6] and exported globally – is not always a straight line. There are variants, amendments, qualifiers, and additions which creep in along the way, sometimes with overt action sometimes with less than overt knowledge. There are varieties of theological schools that emerge, varieties of liturgical understandings and practices, there are varieties of nuances on polity, there are varieties of cultural understandings, all making for an incredibly complicated historical story to follow.[7] When this is added to the mix of nations sending forth into mission and the mix of tribes and peoples, it means a history is uncovered which is nuanced with literally hundreds of unique stories in this genealogical family called Presbyterian.

Mission History: Historic Beginnings c.1790s to c.1930s

These books are focused upon the history of the vast array of Presbyterian missions and churches on the continent of Africa. In terms of this subject focus, what we have tried to do is threefold in terms of overall organisation: in *Volume One*, we trace the *historic beginnings* of Presbyterian missions in Africa. Thus, three parts in *Volume One* of this book refer to these *historic beginnings*. Generally, these have been limited to pre-World War Two (WW2). On occasion for some of these historic beginnings the writer has traced the story beyond WW2 and may take it through to national independence or another significant date or provide a very short historic postscript. *Volume One* overlaps more-or-less with Kenneth Latourette's timeframe for the greatest century of missions.[8] It begins a little before Latourette and ends slightly after, but the main focus will be parallel with the Latourette formulation of geographical expansion during this "greatest century." Sundler and Steed refer to this as the long nineteenth century and use the dates 1787 to 1919 for this period of historic mission activity.[9] We have elongated that on occasion through to the eve of the Second World War. Thus, *Volume One* will be c.1790s to c.1930s more-or-less. Each story will endeavour to establish basic context for mission and location; key leaders both foreign and indigenous; issues of development; and, on occasion, controversies and institutional developments of significance.

---

6 Note the words "related societies." Much of presbyterian mission history is not necessarily that of church courts, boards, or committees, but also included many more complexities with societies etc,. or para-church/interdenominational entities.

7 For example, even as early as 1690 we can see at least five parties of Presbyterians in Scotland, Nathan P. Feldmeth, S. Donald Fortson III, Garth M. Rosell and Kenneth J. Stewart, *Reformed & Evangelical across Four centuries: The Presbyterian Story in America*, 78–79, grouping four within the CofS and one outside to make for five parties.

8 Kenneth Scott Latourette, *A History of the Expansion of Christianity. Volume IV, The Great Century, A.D. 1800–A.D. 1914: Europe and the United States of America*. Original (New York: Harper and Brothers, 1941).

9 Bengt Sundkler, & Christopher Steed, *A History of the Church in Africa* (Cambridge: Cambridge University, 2000), viii.

The most challenging issue faced here in *Volume One* was the way to organise all these historic beginnings. Generally, we have adopted *a chronological approach* more-or-less in each subsection to organise that section's chapters. It is far from perfect, but we concluded this approach works better than adopting an organisational approach by country of mission origin as that can create an imbalanced methodology and perception in today's context of over 225 years of Presbyterian mission involvement on the Continent of Africa. The first three parts (Part One: Western and Southern; Part Two: Eastern and Central, Part Three: The Nile Corridor) within *Volume One* are organised in broad geographic categories, and we realise there is some fluidity here. The approach has been rather broad and is not technically tied down to one modern defining geo-political approach, such as UNESCO.[10] For example, in Part One beginnings are *both* Western *and* Southern so things do not neatly fit into modern geo-political categories and thus the organisational approach here tries to be reflective of some of these complexities. No organisational system on such a large subject will be perfect. A fourth selective, thematic part is also included in *Volume One*.

Mission History: Modern Beginnings c.1940s to c.2023

Next, in *Volume Two*, we have endeavoured to also deal with the new era in mission history and to also include newer Presbyterian mission beginnings after WW2, (which is a fault line for mission history), through the second half of the twentieth century and into the first two decades of the twenty-first century. Thus, *Volume Two* will basically look at c.1940s to c.2023.[11] There are many reasons for this emphasis of new beginnings: one, there are "new players" involved in Presbyterian missions who were not there before WW2 or, if there, they have

---

10 For example, Todd M. Johnson, Kenneth R. Ross & Kenneth R. Ross, eds. *Atlas of Global Christianity 1910–2010* (Edinburgh: Edinburgh University Press, 2009), uses the categories, Christianity in Eastern Africa, Christiani-ty in Middle Africa, Christianity in Northern Africa, Christianity in Southern Africa, and Christianity in Western Africa, 112–133. This seems close if not the same as the geo-political lines of UNESCO.

11 Scott W. Sunquist and Caroline N. Becker, eds. *A History of Presbyterian Missions 1944–2007* (Louisville, KY: Geneve Press, 2008), 2–3. Though with differences, there are many parallels here with the dating of the edited volume of Sunquist and Becker. The 1940s would see a new rise in ecumenical activity in two directions it can be argued, and the paradigm of language was shifting from the 1940s forward to partnership in mission. Contrasts and similarities will need to be realised in this period between WCC and the Lausanne Movement and Presbyterians and missions. See, Theodore A Gill, Jr. "Historical Context for Mission, 1944–2007," in *A History of Presbyterian Missions*, 13–35. Also, Bernard Thorogood, ed. *Gales of Change: Responding to Shifting Missionary Context: The Story of the London Missionary Society, 1945–1977* (Geneva: WCC, 1994). The title alone sums up the point here. Kenneth R. Ross has provided in a short article helpful references to these changes taking place in historic mission fields by the late 1940s, see, "The Legacy of James Dougall," *IBMR* 32.4, 208.

regrouped or realigned; two, there are also theological trajectories which emerge and show that Presbyterianism in Africa, as also in the West, broadly defined, was fracturing and experiencing theological divides (mainline mission boards into the 1930s were still operating under the conversionist paradigm, that would start to change or sometimes even fracture and after WW2 we see new paradigms emerging or at least new tensions emerging in mainline boards[12]); three, the acknowledgement of these newer Presbyterian missions has often been muted, ignored, or marginalised as the older historic missions have received the bulk of the story line;[13] and four, these new beginnings are not always fully aware of one another – it might be a "global village," but sometimes in mission work it may be more like guarded forts – so hopefully this will also prove historically and missionally helpful. These "newer" Presbyterian missions are distinct entities and developments from the historic mission period. These we have classified by the term "modern" in the title for *Volume Two*. This is a word which we recognise as less than perfect. Broadly speaking, we see it as post-WW2 as modern or new missions in contrast to the historic period. A lovely word that encapsulates this period – modern or new – is "neoteric" which means, modern, contemporary, or more recent, but we suspect it is a word that is not in common parlance and therefore not the best word to use, so we have reverted to speaking of this as the modern or newer Presbyterian missions. Word fanatics may use the word *neoteric*!

Themes

Finally, we have opened the door on *select themes*. This theme section in both volumes is not exhaustive but attempts to round out and develop the stories and histories surveyed and allows for some key aspects to be focused on. Some

---

12 Jeffrey C. Burke, "The Establishment of the American Presbyterian Mission in Egypt, 1854–1940: An Overview" (unpublished PhD thesis, McGill University, Montreal, 2000), 61. See also Feldmeth, Fortson, Rosell, and Stewart, pages 268-269 which discusses the 1930s and re-*thinking missions* and such individuals as Pearl Buck and how this worked itself out post-WW2. Nathan P. Feldmeth, S. Donald Fortson III, Garth M. Rosell and Kenneth J. Stewart, *Reformed & Evangelical across Four centuries: The Presbyterian Story in America*, 267. The essay by Bernard Thorogood, "The Gales of Change," though speaking concerning the LMS context, applies much broader to this reality of mission change, in, *Gales of Change: Responding to a Shifting Missionary Context: The Story of the London Missionary Society 1945–1977* (Geneva: WCC, 1994), 1–18. For a survey see, Timothy Yates, *Christian Mission in the Twentieth Century* (Cambridge: CUP, 1994).

13 This is now starting to be acknowledged by historians that evangelical Presbyterianism especially after WW2 has been marginalised, but it must be brought into the narrative. Interestingly the final chapter in the new work by, Feldmeth, Fortson III, Rosell and Stewart, *Reformed & Evangelical across Four centuries: The Presbyterian Story in America*, 304–318, chapter 19 is entitled "Evangelical Marginalization and Resurgence."

themes are chronologically diverse and encapsulate at times both the historic and the modern as defined above for these two volumes. However, generally the themes relate historically to the time periods of each volume. Here under themes is where we also pick up the theme of the global *new diaspora* of African Presbyterians in *Volume Two*.[14]

A Survey

This work is not exhaustive. It is not a full encyclopaedia of Presbyterian mission history and church development, nor does it claim to explore all themes related to Presbyterian mission history and Africa. We have endeavoured to survey as many trajectories as possible – historic and modern. We know there will be gaps and readers will find them, and we would ask that they communicate with us and help us to become aware of these gaps and missed stories. It is hoped in time a second edition will emerge. Likewise, it would be wonderful to see a third complementary volume appear to go alongside this two-volume mission history survey which would explore more themes and theologies at a much more in-depth analytical level. There is much yet to be done!

This work is a close cousin to *handbooks, companions, and guides*. As such it works from the perspective of an engaging reference text to start with on a vast subject. Surveys are invaluable resources and can blend being reference guides and textbooks at the same time, allowing one to see an overview of the vistas of a subject in an organised fashion. Thus, this work will survey, mark-out, guide and direct the reader and also point the reader where to read, research, and study further. The hope is that it is a kind of first "go-to" work. The lines between a companion versus a handbook or even a survey work of a subject field is somewhat flexible or even mysteriously the preserve locked in an editor's mind or a publisher's world. We have opted for the word survey and hope that it will be a benefit to students, to lecturers, for libraries, and for exchange in the global Presbyterian community.

Finally, though the work is a survey study within a certain tradition within the Christian families of denominations, namely the Presbyterian tradition, no doubt comparisons will arise whether Anglican or Pentecostal etc. This book cannot engage in such vast comparisons, although many authors have been tempted, but it hopefully will help the interested reader to do so. On occasion certain writers offer or tease out some of these comparisons, but that is not

---

14 Since the 1970s onwards African migrants to Western industrialised countries has been a constant theme and often with this has been with the establishment of new congregations. Jehu Hanciles, "Missionaries sent and received, Africa, 1910–2010" in *Atlas of Global Christianity*, 264–265.

the focus of these two volumes. It very well could be a good assignment task for student work. We would love to see such comparisons included in a third volume.

Some matters of style and attempts to be user-friendly

A few comments on style will perhaps help readers before they commence the dive into these books.

- Where it is logical, we have tried to draw *cross-references* (usually placed within the footnotes) to other chapters in the collection. Hopefully this will also show unity of the subject. It will generally read as follows: *See chapter 4 in this volume* (the demonstrative adjective *this* refers to, *A Survey of Presbyterian Mission History in Africa: Historic Beginnings (c.1790s to c.1930s) – Volume One*).

- We are using ample *illustration* to be as engaging as possible for readers. Every attempt has been made to verify that there is no copyright infringement, and, with images, we realise this is not always without some degree of uncertainty.

- We believe *maps* are still great teaching tools, so we have endeavoured to include these as much as possible.

- *Charts* have also been created of key factual matters usually in the form of lists. We encourage the study of these charts.

- Select *Timelines* have also been developed for some chapters. Also, we have endeavoured to make sure as much as possible timelines could be made for chapters as an assigned question as well for some chapters. Thus, the goal has been an attempt to provide as much as possible orderly accounts which are chronologically developed.

- Every chapter includes a *Select Bibliography*. These *select bibliographies* will hopefully allow lecturers and students to gain an opening further into the world of Presbyterian mission history in Africa. Obviously, *selective* means it is not *exhaustive*. Only once or twice have we broken that rule of convention. That was to accommodate primary sources that were referenced to such an extent we could not select.

- Generally, we use *short-form footnotes* where only the basic information is given and then the reader can find the full information in the Select Bibliography. This system helps to keep the footnotes as brief as possible and is a standard system in many published works.

- However, there are exceptions, and these concern full bibliographical entry for some sources in the footnotes which will not be included in the Select Bibliography as they are not germane to the overall information of the chapter but suggest rather a side-issue or side-line of studies. The other exception is chapters such as the introduction where no Select Bibliography is included.

- We have opted to use *chapter outlines* at the beginning of each chapter to see the contents *at-a-glance*. It is not an abstract but visually a quick overview we hope for readers. These are very simple and just use the words of the main sub-headings of that chapter.

- On occasion in some chapters there may be included *biographical appendices or charts* giving attention to a particular person in a chapter or a grouping. Some of these may be written or compiled by contributors other than the author of the chapter. All insets or appendices are author-identified as well and are included in the List of Contributors for each volume.

- We acknowledge that many proper names have changed and that *spelling* may have changed in the course of the last three centuries. We have tried to start with the current proper name and introduce the historic names. Often in a chapter the writer will explain by way of a footnote the various spellings of names. No doubt we have missed some name changes or spelling variants.

- History contains *language and names* which may be offensive to the modern reader. We have tried to follow the following custom: if something is in a primary source and quoted, it has been retained for accuracy of history.

- *Abbreviations* have been used in these volumes. Most of these are now quite common, but there are some which are not; we have had to establish a method to create these based upon standard convention. There is also a duplication of abbreviations for certain denominations or organisations. In those cases, in the abbreviation's list, we have used the alpha letters in lowercase, a) b) c) for example with PCA which is a duplication in the abbreviation list. We have found this supplementary method is used in a couple of recently published historical books facing a similar problem of duplication of abbreviations, so we have decided to adopt this method in the full List of Abbreviations. The reader then will need to determine the abbreviation by context in the chapter they read if it is a duplication entry – a good exercise in basic hermeneutical principles!

- In *Volume One* we have also included a series of *fact and reflective questions* at the end of each chapter which lecturers are free to draw upon.

Our aim is *to inform, to guide,* and *to encourage more writing and reflection,* but we also hope *to inspire* – through this account of those who have gone before us and to learn the good, and in humility the less-than-good, and to be reminded that the regional Church possesses an ever-engaging series of stories and its narratives weave together a very complex fabric that constitutes part of the grand story of the global Church. The summation of this project can be found in the scripture texts which are used on the dedicatory pages of these two volumes.

> *Then those who feared the LORD spoke with one another. The LORD paid attention and heard them, and a book of remembrance was written before him of those who feared the LORD and esteemed his name.* Malachi 3:16 ESV.

We invite you to come, to engage, and to review this compilation of mission history. We hope many will also be inspired to keep writing the narrative for future generations to read.

Part One:
Western & Southern Africa: Historic Beginnings & Developments

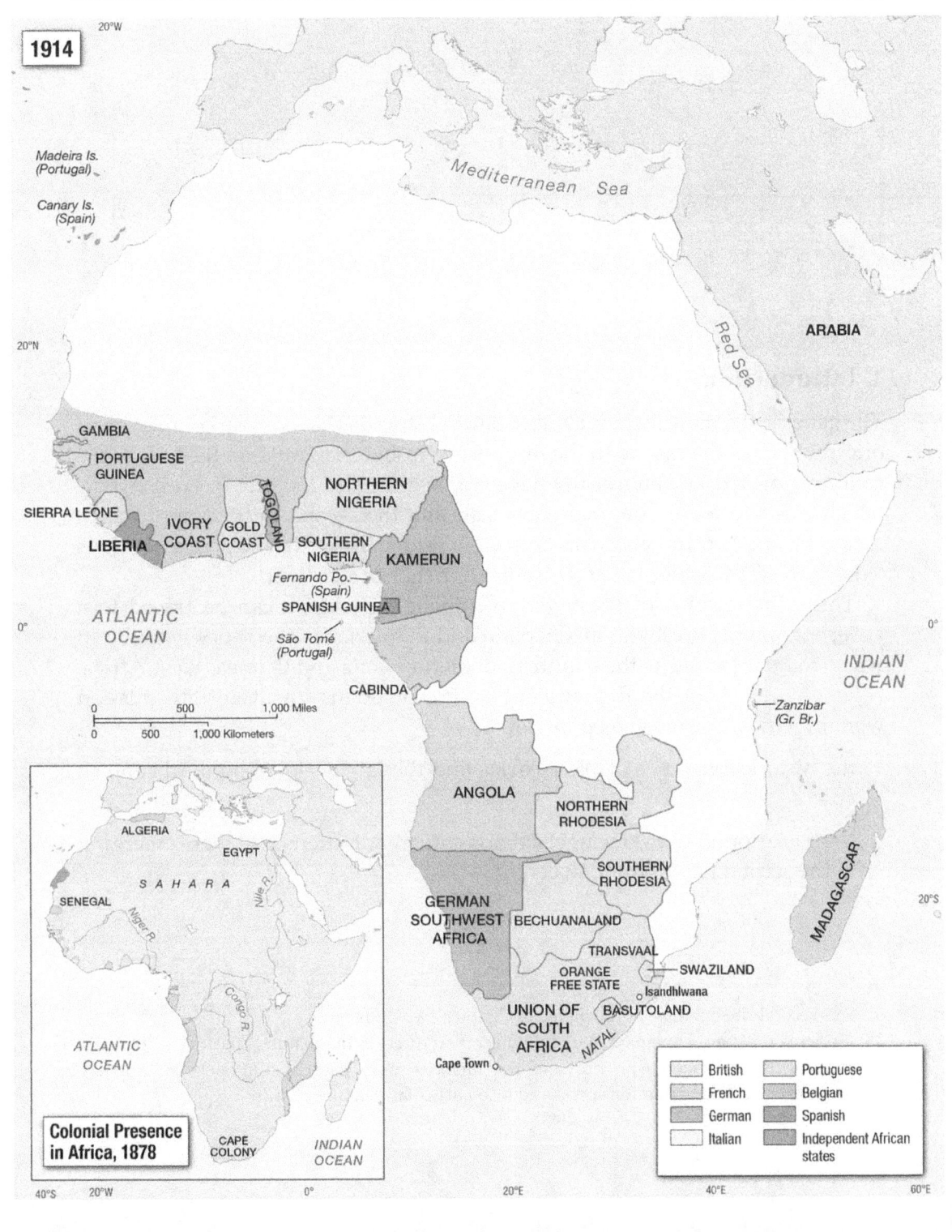

Chapter 1

Beginnings, Part One: West Africa c.1790s, First Efforts

J. C. Whytock

Chapter Outline
1. Introduction
2. A Governor and a Presbyterian Chaplain
3. The Societies and Presbyterians
4. Summary Conclusion

1. Introduction

The genesis of a movement may have several strands that create a complexity of origins. Such is the case with the origins of Presbyterian mission history on the continent of Africa, which really have two beginnings: the first in West Africa, which was aborted by the main agencies, and the second in the Cape,[1] which took root. The two are related, as both were primarily *society* and *patron* missions – not *ecclesial*[2] missions, yet at the same time they are distinct.

These first origins of Presbyterian influence in Africa can be traced to a governor and his Presbyterian chaplain and to missionary societies working in what we know today as the countries of Sierra Leone and Guinea, West Africa. As one reads about the first attempt by Presbyterians involved with mission work in Africa, one must keep in view:

- the historical realities of West Africa and the larger global political context, and
- the background to the evangelical mission organisations that were emerging in the second half of the 18th century.

---

1 This second "beginnings" is the theme of Chapter Two of this work.
2 "Society" mission – explained more fully in section three of this chapter, "patron" – generally meaning the person(s) who provides the finances for a particular mission or chaplain, "ecclesial" – meaning mission sponsored by a particular denomination(s).

These two points will be discussed below.

Often this West African Presbyterian mission narrative has been ignored or forgotten. This is regrettable as it is an important part of the story to understand the flow of Presbyterian mission history on the continent of Africa. Themes that are found in this chapter will reoccur throughout this survey text – e.g., evangelism, education, translation work, sacrifice, finances, personality conflicts, etc. – and thus it is worthwhile to introduce them here as we begin.

2. A Governor and A Presbyterian Chaplain

The Context

Our story begins in England in the 1770s and then moves to the then Thirteen Colonies in North America and the American Revolutionary War. It is a story about the return of the original diaspora Africans (now freed) back to Africa and a new type of colony and a new mission. If one thinks of a triangular relationship between England, North America, and West Africa, one gains a perspective of the complexity of this first mission where Presbyterians began their involvements in Africa.

In 1772 in England, Lord Mansfield's decision in the Somerset Case in effect ended chattel slavery in the British Isles. This was a critical decision in the long road to end slavery. One result of this was that within a few years there were perhaps as many as 15,000 former "African slaves" or "African American slaves" in Great Britain – many of whom were unemployed and destitute. Adding to that number, more former slaves (African Americans) arrived in London after the American War of Independence[3] (1776–1783). These "Black Loyalists," induced by Lord Dunmore's promises of freedom, had escaped from Revolutionary masters, and had crossed to the British lines. After the War, Black Loyalists in the former colonies to the south were evacuated to Nova Scotia, from where some made their way to Britain.

The colony

By 1786, conditions for the black community in London had deteriorated to such an extent that a Committee for the Relief of the Black Poor was formed; and, by 1787, a plan was in place to start a colony (Province of Freedom) of former slaves in West Africa. This unique colony, named Granville Town after Granville Sharp,

---

3   The American Revolution was the war in which the American Thirteen Colonies in North America rebelled against King George III and sought their independence resulting in the formation of the independent country, the United States of America. Not all black people fought for independence and those who sided with King George III were known popularly as Black Loyalists.

failed to take hold due to disease and attack by the neighbouring Temne people. In 1790, the St. Georges Bay Company re-established a colony at Granville Town. Then, in 1792, The Sierra Leone Company resettled over 1100 Black Loyalists from Nova Scotia at Freetown, West Africa.

Many of those involved in the founding and administration of The Sierra Leone Company in the UK were Evangelical Anglicans and members of the Clapham Sect.[4] The Nova Scotian Black Loyalists (one grouping of the colonists) were Baptists, Methodists, Countess of Huntingdon Connexion (Calvinistic methodist), and Anglicans. Presbyterian involvement came with the colony's third governor, Zachary Macaulay (1768–1838).

▲ Historic engraving of Freetown

A Governor and his Chaplain: Macaulay and Clarke

Zachary Macaulay (1768–1838) was born at Inveraray, Argyll, Scotland. He was the son of John Macaulay, a Church of Scotland [Presbyterian] minister, and the father of Thomas Babington Macaulay, the historian. After a brief career in the Jamaican sugar trade, which exposed him to the dehumanising effects of slavery, he returned home an ardent abolitionist. While living with his sister, Jean, and her husband, Thomas Babington, in 1789, Macaulay was converted and introduced to the Clapham Sect of which he became a prominent member. His connection with Sierra Leone began in 1790. By 1792, he was a council member of The Sierra Leone Company, and from 1794 until 1799, he was the colony's governor.

---

4   The Clapham Sect was named after an area then near London called Clapham and was a reformist and abolitionist group of evangelical Christians. Macaulay was a member and editor of its paper *The Christian Observer*. The most prominent member was William Wilberforce. The Clapham Sect interacted with several missionary and other philanthropic societies.

In 1796, Macaulay brought out the Rev. John Clarke, a Church of Scotland minister,[5] to be his chaplain as well as the company chaplain (Sierra Leone Company). Clarke had taken his divinity course at the University of Edinburgh and had been recommended by Dr John Erskine as a missionary for Sierra Leone to Zachary Macaulay. He was ordained by the Scots Presbytery London (CoS)[6] at the Scots Church, Crowne Court, Covent Garden on 22 January 1796. Dr John Love, one of the LMS founders and CoS minister in Spitalfields, was the preacher for the service. Henry Thornton, a prominent evangelical, M. P., and member of the Clapham Sect attended the ordination and provided dinner for the clergy following the ordination service.[7]

▲ Governor Zachary Macaulay

Clarke served in Sierra Leone until his death there in 1799. His ministry met with much trouble from the beginning. On the voyage out, there were disputes among the Scotsmen over how closely the church in West Africa would mirror the church in Scotland; Clarke supported a less rigid tie by promoting the use of Watts' *The Psalms of David Imitated* rather than the 1650 Scottish Psalter. Later, he found difficulty in adapting the content of his sermons to accommodate his less educated hearers. Although he did much to develop a Sunday School, extend missions work, and foster harmony among the various Christian groups in the colony, he was caught in denominational rivalries and jealousies and settler (colonist) and company rivalries.

Reading of Clarke's ministry in Macaulay's letters, there is a sense of pity and sadness. Clarke was a man who humbly did his best to heed Macaulay's advice for improvements, yet he saw little success with the settlers, the dissenting preachers, and others. Macaulay made this entry in his journal in June 1796:

---

5 As far as we are aware Rev. John Clarke was the first settled Presbyterian chaplain in Africa. (Note: sometimes also spelled Clark). He is not to be confused with the other Rev. John Clarke (1802–1879) the Scottish Baptist missionary to Jamaica and Fernando Po, West Africa.
6 CoS in a broad sense as some Secessionists also were involved in various ways. Kenneth M. Black, *The Scots Churches in England* (Edinburgh: William Blackwood, 1906), 179.
7 "Ordinations," *Evangelical Magazine* 4 (1796): 163–164. See also, *Minutes of the Scots Presbytery of London, 5 August 1772 to 19 March 1823*, [MS] Vol. 1, at the Archives of the United Reformed Church History Society, Westminster College, Cambridge. See pages 139–142. Appointed to be taken under trials and assigned a lecture, a homily, and a popular sermon (14 January 1796), delivered such and sustained (16 January 1796) and was ordained when reported such at the 3 February 1796 meeting of the presbytery.

"Clarke lectured in the evening. In his proof of the truth of Scriptures he was ingenious, but far beyond the comprehension of his hearers. This is an error his academic education exposes him to, but he tries to correct it, and I take care to remind him of it whenever I find him soaring out of sight."[8] In fairness, Macaulay's strident restrictions on marriage services may have been a major contributing factor to Rev. Clarke's lack of popularity over time with dissenters. It seems that Mary Perth the Black Loyalist woman regarded him with respect.

3. The Societies and Presbyterians

John Clarke's ministry overlapped in part with that of the Scottish missionary societies whose members came the year after his arrival in West Africa. The 1790s was a period of rapid expansion of new missionary societies. Five, amongst others, were formed in rapid succession in the 1790s in the United Kingdom: the Baptist Missionary Society 1792, the London Missionary Society (LMS) 1795,[9] the Edinburgh Missionary Society (EMS) and the Glasgow Missionary Society (GMS) February/March 1796,[10] and the Church Missionary Society 1799 (originally named the Society for Missions to Africa and the East). Missionary societies were volunteer organisations for mission endeavours with established procedures, common theology and ethos, and organisational channels to achieve mission work. The dating of the EMS and the GMS in early 1796 is significant as these societies were founded before the famous May 1796 General Assembly in the Church of Scotland which debated foreign missions and rejected such, due to finances at that time. Hence it fell upon the mission societies (GMS & EMS), who were often seen with ridicule by many within both the Church of Scotland and some branches of the Secession Presbyterian Churches, to carry the flame for foreign missions. These societies raised money and found recruits to serve under their organisations and thus commenced an incredible period in Scottish missions in Africa as the 19th century emerged.[11] These Scottish Societies could be described as interdenominational, evangelical Presbyterian/

---

8   Macaulay, *Life and Letters*, 141. Further, I have only found one printed work to date by Rev. John Clarke, a letter about Mary Perth, a Methodist and a Black Loyalist woman in Freetown. "Singular Piety in a Female African" [29 July 1796] *Evangelical Magazine* 4 (1796): 460–464.
9   The LMS brought together those who were paedo-baptistic and Reformed/Calvinistic evangelicals.
10 The EMS and GMS in the words of David Alan Currie, "began as miniature versions of the LMS," (150). The EMS name was later changed to the Scottish Missionary Society.
11 The GMS & EMS found support from evangelicals in the Church of Scotland and from many of the Associate Church (Burghers) and to a lesser extent from the Relief Church. Thus, these societies were a place where evangelical Presbyterians from three different denominations of Scottish Presbyterians could labour together.

Calvinist, voluntary mission agencies working outside the ecclesial frameworks by necessity.

Clarke's ministry had been primarily to the colonists – a very mixed grouping of people much different than our modern-day perceptions. Most colonists of Granville Town and Freetown were former slaves from Britain, destitute white women, Black Loyalists, or Jamaican Maroons. The success of the colony depended on a balance of genders; it seems that the organisers thought more in terms of economic strata than in terms of race. The Maroons were communities of escaped African slaves and indigenous Jamaicans who were removed from their villages as plantations expanded. Thus, the Creole culture was established, which was to have a disproportionate influence in the future of Sierra Leone. The missionary societies, on the other hand, worked chiefly among the indigenous peoples.

The GMS and EMS began their foreign mission endeavours in the Sierra Leone area of West Africa in 1797 in co-operation with the LMS.[12] West Africa was the chief centre of mission concern at this time and was a critical mission field as it was the place of freed slaves returning to Africa. The hope was this would become a great missionary sending location across Africa. The first two Scottish missionaries to be sent were from the GMS, March 1797: Duncan Campbell and Alexander Henderson. Both were artisan missionaries. Henderson, a tailor, established two schools in Africa and Campbell, a weaver, helped as an industrial missionary in Africa. They ministered in Rokon on the Rokel River in the interior of Sierra Leone (Temne country). They were less than cordial to one another and, though certain aspects of mission work were commenced, an enduring legacy of an outstanding nature did not occur. As an educator, Henderson was in the early first wave of educational missions to Sierra Leone; he represented the commencement of an abiding Scottish Presbyterian tradition of mission work in Africa focusing upon education. Henderson returned to Scotland and unfortunately latterly departed from the faith. Campbell left Christian mission work in Sierra Leone and became a trader there. Governor Macaulay was grieved by the way these two Presbyterian missionaries treated each other and concluded that little good would come from such fractious attitudes.

In October 1797 two more artisan missionaries were sent out from the GMS, Peter Ferguson and Robert Graham, and two missionaries from the EMS, Henry Brunton and Peter Grieg, and two from the LMS, Alexander Russel and George Capp.

Peter Greig and Henry Brunton were both Secession Presbyterians connected to

---

12 The Baptist Missionary Society had briefly done mission work in Sierra Leone for several months in 1796 overlapping briefly with Clarke's recent arrival. See, K. R. M. Short, "A Note on the Sierra Leone Mission and Religious Freedom, 1796," *The Baptist Quarterly* 28.8 (1980): 355–360.

the EMS; Greig was a gardener and was sent as a catechist, and Brunton was more the teacher/linguist (although also sent out as a catechist) who had studied theology under Professor Lawson in Selkirk. They were to commence work with the Susa peoples at Rio Ponges, inland in Susaland (within what is modern Guinea) 120 miles from Freetown. Brunton laboured in translation work, evangelism and also as chaplain for Zachary Macaulay, being Rev. Clarke's successor from 1798 to 1800. His translation work was most significant for West Africa as he produced a grammar and dictionary for the Susa language and this was one of the first ever printed in Britain.[13] He also produced catechisms and tracts and did pioneering work concerning evangelising semi-Islamic peoples.[14] Some of the catechisms were based upon Isaac Watts' various catechisms and Governor Macaulay prepared one of these and Brunton rendered the translation. Brunton's extensive catechism work needs more research and study. Further Brunton's assistant on these translation projects was Jellorum Harrison from the Pongo – one of the Susa youths that Brunton brought to London to study at the African Academy in Clapham[15] (other students likely helped Brunton as well). Greig became the first Scottish

▲ Susa Grammar title page, 1802, first Presbyterian contribution publication for an African language

---

13 Brunton, *Grammar and Vocabulary of the Susoo*, 1802. Brunton returned to Scotland to convalesce and work on his writing projects. Brunton represents the first of a long line of Presbyterians involved in literacy work in Africa. See also, William Brown, *The History of the Propagation of Christianity Among the Heathen*, Second Edition. (Edinburgh: Fullarton, 1823), volume 2, 501–509. Brown had letters of Brunton to create his account. I have been unable to locate those letters today. Some material relating to the SMS is held at the National Library of Scotland, Edinburgh but unfortunately not all records/letters are there.
14 Flynn, *Western Christian Presence*, 258–315.
15 Connected to the Society for the Education of Africans and also the Clapham Sect. He eventually became a missionary with the LMS and would spend time at the Cape.

Presbyterian martyr in Africa when he was brutally murdered in 1798 at Kubia, on the Fattalah River, by a group of Fullahs. Greig was an evangelist and teacher and had several Susa youths whom he was teaching and training when he was martyred.[16] He possessed a most virtuous Christian disposition and piety and was very much the conciliator amongst the Christian missionaries. Another EMS missionary, Rev. Robert Alexander, was sent out to Sierra Leone, but he stayed only a brief time and returned to Scotland.

After about four years in West Africa, Brunton returned to Scotland and England (1801) and laboured on his writing projects for the CMS before going in 1802 to the Karass Mission in the Caucasus (between the Black and Caspian Seas) as a missionary, where he was also accompanied by the same Susa youth, Jellorum Harrison, a lay catechist who had been with him in the UK. Brunton had availed himself of the African Academy in south London (Clapham) to continue with his language work.[17]

The African Academy, also called the Clapham Academy, deserves special mention here. The origins of this academy can be traced back to John Campbell, the one-time secretary of the EMS. Eventually the Academy was situated in Clapham and became much more oriented with the Clapham Sect. Campbell's rationale for such as academy was as follows: "Might we not bring *over* Africa to England; educate her; when some through grace and gospel might be converted, and sent back to Africa, – if not any converted, yet they might help to spread civilization, so all would not be lost."[18] The youth who were brought from Sierra Leone and environs were a diverse grouping of children of black colonists, tribal heads and traders. The number of youths brought to the Academy is hard to document conclusively. It could be from 24 upwards and perhaps as high as 40. Research has recently helped to create a better understanding of the Academy and its work. Local white children also attended the Academy. It was thus not totally African as often has been popularly thought. The Academy may have only existed seven years and fulfilled its original mandate in that timeframe.[19]

The two other missionaries sent by the GMS, Peter Ferguson, and Robert Graham, were stationed on the Banana Islands along the coast. Again,

---

16 George Smith, "Peter Greig: First Scottish Missionary Martyr," in *Twelve Pioneer Missionaries* (London: Thomas Nelson, 1900), 122–136. Greig's minister was Ebenezer Brown, Inverkeithing. Greig and Brunton were commissioned as catechists at a special service on 22 September 1797 at Bristo Street (Associate Secessionist) Church, Edinburgh.

17 J. Baxter, "Scots in the Caucasus. A curious missionary enterprise," *The Scots Magazine* (Edinburgh), New Series, 16.1 (October 1931), 1–9; Lydia Krasnokutskaya, *Edinburgh Missionaries in Northern Caucasus in XIX Century,* ed. M. Filippov, trans. Katie Yuryeva (London: M. Filippov, 2014).

18 *Life and Times … John Campbell*, 160–161.

19 The best overview is the article by Mouser, "African Academy."

unfortunately their mission did not materialise as both died of fever shortly after arriving there. Alexander Russel and George Capp (LMS) focused their mission endeavours on the Bullam Shore. Russel took ill and had to return to Free Town (current Freetown) and died there in July 1798. The next month, Capp returned to England.[20]

4. Summary Conclusion

The location in West Africa of Sierra Leone and Guinea was critical as concerns the abolishment of the slave trade, freed slaves/recaptives and missions, literacy/education and commerce, and a unique type of colony. Thus, it is understandable why the Scottish societies decided to focus on this region as their first African foray into missionary endeavour.

The earliest attempt at Scottish Presbyterian involvement in missions through the role of Macaulay and his chaplain Rev. Clarke and the united effort of these three societies (GMS, EMS, LMS) did not lead to a permanent Presbyterian church being established in Sierra Leone and modern-day Guinea. Macaulay was certainly committed to educational mission work, and this was in many ways a lasting legacy in Africa for Scottish Presbyterians, yet it did not last here. However, such educational endeavours will be a constant theme throughout many chapters of this book.

We can see Brunton's work as preparing the way for further Church Missionary Society work as they took over that mission station in 1804 in Susaland.[21] Further, Brunton contributed to linguistic and mission strategy in West Africa and beyond and his involvement with Jellorum Harrison from the Pongo certainly makes the story much wider than has so often been explored. The intersection here with the African Academy in Clapham cannot be ignored. It does seem that Brunton was connected in a linguistic way to the Academy. Henry Brunton (c.1770–1813) must be commended as one of the significant early missionaries of the Scottish Societies.

Greig's martyrdom is a reminder of the potential cost of the labours of the cross for Christ and the spread of the Gospel. Greig's life has been often ignored and marginalised in Presbyterian mission history and this should not be the case.

Finally, not all who will go forth as missionaries or pastors will prove to be persevering and servant-like and issues of unity and forbearance are often a theme in Christian work. The societies were at their genesis in the 1790s as well and were learning much about recruitment, strategy, teamwork, and promotion of the mission. This mission thrust was a society-directed mission with like-

---

20 *Register of Missionaries [LMS]*, 2.
21 Mouser ("Origins") argues that Brunton's publications were instrumental for the CMS commencing their missions in the Pongo area amongst other reasons (378).

minded convictions, a catholic spirit, yet denominational tensions can still be found to cause disunity as that seems to have been one of the underlying causes of tension with the early missionaries that were sent. In fact, this appears to be one of the contributing factors as to why no permanent Presbyterian church emerged in this area of West Africa in the 1790s. However, the factors really point in several directions. The denominational make-up of those who went to Sierra Leone in the 1790s brought established ecclesial patterns: for example, Baptist, Huntingdonian, Methodist, and Church of England. The other complexity is really the diverse tensions between peoples both from the African original diaspora (the new colonists who "returned" to Africa) and the native peoples. When all these factors are combined, it is clear that it was not an easy road to achieve unity and concord.

Questions for study (fact type):

1. Name the four new evangelical organisations which were critical to the early mission history of Sierra Leone and Guinea for Presbyterians.
2. Who was the first Presbyterian chaplain to Africa?
3. Who was the first Presbyterian martyr in Africa?
4. What was the name of one of the first published books by a Presbyterian missionary to Africa?
5. In this chapter how is the word *"colonist"* defined?
6. Define what is meant by the term, *artisan missionary*.

Questions for study (reflection type):

1. Explain the diverse nature of the people groups to whom the early Scottish missionary societies endeavoured to work. Explain this same challenge as it relates to the first Presbyterian chaplain. Why was this diversity of people so challenging?
2. Write a two-paragraph summation to answer the question, "What was the Clapham Sect?"

Select Bibliography

Brunton, Henry. *A Grammar and Vocabulary of the Susoo Language to which are added, the names of some of the Susoo towns, near the banks of the Rio Pongas: a small catalogue of Arabic books, and a list of the names of some of the learned men of the Mandingo and Foulah countries, etc.* Edinburgh: J. Ritchie, 1802.

Brunton, Henry. *Mawhoring se siring Susu dimēdiëk bè se ra. Second Catechism for the Susoo Children.* Edinburgh: J. Ritchie, 1801.

Clarke, John. "Singular Piety in a Female African." [letter 29 July 1796] *Evangelical Magazine* 4 (1796): 460–464.

Currie, David Allan. "The Growth of Evangelicalism in the Church of Scotland, 1793–1843." PhD thesis, University of St. Andrew's, 1990. Good on the Societies.

Flynn, Thomas. *The Western Christian Presence in the Russias and Qājār Persia, c.1760–c.1870.* Leiden: Brill, 2017. Overview of Brunton's work as a missionary.

Hair, P. E. H. "A West African in Tartary: Story of Jellorum Harrison." *West African Review* (March 1962): 45–47.

Killingray, David. "Godly Examples and Christian Agents: Training African Missionary Workers in British Institutions in the Nineteenth Century." In *Europe as the Other: External Perspectives on European Christianity*, eds., Judith Becker and Brian Stanley. Göttingen: Vandenhoeck & Ruprecht, 2014. Jellorum Harrison reference.

Life and Letters of Zachary Macaulay. Edited by Viscountess Knutsford. London: Edward Arnold, 1900. Helpful primary source materials.

London Missionary Society: A Register of Missionaries, Deputations, etc. From 1796 to 1923. Compiled by James Sibree. London: LMS, 1923.

Mouser, Bruce L. "African academy – Clapham 1799–1806." *History of Education* 33.1 (2004): 87–103.

Mouser, Bruce L. "Origins of Church Missionary Society Accommodation to Imperial Policy: The Sierra Leone Quagmire and the Closing of the Susu Mission, 1804–17." *Journal of Religion in Africa* 39 (2009): 375–402.

Philip, Robert. *The Life, Times, and Missionary Enterprises of The Rev. John Campbell.* London: John Snow, 1841.

Smith, George. "Peter Greig: First Scottish Missionary Martyr." In *Twelve Pioneer Missionaries.* London: Thomas Nelson, 1900, 122–136.

Tomkins, Stephen. *The Clapham Sect: How Wilberforce's Circle Transformed Britain.* Oxford: Lion, 2010.

Walls, Andrew F. *Crossing Cultural Frontiers: Studies in the History of World Christianity.* Maryknoll, NY: Orbis, 2017.

Whyte, Iain. *Zachary Macaulay 1768–1838: The Steadfast Scot in the British Anti-Slavery Movement.* Liverpool: Liverpool University Press, 2011.

Walls, Andrew F. "Sierra Leone, Afroamerican Remigration and the Beginnings of Protestantism in West Africa (18th–19th Centuries)." In *Transcontinental Links in the History of Non–Western Christianity*, ed. Klaus Koschorke, 45–56. Wiesbaden: Harrassowitz Verlag, 2002.

Walls, Andrew F. "A Christian Experiment: The Early Sierra Leone Colony." *Studies in Church History* 6 (1970): 107–29.

Chapter 2

Beginnings, Part Two: The Cape, c.1800–c.1840s, Taking Root

J. C. Whytock

Chapter Outline
1. Introduction
2. Cape Town Beginnings: A motherkirk
3. The Frontier Settler Church of the Cape Colony
4. Missions in the Eastern Districts of the Cape
5. Chapter Summary Conclusion

1. Introduction

It looked like society-led, interdenominational Presbyterian mission work in Africa was over by the early years of the 19th century as the successful establishment of a lasting Presbyterian mission work did not materialise in West Africa. (As we have noted, there were certain lasting themes and influences but no enduring structural or ecclesial works.) Yet, providentially, a second beginning emerged further south in Africa, at the Cape. This can be separated into three distinct yet intertwined strands across the Cape (in a broad sense): the formation of a congregation in Cape Town, settler congregations further east in the Cape Colony, and a society-directed mission – also in the far eastern districts of the Cape and into the borderlands.

This second beginning had many Scottish connections that involved lay initiative, a clerical presence, diaspora immigrants, and mission societies (not of a Scottish General Assembly-directed mission). What follows now are the stories of these three strands that began in the early 1800s and led to the establishment of the first permanent Presbyterian churches/missions in Africa across the Cape Colony. In fact, by 1830 there was a structure and a mission established. This chapter will thus focus on these early years of the second "beginning" by Scottish Presbyterians.

2. Cape Town Beginnings: A *motherkirk*[1]

A Scottish Regiment and Rev. George Thom

In 1806 the British occupied the Cape for a second time to prevent the French from using the Cape as a refreshing station. As a result, the Cape became a garrison for British soldiers; one of the regiments was the 93rd [Sutherland] Highlanders. Within this regiment were men of pious, evangelical, and Reformed convictions, and they formed themselves into a society in 1808. It was known as The Calvinist Society and was a reviving of an earlier society from the first occupation time when they had been encouraged to form such a society by an LMS missionary who preached for them, William Read before he went to Ceylon.[2] As a society, they worshipped, prayed, studied, and collected money for gospel work.

When Rev. George Thom (1789–1842) arrived in Cape Town on 24 October 1812 on route to India, he met with The Calvinist Society and began preaching for them. Rev. Thom was a Church of Scotland minister, having been ordained by the Scots Presbytery London at the Scots Kirk, London Wall[3] to work as a missionary with the London Missionary Society (LMS). He had travelled out with John Campbell, also with the LMS. It was decided that Thom would remain at the Cape and in effect become the agent for the LMS and work with the slaves, KhoiKhoi, and prisoners.

▲ George Thom

In addition to this work with the LMS, Thom proceeded to organise the first Presbyterian congregation in South Africa by receiving forty members of The Calvinist Society into a new church with a proper constitution and with local presbyterian church government. One may well debate, which was Thom's primary job, but in all likelihood the bulk of his financial support came from the newly organised congregation, akin to a chaplaincy arrangement. Thus, on 6 May 1813, a church constitution was adopted. The first article reads as follows:

---

1   I have used motherkirk as a single word, not as two words, more reflective of the Afrikaans context, *moederkerk*. Occasionally *moedergemeente* is used by some writers.
2   Read is also sometimes spelt Reid, but the *Register of Missionaries [LMS]*, uses the spelling Read, page 5, entry # 75.
3   Again, CoS in a broad sense as this Presbytery also was tolerant of Secessionists. Kenneth M. Black, *The Scots Churches in England* (Edinburgh: William Blackwood, 1906), 179 and 55 for London Wall congregation.

> 1. *Doctrine. The doctrines contained in the Catechism of the Westminster Divines, which, in sum, is that which is believed by the Reformed Churches on the Continent of Europe and the Kirk of Scotland.*

The first communion service was held on the first Sabbath in July 1813 and ninety sat at the table. Then on 5 August 1813, six elders were elected "according to the Westminster Confession of Faith;" two weeks later two became elders. It would appear the others became deacons at that time. There is some confusion about the numbers appointed and some literature refers to some of these as "assistants." Members of the congregation were gathered from the public in Cape Town and from the regiment.

The church grew and embraced those with a diversity of backgrounds – Church of Scotland, Scottish Secessionist Presbyterians, Scottish Baptists, Scottish Congregationalists, and Church of England – about 200 congregants within the year. However, in 1814 the congregation shrank dramatically to a mere twenty-seven members (both civil and military) as the 93rd Regiment was removed to Britain for service, then to North America. Thom wrote in a letter from the Cape in 1814 (which is quoted in part by Gordon Balfour in his *Presbyterianism in the Colonies* about the first "British Presbyterian Church in Cape Colony"):

> When the 93rd Highlanders left Cape Town last month there were among them 156 members of the Church (including three elders and three deacons) all of whom, so far as man can know the heart from the life, were pious persons. The Regiment was certainly a pattern for morality and good behaviour to every other corps. They read their Bible; they observed the Sabbath; they saved their money in order to do good; 7000 rix dollars (1,400 pounds currency) the non-commissioned officers and privates gave for books, societies, and support of the Gospel – a sum perhaps unparalleled in any other corps in the world, given in the short span of 17 or 18 months . . . but if ever apostolic days were revived in modern times on earth I certainly believe some of these to have been granted to us in Africa.[4]

Rev. Thom continued to serve as the minister for this congregation and as an agent for the LMS. This arrangement continued until 1818, when Rev. Thom accepted a call to become the minister of the Dutch Reformed Church (DRC) in Caledon, Cape

---

4   Balfour, *Presbyterianism*, 283–284.

Colony and to undertake mission work amongst the slaves and KhoiKhoi. It would appear the reason for this change was twofold. First, there were tensions in the LMS in 1817–1818 at the Cape over missionary lifestyles and over slavery.[5] Second, it was now obvious that the local Scottish Church was not in a financial position to fund Thom. This left the Scottish Church vacant for two years until the arrival of Rev. John Philip and his appointment in 1820 to the church, again combining it with work for the LMS. John Philip was a Congregationalist who knew Thom well (Thom had once been a member of Philip's Belmont congregation in Aberdeen). Philip led the congregation to formally adopt a Congregational polity, where all appeals were to go to the congregational meeting. The Presbyterians were a minority after the 1820 reorganization yet remained within this reorganized congregation and worshipped there, hence the name "Union" Chapel – reflective of being Congregational *and* Presbyterian.

Therefore, technically the first Presbyterian Church in South Africa lasted for seven years, 1813–1820 and then as a "union" congregation for four years before a second birth. In 1824, a provisional committee was formed to "re-establish" or "resuscitate" a Presbyterian church in Cape Town, its second birth. This committee was likely induced for three reasons: immigration from Britain in the ensuing four years; employees coming to the Cape from the East India Company who advocated for a separate Presbyterian Church; and the prospect of soliciting government funds.

The names of the work both in 1813 and in 1824 appear variously as the Scotch Church, the Scottish Church, or the Scottish National Church, thus reflecting ethnicity and affinities to the established Church of Scotland. The 1824 committee knew that this time they needed government money to make the work succeed.

Rev. James Adamson

The provisional committee was given permission by the governor (Somerset) to hold a public meeting in the Lutheran Church on Strand Street on 25 November 1824, under the chairmanship of Mr Alexander MacDonald. Advisors at this meeting included DRC ministers Rev. Andrew Murray, Sr. of Graaff-Reinet and Rev. Smith of Uitenhage, who addressed the public gathering about Presbyterian church government. Other matters dealt with at the meeting included making resolutions to be "connected" with the Church of Scotland, to begin a subscription to build their own church building, and to communicate with presbyteries in Scotland and the General Assembly to promote the work in Cape Town.

---

5   For further discussion about some of these issues, see, Richard Lovett, *The History of the London Missionary Society 1795–1895*. Vol.1 (London: Henry Frowde, 1899), "Thom was a well-meaning but highly opinionated man, more eager to listen to charges … than to sift and weigh the evidence upon which the charges were based …," 535.

This provisional committee lasted from 25 November 1824 until 1828, when a session was formed. Land was acquired for the Scotch Church in April 1825 on Somerset Street. The government pledged one third of the cost of the building. An architect was secured, Henry Willey Reveley (1789–1875), and he designed a building in the Greek Revival style with a prominent Doric portico – not a hint of any neo-Gothic in this building! The foundation stone was laid on 20 October 1827 and the building opened officially in May 1829. It can still be seen today in Cape Town. Though the building did not "make" the congregation, it was a great aid for ministry and mission and convenience. From 1813 until this building was opened, the Presbyterians had met in *Die Groote Kerk*, the Lutheran Church, the South African Missionary Society premises, and the LMS/Union Chapel premises.

▲ (St. Andrew's) Scottish Church, Cape Town

The provisional committee also made efforts to secure a minister. This request was finally remitted by the General Assembly in Scotland to the Presbytery of Edinburgh. They located a candidate, James Adamson (1797–1875) of the Presbytery of Cupar, and he was ordained "as a minister of the Gospel and as Pastor of the Scottish Church at Cape Town, Cape of Good Hope." Adamson arrived at the Cape in November 1827 and began preaching immediately. Services were held in the Lutheran Church building. He formed a session with assessors; one was a minister in the DRC (Rev. James Edgar). In May of 1829, a full Kirk session was formed.

In August 1829 the trustees adopted the new name of St. Andrew's. This name change was not without controversy. Mr James Abercrombie protested the use of this name as "a relic of Popery." For several years after, the name seems to have gone back and forth between the Scottish Church and St. Andrew's but with the dominant name being The Scottish Church or The Scottish Presbyterian Church. Only after the later 1880s was it consistently called St. Andrew's. One scholarly paper uses both names together as one name – "St. Andrew's Scottish Church," which evidently was also a name the congregation was referred to as in the mid-19th century. If one looks to Australia or Mauritius and some of the first names for Presbyterian churches there, one finds striking parallels. First, the word "Presbyterian" is not often used and the word "Scots" and even "St. Andrew's Scots Church" appears frequently. Hence, there was nothing very unusual here in Cape Town.

Mission Congregation and School, Cape Town

Rev. Adamson continued to fan the flame for local mission work. This was accelerated greatly after Emancipation.[6] Appeals were made to Scotland for the General Assembly to send out a missionary to help with the St. Andrew's Mission but to no avail. Thus, it was decided to employ Rev. G. W. Stegman(n), minister of the Lutheran Church at the time, to conduct the mission to the emancipated slaves, coloured peoples, and the Muslim community in 1838. Mr W. Gorrie was also appointed as a lay assistant, and support came from the Dutch Reformed Church, the Lutheran Church, and St. Andrew's – a unique three-fold mission endeavour in many ways parallel to the societies as here all three parties were paedobaptists.

This mission work increased, and in time there was a re-alignment, not without acrimony, whereby the bulk of this mission became an independent congregation (St. Stephen's) and other missions emerged forming The Apostolic Union of missions around Cape Town and further afield.[7] Latterly, St. Stephen's joined the Dutch Reformed Church under Rev. Stegman, who also joined the Dutch Reformed Church. The Scottish Mission and its congregation and school under St. Andrew's continued a smaller scale with a mission school attached to the Church until 1896 (when the mission school was turned over to the public

---

6 On 28 August 1833 the Slave Emancipation Act was passed granting slaves in the British Empire freedom. It was to come into effect on 1 August 1834. It thus was illegal to own and sell humans as property.

7 The Apostolic Union (AU) at its height had about 10 missions under its auspices. In 1850 the AU approached the Free Church of Scotland to affect a handover to that body for a mission field but the Free Church due to financial limitations did not accept the proposed handover. Dalziel, "The Origin and Growth of Presbyterian Ordinances," 92.

educational system). Adamson's successor, Rev. George Morgan, was directly involved in the Scottish Mission by preaching in Dutch for the mission services.

Rev. Adamson was not only pastoring the Scottish Church but was also very involved with the South African College. He had a great burden for that institution and did all that he could to ensure that it did not collapse. Thus, in a certain sense the story of the Scottish Church is also connected to the history of higher education in the Cape.

Rev. Adamson resigned as minister of St. Andrew's in 1841 yet remained as "assistant" for some time until he eventually went to Oxford, Pennsylvania for educational work there before returning to the Cape Colony. Rev. Morgan had come out to Cape Colony as one of George Thom's recruits and served the Dutch Reformed Church in Somerset East from 1824 to 1841 and the Scottish Church, Cape Town from 1841 to 1871. Under his ministry the congregation prospered numerically to the extent that a seating gallery was added, and a mission day school building was built next to the church. This mission day school gained a strong reputation in Cape Town.

The Scottish Church, Cape Town experienced some division when the Disruption occurred in Scotland, as some charged the Church here with local patronage and Erastianism.[8] The result was that a Free Church of Scotland congregation and mission emerged in Cape Town in 1846. The matter of patronage and Erastianism was not exactly clear in all regards in the Cape Town work. Rev. Morgan took up his pen to defend the cause of the local Scottish Church by claiming freedom from patronage, while at the same time extolling the benefits of the Establishment for the Scottish Church in Cape Town. A summary of Morgan's arguments reads as follows:

> ... the said Scottish Church [Cape Town] was an isolated Presbyterian congregation, that it was not under the jurisdiction of the Church of Scotland, and that the Government, though giving pecuniary aid, had never claimed the right of patronage with regard to the appointment of the ministers.[9]

When Rev. Adamson was ordained for the work in Cape Town, he had been ordained for the congregation there; but the Presbytery of Edinburgh had no jurisdiction over the congregation and never inducted him. Was the Scottish Church, Cape Town thus under the Church of Scotland, and could it be charged with Erastianism? Not all agreed, and so a Free Church of Scotland congregation

---

8   A position held by some which says the state has supremacy in ecclesiastical matters.
9   *St. Andrew's Presbyterian Church, Cape Town: A Centenary Record*, 14.

and mission were formed in Cape Town in 1846 under Rev. W. Gorrie and Rev. E. Miller. Rev. Gorrie was ordained at Free St. George's, Edinburgh in 1846 for the work in Cape Town. However, large sympathies were never there in Cape Town for the Free Church, and it was a hard task to establish another Scottish Presbyterian mission work there. The result was that, due to financial constraints, in 1851 the General Assembly of the Free Church of Scotland closed the work in Cape Town and sold the property there to pay for debts incurred. Gorrie had once worked with the Scottish Church, Cape Town before the Disruption as a lay-assistant missionary and also taught at the South African College. Thus ended a short chapter of Free Church of Scotland work in Cape Town in the 1840s and early 50s.

Though the Scottish Church, Cape Town was a Presbyterian entity without a presbytery, it did have close fraternity with the evangelical movement within the Dutch Reformed Church. A summary review of these connections is helpful. Recall that Revs. Smith and Murray of the DRC had addressed the public meeting in which Presbyterianism was re-established in Cape Town in 1824. In fact, it was from the DRC where at least one assessor elder came under Adamson for about two years (1828–29). But it went beyond this. Thom, of course, was key for all of this initially, but this close affinity remained a constant with Adamson and Morgan. For example, Rev. Adamson was at the famous Worcester Conference 18–19 April 1860 and while there spoke about revival in America. Likewise, at the opening of the Huguenot School in Wellington, South Africa in 1873, Rev. Morgan was there and spoke about the French Huguenots. The close ties with the Scottish evangelical group within the Dutch Reformed Church continued for many years by the Presbyterian Motherkirk and her ministers. In some senses one can argue the relationship to the Scottish ministers in the DRC and to the Scottish Church was a *"quasi-presbytery"* to this very isolated mother Presbyterian congregation and its daughters around the Cape Town area. A Cape Town Presbytery was not formed until 1893. This Presbytery consisted of St. Andrew's, with a separate preaching point at Gardens, plus the separate charges of Woodstock, and Clifton Hill and had four ministers in 1893: Revs. Russell, Maver, Yule, and Taylor. Missions would be developed at Ndabeni, Touws River, and Matjiesfontein.[10]

Summary Conclusion

It is good to remember how and where in God's providence the first Presbyterian Church in South Africa and all of Africa was established. Its roots were not with a carefully developed mission strategy nor with a sending society as such.

---

10 Dalziel, "The Origin and Growth of Presbyterian Ordinances," 107, 114.

Rather, the core foundation was laid by laymen who gathered as a local society of like-minded believers to do good and to nurture one another. They needed shepherding and a young twenty-four-year-old Scot stepped into that gap. It is also a reminder that church planting is not always a straight road of continuous growth and development. Thom's time with this new congregation spanned about six years; and then there was a vacancy for two years followed by absorption for four years into a Union Chapel context, which was of course closely related yet still distinct from an evangelical Presbyterian church. Then came about the "resuscitation," and here we find Establishment issues as part of the history in the colonial African context and eventually a short-lived division over this. Also running together in this brief overview of the beginning years of the Motherkirk's development was local missions work. This work certainly never developed to the extent that was seen in the Eastern Cape by Scottish Presbyterians there, but it was clearly a significant local mission undertaking which must be properly acknowledged.

Today there are many Presbyterian churches throughout various regions of Africa, yet there must always be a first. The history of the Presbyterian Motherkirk in South Africa is a story that intertwines the colonial/imperial and the missionary/chaplain, the transitional and the permanent, the ecclesiastical controversies of home and the realities and complexities of a new context.

This chapter also raises the question concerning who may be called the founder of Presbyterianism in South Africa? Some have claimed James Adamson. This is very questionable for several reasons, not least being that there were Scottish Presbyterian missionaries and settlers in the Eastern Cape who had predated Adamson's arrival. Was it George Thom? Was it laity? Each of the above may be correct in some sense.

3. The Frontier Settler Church of the Cape, 1820

Another beginning stream which shared both continuity and discontinuity with what was formed and developed in Cape Town, was the settler/immigrant Presbyterian church on the frontier of Cape Colony. This stream brought together a complexity of realities, a predominately civilian diaspora people bringing their church and traditions with them and replanting such in a new land. At the heart of this was ministry to the diaspora community. Indigenous mission was in view by some but not universally. The settler community was greatly enlarged in 1820 with the arrival of 4,000+ British settlers.[11]

---

11 There were scattered British settlers in Cape Colony and the frontier area prior to 1820 some of whom were Presbyterians such as Robert Hart. See, David Hilton-Barber, *Robert Hart, the first English-speaking settler in South Africa.* (Pinetown, KZN: Footprints Press, 2018).

A Survey of Presbyterian Mission History in Africa

The first Presbyterian congregation on the frontier can be traced to the work of Thomas Pringle (1789–1834), the leader of the Scottish Party of the 1820 settlers. Pringle took the Scottish settlers inland to the Baviaans River Valley, north of what is now Bedford, in the Eastern Cape. A record of the first worship services which he conducted there on 2 July 1820 reads as follows:

▲ Thomas Pringle

The next day, July 2nd, was our first Sunday on our own grounds. Feeling deeply the importance of maintaining the suitable observance of this day of sacred rest, it was unanimously resolved that we should strictly abstain from all secular employment not sanctioned by absolute necessity; and at the same time commence such a system of religious services as might be with propriety maintained in the absence of a clergyman or minister. The whole party were accordingly assembled after breakfast, under a venerable acacia tree, on the margin of the little stream which murmured around our camp. The river appeared shaded here and there by the graceful willow of Babylon, which grows abundantly along the banks of many of the African streams, and which, with the other peculiar features of the scenery, vividly reminded us of the pathetic lament of the Hebrew exiles: – "By the rivers of Babylon, there we sat; yea we wept when we remembered Zion. We hanged our harps upon the willows in the midst thereof" [Psalm 137] ... It was, indeed, an affecting sight to look round on our little band of Scottish emigrants, thus congregated for the first time to worship God in the wild glen allotted for their future home and the heritage of their offspring. Having selected one of the hymns of our national church, all united in singing it to one of the old pathetic melodies with which it is usually conjoined in the sabbath worship of our native land. The day was bright and still, and the voice of psalms rose with a sweet and touching solemnity among those wild mountains, where the praise of the true God had never, in all human probability, been sung before. The works of the hymn (composed by Logan) were appropriate to our situation, and affected some of our congregation very sensibly: – "O God of Bethel by whose hand thy people still are fed: Who through this weary pilgrimage hast all our fathers led: Through each perplexing path of life our wandering footsteps guide; Give us each day our daily bread, and raiment fit provide: O! spread thy covering wings around, till all our wanderings cease, And at our Father's loved abode our souls arrive in peace."[12] We then read some of the most suitable portions of the English Liturgy, which we considered preferable to any extempore service that could be substituted on this occasion; and concluded with an excellent discourse from a volume of sermons presented to me on parting by my honoured relative the Rev. Dr. Pringle of Perth. We had a similar service in the afternoon; and agreed to maintain in this manner the public worship of God in our infant settlement, until it should please Him, in his good Providence, to privilege it with the ecclesiastical dispensation of religious ordinances.[13]

Pringle saw the settler entrance into the valley as part of a threefold undertaking to establish a settlement to provide a livelihood for people, to aid civilising influences, and to help spread the Gospel to others, whatever the people group that one might encounter. Shortly after he was there, he also began services in Dutch so that he could minister to a wider community as many – black, white, and coloured – knew that language. His concern was to reach out with the gospel. He was a friend of many missionaries, and when he returned to England, he became secretary of the Anti-Slavery Society in league with Zachary Macaulay with whom he shared friendship and the same convictions.

A church building was erected in 1828 and still stands at Glen Lynden. Technically, it was completed while the St. Andrew's Scottish Church was being built in Cape Town.[14] Pringle recruited Rev. John Pears (1790–1866) from the UK to come and serve as the minister of this Presbyterian Church in Glen Lynden. He only stayed one year (1829–30) before moving onto Cape Town and then Somerset East. The make up of the Glen Lynden congregation was augmented with local Boer farmers also joining such that the congregation became associated with the DRC for ministerial help and really became a bilingual English and Dutch

---

12 Scottish Paraphrase 2.
13 Pringle, *Narrative*, 35–38.
14 This challenges the common misconception that St. Andrew's in Cape Town was the first building.

congregation quickly – almost a type of "union" charge, DRC and Presbyterian. Its second minister was ordained by the Presbytery of St. Andrews, Scotland, Rev. Alexander Welsh. He then also joined the DRC when at Glen Lynden, so some type of informal Presbyterian and DRC arrangement existed very early on in Glen Lynden. Other "settler" or immigrant Presbyterian churches emerged, such as in Grahamstown in 1827, Glenthorn in 1840. The latter was more a mission station ministering to a diversity of people groups including the settlers. Scottish Presbyterians also established union congregations on the frontier with Congregationalists during the first half of the 19th century. Financial and demographic realities in many of these rural areas necessitated such cooperation. The story of these settler Presbyterian churches will continue in the story of Presbyterian tributaries and unions later in the 19th and 20th centuries.[15]

We close here by quoting from the memorial stone of Thomas Pringle who was buried in London and reinterred in the Baviaans River Valley in Eildon. It is a fitting tribute which connects the legacy of Macaulay and Pringle:

> *In the wide sphere of humanity he was revered*
> *As the advocate and protector of the oppressed ... Having lived to witness the cause in which he Had ardently and energetically laboured, triumph In the emancipation of the Negro,*
> *He was himself called from the bondage of this world To the enjoyment of eternal liberty*
> *Through the merits of His redeemer.*

Summary Conclusion

Diaspora settler/immigrant Presbyterian congregations were established in the frontier area from 1820 onwards. A key leader for this in the initial stage was the lay Presbyterian leader Thomas Pringle who shared evangelical convictions with many others of his time which were often out-of-step with contemporaries in the colonial Cape community. Alliances with both Afrikaner Reformed and English Congregationalists were formed in many locales. Settler Presbyterian churches emerged on the frontier with mixed results and efforts in indigenous missions. By-and-large, it was a church community for the diaspora settlers.

---

15 See chapter four.

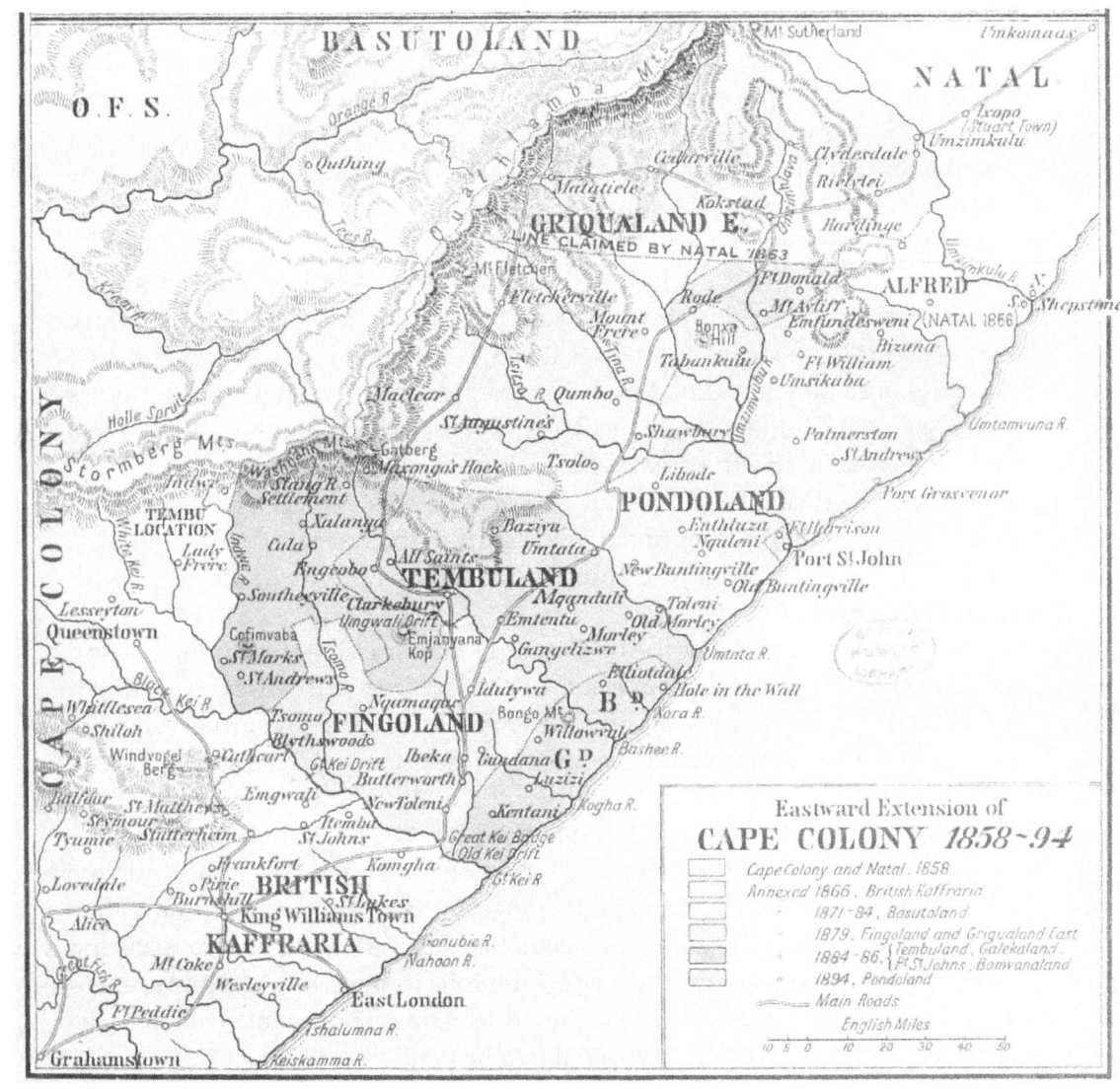

▲ Map of Eastward extension of Cape Colony

4. Missions in the Eastern Districts of the Cape
Planting Seeds and Watering Them
In 1821 the first missionaries of the Glasgow Missionary Society arrived at Tyume (Chumie)[16] in the Eastern Cape. The backstory to the arrival of the GMS here must however acknowledge the seeds that were first planted earlier by the LMS.

---

16 Chumie was an older spelling, but it can also be Tyumie and more popularly today, Tyume.

In 1799–1800, Dr Johannes van der Kemp of the LMS had a mission in what is now the Alice area on the Chumie and Keiskamma rivers for 16 months. He had met King Gika and baptised a SanKhoi woman somewhere on the Keiskamma River where it seems he ran a small school. He roamed from the Katbergs as far east as the Buffalo River. Thus, Shepherd writes: "The great fact remains that he was the first missionary to the Bantu tribes of Southern Africa. He blazed the trail that his successors followed ..."[17]

Next came Rev. and Mrs Joseph Williams, 1816, LMS missionaries who established a school and church on the Kat River, north of today's Fort Beaufort. Williams had ministered from the Kat through to the Chumie. It was a mixed mission to Xhosa and SanKhoi. Rev. Williams died in 1818, but the gospel seeds had been planted. Williams influenced the noted Ntsikana, author of *Ulo Thixo omkhulu ngosezulwini* (He the great God, high in heaven).

Rev. John Brownlee was sent by the LMS as Williams' replacement. He settled at the Chumie (Gwali Mission), about 15 miles from the Kat Mission in June 1820. Several from the Kat moved to Chumie to be under Brownlee's tutelage, with Ntsikana's urging.

It was into this context that the GMS sent its first missionaries to the Eastern Cape. It was to be the second mission of the GMS to the African Continent and was to become its most significant mission in many regards. Why the Eastern Cape? The answer really goes back to Rev. George Thom who in 1820 was in Scotland and was asked to address the GMS. Thom urged the GMS to send missionaries to the Eastern Cape and to Tyume. Though Thom was now with the DRC, he maintained strong connections with the GMS and thus his recommendation for the GMS to come alongside the mission in Tyume Valley was completely understandable. The seeds had been planted – more watering was needed. Rev. Thom conducted a speaking tour in the UK to raise awareness and collected funds for this new GMS mission. Thus, Thom's involvement was critical to the raising up of this new field for the GMS.

The first two missionaries selected by the GMS for the mission at the Tyume were William Ritchie Thomson (1794–1891) and John Bennie (1796–1869); both were recommended by Thomas Chalmers and John Love. Thomson was ordained in London by Presbyterian ministers, of the Kirk, Secession, and the Genevan Church (C. Malan) before being sent. Bennie was sent as a lay catechist. They reached Tyume station on 15 November 1821. Bennie was put in charge of the school for Xhosa and SanKhoi children and adults. Very quickly he proved to be a capable linguist and laid a foundation which would be used by other missionaries. The three missionaries worked together and developed a strategy

---

17 Shepherd, *Where Aloes Flame*, 87.

whereby Bennie met with the children for devotions each morning and evening, Thomson with the women, and Brownlee with the men. In many ways it was a Salem community parallel to the Moravian strategy.

In 1823, Rev. & Mrs John Ross were sent out under the GMS but with the official sanction of his presbytery in Scotland. In many regards, this marked a first of the Church starting to take on more fully its role in missions and working in cooperation with a mission society, perhaps a transitional phase of ecclesial missions with society missions. On route (under John Brownlee who met them in Cape Town) the party visited Genadendal and observed the methodology of that Moravian station. The party arrived at Tyume in December of 1823. Earlier (on June 30, 1823) the first baptisms had occurred – five adults – and then in July seven children were baptized by Rev. Thomson.[18] The five adults all attributed their first hearing of the gospel under Rev. Williams' ministry – one waters and another reaps.[19] The GMS missionaries reported *"We have entered into the labours of our departed brother ..."* and *"Now, then, the foundation of a church is laid in Caffraria; and O that Zion's God would give us strength to go forward in the erection of a noble edifice on it, may it endure as long as the sun, and be a glory and a desire, to the tribes on our north! May He watch over this infant church, feeding and defending it, by His grace and power! May it be one of His jewels, in which He has pleasure, and which he has honour."*[20] Then in November 1823, the first communion service was held in the Tyume Valley.

With the Rosses came a Ruthven printing press. By the end of December 1823, the first Xhosa literature had been printed by John Ross under John Bennie's linguistic hand. Bennie has often been nicknamed the "father of Xhosa literature." He translated the Lord's Prayer, catechisms,

▲ John Bennie

---

18 Rev. Thomson left for Balfour to work amongst the KhoiSan in 1830 with the DRC and remained there until he died in 1896. R. W. Barbour's title, "The First Scottish Missionary in South Africa," in *The Catholic Presbyterian*, (August 1880), 101–109, though helpful, is a most unfortunate title for the article and is misleading.
19 In June 1823, three of those baptised composed a Christian letter in Xhosa of greetings and thanks to the GMS in Scotland through their teacher John Bennie. *Report GMS 1824*, 13–14.
20 *Report GMS 1824*, 12.

51 hymns, and slowly worked through the translation of the scriptures as well as developing grammars.²¹

More mission stations were added in the 1820s to c.1840. This meant a school and a church plus outlying schools and churches were connected into a district. More missionaries arrived – ordained ministers, artisans, teachers, and catechists – to labour in this mission for the GMS. These new stations were Ncera (renamed Lovedale), Balfour, Burnshill, Pirie, Igqibigha and Glenthorn in the Mankazana Valley with missionary names, Chalmers, McDiarmid, Weir, Laing, Niven, Cumming, M'Laren,²² and Govan in this early period up to c.1840. These were all connected with the Glasgow mission societies and represented different strands of Scottish Presbyterian denominations: Relief, Secession, and Kirk or Church of Scotland. Native teachers and evangelists were also added to the ranks. Particular mention is made here of Robert Balfour and Charles Henry, two from the 1823 baptisms.

▲ Burnshill Missionary Station, painting by Thomas Bowler

The Presbytery of Kaffraria, 1824

With Rev. John Ross' arrival, it was immediately decided to form a presbytery. This was to be the first presbytery on the Continent of Africa under subscription to the Westminster documents.

---

21 See charts in chapter 27 in this volume for details on Bennie and early Xhosa hymnals.
22 Miss M'Laren established a girls' school at Igquibigha in 1840 and she was supported by the Glasgow Ladies' Kaffrarian Society (GLKS) as its first society missionary in the Eastern Cape. This Society would later open another larger mission school at Mgwali.

Minutes of the first *Presbytery of Kaffraria* meeting[23]

Chumie Missionary Institution

1 January, 1824

The following individuals William Ritchie Thomson and John Ross ministers and John Bennie, elder, missionaries of the Glasgow Missionary Society or in connection with it being met the Rev. W. R. Thomson opened the meeting by prayer. It appeared that the nature and object of our mission called for the following declaration:

Whereas the Glory of God, the salvation of the souls of men, and the commandment of the exalted Redeemer by His Apostle, to do all things, in His Church, decently and in order require that we, the aforesaid individuals, and those who may be added to our number should, and do thus recognise The Doctrines contained in The Confession of Faith, the Larger and Shorter Catechisms agreed upon by the Assembly of Divines at Westminster and approved by the General Assembly of the Kirk of Scotland, and likewise the Directory of Public Worship of God, and the humble advice of the Assembly of Divines, which has by ordinance of Parliament at Westminster to the Right Honourable the Lords and Commons Assembled in Parliament, concerning Church Government as we believe the same to be expressive of the meaning of the Holy Scriptures and agreeable to the practice of the Apostles and primitive Church; and the rule that we as ministers of the gospel or servants in the Church of God resolve to walk by.

It seemed good unto us that William Ritchie Thomson, minister be Moderator, and John Ross, minister, Clerk, and that a book of Records be kept.

It seemed good unto us that we said Brethren meet together for the purpose of forwarding the glorious Gospel of the Blessed God which was committed to our trust and that our ordinary Meetings, as the Lord may give opportunity, be on the first Thursday of each month.

It seemed good unto us that the country around this Institution be apportioned into districts. On Tuesday, 6th mtg. and that these districts be regularly visited by two of the brethren going out to observe of them each Lord's Day, and one or more of the Brethren every Tuesday and Thursday: And to prevent the interruption of the daily instructing

---

23 *Minute Books of the Presbytery of Kaffraria, Volume one, 1824–1836*, MS. Cory Library, Rhodes University, MS 9037 [pages 1–2].

> the people of the Institution in the art of reading on the two latter days it seems good that the place of the Brother or Brethren whose duty it is to visit should be supplied by another.
>
> On the representation that Mr John Brownlee, Agent for the Colonial Government, holds sentiments which prevent him associating with us in the above manner it seemed good that W.R. Thomson, Minister, should acquaint him with our intentions as contained in the foregoing minute, and that he be called on to assist therein in as far as is consistent with his principles.
>
> It seemed good unto us that an open Journal be kept for recording what passes in these visits and at the Institution.
>
> It seemed good unto us that a monthly correspondence with the Glasgow Missionary Society should be carried on by each of the Brethren in rotation.
>
> *Meeting closed by prayer.*
> *W. R. Thomson, Moderator*

Since this first presbytery was constituted by missionaries of the GMS and "as its members belonged to different sections of the Scottish Church, it took up an independent position, unconnected with any of the Church Courts in Scotland" wrote Gordon Balfour.[24] It was basically to retain this independent status for about twenty years.

In reviewing the early minutes of the Presbytery of Kaffraria some matters of interest include: the original three presbyters often rotated the chair as moderator, which included Bennie the catechist as well; notations on proof printings and corrections for printing Xhosa literature are included in the minutes, including also Xhosa hymns of Bennie and revisions of these for worship services; information about schools in the districts and assigning teachers and the introduction of native teachers are recorded; discussion is noted on the diversity of people groups involved in the mission stations – Xhosa, Mfengu/Fingoes, Coloured, SanKhoi, Mozambicans, and Europeans and also the tensions between Xhosa and Fingoes and how one would leave if the other moved into the territory; destruction of stations is described; establishing irrigation systems and finding the best locations for such is debated; and the establishment of new stations is planned. The clear priority was evangelism, discipleship, and Christian educational training of the local peoples.[25] However, ministry was not excluded to the Settler community

---

24 Balfour, Presbyterianism, 284. Similar wording in volume 7, *Fasti Ecclesiae Scoticanae,* 560.
25 "The kraal-going missionary has made the kirk-going people" was a common expression that emerged about missions in the Eastern Cape amongst the Presbyterians.

either, such as instructions about supply preaching of Robert Niven to Glen Lynden. The presbytery very much ministered to all peoples with whom they came into contact.[26]

c.1837 to c.1847 Realignments

In 1837 the Glasgow Missionary Society divided and became two societies and over time this would impact the mission work in the Eastern Districts of the Cape. The continuing portion retained the name Glasgow Missionary Society and adhered to the establishment principle of the Church of Scotland. The other party, which was voluntarist in sympathy, changed the name to Glasgow Africa Missionary Society. The two missionaries in the Eastern Cape, Revs. William Chalmers and Niven sided with the new Glasgow Africa Missionary Society and were classified as its missionaries.

The Presbytery of Kaffraria remained a united Presbytery at this time in 1837 and to a degree took a neutral course for a few years. Then, on 30 August 1843, the Presbytery of Kaffraria had discussions about the "Free Protesting Church of Scotland" (Free Church) and showed its concurrence with this body. The result was that in 1845 the Free Church of Scotland Mission Board took over the Glasgow Missionary Society work in Kaffraria and hence the Presbytery of Kaffraria became identified with the Free Church in the years to come.

Also, (back in Scotland in 1847) when the Relief and Secession Churches united to form the United Presbyterian Church, they ended up assuming the work of the Glasgow Africa Missionary Society and this became their mission work in Kaffraria. The period from 1837 to 1847 marked a transitional period from the societies to denominationalism or more fully it marked a transitional period from interdenominational evangelical Reformed/Calvinist societies to a much more ecclesial mission approach and this became the nature of the next period.[27] In 1847 a separate United Presbyterian Presbytery of Kaffraria was formed.

Summary Conclusion

The decision of the Glasgow Missionary Society to enter the Eastern districts of the Cape at Thom's urging proved to result in one of the Societies' largest mission endeavours. It stood in direct contrast to their initial labours in West Africa which proved to be a short-lived field for the GMS. The scores of missionaries

---

26 This is not meant to be exhaustive but only a summation based upon select items from the MS minutes for these years 1824–1843.
27 Brian Stanley, "The Theology of the Scottish Protestant Missionary Movement," in *The History of Scottish Theology, Volume 3, The Long Twentieth century*, eds. David Fergusson and Mark W. Elliott. (Oxford: Oxford University Press, 2019), 55.

and native missionaries who served in this field of the Eastern Districts of the Cape have been noted above, yet each story has not been fully told. The reality that this mission built upon a foundation of previous LMS work must not be ignored. It certainly appears that at the first baptism service and first communion service there was a real sense of this unity. The initial period of establishment and development was a costly endeavour; the tensions of the region were a perennial issue. The establishment of the first presbytery in Africa connected to the Westminster documents stands as an historic milestone in mission history for Presbyterians.

5. Chapter Summary Conclusion

This chapter has attempted to identify the key organisations and names involved in the second beginning of Presbyterian mission work on the Continent of Africa in Cape Town, the Cape Frontier, and the Eastern Districts of the Cape, in essence three strands. Each area presented its own challenges, and each challenge is also worthy of reflection for contemporary ministry and church planting. By c.1830, Presbyterian missions and churches were established in Africa and a clearly identified organisation and work was established. Pastoral care, evangelism, discipleship, literature, and Christian education were key components of this mission work. The period of c.1800 to c.1840 intersects with many contextual matters such as economics/commerce, colonial expansion, imperialism, and evangelisation. Amid all of these complexities, the Lord's Church did advance.

Questions for study (fact type):

1. Write one paragraph giving five facts about George Thom.
2. Who was Thomas Pringle?
3. Name the first two missionaries sent in 1821 by the Glasgow Missionary Society to what is now the Eastern Cape.
4. What year was the first presbytery in Africa constituted?
5. What year did the Glasgow Missionary Society divide into two societies?

Questions for study (reflection type):

1. Discuss what it means when it is said that the 1840s were a "transitional period from interdenominational evangelical Reformed/Calvinist societies to a much more ecclesial mission approach which was to become the nature of the next period."
2. Review the minute of the first presbytery meeting and comment upon the mission strategy that was encapsulated in that minute.
3. Discuss the parallels between the historic settler/immigrant diaspora congregations in the Cape and modern African diaspora congregations in Europe.

Select Bibliography

Cape Town

Balfour, G. *Presbyterianism in the Colonies.* Edinburgh: MacNiven & Wallace, 1899.

Bower, Douglas K. "The Christian Witness of the Presbyterian Church of South Africa against Apartheid between 1948–1994." HonsBA thesis, University of Pretoria, 2013.

Cuthbertson, G. C. "The St. Andrew's Scottish Church Mission in Cape Town, 1838–1878." *Contree* 9 (January 1981): 12–18.

Dalziel, John. "The Origin and Growth of Presbyterian Ordinances of Worship among English speaking European South Africans Prior to the Formation of the Presbyterian Church of South Africa in 1897." PhD thesis, University of Edinburgh, 1957.

Duncan, Graham A. "The Migratory Dimension of Scottish Presbyterianism in Southern Africa." *African Historical Review* 47.2 (2015): 89–118.

"George Thom Collection MS160." J. S. Gericke Library Document Centre, University of Stellenbosch.

Jardine, Alexander J. A. *A Fragment of Church History at the Cape of Good Hope.* Original 1827. Reprint, Cape Town: South African Library, 1979.

[Rodger, J. ed.] *St. Andrew's Presbyterian Church, Cape Town: A Centenary Record.* Cape Town: Presbyterian Bookroom, 1929.

Sass, Frederick William. "The Influence of the Church of Scotland on the Dutch Reformed Church of South Africa." PhD thesis, University of Edinburgh, 1956.

Scott, Hew, comp. *Fasti Ecclesiae Scoticanae.* Vol. 7. Original 1866. New Edition, Edinburgh: Oliver & Boyd, 1928.

Whytock, Jack C. "A Forgotten Anniversary (1813–2013): The Presbyterian Motherkirk in South Africa. *Die Presbiteriannse Moederkerk in Suid-Afrika.*" *Haddington House Journal* 16 (2014): 31–38.

The Frontier Settler Church

Duncan, as above.

Glen Thorn Presbyterian Church: Its Influence on the spread of the Gospel in the Mankazana Valley … [1840–1990]. No pl. no pub. 1990.

Hilton-Barber, David. *Robert Hart: The first English-speaking settler in South Africa.* South Africa: Footprint Press, 2018.

Hofmeyr, J. W. and Gerald J. Pillay, eds. *A History of Christianity in South Africa.* Vol.1. Pretoria: HAUM Tertiary, 1994.

Pringle, Thomas. *Narrative of a Residence in South Africa*. New Edition. London: Edward Moxon, 1835.

Sass, Frederick William. "The Influence of the Church of Scotland on the Dutch Reformed Church of South Africa." PhD thesis, University of Edinburgh, 1956.

Missions in the Eastern Districts of the Cape

Bennie, John. *A Systematic Vocabulary of the Kaffrarian Language in two parts to which is prefixed an Introduction to Kaffrarian Grammar.* Lovedale: GMS, 1826. Plus, Dictionaries, 1831; Mark, 1837; reader, 1839; Xhosa hymnal, 1839.

Hewat, Elizabeth G. K. *Vision and Achievement 1796–1956: A History of the Foreign Missions of the Churches uniting in the Church of Scotland*. Edinburgh: Thomas Nelson, 1960.

Minute Books of the Presbytery of Kaffraria, Volume one, 1824–1836. MS. Cory Library, Rhodes University, MS 9037.

Minute Books of the Presbytery of Kaffraria, Volume two, 1836–1845. MS. Cory Library, Rhodes University, MS 9038.

Minute Books of the Presbytery of Kaffraria, Volume three, 1845–1865. MS. Cory Library, Rhodes University, MS 9039.

Report of the Glasgow Missionary Society, for 1822. Glasgow: Andrew Young, 1822. Also, for 1823, 1824ff.

Ross, John S. "The trivial round, the common task: minutes of the Missionary Board of the Glasgow Missionary Society (1838–1843)." *In die Skriflig* 43:3 (2009): 563–583.

Scott, Hew, comp. *Fasti Ecclesiae Scoticanae*. Vol. 7. Original 1866. New Edition. Edinburgh: Oliver and Boyd, 1928.

Shepherd, R. H. W. *Where Aloes Flame: South African Missionary Vignettes*. London: Lutterworth, 1948.

Shell, Sandra C. T. W. "A Missionary Life Among the AmaXhosa: The Eastern Cape Journals of James Laing, 1830–1836." MA thesis, University of Cape Town, 2006.

Slowan, William J. *Missions of the United Presbyterian Church: The Story of Our Kaffrarian Mission*. Edinburgh: United Presbyterian Church, 1894.

Thomson, William Ritchie. "Draft Memorandum on the increase of Native Agency" (1831). Cory Library, Rhodes University, MS 17,137.

Vazi, Clifford Mandeli. "The History of Pirie Mission and Amaheke Chiefdom." MA thesis, Rhodes University, 1988.

Williams, Donovan. *When Races Meet: The Life and Times of William Ritchie Thomson, Glasgow Society Missionary, Government Agent, and Dutch Reformed Minister, 1794–1891*. Johannesburg: A. P. B. Publishers, 1967.

Chapter 3

Presbyterian Missions and a New Nation: Liberia, 1833–1894

Steve Curtis

Chapter Outline
1. Introduction
2. Background: Repatriation or Colonisation?
3. The Early Years (1833–1847)
4. The Later Years (1847–1894)
5. The Racial Dynamic: Slavery and Schism
6. Leaving Liberia
7. Postscript: Presbyterianism in Liberia in the 20th Century
8. Conclusion

1. Introduction

The history of Presbyterian missions in Liberia is closely connected with the very establishment of this West African nation. In the early 19th century, the American Colonization Society (ACS) was formed with the controversial aim of resettling black people from the United States to what would become Liberia. Charles Fenton Mercer, U.S. Representative from Virginia, is credited with originating the idea and gaining support for it from his brother-in-law, Robert Finley, a Presbyterian pastor. However, Finley, who studied at Princeton (then the College of New Jersey) under founding father John Witherspoon, had written of a desire to resettle freed blacks to Africa, even before Mercer devised and formalized such a plan. As early as 1815, Finley wrote that

> ... the state of the free blacks has very much occupied my mind ... Could not the rich and benevolent devise means to form a colony on some part of the coast of Africa, similar to that of Sierra Leone, which might gradually induce many free blacks to go and settle, devising for them the means of getting there, and protection and support until they were established?[1]

---

1 Alexander, *History of Colonization on the Western Coast of Africa*, 78. Note spelling: "colonisation" unless quoted as "colonization."

The idea was supported, initially at least, both by slaveholders who sought to have free blacks removed from the United States to minimize the potential that they could instigate rebellion and, in some instances, by those opposed to the very idea of slavery. To this end, the ACS was formed in 1816, with several notable members, such as Francis Scott Key, Henry Clay, Daniel Webster, and supported by presidents Jefferson, Madison, and Monroe. Another founding member was the Presbyterian minister, Ralph Randolph Gurley, chaplain to the U.S. House of Representatives. After his instrumental role in the founding of the ACS, Finley would die the following year.

From its inception, there were those who promoted the colony for purely social and economic reasons. There were others, however, who professed that such a migration would be tantamount to the biblical promise of the expansion of the gospel to the uttermost parts of the world.

In April 1822, the ACS established a colony of manumitted, or freed, slaves in the region and governed it for 25 years until the Republic of Liberia was established on 24 August 1847, with the capital at Monrovia. The American Presbyterian mission to Liberia commenced in the Monrovia area in 1833 and would ultimately be withdrawn in 1894. In 1834, a second mission was established by Presbyterians by working with the ABCFM in Cape Palmas and was transferred to the oversight of the Episcopalian mission in 1841. This chapter will consider the background to the decision to establish the settlements in Liberia; explore the lives and ministries of some of the Presbyterian missionaries who served there, including discussions of the unity and disunity among them regarding such issues as racial dynamics; and consider reasons for the withdrawal of the one mission and the transfer of the other. A brief survey of Presbyterian involvement in Liberia since 1894 will also be presented as a postscript.

2. Background: Repatriation or Colonisation?

The idea of repatriating[2] free blacks long predated the founding of the settlement of Liberia. This was not the first such undertaking. The Sierra Leone colony was established by resettling free blacks from the United Kingdom, Nova Scotia, and Jamaica.[3] Further, Ann Mifflin, a Quaker abolitionist, had conceived of a similar plan, which had reached the halls of the US Congress and the presidency itself, as Jefferson wrote in response: "[T]hat [is] the most desirable measure that could be adopted ... Going from a country possessing all the useful arts, they might be the means of transplanting them among the inhabitants of Africa ..."[4] Over

---

2   Repatriate means to return someone to their homeland or region.
3   See Chapter One in this volume.
4   Thomas Jefferson (1811, January 21). From *The Works of Thomas Jefferson in Twelve Volumes*. Letter from Thomas Jefferson to John Lynch.

the ensuing decades, and after witnessing the establishment of the Freetown settlement of Sierra Leone by the British, the consensus arose that colonisation might be the best approach to repatriation. With more than 250,000 free blacks in the United States, a movement to that end began with Finley, who wrote:

> The great desire of those whose minds are impressed with the subject is to give opportunity to the free people of color to rise to their proper level and at the same time to provide a powerful means of putting an end to the slave trade, and sending civilization and Christianity to Africa.[5]

Once the ACS had been formed, it was expedient to embark on the exploration of the west Africa region where the colony would settle. Thus, in 1818, Samuel Mills of the American Bible Society, and Ebenezer Burgess of the University of Vermont, set out to Sierra Leone and Sherbro to explore possible sites for the colony. However, neither of these locations proved acceptable and so, somewhat by force,[6] a local leader to the south, King Peter, was convinced to hand over to the Americans what would be called Liberia ("Land of the Free") and which would become the base for both repatriation and colonisation. The town they established, at the mouth of the St. Paul River, was named Monrovia, after the US President, James Monroe, who had strongly advocated for the West African colony. Regrettably, because of the coercive nature of the transfer of land, there would long be tensions, and even violence and battles, between the indigenous population and the colonisers such that, despite the best intentions of the white missionaries that went out among them, the fruit of their evangelism was minimal.

3. The Early Years (1833–1847)

The settlement of what would become Liberia began in earnest on 21 April 1833, when a ship sailed from New Orleans with 150 blacks on board, more than 90 of whom were slaves who had been manumitted for the purpose of this journey. Twenty-nine of them quickly died of cholera. Soon after, on 10 May, a ship sailed from Philadelphia, and on 5 November, 50 blacks from Norfolk arrived, including 44 freed slaves from Virginia. This last, the *Jupiter*, was the ship that carried the first Presbyterian missionaries to Africa.

---

5   Miller, *Search for a Black Nationality: Black Immigration and Colonization, 1787–1863*, 45.
6   Bayard, *A Sketch of the Life of Commodore Robert F. Stockton*, 46.

Presbyterian Sending Boards

In 1817, in a collective effort to engage in mission activities among the indigenous tribes of North America, as well as throughout "the heathen and anti-Christian world," the General Assembly of the Presbyterian Church (PCUSA) joined with the Dutch Reformed and Associate Reformed denominations to form the United Foreign Missionary Society (UFMS). In 1826, the UFMS was brought under control of the American Board of Commissioners for Foreign Missions (ABCFM), an organization perceived by many as the domain of the Congregationalists yet supported by many other paedobaptist churches. In 1834, the Presbyterians in America numbered 233,580, while the Congregationalists (at 126,714) and the Dutch Reformed (at 20,186) represented a much smaller contingent.[7] Thus, in 1831, Rev. Elisha Pope Swift, pastor of Second Presbyterian Church in Pittsburg, Pennsylvania, rose at the Synod of Pittsburg to point out that the foreign missions of the Presbyterians were almost wholly engulfed within the ABCFM. Swift argued that Presbyterians should be in control of their own missionaries and mission efforts, as were the Baptists and Methodists, and that this control required that Presbyterians form their own mission board. In response, the Synod formed the Western Foreign Missionary Society (WFMS) later that year.[8] Shortly after its inception, the WFMS began the Presbyterian mission in Liberia (February 1832) with the commissioning of Rev. John Brooks Pinney as its first foreign missionary. Not long after Pinney arrived in Liberia, the ABCFM would send its own missionary to Liberia, the Presbyterian John Leighton Wilson.

Presbyterian Missionaries

John Brooks Pinney (1806–1882)

Pinney was converted in his senior year of college at the University of Georgia, where he had studied law and was admitted to the bar. Being convinced of the call to ministry, however, he taught for a year in South Carolina to raise tuition to attend Princeton Theological Seminary where, as a young student, he read accounts of travellers to Africa. These accounts told of innumerable villages of thousands of people – most of whom had become followers of Islam. Therefore, it was his intention to reach the souls in these lands with the gospel.

Pinney and Joseph W. Barr were ordained by Archibald Alexander, the founding father of Princeton Seminary, and were set to sail on 5 November 1833 aboard the *Jupiter* from Norfolk; however, Barr died on the eve of their

---

7   "Organization, Relations, and Responsibilities of the Board," *The Missionary Herald*, 3 (1884), 31.
8   The General Assembly would assume control in 1837, renaming it the Presbyterian Board of Foreign Missions (PBFM) in 1837.

departure. Pinney went on, accompanied by John Cloud, Matthew and Harriet Laird, and James Temple, arriving in Monrovia on 31 December 1833. Cloud, born in 1801, was a graduate of Allegheny Seminary and had been ordained at Brick Presbyterian Church in New York City.[9] Matthew Laird was a graduate of the College of New Jersey (later to be renamed Princeton University) and had also just been ordained in 1833. Cloud, as well as Matthew and Harriet Laird all died of dysentery less than four months after they arrived. Temple was assigned the role of "Negro assistant missionary" by the Presbytery of Philadelphia. He would return to America the following summer, after the deaths of all the others except Pinney.

Originally, Pinney had thought to "tarry but a moment to rest" at the colony in Monrovia before continuing to the continent's interior for his proposed mission. However, upon his arrival at the colony, he noted the challenges that would attend a missionary journey to the interior and resolved to create at the coast "a gate of entrance and a place of protection" for future missionaries who would arrive to serve throughout western Africa. While he was called to minister among the colonists, he was particularly concerned with the aborigines.[10] In addition, he was soon asked by the ACS to serve as the "colonial agent," or Acting-Governor of Liberia and this settled his changed plan to stay at the colony. Pinney was the first Presbyterian missionary from America in all of Africa.[11]

▲ John B. Pinney

Pinney would eventually be offered the position of Governor of Liberia, which he turned down to focus on the work of the mission. However, health challenges led to his return to the United States after only two years. Over the ensuing decades, Pinney would continue to work for the ACS (and, later, the New York Colonization Society), as well as serve as a minister and a missionary, returning to Africa on several occasions, even serving as the Consul-General of Liberia from 1853–1865, after Lincoln had formally recognized Liberia as an independent nation.

---

9 Brown, *One Hundred Years*, 205.
10 Nassau, *Historical Sketch of the Missions in Africa*, 6.
11 Presbyterian Heritage Center, Biographical Index of Missionaries – Africa: Pinney, Rev. John Brook. https://www.phcmontreat.org/bios/Bios-Missionaries-Africa.htm.

His lifelong vision was for the improvement of blacks, whether in the United States or in Africa, particularly in Liberia. In addition to his commitment to the propagation of the gospel, he was convinced of the importance of education. Three years after he first visited Liberia, he noted: "these colonies cannot advance upon sure and proper principles, unless education and religion keep pace with emigration." Consistent with that conviction, he was involved with the College of Monrovia, serving briefly as its president. At 75 years old, he and his wife of 45 years, Ellen Seward, settled in Florida. Until his death the following year, Pinney continued to teach and preach to blacks in his community.

John Leighton Wilson (1809–1886)

In August of 1833, Pinney spoke about Liberia to a crowd gathered at the First Presbyterian Church in Columbia, South Carolina. Some of the whites present took umbrage at the address being given in the presence of blacks, presumably because they might be inclined to seek the freedom that was held out in the prospect of the settlement. The uproar became so intense that Pinney was "driven off … by a mob! And for what? For the great and unpardonable crime of speaking about the Colonization society in a public address where there were Negroes!" The author of that incredulity was John Leighton Wilson, a young man who had hoped to meet Pinney in Columbia yet arrived a day after the "rabble" drove him off.

▲ John L. Wilson

John Leighton Wilson[12] was descended from Scotch-Irish families that arrived in South Carolina in the early eighteenth century. Notable figures in the Revolutionary War and godly figures in the Presbyterian tradition populated those ancestors. Among them was William James, on his mother's side, who had served as one of the original elders in the Williamsburg church and Robert Wilson James, a founder of Columbia Seminary and pastor of the Presbyterian church in Williamsburg County, where the large Wilson clan was already well-established as landowners and farmers. From that James clan, John Leighton Wilson's father, William Wilson, would marry Jane E. James. Young John Leighton Wilson was raised amid an

---

12 A helpful overview of Wilson is chapter three in David B. Calhoun, *Swift and Beautiful: The Amazing Stories of Faithful Missionaries*. (Edinburgh: Banner of Truth, 2020), 37–54.

extended family that was known for their piety and godly character. However, it wasn't until a 21-year-old Wilson was attending a series of revival services, as the Second Great Awakening reached Charleston, that he began to be burdened by a vision of an eternity of utter aloneness waiting for him beyond the judgement seat of God. For several weeks, he was overwhelmed with the agony of this vision until he encountered the love of Christ. In light of the depth of his pre-conversion distress, the corresponding heights of the transformation of his conversion compelled him toward an honest and total relationship with God. To this end, he began his journey on what would be a lifetime of sacrifice and service in mission and ministry.

He began by enrolling in Colombia Seminary, one of just seven students in the inaugural class. Upon graduation, he was ordained in the Synod of South Carolina and straightway inquired with the ABCFM whether he could serve as a missionary in West Africa. Under the direction of the Maryland Colonization Society (MCS), a branch of the ACS, a colony was set to be established at Cape Palmas, about 250 miles south of Monrovia. For their part, the ABCFM had been hopeful that there would be a missionary candidate for this project from the American South, as they supposed such would be better able to tolerate the West African climate. Before Wilson set off to live and serve in Liberia, however, he wanted to find a wife to join him there. Thus, he travelled to Savannah, Georgia, where, through the introduction of a mutual friend, he met Jane Elizabeth Bayard.

Jane was of laudable stock in her own right, with her forebears serving nobly as officers in the Revolutionary War. She was also a cousin to Charles Hodge, the Princeton professor, who was already being recognized as a budding but influential theologian. As with Wilson, Jane was inclined toward African missions and, also like Wilson, had inquired of the ABCFM about the possibility of serving in West Africa. Unlike Wilson, however, she was met with a qualified denial – with the qualification being that the Board did not send single females into the field. Thus, she could only go if she were to marry someone who would also be accepted as a missionary by the ABCFM. The union, then, of Wilson and Jane, was more than merely a matter of love, though it was that to be sure, but also a shared passion for the gospel work of missions in West Africa. Upon their marriage, they were commissioned by the ABCFM and, concurrently, by the MCS.

In December 1834, the newly married couple reached the coast of Liberia and made their way to Cape Palmas. Despite serious bouts with malaria and other cultural challenges, Wilson dove straightway into the difficult task of learning the Grebo language. His careful study produced the first written works in the language: first, a dictionary and then, a rudimentary grammar. His work would lay the foundation for the Grebo dialect that would eventually prevail in the schools and government.

In the early years in the colony, mission schools were established, where Jane and Wilson served alongside a number of others who came to the Cape, both to promote the colony and preach the gospel. While passionate about the latter, Wilson was increasingly outspoken about what he perceived as the primary purpose of the colony vis-à-vis the MCS, declaring in several letters that the Society was more concerned with the removal of blacks from Maryland than it was with the establishment of a healthy colony in Liberia. Further, he rejected the notion that the mission was under the control of the colony.[13] For these positions, his relationship with the MSC began to falter.

Along the way, the Wilsons endured myriad hardships. They were caught up in the struggles between colonists and the Grebo and between the white missionaries and the black settlers. They encountered angry mobs frustrated with the mistreatment of the Grebo; they suffered through bouts of ill health; and they even came across cannibals.[14] Adding to these challenges was the split, in 1837, of the Presbyterian Church in the United States, with the "Old School" electing to establish and support the PBFM, leaving only the "New School" churches to support the colony. This, even though the "Old School" was championed by none other than Jane's cousin, Charles Hodge. Consequently, ships continued to arrive with more immigrants but fewer stores. This led to a financial crisis and Wilson was forced to scuttle plans for more schools and even contract the size of the existing schools. Nevertheless, after seven years in the colony, Wilson could report this level of success:

> A church of forty members organized; more than a hundred youth educated; the Grebo language reduced to writing; a grammar and dictionary of the language published; the Gospels of Matthew and John translated, and six or eight other small volumes published in the native language.[15]

For her part, Jane had been actively involved in the work of the schools, training both black settlers and native Grebo to be teachers. Cognizant of the language, as well as the cultural challenges, she wisely taught English to the Grebo and the Grebo language to the immigrants.

Because of the aforementioned conflict with the MCS, together with an ongoing conflict with the governor of Liberia over the role of the immigrants in Liberian society, Wilson began to look for a new place to establish a mission away from the intervention of the colonial powers – both in the States and in Liberia. Thus, in 1842, Wilson established a new mission south along the coast

---

13 Clarke, *By the Rivers of Water*, 144.
14 DuBose, *Memoirs of Rev. John Leighton Wilson*, 82.
15 Dubose, *Memoirs of Rev. John Leighton Wilson*, 78.

in Gabon. The mission at Cape Palmas was then transferred to the nearby Episcopal mission, which had moved just outside of the colony in order to maintain independence from MCS oversight. Later in life, after leaving Gabon in 1852, he served as a Secretary of the PBFM, while publishing numerous books and articles on missions and African culture, generally.

Others who served in the early period

Amos Herring (1794–1873) was born a slave in North Carolina, though he was raised in Virginia, attending a Presbyterian church there until he was freed in 1826. In 1833, he led his family to the Liberian colony, only to lose his wife and two of their five children to disease shortly after landing. He served as a pastor in Monrovia for several years. In 1847, he served as a delegate to the Constitutional Convention, representing Grand Bassa. In that capacity, he signed Liberia's Declaration of Independence and her Constitution.

In 1834, *Josiah F. C. Finley* (1807–1838), the son of ACS founder, Robert Finley, arrived in Liberia. Finley would serve at the Greenville settlement on the Sinoe River. In 1838, while en route from Greenville to Monrovia, he was killed by a native tribe that objected to the settlers plying the riverways, which they deemed to be under their control.

Ephraim Titler, a black licentiate of the Presbytery of Philadelphia, arrived early in 1837, and proceeded to the station situated at Greenville. He reported that he found the natives to be "friendly, but capricious; and most ignorant, superstitious, and degraded."[16] He was stationed at Boblee among the Bassa tribe on the John River.[17] Together with Herring, Titler was also a delegate to the Constitutional Convention, signing the Declaration of Independence and the Constitution.

In 1841, *Rev. O. K. Canfield* and *Rev. J. P. Alward* arrived with their wives, accompanied by Cecilia Van Tyne, a black teacher who would assist in the establishing of the Settra Kroo Mission of the Presbyterian Church. Canfield and Alward died within months of arrival and their wives returned to the States. Van Tyne remained until 1844, at work in the mission, until her health required her to return home. Also in 1841, *Rev. Robert and Mrs Sawyer* arrived and stayed with Canfield until his death, after which they worked alongside *Van Tyne* at the Settra Kroo mission. Robert Sawyer would die in 1843 and Catherine Sawyer would remarry newly-arrived Presbyterian minister, *John M. Connely*, who served until declining health caused his return home in 1849.

James M. Priest (1819–1893) was born a slave in Kentucky. His owner, Jane Meaux, educated him, freed him, and sent him to Liberia to assess the colony. After

---

16 American Presbyterian Board, "Western Africa," *The Missionary Register*, 28 (1840), 22.

17 Board of Foreign Missions of the Presbyterian Church, "Survey of Missionary Stations," *The Foreign Missionary Chronicle*, 11 (1838), 6.

A Survey of Presbyterian Mission History in Africa

▲ James M. Priest

his return, he studied at McCormick Theological Seminary and was ordained by the Presbytery of New York. He was then sent to Liberia as a missionary in 1843. He rose in prominence in the colony and would eventually serve as Vice-President from 1864–1868, before serving as a Supreme Court Justice.

Also serving in those early years in Liberia was *Rev. James Eden*, a free black, born in Charleston, South Carolina. Originally a minister in the African Methodist Episcopal Church, he and other blacks had left their denomination to join the Presbyterian Church. Upon learning of the Presbyterians offering passage to Liberia, he, his wife, and their six children, joined the voyage. Eden served as the pastor at Monrovia until his death in 1848 of the African fever, which claimed the lives of so many missionaries.

Harsh Conditions

From the very beginning, those who sought to answer the call to missions in Liberia learned that the climate and the prevalence of disease would take their toll. Foreshadowing the tragedies that would befall the early missionaries, three of the first four who ventured on the journey died within a few months of arrival. Pinney, too, would return to the States in the spring of 1834. These challenges led to the decision by the Board to increase the sending of black missionaries, as they wrongly concluded that their African heritage would provide some constitutional defence against the African environment. One writer at the time argued:

> The early graves of most of the early Missionaries already sent there, afford affecting evidence that the climate has hitherto been injurious and fatal to the White Man. Shall the Board, therefore, encourage White Missionaries to go thither? or, shall they rest the hopes of Africa, as far as their agency is concerned, on preparing and sending out, as Missionaries, Coloured Men, whose constitution is so much better adapted to that climate? ... Surely, among the many thousands of Coloured Communicants in the Presbyterian Church, there must be many, who, if properly educated, would make efficient Missionaries to the land of their forefathers.[18]

---

18 *Missionary Register*, 23.

This judgment would, in fact, lead to the decision of the PBFM in 1842 to send only black missionaries to Liberia.[19] By the middle of the century, blacks would account for 59 of the 75 missionaries in the country.

4. The Later Years (1847–1894)

Independent Republic of Liberia

The founding of the new Republic was a significant development on the African continent, as it was the first democratic republic in Africa. For its part, the missionary effort was integrally connected with the political developments of the new republic. With Titler and Herring as signers to the Declaration of Independence and Constitution, and with Pinney serving as Consul-General, Priest as Vice President and Supreme Court Justice, and Blyden (discussed below) as Commissioner to Britain and the United States, it is little wonder that, in 1870, the fifth moderator of the Presbyterian Church of Liberia would write to the New York Presbytery:

> In announcing the fact that I have been nominated by an almost unanimous vote of the Board of Trustees to the Presidency of Liberia College, I cannot help calling your attention to the influence which Presbyterianism has exerted and is still exerting in Liberia. All the leading men of the country are now either Presbyterians or have been educated by Presbyterians.[20]

While these were illustrious accomplishments indeed, the labour continued unabated with the work of others who answered the call to reach both the colonists and the indigenous people with the gospel.

---

19 Another tributary often forgotten within American Presbyterian mission involvement in Liberia was with the Associate Reformed (Presbyterian) Synod of the South. A Liberian mission was financially supported by this Synod between 1845 and 1855. The ARP Synod of the South evidently acquired some land in Kentucky, Liberia in the 1840s. It initially partnered in helping fund a school there under Thomas Ware's direction and the American Colonization Society; upon Ware's death, the ARP Synod partnered with Rev. H. W. Erskine, a Presbyterian minister and educator in Kentucky, Liberia for the training of ministers. See, Robert Lathan, *History of the Associate Reformed Synod of the South* (Harrisburg, PA: author published, 1882), 381–384; *The African Repository*, 26 (1850): 118.

20 Presbyterian Church of Liberia. https://sites.google.com/site/presbyterianchurchofliberia/ (Accessed 7 June 2022)

Harrison W. Ellis

After Eden's death in 1848, Rev. H. W. Ellis succeeded him as pastor at the Presbyterian church in Monrovia. Ellis was born a slave in Virginia, sold into Tennessee and then into Alabama. As a young boy, he heard ministers preaching from the Bible and was inspired to learn to read it. Principally self-taught, he mastered that task, and then went on to learn to read Latin, Greek, and Hebrew. He read not only the Bible but works of theology and ministry as well. While living – still as a slave – in Alabama, the synods of Alabama and Mississippi came together to purchase his freedom, and that of his wife and two children, for $2500. He was ordained by the Presbytery of Tuscaloosa and, of his examination, it was said:

> ... for precision on the details of religious experience; for sober, rational views of what constitutes a call to the ministry; for sound, consistent, scriptural views of the leading doctrines of the Gospel, few candidates for the office have been known to equal him.[21]

While serving in Monrovia, Ellis learned the languages of two local tribes, so that he might preach to them in their native tongue.

Edward Wilmot Blyden (1832–1912)

Another black man who figured prominently among the Presbyterian story in Liberia after its independence – especially in the connection between Presbyterianism and education – is Edward Blyden. Born in the Virgin Islands, Blyden was raised in the Dutch Reformed Church. By 1850, he was convinced of a calling to ministry and, consistent with that calling, he journeyed to the United States to seek training at Rutgers Theological College, However, he was denied admission there and elsewhere. While in the US, however, he met John Pinney and became aware of, and engaged with, the efforts of the Liberian colonisation movement. This led to his relocation to Monrovia, where he would attend the Presbyterian-established Alexander High School in Monrovia, with Reverend David A. Wilson as principal.

---

21 E., "Negro Intellect. – Ellis and Douglass, and Uncle Tom," *Frederick Douglass' Paper*, 15 July 1853, in Railton, Stephen. 1999. Uncle Tom's Cabin and American Culture: A Multimedia Archive. Charlottesville, VA: Stephen Railton and the Institute for Advanced Technology in the Humanities, Electronic Text Center, University of Virginia. http://utc.iath.virginia.edu/africam/afar03yt.html (accessed 7 June 2022).

Wilson was a white graduate from Princeton who tutored Blyden in the doctrines of Old School Presbyterianism. This led to Blyden's ordination in the Presbytery of West Africa in 1858. That same year, he succeeded Wilson as principal at Alexander High School. He left this post in 1861 to serve as Professor of Classics at Liberia College and, simultaneously, as Liberian Commissioner to both Britain and the United States. He would increasingly promote, from the pulpit and the press, the philosophy later codified as Pan-Africanism, whereby he sought the universal improvement of blacks. Throughout the 1870s and 1880s, Blyden would progressively distance himself from the Presbyterian missions movement in West Africa, developing, at the same time, an apparent appreciation for Islam and what he viewed as its positive contribution to the native Africans. Consequently, in 1886, he resigned from the Presbyterian Church.

▲ *Edward W. Blyden*

5. The Racial Dynamics: Slavery and Schism

While the mission was underway in Liberia, the United States was increasingly engaged in the conflict over the issues that would lead to the Civil War – most relevant among them for the present discussion was the matter of slavery. Slavery was dividing not only the states; it was also dividing the churches. Following the schism in the Presbyterian Church in 1837 (around the issues of slavery, theology, and other divisions) into the "Old School" and "New School" Presbyterian Church, the Old School took over the WFMS, renaming it the Presbyterian Board of Foreign Missions (PBFM). The division wasn't limited to the United States. One author argues, "… the story of Presbyterian missionary efforts in the Republic of Liberia in the three decades before the American Civil War was filled with tension, rife with conflict, and scarred by tragedy."[22] Whether or not this is a wholly accurate assessment, there does appear to have been racial challenges among the missionaries in Liberia.

Virtually all the missionaries were opposed to slavery. One notable exception was Edward T. Williams, who arrived in 1856, and stayed with David Wilson, the principal of Alexander High School. Williams believed that to release his slaves would be harmful to them, as they would be left with no means of provision. At

---

22 McArver, "'The Salvation of Souls' and the 'Salvation of the Republic of Liberia': Denominational Conflict and Racial Diversity in Antebellum Presbyterian Foreign Missions," in *North American Foreign Missions, 1810–1914: Theology, Theory, and Policy*, 134.

one point, he wrote, "If Liberia is to be enlightened, & the heathen tribes, in and around her(e), are to be Christianized, white men are indispensable." Because of such expressions, some have expressed the view that the white missionaries viewed black missionaries as inferior. Nevertheless, Williams appears to have been quite well-loved among both his white and black colleagues.[23]

Other remarks, however, do bear out the racial tension, as when Titler wrote that the board "expects a man of colour to do more with less means than a white one. Yes, I sometimes fear that they expects [sic] more than Jehovah Himself requires."[24] Likewise, Priest wrote of his desire to "show the people in Africa that Presbyterians do not believe in the doctrine, namely that collard [sic] men in Africa must all have masters in order that matters may go right."[25]

While there was obviously tension surrounding the racial divisions in the United States and within the Presbyterian churches there, and while there were certainly episodes of racial disparity with the Liberian colony, there appears to have been comity on the issue of education as a means both to improve the lives of the people living in Liberia *and* to reach them with the gospel.

Both white and black missionaries sent out by the PBFM were convinced of the importance of both Christian theology and American culture if the Liberian experiment was to be a success. For those goals to be achieved, however, they likewise understood that education was essential – both for the free black settlers and for the indigenous population.

White and black missionaries also both disapproved of the native's heathenism – and of many of the colonists, for that matter, who had in many cases abandoned any pretense of the Christian faith that they may have claimed in the States. In this vein, Sawyer even expressed chagrin that the colonists weren't active partners in the mission work with the missionaries, saying,

> I was very much of the opinion that the Colonists were almost like so many missionaries to the Heathen, consequently I was opposed to receiving any impressions at variance with that oppionin [sic]; but it is my serious & solemn conviction that the truth lies directly in the opposite.[26]

---

23 McArver, "'The Salvation of Souls' and the 'Salvation of the Republic of Liberia,'" 157.
24 Ephram Titler to Walter Lowrie, 10 April 1839, *Presbyterian Church in the U.S.A.: Board of Foreign Mission Correspondence and Reports, Africa* (hereafter, *BFMCR*), vol. 1.
25 James Priest to Walter Lowrie (no other date) 1843, *BFMCR*, vol 1.
26 McArver, "'The Salvation of Souls' and the 'Salvation of the Republic of Liberia,'" 151.

Wilson expressed a similar frustration:

> We regard it as one of the chief failings of the Liberians, and one of the most serious hindrances to their improvement, that they are too willing to be taken care of … very little has been done to support the Gospel among themselves …[27]

Thus, there were multiple overlapping and contradictory tensions – between blacks and whites; between missionaries (black and white) and non-missionary colonists. Yet, all parties agreed in the value of education. To that end, a number of schools, such as the Alexander High School, were established for the purpose of educating the colonists and the indigenous population.

6. Leaving Liberia

The end of the Presbyterian mission in Liberia coincided, in part, with the end of the ACS's efforts at colonisation in Liberia, reflecting, in some way, the intrinsic nature of the two endeavours from the outset: the ACS had a vision to create a new colony; the PBFM had a vision to use that colony as a mission outpost to reach the indigenous people of West Africa. As support for the resettling of free blacks in Africa became far less popular in the US, however, it led to dramatic decreases in both funding and interest. A similar disinterest developed among the PBFM. Requests from the field for funding missions and schools were largely rejected. Salaries were summarily reduced and a lack of communication from the PBFM added to the missionaries' frustration, until it was thought that the Board "neither trusted them, respected them, nor had any deep concern for them."[28]

In 1891, the PBFM saw a new leader, Robert Speer, who would be instrumental in the termination of the mission. A missionary, A. C. Good, had been sent to investigate the work in Liberia. In essence, he reported that, for the most part, the missionaries were poorly trained; lacking in evangelistic fervour; ministering primarily among the settlers while neglecting the indigenous peoples; and, in some cases, more engaged in secular pursuits than mission endeavours. Good concluded that the only solution would be a significant infusion of funds to provide training, build schools, and send out new missionaries to lead in the work. In his review of the mission, Speer interpreted the findings to demonstrate that it was "no nearer self-support than it was at the beginning. Its evangelistic work has not reached beyond the Liberian settlements, and its schools have not

---

27 Wilson, *Western Africa: Its History, Condition, and Prospects*, 410.
28 Hodgson, "The Presbyterian Mission to Liberia, 1832–1900," 338.

attained the ends which it was desired that they should. In other words, there is dissatisfaction."[29]

The Board was convinced that the Liberia church was too dependent, while the missionaries were convinced that they needed more funding – for training, building, et cetera – to enable the church to become independent. Speer again responded unsympathetically, writing that "Christian work is not dependent only for its success upon funds, it is dependent only upon our willingness to let God use us." He was convinced that "[l]iberal appropriations have been made for Liberians" and that the problem lies in "a lack of grasp upon the missionary purpose and the unflagging zeal of the missionary spirit." He concluded that funds "must be expended elsewhere where they can be made to tell on the evangelization of non-Christian peoples."[30]

At first, in 1894, a plan was implemented to gradually reduce the presence of missionaries and, simultaneously, encourage the Liberia church to become self-supporting. However, within three years, only three men in Liberia were receiving any support from the PBFM and even that ended in 1900.

7. Postscript: Presbyterianism in Liberia in the Twentieth Century

A national denomination, the Presbyterian Church of Liberia (PCL) eventually grew out of the mission work of the PFMB, becoming independent in 1928. In 1980, the PCL came under the auspices of the Cumberland Presbyterian Church (CPC) and remained in that relationship until 2006 when, at the annual Synod of the PCL, it was decided that all ties to the CPC be severed.

There are presently 15 Presbyterian congregations in the PCL, serving approximately 3,000 members. There are three schools in operation. Separately, the First Presbyterian Church of Monrovia, which traces its roots to 1888, merged with the Monrovia Congregational Church in 1918 and is presently associated with the Evangelical Covenant Order of Presbyterians (ECO). Finally, there are Presbyterian missionaries at work in Liberia from the PC(USA) as well as from the Evangelical Presbyterian Church (EPC).

8. Conclusion

One author offers a succinct, if pessimistic summary of the Presbyterian mission efforts in Liberia:

---

29 Speer to Liberian missionaries, 24 Jan. 1893, cited in Hodgson, 340.
30 Speer to the West African Presbytery, 22 April 1893, cited in Hodgson, 344.

> Seldom have we known a mission commenced with more deliberate and well-informed judgment, conducted by more devoted and thoroughly qualified men, and resulting in more disastrous and apparently fruitless events.[31]

Indeed, it is difficult to survey this history without a sense of exasperation. And yet, the author who penned those words goes on to refute his own judgment:

> Yet the events have not been fruitless ... The piety of so many of Christ's servants, their self-denial, their willingness to peril life itself for the salvation of the heathen, their happy though brief missionary life, their peaceful death – all these have yielded fruit surely in the churches at home if not among the hardened Kroo people and their record is on high – their crown of rejoicing is the brighter after being gained in the dark land of Africa.[32]

In fact, there was fruit born in Africa, as well. These words from Liberia's Declaration of Independence are a reminder of the mark left on that nation by the many Presbyterians who ministered there, educated there, and navigated the country through her infancy:

> Our churches for the worship of our Creator, everywhere to be seen, bear testimony to our piety, and to our acknowledgement of his Providence. The native African, bowing down with us before the altar of the Living God, declares that from us, feeble as we are, the light of Christianity has gone forth ...[33]

---

31 Lowrie, *Manual of the Foreign Missions of the Presbyterian Church in the United States of America*, 74.
32 Lowrie, *Manual of the Foreign Missions of the Presbyterian Church in the United States of America*, 74.
33 *The Independent Republic of Liberia; Its Constitution and Declaration of Independence; Address of the Colonists to the Free People of Color in the United States, with other Documents. Issued Chiefly for the Use of the Free People of Color.* (Philadelphia: William F. Geddes, 1848), 9.

A Survey of Presbyterian Mission History in Africa

Questions for study (fact type):

1. What was the purpose of the American Colonization Society?
2. What does the country name 'Liberia' mean?
3. a) Name the first permanently settled ordained Presbyterian missionary to begin mission work in Liberia at Monrovia.
   b) Name the others in his team and explain what happened to them.
4. a) Name the first ordained Presbyterian missionary to begin mission work in Cape Palmas.
   b) What mission agency did he serve under? c) What indigenous language did he help to develop in written form?
5. Name several of the early African American missionaries who served in Liberia.

Questions for study (reflection type):

1. Describe the tensions which developed between the colonists and the indigenous population.
2. Using section 5, discuss the personnel responsible and the rationale for the withdrawal of the PBFM of the PCUSA from Liberia.

Select Bibliography

Alexander, Archibald. *A History of Colonization on the Western Coast of Africa*. PA: William S. Martien, 1846.

American Presbyterian Board. "Western Africa," *The Missionary Register*, Vol. 28. London: L & G Seeley, 1840.

Bayard, Samuel J. *A Sketch of the Life of Commodore Robert F. Stockton*. New York: Derby & Jackson, 1856.

Board of Foreign Missions of the Presbyterian Church. "Survey of Missionary Stations," *The Foreign Missionary Chronicle*, Vol. 11. New York: Robert Carter, 1838.

Brown, Arthur Judson. *One Hundred Years*. New York: Fleming H. Revell Co., 1936.

Clarke, Erskine. *By the Rivers of Water: A Nineteenth-Century Atlantic Odyssey*. New York: Basic Books, 2013.

DuBose, Hampden C. *Memoirs of Rev. John Leighton Wilson D.D*. Richmond, VA: Presbyterian Ministry of Publication, 1895.

Hodgson, Eva Naomi. "The Presbyterian Mission to Liberia, 1832–1900." PhD dissertation, Columbia University, 1980.

Jefferson, Thomas (1811, January 21). From *The Works of Thomas Jefferson in Twelve Volumes*. Letter from Thomas Jefferson to John Lynch. Federal Edition. Collected and edited by Paul Leicester Ford. http://memory.loc.gov/service/mss/mtj/mtj1/045/045_0075_0077.pdf.

Lowrie, John C. *A Manual of the Foreign Missions of the Presbyterian Church in the United States of America*. New York: William Rankin, Jr., 1868.

McArver, Susan Wilds. "'The Salvation of Souls' and the 'Salvation of the Republic of Liberia': Denominational Conflict and Racial Diversity in Antebellum Presbyterian Foreign Missions." In *North American Foreign Missions, 1810–1914: Theology, Theory, and Policy*, ed. Wilbert R. Shenk. Grand Rapids: Eerdmans, 2004, 133–160.

Miller, Floyd J. *The Search for a Black Nationality: Black Immigration and Colonization, 1787–1863*. Urbana, IL: University of Illinois Press, 1975.

Nassau, Robert H. *A Historical Sketch of the Missions in Africa*. PA: Women's Foreign Missionary Society of the Presbyterian Church, 1881.

"Organization, Relations, and Responsibilities of the Board," *The Missionary Herald*, Vol. 3. Boston: Crocker and Brewster, 1884.

Presbyterian Heritage Center, Montreat, North Carolina. Biographical Index of Missionaries – Africa: Pinney, Rev. John Brook. https://www.phcmontreat.org/bios/Bios-Missionaries-Africa.htm.

Wilson, John Leighton. *Western Africa: Its History, Condition, and Prospects*. New York: Harper and Brothers, 1856.

Wynkoop, Stephen. "Extracts from the Journals of Messrs. Wilson and Wynkoop," *The Missionary Herald*, Vol. 3. Boston: Crocker and Brewster, 1884.

Chapter 4

Survey of Presbyterian Churches of Southern Africa, 1841–2000: With a focus on the tributary streams of the UPCSA

Douglas K. Bower

Chapter Outline
1. Introduction
2. The foundation of the Presbyterian Church in the Cape
3. The continued growth and expansion of the Presbyterian Church in the Cape
4. Beyond the Cape: The spread of Presbyterianism throughout South Africa
5. The establishment of the PCSA as a denomination
6. The expansion of the Church in South Africa, Zimbabwe, and Zambia 1910–1994
7. The formation of the Bantu Presbyterian Church (BPC)
8. The creation of The Uniting Presbyterian Church in Southern Africa (UPCSA) 1994–2000
9. Conclusion

1. Introduction

The history of the Presbyterian churches in Southern Africa is complex, to say the least! This chapter seeks to build from chapter two in this book by taking us on chronologically from circa 1841 and by expanding our geographical base to be inclusive of Southern Africa, not just the Cape. In order to do this, we start with a brief review of how Presbyterianism arrived in South Africa and extended into Zambia and Zimbabwe, and finally how the Uniting Presbyterian

Church in Southern Africa (UPCSA) was created.[1] Others have written in-depth histories and analyses of the development of aspects of Presbyterianism in Southern Africa and of particular congregations or presbyteries. Though this survey takes note of the various Presbyterian churches which have emerged during this time frame in this geographic region, it will primarily focus on the story-line of what in 1999 became known as the UPCSA, thus tracing it from its antecedents. The multiple Presbyterian churches cannot all receive attention, so it is my intention to draw together the most important events to show how the Presbyterian church was planted in South Africa and continued to grow and bear good fruits in the stream now known as the UPCSA.

Now, nothing exists in a void – the Church does not exist completely separate from political, social, economic, cultural, racial, and linguistic realities. Thus, where relevant, reference has been made to historical circumstances and events. Again, for the sake of brevity, these have been kept short.

As indicated in the chapter outline, the chapter will cover the following topics:

- Foundation of the Presbyterian Church in the Cape: the arrival of the first Presbyterians at the Cape, early congregations, and missions work;

- The continued growth and expansion of the Presbyterian Church in the Cape: the work continues;

- Beyond the Cape: The spread of Presbyterianism throughout South Africa: the spread of Presbyterian Churches and congregations throughout the Eastern Cape, Natal and even through modern-day Gauteng;

- The establishment of the PCSA as a denomination;

- The expansion of the Church in South Africa, Zimbabwe and Zambia 1910–1994: establishment of PCSA Churches and congregations in the countries neighbouring South Africa, their growth and work;

- The formation of the Bantu Presbyterian Church (BPC): reasons for the formation of the BPC, the inaugural General Assembly and the expansion of the BPC;

---

1 It should be noted that this chapter is, to some extent, dependent on key, unpublished – or soon to be published – secondary sources. Authors of these works have generously, through their quotations and assistance, provided invaluable access to primary sources, some of which were handwritten or stored in remote denominational archives. This chapter would not have been possible without these invaluable contributions and sources. Thus, I wish to acknowledge with thanks the following ministers and scholars who allowed access to their research and sources: Douglas Bax, Graham A. Duncan, and Alastair Rodger. See select bibliography for further details.

A Survey of Presbyterian Mission History in Africa

- Finally, the creation of the Uniting Presbyterian Church in Southern Africa (UPCSA) 1994–2000: the different Presbyterian Churches in Southern Africa joined together to form the Uniting Presbyterian Church.

▼ Timeline showing notable events in Southern Africa and in the Presbyterian churches:

Early 1800s	Scottish regiments arrive at the Cape
1801	Rev. William Read (LMS) conducted services at the Cape
1812	Dr G. Thom arrived at the Cape; first Presbyterian congregation established 1813
1820	4000+ Settlers arrived in the Eastern Cape
1824	First Presbytery (Kaffraria) formed in Eastern Cape
1827	Foundation stone for St. Andrew's (Scottish)Presbyterian Church, Cape Town laid
1828	First Presbyterian Church at Glen Lynden built and completed
1829	St. Andrew's Church building completed in Cape Town
1852	Presbytery of Natal formed
1867	Discovery of diamonds and gold in South Africa
1890	Presbytery of Transvaal formed
1893	Presbytery of the Cape formed
1896	First congregation established in Bulawayo, Zimbabwe
1897	Federal Council met and voted to establish PCSA as denomination, First General Assembly
1898	Rev. Mzimba and formation of the Presbyterian Church of Africa
1899	South African War (Anglo-Boer War) started, ended 1902
1900	Union in Scotland of the FCS & the UPCS, creating the United Free Church of Scotland
1903	Congregation established in Harare, Zimbabwe
1923	PCSA – name changed to Presbyterian Church of Southern Africa BPC formed in South Africa
1925	Rev. Yekelo Mbali elected as Moderator of the BPC
1926	First PCSA congregation established at Livingstone, Zambia

1948	Nationalist government elected in South Africa, Apartheid (1948 to 1990)
	Presbyterian Church of Southern Africa (PCSA), incorporating congregations from South Africa, Zambia, and Zimbabwe
1964	Zambia independence, became a republic
1979	BPC name changed to Reformed Presbyterian Church of South Africa (RPCSA)
1980	Zimbabwe independence
1994	Democratic elections in South Africa
1999	PCSA and RPCSA united as Uniting Presbyterian Church of Southern Africa (UPCSA)
2000	UPCSA: 15 South African presbyteries, one Presbytery in Zimbabwe, and two presbyteries in Zambia

As should be clear from this overview, this chapter hopes to provide a broad picture of how the Presbyterian Church in Southern Africa (UPCSA stream) was planted, grew, expanded, and continued to work for the glory of God.

2. The foundation of the Presbyterian Church in the Cape

Presbyterianism developed at the Cape during the early 1800s with the arrival of Scottish regiments. The reason for their arrival was within the wider context of British colonialism. France and Britain were at war, and this led to the British occupation of the Cape from 1795 to 1803 and again in 1806. This was done as a pre-emptive strike in order to prevent the French from using the Cape as a resupply station for their ships. It was during this occupation that the Argyll and Scottish Highlanders regiments came to the Cape. Being staunchly Presbyterian, the regiments formed an association for "worship and fellowship" which met regularly for Bible study and prayer.[2] In 1800/1, a missionary of the London Missionary Society (LMS), the Rev. W. Read conducted services with the regiments and encouraged them to start the Calvinist Society before Read went to India. However, in 1802, the peace of Amiens was negotiated with the French, and the Cape was handed back to the Dutch in 1803. With this peace, the Calvinist Society collapsed due to the withdrawal of troops from the Cape. However, in 1806, war broke out afresh and the Cape was re-occupied by the British. It was during the second occupation that the first Battalion of the 93rd

---

2   Galloway, *Your Church. Presbyterian Church of Southern Africa*, 6.

Regiment or Sutherland Highlanders revived the Calvinist Society, public worship, Bible study, and prayer.

Dr George Thom, a Church of Scotland minister, arrived in 1812 at the Cape on his way to India as an LMS missionary. As he was waiting for a ship, he conducted services for the soldiers and met with the Calvinist Society. This led to his decision to remain at the Cape as both a minister and a missionary. It was under his ministry that the first Presbyterian congregation was constituted on 6 May 1813. They used the premises of the South African Missionary Society chapel in Long Street. Therefore, the first Presbyterian congregation in South Africa was birthed out of the necessity of the Scottish military regiment stationed at the Cape, but the earliest Christian outreach was done through chaplaincy and then reached out to civilian settlers and the local population. Thom is notable for having written to William Wilberforce, the famous British politician, philanthropist, who was the leader of the movement to abolish the slave trade. Thom appealed to Wilberforce for help against the slave trade at the Cape.

In 1814, the Scottish regiments left the Cape and, with them, the majority of the congregation. Rev. Thom therefore accepted a call to a Dutch Reformed Church in Caledon in 1818. Two years later, in 1820, Thom was sent to Scotland by the Dutch Reformed Church to recruit ministers and teachers for the work in South Africa.

In 1819, Dr John Philip came to the Cape as director of the LMS mission to Africa. The remaining members of the Presbyterian congregation at the Cape asked Rev. John Phillip if he would conduct services for them; in 1820 they called him as a minister. Phillips was a staunch congregationalist and insisted that the polity of the church be changed from the authority of the Kirk session to quarterly meetings of the local congregation. Thus, seven years after its inception, the first Presbyterian Church became the first Congregationalist church.

This left many Scottish Presbyterians exceptionally unhappy. However, in 1824 they became aware that the British government was prepared to offer financial assistance to Presbyterians in the colonies. With this news, the Presbyterians set about forming a committee to raise funds for the building of a church. They requested financial aid from both the British government and the Church of Scotland. In 1827, Dr James Adamson, a highly intellectual man (and cousin of Thomas Chalmers, the noted Scottish minister) filled with missionary zeal, arrived at the Cape from Scotland to be the new congregation's first minister. In October of that same year, the foundation stone of 'Scottish Church' was laid. It was completed in May 1829. Regular services were conducted in the building, and it was later renamed St. Andrew's Presbyterian Church. St. Andrew's is regarded as the mother church, or flagship church, of Presbyterianism in Southern Africa. This church had strong links with British colonialism from its inception.

In 1838, Rev. Adamson, with the support of his session, started missionary work among the coloured slaves. The members of the Mission met for separate services and Bible study in St. Andrew's Church. Those who attended worshipped in Dutch and needed basic Biblical instruction. With the emancipation of slaves taking effect in 1838 throughout the British Empire, the session appointed G.W. Stegman, then second Minister of the Lutheran Church, to head up the Mission, as he was fluent in Dutch. Members of the Dutch Reformed Church, the Lutheran Church, and St. Andrew's supported him. These three churches working together showed a truly ecumenical spirit, which was revolutionary for its time. St. Andrew's was the first English church to both marry and accept freed slaves onto its membership rolls. The Mission had over 1000 members; between 1838 and 1841 they also baptised 134 who became full members. Other than biblical instruction and marriages, the mission provided alms for the poor and free medical care. This helped to save many lives during the great measles and smallpox outbreak in 1840–1841.

3. The continued growth and expansion of the Presbyterian Church in the Cape

Besides many other public upliftment endeavours, Adamson almost single-handedly helped to establish the South African College, later to become the University of Cape Town. In 1841 the college nearly closed, and Adamson resigned from his post at St. Andrew's to serve as a full-time professor. As a professor he taught mathematics, science, and several other subjects. Nearly his full salary earned as a professor went to the mission. Also in 1841, G. W. Stegman began a Mission to provide basic education for 500 children and by 1842 the congregation built a hall for this purpose.

While Rev. Thom had been recruiting ministers in Scotland in 1820, he had met and recruited Rev. George Morgan. Morgan served the Dutch Reformed Church in Somerset East for 17 years before arriving at St. Andrew's as Adamson's successor. However, tensions arose between Morgan and Stegman in 1842, leading the latter to leave St. Andrew's, tragically taking most of the Mission and its Lutheran teachers with him. After that, numbers at the church and its mission steadily declined until there were only 75 English-speaking and 44 Dutch-speaking people.

Due to ill-health in 1871, Morgan was forced to resign. Another Scot, Rev. James Russell, was appointed the minister of St. Andrew's in 1872. The church's work then steadily expanded. Unfortunately, the economic depression of the time caused numbers to further plummet in both congregations and in 1878, the church closed its mission. The remaining members of the mission congregation were invited to join St. Andrew's, but those who could not speak English soon joined other mission churches. The Mission school continued to be one of the best primary schools at the Cape, and in 1896 it was grafted into the public school system. Presbyterianism never fully recovered from this loss, and even today, many of the existing congregations do not have a large Coloured constituency. The closing of the mission was one of two devastating events which led to the PCSA not being as multiracial and representative of the country as a whole.

4. Beyond the Cape: The spread of Presbyterianism throughout South Africa

The discovery of diamonds and gold in the North in early 1867 led to greater numbers of British settlers coming to South Africa. First Sunday schools were established in various parts of Cape Town and these grew into churches in their own rights. There were also missions towards Africans started in the city. As Scottish settlers moved further northwards and eastwards, they took Presbyterianism with them.

Presbyterianism spread in the Eastern Cape in large part because of the Wars of Dispossession which forced the amaXhosa further and further away from the conflict to create a buffer zone between the Fish and Keiskamma Rivers. This movement laid the groundwork for the arrival of 4000+ British settlers in 1820 in the Eastern Cape. The British government's plan was to boost the English-speaking population and prevent further incursions into colonial territory by the amaXhosa. The 1820 Settlers included a Scottish party who built the first Presbyterian Church at Glen Lynden, north of Bedford in 1828. This endeavour was partly financed by the British government and partly through the fundraising efforts of Thomas Pringle, leader of the Scottish settlers. This church, and not St. Andrew's in Cape Town, was the first Presbyterian Church building in the country. It was completed a full year before St. Andrew's was finished. However, by 1830, because the congregation was isolated, they were incorporated into the Dutch Reformed Church. The building is still standing but is no longer in use. Presbyterian settler churches were established in Alice, Adelaide, Fort Beaufort, King William's Town and East London. These Presbyterian churches were often referred to as 'Scottish.' But a large percentage of churches were made up of both Presbyterian and Congregational members and so became largely independent "Union Churches." Later some of these union churches formed the Congregational union of South Africa, while a few decided to remain Presbyterian in polity and keep their connection to the settler churches.

Presbyterianism came to Natal through Rev. Philip's request to the American Board of Commissioners for Foreign Mission (ABCFM), who in 1835 sent six missionary couples to Natal. However, the war between the Zulu's and the Boers put the lives of the missionaries in danger, and only two couples remained in South Africa while the rest departed. Daniel Lindley and his wife, Lucy, were one of the missionary couples who decided to stay. Daniel Lindley's ministry continued amongst the Dutch farmers in the Pietermaritzburg area from 1842 to 1847 where he served as a minister. (See chapter six in this book on Lindley). Alongside his ministerial duties to the Boers, he also began to conduct Presbyterian services for the British colonists who were coming in ever-increasing numbers to Natal. So, it was in 1850 that the Presbyterians in Pietermaritzburg formally constituted 'the Presbyterian Church of Natal.' The first minister to serve this congregation was Rev. William Campbell (1801–1873) of the Free Church of Scotland, and they constructed the first Presbyterian Church in Natal. By 1850, Presbyterians were worshipping in Durban; they were soon joined by the Congregationalists. The next congregation was established in 1862 and more congregations followed.

Presbyterianism continued to grow rapidly in South Africa particularly with the discovery of diamonds in Kimberley in 1870, and gold in Witwatersrand in 1886. Congregations were founded in Kimberley in 1871, Johannesburg (St. George's) in 1888, and St. John's in Bloemfontein in 1896. After the cessation of hostilities caused by the Anglo Boer war of 1899–1902, Presbyterianism expanded rapidly, especially along the Witwatersrand. Presbyterianism was established wherever British colonialism seemed to take root, characterising it very much as a diaspora church. The Presbytery of Transvaal was formed in 1890 out of the Presbytery of Natal.[3] In 1899 the Presbytery of the Orange River was likewise formed out of the Presbytery of Natal but this time under the new GA's authorisation.[4]

This is true for beyond South African borders as well: the first Presbyterian congregation in Zimbabwe was established in 1896 in Bulawayo, and the second in 1903 in Harare (Salisbury). The first Presbyterian congregation established in Zambia took root in 1926 at Livingstone and more followed. So, by 1948 the Presbyterian Church of South Africa became the Presbyterian Church of Southern Africa encompassing South Africa, Zimbabwe, and Zambia.[5]

5. The establishment of the PCSA as a denomination

With the expansion of Presbyterianism throughout the length and breadth of South Africa, a decision was taken to try to unite the various presbyteries and individual congregations into a denomination. St. Andrew's Presbyterian Church took the initiative at a meeting held on 19 April 1892 towards establishing a united Presbyterian Church in South Africa. Through a unanimous vote,

---

3 Dalziel, "The Origin and Growth of Presbyterian Ordinances," 618.
4 Dalziel, "The Origin and Growth of Presbyterian Ordinances," 620–621.
5 Duncan, "A Brief History of Presbyterianism in Southern Africa," 1–4; Hofmeyr & Pillay, *A History of Christianity in South Africa*, 67–70.

the church session was instructed to reach out to the various congregations and presbyteries with the idea of uniting as a body to create a South African Presbyterian Church or, failing that, a Presbyterian union or conference. Their dream and vision for the church was for a united denomination made up of settler communities and indigenous mission churches. In October of 1892, delegates from the various churches and presbyteries met in Kimberley and formed the Federal Council. The Federal Council met annually for six years and consisted of representatives from all seven presbyteries, the Scottish missionary work, and the congregation of Port Elizabeth (later renamed Gqeberha) which was not connected to any presbytery. The primary focus of the Council was to draft a document for the basis of union.

During its fourth meeting in 1895 in Port Elizabeth (Gqeberha), the Council received word from the Free Church of Scotland through the colonial committee. The General Assembly of the Free Church of Scotland endorsed the concept of union, believing there should be one church in South Africa made up of all the races. They also believed this would reduce the financial burdens of their mission churches in the Eastern Cape. So, on 17 September 1897, the Federal Council met for the sixth and final time in Commercial Road Presbyterian Church in Durban. The presbyteries commissioned sixteen ministers and nine elders to attend the meeting, but five ministers and one elder did not attend. In total, 54 congregations, two educational institutions, and two mission stations were represented at the assembly. All the presbyteries represented at the conference were in favour of the union. However, three of the presbyteries, those of Kaffraria Free Church of Scotland, Transkei FCS, and Adelaide United Presbyterian, chose to remain out of the union. Thus, in the end it was the Presbyteries of Cape Town, of Transvaal, of Natal, and of Kaffraria (UP), and the congregation in Port Elizabeth which formed the union Church.[6] The reason given for remaining aloof was the fear of white minority domination over a black majority church, which is what would have occurred, had these presbyteries entered the union. The Council decided to find a way of balancing the Mission churches and the colonial/settler churches. This was done by "requiring separate majorities of white and of black votes at the General Assembly 'to pass a proposed measure into law' and setting up 'a

---

6 *The Manual of Law, Practice and Procedure in the Presbyterian Church of Southern Africa* (Johannesburg: PCSA, 1971), 1, on "The First General Assembly." It should be noted that earlier attempts (prior to the Conferences) at selective "unions" had been discussed. For example, in 1883 a union discussion occurred between the two presbyteries – the Kaffraria Presbytery (UP) and the FCS Kaffraria Presbytery (FCS) and this was sent to the superior courts of both denominations, but it did not happen. *Quarterly Register of the Alliance for Reformed Churches* (1883), 22.

final Court of Appeal' for dealing with 'certain questions.'"[7] Many missionaries, and particularly Rev. James Stewart of Lovedale College, supported the idea. Sadly, many black ministers felt that they would never be on equal footing with their white counterparts and so insisted on remaining out of the union even though they supported it in theory. The colonial churches failed in alleviating such fears, as it should be noted that, at the assembly, both sides were represented only by white ministers. The tragedy is, had the black congregations chosen to join the union, within a few years, they would have been the majority within the church. The picture of the PCSA might then have been very different. But as it is, from its inception, racial division was already beginning to solidify. In 1897, on the final evening of the conference, the General Assembly voted unanimously for union and the Presbyterian Church of South Africa was established as a denomination. The first moderator of the general assembly was Rev. John Smith of Pietermaritzburg. The Basis of Union of the Assembly went on to adopt:

1. The name of the United Church is 'The Presbyterian Church of South Africa'.
2. The Word of God as contained in the Old and New Testaments is the supreme Rule of Faith and Practice in this Church. Adhering to the system of doctrine contained in the Westminster and other Confessions of the Reformed Church, we accept and hold as our Subordinate Standard the XXIV 'Articles of the Faith' of the Presbyterian Church of England [PCE] as a statement of the leading doctrines taught in Scripture.
3. The Presbyterian form of Church Government is held to be founded and agreeable to, the Word of God.[8]

Although there was an early aspiration to be multiracial, it needs to be noted that the primary focus and reason for the existence of the PCSA at the time was to service the spiritual needs of the British settler community. Another reason for the lack of a multiracial church was the decision of the Scottish mission churches to stay out of the PCSA when it was established as a denomination in 1897. Their reason for staying out of the union was that they wanted to develop as a black church without paternal white domination, which was the reality in many churches.

With the PCSA now duly constituted as a denomination, it could get on with

---

[7] Bax, "UPCSA Edition: History of UPCSA," 20.
[8] Bax, "UPCSA Edition: History of UPCSA," (unpublished manuscript), 19.

the work of ministry. The next general assembly was held at St. Andrew's Church in Cape Town. It went from 33 congregations to 68 congregations within one year. After the South Africa War, Presbyterian Churches in Zimbabwe became part of the PCSA. By 1903, the PCSA consisted of 24 European congregations and 10 Native congregations, 100 European elders, 101 native elders, 86 schools, and 100 mission stations. A few years after its inception, the PCSA was a black majority church. However, all the presbyteries within the PCSA, except for one, were white dominated.

As has already been noted, and which the statistics provided underscore, the PCSA was plagued by racial divisions from its establishment. The native congregations were accustomed to services being conducted in their own language, whereas English was the dominant language in the settler churches. Also, the work of establishing new churches was divided. A colonial committee was set up for the establishment of white churches and the missions committee for the establishment of native churches. Although tension and division existed, the early 20th Century relations between the PCSA and the Free Church Missions (later called the Bantu Presbyterian Church – BPC) were quite amicable. Most of the Free Church Missions during the early part of the century could be found in the rural areas of South Africa. Thus, an agreement was reached between the Free Church Missions congregations and the PCSA: when BPC members came to live and work in towns and cities the PCSA churches would minister to these members. When the members returned to their rural homes, they would be able to resume their membership at their BPC home-churches. As towns and cities grew, and a general trend towards urbanisation took hold, more and more Africans became permanent urban residents. The BPC decided to establish congregations within these urban areas, however this led to some friction with the PCSA.[9]

As the PCSA began to expand and grow, and as the political situation became more fixated on racial separation, racial lines became entrenched between the two parts of this church. Therefore, it appeared that the fears voiced by those presbyteries and congregations who remained outside the union had come to pass. Unfortunately, the political situation in South Africa, where racial segregation under the flag of 'separate development' and later official policy as Apartheid (from 1948 to 1990), only exacerbated the existing division between different race groups. The PCSA entered the apartheid years as a racially divided church, and this would greatly hamper their witness.

In 1923, the first Presbyterian Church in Zambia joined the PCSA. At that time, the church changed its name to the Presbyterian Church in Southern Africa. The PCSA encompassed three countries by 1948 and had 11 presbyteries.[10]

---

9 Rodger, 2022.
10 Bax, "UPCSA Edition: History of UPCSA," 18–20.

6. The expansion of the Church in South Africa, Zimbabwe, and Zambia 1910–1994

It was with great vigour and zeal that the PCSA set out with its continued trajectory of growth. Their programme of expansion reached new heights from 1910 to 1994. Wherever there were settler communities or European expatriate communities, the Church sought to establish itself. The Church began to grow most rapidly in the urban centres and around the goldfields. On the West and the East Rand, in almost every town, a Presbyterian Church could be found. This was largely due to the influx of Scottish immigrants from the United Kingdom. By 1926, there already were many Presbyterian churches in and around South Africa, as already noted. Over 68 congregations had already been established and the numbers were consistently growing.

Growth of the church outside of South Africa

The church then began to break new ground as it continued to extend its influence beyond the borders of South Africa. Already in 1896, the first Presbyterian Church was planted in Zimbabwe, in the city of Bulawayo, and by 1903, the next Church was planted in Salisbury (today Harare). From there, more and more Churches were planted across Zimbabwe. And then, in 1926, the first Presbyterian congregation was established in Zambia. Known as the David Livingstone Memorial Presbyterian Church, it was named after Dr David Livingstone, the famous missionary doctor.[11]

Due to this rapid expansion, it was deemed necessary the denomination should change its name from the 'Presbyterian Church of South Africa' to the 'Presbyterian Church of Southern Africa.' This reflected both the transnational and aspirational transracial identity of the Presbyterian Church founders. By 1982, the church consisted of 70,000 communicant members of all races, 180 ministers, and 12 presbyteries spread across the three countries.[12]

Expansion and growth of the PCSA in Zambia

The expansion of the PCSA into Zambia was not as rapid as its counterpart in Zimbabwe. For nearly 30 years, the Livingstone congregation was the only PCSA church in Zambia. This congregation was part of the Presbytery of Southern Rhodesia and was subsequently subdivided into two presbyteries, those of Matabeleland and Mashonaland. By 1950, the urban populations of these

---

11 Pons, *The Southern and Central Streams of Presbyterianism in Africa*. 3.
12 Pons, *The Southern and Central Streams of Presbyterianism in Africa*, 4.

presbyteries were growing exponentially, which necessitated the need for the Minister of Livingstone congregation, Rev. Hugh Squair, to begin to pastorally care for people in the towns and along the railway lines which criss-crossed between Zimbabwe and Zambia. In 1956, he was required to visit Lusaka, and he planted a Presbyterian congregation there, which is now called St. Columba. The Lusaka congregation was small initially, only six members, and they asked their minister to travel monthly from Livingstone to conduct services for them. This was a round trip of approximately 600 miles! Soon their faith was rewarded as within a year they were able to call their own minister to pastor their 200 strong congregation.[13] Another congregation, also named St. Columba, was soon established at Kabwe (formerly known as Broken Hill). By 1959, St. Andrew's Presbyterian church was established along the Copperbelt in the town Kitwe.[14]

Zambia gained independence and became a republic in 1964. During the years preceding independence, the church scene was quite fluid and dynamic. Many of the previous missionary churches sought to amalgamate, abandon their individual ecclesiastical identities, and create a new denomination known as the United Church of Zambia (UCZ). As the PCSA work continued to expand in Zambia, it found fertile ground for growth – particularly amongst those Presbyterian congregations which did not feel completely at home in the United Church of Zambia, or who were seeking a particular Presbyterian ethos, or even those who had backslidden and were not worshipping anywhere at all. The PCSA found a welcoming environment for the establishment of this new work. Initially the church mainly focused on Europeans resident in Zambia, however it very quickly began to affect other race groups. When Tumbuka-speaking Presbyterians, from the eastern province, bordering Malawi, saw the impact of the church within the Midlands and the Copperbelt, they asked to be brought under the church's covering. This began in Lusaka in 1958, and then was followed in quick succession by churches being planted in Wusakili in Kitwe, Kabushi in Ndola and Kabwe. In 1970, an independent Presbyterian Church, along with the entire congregation, building, and their aging minister from Luanshya was admitted to the denomination. During 1970 this congregation was mainly served by ministers of the PCSA, both black and white. Sadly, by the end of 1970, these ministers had left the Luanshya congregation. However, the church managed to maintain its work thanks to the help of Rev. S. K. Nkowne, a former minister of the Church of Central Africa Presbyterian Church (CCAP), who joined the United Church of Zambia and was seconded to the Luanshya congregation.[15]

---

13 Galloway, *Your Church. Presbyterian Church of Southern Africa*, 7.
14 Pons, *The Southern and Central Streams of Presbyterianism in* Africa, 4.
15 Pons, *The Southern and Central Streams of Presbyterianism in Africa*, 4–5.

The "Presbyterian Church in Zambia," or the PCZ as it came to be called, continued its upward trajectory through rapid development. In Lusaka, both the Kabwata and Matereo congregations began to plant a number of preaching stations, several of which at the time began to experience phenomenal growth and soon became full status congregations. The Kabwata congregation alone had over 1500 communicant members at one time. These churches were able to build solid Church structures, which still exist today, at Livingstone, St. Columba's Kitwe, St. Columba's Kabwe and John Knox in Luanshya. Further buildings were erected at Kabwata, Chawama in Lusaka and Kabushi in Ndola. In 1980, the PCSA took a bold step by appointing one of its senior ministers, the Rev. Edwin Pons, as minister of the Church Extension Committee for the presbytery of Zambia. This newly formed committee aimed to further develop and grow the church in Zambia. This was done through an aggressive recruiting process of young Zambians for the ministry, as well as vigorous eldership and stewardship training programs. Extensive fundraising drives, to fund building projects and to pay for students for the ministry to complete their theological studies in Zambia, were undertaken.[16]

During the late 1970s and early 1980s, a great change came to two of the congregations in Zambia which had previously only consisted of European members. St. Andrew's Kitwe and St. Columba's Lusaka both became completely racially mixed, something which was quite unusual for the area and time. These congregations now welcomed Europeans, Zambians, Asians, Ghanaians, Kenyans, Tanzanians, and others. Although these congregations remained predominantly English-speaking, another church, St. Columba's Kabwe, was transformed into a Tumbuka-speaking congregation.[17] These changes were notable at the time, as the Church in other parts of Africa, notably in South Africa, was increasingly segregated.

It is important to note at this juncture that the harmonious integration of the congregations and members of all races, nations, and creeds had been the ultimate hope of many early Presbyterian ministers and missionaries in Africa, although it was often seen as undesirable or impossible by various members or leaders. Initially the separate congregations had been deemed necessary, as church leaders had feared

▲ James J. R. Jolobe

---

16 Pons, *The Southern and Central Streams of Presbyterianism in Africa*, 5.
17 Pons, *The Southern and Central Streams of Presbyterianism in Africa*, 5.

that integrated missionary churches would become a disregarded sub-group of the European congregations. However, the integration of the churches mentioned in the paragraph above provided hope for a united and uniting body of Christ. Unfortunately, the same view was not supported in South Africa, where apartheid and 'separate development' policies largely dominated the composition of the congregations for many more years to come.[18]

7. The formation of the Bantu Presbyterian Church (BPC)

In 1900, in Scotland two former entities which had separated from the Church of Scotland, namely the Free Church of Scotland and the United Presbyterian Church of Scotland, merged to become one new denomination: the United Free Church of Scotland (UFCS). Bax writes that the "two former Churches' work in South Africa remained separate, however. This was largely because by now the UPC missions were formally part of the PCSA whereas the missions of the FC had remained outside the PCSA, as the largely self-governing Synod of Kaffraria (sic), which now fell under the General Assembly of the UFC."[19]

Many of the black clergy and congregations in old Free Church missions were sceptical of such a union as they still feared white domination and paternalism and that the black church would merely become an appendage of the white-led PCSA. In 1920, the United Free Church sent out two Assessors from Scotland. They consulted with both clergy, congregations, and the majority of the mission stations. At a conference of missionaries held at Blythewood Mission, a decision was taken that during this interim period, it would be beneficial for Black Presbyterians to have their own church, rather than joining the PCSA, which was likely to be white dominated for a long time.[20]

It was believed that the formation of the Bantu Presbyterian Church (BPC), later known as the Reformed Presbyterian Church of South Africa (RPCSA), would help develop black leadership, promote culturally sensitive styles of worship, ministry, mission, and church development. This seemed like the logical and the best step forward for the empowerment and continuation of black Presbyterians. This sadly was because there was not a tradition in South Africa at the time

---

18 Pons, *The Southern and Central Streams of Presbyterianism in Africa*, 5.
19 Bax, "UPCSA Edition: History of UPCSA," 20. To complicate matters, we note a remnant Free Church in South Africa would be resuscitated after the 1900 union (see chapter seven in this volume); and a United Free Church Mission would also commence in 1932 in what is today Botswana after the 1929 union by the *continuing* United Free Church (see the section under smaller Presbyterian missions in Southern Africa in *Volume Two*) so that continuing denomination did not totally end its involvement in Southern Africa after 1929.
20 Bax, "UPCSA Edition: History of UPCSA," 20.

of White's sharing power with Blacks, nor, indeed, with any other race. The Presbyterian Church in Southern Africa agreed at a conference in 1921 to allow any black members, who did not wish to stay, to join this fledgling denomination, and gave them its blessing. In 1923, the Bantu/Reformed Presbyterian Church was born. All the black congregations of the old Free Church and the majority of congregations from the old United Presbyterian Church were received into this new denomination. When the BPC was constituted, it began with 22,000 members, 45 congregations, 48 ordained missionaries and ministers, and 385 schools with 24,000 pupils.[21] The PCSA lost half of its black membership, a presbytery, and many congregations, mostly in the Synod of Kaffraria. These congregations made up the majority of what was the Bantu Presbyterian Church. A large portion of the African membership elected to remain part of the PCSA when the BPC was formed. Many prominent African ministers were active in the PCSA at the time, for example Rev. Dr James Jolobe and Rev. Dr George Molefe. It must be noted that not all BPC ministers were in favour of a separate denomination, because they saw it as a perpetuation of the underlying current of separate development policy and structures being perpetuated in South Africa at the time.[22] The decision to create the BPC was met with harsh criticism, as it was seen as an extension of apartheid or 'separate development' policies. The PCSA was vocal in its decision to remain a multi-racial church, even under severe pressure and when facing many obstacles and opposition. Pons notes that the "PCSA ... sought to witness to the unity of the Body of Christ and has often stood up to be counted as a consistent opponent of the ideology and practice of 'apartheid.'"[23] This was a truly remarkable ideological aspiration, but oftentimes this was not witnessed at grass-roots level, and many individual congregations within South Africa remained or became divided, especially as apartheid laws came into further, and devastating, effect.

The Inaugural General Assembly of the BPC

It was deemed necessary and agreeable that "the Synod and Presbyteries meet immediately before the convocation and General Assembly to resolve to dissolve with a view to uniting in the new church."[24] At this convocation, the Presbyterian missions met at Lovedale on the evening of 4 July 1923, with Rev. P. L. Hunter as the Chair. At this meeting, the Synod of Kaffraria resolved to

---

21 Bax, "UPCSA Edition: History of UPCSA," 21.
22 Bax, "UPCSA Edition: History of UPCSA," 21.
23 Pons, *The Southern and Central Streams of Presbyterianism in Africa*, 6.
24 As quoted in Duncan, *The Bantu Presbyterian Church of South Africa* (forthcoming) 2022, Commission on Union, 6 February 1923, Box 12, F91–100, NAHECS, UFH.

convey all properties to the new church, along with the disjunction certificates of all its members and presbyteries. The Presbytery of Mankazana also tabled its disjunction, while it was reported that the Mission Council of Natal had been unable to meet and would report subsequently to the Assembly. Therefore, at the opening of the very first General Assembly of the Bantu Presbyterian Church in South Africa, this denomination began with 25,000 souls under its care. The first Moderator of the BPC was the Rev. William Stuart of Burns Hill mission, who was elected unanimously in 1923.

Rev. Stuart formally constituted the gathering of the assembly and delivered his Moderatorial Address. He commented that this was a watershed moment for the church, with the uniting of the FC and UP missions along with the Mission Council of Natal. Rev Stuart said:

> [L]ittle wonder if the taking of this step had occasioned doubts, fears and anxieties in the minds of some of our people. ... It has been well for ourselves and for these communities that the taking of this step has been matter of long continued earnest deliberation, much consultation and many earnest prayers ... a forward step in the line of natural development' and a result of 'earnest and prayerful deliberation, full and careful consideration of the many interests involved and persons specially concerned'. The highest office was open to black people 'as it ought to be', so the new church retained the concepts of equality and parity. 'The Church of Christ is for any and everyone, ... irrespective of nationality, colour or tongue.[25]

This is what the church set out to be at its inception: a place where black leadership, ministry, mission and worship could flourish and bring glory to God.[26]

The expansion of BPCSA 1923–1994

In 1925, two years later, at the second General Assembly of the BPC, the first black Moderator was elected – the Rev. Yekelo Mbali.[27]

In 1929, the United Free Church of Scotland merged with the Church of Scotland. This meant all the BPC's missionary ministers now fell under the

---

25 As quoted in Duncan, *The Bantu Presbyterian Church of South Africa* (forthcoming) 2022. "Rev. W. Stuart, Moderatorial Address at 1st General Assembly, BPCSA 1923," 35, 39.
26 Duncan, *The Bantu Presbyterian Church of South Africa* (forthcoming) 2022.
27 Duncan, *The Bantu Presbyterian Church of South Africa* (forthcoming) 2022.

care and discipline of the Church of Scotland. In the years following, it became apparent that, although the missionaries themselves were in support of black self-rule in theory, in practice the BPC was still dominated, to a large extent, by white colonial mission ideology through Mission Councils. So, in theory, they were an independent Church, in practice, the BPC which grew out of the Scottish missions, ended up becoming subordinate to the Mission Councils. The Mission Councils controlled the finances and missionary personnel, thus controlling the practical necessities for ministry. The BPC's independence was restricted, as Duncan states:

> because the Mission Councils were exclusive, they existed taking no great account of the views of Blacks possibly not expressed in the presbytery as the result of 'intimidation' by missionaries 'who knew better' but understood less.[28]

Despite these inequalities, within the BPC this does not make their achievements and their development any less distinguished than those churches with a longer history and a more diverse experience. Regardless of the lack of resources, the mission work which grew before 1923, and the church which came after, has survived! It grew rapidly from its formation. This was only possible through the powerful witness of many faithful African members who, with great courage and zeal for the gospel, proclaimed the saving power of Jesus Christ throughout their wider communities. As Duncan reminds us, even though there were "reservations about the ability of … [Black Presbyterians] to handle their own church affairs, the birth of the BPCSA was a triumph of realism in the South African context."[29]

By the late 1950s, the BPC consisted of seven presbyteries, which were formed to care and supervise the work of the church. These presbyteries were as follows: Kaffraria (its designation during the Apartheid era), Mankazana, Transkei, Griqualand East, Umtata (Mthatha), Natal, and Zoutpansberg. There was discussion around merging two of the presbyteries – those of Kaffraria and Mankazana – but this was considered hasty at the time. Later these presbyteries united to become one presbytery. In the years following, more presbyteries were added: the Western Cape, Ciskei, Southern Natal, Southern Transvaal, and Orange Free State.

The BPC, along with its ministers, did an outstanding job of caring pastorally for its congregations, while also remaining politically active. BPC ministers spoke out against unjust laws, which restricted the rights and aspirations of the

---

28 Duncan, *The Bantu Presbyterian Church of South Africa* (forthcoming) 2022.
29 Duncan, *The Bantu Presbyterian Church of South Africa* (forthcoming) 2022; Bax, "UPCSA Edition: History of UPCSA," 21.

majority of South Africans. The BPC at this point was making great strides. But it was still plagued by a missionary mindset, which inhibited greater autonomy. There was a belief that the church should conform to the rights and practice of the mother church, which before 1929 was the United Free Church of Scotland, and afterwards the Church of Scotland. This meant on paper the BPC was independent, but in practice it was neither autonomous nor self-governing. As already mentioned, the church continued to be held by the shackles of financial support coming from the foreign missions committee of the Church of Scotland. This meant it remained dependent on the mother church in terms of both staffing, finance, and theological training. This became an increasing source of frustration and distrust, and actually hampered the outreach of the BPC within the South African context at this point.[30]

The missionaries did sterling work, and they made great sacrifices both for themselves and their families. Unfortunately, despite this significant contribution to the global mission, they produced paradoxical responses of both conformity and resistance. This was largely due to mission education. Some responded to this education through faith and conformity. Others resisted, as an expression of their faithfulness to God, but not in accord with the missionaries' wishes or aspirations. Nonetheless the BPC would not have existed, had it not been for the establishment of these mission stations, which offered education and upliftment to its people. There was no resistance against the appointment of new missionaries, and their desire to come and serve the church. In fact, many missionaries were encouraged to remain and serve even after 1980, when more autonomy was being handed from the mother church to those within the leadership of the BPC. In 1979, the denomination took a bold step, reflecting this new-found independence, and changed its name to the Reformed Presbyterian Church of Southern Africa (RPCSA). It was this maturity within the denomination, which led the RPCSA to open dialogue with the PCSA about becoming one new denomination. This led to discussions by both churches about the possibility of forming one new Uniting Presbyterian Church in Southern Africa.[31]

8. The creation of The Uniting Presbyterian Church in Southern Africa (UPCSA) 1994–2000

Although the founders of the Presbyterian church in South Africa had hoped and aspired towards multiracialism, the reality failed to live up to this mighty desire. For many years the political, economic, and social realities of Apartheid

---

30 Duncan, *The Bantu Presbyterian Church of South Africa* (forthcoming) 2022.
31 Duncan, *The Bantu Presbyterian Church of South Africa* (forthcoming) 2022.

fed the friction between the BPC, PCSA and other churches. Even when good relationships were established on individual or congregational levels, the political situation made it increasingly difficult to maintain these links.

Two attempts were made to bring together the PCSA, RPCSA, the Evangelical Presbyterian Church of SA (formerly the Swiss Mission), and latterly the United Congregational Church of Southern Africa. The first attempt was made from 1959 to 1972 and the second from 1973 to 1981. Unfortunately, due to a lack of support for union, the RPCSA chose to withdraw during both attempts. Both early attempts ended in failure.

During the 1980s the situation in South Africa worsened as international sanctions, internal violence, unlawful detention, arrests, political murders, and protests took hold of the country. However, during the late 1980s, there was a renewed interest to form a union, initially spearheaded by the PCSA. Various informal contacts led to a number of meetings between the Ecumenical Relationships Committees of the two Churches. Although presbyteries and congregations were encouraged and various steps were taken to facilitate the process, only a limited number became involved. In 1990, the meetings between the two Committees culminated in the adoption of a 'Basis of Agreement' by both General Assemblies. This document

- "reviewed the difficult history of the relationship, while acknowledging that there were exceptions;
- stated the conviction that God was calling these Churches to rebuild good relationships, though union was not a realistic possibility at that time;
- set out guidelines and practical ideas for increased contacts and cooperation on various levels; and
- stressed the importance of going beyond adopting resolutions to implementation."[32]

Meanwhile, the political situation in South Africa had slowly improved during the early 1990s. Meetings between the Apartheid government and the ANC (African National Congress) were being held, political prisoners (including Nelson Mandela) were released, liberation organisations were unbanned, and negotiations for a new democracy all culminated in the first free and fair democratic elections in South Africa in 1994.

It has been said that change is inevitable, and that God's timing is perfect. This is never truer than with the creation of the uniting Presbyterian Church in Southern Africa. With the advent of democracy, the birth of a new nation,

---

32 Rodger, 2022.

free and independent, where every single citizen's rights and aspirations were acknowledged, with freedom of religion ingrained into the fledgling nations' constitution, it was now time for the barrier which had separated so many Presbyterians across the racial divide to come crashing down. In 1994, the RPCSA Assembly decided to propose the reopening of union talks. With the changing political situation, the RPCSA were hopeful that a union of equal partners could now be created, and fears of being dominated by one party were fading.

The PCSA responded positively. Soon a joint committee was constituted and the practical work towards establishing a union began without delay. In 1997, a draft 'Basis of the Union' was presented to the Assemblies. This was sent to the various presbyteries for comment and approval/disapproval. From that time on, much missional energy was invested in securing the union. At the 1998 Assemblies, a final draft was tabled and, after some minor changes were made, became the official 'Basis of Union.' A joint Special Commission on Union was set up to prepare the way for union. Finally, on 26 September 1999, a joyful celebration took place in Gqeberha (then Port Elizabeth), as the two Churches united to form the Uniting Presbyterian Church in Southern Africa. Present at this happy occasion were representatives of the Church of Scotland and a number of other churches.[33]

Although the years since 1999 have not been without friction, the Union of these Churches stood as a symbol of hope.[34] Hope in the unity of the body of believers, hope for true reconciliation and collaboration, and hope in the triumph of peace.

In the early 2000s (the first full list of presbyteries available), the UPCSA had 18 presbyteries; 15 presbyteries in South Africa, one in Zimbabwe and two in Zambia. These presbyteries were as follows: Amatola, Central Cape, Central Zambia, Copperbelt, Drakensberg, East Griqualand, Egoli, Free State, Highveld, Lekoa, Limpopo, Thekwini, Thukela, Transkei, Tshwane, Umtata, Western Cape, and Zimbabwe.

9. Conclusion

It is helpful to see the path of Presbyterianism in South Africa as an elongated diamond shape: at first there was a single Presbyterian stream in the country, later to be joined by various smaller streams to form the PCSA. However, there the paths diverged: the PCSA continued one way and the BPC/RPCSA followed a different path. Finally, though, these streams met up as these Presbyterian Churches in South Africa became united as the UPCSA.

---

33 Duncan, *The Bantu Presbyterian Church of South Africa* (forthcoming) 2022; Rodger, 2022.
34 After the chronological period of this chapter, it can be noted as a postscript that in 2003/2004 the RPCSA was reconstituted by a minority group.

Presbyterianism in Southern Africa was deeply influenced by the historical Reformation roots of church polity, the historical events of the era, as well as social, racial, and economic factors. It is fair to state that many of the Southern Africa churches and congregations would not have existed if not for the tireless and passionate work of various individuals, ministers and missionaries, whose commitment to God's call helped to shape the Presbyterian Church in South Africa. This includes the various ministers and leaders who were willing to stand up against political injustices and whose hope for a United and Uniting Church was brought to fruition. As with many churches and individual congregations the world over, there remains many internal and external obstacles for Presbyterian Churches in Southern Africa – including continuing racial, social, and economic inequalities, financial pressures, divergent theologies, leadership voids, and many other challenges – yet the hope in the ideals of a Uniting faith and denomination remains.

Questions for study (fact type):

1 This chapter has two critical ecclesiastical unions. Describe the process which culminated in the 1897 Union and how this union was worked out. Use the information questions – Who, What, When, Where, How, and Why – to prepare your answers for questions #1 and #2.
2 Next, describe the process which led to the Union of 1999 and how this union was worked out.

Questions for study (reflection type):

1 "the Church does not exist completely separate from political, social, economic, cultural, racial, and linguistic realities"

 Discuss this quotation from the introduction by giving one example from this chapter of each of these realities – political, social, economic, cultural, racial, and linguistic realities – and how they have affected the development of what eventually became The Uniting Presbyterian Church in Southern Africa.

2 *"Although the years since 1999 have not been without friction, the Union of these Churches stood as a symbol of hope. Hope in the unity of the body of believers, hope for true reconciliation and collaboration, and hope in the triumph of peace."*

 This quote refers to the establishment of the UPCSA. Why is it important to know the history of a denomination as you face present challenges? How can knowing the history bring encouragement and perspective for the future? Discuss.

Select Bibliography

Bax, Douglas S. "UPCSA Edition: History of UPCSA. unpublished manuscript." 1999: 3–38.

Bantu Presbyterian Church of South Africa (BPCSA), *Proceedings of the General Assembly. Incwadi yamaculo amaXhosa (Ehlaziyiwo): Egunyasiswe ngamabandla aseRhabe.* Lovedale: Lovedale Press, 1923. Rev. W. Stuart, Moderatorial Address at 1st General Assembly, BPCSA 1923. (Quoted in Duncan, 2022).

Bantu Presbyterian Church of South Africa, Archives, Cory Library for Historical Research, Rhodes University, Grahamstown.

Bower, Douglas K. "The Christian witness of the Presbyterian Church in Southern Africa against Apartheid between 1948–1994." BAHons thesis, University of Pretoria, 2013.

Commission on Union, 6 February 1923, Box 12, F91–100, NAHECS, UFH. (Quoted in Duncan, 2022).

Dalziel, John. "The Origin and Growth of Presbyterian Ordinances of Worship among English speaking European South Africans Prior to the Formation of the Presbyterian Church of South Africa in 1897." PhD thesis, University of Edinburgh, 1957.

Duncan, Graham A. "A Brief History of Presbyterianism in Southern Africa." Pretoria: unpublished work, 2008.

Duncan, Graham A. *The Bantu Presbyterian Church of South Africa: A history of the Free Church of Scotland Mission.* Edinburgh: Edinburgh University Press, 2022 (Forthcoming).

Duncan, Graham A. "The Presbyterian Church of South Africa: The early years, 1897–1923, and future prospects." *Verbum et Ecclesia*, 43.1 (2022): 1–9. https://dx.doi.org/10.4102/ve.v43i1.2395

Galloway, L. *Your Church. Presbyterian Church of Southern Africa.* [Booklet] PCSA, 1965.

Hofmeyr, J. W. & G. J. Pillay, eds., *A History of Christianity in South Africa Vol 1.* Pretoria: HAUM Tertiary, 1994.

The Manual of Law, Practice and Procedure in the Presbyterian Church of Southern Africa. Johannesburg: PCSA, 1971.

Pons, E. S. *The Southern and Central Streams of Presbyterianism in Africa.* Kitwe, Zambia: Presbyterian Church of Southern Africa, 1982.

Reformed Presbyterian Church in Southern Africa, archives, Cory Library for Historical Research, Rhodes University, Grahamstown.

Rodger, Alastair. [Personal communication]. 30 January 2022.

South African history Online. 2012. States of Emergency in South Africa: The 1960s and 1980s. Available from: https://www.sahistory.org.za/topic/state-emergency-south-africa-1960-and-1980s (Accessed 28 December 2021).

South African History Online. 2012. A history of apartheid in South Africa. Available from: https://www.sahistory.org.za/article/history-apartheid-south-africa (Accessed 28 December 2021).

Wark, D. "After forty years: A sketch of the growth of the Presbyterian Church of South Africa from 1898 to 1938." Reprinted from *The Presbyterian Churchman* of December 1939. Citadel Press and Finance Committee of the General Assembly, 1940.

Chapter 5

Sound the Trumpet: The Life and Ministry of Tiyo Soga, 1829–1871

John S. Ross

Chapter Outline
1. Introduction
2. The Early Years: 1829–1846
3. The First Visit to Glasgow: 1846–1848
4. Uniondale: 1848–1850
5. The Second Visit to Glasgow: 1850–1856
6. The Mgwali Years: 1857–1868
7. Tutura and the End: 1868–1871
8. Conclusion

1. Introduction

Tiyo Soga was the first black South African to be ordained as a Presbyterian minister, a great African intellectual, a pioneer journalist, translator, and hymn composer. Married to a Scotswoman, Janet Burnside, their children made significant contributions to Africa: William Anderson (1858–1916) was an ordained United Presbyterian minister and the first qualified black medical doctor in South Africa; John Henderson (1860–1941) was also a United Presbyterian minister, translator and ethnologist; Alan Kirkland (1862–1938) was a lawyer, journalist, editor of *Izwi Labantu*, politician, and a founder of the South African Native National Congress (now the African National Congress); of Isabella McFarlane (1864–1884) little is known, she was born at Inverkip in Scotland and died at Cunningham Mission, Toleni, Transkei; Jotello Festiri (1865–1906) was South Africa's first black veterinary surgeon who played a leading role in eradicating rinderpest; Frances Maria Anna (1868–1942) worked for the United Free Church of Scotland mission in South Africa; Jessie Margaret (1870–1954) was the only Soga child to settle in Scotland, she was a contralto singer, music teacher, and suffragiste.

2. The Early Years: 1829–1846

Tiyo Soga was an aristocrat, descended from a line of great leaders, wise counsellors, and brave warriors of the Rharhabe clan of the Xhosa people living in what is now the Eastern Cape of South Africa. His grandfather, Jottelo, a leading adviser of Ngqika, the head of the western or Rharhabe Xhosa, fought and, it is said, died, in the battle of Amalinde in 1818.[1] Tiyo's father, usually referred to with great respect as Old Soga, was also a counsellor to Ngqika and his son and heir, Mgolombane Sandile, as well as a loyal and courageous soldier.

Not far from Old Soga's kraal was the home of Ntsikana (c.1780–1820) also one of Ngqika's councillors and probably the first Xhosa convert to Christianity. As a teenager he had heard the gospel from the Dutch missionary Johannes van der Kemp (1747–1811) of the London Missionary Society. What he heard, combined with certain mystical experiences, led him from traditional Xhosa religion and his calling as a diviner, to discover more of 'Thixo [God] and his son.'[2] Ntsikana sought instruction, first from Joseph Williams (1780–1818), the missionary at Kat River, and then from John Brownlee (1791–1871) of the London Missionary Society at the Tyumie (old spelling: 'Chumie') mission. For Ntsikana this life-transforming encounter with the gospel was more than personal; it was to be shared. One with whom he shared it was Old Soga.

Old Soga's great wife, Nosutu, was a Christian from the Amantinde clan, who gave birth to a boy in 1829 and gave him the birth name of Zisani, later shortened to Sani. It was his father who called him Tiyo, in honour of a great counsellor and brave warrior, hoping that his son would play an equally important role in the story of his people.[3] Tiyo's wisdom, however, would be spiritual rather than human, and his courage though not proved militarily would result in sacrificial service for Christ, his Lord.

The Soga family kraal at Gwali was near to the Tyumie mission station which had been founded by Rev. John Brownlee of the London Missionary Society in 1820.[4] As Tiyo was reaching manhood, the mission was under the guidance of Rev. William Chalmers (1802–1847), a minister of the Glasgow

---

1 Milton, *The Edges of War*, 68f.
2 The amaXhosa name for God is 'u-Dali,' but 'Thixo,' a word possibly of Khoikhoi or San origin, has been used at least since the coming of the first missionaries as expressing a concept of God more compatible with Christian teaching. Tiyo's son, John Henderson Soga, discusses this in his important anthropological work, *The Ama-Xosa: Life and Customs* (Lovedale: Lovedale Press, n.d.), 150.
3 Cf. Donovan Williams, ed. *The Journal and Selected Writings of the Reverend Tiyo Soga*, 1. Williams implausibly speculates that 'Tiyo' is derived from 'Theo', an abbreviation of 'Theodore,' but this is improbable in view of John Chalmers' explanation. John A. Chalmers, *Tiyo Soga: A Page of South African Mission Work*, 10.
4 For Brownlee's missionary activity see Basil Holt, *Greatheart of the Border: A Life of John Brownlee Pioneer Missionary in South Africa*.

Missionary Society, whose son, John Aitken Chalmers (1837–1888), though Tiyo's junior, proved to be a good friend, ministerial colleague, and faithful biographer. Tiyo's eldest brother, his father's great son, Festiri, seeing the benefits of the education offered by the missionaries, neglected the cattle he was supposed to be herding and went to school to learn to read. At first, his father was angry and punished him for his carelessness, but seeing his heart was set on receiving an education, and knowing he was fully supported by his mother, he yielded.

Festiri was Tiyo's first teacher, passing on what he had learned to the junior members of his family and to others eager to learn. Under the supervision of William Chalmers, and with the help his mother, Festiri constructed a thatched schoolhouse, which was named *Struthers*, for Rev. Gavin Struthers of the Scottish Relief Church. The school bell was the iron tyre of a wagon wheel, suspended between two posts and rung by striking it with a stone. Recognising their potential, William Chalmers sent Festiri and Tiyo to the central school at the mission station further down the valley. Not far away was the Lovedale Seminary, a secondary school, where in 1844, the fifteen-year-old Tiyo commenced his formal education.[5]

Though only a few miles distant, Lovedale was, in reality, worlds away. Coming to terms with this new world would cause Tiyo many struggles. Run by the Free Church of Scotland, Lovedale's educational policy was multiracial: Xhosa students and the sons of settlers and missionaries sat side by side in the same class. The senior students, both black and white, reminded Tiyo that as a newcomer he was the lowest in the class, but this did not worry him; over the coming months he worked steadily, passing the others to become top of the class in every subject, except mathematics, in which he came second.

3. The First Visit to Glasgow: 1846–1848

In 1846 the seventh of the Cape Frontier Wars, the so-called War of the Axe, broke out. With the earlier treaties breaking down, settlers pressed the leaders of the Colony to find a pretext for a war which might open Xhosa country to settlement. They found it when, in the middle of March, a Xhosa, arrested for the theft of an axe, was sent for trial to Grahamstown under escort of a small contingent of Cape Mounted Rifles. The party was ambushed, the prisoner liberated, and the man to whom he had been shackled was killed, necessitating, in the minds of the authorities, retaliation. On 11th April a large colonial force, including Imperial troops, Boer commandos, and Mfengu irregulars, under the command of Colonel

---

5   For Lovedale's founding and multiracial mission, and its deliberate subversion by the passing of Henrik Verwoerd's notorious Bantu Education Act 1953 (No.47), see Shepherd, *Lovedale*.

Henry Somerset (1794–1862), crossed the border at Block Drift to invade Xhosa territory, making Sandile's kraal at Burnshill their objective.

Lovedale was vulnerably situated on the border; at the outbreak of war the school closed, and the students were sent home. Most of the Scottish missionaries, and Tiyo's mother, Nosutu, fled to Fort Armstrong for safety. Lovedale's principal, Rev. William Govan, however, used this opportunity to return to Scotland, inviting Tiyo to go with him to complete his education in Glasgow. Tiyo's father could not be consulted as he was in the Amathole mountains fighting, so Tiyo's mother was asked to give her permission. Nosutu's response was swift and simple.

> My son is the property of God; wherever he goes, God goes with him. If my son is willing to go I make no objection, for no harm can befall him even across the sea; he is as much in God's keeping *there* as near to me.[6]

Such was her spirited and trusting answer, but the final decision she left to her son, who speedily and eagerly consented. Tiyo together with the Govans, and with Bryce and Richard Ross, the two sons of the missionary, Rev. John Ross of Pirie, set out by ox-waggon for Port Elizabeth to embark for Cape Town and the long voyage to Britain.

The large John Street United Presbyterian Church in Glasgow, which Tiyo attended, took financial responsibility for his education. The minister, Dr William Anderson (1799–1872), showed him much kindness, not only understanding his loneliness in the city and need for encouragement and support, but affirming his identity as a black man. Through Anderson's help, Tiyo was saved from many temptations and dangers that could have led him astray, so that the seed of the gospel, planted in his heart by his mother, was able to germinate and flourish. On 7 May 1848, he made public profession of his faith by being baptised by Dr Anderson and received as a communicant member of the congregation.

For Tiyo Soga, becoming a Christian was no superficial change of religious affiliation. He was not 'converting' to Christianity in the sense of rejecting his former culture by embracing the traditions of those who had made provision for his education, rather he was professing what he actually believed to be true, that he had been converted by the power of the Holy Spirit. Henceforth, as Donovan Williams commented, Tiyo Soga 'always saw himself as a Christian first; from this all else followed.'[7] How he reconciled that to his Xhosa heritage and culture we shall discover.

---

6   Chalmers, *Tiyo Soga*, 39.
7   Williams, *Journal … Soga*, 7.

4. Uniondale: 1848–1850

On 24 October 1848, Soga, accompanied Rev. George Brown, a new recruit for the Tyumie mission, left Glasgow by express train for London, where they were to board the *Jane*, a sailing barque that would bring them slowly back to Africa. On the platform at Glasgow to bid them Godspeed was Dr Struthers, then moderator of the United Presbyterian Synod, after whom the little school at Gwali had been named. An untroubled three-month voyage brought them into Port Elizabeth on 31 January 1849. Shortly after returning home, Soga, who had been appointed as catechist (a religious teacher) on an annual salary of £25, was given the responsibility, with a colleague, Robert Niven, of opening a new mission station at a place they called Uniondale, originally known in Xhosa as Qoboqobo (a fragile thing) and later called Keiskammahoek, approximately twenty-five kilometres east of his home near Tyumie. It was here that he first preached before a congregation and here too that he began to write hymns for a Xhosa hymn book he would publish.[8]

Uniondale was also the place where Soga first faced strong opposition to his Christian convictions from his own people. When it became known that he had not submitted to circumcision, the most important coming of age ritual for Xhosa men, fathers, disgusted, took their sons away from his school. Some of his contemporaries threatened his life if he did not submit to circumcision, but even after his home had been broken into and his property stolen, he refused to compromise his Christian convictions. In later life he was able to encourage Xhosa Christian young men to disentangle the neutral and cultural elements of circumcision from those intimately related to traditional religion and the worship of the ancestors.[9]

As the work went on at Uniondale, the unstable frontier was again teetering on the edge of war. This eighth war, the War of Mlanjeni, was triggered by the high-handed theatricality of the Governor of Cape Province, Sir Harry Smith. Not only had he earlier humiliated in public the great Xhosa chief and military strategist Maqoma, but he had forced Sandile, when detained in Grahamstown, to kiss his boot. Understandably, the Xhosa disliked and distrusted him. On 23rd December, Smith gathered Xhosa leaders at Fort Cox to proclaim a new territory,

---

8   See chart in Chapter 27 in this volume for more on Tiyo Soga's contribution in hymn writing.
9   Circumcision is regarded as an important rite of passage for Xhosa young men. After circumcision the initiates (*abakwetha*) live together in seclusion to allow time for the healing process, during which they smear white clay on their bodies, eat a prescribed diet, observe numerous rituals and undergo instruction. Circumcised men are qualified to marry, inherit possessions and officiate in ritual ceremonies. Tiyo Soga did not object in principle to circumcision for Christian young men, but insisted it be separated from its traditional religious overtones and treated as a civil rite. Cf. Chalmers, *Tiyo Soga*, 264ff.

British Kaffraria, and to announce the dismantling of the Neutral Territory, a buffer strip between Xhosa lands and the Colony, which would in future be given over to colonial settlement, though the Xhosa would be permitted to remain in their homes. Smith now deposed their respected chief, Sandile, who had refused to attend the meeting, declaring that he, Smith, would, henceforth, rule under martial law as their supreme chief, their 'Inkos Inkhulu!' (Great Lord). The gathered chiefs were then required to indicate their assent by coming forward exclaiming 'Inkos Inkhulu!' and engaging in the by now customary bootlicking, while the imperious but very short-statured Smith, remained seated upon his horse.

On Christmas Eve 1850, the much provoked and deeply humiliated Xhosa sought retribution. Seizing the initiative, they opened hostilities by ambushing in the Booma Pass a column of six hundred troops under the incompetent and cowardly Col. George McKinnon, who had been ordered by Smith to patrol the Amathole mountains, the heart of Sandile's territory.[10] Then, on the following morning, Christmas Day, the Xhosa fell on the military villages of Auckland, Woburn and Juanasburg (named after Smith's Spanish wife). These settlements had been established in the Tyumie valley, within Ngqika territory, by retired military veterans who wished to live in the colony. At the time, Woburn was occupied by sixteen men, though no women; all sixteen were killed. At Auckland twenty-eight men fell, but the Xhosa, as was customary, permitted the women to escape, after robbing them of virtually all they had. Traumatised, they and their small children found refuge in the Gwali mission. In the meantime, the settlers at Juanasberg, by now fully aware of their peril, escaped with their lives, though their homes were burned down.

With Uniondale at the centre of the unrest, Niven and his family speedily departed to seek safety, but Soga and an elder, a man named Busak, remained behind. That afternoon, as the mission station was attacked and burned to the ground, Soga and Busak grabbed a few of their things and ran for their lives to a nearby kraal where they knew they would be safe. This was a hard time for Xhosa Christians. Busak lost everything he owned and, about a year later, was found dead with assegai wounds. Other local Christians, afraid to be denounced as traitors, hid in a cave in the Amathole mountains, until in 1853 over a hundred of them made their way to Rev. Richard Birt of the London Missionary Society, at Peelton mission station, near King William's Town. In the aftermath, Uniondale and Igquibigha had both been turned into military posts, and the missionaries forbidden to reoccupy them.

---

10 For McKinnon's incompetence and cowardice see Keith Smith, *Harry Smith's Last Throw: The Eighth Frontier War, 1850–1853*, 57–58.

The outbreak of fighting had so badly shaken Mrs Niven's nerves that the family decided to return to Scotland, offering to take Tiyo with them, thus opening up for him the possibly of training for ordained ministry. Sad at heart for his country and his people, now, for a second time fleeing conflict, Soga left Africa for Glasgow. But before the party embarked at Cape Town, he was tempted to remain, having been offered, at a very good salary, the post of a government interpreter. This temptation he resisted, saying that he would rather beg in the streets of Glasgow for his fees for the Theological Hall. He did not have to beg on the streets, for although his father refused to make any contribution towards his ministerial training, the John Street Church made generous provision for him.

5. The Second Visit to Glasgow: 1850–1856

To prepare for ordination in the United Presbyterian Church, a student was required first to graduate Bachelor of Arts at Glasgow University and then complete the prescribed course at the Theological Hall. Hard at his books during the hall's sessions, on Sundays, Soga taught in a Sunday school in one of the poorer parts of the city. He made many friends, influencing some to consider missionary work in South Africa and inducing others to support the growing Xhosa church.

Who were the people who influenced him? These were mainly, though not exclusively, United Presbyterians, who among all Scottish Presbyterians of the time, showed themselves more sympathetic towards cultural diversity than any others. One of the most influential in this regard happened to be a teacher at the Theological Hall, Prof. John Brown. Brown taught that on becoming a Christian one did not abandon ones' ethnic identity or culture. Although it was necessary to distinguish what was or was not compatible with Christianity within that culture, it was important only to renounce such elements as were incompatible, affirming what remained. Brown had expressed himself very clearly on the matter in his commentary on Romans. Commenting on chapter 10, Brown wrote of St Paul's post-conversion loyalty to his Jewishness and to his people Israel:

> Christianity does not unhinge the relations formed by nature; it draws them closer. It does not extinguish the affections which grow out of these relations; it regulates and sanctifies them, and, connecting them with religious duty, secures a healthful strength and a steady operation. Paul, when he became a Christian ... did not cease to be a Jew. He ... continued a patriot. Before his conversion, his patriotism manifested itself in his wishes and exertions to promote the worldly prosperity and glory of his race. It is their salvation now that he is chiefly

> anxious about. For this he lives; for this he is willing to die …
> It is his heart's desire and prayer to God, that all men may be
> saved; but the salvation of Israel excites a peculiar intensity of
> desire – draws forth a peculiar fervency of supplication.[11]

Soga was to discover that United Presbyterian cultural sympathy extended to extraordinary lengths when, after completing his theological studies, on 23 December 1856, six years to the day since the events that had displaced him from his home in the Amathole mountains, he was ordained by the United Presbyterian Presbytery of Glasgow as a minister of the John Street church on equal terms with his white colleagues. A most remarkable ordination prayer was offered by the senior minister, Rev. William Anderson. With his hand resting on Soga's head, he earnestly prayed for God's blessing for his young African friend, then eloquently asked God to make the British government change its colonial policy, and finally sought God's blessing on 'the noble chieftain Sandile,' at that very moment considered by the British authorities at the Cape to be a fugitive from justice.

▲ Rev. Tiyo & Janet (née Burnside) Soga

The claim is often made that Tiyo Soga was the first black South Africa to be ordained to Christian ministry, this, however, is open to challenge, unless we adopt South Africa's apartheid era racial classifications, as Soga's near neighbour,

---

11 John Brown, *Analytical Exposition of the Epistle of St. Paul the Apostle to the Romans*, (Edinburgh: William Oliphant and Co, 1857), 301. Cf. "The Reverend Tiyo Soga: Negotiating Culture, Race and Nationality among the Embattled Xhosa of South Africa" in Peggy Brock, Norman Etherington, Gareth Griffiths, and Jacqueline Van Gent, *Indigenous Evangelists and Questions of Authority in the British Empire 1750–1940*, 45–57.

at Blinkwater, Fort Beaufort, Rev. Arie van Rooyen, of Khoisan descent, was ordained seven years earlier, in 1849, to the Congregationalist ministry of the London Missionary Society.[12] As far as we know, Soga was the first black South African to be ordained to Presbyterian ministry.

Among other friendships Soga established in Scotland by far the most important was a romantic attachment to Janet Burnside. How, where and in what circumstances they met we do not know. Janet, two years older than Tiyo, was the eldest daughter of Alan and Isabelle Burnside, then living with her parents at Craignestock, in the Calton district of Glasgow, famous for its cotton weaving. Janet's mother was a dressmaker. Her father was a yarn warper, a relatively poorly paid job preparing looms for the weaving of cotton cloth. The marriage took place in Ibrox United Presbyterian Church, Ibroxholm, on 27 February 1857, with Rev. John Ker officiating. Poor they may have been but judging from the invitations Tiyo sent out to his friends, playfully announcing his being 'launched into the horrors of matrimony,' their wedding seems to have been a light-hearted and happy event.[13]

Although the newly married couple suffered no embarrassment or criticism in Scotland on account of their inter-racial marriage, it was a different story when they returned to the Cape. Walking in the streets of Cape Town and Port Elizabeth they often suffered the loudly expressed disapproval of ill-mannered racially prejudiced colonists; however, the couple refused to be troubled by this small-mindedness. One day, after their being stared at disapprovingly by unfriendly people, Soga wrote that the principle of the equality of the races had triumphed: he had stared down his critics.[14]

The Sogas arrived home to British Kaffraria to discover the country, already laid waste by war, further devastated by the Cattle Killing.[15] In the winter of 1856 it was put about that the spirits of the Xhosa ancestors had told a young prophetess called Nongqawuse to instruct the people to destroy all their crops and kill their cattle: in return, the ancestors would sweep the settlers into the sea. After eighty years of colonial aggression and seeing no way to regain their status as an independent people, many Xhosa people were only too ready to believe the

---

12 Joanne Ruth Davis, *Tiyo Soga: A Literary History*, 3. Van Rooyen's son, James, was at Lovedale with Soga's son, William Anderson. See T. Simon N. Gqubule, "An Examination of the Theological Education of Africans in the Presbyterian, Methodist, Congregational and Anglican Churches in South Africa from 1860 to 1960." (Unpublished PhD thesis, Rhodes University, Grahamstown, 1977), 51.
13 The marriage certificate may be viewed and downloaded from, http://www.scotlandspeople.gov.uk
14 Chalmers, *Tiyo Soga*, 131f.
15 For a definitive account of the Cattle Killing episode see Jeff Pieres, *The Dead Will Arise: Nongqawuse and the Great Xhosa Cattle-Killing of 1856–7*.

prophecies. All across the region cattle were slaughtered, their carcasses left to rot. Granaries were emptied and the ground left unplanted. The ancestors' promise, it was said, would be fulfilled on 18 February 1857, when the sun would rise red. But that day the sun rose the same as it had on every other day and proved the prophecy false. The result was not only great disillusionment, but a catastrophe of immense proportions, in which the Xhosa people were both perpetrators and victims. The population of British Kaffraria is said to have plummeted from around one hundred and five thousand to fewer than twenty-seven thousand, with corpses littering the land, even as the surviving hungry desperately sought food and help.

For the Xhosa, now well and truly under the colonial heel, it was scant comfort to recall the recent victories of Maqoma and his two hundred warriors who defied for over eighteen months four thousand crack imperial troops, keeping large parts of the north of the Colony ungovernable and uninhabitable by white people. Nor did it matter that they had been revenged on the conceited Governor, Sir Harry Smith, who, having exhausted the patience of his superiors, had been recalled to England in disgrace. The Xhosa survivors were now herded by the colonial authorities into villages located on poor unproductive land to eke out whatever living they could scratch from the soil or bind themselves in discriminatory and exploitary labour contracts deep in the Colony, far from home.

6. The Mgwali Years: 1857–1868

In December 1857, Tiyo and Janet Soga, joined by Rev. Robert Johnston, moved to a new mission station at Mgwali, near Stutterheim, and set to work providing food and shelter for the starving and homeless people flocking to them. Soga appealed to friends in Scotland for financial aid, telling how they were 'seeing sights that are making our hearts bleed and our eyes weep. It was only yesterday that … with my own hands … I dug the grave of a mother and two children who had died of sheer starvation.'[16] Terrible as this was, worse was to come, for when the time for sowing came many were too weak to cultivate their land and a severe prolongation of the famine threatened. But there were good stories too. A young lad of around twelve had been brought in unconscious and close to death, but kindness and good food 'are working wonders for him.'[17] Such stories when related in the *United Presbyterian Missionary Record* encouraged generous donations from the churches in Scotland.

---

16 Chalmers, *Tiyo Soga*, 142.
17 Chalmers, Tiyo Soga, 143.

With their own hands, Soga and Johnston built two small mud-walled cottages and a tiny church. As Johnston painted the woodwork, Soga cut and fitted the glass for the windows. Each Sunday, they took it in turns to conduct services: one in English for the few settlers in the area, the other in isiXhosa. Soga had thought that disillusionment with the failed prophecies might open Xhosa hearts to the Gospel, but at first there was resistance. On 21st January, in his mission journal he wrote, 'Conducted a service in the morning...there [were] a few Xhosas present.'[18] Then, as confidence rose, attitudes began to soften. In March he could write, 'There were three red Xhosas present in our services.'[19] On Sunday 10th April the little church was opened, and the Lord's Supper was celebrated with forty communicants. By the end of May attendance had reached around one hundred and fifty. Soga and Johnston now felt optimistic: 'our little Sanctuary was quite full and attention sustained in all the Services.'[20] By September the church was too small. On Sunday, 16th September, Soga wrote, "Another splendid day in attendance – No room at all – some had to stand outside – a good company of fine young people."[21]

In July 1861 the foundation for a new Mgwali church was laid. Intended to accommodate a congregation of six hundred, it was opened a year later, on Sunday 15th June. This was a day of great rejoicing, hearty feasting, good fellowship, and fine preaching. The seventy-one-year-old Tyumie pioneer, Rev. John Brownlee, rode over from King William's Town to preach at the morning Xhosa service. Soga's former teacher, Rev. William Govan, principal of Lovedale, preached in English at noon. His close friend, Rev. Bryce Ross of Pirie, preached in the afternoon in Xhosa, from the text Matthew 5.9, 'Blessed are the peacemakers,' an allusion to Soga himself. It was Ross' sincere hope that the promised benediction would rest upon his friend. Rev. James Read of Kat River, colleague of Rev. Arie van Rooyen, preached from Acts 16 in Dutch, reminding the Dutch settlers in the congregation what many resented to hear, that all men were equal: all needed to ask, 'What must I do to be saved?' and all needed to heed the answer, 'Believe on the Lord Jesus Christ and you will be saved.' Soga's United Presbyterian colleagues, Rev. James Laing and Rev. John Chalmers, were both present, as were his neighbours, Rev. Johann Kropf of the Berlin Mission at Bethel, and Revs. Thomas Brockway and Henry Kayser of the London Missionary Society at Peelton.

---

18 Williams, *Journal ... Soga*, 16.
19 Williams, *Journal ... Soga*, 17. 'Red Xhosa' were the conservative Xhosas who followed traditional African religion and wore blankets coloured with red ochre.
20 Williams, *Journal ... Soga*, 19.
21 Williams, *Journal ... Soga*, 21.

▲ Mgwali Church

With the church building now complete, Soga dedicated his time to writing, especially the completion of *Uhambo loMhambi*, his literal translation of John Bunyan's *Pilgrim's Progress*, which he had begun as a student in Glasgow.[22] This he finished on 21 November 1866, noting in his journal, "Quarter past nine o'clock, night. Finished, through the goodness of Almighty God, the translation of the first part of the Pilgrim's Progress, my fingers aching with writing."[23] He dedicated the volume to Lovedale's principal, Dr. William Govan, who had it printed and published by the Lovedale Press.

---

22 See Thulani Nxasana, "The Journey of the African as Missionary: The Journal and Selected Writings of the Reverend Tiyo Soga," in *English in Africa* 38. 2 (2011), 61–76.
23 Nxasana, "The Journey of the African as Missionary," 340.

UHAMBO LO MHAMBI,

OWESUKA KWE LILIZWE,

WAYE ESINGA

KWELO LIZAYO.

IMBALI EZEKELISWE NGE PUPA,

NGU

John Bunyan, Isicaka sika Tixo.

IGUQULWE KWINTETO YA MANGESI,
NGU MFUNDISI, UMFO KA SOGA.

LOVEDALE:
ISHICILELWE NGE SISHICILELO SESA KIWO
SABA FUNDISI.
1868.

TO

The Rev. William Goban,

THE FOUNDER

And Superintendent

OF THE

Lovedale Free Church Missionary Institution,

ONE OF THE LONG-TRIED, UNWEARYING, CONSTANT FRIENDS
AND BENEFACTORS OF THE

Native Races of South Africa,

THIS TRANSLATION INTO THE KAFIR LANGUAGE

OF

JOHN BUNYAN'S RENOWNED WORK

IS DEDICATED,

WITH MUCH AFFECTION, ESTEEM AND ADMIRATION,

BY HIS FRIEND AND PUPIL,

TIYO SOGA.

▲ *Pilgrim's Progress* title page and dedication page

Soga, who had bestrode two worlds, had a great ability to unite people, his ministry transcended race with many Xhosa people and local settlers attending his services. He also rose above narrow Christian denominationalism. Presbyterian, Methodist, and Anglican congregations in Port Elizabeth, Uitenhage, Grahamstown, Bedford, Alice, King Williams Town were all open to him; he even preached in the Dutch Reformed Moederkerk in Cape Town. As a result, most of the early prejudice against himself and his wife disappeared. Indeed, one old white resident of King William's Town presented him with two beautifully bound books, inscribed: "To the Rev. Tiyo Soga, upon hearing the first sermon preached by him at King William's Town."[24]

Busy writing Xhosa hymns for inclusion in a school hymnbook, which was published in 1864, Soga also found himself embroiled in a farcical controversy concerning the revision of the Xhosa Bible. By 1859 the Wesleyan missionary,

---

24 Collection of the Amathole Museum at King Williams Town.

Rev. John W. Appelyard, had translated the whole Bible, which was published in 1864. Many missionaries and churchmen, including Soga, were not at all satisfied with the quality of the translation, and, much to Appleyard's chagrin, suggested a revision. Soga was now at the height of his literary ability: his mother tongue was isiXhosa, the translation's target language; he was a fluent English-speaking author; a scholar trained in the biblical languages of Hebrew and Greek; and was working on an improved Xhosa orthography. Not only was he a most obvious choice as a member of any revision committee, but, owing to his education, ability, and experience, he deserved precedence as a translator. What in fact happened, was that his death before the completion of the revision, allowed others to disparage his ability, even as a Xhosa speaker, writing him out of a predominately white narrative and denigrating with faint praise his work on the Acts of the Apostles.[25]

In 1862 Soga began to get involved in journalism, writing under the pseudonym, *Nonjiba Waseluhlangeni* (Dove of the Nation) in the Lovedale monthly bilingual English-Xhosa newspaper, *Indaba* (The News). This platform allowed Soga to develop clear ideas about, what came to be called, Black-consciousness, which would be taken up and developed by thinkers and anti-apartheid activists such as Steve Biko (1946–1977). In June 1864, drawing on the teaching of Romans 13:7, and his own practice, he called on all Christians to give "respect to whom respect is owed, honour to whom honour is owed," irrespective of colour or ethnicity: a courteous raising of the hat to traditional leaders, and a nod to deserving white men, but all without obsequiousness:

> We want to know if you greet your chiefs with their traditional salutations – you who are converts to Christianity, you the dwellers in Mission stations. If you no longer do this what caused you to abandon this fine practice? Raise your hats to chiefs and respectable people. To White gentlemen bow your heads gently even though you do not utter a word. Do that to White people who deserve this ... But we do not advise this to [Whites] who are no better than yourselves. This 'Morning Sir' of the Xhosa people whenever they see a White face is very annoying.[26]

For Soga, though, this was not a happy time, unpleasant tensions, including those over the Bible translation, culminated in 1864, when his friend, John Chalmers,

---

25 For a scholarly review of this unseemly farrago see Davis, *Tiyo Soga*, 170–210.
26 *Indaba*, vol.2, no. 6, June 1864, 353–354. English translation in Williams, *Journal ... Soga*, 174–175.

published a hurtful and derogatory article entitled 'The Kaffir Race.' Originally carried by *Indaba*, and then on 25th April by the *King William's Town Gazette and Kaffrarian Banner*, the article expressed Chalmers' jaundiced view of Africans. In it he reiterated tired old racist tropes, suggesting that the Xhosa people would be obliterated by history unless they made what whites might consider a full contribution to the life of the Colony. Chalmers' attitude deeply angered Soga. Writing anonymously to the *Gazette* under the pseudonym *Defensor*, he challenged his friend's assumption that black people were inherently 'indolent,' 'drunken,' 'averse to change,' and consequently 'doomed to extinction.'

The importance of this public debate for racial equity cannot be overstated, for despite a strong difference of opinion, their literary battle did not result in personal animosity between Soga and Chalmers. As Williams remarks, "As far as can be ascertained, the letters are the first of their kind by a black man in South Africa, and contribute to making 1865 the great year for the emergence of Black consciousness."[27]

Putting his preaching into practice, Soga, reminded his children of their precarious future as children of a biracial family, but added: "For your own sakes never appear ashamed that your father was a Kaffir, and that you inherit some African blood ... take your place in the world as coloured, not as white men, as Kaffirs, not as Englishmen."[28]

7. Tutura and the End: 1868–1871

In 1868 the United Presbyterian Church appointed Soga to a new mission station named Somerville, after the ex-secretary of the United Presbyterian Foreign Missions Board, at Tutura, sixty miles northeast of Mgwali, near the growing trading centre of Butterworth. In all humility, Soga was pessimistic of the outcome, knowing that it had been political reasons alone that had motivated the locally-based Sarili ka Hintsa, chief of the Gcaleka, paramount chief of the Xhosa, and his counsellors, all of whom were resistant to Christianity, to ask for a missionary. Yet the reality was not as bad as he anticipated. By 1870 about a hundred people were regularly attending his little mud-walled church, and

---

27 Williams, *Journal ... Soga*, 178. See, Nxasana, "The Journey of the African as Missionary," 70.

28 Chalmers, *Tiyo Soga*, 430. The term 'Kaffir,' various spelled as Caffre, Kafir, etc., was always a derogatory term, being derived from an Arabic word meaning a person without religious beliefs. In mid-nineteenth century South Africa, the term was used widely with little or no offence as more or less synonymous with Xhosa. Soga frequently uses it of himself, his family and his people. Today, however, owing to its use in the apartheid era, it is regarded as highly offensive. Throughout this article 'Xhosa' has been substituted, except in two places where it is reluctantly retained for authenticity.

Soga was preparing a group of enquirers for baptism. On 16 April 1871, a new church building was opened, attended, as had been the Mgwali opening, by missionaries of many different denominations. Bryce Ross came from Pirie, one hundred miles distant, and John Chalmers was also there to preach the opening sermon. What, however, most struck Soga was a thought in a prayer by a Xhosa Christian who noticed that by going first into the old, now dilapidated, hut in which the services had up until then been held, they were taking with them "the blessing of the old house into the new, as otherwise we should have left it behind. No good ever came of people who did not give old age its due."[29]

Two months later, on a chilly midwinter June day, Soga set out on horseback to establish an outstation at Mapassa's kraal, but as Mapassa was away from home he had to wait. The weather turned colder and wetter, trapping him for a number of days in a damp hut with no food and no-one willing to take care of him. On the Saturday, cold, hungry and dispirited, he rode back to Tutura in the pouring rain, only to discover his wife and family had gone the twenty miles into Butterworth and would not return for a few days. Shivering with fever, he lay on a sofa and covered himself with a blanket to try to keep warm. By Sunday morning, he had recovered sufficiently to force himself to preach, but remained seriously ill for a further two weeks.

At the beginning of July, feeling a little stronger, he agreed to vaccinate villagers, worried about an outbreak of smallpox, who had lined up on his veranda seeking help. Once more he overworked, and the fever returned. A doctor was sent for, but little could be done. On 12 August 1871, sitting at his bedside was his close friend Richard Ross of Pirie, who had been with him at Lovedale and in Glasgow, and with whom he had often shared the joys and struggles of Christian ministry. As Ross helped his friend to change his position in bed, he felt his body go limp. Looking into his face, he saw him 'calmly, gently, as an infant falling asleep' breath his last breath.[30] He was only forty-one years of age.

Three days later simple funeral services were held in Xhosa and English. His worn-out body was laid to rest in the orchard he had planted himself. Six Xhosa Christians carried the coffin. At the graveside was his widow, Janet, and their seven children: the thirteen-year-old William Anderson, eleven-year-old John Henderson, nine-year-old Allan Kirkland and six-year-old Jotello Festiri, and the little girls, Bella, Frances, and Jessie Margaret. There too was his elderly mother, Nosutu, with words of Christian comfort for all.

---

29 Williams, *Journal ... Soga*, 144.
30 Williams, *Journal ... Soga*, 485.

8. Conclusion

A number of memorials commemorate Tiyo Soga's life and work. More than one church has been named in his honour, and at least one branch of the African National Congress political party. St. Andrew's Presbyterian Church in King William's Town (now known as Qonce), a congregation which he helped to establish, commemorates his life in a stained-glass window. In October 2001, at the inaugural Z. K. Matthews Memorial Lecture, at the University of Fort Hare, South African President, Thabo Mbeki, listed Tiyo Soga first in a catalogue of black intellectuals. Soga's contribution to South Africa's national life was formally recognised on 20 April 2006 when he was posthumously awarded his country's highest civilian honour, The Order of Ikhamanga in Gold.[31] In 2013 Tiyo and Janet Soga were commemorated in an embroidered panel of the Scottish Diaspora Tapestry.[32] Tiyo Soga was much more than an intellectual. The English translation of the Xhosa epitaph on his memorial stone at Tutura aptly summarises his life and contribution to his own generation and those that succeeded. He was:

> A friend of God, a lover of His Son, inspired by His Spirit, a disciple of His Holy Word. A zealous churchman, an ardent patriot, a large-hearted philanthropist, a dutiful son, an affectionate brother, a tender husband, a loving father, a faithful friend, a learned scholar, an eloquent orator and in manners a gentleman. A model Xhosa.[33]

Questions for study (fact type):

1. Draw a timeline for Tiyo Soga's life that includes the following dates: Birthdate, commencement of his formal education at Lovedale, first visit to Glasgow, Uniondale, second visit to Glasgow, date of marriage and wife's name, Mgwali years, Tutura years, and death date.
2. List the names of Tiyo Soga's children. Beside each name, write something significant about their life.
3. Name Tiyo Soga's most famous translation work (besides the Scriptures) and also his most famous hymn.

---

31 http://www.thepresidency.gov.za/national-orders/recipient/tiyo-soga-1829–1871 Accessed 7 April 2021.
32 The panel was stitched by Zukiswa Zita and Nozibele Nxado of the Keiskamma Art Project, Hamburg, Eastern Cape, South Africa. To view online see, https://scottish-diaspora-tapestry.web.app/#
33 Chalmers, *Tiyo Soga*, 488.

Questions for study (reflection type):

1 One of Tiyo Soga's professors at the Theological Hall in Glasgow taught him that "*on becoming a Christian one did not abandon ones' ethnic identity or culture. Although it was necessary to distinguish what was or was not compatible with Christianity within that culture, it was important only to renounce such elements as were incompatible, affirming what remained.*" Explain what this means and provide examples from Soga's life to show that as a Christian he remained a Xhosa man in his culture.

2 In June 1864, in the newspaper *Indaba*, Tiyo Soga commented on the teaching of Romans 13:7 and his own practice by writing,

> We want to know if you greet your chiefs with their traditional salutations – you who are converts to Christianity, you the dwellers in Mission stations. If you no longer do this what caused you to abandon this fine practice? Raise your hats to chiefs and respectable people. To White gentlemen bow your heads gently even though you do not utter a word. Do that to White people who deserve this ... But we do not advise this to [Whites] who are no better than yourselves. This 'Morning Sir' of the Xhosa people whenever they see a White face is very annoying.

Explain the Biblical principle of Romans 13 and how Soga was trying to apply this teaching in his own context in the above paragraph.

Tiyo Soga's Hymn: *Lizalis' idinga lakho* (Fulfill your promise)[34]

Lizalis' idinga lakho,	Fulfill your promise
Thixo Nkosi yenyaniso!	Faithful God!
Zonk' iintlanga, zonk' izizwe,	All races, all nations
Ma zizuze usindiso.	must be saved.
Amadolo kweli lizwe,	All knees in this world
Ma kagobe phambi kwakho;	Must bow before you,
Zide zithi zonk' iilwimi,	So that all tongues
Ziluxel' udumo lwakho.	May proclaim your glory.

---

34 There are various Xhosa textual variants of this hymn and various English translations of it. This particular translation appears to be anonymous or a compilation of several translations. It is literal and may miss the poetic features present in Xhosa.

Law'la, law'la, Nkosi, Yesu!	Prevail our God,
Koza ngawe ukonwaba;	Happiness can only come through you.
Ngeziphithi-phithi zethu,	Because of our struggles
Yonakele imihlaba.	This world is damaged.
Bona *izwe lakowethu,*	Look at our world,
uxolel' izono zalo;	Forgive our sins.
Ungathob' ingqumbo yakho,	Do not send your wrath
Luze luf' usapho lwalo.	To kill you children.
Yaala, Nkosi, singadeli	Stop us Lord from disobeying
Iimfundiso zezwi lakho;	The teachings of your Word.
Uze usivuselele,	Revive us
Sive inyaniso yakho.	So we can hear your Truth

Select Bibliography

Bradford, Tolly. *Prophetic Identities: Indigenous Missionaries on British Colonial Frontiers, 1850–75.* Vancouver: University of British Columbia Press, 2012.

Brock, Peggy, Norman Etherington, Gareth Griffiths, and Jacqueline Van Gent. *Indigenous Evangelists and Questions of Authority in the British Empire 1750–1940.* Leiden: Brill, 2015.

Chalmers, John A. *Tiyo Soga: A Page of South African Mission Work.* Edinburgh: Andrew Elliot, 1877. This primary source of Soga's life and ministry is available online at: https://archive.org/details/tiyosogapageofso00chal

Davis, Joanne Ruth. *Tiyo Soga: A Literary History.* Pretoria: University of South Africa, 2018.

Holt, Basil. *Greatheart of the Border: A Life of John Brownlee Pioneer Missionary in South Africa.* King William's Town: South African Missionary Museum, 1976.

Milton, John. *The Edges of War: A History of the Frontier Wars, 1702–1878.* Cape Town: Jutta, 1983.

Mostert, Noel. *Frontiers: The Epic of South Africa's Creation and the Tragedy of the Xhosa People.* London: Jonathan Cape, 1992.

Ndletyana, Mcebisi, ed. *African Intellectuals in 19th and early 20th century South Africa.* Cape Town: HSRC Press, 2008.

Nxasana, Thulani. "The Journey of the African as Missionary: The Journal and Selected Writings of the Reverend Tiyo Soga." *English in Africa* 38. 2 (2011): 61–76.

Pieres, Jeff. *The House of Phalo*. Cape Town: Jonathan Ball, 1981.

– *The Dead Will Arise: Nongqawuse and the Great Xhosa Cattle-Killing of 1856–7*. Cape Town: Jonathan Ball, 1989.

Price, Richard. *Making Empires: Colonial Encounters and the Creation of Imperial Rule in Nineteenth-Century Africa*. Cambridge: Cambridge University Press, 2008.

Shepherd, Robert. *Lovedale: The Story of a Century, 1841–1941*. Lovedale: Lovedale Press, n.d.

Smith, Keith. *Harry Smith's Last Throw: The Eighth Frontier War, 1850–1853*. London: Frontline Books, 2012.

Williams, Donovan. *Umfundisi: A Biography of Tiyo Soga 1829–1871*. Lovedale: Lovedale Press, 1978.

Balkema, A.A. ed. *The Journal and Selected Writings of the Reverend Tiyo Soga*. Cape Town: 1983.

Chapter 6

Daniel Lindley, the American Board of Commissioners and South Africa

Dale W. Johnson

Chapter Outline
1. Introduction
2. The Lindley family and Daniel's Early Years
3. Lindley and the American Board of Missions
4. From Bachelor Pastor to Married Missionary, 1834
5. The Inland Trek in South Africa, 1835–1836
6. The Boers of South Africa
7. Daniel and Lucy Lindley serve in the American Mission in Natal, 1836–1839
8. Lindley's School for Boer Children, 1840
9. Rev. Daniel Lindley, Pastor to the Boers at the Church of the Vow, 1839–1846
10. Tensions between the Dutch and the British
11. Labours Resume in Natal, 1847–1859
12. Return to America, 1859–1862
13. The Lindley's mature years in Natal, 1863–1872
14. Summary Conclusion

1. Introduction

The history of the early church followed the Acts 1:8 roadmap to spread the message of Jesus and his triumph over death. From Jerusalem the message travelled to Judea and Philip introduced the good news to Samaria. An angel of the Lord told Philip to go south on the desert road that connects Jerusalem with Gaza. There, Philip encountered a government official, an Ethiopian eunuch reading the prophet Isaiah (chapter 53) from a scroll. Philip shared the good news, the man believed what was explained to him and he received baptism by Philip. This is the Bible's account of how the gospel was introduced to Africa. This gospel introduction to the continent of Africa has enormous implications for the history of Christianity. In the centuries to come, great Christian leaders emerged from Africa. They include Cyprian of Carthage, Tertullian the "founder" of Western or Latin Christianity and St. Augustine, Bishop of Hippo Regius, one of the four doctors of the Latin Church. This distinguished pedigree of Christian leaders and thinkers in Africa began in Acts chapter eight with the obedience of Philip the Evangelist.

2. The Lindley Family and Daniel's Early Years

By contrast to Philip the Evangelist, Daniel Lindley's call to spread the message of Christ to Africa followed a more traditional route. It is to this story that we now turn. Daniel Lindley (1801–80) grew up in the home of pious Presbyterians. His great-grandfather Demas Lindley, an elder for 60 years, attended the first meeting of the Redstone Presbytery in September 1781.[1] Daniel's father, Jacob Lindley, began his college education at Princeton in 1798 when Dr Samuel Stanhope Smith was president of the school.

Daniel Lindley did not follow his father's steps to Princeton. Daniel Lindley's conversion came at age 23, just prior to his college graduation. He soon believed God was calling him into the Presbyterian ministry and entered Union Theological Seminary, which opened on a property opposite Hampden-Sydney College in Virginia.

He graduated from seminary in June 1831. He was licensed and then ordained to serve as the pastor of Rocky River Presbyterian Church (PCUSA) in North Carolina. He served there for two years before he experienced God's call on his life to the mission field in Africa. Two factors prompted this rather dramatic move. While in his pastor's study he read the newspaper, the *Missionary Herald*, a publication of the American Board of Commissioners for Foreign Missions (hereafter American Board) and felt an irresistible call to respond. The author of the article urged settled pastors to consider resigning from their charge and joining the cause of foreign missions. Lindley later explained his new call to missions with this terse statement: "I gave heed to the appeal, resigned and went."[2] When Lindley responded to this call, he became one of the first Americans to present the claims of Christ in Africa. Lindley was not running from a failed pastorate at Rocky River. In two short years 250 members were added to the congregation with a total of 550 members.

▲ *Daniel Lindley*

---

1 Smith, *The Life and Times of David Lindley*, 11–12. Smith's biography contains many primary source extracts of letters and diary entries. This book will be used extensively in this chapter.
2 Smith, *Daniel Lindley*, 44.

3. Lindley and the American Board of Missions

The American Board (ABCFM), with whom Daniel Lindley worked for fifty years, began in 1810 when Lindley was 9 years old. As early as 1816 the American Board made plans for Africa, which were not commenced until 1833 on Cape Palmas on the Guinea Coast (see chapter three).[3] After seven years, the Board began exploring a more promising location, settling on the Gaboon River in 1842 (see chapter ten). Subsequently they focused on a healthier location than the equatorial regions of Africa. This was the first effort of the American Board to enter Southern Africa with the Gospel.

Undeniably, one powerful motivation for the American Board to focus on African missions grew out of guilt, and a somewhat clumsy, though well-intentioned attempt at a "pay back." America took slaves from Africa for two centuries and profited handsomely from it. The response by the American Board was in some way to give back to Africa in payment for what had been taken. The technical name for this philosophy was the doctrine of recompense. The American Board wanted Christian churches to partner with them in the mission of healing in Africa. The Board believed the greatest gift they could bring to the African people was the gospel of grace in Christ Jesus. In 1833, the Board officials wrote these words: "We owe an immense debt to Africa, and nothing short of the blessings of the Gospel will pay for it."[4] What reads to us today as paternalism, the well-intentioned strategy towards Africa was "Christianity and Civilization." This was the very language and advice given by Dr John Philip, the Superintendent of the London Mission Society in South Africa. He told the American Board: "Civilization is to the Christian religion what the body is to the soul ... the Gospel can never have a permanent footing in a barbarous country unless education and civilization go hand in hand with our religious instruction."[5] John Philip pointed the American Board toward the Zulus in South Africa.[6]

---

3 Christofersen, *Adventuring with God: The Story of the American Board Mission in South Africa*, 11–12.
4 John B. Boles, *The Great Revival: Beginnings of the Bible Belt* (Lexington, KY: University Press of Kentucky, 1996), 37.
5 Smith, *Daniel Lindley*, 48–49. Other popular explanations include the ideas of the "errand in the wilderness" motif of the Puritan enterprise in New England, and an extension of the "manifest destiny" in American empire building. See, Norman A. Etherington, "An American Errand in the South African Wilderness," *Church History* 39 (1970), 62–71.
6 Smith, *Daniel Lindley*, 50.

4. From Bachelor Pastor to Married Missionary, 1834

When Daniel Lindley answered the call to foreign missions, he was a bachelor. After his acceptance by the American Board and appointment to service in Southeast Africa, he wrote the Board asking them to amend his appointment and include the name of Miss Lucy Allen who would accompany Daniel as his wife to the mission field. The couple married on 20 November 1834 in Hartford, Connecticut. On Sunday 23 November 1834, Daniel, Lucy and four other missionaries were commissioned for missionary service at the historic Park Street Church, Boston, and soon sailed for Cape Town, South Africa on a 64-day voyage.[7]

5. The Inland Trek in South Africa, 1835–1836

The American Board, with close consultation from Dr John Philip in Cape Town, directed the three missionary couples – the Lindleys, Wilsons, and Venables – toward an inland mission. The mission inland required a 1,000-mile trek northeast from Cape Town to a splinter group of Zulus called the Matebele (Northern Ndebele), led by Chief Mzilkazi.[8] The couples travelled in a heavy, springless wagon pulled by a team of 14–16 oxen per wagon. If conditions were perfect, they could cover upwards of 20 miles per day. When water washed out the terrain and they travelled through deep mud, they might make five miles, or even a single mile in a day.[9] Daniel Lindley summed up the difficulty of the trek: "in an ox-wagon every mile is difficult."[10]

After weeks of tedious bone jarring travel, the party arrived at its first respite. Three hundred and fifty miles into the trek, they stopped at a village called Beaufort West on the edge of the Great Karroo, a semi-desert region. Both travellers and oxen found much needed water and rest. They continued their trek north. They were led by veteran missionary with the London Society Rev. Peter Wright, who guided them since Cape Town. In mid-May 1835, after eight weeks of travel by wagon, they arrived at Griqua Town where the London Society had a station. The missionaries made this their home for nearly eight months and began to study the two languages of Mzilikazi's people, Tebele and Chanana.[11] Both of these were Bantu languages with their distinctive clicks.[12]

---

7 Smith, *Daniel Lindley*, 61.
8 Christofersen, *Adventuring with God*, 13.
9 Smith, *Daniel Lindley*, 65–66.
10 Smith, *Daniel Lindley*, 62.
11 Christofersen, *Adventuring with God*, 13–14.
12 Smith, *Daniel Lindley*, 81.

Mrs Lindley explained another reason for the extended stay in Griqua Town: "The feet, the flesh, and strength of a great part of the oxen are gone and must be brought back by rest and food before we can proceed on our way."[13] They also learned Lucy Lindley was pregnant. Oxcart travel and the uncertainty over the supply of water prompted their extended stay in Griqua Town. The Lindley's first child, Mary Elizabeth, made her appearance 9 October 1835. After months of rest and study, the missionaries headed north 110 miles to Kuruman (a mission post founded by Dr Robert Moffat, the father-in-law of Robert Livingstone).

From Kuruman, Lindley and Venable set out for Mosega for the purpose of selecting an inhabitable site for their mission to the Matabele. They settled on an old, abandoned site settled originally by French missionaries. With the help of local labourers, they pulled down some of the French structures and from the wooded mountains, cut timber for rafters and planks, and made clay bricks for a structure that could house all three families.[14] After several delays, the missionaries were given an audience with Chief Mzilikazi in Mosega who received them cordially.[15] It was essential that the missionaries receive the Chief's approval and blessing on their mission. The Chief's word held enormous power over the people and the land he governed. Chief Mzilikazi (through an interpreter) gave his permission for the missionaries to teach his people to read. With a very limited vocabulary of the language, Mrs Lindley poured out her personal thoughts in her Diary after some women visited her. "O how I long to be able to converse with the females about the concerns of their immortal souls!"[16] In Griqua Town one of the British missionaries helped them prepare a grammar and vocabulary of two or three thousand words as a primer for their communication with the people.[17]

The missionaries found their new quarters uninhabitable because the clay floors they installed would not dry properly. They were forced to sleep outside in the wagons with frost at night and temperatures around 30 degrees Fahrenheit. The cold weather forced them inside but in these poor conditions everyone became sick with chills, high fever, and sore joints making any movement extremely painful. Some of the missionaries suffered from these mysterious ailments for months. Dr Wilson's wife Jane died from her illness leaving her husband, an eight-month-old daughter, and a completely distraught team of inexperienced missionaries. Believing her death was imminent, Jane Wilson offered her parting words: "I find Jesus to be an all sufficient savior … Tell my mother, sister and friends that I have

---

13 Smith, *Daniel Lindley*, 69.
14 Smith, *Daniel Lindley*, 70, 83, 87–88.
15 Smith, *Daniel Lindley*, 88–90.
16 Smith, *Daniel Lindley*, 90.
17 Smith, *Daniel Lindley*, 81.

never regretted coming to Africa."[18] Jane Wilson was "the first white woman to die within the Transvaal."[19] Veteran missionary Robert Moffat aptly summed up the shock of the American missionaries: "they were so dispirited by the effects of disease as to be scarcely able to judge how they should act."[20]

6. The Boers in South Africa

About the same time Lindley and others were recovering from their illness, the Dutch Boers and the Matebele fought a number of bloody battles. The Dutch resented the intrusive policies passed by the British Parliament regarding slavery in South Africa. In 1808, two years after the Cape Colony became part of the British Empire, Parliament ended the slave trade. In the 1820s a series of laws extended additional "rights" to slaves and freed slaves in the colony. The Parliament set aside millions of pounds sterling to compensate former slave owners, but in fact they received only partial payment or nothing at all.[21] Anna Steenkamp, one of the Voortrekkers, explained the grievances of the Dutch this way: "It was not so much the freeing of the slaves ... as much as their being placed on an equal footing with Christians, contrary to the laws of God and the natural distinction of race and religion ... we rather withdrew in order to preserve our doctrines in purity."[22] Each year the Boers who depended on cattle for their living would spend some weeks or months in their wagons searching for grazing land for their cattle. When the British government began imposing restrictions on slavery, some of the Dutch cattlemen decided to head north into the interior of South Africa, away from the meddlesome British policies.

In January 1837 the Boers attacked 13 villages. Their stated purpose was the recovery of livestock taken from them in earlier raids. In the Boers' attack, some of the bullets hit the missionaries' house, but no one was harmed. A short extract from Daniel Lindley's letter to the American Board describes the terror the missionaries felt. "The fire of one gun followed that of another ... the thought would rush ... there fell one and another and another ... of the poor heathen of whose salvation we once had some hope. Our hearts became sick again for in a few minutes we were in the midst of a slaughter."[23] The Boer's attack was not aimed at the Matebele warriors, but rather the most vulnerable, the old, the infirmed and children. An account by Dr John Matthew, later the

---

18 Smith, *Daniel Lindley*, 95–96.
19 Smith, *Daniel Lindley*, 96.
20 Smith, *Daniel Lindley*, 98.
21 Smith, *Daniel Lindley*, 78–79.
22 Smith, *Daniel Lindley*, 79.
23 Smith, *Daniel Lindley*, 103.

Lindley's son-in-law, claimed Mrs Lindley's bedroom became crowded with bleeding victims.[24] Some hours later the Boers returned hungry, looking for food. They stole what food the missionaries had, destroyed their garden, and burned their house. The grand irony of this attack, looting and pillaging is that a few years later some of the same Boers invited Daniel Lindley to become their pastor.

The Boers now claimed ownership of the vast territory previously controlled by Mzilikazi. The missionaries loaded their possessions and retraced their steps. They greatly feared reprisals from marauding Matebele warriors. In their removal they experienced much assistance and acts of kindness by the Boers and by Wesleyan missionaries once they reached Thaba Nchu.[25] Rather than wait for instructions from the American Board in Boston, the short-lived inland mission came to an end. The missionaries decided to head east and join their colleagues at the Maritime Mission in Port Natal. After weeks of perilous travel and overturned wagons, they arrived in Natal in late July 1837.[26] The Maritime Mission in Natal began with three couples, affiliated with the American Board, Dr and Mrs Newton Adams, Mr and Mrs George Champion, and Mr and Mrs Aldin Grout. Upon the arrival of Lindley and company, various work assignments were given. The Lindley's began building at Imfume on the Ilovu River, south of Durban.[27]

7. Daniel and Lucy Lindley serve in the American Mission in Natal, 1836–1839

Beyond the physical building of structures, the work of the Lord was taking root in Natal. Daniel Lindley preached his first sermon through an interpreter to the Zulus. Dr Adams preached regularly on Sundays to four hundred Zulus while Mrs Adams instructed the children in Sunday School. Some Zulus, including Chief Dingane, took the beginning steps toward literacy.[28] Dr Adams opened a medical clinic to serve the Zulus and operated a printing press to produce booklets and tracts in the Zulu language. The work of the ABCFM in Zulu printing, translation, and literature distribution was one of this mission's greatest contributions in Natal.[29] Within a few years Mr Champion's press

---

24 J. W. Matthews, *Twenty Years' Personal Experience in South Africa*, 1887, 27, quoted in Smith, *Daniel Lindley*, 105.
25 Smith, *Daniel Lindley*, 111–112.
26 Christofersen, *Adventuring with God*, 15.
27 Smith, *Daniel Lindley*, 123; Christofersen, *Adventuring with God*, 20.
28 Smith, *Daniel Lindley*, 130–131.
29 Du Plessis, *History of Christian Missions in South Africa*, 306.

produced small books for schools and Dr Adam's press at Umlazi printed nearly 56,000 pages by the end of 1840 without a dictionary or grammar to consult.[30]

Piet Retief, the newly elected governor of the Boers, wrote to Chief Dingane desirous of a personal interview. By this date Chief Dingane would have known of the Boers fighting prowess and their defeat of Chief Mzilikazi. The Boers sought a land gift within Natal territory – something Dingane had no intention of granting. Retief also wrote a letter to Dingane containing a "not-so-veiled" threat. He told Dingane that the Bible warned that kings who acted as Chief Mzilikazi could expect vengeance. After securing some of Dingane's stolen cattle, the Chief appeared to grant certain land of Natal to the Boers. Returning a few days later to seal the deal, Retief and the Boers left their guns outside of town. As the Boers assembled Dingane allegedly shouted, "kill the villains" and the carnage began. That night the Zulus followed up with an attack on a Boer encampment killing about 200.[31] Dingane ordered his Zulu warriors to kill without distinction any white people they found. Lindley wrote, "Natal is now a miserable desolation, for Dingane has nearly realized the utmost of his wishes concerning this place and people."[32] Lindley's mission station at Imfumi was looted and largely destroyed.

The prospect for missions appeared bleak. The Lindley's found safety for a year living in Port Elizabeth, where Daniel preached in area churches. Of the twelve missionaries sent by the American Board to South Africa in 1835, only four stayed in Africa, the Lindleys and the Adams.[33] For different reasons, conditions in America appeared equally dismal. The American Board found itself deeply in debt and few people offered themselves for missionary service. Under these dire circumstances the Board gave several options to the missionaries. They could return to the United States, transfer to India and join American Board missionaries there, or patiently remain in South Africa and pray for improved conditions.[34] They chose the latter.

With this peace settlement in place between the Zulus and the Boers, Dr and Mrs Adams and Daniel Lindley returned to Natal to resume their mission work from Port Elizabeth. Mrs Lindley and her two daughters stayed back in Port Elizabeth, all suffering from an outbreak of measles. Lindley decided to open a school for the Dutch children. In his visitation of the Boer encampments, Lindley

---

30 Christofersen, *Adventuring with God*, 19.
31 Smith, *Daniel Lindley*, 137–138.
32 Smith, *Daniel Lindley*, 144.
33 Smith, *Daniel Lindley*, 147.
34 Smith, *Daniel Lindley*, 147.

discovered that only about half of the Dutch population over age ten could read.[35] He wrote to his wife explaining his rationale. "The Dutch need help and I will help them if the Lord so will."[36] This sentiment also betrayed a grander, gospel strategy for the Boers. Lindley expressed this plan to reach both the Boers and the native people in a letter to Henry Venable: "The Boers also need a great many teachers of all sorts except teachers of evil. It is my … opinion that the salvation of many of the Aborigines here can be secured only by giving a good measure of light to the newly arrived emigrants of this country …"[37] In a very telling claim, Lindley explained his strategy. "I sincerely believe that the cheapest, speediest, easiest way to convert the heathen here is to convert the white ones first …"[38] This represents a changed strategy for Lindley, based not on an ivory tower theory, but on his personal experience and the changed conditions in South Africa. He was struck by the irony that the Boers possessed a "deep reverence for the Word of God," but were actually completely ignorant of its teaching.[39] He explained, "The Boers are all matter-of-course members of the Reformed Church to which they have a bigoted, rather than intelligent attachment."[40] The biggest challenge Lindley faced was Boer resistance to the Gospel because they already considered themselves faithful Christians. He opined in a letter to Rufus Anderson, the Secretary of the American Board, "they are about as good Christians as Nestorians."[41] At this juncture, Daniel Lindley took stock of his life and felt profound discouragement. Nearly 40 years old, Lindley had invested five years in Africa with essentially no tangible results. These thoughts no doubt contributed to this developing strategy of working more directly with the Boers as a means of reaching the Zulus.[42]

Following the withdrawal of British troops from Port Natal in late December 1839, the Boers took quick advantage. They established the so-called "Republic of Natalia," raised their flag and set their eye on removing the last impediment to settlement in their way, namely, Chief Dingane. Now in league with Dingane's brother Mpande, the Boers planned to march on Dingane's capital Mgungunlovu with their respective armies. Most of the fighting and casualties were from the feuding Zulu brothers. In the fighting that ensued, Dingane fled, and the Boers liberated 41,000 head of cattle from Dingane's villages. Lindley estimated the

---

35 Smith, *Daniel Lindley*, 160.
36 Smith, *Daniel Lindley*, 154.
37 Smith, *Daniel Lindley*, 154.
38 Smith, *Daniel Lindley*, 160.
39 Smith, *Daniel Lindley*, 162.
40 Smith, *Daniel Lindley*, 162.
41 Smith, *Daniel Lindley*, 163.
42 Smith, *Daniel Lindley*, 165.

combined loss of Zulus between 8,000–12,00 warriors.[43] The Boers now held vast portions of land with Mpande, who was declared king of the Zulus, but served only in a figurehead role.[44]

8. Lindley's School for Boer Children, 1840

Lindley's work now focused more directly with the Boers. In January 1840, he opened a school in Umlazi for Boer children under age eight with 90 pupils. He taught them to read and catechized them using the Heidelberg Catechism (which he considered inferior to the Westminster Shorter Catechism). Daniel did most of the teaching, with Mrs Lindley helping part-time each day.[45] In his visitation of the Boer encampments, Lindley found one man who had served as an elder, and another officer, an ordained deacon. He identified two other men who stood out for their piety and leadership whom he subsequently ordained, and organised a church complete with a session. The Boer's built the Lindley's a small house replacing the one destroyed some months earlier in the battles. Lindley's relations with the Boer community were growing ever stronger, and he informed the American Board of his recent labours and his distinctive new strategy to his mission in South Africa. It seems the Board gave Lindley their reluctant approval to labour part time with the Boer community. Support for his labours picked up pace. The Boers helped to subsidise the school and the mission Board of the Reformed Church in America also promised to offset Lindley's expenses. In Lindley's annual report to the American Board dated 26 January 1841 he wrote: "The past year has, on the whole, been the best one my wife and I have had in Africa."[46]

9. Reverend Daniel Lindley, Pastor to the Boers at the Church of the Vow, 1839–1846

The Boers continued to build the skeleton of their infant Republic of Natalia. The constitution of Natalia mandated that the Dutch Reformed Church was the established church in Natalia.[47] The Dutch community made several appeals to the Cape Synod to secure a pastor, but without success. They described the plight of some 8,000–12,000 Dutch emigrants "having forsaken hearthstone and altar … going out into the desert without a Moses or Aaron, without sign or guidance to

---

43 Smith, *Daniel Lindley*, 168–169.
44 Smith, *Daniel Lindley*, 168.
45 Smith, *Daniel Lindley*, 172, 191.
46 Smith, *Daniel Lindley*, 173.
47 Smith, *Daniel Lindley*, 175–177.

seek a land for themselves."[48] They turned to Rev. Daniel Lindley, the missionary and schoolteacher to be their Moses. After examination of his credentials and his doctrine by the Dutch, Lindley sought and received an "honorable release" from his affiliation with his mission agency the American Board.[49] Lindley and his family moved inland to Pietermaritzburg to serve the Lord at the Church of the Vow. He described the boundaries and thus the immensity of his duties as pastor to the Boers. "I had for my parish all the country embraced in the district of Natal, the Free State and the Transvaal republic. I made several long trips into the interior and held religious services ... I have ... the cure of, I suppose, not less than 20,000 souls."[50] In his seven years with the Boers, Lindley organised five churches and baptised nearly 7,000 children.

10. Tensions between the Dutch and British

In August of 1841 the *Volksraad* proclaimed the Zulus had no rights to land in Natal. About 50,000 Zulus were driven into Pondoland under the rule of Chief Faku.[51] Alarmed by these outrageous developments, the Governor of Cape Colony, Sir George Napier denounced the high-handed actions of the *Volksraad* and under orders announced the return of British troops to Natal. The Boers retaliated against the British in a military strike causing fatalities, but they submitted in the face of British reinforcements. Napier wrote to Lord Stanley claiming that British inclusion of Natal into the British Empire as a colony was the only way to end the enslavement of Zulus by the Boers.[52]

After months of foot dragging, the *Volksraad* members signed a document in August 1843 affirming "equality without regard to color or race, a ban on slavery, and recognition of the Queen's authority."[53] A British Commission began drawing up plans to distribute land to Africans in groups of 10,000–12,000 each on 100,000 acres. This marks the beginning of a complex, controversial and perhaps insoluble challenge of land distribution that went on for decades. Given the new realities, the Boers continued their flight north across the Vaal River to establish large farms and build their cattle herds.

At this time Daniel Lindley and Newton Adams suffered a severe blow from the American Board in Boston. The Board, against counsel from the missionaries

---

48 Smith, *Daniel Lindley*, 178.
49 Smith, *Daniel Lindley*, 182.
50 Smith, *Daniel Lindley*, 184.
51 Smith, *Daniel Lindley*, 223.
52 Smith, *Daniel Lindley*, 232.
53 Smith, *Daniel Lindley*, 237.

on site in South Africa, decided to close the South African Mission.[54] Two factors shaped their decision. First, the American Board faced huge financial challenges they could not sustain. Secondly, the Board believed South African missions under British rule would prosper under British missionaries. "Better now," the Board concluded," to retire from a field which has caused so much anxiety and produced so little fruit."[55] Undoubtedly, the American missionaries found this a bitter pill to swallow. The Board said they could come home or move to India and join the American Board missionaries there.

News of the missionaries' imminent expulsion quickly circulated, and a united front of British, Boer and native support arose to keep the Americans in Natal. Friends offered both moral and financial support to the missionaries.[56] Sir Peregrine Maitland, the new Governor of Cape Colony, told the American missionaries to remain in Natal and continue their work. They should "endeavor to teach the natives the truths of the gospel according to the harmony of the Protestant professions of faith and to induce them to live in the practice of Christian morality."[57] The British proposed to pay for school construction and for rebuilding the mission stations. In March 1844, responding to an organised pressure campaign, the American Board reversed their earlier instructions and allowed the American missionaries to continue their labours in South Africa. The Board, however, forbade the missionaries from taking British money.[58]

11. Labours resume in Natal, 1847–1859

Inanda Station

After his release from his pastorate to the Church of the Vow in Pietermaritzburg, Daniel Lindley returned to missionary service within the ABCFM in Inanda, 15 miles northwest of present-day Durban, and 10 miles from the sea.[59] Here he would spend his final years in Africa. Assisted by Hottentots and both skilled and unskilled labourers, Lindley built a house 40 x 20 feet of unburnt brick, large enough to accommodate Daniel, Lucy and seven children.[60] The Lindley children eventually grew to eleven. The children jokingly called themselves the "tribe of Dan."[61] All eleven children learned the Westminster Shorter Catechism, and

---

54 Smith, *Daniel Lindley*, 238.
55 Smith, *Daniel Lindley*, 239.
56 Smith, *Daniel Lindley*, 240.
57 Smith, *Daniel Lindley*, 240.
58 Smith, *Daniel Lindley*, 241.
59 Christofersen, *Adventuring with God*, 32.
60 Smith, *Daniel Lindley*, 274.
61 Smith, *Daniel Lindley*, 275, 286.

all learned the Zulu language.⁶² Like every other missionary, Lindley became a "jack of all trades." On occasion he performed the duties of hunter, wood cutter, carpenter, brickmaker, bricklayer, preacher, teacher, administrator, shoemaker, farmer, doctor, and sometimes, dentist. Lindley gave hundreds of vaccinations to natives over the years. Governor Napier had appointed Lindley a member of the Land Commission involving equitable land distribution to the Zulus in the Inanda reserve.⁶³

▲ *The Daniel Lindley family*

Rev. Lindley founded a church in Inanda with 9 members in January 1849. Six years later the church membership numbered 31. Though this number seems meagre, it represents significant success. Lindley's biographer says at this period the Zulus were not responsive. Providentially, this was to change by the blessing of God and Lindley's faithful persistence. Lucy Lindley recorded in her diary a revealing entry for 27 November 1857. In a season of prayer, "Mr Lindley made a fresh dedication of our whole remaining selves to the mission work and prayed earnestly that here many might come up to inquire after the Lord our Saviour."⁶⁴

The same year (1857), with a new house under construction, Lindley himself reflected on the past and made plans for the future. There were now 50 members at the Inanda church. He measured his "success" among the Zulus in terms of

---

62 Smith, *Daniel Lindley*, 289.
63 Christofersen, *Adventuring with God*, 31.
64 Smith, *Daniel Lindley*, 319.

morality and behaviour. He told the Board of the Zulus' improvement in literacy, the wearing of clothes, appearance, and civility. Lindley and other missionaries put the language of the Zulus into writing, translated portions of the Bible, and preached faithfully every Sunday. Missing in his report to the Board is any mention of doctrine, theology, or conversions to Christ.[65] Depending on the Lord for strength and wisdom, Lindley's task involved the slow process of line upon line, precept upon precept. He faithfully sowed the seed and prayed that the Lord would send the harvest.

Pioneer work for the Presbytery of Natal

Workers with the ABCFM often exhibited an ability to labour across denominational lines whether Congregational, Presbyterian, and (in Lindley's case) also Dutch Reformed. We have seen his involvement as an ordained PCUSA missionary with the ABCFM labouring with the Voortrekkers to establish Dutch Reformed Churches. We have also seen his involvement to help establish churches which became Congregational. There is one last ecclesiastic piece to the ministry of Daniel Lindley and that is his involvement to encourage the development of English-speaking Presbyterian congregations in Natal. Lindley saw the spiritual need of the new English-speaking colonists who were coming in large numbers between 1848 and 1850 (and soldiers who were there as well) and began to also minister to them and helped them towards forming a Presbyterian congregation in Pietermaritzburg. He then turned this work over to a new immigrant minister (FCS), Rev. William Campbell (1801–1873), who came out from Scotland in 1850 with free passage in exchange for ministering to immigrants in Natal (basically as a chaplain for the J. C. Byrne Scheme).

Campbell was an ordained Free Church of Scotland minister who had served in both Scotland and Ireland. With Lindley's encouragement, he brought together a united Presbyterian congregation in Pietermaritzburg and was inducted into this work by Rev. Daniel Lindley. An *ad hoc* Presbytery was also formed in part to meet the need for a Presbyterian minister in Pinetown (near Durban). The FCS probationer and teacher Charles Scott was ordained by this Presbytery of three ministers, Rev. Daniel Lindley, Rev. William Campbell, and Rev. Karl Wilhelm Posselt on 11 May 1852.[66] It appears later that same day in May 1852, the Presbytery of Natal was *formally formed* with the three ministerial members being now Revs. Lindley, Campbell, and Scott:

---

65 Smith, *Daniel Lindley*, 329.
66 Posselt was a missionary in Natal with the Berlin Missionary Society which had good relations with the ABCFM. He was a Lutheran minister.

After the above proceedings [the ordination of Charles Scott] the Revd. C. Scott having been admitted as a member of the presbytery: It was resolved that the Revd. Messrs. D. Lindley and Wm. Campbell and C. Scott form themselves into the first Presbytery of the Presbyterian Church of Natal.[67]

From the beginning, this Presbytery exhibited a catholicity of spirit, attempted not to draw itself into the disputes of Scotland, and thus reached out to a variety of Presbyterian streams amongst the immigrants.

12. Return to America, 1859–1862

For three years, 1859–1862, the Lindley's lived in the United States. The primary purpose for returning to the States involved meeting with the American Board, visiting supporting churches, and resting from their labours. Daniel Lindley developed into an engaging speaker and received countless invitations. On two occasions he planned to return to Africa, but the American Board prevailed upon him to continue his travel and speaking engagements on behalf of the Board.[68] In some places Lindley went away dismayed because of the lack of interest in missions in general.[69] While Lindley wished to return to Africa so too did his Zulu friends. He received many letters in America from Africa urging him and the American Board to permit Lindley to return to his congregation in Natal. Some Zulus organised a fund raiser and sent him 150 British pounds to defray his expenses on his return voyage to Africa. He also received the shocking news that his new unoccupied house in Inanda burned to the ground when the thatched roof caught fire due to negligence from one of the caretakers. The American Board gave the Lindley family $700 and they received an outpouring of cash gifts and furniture to replace what was a complete loss of the house and its contents, totalling over $2400.[70]

---

67 *Twentieth Century Impressions of Natal: Its People, Commerce, Industries, and Resources.* (Natal: Lloyd's Greater Britain Publishing Company, 1906), 143–145. Balfour, *Presbyterianism in the Colonies*, 285; Dalziel, "The Origin and Growth of Presbyterian Ordinances," 386–392 and Dalziel 383 quoting from the "Minutes of Natal Presbytery" page 2. The formation of the Presbytery of Natal was actually decided at the first ad hoc meeting for the ordination service and was minuted at that meeting. The ABCFM would often supply the pulpit for Campbell when he was away fund-raising overseas or in the Cape. Lindley would also assist Campbell at Communion services in Pietermaritzburg. Thus, Lindley's involvement with the English-speaking Presbyterians is another dimension of his mission work.
68 Smith, *Daniel Lindley*, 343.
69 Smith, *Daniel Lindley*, 349.
70 Smith, *Daniel Lindley*, 352.

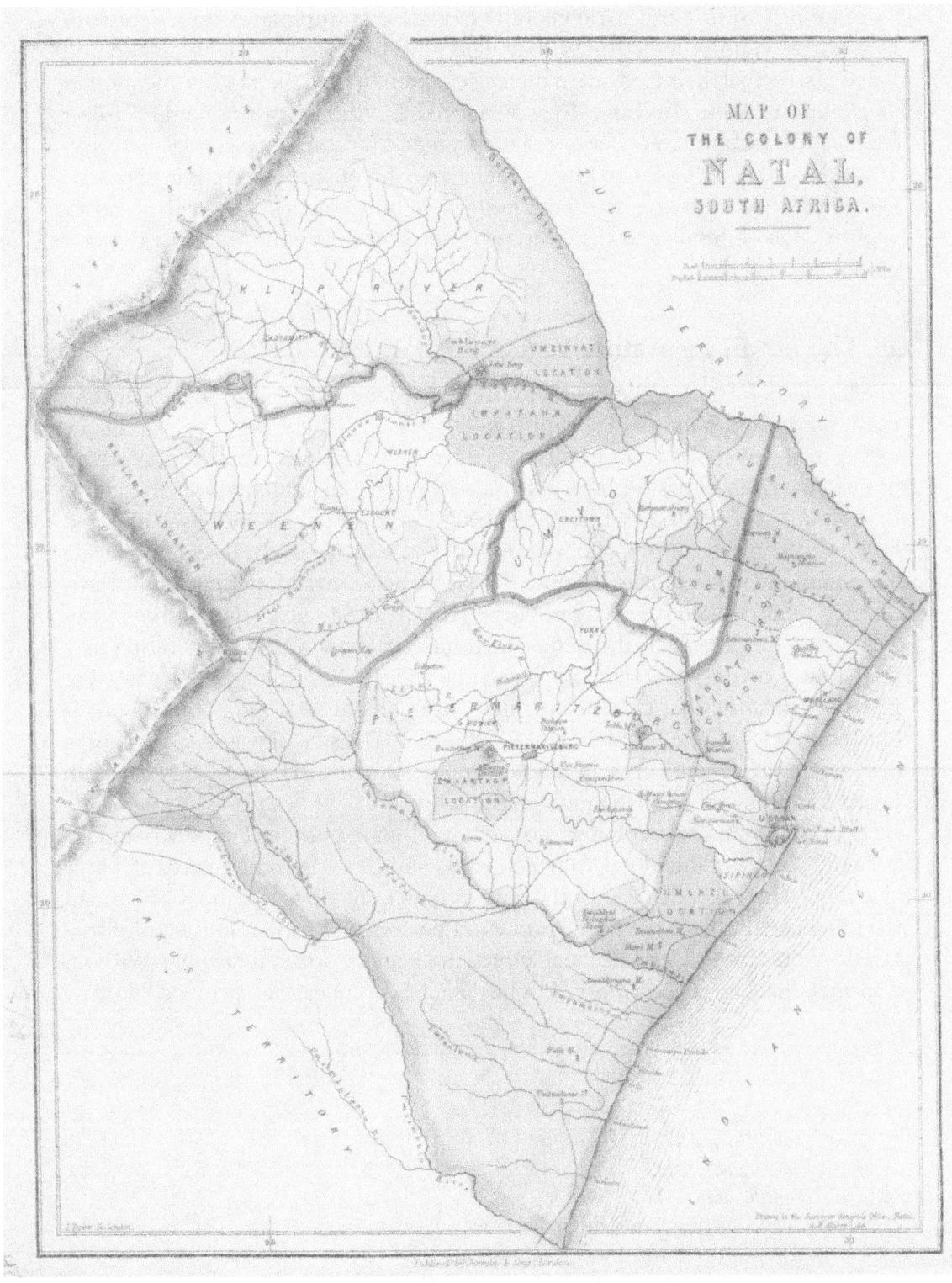

▲ *Map of Natal Colony*

Upon arrival in Africa, friends of the Lindley family planned a celebratory feast. After a sumptuous dinner they held a prayer meeting. Many prayed and "gave thanks that their God heard their cries and returned their father and mother and many of their children. They honoured Lindley with the name "*U-Bebe omhlope*" (i.e., white *Bebe*) after one of their great Zulu chiefs of legendary status.[71] This honour from those who knew him best no doubt surpassed conferral of the Doctor of Divinity degree given to Lindley by Ohio University in 1860.[72] Lindley was an Ohio alumnus and his father was one of the founders and first director of the university.

13. The Lindley's Mature Years in Natal, 1863–1872

The last ten years of Lindley's service in Africa came after his return to Durban from America in January 1863. Spiritually speaking, these next years were the most productive years of his life. The seeds he had sown and watered now began to bear fruit. The mission built a female seminary in Inanda, with the entire undertaking supervised by Lindley. The logic of the girls' school was well stated by James K. Aggery. "Educate a man and you educate an individual; educate a woman and you educate a family."[73] The school opened with 19 Zulu girls. Lindley fondly called his charges, "black, dirty little angels."[74] As of the date of this writing in late 2021, the female seminary in Inanda is still operating as a Christian boarding school, coping with the COVID-19 virus and a devastating fire in the historic chapel. This ongoing Christian education may be one of the outstanding legacies of Daniel and Lucy Lindley. The school was also the source of some disagreement between Lindley and the American Board. The American Board did not want English taught at the school.

Zulu Christians were coming into their own, having formed Home Missionary Societies. They ordained two Zulu men who would soon become pastors of native churches. They also dealt with the contentious issue of polygamy and banned the practice.[75] By 1869, the number of Zulu pastors had grown to the point that Lindley could report 9 or 10 capable preachers and a dozen assistants. Without a formal theological seminary, Lindley and two colleagues provided formal

---

71 Smith, *Daniel Lindley*, 355.
72 Smith, *Daniel Lindley*, 343.
73 Smith, *Daniel Lindley*, 383.
74 Smith, *Daniel Lindley*, 383.
75 Smith, *Daniel Lindley*, 391. Regarding the polygamy controversy, see also, Phillips, *Protestant America and the Pagan World: The First Half Century of the American Board of Missions, 1810-1860*, 231. This work originated as a doctoral dissertation. Chapter seven is titled, "Africa and the Evangelicals." Regarding Home Mission Societies see also, Dinnerstein, "The American Zulu Mission in the Nineteenth Century: Clash over Culture," 240–242.

theological instruction for seven men in an intensive manner in the winter of 1870.[76] Dr Nathaniel George Clark, a graduate of Halle and Berlin Universities replaced the retired Rufus Anderson as Secretary of the American Board told the missionaries, "We must not expect to bring up our native Christians to our standards at once. Your work is not to make American but Zulu Christians ... The great thing is to bring men to Christ, not to change their social customs ..."[77]

During much of 1868, Daniel Lindley's voice steadily deteriorated making it impossible for him to preach. Theologically trained and licensed Zulu men filled the pulpit admirably. Lindley believed some of the men preached better sermons than he preached. Assessing the modest progress of some of the Zulus over thirty years, he opined to the American Board: "their darkness has been changed to twilight, not to perfect day..."[78] The churches organised with African pastors used a congregational polity with each church operating as a self-governing body. Over time, however, the congregational system broke down. When the African Congregational Church gained its autonomy in 1900, its hybrid polity was called *"episcopresbygational."*[79] The growth of the church was slow but steady. In 23 years the Inanda church grew to 104 members. When the time came for Daniel Lindley to step down as pastor, James Dube, whom Lindley mentored and considered a beloved son, was ordained and replaced him as pastor. Lindley called the ordination, "the high-water mark of his career ... the gladdest day of my life."[80]

About this same time, Mrs Lindley's health began to decline. The diagnosis of heart disease changed Lindley's plans. They intended to live the rest of their lives and die in Natal, but failing health necessitated expert medical care. Lindley announced his retirement to the American Board in October 1872. He was now 70 years and the Lindley's completed 37 years in service for Africa.

14. Summary Conclusion

When the Boers heard of Lindley's impending retirement, they offered their beloved former pastor a large farm in Orange Free State. He refused their generous offer, requesting instead that they simply name a farm for him if they wished. He said, "From you my old friends, all I ask is that you remember my

---

76 Smith, *Daniel Lindley*, 400. On Seminary education see, Dinnerstein, "American Zulu Mission," 239–240.
77 Smith, *Daniel Lindley*, 389, 392.
78 Smith, *Daniel Lindley*, 399.
79 Smith, *Daniel Lindley*, 400. On Congregational polity see, Dinnerstein, "American Zulu Mission," 246.
80 Smith, *Daniel Lindley*, 401.

teachings and give me the assurance that you serve the Lord God and cherish a warm love for the Saviour."[81] Lindley's affiliation with the American Board did not end with his final move to America. The Board hired him as one of their agents to travel and speak on behalf of the mission agency. In one period of 6 weeks, Lindley spoke 52 times, each time for an hour.

The President of Middlebury College described Lindley's public speaking skills this way: "It may be difficult to explain his power over his audience, but I never knew an audience to tire nor flag … his closing appeal was often one of irresistible pathos and power."[82] Lindley faithfully performed these speaking duties until it was physically impossible to go on. Lindley was no longer serving in Africa, but his memory lingered in Africa long after his return to the States. Zulu Christians collected money and sent $100 to the United States with the instructions that it be used "to bury their father and mother."[83] The close of this spiritual warrior's career came on 3 September 1880, at age 80. He was laid to his earthly rest at the family plot in Tarrytown, New York.[84] Daniel Lindley's life is well summed up in a letter written in 1867 by the American Board in Boston regarding the prospects for the gospel in Africa, it reads: "Let us never despair of Africa … She also belongs to Christ."[85] Despite many lean years, setbacks, reversals and steep challenges, Lindley's commitment to his Lord and his desire to spread truth, light and hope in Africa never waned.

Questions for study (fact type):

1. What was the ABCFM?
2. Why did the ABCFM commence mission work in Natal?
3. What three ecclesiastical entities did Lindley help to develop in South Africa?

Questions for study (reflection type):

1. Explain Lindley's mission strategy in working with the Boer Trekkers. Do you agree with this strategy? Why or why not?
2. "Educate a man and you educate an individual; educate a woman and you educate a family."

Write a paragraph about the Inanda Seminary for Girls. Use the information questions – Who, What, When, Where, Why and How? – to assist you in your answer.

---

81 Smith, *Daniel Lindley*, 415. There is a town in the Free State named after him, Lindley, South Africa.
82 Smith, *Daniel Lindley*, 428.
83 Smith, *Daniel Lindley*, 419.
84 Smith, *Daniel Lindley*, 442.
85 Smith, *Daniel Lindley*, 358.

3. "When the Boers heard of Lindley's impending retirement, they offered their beloved former pastor a large farm in Orange Free State. He refused their generous offer, requesting instead that they simply name a farm for him if they wished."

"Zulu Christians collected money and sent $100 to the United States with the instructions that it be used 'to bury their father and mother.'"

Rev. & Mrs Lindley were able to give and receive that love of Christians from different cultures.
Using Christ's prayer in John 17:15-25, explain how and why this was possible. What can we learn from the testimony of the Lindley family?

Select Bibliography

Secondary Sources:

Balfour, R Gordon. *Presbyterianism in the Colonies*. Edinburgh: MacNiven & Wallace, 1899.

Bartlett, Samuel C. *Historical Sketches of the Missions of the American Board*. New York: Arno Press, 1972 reprint edition first published in Boston, 1876. The first chapter pp. 1-15 is titled, "Missions in Africa."

Christofersen, Arthur F. *Adventuring with God: The Story of the American Board Mission in South Africa*. Durban: Robinson & Co., 1967.

Dalziel, John. "The Origin and Growth of Presbyterian Ordinances of Worship among English speaking European South Africans Prior to the Formation of the Presbyterian Church of South Africa in 1897." PhD thesis, University of Edinburgh, 1957.

Davies, Horton. *Great South Africa Christians*. Cape Town: Oxford University Press, 1951, 40-48.

Dinnerstein, Myra. "The American Board Mission to the Zulu, 1835-1900." PhD dissertation, Columbia University, 1971.

.... . "The American Zulu Missions in the Nineteenth Century: Clash over Customs." *Church History* 45.2 (June 1976): 235-246.

Du Plessis, Johannes. *A History of Christian Missions in South Africa*. London: Longmans, Green and Co., 1911.

Etherington, Norman A. "An Errand into the South African Wilderness." *Church History* 39.1 (January 1970): 62-71.

Houle, Robert J. "Constructing an amakholwa Community: Cattle and the Creation of a Zulu Christianity." M.A. thesis, University of Wisconsin-Madison, 1998.

Phillips, Clifton Jackson. *Protestant America and the Pagan World: The First Half Century of the American Board of Commissioners for Foreign Missions, 1810–1860.* Cambridge, MA: Harvard University Press, 1969, chapter seven, pp. 206–232 is titled, "Africa and the Evangelicals."

Ross, Andrew. *John Philips (1775–1851) Missions, Race and Politics in South Africa.* Aberdeen: Aberdeen University Press, 1986.

Scheepers, Meagan. "A comparative Study between two American Missionaries, namely Rev. Daniel Lindley and Dr. Newton Adams in the Frontier Society of Port Natal." BAHons thesis, University of Natal, 1988.

Smith, Edwin W. *The Life and Times of Daniel Lindley, 1801–80: Missionary to the Zulus, Pastor of the Voortrekkers, ubebe Omhlope.* New York: Library Publishers, 1952. This is a meticulously researched biography filled with extracts of letters by Daniel Lindley to the American Board and entries from the diary of Lucy Lindley.

Strong, William Ellsworth. *The Story of The American Board: An Account of the First Hundred Years of the American Board of Commissioners for Foreign Missions.* New York: Arno Press, 1969, reprint of 1910 edition.

Manuscripts and Primary Sources:

Biographer Edwin W. Smith mentions on p. x, Mrs Anson Philips Stokes had in her possession a large box of family correspondence. Smith used these letters extensively.

American Board of Commissioners for Foreign Missions Papers, (ABC), housed at the Houghton Library, Harvard University, Cambridge, MA.

Annual Reports of the American Board for Foreign Missions, 1812–1860, housed at the Divinity Library of Yale University, New Haven, CN.

The Missionary Herald, 1821–1860. This was the official organ of the American Board of Commissioners. Many of Daniel Lindley's letters to the Board were printed in this publication. Full text access available: http://findit.library.yale.edu/catalog/digcoll: 446226 Also, available through the American Antiquarian Society (AAS), Historical Periodical Collection, series 2-5, (1821–1879).

Chapter 7

Alexander Dewar, The Free Church in South Africa, and its Resuscitation post-1900

Nelson Pilile Mpayipeli [1]

Chapter Outline
1. Introduction
2. Resuscitation – the Remnant Calls Out from Macedonia
3. Developments – First Missionary Family, preaching points, schools, etc.
4. Postscript: 1970s & 80s: training, youth work, the General Assembly
5. Conclusion

1. Introduction

This chapter explores the post-1900 Free Church of Scotland mission which continued in South Africa after the 1900 Union in Scotland of two Presbyterian bodies there. In this chapter, central place will be given to the first missionary Rev. Alexander Dewar and thus a short biographical sketch will be included. Readers will come to grasp why this remnant stayed out of the 1900 union and how it slowly re-established itself chiefly through to the mid-1940s. A short postscript will be included with some highlighted developments post-World War Two.

2. Resuscitation – the Remnant Calls Out from Macedonia

The Situation in the South African Mission Stations

In 1900 there was a union between the United Presbyterian Church of Scotland and the majority of the Free Church of Scotland. While not all were in favour of the union, it was unfortunate that all the missionaries in all of the mission fields in Africa were in favour of the union. Initially this even included Rev. Alexander

---

[1] This material was originally gathered for a dissertation submitted for the diploma in post-graduate studies at the Free Church of Scotland College, Edinburgh, Scotland, May 1994. Rev. Mpayipeli died during the writing of the present volume – March 2022. Additional footnotes and comments have been added occasionally by the editors.

Dewar (see section 3 of this chapter) who was busy in his Mission Station at Mwenzo (situated in modern-day Zambia) during this time and who remained in that newly formed Church which was the United Free Church of Scotland.[2]

Consequently, in 1900 the Free Church of Scotland was bereft of all the mission property and funds, the reason for this being that all the missionaries who were in South Africa during that time joined the United Free Church of Scotland. When the Union of 1900 was effected, it was carried out without the cognizance and so without the concurrence of the congregations in the mission districts. There was a sentiment by many that proper consultation should have been done with the mission churches, rather than all being determined in Scotland. Things were carried on as though there were no changes, but people were deceived about the Union from the perspective of the remnant who remained out of this union.[3]

However, the missionary ardour of the remnant of the Free Church of Scotland was still strong, and as it began to recover from its wounds, it sought an outlet for its missionary zeal. The Free Church of Scotland had no desire to bring to Africa the ecclesiastical dissensions that had rent Scotland from end to end and it reported to the Executive Commission set up by Parliament that it did not desire to intrude upon any sphere formerly occupied by the Free Church now taken over by the United Free Church. The desire, however, to engage in missionary work in some part of the African Continent with which the Free Church had been so long and honourable associated, was frequently expressed by the General Assembly.[4]

Rev. J. D. McCulloch's Visit to South Africa

In 1905, the then Convener of the Foreign Missions Committee of the Free Church of Scotland, Rev. McCulloch, was sent to South Africa to visit and convey the Church's brotherly greetings to the Presbyterian Churches there. On his return, McCulloch brought back a detailed report on the situation and suggested Rhodesia (modern-day Zimbabwe and Zambia) as the most suitable field for fresh missionary enterprise; but he also brought with him a petition containing about 4,000 signatures from native churches in the South African field, formerly occupied by the Free Church, asking for recognition by the Free Church of Scotland whom they regarded as their mother church.[5]

---

2 *Acts of the General Assembly*, 1901, 356. Some interesting background material on Dewar and relations with Robert Laws of the Livingstonia Mission is given in John McCracken, *Politics and Christianity in Malawi 1875–1940: the Impact of the Livingstonia Mission in the Northern Province.* Original 1977. (Zomba: Kachere Series, 2000), 173–174.
3 *The Monthly Record of the Free Church of Scotland*, June 1908, 100–101.
4 *Free Church of Scotland Missionary Enterprise*, issued by the Foreign Missions Committee, Edinburgh, 1949, 10.
5 *Free Church of Scotland Missionary Enterprise*, issued by the Foreign Missions Committee, Edinburgh, 1949, 10.

Two Deputies Sent to South Africa Again

As communications continued between the African (native) congregations in South Africa and the Free Church of Scotland, the General Assembly of 1907, feeling, to use its own words, "unable to come to a right conclusion without more information than could be gather by correspondence,"[6] resolved to send two deputies to South Africa. These deputies were Principal McCulloch and Professor John MacLeod. After a thorough investigation of conditions there, the deputies cabled to the ensuing Commission of Assembly for permission to resuscitate the Free Church Presbytery of Kaffraria and ordain two African pastors by the names of Ntsikana Gaba and Burnet Gaba.[7] One was to look after the Pirie stations and the other after the Burnshill stations.[8] This was granted, though not without dissent on the ground of procedure.[9] The Gabas were ordained on 29th August 1907 by the resuscitated Presbytery of Kaffraria.

3. Developments – First Missionary family, preaching points, schools, etc.

When the deputies had returned to Scotland from South Africa, a full, detailed and encouraging report was presented to the Foreign Missions Committee and was gladly accepted.[10] It became evident that there was a great need for a missionary who would be the superintendent of the Free Church of Scotland Mission in South Africa. An appeal was made to anyone who thought that he would be suitable for the work. This was made by the Convener of the Foreign Missions Committee of the Free Church of Scotland, Rev. C. A. Bannatyne.[11] Several applied but the Committee considered Rev. Alexander Dewar's application and he was nominated as a man suitable for the work.

Rev. Alexander Dewar

Alexander Dewar (1864–1943) was born in Lochgilphead, Scotland and studied at Glasgow University and Glasgow Free Church College. He had come under conviction to become a missionary at the evangelistic meetings of Moody and Sankey held in Glasgow and thus he applied to study to become a minister and missionary. Dewar was ordained in 1893 and was sent as a missionary of the

---

6 *The Monthly Record of the Free Church of Scotland*, June 1907, 101.
7 *Free Church of Scotland Missionary Enterprise*, issued by the Foreign Missions Committee, 11.
8 *The Monthly Record of the Free Church of Scotland*, June 1908, 100, under "Presbytery of Kaffraria."
9 *Free Church of Scotland Missionary Enterprise*, issued by the Foreign Missions Committee, 11.
10 *The Monthly Record of the Free Church of Scotland*, June 1908, 100–101.
11 *The Monthly Record of the Free Church of Scotland*, January 1908, 2–3.

Free Church to Livingstonia, Nyasaland (modern Malawi).[12] Dewar gained much experience in actual missionary work at Livingstonia. For several years he had laboured in Livingstonia in both what is now Malawi and also Zambia where his efforts in pioneering work were marked with special success. He founded the mission station at Mwenzo in Zambia (1894) and was deeply involved there in industrial work, agriculture, establishing a school, and a church. The first communion service was held at Mwenzo in May 1896. The Dewars were also involved in adopting orphans while at Mwenzo. These had lost their parents due to wars and the slave trade which was still operating in the area. Many of these orphans became invaluable assistants in the mission station at Mwenzo. Alexander Dewar, together with the Scottish ministers W. A. Elmslie and A. G. Macalpine, constituted the first meeting of the (North) Livingstonia Presbytery at the Overtoun Institution, 15 November 1899.[13]

The Dewars entered into the United Free Church of Scotland in 1900 and remained with it until 1905 when his sympathies towards the 1900 Union changed and he resigned from the Livingstonia Mission now connected with the UF Church. His eleven years connected to the Livingstonia Mission were invaluable training and preparation for what he would be called upon later to do in South Africa. Resigning on 9 March 1905,[14] he then went to Burma for about three and a half years where he assisted in dealing with his sister-in-law's uncle's estate as a teak merchant there and as a chaplain to the Burmah [Burma] Oil Company. He returned to Scotland from Burma in August 1908, having already been appointed a missionary to South Africa for the Free Church. He was described as a man still in his prime of life

▲ *Alexander Dewar when Moderator of the FCS GA*

---

12 Alexander Dewar was married twice. His first wife, Emmeline Harvey, was a single missionary in the Livingstonia Mission and they married there. Emmeline compiled and translated, *Chinamwanga Stories*, published in Livingstonia by the Mission Press, 1900 (see chapter 14 in this volume). This was a book of local folklore stories for children that she hoped would be used to entice the children to come to school. The book can be found at SOAS and also an electronic version at: https://archive.org/details/dewar-chinamwanga-stories-1900/page/n1/mode/2up She was the mother of two of Alexander's children – Alexander and Margaret. Emmeline died tragically in East London, SA in 1918. Alexander married his second wife, Charlotte, in King William's Town in 1923. They were blessed with a son, Ian, born in 1930.
13 McCracken, *Politics and Christianity in Malawi*, 243.
14 *Fasti of the United Free Church of Scotland 1900–1929*, ed. J. A. Lamb (Edinburgh: Oliver & Boyd, 1956), 561.

and with a distinguished record as a student. The Foreign Missions Committee had concluded that since he had an intimate knowledge of the Africans, their customs and language and had already rendered notable service in translating several portions of scripture into the native dialects when at Mwenzo, he was the man for this mission. His attainments in translation were plainly of a special value in view of the necessity of an adequate metrical version of the Psalms for the missionary requirements of the Free Church. Dewar's theological sympathies were in complete agreement with the standpoint of the Free Church and of her position with regard to the conduct of public worship; he had signified his unqualified approval.[15]

The Foreign Missions Committee could not refrain from expressing their belief that the hand of a kind Providence could be plainly traced in enabling them to bring before the General Assembly the name of one so exceptionally qualified to engage in their work in the South African field.[16] He arrived in King William's Town/Qonca in November 1908, along with his wife, Emmeline, and their two children, Alexander (Rex) and Margaret (Queenie).

Mission Stations

Pirie

Before the Union, this was the main station which occupied a place all its own in the history of the Free Church in South Africa, for it was there that the Rev. John Ross finally settled. In this area, there were remnants who remained true to the cause of the Free Church and did not join the Union of 1900. The arrival of the first missionary from Scotland after 1900 in the person of Rev. Dewar was a great encouragement to them. It was appropriate therefore that when he arrived, this was the first station to be visited by him. On Monday, 30th November 1908, Rev. Dewar visited Pirie accompanied by Mr Makubalo, who had offered to drive him with his horse and trap. Quite a number of men on horseback joined them on their way. There were elders and members who had come in from Pirie that morning to escort Dewar to their station. He was heartily welcomed by Rev. Ntsikana Gaba and the great crowd of church members and adherents. Pirie had at the time the main station and seven out-stations.

Knox was an out-station of the Pirie District but though that was the case, it had its own interesting history as a station. It was at Knox that Rev. Principal McCulloch and Rev. Prof MacLead reconstituted the Free Church Mission in South Africa on 21 August 1907. The moving spirit in this determined adherence to the Free Church was Mr Neku, the headman who was also a teacher and

---

15 *The Monthly Record of the Free Church of Scotland*, June 1908, 100.
16 *The Monthly Record of the Free Church of Scotland*, June 1908, 100.

elder, and he had the assistance of other fellow Christian Office-bearers such as William Gaba and his two sons Ntsikana and Burnet.[17] It was through the efforts of Mr Neku and Mr William Gaba that some other congregations were formed and petitions forwarded to Edinburgh begging the Free Church to reconstitute its missionary work in their midst. Subsequently, the first Presbytery meeting held in Rev. Dewar's presence was in this station.

Burnshill

Mr Burnet Gaba was the pastor of Burnshill congregation and its ten out-stations. As arranged previously, Dewar visited Burnshill station with a number of men from King William's Town, all of them on horseback. As they appeared at the Mission Station, loud shouts of welcome were heard. What happened at Pirie the previous day was repeated at Burnshill. From what Dewar had seen and heard from Pirie and Burnshill, he felt that God had done great things in permitting them to take part in such a service and prayed that God would bless them in the days to come and make them worthy of this great work.[18]

Transkei and Griqualand East

At the meeting of the Presbytery at Knox on 16 March 1909, members of the Presbytery from Transkei and Griqualand East were eager that Rev. Dewar would soon visit them. As a result, Rev. Dewar accompanied by Ntsikana Gaba and Philemon Mpunzi went to visit Ngcingwana in Transkei near Idutywa. A public meeting was arranged by Mr Sangqu and his men on Saturday. They were glad there was a missionary among them and that Rev. Dewar managed to visit them at Ngcingwana. The headman, Mr Sagqu, told how they and their fathers had been brought up in the Free Church and wished to remain in it and that all the people on Ngcingwana with the exception of two families had refused to join the United Free Church. They had continued sending their children to the old school which was in the possession of the United Free Church and supervised by them. This meant that out of 106 children on the roll, only ten belonged to the United Free Church, yet the people who adhered to the Free Church were forced to be under the United Free Church superintendentship. That was a pathetic state of affairs. In this matter, they felt that they had a just grievance.[19] Next day, a regular service was held in the hut and although the people had to travel great distances to the Church, they managed to come. People were very encouraged and felt that the work would go again as before.

---

17 *Free Church of Scotland Missionary Enterprise*, 13–14.
18 *Monthly Record of the Free Church of Scotland*, February 1909, 28.
19 *The Instructor: Youth Magazine of the Free Church of Scotland*, August 1909, 216.

When it became time for Rev. Dewar to visit Griqualand East, he was accompanied by Mr Ntisikana Gabe and another elder. On their arrival, they were warmly welcomed by Chief Jamangile himself. On the next day, they visited the Chief and discussed business with him. Rev. Dewar also went to see the Church school which was built by Chief Jamangile and his people. The Chief and his people were deprived of the use of this building because they refused to join the Union. The deprivation of the building was a great grief to the Chief.[20] Because of that confusion, some of Jamangile's people joined the Presbyterian Church of Africa (Mzimba).[21]

Gqumahashe Station

Besides Pirie and Burnshill Stations there was a separate station near Lovedale called Gqumahashe. It seems this station was smaller and had fewer out-stations in the early period. Latterly it will be known as the Dewar District in honour of Rev. Dewar.

Properties

Attempts were made to regain the Church properties which belonged to the Free Church before the Union where the Free Church was in the majority but unfortunately these did not succeed. In order to be able to build again, new sites had to be applied for. That in itself was a long process but at last sites were granted to the Free Church. When these sites were granted, there was a desire among African Christians that the titles of these news sites should be made out in the name of local trustees. Dewar asked for advice on this matter from the Foreign Missions Committee. The Committee did not accede to this proposal and made it clear that the law and practice of the Church required that all such buildings should be held in the name of the General Trustees.[22]

Summation

Due to the greatness of the work in South Africa under Rev. Dewar, about twenty church schools were to be erected. The two main stations were Pirie, under the pastoral charge of Rev. Ntsikana Gaba and in connection with which there were seven out-stations, and Burnshill, which was under the care of Burnet Gaba and embraced ten outlying stations of a similar kind. Besides these two, there was a station at Gqumahashe near Lovedale, and several stations in Transkei and

---

20 *Monthly Record of the Free Church of Scotland*, February 1910, 28.
21 *Monthly Record of the Free Church of Scotland*, February 1910, 29.
22 *Acts of the General Assembly*, 1911, 632.

Griqualand East further north.[23] On the question of Church buildings, it was decided that temporary buildings of mud bricks should be erected. It was the policy of Rev. Dewar to try to obtain sites and build churches on raised ground or hill tops so that these could be seen by people roundabout.[24] Examples of these were Knox, Gquamahashe, Muyameni, Ngcingwana, and Jafta.

Pastors

When Rev. Dewar arrived in South Africa, there were already two African pastors who were ordained by the two deputies from Scotland in 1907. There were brothers, Burnet and Ntsikana Gaba. One was to be in charge of Pirie and the other in charge of Burnshill. These men welcomed Dewar on his arrival and showed him the different mission stations. According to the direction of the Foreign Missions Committee, Dewar was to be the superintendent of the whole mission work in South Africa. Burnet Gaba resigned from the Free Church and started an independent Church known by his name as he found the oversight of the Free Church in Scotland through Dewar to be oppressive. Ntsikana Gaba continued working in the Pirie district under the supervision of Rev. Dewar.[25]

Evangelists

Among the assistants of Rev. Dewar in the Mission Field in South Africa were evangelists. Due to the fact that Rev. Dewar could not be in many different places at the same time, it was proper for him to use the services of these men. In fact, one of them was appointed before he undertook the work in South Africa. This was William Matayo who was an evangelist in the Burnshill district and was stationed at Mnyameni. He remained faithful as an evangelist of the Free Church, even after suffering much as he was dismissed from his teaching post because he would not enter the Union. He was doing a great work and for this reason Dewar was able to appeal to Scotland for him to be assisted with Christian books which would help him in the preparation of his sermons.[26] There were others who were used in the different districts. At Pirie, Mr Philemon Mpunzi was an evangelist. He also accompanied Dewar in his travels in Transkei. On another occasion Mr Mpunzi and a man identified only as *David* from Mwenzo Central Africa (modern Zambia) who was one of Rev.

---

23 *Acts of the General Assembly*, 1911, 632.
24 A letter from Mr I. [Ian]. Dewar, 402 Sonnenkus, Camps Bay, Cape Town, dated 20th March 1994, page 4, to the author.
25 *Monthly Record of the Free Church of Scotland*, September 1911, 146; *Acts of the General Assembly*, 1912, 816.
26 *The Monthly Record of the Free Church of Scotland*, November 1909, 190.

Dewar's first pupils in Livingstonia, were left behind by Dewar conducting services at Chief Jamangile's place with encouraging results.[27] Those were the men who contributed much to the expansion of the work of the Free Church. The services of such men were not only confined to the beginning of the twentieth century, but they were in use even by the end of the twentieth century. In fact, when Dewar went back to Scotland in mid-1920 until 1922, Rev. William Murray (Free Church of Scotland missionary sent to South Africa in 1912,[28] assumed the sole responsibility for the oversight of the work. During this period, he expressed the conviction that the church needed to train African men for the work (initially as Evangelists) for "better work, and deeper and more lasting could be done if we had the right class of man as Evangelist to live for a time with the people and help them in their homes. The European Missionary is in too much of a hurry for this." [29]

▲ *Ox wagon crossing Keiskamma River*

---

27 *Acts of General Assembly*, 1912, 817. It is most interesting to learn about the involvement of a native evangelist from Mwenzo serving the Free Church in the Transkei.
28 Graham, *Ochre and The Blue*, 53.
29 Graham, *Ochre and The Blue*, 66. See also, *Annals of the Free Church of Scotland 1900–1986*, ed. G. N. M. Collins, (Edinburgh, n.d.), 59. During the Dewar era the following FCS missionaries also served: Rev. William Murray (1912–1922), Rev. Adam A. MacPherson (1925–1929), Rev. John A. Macdonald, (1927–1929), and then following Rev. Dewar's death, Rev. Joseph McCracken (1945–1974), was the first successor, as per comparing dates in *Annals* as above, 20, 31, 35, 59.

Teachers

The work of teachers as assistants to Rev. Dewar should not be underestimated. These men did their task at difficult times. Some of these teachers had to suffer because they adhered to the Free Church. An example of this was Mr Matayo, as already noted. It was not Matayo alone who suffered. In the Pirie district Mr Henry Ntshona experienced the same fate. He was dismissed as a teacher in the school of the United Free Church because he adhered to the Free Church. Dewar appealed for him to Scotland, so that he could be employed in the Free Church school. The reason for this was that the Free Church children had been withdrawn from the school of the United Free Church since the missionary of that Church had dismissed Ntshona. In the meantime, Dewar took responsibility for the part of Ntshona's salary which, while he was in office, had been paid by the government. Ntshona was a staunch Free Church man and a competent teacher with sixteen years' experience, and he enjoyed the confidence of the people at Dyafta in whose school he had been teacher for twelve years. His salary was £42 a year, on which £30 was paid by the government grant and the balance by fees payable by the parents.[30]

Assistants from Scotland

It was good news to Rev. Dewar and to the people of the Free Church in South Africa when they heard that William Murray, who had been a missionary in Livingstonia, had applied to the Free Church of Scotland to be accepted as a missionary to South Africa. Murray had served for 22 years as an artisan missionary in Livingstonia and was ordained by the Free Church Presbytery of Glasgow in 1912, now for the work in South Africa. His arrival in South Africa was a relief to Dewar as he would help him. When he arrived in 1912, he was stationed in Keiskammahoek to be in charge of the Burnshill district with its out-stations. He did great work in the Burnshill district, and he was encouraged by the work at Emnyameni where the congregation became stronger, and the schoolwork was also encouraging. After eleven years of devoted service for the cause of Christ in the Burnshill district he passed away in 1923, two months after he had arrived in Scotland on furlough.[31] Rev. Dewar was very grieved on Rev. Murray's death, and he was again left alone with the work.

It was not until 1925 that another assistant from Scotland arrived in South Africa in the person of Mr Adam MacPherson. During this time, people came to join the Free Church when they noticed that there was a Free Church missionary. Rev. Damane from the Presbyterian Church of Africa (Mzimba) and Rev. H.

---

30 *Acts of General Assembly*, December 1910, 200.
31 *Free Church of Scotland Missionary Enterprise*, 15; *Acts of the General Assembly*, 1912, 820.

Mazwi from the same church, asked to be received into the Free Church with their congregations. Both of these men in later years assisted Rev. Dewar in the Transkei. It was a pity that Mr MacPherson and his wife were not able to continue their work in South Africa due to poor health. They returned to Scotland in 1929 after spending a period of five years in South Africa.

Schools

Rev. Dewar's work was not confined to the Church alone. He had to be in charge of the Free Church Schools. These schools were not recognised by the government. This meant that they were not able to receive a grant from the government and secondly that even a school inspector could visit them. That opened another area of service for Dewar because it meant that for some time he had to act as an inspector of these schools. When he was involved in this inspection, he noticed that children had no Bible instruction and did not know the Bible. The Free Church teachers were encouraged to teach the Bible in all the Free Church Schools.[32]

Eventually these Free Church of Scotland schools passed into the control of the South African Parliament following the enactment of the 1954 Act that put mission schools into the hands of the Department of Native Affairs and local school committees and boards.[33]

Women's Work

The missionary wives together with women throughout the mission stations, ministered to the women not only of the Free Church but in the various villages in the districts. In the July 1929 *Instructor*, there is a letter from Mrs Charlotte Dewar. She tells about four journeys to outlying stations of the Mission, where she held the Women's Quarterly Meetings and examined a number of Sabbath Schools. She says:

> It was gratifying to see some few boys present at these examinations. We are indebted to the elder of Macfarlane for the happy idea of having a class for herd-boys at 6 am. Then Mrs Dewar appealed for money to buy Bibles to give as prizes each year to the children in every Sabbath School, 27 to 30 in all. The Sunday Schools were a promising feature of the work. There were 627 children enrolled. Stephen Zondani of Gqumahashe was an excellent Sunday School teacher and trained other teachers.[34]

---

32 *The Monthly Record of the Free Church of Scotland*, August 1909, 137.
33 Graham, *Ochre and The Blue*, 154.
34 Graham, *Ochre and The Blue*, 86–87.

4. Postscript: the 1970s & 80s: training, youth work, the General Assembly is born

Some of the early Free Church developments (pastors, evangelists, teachers, schools, women's work, etc.) were further developed in later years through some key events. A very select postscript has been included here.

Dimbaza Reformed Bible School

In March 1978, a group of leaders met together in East London at Die Gereformeerde Kerke in Suid-Afrika (GKSA) to form a four-way partnership to start a Bible School in Dimbaza (about 20 kilometres from King William's Town). The four partners were: the Gereformeerde Kerk East London (GKSA), the Gereformeerde Kerk eMonti (GKSA), the Free Church of Scotland (FCS), and the Free Church of Southern Africa (FCSA). Appeals were sent throughout South Africa to the GKSA congregations to help with expenses to begin the Bible School and to the FCS. Support came from these sources and beyond.

During the first year (1979) alone, several conferences and "short courses" were held for ministers, evangelists, schoolteachers, young people, and women. Most were held on location in Dimbaza, but some also were held in the Transkei. A weekly evening course was also held that year, and the Bible correspondence programme began. The Bible School became known for its Christian literature work. At the end of 1986, the school moved to King William's Town/Qonce and was renamed Dumisani (Xhosa for "praise") Bible School.[35] Gradually, local indigenous leadership at all levels was being raised up.

Developments in Youth Work

By the late 1980s, there was a growing awareness within the FCSA of the importance of youth ministry. Youth Conferences became an annual feature of the Free Church calendar. Several choirs of young people gather for fellowship and teaching. In 1994, a youth worker, Mr Eric Mekute, was commissioned by the FCSA assembly to work amongst the youth of the denomination. Such developments highlighted the growing independence of the young denomination.

---

35 For a survey story of the first 40 years of the history of Dumisani Theological Institute and Bible School, see "An Overview of the Dumisani Story," in *Voices of Thanksgiving*, eds. Jack & Nancy Whytock (Charlottetown, PE: Haddington House Trust, 2019), 9–19. In the 1930s and 40s some FCSA evangelists trained at the Lovedale Bible School but by the late 1950s it was closed.

The General Assembly is born

Looking back to the early 1980s, perhaps the climax of the longer-term significance of Mr Alexander Dewar's work (from 1908 until his death in 1943) was reached when in 1983 the Free Church in Southern Africa was born, and the first General Assembly met at Dimbaza with Rev. B. M. Taho (d.29 Dec. 2022) as its Moderator – 9 July 1983. The work in South Africa was organised into two Presbyteries, the Presbytery of Transkei and the Southern Presbytery which consists of the congregations in the then Ciskei and the townships of Cape Town, Somerset East, Port Elizabeth, Dordrecht, and Mdantsane (East London).

The dream of Rev. Dewar of an African Church which he spoke about in his speech when he was the Moderator of the Free Church of Scotland in 1927 was fulfilled. For he had said that the time had come when the natives, fired with a sense of ambition and a belief in their own ability, were seeking to have missionary churches brought more directly under their own control. The demand appeared to be well-nigh universal. While the above must be the ideal to which all missionary organisations should aspire, the situation was involved and circled with difficulties. A judgement could only be passed as to whether a group of natives were ready to control their ecclesiastical matters or not after thorough, sympathetic appreciation and understanding of the local circumstances involved. The ideal in the Gospel enterprise was to pioneer virgin country, evangelise native tribes and through time bring them to the stage where they would be able to conduct their own church affairs and be sufficiently strong to send out parties to being in those out with the Gospel circle.[36]

5. Conclusion

The resuscitation of the Free Church of Scotland mission in South Africa post-1900 was accomplished by God's grace and the dedication of many – in both Scotland, elsewhere overseas, and South Africa. The historic bonds of this partnership produced an open door through which Alexander Dewar ably walked to provide leadership, encouragement, and training for 35 years. As the denomination produced the fruit of its own leadership, the FCS and the FCSA were able to transition from a "parent/child" relationship to that of "brothers and sisters" in Christ in mutual encouragement and support. The Free Church of Southern Africa today has the opportunity to build on that legacy to the glory of God and the increase of His Kingdom.

---

36 *The Monthly Record of the Free Church of Scotland*, June 1927, 129. For a list of missionaries who served in the FCSA (1900–2000) and African Ministers of the FCSA (1900–2000), see Graham, *Ochre and The Blue*, 377–378.

Questions for study (fact type):

1 Name the first appointed missionary after the 1900 resuscitation and write one paragraph about his ministry.
2 Name the first indigenous ministers appointed after the 1900 resuscitation and write one paragraph about their ministry.
3 List the day schools that were established during Rev. Dewar's ministry. Make a separate list of the key indigenous teachers.

Questions for study (reflection type):

1 Why do you think the remnant of Free Churches did not enter the 1900 Union in South Africa? Discuss and evaluate.
2 Discuss the role of the Christian day school in Christian mission.

Select Bibliography

Graham, Bill and Elizabeth, *The Ochre and the Blue: The Story of the Mission Work of the Free Church of Scotland in South Africa in the Twentieth Century*. Edinburgh: Free Church of Scotland Public., 2009.

Mpayipeli, Nelson Pilile, "Alexander Dewar and the Free Church of Scotland Mission in South Africa." PGDip dissertation, Free Church of Scotland College (now Edinburgh Theological Seminary), Edinburgh, 1994.

Papers of Rev. Alexander Dewar, MSS. Edinburgh University Library Special Collections, Edinburgh. GB 237 Coll. 887, E 2004.5 https://archiveshub.jisc.ac.uk/data/gb237-coll-887

"South Africa Presbytery Notes 1907–1964. Free Church of Scotland Presbytery of Kaffraria." (Booklet). No place, no publisher and no date. 16 pages.

Chapter 8

"*The Lovedale Method*," Context, Development, & Transmission

J. C. Whytock

Chapter Outline
1. Introduction
2. Antecedents and a Name
3. First Principal, Ideals and Realities: William Govan
4. Second Principal, Changing of the Guard: James Stewart
5. Survey c.1906–c.1950s
6. Sub-stories: Oromo slaves, Malawi and Kenya, Printing Press, Bible School
7. Conclusion: Impact, Transmission and Shadows of What Once Were

1. Introduction

In African mission history there is a certain aura of nostalgia, glory, and sadness around the word Lovedale. In literature one will find such things as Lovedale "the Christian Colossus." It was in many ways the premier institution which Presbyterians in the 19th century and early 20th century saw as their greatest achievement in educational missions on the continent of Africa, or as Brian Stanley wrote "the most famous Scottish mission station in Africa."[1] It is thus not an easy task to unpack the story of Lovedale. In this chapter, the development will not encompass every aspect of that story, but we will endeavour to draw the lines through many of the significant historical aspects and leaders of its development.

▲ Lovedale stamp

---

1 Stanley, "The Theology of the Scottish Protestant Missionary Movement," 52.

2. Antecedents and a Name

Lovedale did not just drop out of heaven. There are matters behind it, or antecedents. One such concept would be the Scottish Presbyterian philosophy that education and mission work go together or are handmaids to each other. Andrew Walls argues that Lovedale was influenced by the educational mission methods of Alexander Duff and John Wilson in Scottish Presbyterian work in India, especially upon Lovedale's first principal, William Govan. Duff went to India in 1830 and founded the General Assembly's Institution with English as the primary medium of instruction together with teaching in the vernacular Bengali. He was firmly committed to it being non-sectarian in the student body, and to move students from the elementary classes to the collegiate level. Success led to branch schools being established from the mother institution. The Christian faith was to be taught but so were a multitude of subjects including economics, something which was not positively taken by the church back in Scotland since it was viewed as non-spiritual. This raises several points but the last notes that there were various stresses and strains within Scottish Presbyterian circles as to just what types of education and the nature of such should be best developed on the mission field.[2] So, technically when Lovedale would formally commence in 1841, it did have precedents to draw upon and that circle of influence runs deep to Chalmers and even back to the Scottish First Book of Discipline and parish education.[3]

The other antecedent to recall is that since 1841, Lovedale was really building upon the foundation of John Bennie and John Ross dating back to their initiatives of the early 1820s in informal education and elementary formal educational endeavours in the Eastern Cape. Bennie was preparing basic materials in Xhosa and then Ross was the printer. Catechistic work by helping prepare candidates for baptism was all part of the development of informal Christian education. Bennie almost immediately had gathered around him pupils and started a school. Lovedale of 1841 would not have been able to happen without the almost twenty years of groundwork and infrastructure that had been done in informal education, translation work, printing, linguistics and attempts in a complex environment with formal elementary schooling. For example, in 1838, Lovedale as a school had 134 pupils registered with it, doing academic and vocational

---

2   A helpful summary of this Scottish approach of Christian missions through school, the Bible, and mission and civilising effects for both home and overseas, see, Ian Shaw, *Churches Revolutions & Empires 1789–1914* (Fearn, UK: Christian Focus, 2012), 116 and Claire Kaczmarek, "Mission Education and the Evangelical Missiology of James Stewart in Lovedale," 5–7.
3   Walls, *DSCHT*, 579 and Paton, *Alexander Duff*, 68–77, 156ff.

work. It really can be argued correctly that the Lovedale Press, which would be most significant for the advance of the Lovedale Institution, began in 1823 long before Lovedale actually was formally declared an Institution.

Next, what about the name? There were two or three names that have commonly been used: Lovedale Institution or Lovedale Missionary Institution,[44] Lovedale Seminary, and Lovedale Missionary School. The first portion of the name is the easiest to define: it was named after John Love (1757–1825) a leading evangelical Church of Scotland minister and advocate of missions who was deeply involved in both the London Missionary Society and the Glasgow Missionary Society. His name was given to the missionary station in the Eastern Cape in 1824. As a station it covered the whole range of mission activities which included informal and formal aspects of Christian evangelism, nurture, and education. It was situated in the Thyume Valley and due to conflict was relocated over the early years until it settled by the west bank of the Thyume River in what is today, Alice, its location when it was formalised in 1841.

The second part of the name, starting with *Institution*, seems to have been a common way of describing both missionary stations in some instances and educational endeavours, as already noted in India with Duff. It is a broad way of conveying a place of instruction, in this case Christian teaching. *Seminary* to the modern ear sounds like a graduate or postgraduate theological school or to some the original usage as a Roman Catholic counter-reformation school for priests. Such was not the case. Yes, the Bible or theology broadly defined was in the curriculum and training for Christian work or ministry but not a modern definition of seminary. A much broader term in older usage, more like a training high school, was meant. Finally, the name of *Missionary School* – that encapsulated what Lovedale was for us today – established as a missionary enterprise but also training for mission and work. It was a school but one with many parts for mission training in the broadest sense.

Summary

The two antecedents of Lovedale are: it was rooted in Scottish Presbyterian missions and education as partners and secondly, Lovedale existed for almost twenty years before it was formalised and expanded in 1841.

---

4 On occasion the word Institution is changed to the word *Institute* and this name can be found in some of the Stewart papers.

3. First Principal, Ideals and Realities: 1841–1870, William Govan

William Govan (1804–1875) was the first principal serving from 1841 to 1870 at the Lovedale Institution. An ordained minister of the Church of Scotland and also a schoolteacher having taught classics for ten years, he was appointed to the position by the Glasgow Missionary Society, the section which sided with the establishment principle. Latterly, he and this society would realign with the Free Church of Scotland and labour with its foreign mission's board and thus Lovedale became associated with the Free Church of Scotland after the Disruption though to 1900 (and then from 1900 to 1929 with the United Free Church of Scotland and after 1929 to closing with the Church of Scotland).

Govan's vision was an institution open to all races and thus the opening class was both white and black students studying in classes together. Education was to be in English predominately and some Xhosa. It included Latin and Greek in the higher levels. It was not to be for only one denomination, but open to all. His vision was for Lovedale to eventually have various divisions, an elementary school division and a teacher training school, a preparatory school (basically a high school) which would include classical education, and a college, and a theological hall. It was an ambitious vision with a strong ideal for moving all to a very high level of learning. He was committed to evangelism, Christian nurture, and developing a Christian perspective in applying the faith. There was also to be a commitment to practical skills development, which were done through each student doing manual labour to support the Institution. In the 1850s several trades were added: carpentry, wagon making, smithing, agriculture, printing, and bookbinding. Yet, as Andrew Ross stated, all underscored by Govan's primary vision "to produce a Christian academic elite (black and white) to lead the nation."[5]

▲ William Govan

Govan was a committed evangelical Christian who emphasised evangelism, conversion, and nurture through education. Such an emphasis will lead to cultural conflict of worldviews and different interpretations have developed of such amongst historians.[6] From all accounts he attempted to be fair, and respectful to all and to maintain his evangelical

---

5   Ross, "Govan, William," 253.
6   See, Duncan, "Coercive agency in mission education."

theological convictions. Was he blind to some things? No doubt he was just as it will likely be said of all of us.

He has been greatly overshadowed by the next principal at Lovedale, James Stewart. It has often been forgotten that Stewart built upon the work of Govan and secondly though there were educational philosophical differences. Govan's vision in-part, it can be argued, did reach fruition years later with the establishment of what would become the South African Native College and latterly the University of Fort Hare.

It was under Govan's principalship that Tiyo Soga was a student at Lovedale and also accompanied Govan to Scotland (See chapter on Soga). The first class under Govan's principalship saw 20 students, 11 black and 9 white. By 1902, Lovedale would have 6,000 students pass through its doors. In his final year, Govan began the process of training at a level for ordination for Free Church ministers at Lovedale with a three-year course. The first class would finish their studies when Stewart became principal. The initial intake of ministerial students had all completed their literary course at Lovedale first before 1870 under Govan's principalship.

Govan had many storms to weather as the first principal of Lovedale. In 1848 the Free Church Foreign Missions Committee recommended closing its South African mission, but "friends" rallied behind Lovedale, and they carried the finances of Lovedale with the proviso that Lovedale remain part of the Mission work of the Free Church. Aside from major financial pressures, there were wars and famine and constant tensions in the region.

4. Second Principal, Changing of the Guard, James Stewart

James Stewart (1831–1905) looms large in 19th century African Presbyterian mission history, symbolic in his monumental grave marker atop a large hill (Sandile's Kop) seen from a distance in Alice, SA.[7] Stewart joined David Livingstone in the famous Zambesi expedition (Stewart being on the expedition 1862–1863 for fourteen months) to investigate the possibilities of a Christian mission in this interior region of Africa. This is where the noted phraseology will become widely known: "to introduce Commerce, Civilization, and Christianity to the lands of Zambezi River and Lake Malawi." Stewart did not end the expedition on good terms with Livingstone. There are perhaps a multitude of reasons, one being Livingstone's wife's death and the other a conflict of leadership vision and practice. The expedition, despite all its problems did identify many issues concerning this region of Africa one of which was to locate Lake Nyassa.

---

7 As a student, Stewart's nickname was *Stewart Africanus* due to his obsession for Africa.

James Stewart

Stewart's extensive travels in the shires would help him later to establish the Livingstonia mission.[8]

Stewart was a minister of the Free Church of Scotland and also trained in medicine.[9] He was appointed to the Lovedale Institution in 1867 having first visited it in 1863 when involved with the Zambesi Expedition. He came into conflict almost immediately with Govan's vision. Shepherd summarised it in these words: "Govan was sacrificed because of his conviction that a primitive people could best be elevated first by the highest education of the few and Stewart took his place as Principal because he advocated first the elementary education of the many."[10] The Free Church Foreign Missions Committee under Duff's chairmanship sided with Stewart and the result was that Govan resigned and returned to Scotland, making Stewart principal in 1870.

It can be summarised that Stewart stressed a broader educational model (a comprehensive approach) adapted to what he considered the context. It was also to be practical or in the language of the day, industrial. However, ever central was the undergirding of a Christian ethos and Bible-centred life. Spiritual formation and character development in terms of today's language were central. Lovedale was to provide what Stewart often described as a combined comprehensive system of education: religious instruction (the Christian faith and life), general education, and industrial training "conjoined with the preaching of the Gospel or the purely evangelistic method. The latter must always take the chief and most honoured place."[11] From this would arise teachers, preachers, catechists and evangelists, artisans, and workers all leading to the development and growth of church and society. English was to be the focus and the classical languages would only be reserved for theology students not for all in the higher levels.

Stewart was a man constantly on the move and energetic for the advancement

---

8   J. P. R. Wallis, ed., *The Zambesi Journal of James Stewart 1862–1862* (London: Chatto & Windus, 1952).
9   Stewart was the last moderator of the General Assembly of the Free Church of Scotland 1899–1900 just before the union with the United Presbyterian Church. He was an active churchman, prominent missionary statesman who chaired the first General Missionary Conference (1904) in South Africa, and he was a well-trained and competent surgeon and botanist.
10 Shepherd, *Lovedale, South Africa*, 32.
11 Stewart, *Lovedale, South Africa Fifty Illustrations*, viii, 5–7. A very concise statement by Stewart as to his comprehensive method and commitment to Christian mission of education and evangelism.

and development of Lovedale. When he died in 1905 enrolment at Lovedale stood at 750. In the early 1870s he prioritised a better integration of the industrial with the academic work of Lovedale and oversaw the refurbishment of the industrial training facilities.

It was during his time as principal that the first Free Church candidates did the ministerial three-year course, Elijah Makiwane and Pambani Mzimba and also one Congregationalist, James van Rooyen.[12] In 1884 Stewart invited the United Presbyterians and the Congregationalists to join with the Free Church to train ministers at Lovedale and such occurred through to 1920, when it was then transferred over to the department of divinity at the new Native College where Kerr was the principal. The systematic theology text at Fort Hare for the first several years was Charles Hodge's three volume *Systematic Theology*.

The advancement of co-educational work technically was to be established under Govan's principalship in 1866 but really under Stewart's eye as he and his wife travelled out from Scotland with Jane Elizabeth Waterston to Lovedale in 1867. Waterston was to be in charge as superintendent of the Girls' Institution or Seminary at Lovedale which formally commenced in 1868. The arrangement was that Ladies' Societies in Scotland in the Free Church would raise support for Waterston and others, but these societies/committees would be under the headship of the Free Church Foreign Missions Committee. In the early 1870s this Girls' Institution expanded rapidly at Lovedale and became a vital part of the work there. Waterston served at Lovedale from 1868 to January 1874 when she left to seek medical training. She served briefly in Livingstonia in 1879–80 but was not compatible working with Roberts Laws and returned to Lovedale where she established a dispensary and cared for the medical needs of students for three years before leaving to establish her own practice in Cape Town. Waterston's vision really would bear fruit many years later when Victoria Hospital

▲ Cecilia Makiwane stamp

---

12 Two other students joined these early classes, one James Scott who did part of his ministerial training at Lovedale before going to Scotland and likewise for David Gezani who did the ministerial course at Lovedale and finished at the Dutch Reformed Seminary in Stellenbosch. See, Abrahams, Punt, Williams, eds., *Theology on the Tyume*, ii–iii.

was established at Lovedale in 1898 and the training of nurses was added. One of first Lovedale nurses, Cecilia Makiwane completed her course the year following Stewart's death. Stewart, like Livingstone, had as his motto: "God had only one Son, and He was a missionary and a physician. A poor imitation of Him I am, or wish to be." Stewart's plan was in time to develop the medical side at Lovedale, but he realised the enormous cost involved in such an undertaking.

Stewart established the monthly *The Kaffir Express* in 1870, renamed *The Christian Express* in 1876. This newspaper was to have wide influence for Lovedale and its vision and ministry. Often the theme of equality of the races has been picked up by historians but often fails to emphasise also the evangelical nature of the publication. For example, Andrew Murray was requested to write a series of articles for *The Christian Express* on the theme of "Aids to Christian Devotion" (still in print today as, *The Believer's Call to Commitment*). Murray also preached at Lovedale for Christian conventions with staff and students during Stewart's principalship. Thus, the evangelical tone of the mission must not be downplayed or ignored.

Finally, Stewart must be seen as an exporter of the Lovedale model as he saw it. The closest replica was at the Blythswood Institution established in 1877 near Butterworth, often called "the child of Lovedale." The seeds went back to 1873 for this new institution to do in the Transkei what Lovedale was doing in Alice. The Fengu contributed generously and with additional funds raised, Blythswood opened in 1877 to provide co-educational elementary education and industrial training, perhaps thus also in part a feeder-school to Lovedale for the higher level and also on a multi-racial model like Lovedale. As in the case with Lovedale a girl's division as an attached seminary boarding block would also in time be established. Blythswood did not ever reach the enrolment size of its mother institution yet did have a steady stream of students. The same evangelical Christian emphasis was to undergird this work and similar spiritual exercises which were found at Lovedale were inculcated at Blythswood. The institution was to be under Lovedale's governance, and this caused conflict with the first principal of Blythswood, Rev. James MacDonald. John Bennie the son of the noted John Bennie (see chapter two) was appointed for two years as acting principal to reorganise matters and following this the next principal, Rev. James MacLaren was answerable not to Lovedale but directly to the Foreign Mission Committee of the Free Church of Scotland.

Shepherd argues that Stewart's vision was a federation of institutions: Lovedale, Blythswood, Livingstonia, and Blantyre, with Lovedale as the centre, and in time rising to a native university and divinity hall as well. The reality was that such did not exactly occur. The Lovedale modal may have been reproduced but the issue of control was challenged, and each model would in the end have its own autonomy and internal divisions with supporting mission agencies.[13] Perhaps in a certain way Lovedale did give birth to the Native College which did rise to become a university with its own faculty of theology. We will pick up Stewart's involvement in Malawi and Kenya in section six of this chapter.

▲ Class Photo, c.1890s

5. Survey c.1906–c.1950s

Lovedale had three principals after Stewart, from 1906 to 1955, Henderson, Wilkie, and Shepherd.

The Principals of Lovedale	
Years of Service	Name of Principal
1841–1870	William Govan
1870–1905	James Stewart
1906–1930	James Henderson
1932–1942	Arthur Wilkie
1942–1955	R.H.W. Shepherd

---

13 Rodger, "Blythswood," 27–28, referring to Shepherd but not noted where in Shepherd. Further, page 45 citing from Brook, pages 85–90.

James Henderson (1867–1930) was a Free Church of Scotland missionary appointed to the Livingstonia Mission in 1895. He became head of the Overtoun Training School at Khondowe, Malawi before taking up his post at Lovedale in 1906. Under Henderson (now United Free after the 1900 union), Lovedale kept basically much to the vision and patterns established by Stewart and his model with the exception perhaps that Henderson emphasised vernacular language development more than Stewart had. Henderson actively helped pursue a university level institution to be established in line with Stewart's thinking and he chaired the committee to help establish such and in many ways his hand in the creation of what became the University of Fort Hare has often been marginalised. Henderson also maintained the liberal perspective on race relations in a period of time in which this was becoming an increasing issue. Like Stewart, Henderson maintained contacts with African American institutions in the United States such as Tuskegee in Alabama. It seems that Henderson had a particular interest in Booker T. Washington.[14] In 1930, Henderson's last year as principal at Lovedale, the student enrolment had grown to 1,063. It was viewed by many as the most important of the institutions of education in Southern Africa for black Africans, yet tension between Lovedale and the state was also increasing.

Arthur Wilkie (1878–1958) was not appointed until 1932. The position of principal had become enormous as it was over the entire Lovedale operation which included the educational division, the hospital, the farm, and the press, not to mention several other tasks all woven within the entire complexity of the Institution as a Christian entity. Various candidates were proposed, and discussion centred around whether the principal should be from Scotland. In the end a Scot was appointed, Arthur Wilkie,[15] but whose knowledge of West Africa was extensive. Wilkie's term as principal shows again the meeting of the circles of Scottish Presbyterians involved in Africa especially given the early 20th century unions in Scotland.

Wilkie first began his missionary labours with the United Free Church of Scotland in Calabar, 1901 to 1917, and then was moved onto the Gold Coast and Togoland, 1917–1930, and then concluded at Lovedale, 1932–1942, by now a Church of Scotland missionary after the 1929 union.[16]

Henderson had been involved with Livingstonia like Stewart, this time it is

---

14 An unexplored area is Stewart and Henderson's tours and correspondence with African American institutions such as Fisk, Tuskegee, and Hampton. It does present another global line of connections to consider.
15 Wilkie's parents were Scots and Wilkie studied in Scotland but was born in Cheshire, England and was raised in the UP Church.
16 See, White on Wilkie, "Lovedale Press," 17–20.

from the Scottish missionary work in West Africa that the principal was drawn from. It is interesting that one of the other candidates proposed by the Scottish Church was Rev. James Dougall the missionary/principal in East Africa (Kenya) at the Jeanes Training School, but he refused to leave this appointment.[17] Thus, the Scottish Church was doing a shuffleboard approach with leading missionary educationalists it seems translating them around the continent of Africa.

Wilkie came with incredible experience to the position at Lovedale and much connectedness. He had conducted the funeral of Mary Slessor in Calabar amongst his many missionary tasks. His handling of a very complex situation in the Gold Coast and Togoland during the First World War earned him the epitaph of the Christian conciliator. He came to Lovedale at a trying time – the winds were clearly changing. There were incredible financial challenges during the thirties, there were major challenges in the industrial department and farming department and with issues of certification of apprentices, and there were increasing tensions with society as a whole in South Africa relating to antagonism towards missionary schools, racial tensions, and government challenges.

Wilkie's chief contributions in other ways to Lovedale during his principalship were the establishment of a Bible School in 1932, extensive building programmes despite the financial issues, developments in the high school level, and the expansion of the Lovedale Press. The Bible School and the Press were avenues which provided ways to develop spiritual work. Also, Wilkie was a strong proponent of the vernacular and so the Lovedale Press would become a means to print books in the vernacular. He retired amidst the centenary celebrations of Lovedale.

R. H. W. Shepherd (1888–1971) was appointed principal of Lovedale in 1942. He was to be the last Church of Scotland minister as principal. Shepherd was ordained by the United Free Church of Scotland and sent to the Transkei (Tembuland) in 1920. In 1927 he was transferred to Lovedale Institution as chaplain and director of the Lovedale Press and as editor of *The South African Outlook*, a monthly paper/magazine which had begun in 1922[18] as a replacement of *The Christian Express* which had begun back in 1870 under Stewart.

Shepherd was in line with Stewart's wide-based approach to education for the many and not the elitist approach. Despite this, Shepherd was to see through one of the most difficult periods on campus. In April 1920, Henderson had faced a riot at Lovedale, which on the surface related to flour, but in August 1946 Shepherd faced a greater riot. Henderson it seems managed to readmit students who agreed

---

17 Excellent work about James Dougall has been undertaken by Kenneth Ross. See, "The Legacy of James Dougall," in *The International Bulletin of Missionary Research*, 32.4 (2008): 206–209. Ross shows how Wilkie was a mentor for Dougall's vision.
18 Shepherd would remain as editor from 1942 to 1963.

to terms for readmittance and expelled others (the ringleaders were dealt with more harshly and not readmitted) and basically was able to carry-on. The 1946 riot/strike was much different. Windows were smashed and property damaged, and some students were held in jail and the decision was made to close Lovedale for nine weeks. The Lovedale governance bodies were divided as to what to do. An Inquiry was set-up and much investigation and questioning occurred.

The context of just after the war is significant, the rising desire for egalitarianism, strike talk throughout SA, the food crisis of the time (sugar and milk related it appears), the drought, and deteriorating feelings between a segment of the student body towards the Lovedale leadership combined and issued in frustration and a feeling of hopelessness for their future. The issue was perhaps in the eyes of Professor J. T. Jabavu not so much the missionary institution but the general feeling of hopelessness in the country for blacks who were becoming educated and yet rejected by-in-large by a white South Africa through the colour-bar system.[19]

It can also be seen that the 1946 riot was all part of the context that would serve the purposes when the new Nationalist Party became the government of South Africa in May 1948. Native education was one of its top concerns. Thus, Shepherd's time as principal faced incredible tensions in the late 1940s and early 1950s at Lovedale and must be read in the wider context of the nation.

White further summarises it as follows:

> But the most important feature of Shepherd's period was the impending clash with the State. The National Party had won the 1948 election and one of their first actions was to appoint a Commission on African education under the chairmanship of W. W. M. Eiselen. This Commission spelt the demise of missionary control over African education and the beginning of total control by the State. Such a scenario was bound to create conflict

and

> The Report of the Eiselen Commission must be considered as one of the most important and controversial documents ever to have come out of this country. It was to give rise to the Bantu Education Act No 47 of 1953.[20]

---

19 White, "Lovedale Press," 134.
20 White, "Lovedale Press," 152.

White's words "the demise of missionary control over African education" are an incredible summation. It was the end of an era. The Nationalist government gave little room for the missionary schools in South Africa. They could close, be taken over, or attempt to be solely private but would face a hard road for registration if they so tried the latter (Adams College in Natal had tried that route and was denied). The Lovedale Governing Council and the Church of Scotland Foreign Missions Board were truly in a tight spot. The government offered that the church could run the hostels but not the schools. The Lovedale Governing body concluded that this was a recipe for constant conflict so quickly opted not to run the hostels. In the end, they went the pragmatic route of the government takeover hoping that at least some of the teaching staff would carry-on and attempt to see the ethos maintained.

In the name of native education, the Nationalist government was really implementing its separateness (apartheid) policy and to deal with the missionary schools which were often viewed as the source of liberal thinking on the races. Opposition voices were raised. *The Outlook* had many who wrote with alarm at what was being proposed. Alexander Kerr, a Presbyterian elder, the principal at the Native College, and a member of the Lovedale Governing Council spoke out, but the voices were overridden. Virtually all the churches expressed their disapproval with the exception of the Dutch Reformed Church which were commending. Some such as the General Assembly of the Bantu Presbyterian Church proposed a compromise of allowing the missionary schools and the government establishing a parallel government-run system. In the end there was no compromise, as White wrote, it was the demise of the missionary schools. There was to be no cooperation between the church and the state for education. The mission could have a chaplaincy type role but that was all. The days of the holistic model and Christian education and mission in all its spheres, in which the church through her missionary endeavours was central, was over.

Lovedale was under the government plan to become an all-boys school and was to focus upon the technical subjects and only at high school level. Printing was not to be done in the industrial training at the reorganised Lovedale. The last point is most telling as this was an area for expression as well as training. Shepherd retired as Principal in December 1955 and did not serve under the state control of Lovedale. The Lovedale Governing Council met for its last meeting on 10 November 1955 and dissolved itself effective December 31st 1955, conveying its powers to the South African Mission Council of the Church of Scotland and that Council was dissolved in 1981.

6. Sub-stories: Oromo slaves, Malawi & Kenya, Printing Press, Bible School

There are four select substories that have been selected as brief narratives within the larger story of the Lovedale Institution. They are important and help to see the wider orbit of the ministry and development of the Lovedale Institution.

Oromo Slaves

In 1888 a British warship captured 200 Oromo[21] children from an Arab dhow of slave traders. These children were from southern Ethiopia and were destined to slavery in the Middle East. Their stories are marked by trauma and suffering. Another group were added to this number and taken to near Aden and the Keith-Falconer Mission Station (Free Church of Scotland), and from these, 64 were taken to Lovedale Missionary Institution. The global connections of the Scottish Presbyterians in the 19th century were immense and are just demonstrated in this one incident.

▲ Oromo girls

These Oromo children arrived at Lovedale in August 1890. They were educated at Lovedale, and many decided to remain in South Africa. 17 returned to Ethio-

---

21 Older accounts will refer to these children as the *Galla* slaves. This is a pejorative term and *Oromo* the preferred name.

pia. Most became tradesmen, domestic workers, or teachers in various locations of South Africa. One went to the United States and one, Gilo, remained the rest of his life at Lovedale, and died there in 1948. Gilo's grave is next to that of the noted John Knox Bokwe in Alice.[22]

Malawi and Kenya

Elsewhere in this book the Livingstonia Mission, Nyasaland, now Malawi and the Industrial Mission in British East Africa, now Kenya is discussed. Here the purpose is to highlight the unity of Presbyterian involvement in late 19th century missions in Africa, the unity around Stewart and Lovedale to mission, and the unity of a comprehensive method and approach in three separate missions.

The Livingstonia mission[23] is unique as Xhosa Lovedale students were also involved with this mission. The focus has often been upon James Stewart, yet it is much larger than this. The Livingstonia Mission was conceived as a memorial mission to David Livingstone to the Lake Nyassa area in 1874 by Stewart who proposed such to the Free Church of Scotland Foreign Missions Committee. Stewart had dreamed of this mission ten years earlier. Roberts Laws, of the Livingstonia Mission, wrote from Lake Nyassa to Stewart at Lovedale, "We have a splendid field here for native catechists or men from Lovedale. In a short time we shall be ready for them." Stewart sought volunteers from the senior class at Lovedale. Fourteen volunteered and from that four were selected: William Koyi, Shadrach Mngunana, Isaac Williams Wauchope, and Mapassa Ntintili. These four, together with Stewart and five others, made up the party which left South Africa for the Livingstonia Mission in 1876. Shadrach Mngunana taught school at Cape Maclear but succumbed to fever after nine months and died. Wauchope also fell ill and was sent back to South Africa not long after arriving at Livingstonia. Ntintili was a wagon maker and served four years at Livingstonia and also at Blantyre as an educator and from all accounts was of great help to the mission.[24] He returned to SA and served as a teacher and an evangelist. Koyi served two terms in Malawi, for a total of about nine years. He was highly regarded for his work amongst the Ngoni.[25]

---

22 Sandra Shell is a prolific writer in this field. See select bibliography at the end of this chapter.
23 James Stewart, *Livingstonia: Its Origin: An Account of the Establishment of that Mission in British Central Africa* (Edinburgh: Andrew Elliot, 1894).
24 One of the students whom Ntintili trained was Kagaso Sazuze who went to continue his studies at Lovedale and then returned to the Blantyre Mission at Zomba as an educator. This is another example of the exchanges between Lovedale and Malawi.
25 Jack Thompson was a prolific writer on this subject. See select bibliography at the end of this chapter. A fifth Lovedale Xhosa evangelist, George Williams, arrived and served from 1883 to 1888 to work with the Ngoni.

The Livingstonia Mission models very closely following Lovedale and conforms to many of Stewart's ideals. Like Stewart, Laws was trained in theology and medicine, and this is only one aspect of similarity. The whole vision of Lovedale as a comprehensive approach to education and evangelism or mission was all exported into the Livingstonia mission. The story of the Overtoun Institution at Khondowe and its branch schools shows remarkable parallels to Lovedale. The Livingstonia Mission became the centre of education and industrial training in Malawi. Laws was recruited to give advice to establish a similar institution in Calabar, Nigeria based upon likenesses to Lovedale and to Overtoun. This would give birth as the Hope Waddell Training Institute in 1895 in Calabar.

In 1891 Stewart was invited to begin a new mission station in British East Africa, now Kenya, to be inland from Mombasa. This new mission station was to be modelled upon that of Lovedale. This mission was called the East Africa Scottish Mission and was connected to the Imperial British East Africa Chartered Company. One member of the party was a former Lovedale student, Dr Robert U. Moffatt the grandson of Robert Moffatt. Thomas Watson, a Free Church probationer was also amongst the team and after 1893 he would become the mission leader. Stewart chose the mission station to be established at Kibwezi about 180 miles from Mombasa. He remained with the team for six months before leaving to return to Lovedale. Before leaving, six houses, a church, two schools, and a workshop had been built. This mission went from tragedy to tragedy until only Thomas Watson was left in 1898 to re-establish the mission at Kikuyu 1898. Watson established a school here and began with seven Kikuyu pupils. These seven went on all to profess faith in Jesus Christ. Watson died in December 1900 from pneumonia.[26] The East Africa Scottish Mission was handed over to the Church of Scotland in 1901. The educational philosophy that would develop mirrored much of the Lovedale model.

In summation, Stewart was the common personage in all of these locations as was also his mission and method. The undertones of Christianity, commerce and civilisation can be found throughout and hearken back to Livingstone's expeditions and vision.[27] These are complex at times and difficult to fully untangle as to motives for all involved but for the vast majority it was evangelical in outlook and the desire for the souls and welfare of humanity to be blessed and enriched. Charges of imperialist oppression will remain and each will have to make their judgement on this. Recall the vision of these missions, a people walking in darkness have seen the light and judge then accordingly.

---

26 A dated yet helpful work is, Brian G. McIntosh, "The Scottish Mission in Kenya, 1891–1923," (Unpublished PhD thesis, University of Edinburgh, 1969).

27 See, Robert Speer's chapter, "The Civilizing Influence of Missions," in *Missionary Principles and Practices: A Discussion of Christian Missions and of some Criticisms upon them* (New York: Revell, 1902), 412–420 for a fairly contemporaneous understanding of this overall topic.

Lovedale Printing Press

Since Lovedale's model was comprehensive and included skills development such as printing and bookbinding a singular focus could be upon the role of skills enhancement, yet with printing there are other focal aspects to consider, such as the development of Christian literature, the development of textbooks for schools, secular printing, developments in vernacular languages, the dissemination through colportage ministry, economic development , journalist development, and political activism and writing. It is really a very large area of consideration not to mention the line between printing and in some way also being a publishing house.

One of the most significant Christian works published must be Tiyo Soga's translation of Bunyan's *Pilgrim's Progress*. Soga's translation, *Uhambo Lomhambi*, into Xhosa was published by the Lovedale Press in 1867 and remained in print by the press through to the 1970s.The press produced an incredible amount of Christian literature and this alone would be a full study.

The Lovedale press was an informal operation from 1823, technically the founding date which many use, until 1861 when it was expanded with a printing department within the Institution and formalised. It helped many Africans develop their literary and writing craft such writers as R. R. R. Dhlomo, Sol Plaatje, Victoria Swaartbooi, H. I. E. Dhlomo, T. B. Soga, and J. J. R. Jolobe amongst others. Music composers were also included in the publications, such as those by John Knox Bokwe, R. T. Caluza and B. Tyamzashe.

The first newspaper can be traced back to 1844, *Ikwezi.* Though short lived, some of the earliest Xhosa writings were in it, by William Kobe Ntsikana and Zaze Soga. Other newspapers followed: *Indaba*, then the bilingual newspaper *Isigidimi samaXhosa* from 1870 to 1888.

▲ Lovedale printing class

Lovedale textbook production reached 500,000 per year in 1953. Apprentice training declined after 1956 as it was now deemed not an industrial training programme suitable under the new Bantu Education Act. Yet as a press it carried on with much opposition and feelings of ill-will by the new government. It became an employee-owned company.[28]

Lovedale Bible School

The Bible School opened in 1932 inspired by Principal Henderson's vision to see evangelists, catechists or lay preachers trained and accepted students from various denominations – Bantu Presbyterian, Methodist, Free Church, Baptist, Anglican, Moravian, and others. The story of the Bible School at Lovedale has often been ignored.[29] It was a way of Lovedale reaching out to those with a diversity of educational backgrounds and involved in the life of the church. It was initially limited to training men and then in 1944 it also was opened to Bible Women. The Bible School had its own building on the Lovedale campus which was a gift of Lord Joseph MacLay of Scotland who also helped later to fund the development of an extension of the training programme to include Bible Women. MacLay had personally visited Lovedale in the 1930s and taken an interest in its ministry and in particular the Bible school. MacLay's other African mission endeavour was with the Southern Morocco Mission and the Central Morocco Mission. From the beginning this was to be an interdenominational Bible School. Primary finance came from the friends in the Church of Scotland, and it fell annually under the principal's report on Lovedale and was viewed as one of the branches of the Lovedale Institution.

The Bible School offered short training courses and also was engaged with preparing appropriate Christian literature – chiefly Sunday School curriculum and preaching notes called *Preaching Helps* for preachers. The latter preaching notes were produced monthly and were translated into various vernacular languages at Lovedale and printed but were also then translated in other countries where they were sent monthly. These were distributed well beyond the Eastern Cape area and were sent across Africa. Sierra Leone and other places in West Africa, to Sudan and to East Africa. In 1944, 5,000 *Preaching Helps* were being produced each month at Lovedale in seven different languages. When one considers the other sites doing translation, it is hard to calculate just what impact these *Preaching Helps* were having across Africa.

The main tutoring course was for the evangelists who would come and board

---

28 As of 2023, its 200th anniversary, (using the commencement date 1823) there are three "employees" struggling to keep the Lovedale Press operational.
29 Shepherd, *Lovedale ... 1841–1941*, 383–391.

at Lovedale for five months in a year. The course focused upon spiritual growth and evangelistic training and Sunday School ministry. In addition, teaching on general educational subjects was also included. Some men came for two sessions and occasionally some came for three. Short training courses were also offered across South Africa and at these each year hundreds would attend who were evangelists, preachers, schoolteachers, Sunday school teachers and others. These travelling schools were considered as field work.

The Bible School usually operated with two or three staff, a head of the Bible School, for many years Rev. Edward W. Grant, and a tutor, Rev. James Ranisi Jolobe[30] (1902–1976), and when the Bible Women five-month course began, Miss Barbour was brought from the Ladies Seminary at Engwali to be the tutor for the Bible Women and pastors' wives and others. In addition, the Bible School was involved with chaplaincy ministry at the Victoria Hospital and organising colportage work into the Transkei with students of the Bible School as colporteurs.

It seems that the Bible School continued through 1958.[31] However, the Bible School was clearly facing challenges both financially and by the Nationalist government by the late 1950s and was "temporarily" closed in 1959 and the premises used as hostel accommodation by the Lovedale Institution under the new government educational reconfiguration. The premises made their way into the College at Fort Hare and there is no evidence the Bible School was able to carry-on into the 1960s leaving a great void in development of leaders and resources for the churches. In many ways the Dimbaza Bible School which began in 1979 in Dimbaza township in the then Ciskei and later took the name Dumisani was akin to what the Lovedale Bible School had done.[32] (This latter Bible School was a joint ministry of the Free Church of Scotland, the two branches at the time of the Reformed Church, and the Free Church of Southern Africa). Church of Scotland missionary involvement greatly declined at Lovedale after 1955. The last CoS missionary appointment was in 1978, with Rev. Graham Duncan to the Lovedale Institution as missionary-in-charge of the Institution, its congregation and district (1978–1981).

Summary

These four substories help enlarge our depth of understanding of the Lovedale Missionary Institution. A substory is likened to the undergrowth of a great forest. These four substories contributed to the growth and development of the greater

---

30 Rev. Jolobe served as the tutor for the Bible School from 1938–1949.
31 If this is the case which appears to be fairly certain, the Lovedale Bible School existed for 26 years of ministry. Personal correspondence from Dilys Howard and Graham Duncan, 21 & 22 July 2022.
32 Jack & Nancy Whytock, eds., *Voices of Thanksgiving: Dumisani Theological Institute & Bible School, 1979–2019* (Charlottetown, PE: Haddington House Trust, 2019).

whole of Lovedale in different ways whether extending its care and education to a dispossessed group of children, seeing the Lovedale footprint and method carried across wider-Africa, the influence of the printed word, and the training of church leaders.

7. Conclusion: Impact, Transmission, and Shadows of What Once Were

Lovedale as it came to its great transition as a missionary enterprise in 1955 was a vast Christian missional undertaking: there were the two schools connected to the two hospitals so that convalescents there were receiving an education (the tuberculosis hospital had patients who were there for long stays), plus there was the elementary school, the high school, the industrial and training departments – woodworking and carpentry, bookbinding and printing, the dairy farm and the girls' industrial school, the Lovedale congregation, the district congregations, the printing press with its various associated works, the teachers' training school, the Bible School, the nurses' training school, the maternity training school (midwifery), the hostels for girls and boys, the staffing houses, the two hospital complexes, the singing school (known also a practising school), chaplaincy services, student Christian associations, colportage work, and special convention seasons and speakers – no wonder it was known as the Christian colossus! Missionary speakers from across Africa it seemed were constantly passing through its gates – from Nigeria, Kenya, Tanzania, etc. not to mention speakers also from overseas, America, Asia, and Europe. A dimension also needing exploration is the cultivation of Christian spirituality and piety at Lovedale.

Until 1920 Lovedale had conducted its own literary courses using English as the classical language and other higher courses for seniors after a high school normal course (basically functioning at BA level). These would be the candidates for the ministry after which they then did their three-year divinity training course, some of whom also did both Greek and Hebrew in their studies in the Free Church. As already stated, this senior literary course and divinity course ended with the new Native College being able in 1920 to take up this role. The Native College was very much the sibling of Lovedale. It is fair to say that out of Lovedale grew the Native College, Fort Hare University.[33]

---

33 As Stewart lay dying, he was planning for the delegation to come and meet at Lovedale for the Lovedale Native Convention and plan a Native College. He died on 21 December 1905, the delegation met on 28 December 1905 and held a memorial service as a delegation at Sandiles' Kop on that day, three days after his funeral on 25 December. It is a story of siblings. The land upon which the Native College was built was given by Lovedale.

Lovedale's impact in terms of transmission and likeness is a fascinating study of comparison. The lines of connection to Blythswood as its child have already been drawn and also reference to Malawi and Kenya. Mention is made by Stewart and Laws to the Calabar Mission in West Africa also adopting the comprehensive method of religious education, general education, and industrial training under the overall concept of education and evangelism. Stewart and Lovedale were raised up as models to Presbyterians and others on the continent of Africa. Closer at hand, both the Methodists and Anglicans would endeavour such a comprehensive plan at Healdtown at various times and at St. Matthew's, Keiskammahoek.

Lovedale stood as the largest missionary centre once in Africa. It had worldwide fame and an interconnectedness globally. Its roots with the Glasgow Missionary Society and then the Scottish Churches, Free, United-Free, and finally Church of Scotland, and its "friends" and donors literally brings hundreds of personnel and supporters into the storyline. The place of "friends" to Lovedale as some of its greatest supporters must not be underestimated and has often been muted by the ecclesial.

The influences of Lovedale through its branch schools and its teachers that were trained through Lovedale extended the Lovedale reach and influence across Southern Africa into Zimbabwe, Zambia, Botswana, Lesotho, Swaziland, Namibia, Kenya and Tanzania, and South Africa through teachers, trained industrialists, and also through students who came from these places to study at Lovedale. The impact of students on occasion also included those from

▲ Boarders, residents and staff, early 1890s

West Africa. It crossed various African tribes well beyond the Xhosa and also crossed numerous white cultures from the colonial Scots, French missionaries in Lesotho, to English, and German. Each of these in the black, coloured, and white communities had their own cultural homes and Lovedale became a place of their meeting. It was not always easy as stories reveal inter-tribal jealousy and conflict. No society is immune from jealousy and strife, Christian or otherwise.

The acceptance of government money had created years of precedence at Lovedale and at the hundreds of branch mission schools. Some have argued that this shows a cooperative colonial enterprise but the other way of seeing this was that it represented the cooperation of church and state to create a Godly commonwealth in society. Yet, it also seems to be a root which was exposed with the state's take-over and control in 1955. The old cliché, "He who pays the piper calls the tune," does not seem far from the mark here. The application of the establishment principle of cooperation versus the ideal of volunteerism of a Christian educational institution is a matter which needs further discussion as it pertains to the Lovedale Missionary Institution and branch schools. What remained after 1955 was in essence shadows of the past days.[34]

Questions for study (fact type):

1. Why was this station called "Lovedale"?
2. Summarise the diverse nature of education and ministry which was offered at Lovedale at the height of its influence.
3. What was the Lovedale Bible School?

Questions for study (reflection type):

1. Explain why this chapter argues that the "Lovedale method" was reproduced in other places.
2. Discuss the transformation of Lovedale post-1955. How and why did it change?

Select Bibliography

Abrahams, S. P., J. Punt, and David T. Williams, eds. *Theology on the Tyume*. Alice: Lovedale Press, 1997.

Bean, Lucy and Elizabeth van Heyningen, eds. *The Letters of Jane Elizabeth Waterston 1866–1905*. Cape Town: Van Riebeeck Society, 1983.

---

[34] Lovedale today after reconfiguration and reopening, is a TVET, a technical and vocational educational and training institution under the department of higher education in SA and has three campuses, Alice, King William's Town, and Zwelitsha.

Brock S. M. "James Stewart and Lovedale: A reappraisal of missionary attitudes and African response in the Eastern Cape, South Africa, 1870–1905." PhD thesis, University of Edinburgh, 1974.

Burchell D. E. "A history of the Lovedale Missionary Institution, 1890–1930." MA thesis, University of Natal, 1979.

Duncan, Graham A. "Coercive agency in mission education at Lovedale Missionary Institution." *HTS* 60.3 (2004): 942–992.

Hewat, Elizabeth G. K. *Vision and Achievement 1796–1956: A History of the Foreign Missions of the Churches united in the Church of Scotland.* Edinburgh: Thomas Nelson, 1960.

"The James Stewart Papers, Manuscripts and Archives." University of Cape Town Libraries, Jagger Library, Libraries' Special Collections BC 106. 678 items in total and a mine of research material here.

Kaczmarek, Claire. "Mission Education and the Evangelical Missiology of James Stewart in Lovedale." In *Missionary Work in Africa in Eugene Casalis's Time and Beyond*, eds. Jamary Mdumeli and Michel Prum. Newcastle-upon-Tyne: Cambridge Scholars Publishing, 2015, 5–28.

"Lovedale Collection," Cory Library, Rhodes University, Grahamstown, SA. An extensive collection of MSS and books related to Lovedale Institution and Press.

Lovedale Missionary Institution Report for 1944. Alice: Lovedale Press, 1944.

McIntosh, Brian G. "The Scottish Mission in Kenya, 1891–1923." PhD thesis, University of Edinburgh, 1969.

Paton, William. *Alexander Duff: Pioneer of Missionary Education.* London: SCM, 1923. Chapter five is key.

Rodger, Alastair. "The Early History of Blythswood Missionary Institution." BD thesis, Rhodes University, 1977.

Ross, Andrew C. "Govan, William", "Stewart, James", "Henderson, James", "Shepherd, Robert Henry Wishart." *BDCM*, 253, 641, 288, 617.

Shell, Sandra Rowoldt. *Children of Hope: The Odyssey of the Oromo Slaves from Ethiopia to South Africa.* Athens, OH: University of Ohio Press, 2018.

Shell, Sandra Rowoldt. "Trauma And Slavery: Gilo And the Soft, Subtle Shackles of Lovedale." *Bulletin of the National Library of South Africa* 71.2 (2017): 141–156.

Shepherd, R. H. W. *Lovedale, South Africa: The Story of a Century, 1841–1941.* Alice: Lovedale Press, 1941.

Shepherd, R. H. W. *Lovedale, South Africa: 1824–1955*. Alice, SA: Lovedale Press, 1971.

Shepherd, R. H. W. *Lovedale and Literature for the Bantu*. Alice: Lovedale Press, 1945.

Stanley, Brian. "The Theology of the Scottish Protestant Missionary Movement." In *The History of Scottish Theology, Volume 3, The Long Twentieth century*, eds. David Fergusson and Mark W. Elliott. Oxford: Oxford University Press, 2019, 51–63.

Stanley, Liz. "Protest and the Lovedale Riot of 1946: 'Largely a Rebellion against Authority'?" *Journal of Southern African Studies* 44.6 (2018): 1039–1055.

Stewart, James. *Dawn in the Dark Continent: Or Africa and its Missions, the Duff missionary lectures for 1902*. Edinburgh: Oliphant, 1903.

Stewart, James. *Livingstonia: Its Origin: An Account of the Establishment of that Mission in British Central Africa*. Edinburgh: Andrew Elliot, 1894.

Stewart, James. *Lovedale and Transkei Missionary Institutions*. December 1874. A pamphlet.

Stewart, James. *Lovedale, South Africa, Illustrated by 50 Views from Photographs*. Edinburgh/Glasgow: Elliot/Bryce, 1894.

Stewart, James. *Lovedale Past and Present: A Register of Two Thousand Names*. Alice, SA: Lovedale Mission Press, 1887.

Stewart, James. *Short Biographies of the Galla Rescued Slaves Now at Lovedale: With an Account of Their Country and Their Capture*. Alice, SA: Lovedale Press, 1891.

Thompson, T. Jack. *Ngoni, Xhosa and Scot*. Kachere Book No. 22. Zomba: Kachere Series, 2007.

Thompson, T. Jack. *Touching the Heart: Xhosa Missionaries to Malawi, 1876–1888*. Pretoria: University of South Africa Press, 2000.

Thompson, T. Jack. "Xhosa Missionaries to Malawi: Black Europeans or African Christians?" *International Bulletin of Mission Research* 24.4 (October 2000): 168–170.

Wells, James. *Stewart of Lovedale: The Life of James Stewart, D.D., M.D.* London: Hodder & Stoughton, 1909.

White, Timothy R. H. "Lovedale 1930–1955: The Study of a Missionary Institution in its Social, Educational and Political Context." MA thesis, Rhodes University, 1987.

White, Tim. "The Lovedale Press during the Directorship of R. H. W. Shepherd, 1930–1955." *English in Africa* 19. 2 (1992): 69–84.

Chapter 9

The Presbyterian Story in Nigeria, c.1846 to Independence

Todd Statham

Chapter Outline
1. Introduction
2. Setting the Scene
3. The Early Years: 1846–1900
4. A Growing Church: 1900–1960
5. Conclusion

Bio Inset: Mary Slessor

1. Introduction

The birth and growth of Presbyterianism in Nigeria is a significant branching of the worldwide Reformed family tree. It is also a very important chapter of the history of Christianity in West Africa.

Presbyterianism in Nigeria dates from the mid-19th century, when a handful of brave Jamaican and Scottish missionaries of the United Presbyterian Church (UPCS) established a mission on the delta of the Calabar River in (what is today) southeastern Nigeria. How the Presbyterian Church in Nigeria (PCN) grew from humble origins on the eastern fringe of the country to become a national church that is one of the world's largest Presbyterian denominations is a fascinating story. This story is not as well-known as it should be among either African Christians or students of the history of Presbyterianism.

Perhaps this is because the story has been overshadowed by scholars' attention to the famous missionary expedition in 1841 up the mighty Niger River, which took place only five years before the Presbyterians chose the small Calabar River for their base. The so-called 'Niger Expedition' laid the seeds of the Anglican Church of Nigeria – the largest Protestant denomination in West Africa – and launched the career of Samuel Ajayi Crowther (1807-91), who is rightfully honoured as one of the great African Christians of modern times.¹ As we shall see in this chapter, which recounts the development of Nigerian Presbyterianism from the mid-1840s until national independence in 1960, the Presbyterian story overlaps the better-known Anglican story in many ways. But it is also unique. Reformed theology and Presbyterian tradition gave the PCN's development a distinct shape and focus, as did the fact that it grew up and then spread from particular cultural settings among the Efik, Ibibio and Igbo peoples of southeastern Nigeria.

2. Setting the Scene

Mission always takes place in a particular context – a place and a time that shapes how the missionaries' proclamation of the gospel is heard and why it's received or rejected by local peoples. So, it is important to know something about both Christian missions in the mid-19th century, as well as the Calabar region in which the UPCS mission was planted in the 1840s, and from which the Presbyterian church spread to other parts of Nigeria.

First of all, like many of the new churches in Africa that were planted by missionaries in the 19th century, Presbyterianism in Nigeria has its origins in the "vital connection between the evangelical revival, the antislavery campaign, and the modern missionary movement."² The evangelical revival that took place in Europe and North America in the 18th century created enthusiasm to deepen the faith of Christians in the West as well as spread the gospel abroad in obedience to Christ (Matt 28:19–20). The evangelical revival also bred a moral earnestness that left many Christians deeply critical of the widespread institution of slavery. By the 19th century, the evangelical revival had created powerful and energetic domestic church movements as well as trans-Atlantic networks of Christians that were advocating *for* mission and *against* the slave trade.

Not surprisingly, then, Africa came into focus. After all, it was the main source of slaves and was largely unevangelised. As slavery diminished in the vast British Empire – the trade was banned in 1807 and slaves in the Empire were emancipated in 1833 – compelling arguments were made by evangelical Christians that Africa should be opened up for Christianity. Not only would missionaries bring the gospel to Africa, but the evil slave trade could also be replaced by legitimate trade between the West and Africa. This argument for 'Christianity and commerce' (or 'the gospel and the plough') was most famously

---

1 See Lamin Sanneh, "The CMS and the African Transformation: Samuel Ajayi Crowther and the Opening of Nigeria," in *The Church Mission Society and World Christianity, 1799–1999*, eds. Kevin Ward & Brian Stanley (Grand Rapids: Eerdmans, 2000), 173–97.
2 Jehu Hanciles, "Back to Africa: White Abolitionists and Black Missionaries," in *African Christianity: An African Story*, ed. Ogbu Kalu (Trenton, NJ: Africa World Press, 2007), 175.

made by the British politician and evangelical leader Thomas Fowell Buxton in *The African Slave Trade and Its Remedy* (1839). Yet it is interesting how Buxton's basic argument had been made decades earlier by the Christian and Nigerian (Igbo) Olaudah Equiano (1745–97). Enslaved as a child, he became a prominent abolitionist upon receiving his freedom. In *The Interesting Narrative of the Life of Olaudah Equiano, or Gustavus Vassa, the African, Written by Himself* (1789), Equiano wrote:

> Africa lays open an endless field of commerce to the British manufactures and merchant adventurer. The manufacturing interest and the general interests are synonymous. The abolition of slavery would be in reality an universal good.[3]

Second, all this helps us understand the choice of Calabar for the Presbyterian mission in the mid-1840s. The delta region of the Cross and Calabar rivers in southeastern Nigeria – what is called Calabar – was strategic. It had been connected to the wider world for centuries.[4] Tens of thousands of slaves were shipped down these rivers from the interior to the coastal kingdoms of Duke Town, Old Town, and Creek Town on the Bight of Biafra, then sent to markets in the Americas. Some estimates suggest that as much as 15% of the total African slave trade passed out of the Bight of Biafra. The 'kings' (i.e., chiefs) of the Calabar kingdoms were savvy traders with a global outlook. They knew the value of learning English and developing close ties to European markets. This connection remained crucial when the end of the slave trade in the British Empire in 1807 shattered the lucrative foreign market for slaves. The Calabar kingdoms maintained a domestic market for slaves but shifted trade focus to new items like palm oil, which was valued in Europe for use in candles, soap and as a lubricant. Close ties to the British were greatly desired, then, to cultivate what missionaries and lobbyists like Equiano and Buxton called 'legitimate trade.' It was, in fact, an invitation from one of the Calabar kings to the Scottish missionaries that provided a firm reason to establish a mission on the delta.

We can see how factors like the ambition of the Calabar rulers, the decline of the slave trade and the turn to legitimate trade, as well as the arrival of Presbyterian missionaries, come together in this fascinating excerpt from a letter written in 1849 by King Archibong of Duke Town to a British naval officer patrolling the Bight.

---

3   Cited in Hanciles, "Back to Africa: White Abolitionists and Black Missionaries," 172.
4   See Randy Sparks, *The Two Princes of Calabar: An Eighteenth-Century Atlantic Odyssey* (Cambridge: Harvard University Press, 2004). Further historical information is drawn from Toyin Falola and Matthew Heaton, *A History of Nigeria* (Cambridge: Cambridge University Press, 2008), 39–84.

> I no will allow any slave-trade; it be bad thing. I will to keep treaty King Eyamba make with Queen of England, and I sign yesterday. I keep heed for what you say about the [Presbyterian] missionaries. Them and me be good friends. I give them place to hold meeting, and ring big bell in marketplace every God day to call all man to hear God's word.[5]

Unlike in western Nigeria, where Yoruba states held more centralised power and influence, the southeastern part of Nigeria had many smaller trading kingdoms and less centralised arrangements of political power. This made it more likely for the rulers of these Efik and Igbo kingdoms – like at Calabar – to reach out to the British as allies rather than enemies. Missionaries thus had an opportunity to enter the kingdoms as invited guests and not intruders.

There is one final item of which to take note. The eminent Sierra Leonean scholar, Jehu Hanciles, reminds us that "the story of modern African Christianity began not with white missionary agency but as the initiative of ex-African slaves."[6] This happened famously in Liberia and Sierra Leone, which were settled and evangelised by former slaves from Canada, Britain, and America as part of the 'back to Africa' impulse. It is also true of the beginnings of Presbyterianism in Nigeria, which was the "offspring" of Presbyterian mission work in the Caribbean.[7] In the 1820s and 30s the Scottish Missionary Society, which was itself the fruit of the evangelical revival, developed a new church among the slaves and freed slaves in the British colony of Jamaica. In the 1840s, Efik chiefs asked the SMS to plant a mission in Calabar. The United Secession Church, an evangelical Presbyterian denomination (that was one of the SMS's supporting churches) agreed, after some negotiation and debate.[8] There was substantial cost involved, of course. The SMS was also painfully aware that the famous Niger Expedition of 1841 tragically saw a third of its white participants die of fever. "Beware, beware the Bight of Benin. There's few come out, though many go in," went a popular saying in the 19th century! Nevertheless, in 1846 a band of

---

5   Recorded in William Marwick, *William and Louisa Anderson: A Record of their Life and Work in Jamaica and Old Calabar* (Edinburgh: Andrew Elliot, 1897), 217.
6   Hanciles, "Back to Africa: White Abolitionists and Black Missionaries," 175.
7   This is the expression used by Hope Masterton Waddell, whose career spanned the Jamaican and Calabar missions. See Hope Masterton Waddell, *Twenty-Nine Years in the West Indies and Central Africa* (London: Nelson and Sons, 1863).
8   The United Secession Church joined the Relief Church to form the United Presbyterian Church [UPCS] in 1847. The Calabar mission was thus connected to the UPCS for a half century; the UPCS joined with the Free Church of Scotland to form the United Free Church [UFCS] in 1900. In 1929 the UFCS (re)joined the Church of Scotland [CoS] and the Presbyterian mission in Nigeria was run by the CoS post-1929.

Jamaican and Scotch-Irish Presbyterians arrived at Calabar. This band included the Irish doctor Hope Waddell, the Scottish pastor William Anderson, and his gifted Jamaican wife Louisa, a schoolteacher and so competent a leader that she became known in Calabar as "de best man for de mission."[9] And thus began the Presbyterian story in Nigeria.

Through the eyes of faith, the planting of the UPCS mission at Calabar was providential. Not only was the Bight of Biafra already connected to the Atlantic world through commerce, the Calabar kingdoms were generally welcoming of both 'Christianity and commerce.' The Cross and Calabar rivers had been channels for the terrible slave trade; now they could be pathways for the gospel from the coast to the Igbo peoples of the interior. Finally, Calabar society was in political and economic transition in the mid-19th century because of the decline of slavery. As historians of Christianity have often observed, societies that are in upheaval often prove receptive to the Christian gospel.[10] When old values, powers and patterns are disrupted or challenged, people turn to a new message to help make sense of a changing world.

▲ Hope M. Waddell

3. Early Years: 1846–1900

The Presbyterian missionaries initially established mission stations on the Calabar delta at Duke Town and Creek Town under the sponsorship of ruling kings. The missionaries lived in these stations, and used them to host small schools, Sunday church services, medical clinics, and other evangelistic meetings. These were also bases from which to launch further mission work upriver and into the interior.

This first stage of Presbyterianism in Nigeria was genuine cross-cultural mission work: it was far from easy! Not only did the Scottish and Jamaican missionaries learn Efik in order to communicate the gospel to locals who did not know the pidgin English used by rulers and traders, they had to try to

---

9   https://dacb.org/stories/nigeria/anderson-louisa/.
10 E.g., Andrew Walls, "Origins of Old Northern and New Southern Christianity," in *The Missionary Movement in Christian History: Studies in the Transmission of Faith* (Edinburgh: T & T Clark, 1996), 68–78.

communicate the gospel in a way that made sense within the Efik worldview. Dr Waddell, who served the Calabar mission until 1858, noted that Nigerians traditionally believed in a great and powerful God, and so could readily understand Biblical monotheism. But important doctrines like 'salvation' and 'personal sin' made less sense to them at first. However, the missionary proclamation of Jesus as Lord and Saviour found a point of contact with the profound sense of the reality of evil in Efik and Igbo culture: hostile spirits, gods, and 'witches' caused terror, harm and misfortune to oneself or others unless they were appeased or controlled through rituals, taboos, and offerings.[11]

There were other local traditions and practices that upset the missionaries. Slavery was pervasive, for example, and both slaves and wives were ritually killed upon the death of wealthy or powerful persons. Twins were considered cursed, so they and their mothers would be killed outright or abandoned in the forest to die. In the first decades of the mission, the missionaries could not yet rely on British colonial authorities to step in and forcefully stop practices with which they disagreed. Rather, they had to persuade the 'Ekpe' – the informal body of rituals, beliefs and laws preserved by the families and clans – to itself be changed. Or, they had to defy it and risk 'blowing Egbo,' i.e., being shunned, for acts like harbouring runaway slaves, rescuing twins from the forest, or criticising the 'chop nut' (poison ordeal) that was often used to settle personal disputes.

Needless to say, this process of persuasion was slow and uneven. There was great opposition among local peoples to the gospel itself and resentment among the elite in society at the missionaries' critique of traditional culture and Epke. Missionary records from this era contain some sorrowful recollections of helplessly watching the ritual sacrifice of slaves or the poison ordeal. Frustration at the slow progress of the gospel in Calabar is clear in the fascinating journal entry from Dr Waddell from around 1850, recounting a conversation between himself and King Honesty Eyo II of Creek Town.

> I remarked that for three years God's word had been preached in Calabar, and as yet we saw no one give himself to the Lord and obey him. The king in reply said, that the Word of God had begun to grow a little in Calabar, and instanced some particulars of improvement that had been effected. He added that England, which had it for more than a thousand years, did not yet altogether believe and obey it; and he hoped that God would be patient in Calabar.[12]

---

11 Waddell, *Twenty-Nine Years in the West Indies and Central Africa*, 278.
12 Waddell, *Twenty-Nine Years in the West Indies and Central Africa*, 397.

This excerpt also makes clear the wit of the remarkable King Honesty Eyo II! King Eyo was never baptised as a Christian although he volunteered as an interpreter for Creek Town church services and evangelistic meetings. He also encouraged his people to observe the Lord's Day (what was very important for Presbyterians in the 19th century) by pausing from work, and he eventually permitted the Presbyterians to move upriver to erect new mission stations.[13] And, significantly, when he died in 1858, he insisted – to his daughter's fury – that he was to be buried "without a drop of human blood being shed on the occasion." Shortly before his death he had thrown his family idols into the river.[14]

There were not a lot of conversions to Christianity at the Calabar mission in the early years. The missionaries themselves had very high expectations for potential converts in terms of morality, Biblical literacy, and orthodoxy. They also seemed to underestimate the cost of following Jesus: baptism violently cut through bonds of belief and family in traditional society. So, the Presbyterian church in Nigeria grew little in numbers apart from some runaway slaves in Duke Town and some members of King Eyo's family in Creek Town. At the same time, the close alliance between the Calabar rulers and the Presbyterian missionaries, which was an advantage in some ways, made it difficult for the mission to expand beyond Calabar. Not only was the king's permission required to move upriver, some clans and kingdoms in the interior distrusted the Efik kingdoms – and by extension their European 'friends' – because of their past role in the slave trade. For this reason, in his authoritative history of Presbyterianism in Nigeria, Geoffrey Johnson calls the period from the mid-1850s to 1880 "the long pause" of the Calabar mission.[15]

Fortunately, the UPCS remained committed to the Calabar mission. Indeed, there was always enthusiasm among the laity in Scotland for the work. When Dr Waddell returned to Calabar from his break in Scotland in 1848, he sailed back on a boat that had been purchased by monies raised by UPCS Sunday school children![16] And, for all the setbacks and slow growth of Presbyterianism in Nigeria during the "long pause," seeds were planted that would later bear fruit. These should be noted and celebrated.

Foremost, on 1 September 1858 the two congregations at Duke Town and

---

13 See the description given of him by Hugh Goldie, *Calabar and its Mission*, new ed. with additional chapters (Edinburgh and London: Oliphant, 1901), 196–98.
14 Waddell, *Twenty-Nine Years in the West Indies and Central Africa*, 643.
15 Geoffrey Johnston, *Of God and Maxim Guns: Presbyterianism in Nigeria, 1846–1966* (Waterloo, ON: Wilfrid Laurier University Press, 1988), 21. This chapter leans heavily on Johnston's fine account.
16 Waddell, *Twenty-Nine Years in the West Indies and Central Africa*, 387.

Creek Town formed "the Presbytery of Biafra, constituted on the basis of the Westminster Confession and Larger and Short Catechisms, as these were received and held by the parent Church."[17] This newly constituted Presbytery would eventually become the PCN. It is of *great significance* that in this new Presbytery Scottish missionary, Jamaican missionary and African Christian sat as equals. We should also celebrate the good work this small church was doing: the gospel was being preached, local children were being educated in its schools and taught to read Scripture, and many orphans – having been saved from death – were being raised by female missionaries like Louisa Anderson and (later) Mary Slessor.

Further, because the number of converts at this time was few, it should be recognized how courageous it was to attend church, and to turn one's back on many of the cherished traditions and beliefs of one's people. Such courage was especially needed at death because of the many important rituals connected to death and the afterlife in traditional African societies. For that reason, Rev. Hugh Goldie, one of the leading Scottish missionaries at Calabar in this period, carefully recorded the day in 1858 when a young woman named Ehru died.

> Hers was the first Christian burial amongst the natives. Her husband dug a small grave in the small yard behind his house, and calling the members of the church together, with a short address and prayer we placed her remains into the narrow house, in 'sure and certain hope of a glorious resurrection'.[18]

We should celebrate too how the missionaries laboured hard and fast to translate the Scriptures into local languages. The New Testament was translated in Efik already by 1850 and into Igbo a decade later; the Efik had the whole Bible in their language by 1868 and the Igbo by 1900.[19] Rev Goldie (1815–95) also published an Efik dictionary at this time. Translating the Scriptures into local languages is necessary to communicate the gospel to individuals but also help God's truth 'find a home' within that culture and convert it from within. During this period, the Presbyterian missionaries began working with young Efik and Ibibio Christians to train them as evangelists and catechists through study of Scripture, biblical theology, and Presbyterian catechisms. These new Christians

---

17 Goldie, *Calabar and its Mission*, 195.
18 Goldie, *Calabar and its Mission*, 194–95.
19 Ype Schaaf, *On Their Way Rejoicing: The History and Role of the Bible in Africa*, rev. ed. (Oxford: Regnum, 2002), 88–89. Robb also translated into Efik *Pilgrim's Progress*, and Goldie translated about 300 hymns and psalms into Efik. See Bruce McLennan, *Mary Slessor: A Life on the Altar for God* (Fearn, Ross-shire: Christian Focus, 2014), 35.

would be (what Andrew Walls calls) "the terminal connection" through which Christianity passed into village society.[20] And while many of the names of these first believers have been forgotten, two well-known converts from this early period deserve mention.

Ensa Okoho became King Eyo Honesty VII of Creek Town in 1874 and ruled until his death in 1892.[21] He had been baptised at the Presbyterian mission in 1858 as one of the very first converts, and, as the Westminster Larger Catechism (Q. 167) put it, 'improved upon his baptism' his whole life long. Alongside his duties as king, which he served with integrity and fairness, King Eyo VII was an elder, clerk of session, Sunday School superintendent and occasional preacher at the Creek Town congregation. He also sponsored the building of a new, larger church in Creek Town in 1879. King Eyo Honesty VII used his influence to encourage his own people to put away practices contrary to the gospel and embrace Christianity, and even shared his faith with neighbouring kings and rulers. With good reason, the missionaries likened him to the godly ruler Nehemiah!

▲ Essien Essien Ukpabio   ▲ Rev Essien Essien Ukpabio with family, c.1900–1910

Pride of place in the early Presbyterian church must go to Essien Essien (Esien) Ukpabio, who was the first baptised convert of the Creek Town congregation (1853). He soon became an elder and catechist, providing the missionaries with invaluable help as an interpreter and teacher. In 1872, Ukpabio became the first ordained Nigerian Presbyterian pastor. Ukpabio was highly respected by his own people and by the missionaries for his upright character, ability, and deep

---

20 Andrew F. Walls, "The Evangelical Revival, the Missionary Movement, and Africa," in *The Missionary Movement in Christian History*, 87.
21 And excellent overview is: https://dacb.org/stories/nigeria/ensa-okoho/

faith. The esteem in which he was held is evidenced by the fact that in the 1890s he officiated the funeral service of one of the 'fathers' of the Calabar mission, Rev. Goldie; in 1897 he became the lead pastor in Creek Town with two Scottish colleagues assisting *him*. That same year, Ukpabio was chosen to represent the Calabar mission at the UPCS jubilee celebration in Scotland. That one of the PCN's institutions today bears the name Essien Ukpabio Theological College is a fitting honour for this Presbyterian pioneer.[22]

4. A Growing Church: 1900–1960

This next episode of the Presbyterian story in Nigeria covers the colonial era. British rule over Nigeria emerged in full force at the end of the 19th century and crystallised in the 1914 union of the southern and northern protectorates as the Colony and Protectorate of Nigeria.[23] Geoffrey Johnston believes that British conquest was "the decisive event in the church's history …."[24] This is not because Johnston believes that colonialism was good. Colonialism's legacy on African culture, politics, and religion has been, of course, very problematic. Rather, the British conquest and colonial rule pushed and pulled the young Presbyterian church beyond its Calabar base. Also, colonial rule provided the context for Presbyterian mission work to develop considerably in fields like education and health, which were prized in the new colony. In 1900 the Presbyterian church, notes Johnson, "was a Calabar church with a few struggling outstations; in 1920, it was a network of churches and schools extending up both sides of the Cross River as far as the great bend and beyond."[25] Finally, colonialism was the negative backdrop for the confident *African* Presbyterian church that emerged as Nigeria moved toward independence in 1960.

This period, then, saw considerable numerical growth of Presbyterianism in southeastern Nigeria as well as its geographic spread across the colony. There was

---

22 I have drawn this biographical information primarily from Goldie, *Calabar and its Mission*. More research and writing needs to be done on Ukpabio – there is, for example, no entry for him in the *Dictionary of African Christian Biography*.
23 For this section, I'm relying on Johnston, *Of God and Maxim Guns: Presbyterianism in Nigeria, 1846–1966*; Ogbu Kalu, "The Battle of the Gods: Christianization of Cross River Igboland, 1903–1950," *Journal of the Historical Society of Nigeria*, vol 10 (1979): 1–18; and Njoku Donatus Igwe, "The Socio-Economic and Cultural Impact of the Presbyterian Mission in North Eastern Igboland (1880–2006)," (Unpublished PhD Dissertation, University of Nigeria – Nsukka, 2007). For a good survey of the wider African context in this period see Ogbu Kalu, "African Christianity: From the World Wars to Decolonization," in *African Christianity: An African Story*, 291–314.
24 Johnston, *Of God and Maxim Guns*, 304.
25 Johnston, *Of God and Maxim Guns*, 4.

also a deepening of its social impact on the nation through church-run schools and colleges, hospitals, and clinics, as well as those individual Presbyterians who were civic leaders in the colony. True, Presbyterianism had begun to grow beyond Calabar already in the late 19th century as the intrepid Mary Slessor and her African colleagues began to push into Igboland. But the British conquest in the early 20th century made it much safer and easier for missionaries to settle among the Ibibio and Igbo villages. At the same time, there was a growing desire in the Colony both for Christian teaching and for western-style education and health care, which the missionaries were able to provide.

Let's look in turn at several aspects of the growth of Presbyterianism in colonial Nigeria.

Evangelism and Conversion

Historians previously focused on white missionaries as the 'heroes' of the spread of the gospel in Africa. This has meant that great Presbyterian missionaries like Hugh Waddell and Mary Slessor overshadowed the role played by Nigerian Christians in creating their own church. Now scholars of African Christianity recognize that while "most of the pioneer mission stations were founded by whites, it was African catechists, teachers, traders and migrant labourers who assimilated the faith and initiated villagers, kinsfolk, workmates and strangers into the new identity."[26] This was true of the expansion of the Presbyterian church into Igboland.

Take, for example, Uchendu Udo (1901–44), who was converted in 1911 by UFCS missionaries when they visited his hometown of Ohafia. Ordained an elder in 1923, Uchendu worked alongside several other evangelists, travelling on foot to preach and teach in new Presbyterian congregations. He led a group of new Christians to exorcize the 'evil forest' in order to build the mission station there, "and converted many of his townspeople to the Lord and fought against ritual murder, the killing of twins, and human sacrifice."[27] Similarly, Otum Onouha (1875–1957) became a Christian in 1911 after learning to read the Bible in Igbo; he helped the missionaries as an interpreter, translator of Scripture, and served as an elder in his hometown of Elu Ohafia from 1917 until his death in 1957.

> He preached vigorously against the killing of twins and the ill-treatment of their mothers. He fearlessly campaigned against the worship of idols and the inhuman practice of head-hunting.

---

26 Richard Gray, "Christianity, Colonialism and Communications," in *Black Christians and White Missionaries* (New Haven: Yale University Press, 1985), 81.

27 https://dacb.org/stories/nigeria/udo-uchendu/

> The church he started has won many converts and still stands today. Elder Otum is still remembered and respected as a faithful Christian leader who endured many insults and abuses from pagan chiefs in his effort to spread the gospel among his people in Ohafia, in Abia State, Nigeria.[28]

We see a similar pattern in the Presbyterian church's spread among the Aro. The oracle at Arochukwu (in present day Abia State) – what the British called "the long Ju-Ju" – was widely feared across southeastern Nigeria through the 18th and 19th centuries. The long Ju-Ju allowed the fearsome Aro to dominate the interior slave market, as well as achieve prestige by settling disputes through the god of the oracle, who would 'eat' the guilty party of a witchcraft or criminal trial. In 1901 the British marched on the Aro, defeated them and destroyed the oracle. Presbyterian missionaries like Slessor quickly followed the British into the area around Arochukwu to set up mission stations. However, the church grew primarily because of the work of new Christians. A fascinating and colourful account is provided by the late Prof. Ogbu Kalu, drawing upon oral testimony from the Aro.

> The early Aro converts, Mazi Okarafor Uro of Amankuru and Mazi Nwafor Ogwuma spearheaded the mission ... aided by local men who had visited Arochukwu. They marched into these communities at the head of a musical band, with kerosene tins serving as instruments. A combination of preaching and icono-clastic destruction of sacred groves and family patron gods won the day. At Utu-tu, the Christians were feared because the indigenous guides were a band of outcasts (hardened criminals) called ndi agu. Ironically, these dreaded men came with the new Christians chanting in bawderized [sic] and incomprehensible Efik a catchy tune urging that 'Jesus loves us, there is no greater love than that of Jesus who died for our sake.'

Kalu notes that this evangelistic work definitely benefited from having a connection to the British, "whose boots had just trampled past." But it was the long, faithful ministries of new Christians like Rev. Ogwuma, who was ordained in 1918 and was the first Igbo to administer sacraments in the Presbyterian church, and Rev. John Ijoma, who served from 1925 to 1948, that helped the

---

28 https://dacb.org/stories/nigeria/onuoha-otum/

Presbyterian church sink roots into new territories.[29] Catechism and church discipline (especially over polygamy and slavery) were prominent aspects of these ministries. There was also constant pressure – sometimes violently so – from those who still held to the Ekpe and bowed to ancient gods.

As the Presbyterian mission church spread throughout the Biafra region in the first half of the 20th century, it is worth considering among *whom* it grew. Who were these first generations of Ibibio and Igbo Presbyterians? In one of the great novels of the 20th century, *Things Fall Apart* (1958), Chinua Achebe writes critically of the new converts. In his fictional Igbo village of Umuofia, set in the time that Presbyterian missionaries were beginning to work in the area, not one of the converts

> was a man whose word was heeded in the assembly of the people. None of them was a man of title. They were mostly the kind of people that were called efulefu, worthless empty men. The imagery of an efulefu in the language of the clan was a man who sold his machete and wore the sheath to battle. Chielo, the priestess of Agbala, called the converts the excrement of the clan, and the new faith was a mad dog that had come to eat it up.[30]

Indeed, new converts often were *efulefu* (or what Kalu calls *ndi agu*). "Brothers and sisters, think of what you were when you were called. Not many of you were wise by human standards; not many were influential; not many were of noble birth" (I Cor. 1:26). The gospel has *always* been good news for the poor and the marginalised. At the same time, we should recall that the Presbyterian church had initially grown among the royal families in Calabar. Further, the venerated Igbo Rev. Awa Ugbaga (1896–1987),[31] who was ordained in 1930 and "established many congregations in urban areas like Umuahia and Aba, and in rural areas" came from a chiefly family, as did other new Christians like Dr Francis Ibiam.

One last point needs to be raised regarding patterns of evangelism and conversion in colonial-era Presbyterianism. This point is essential for understanding the somewhat uneven spread of Presbyterianism across Nigeria, which persists to this day. Because the various European mission churches active in Nigeria in the 19th century pledged to avoid competing with each other, denominational 'districts' of mission churches were created: Presbyterians were active in one part of the country; Anglicans, Methodists, or Baptists, etc.,

---

29 Kalu, "The Battle of the Gods," 7.
30 Chinua Achebe, *Things Fall Apart*. Original 1958. (Anchor Canada, 2009), 143.
31 https://dacb.org/stories/nigeria/ugbaga-awa/

were active in other parts. This was a peaceable solution to the problem of denominationalism. It did, however, encourage church denominations to race into new territories in order to claim it as 'their' turf, which sometimes left the small Presbyterian church with mission stations and schools in the hinterland they were not able to sufficiently staff. This rushed approach depleted resources and morale.

More to the point, the division of Nigeria into denominational territories only made sense when Nigeria was a stable agricultural society in which people were not apt to relocate for work. But colonial rule changed that. It has been well documented how the advent of railways and then roads began to make some market towns more important than others as trade centres. People began to leave their villages to settle in these growing towns. At the same time, the colonial government encouraged educated men and women to resettle in the administrative centres of the colony like Lagos or Port Harcourt. Presbyterianism was not ready for such economic and urban developments. It had taken root in southeastern Nigeria where economic and urban growth happened later than in the country's west. Many educated Efik and Igbo Presbyterians left Presbyterian 'territory' and were not always able to establish Presbyterian congregations in the growing cities and towns. In fact, it was only after WW2 that the churches accepted the idea of 'open towns' for denominations. Even then, Presbyterian polity was not always practical. Congregations created around the country (including Lagos) through migration were still tied to the *eastern* heartland of Presbyterianism. As late as 1959, the new Presbyterian church set up in Kaduna in northwest Nigeria was as an outstation of the Duke Town congregation in Calabar – on the other side of the country! Finally, as historians like Johnson and Kalu have pointed out, the missionary division of Nigeria into denominational jurisdictions had the effect of creating churches that were often 'clannish' or tribal, which would prove a liability in an independent nation often troubled by ethnic and regional division.

Health

A significant gospel witness of Presbyterianism in Nigeria has been in healthcare. Of course, before the discovery of malarial prophylactics and other important treatments, missionary medical work focused simply on keeping themselves alive in (what was for Europeans) an inhospitable climate! The rate of illness and death for white missionaries remained high into the first decades of the 20th century. Yet concern to show the love of God for African bodies as well as souls made healthcare an important part of the growing Presbyterian church – and this development continued with force in the colonial period.

One reason why health was a large feature of Presbyterian witness was due to the *kind* of missionaries that came to serve. Historians have noted that by the late 19th century, missionary identity had expanded beyond a clerical idea (e.g., a pastor) to a wider focus on the kingdom of God in which lay people could more easily find a role. Indeed, by the early 20th century, single lay women made up the largest group of foreign missionaries around the world.[32] In Nigerian Presbyterianism, we see this trend in Mary Slessor and Margaret Manson Graham. They served the kingdom of God in Nigeria as lay persons and did so with great effectiveness. Graham, who arrived in Calabar in 1895, followed the British military expedition into Aro where she served as a nurse and advocate for outcast children and women until her death in 1933.[33] Another reason for the Presbyterian attention to healthcare was its undeniably *spiritual* power in the African context. Because misfortune, ill-health and injury were traditionally interpreted in part as caused by evil spirits or curses, to treat medical problems through prayer and penicillin was to confront these 'gods.' Healthcare, in this sense, could be a direct witness to the lordship of Christ!

Presbyterian mission stations would typically set up small clinics to serve the neighbouring peoples. Some of these clinics developed into hospitals in the colonial era with Scottish missionary doctors in charge. "His hospital was a simple mud building and he had little if any trained assistance," writes Johnston of one of these doctors.

> Despite these shortcomings, he reports over 9,000 outpatients in 1903 and 11,000 in 1904 … His patients were usually women and the complaint was mainly some kind of ulcer.[34]

Presbyterian mission clinics and hospitals were at the forefront of dispensing immunizations and treatment against yaws – the most devastating affliction for children in tropical Africa at that time. In the 1930s and 40s, Mary Slessor Hospital at Calabar was a leading centre for training African medical staff and had an innovative lepers' colony attached to it. In the 1950s, there was a noticeable shift in focus toward encouraging maternal health and preventative treatments, especially after the discovery of antibiotics. Of course, it was never easy for a small church to financially support hospitals, which requires highly trained (and well paid) staff as well as expensive supplies. It is not surprising, therefore, that Presbyterian institutions like Mary Slessor Hospital or the training hospital in Umuahia were eventually taken over by the government. But this should not detract from the impressive Presbyterian contribution to serve Nigerians with Christian compassion.

---

32 See Andrew Walls, "The Missionary Movement: A Lay Fiefdom?" in *The Cross-Cultural Process in Christian History* (Edinburgh: T & T Clark, 2002), 215–35.
33 "Margaret Manson Graham (1860–1933)," in *Biographical Dictionary of Scottish Women*, ed. Rhonda Lane (Edinburgh: Edinburgh University Press, 2005), 142–43.
34 Johnston, *Of God and Maxim Guns*, 194.

In this section, Dr Francis Ibiam (1906–1995) must be mentioned as perhaps *the* outstanding Nigerian Presbyterian of the 20th century. Born in what is now Ebonyi State, Ibiam enrolled at the Presbyterian's Hope Waddell Training Institute, and was baptised in 1919. A gifted student, he graduated as the first African medical graduate of the University of St. Andrews in Scotland.

> On his return to Nigeria in August 1935, Francis chose to be a missionary medical doctor under the auspices of the Church of Scotland Mission. He was inspired to do this by his abiding admiration for the Scottish missionaries who left the beauty and bounty of their homes to serve in remote places like his village in Unwana.[35]

He dedicated his life to healthcare, setting up and overseeing several mission hospitals; he also established the School of Nursing at the hospital in Itu. He was appointed the first Nigerian principal of the Hope Waddell Training Institute in 1957 and advocated for both a Nigerian university and universal primary education.

Esteemed both within Nigeria and Britain for his ability and Christian integrity, in 1960 Ibiam was appointed governor of the eastern province of the new republic of Nigeria. During the terrible civil war (1967–70), in which several million people died (mostly from hunger), he served as an advisor to the Biafra government and used his church contacts abroad to secure desperately-needed provisions. Although he renounced his knighthood to protest Britain's lack of support for Biafra, many accolades followed him through the rest of his long life.

> Ibiam was a key Christian figure, responsible for new initiatives such as the Bible Society of Nigeria and the Christian Medical Fellowship, and serving as president of the Christian Council of Nigeria (1955–1958) and in many other representative capacities. He was also an outstanding African ecumenical figure of the decolonization period, serving as … president of the AACC [All African Council of Churches] and of the World Council of Churches, chairman of the council of the United Bible Societies, and leader of the AACC peace mission to Sudan. In his home area he was a respected traditional ruler, Eze Ogo Isiala I of Unwana and Osuji of Uburu.[36]

---

35 https://dacb.org/stories/nigeria/ibiam-akanu/
36 https://dacb.org/stories/nigeria/ibiam2-akanu/

Education

"Reformation and education had marched together" through Presbyterian history, observed Andrew Walls. The Scottish Reformers were concerned to create a nation of literate believers who could read Scripture for themselves and engage God's world through learning.[37] Education has thus been a priority wherever Presbyterian missions were established: Nigeria was no exception. We have already seen in the preceding section how a Presbyterian mission school system was set up in the first half-century of the church's existence. Indeed, the tandem of church and school was so close that sometimes the schoolhouse preceded the actual church building in a newly evangelised area! Often the church building functioned on weekdays as the village schoolhouse.[38] It is hard to overestimate the social impact of Presbyterian schools: "As school pupils, slaves sat next to their masters, were issued with identical books and materials, enjoyed the same attention, received praise and blame as merited."[39] This was true not only for slaves and free but for boys and *girls*.

Furthermore, because the Presbyterian schools insisted on a religious core to the curriculum, including substantial use of the Bible, the school system steered students towards baptism and faith. Dr Ibiam was a famous example of how Christian schooling prepared students for following Jesus, but there were countless others. Rev. Robert Olugu Ume (1903–1968) became a Christian while in primary school, then a prominent teacher and educator who combined teaching with pastoral work. He is remembered to this day both for winning "many souls for Christ in all the places he served" and "promoting the education of women and the learning of European skills among the youth."[40] It is with good reason that historians like Johnson believe that strong Presbyterian numeric growth in the 1930s and 40s was driven by the effectiveness of Presbyterian schools.

Presbyterian education had two focal points: (1) local primary schools, and (2) institutions of higher education. The primary school system that developed in the colonial era was typically rural and village based throughout Calabar and Igboland. The curriculum focused on literacy and practical skills, as well as Bible knowledge. This model has been criticised by some Nigerians scholars after independence for being 'pietistic' and basic. During the colonial era the authorities, too, often disdained Presbyterian 'bush schools'. They preferred secular schooling that would train Nigerians in the clerical skills needed by the

---

37 Andrew Walls, "The Scottish Missionary Diaspora," in *The Cross-Cultural Process in Christian History*, 259.
38 This section draws heavily from an excellent study by William H. Taylor, "The Presbyterian Educational Impact in Eastern Nigeria," *Journal of Religion in Africa* 14 (1983): 223–45.
39 Taylor, "The Presbyterian Educational Impact in Eastern Nigeria," 230.
40 https://dacb.org/stories/nigeria/olugu-ume/

colonial administration. To that end they encouraged boarding schools with specialised training for gifted students. However, William Taylor defends the Presbyterian concern for universal education through village schools, as well as their resistance to secular and pragmatic education.

> The Presbyterians had an unsurpassed record as teacher-trainers but the growing secularization never deterred them from vetting their teachers' morals as well as their religious beliefs ... This concern for a teacher's character, together with the mission's reticence to accept more than minimal government aid, may explain why its school system did not expand faster or further.[41]

He also notes that the expansion of the Presbyterian church into Igboland did require the church schools to develop in excellence and scope, because the "able, extraverted and ambitious Igbo" demanded it. There could be no question, either, of relying on Scottish missionaries like Slessor to bear the burden of teaching: Nigerian men and women quickly became the main teachers in Presbyterian schools. At the time of independence, as the Presbyterian Church of East Nigeria officially became the PCN, it ran five secondary schools, three boarding schools, four teacher training colleges and over two hundred primary schools – with the vast majority of staff being Nigerians themselves. This was a remarkable achievement.

It should be clear, too, how Presbyterian schools could encourage feelings of African independence and agency among students. Ogbu Kalu is correct to insist that "Anglicans and Scottish Presbyterians who were a part of the establishment were most inclined to accept the hegemony and injustice of colonial rule."[42] But it is also true that education could undermine this 'establishment mentality' by giving a powerful voice to African interests. Historians have noted, for example, that already by the time the 'Great Depression' hit Nigeria in the late 1920s there was an 'elite' class of Christian, educated southern Nigerians – many of whom were Presbyterian schooled – holding the British colonial government accountable, as well as pushing for better opportunities for Africans.[43]

The second focus of Presbyterian education was higher education. A Women's Training Centre was established, for example, in Umuahia in the 1930s. Pride of place must be given to the Hope Waddell Training Institute. Founded in 1895

---

41 Taylor, "The Presbyterian Educational Impact in Eastern Nigeria," 234.
42 Kalu, "Ethiopianism in African Christianity," in *African Christianity: An African Story*, 230.
43 Falola and Heaton, *A History of Nigeria*, 111.

▲ Hope Waddell Training Institution, founded 1895, photo of one of the buildings, c.1951

and located in Calabar, the HWTI was one of Nigeria's most prestigious schools in the colonial era. It drew students from all over west Africa, and under the long leadership (1907–43) of the esteemed Scottish missionary J. K. MacGregor included kindergarten, primary and secondary education, teacher and industrial training. Geoffrey Johnston notes that many of Nigeria's teachers in the first half of the 20th century were trained at HWTI, and its graduates provided "the backbone" of both the school system and ministry of the Presbyterian church, as well as some other churches.[44] Presbyterian leaders of the post-independent church, like Dr Ibiam and the talented Okenwa Ikwan (1914–1989), were graduates of HWTI.[45]

Toward an Independent African Church

The important educational work done by Presbyterians in this period raises a related question: how was the church educating ministers of the gospel? An educated pastorate has been a feature of Presbyterianism throughout its history,

---

44 Johnston, *Of God and Maxim Guns*, 168.
45 https://dacb.org/stories/nigeria/ikwan-okenwa/

and theological education, as traditionally understood by Presbyterians, involved formal study of theology, Bible, pastoral studies, and other topics. As Nigerian Presbyterianism developed throughout the colonial era, theological education aimed to create a clergy for this growing church the Presbytery of Biafra, which became a Synod (1921), then the Presbyterian Church of Biafra (1945), and then the Presbyterian Church of Eastern Nigeria (1952–1960). Frankly, historians have not highly valued Presbyterian theological education in this era, with two gaps especially singled out.[46]

First, the quick growth of Christianity in Nigeria, including in the Presbyterian church, made it difficult to offer more than a very basic and practical theological education. A second reason is rooted in the racist context of colonialism. Especially throughout the first quarter of the 20th century, there was a sad increase in white missionary paternalism toward African Christians, which was a disincentive to educating indigenous clergy. Between 1900 and 1925 just thirteen Nigerians were ordained to Presbyterian ministry – and only two of them had serious training! At the same time, the Mission Council tended to dominate the church, which gave Scottish missionaries a disproportionate amount of power and influence in the wider church. Perhaps the tendency within the PCN even today to view pastors in an almost Anglican (i.e. episcopal) manner has its origins in the fact that for the first half of the 20th century Presbyterian pastors – whether black or white – were always too few, and had to take on many duties of oversight and administration.[47]

By the 1930s, however, the Presbyterian witness in Nigeria was becoming more African. Missionaries were no longer automatically part of a local church session – they had to be invited. And the power of the Mission Council diminished through the 1940s and 50s as Nigerian Presbyterians sought the independence of both their nation and church. One example of this increasing assertiveness was that Presbyterians began thinking about what their church would look like *after* independence. Many thought Nigerian Christianity should not reflect all the denominational differences that the missionaries had brought with them to Africa. As a result, Nigerian Presbyterian leaders were very active in the ecumenical movement and entered into long and serious discussions through the 1940s and 50s with Methodists and Anglicans about creating a single Protestant church for Nigeria. Although this church did not materialise, the creation of Trinity College in the 1940s by these three churches did provide the higher quality theological education that had been lacking in earlier decades, as did the establishment of the Presbyterian's seminary at Akwa (which became Essien Ukpabio Theological College).

---

46 Johnston, *Of God and Maxim Guns*, 128.
47 So argued by Kalu, "The Battle of the Gods," 12.

We can see some of these indigenizing developments reflected in the career of a distinguished mid-century Presbyterian, Rev. Ochu Mbila (1908–1993). Mbila received an education only when the Presbyterian missionaries set up a school in his Igbo homeland; he converted to Christianity in 1921. After training as a teacher, Mbila studied for ministry and was ordained in 1952. He planted and pastored many churches and was a strong advocate for church union.

> He was a man of immense stamina who worked tirelessly. He wrote articles and booklets, conducted seminars, retreats, and revivals for the renewal of local churches. He was a man of strong faith, totally committed to Jesus Christ, who lived a modest lifestyle and had few material possessions.[48]

The *Dictionary of African Christian Biography* also notes, significantly, that Mbila encouraged the use of traditional African musical instruments in church worship. The colonial era in western Africa saw the rise of what scholars call "African Indigenous Churches" [AICs] like the *Aladura*, which were widespread in Nigeria.[49] While the Presbyterians typically resisted the *Aladura* and other AICs, there was certainly common concern at this time to see aspects of African culture like music, traditional names, or dress redeemed for the Nigerian Presbyterian church.

5. Conclusion

On 1 October 1960 Nigeria became independent of Great Britain. That same year, the Presbyterian Church in Eastern Nigeria rebranded itself as a national church: the Presbyterian Church in Nigeria. To conclude our story of Presbyterianism in Nigeria in the year 1960 is to pause on the verge of massive change and upheaval that would characterise the new nation: astonishing population growth, rapid urbanisation, economic transformation through the discovery of petroleum and the expansion of education, ethnic-religious tension between the Christian south and Muslim north, and, of course, the tragedy of the Biafra War (1967–70) and its lingering divisiveness. Since independence, the so-called "Giant of Africa" has become even more of a giant in terms of population and power. And Presbyterianism in Nigeria – while not a giant – has grown substantially into one of the world's largest Reformed denominations. Today, Nigerian Presbyterians

---

48 https://dacb.org/stories/nigeria/mbila-ochu/
49 A good overview is Afe Adogame and Lazio Jafta, "Zionists, Aladura and Roho: African Instituted Churches," in *African Christianity: An African Story*, 271–89.

number approximately 4 million and are a growing global presence through missionaries and immigration to the West and other parts of Africa.[50]

Questions for study (fact type):

1. Describe the 1846 missionary team that began work in Calabar: who? what? why? how?
2. Explain the following statement: "The Calabar Mission was an 'offshoot' of the Caribbean Mission."
3. What was the name and date for the formation of the first presbytery in Nigeria?
4. Who was the first ordinand of this Mission?
5. Who was King Eyo Honesty VII?

Questions for study (reflection type):

1. Discuss the mission work of the Hope Waddell Institution and compare this to the Lovedale Institution in South Africa (see also chapter eight).
2. From the appended inset on Mary Slessor with this chapter, discuss the philosophy of "wholistic missions" in the life and labours of Mary Slessor.

Select Bibliography

Goldie, Hugh. *Calabar and its Mission*. Edinburgh and London: Oliphant, 1901.

Goldie, Hugh. *Dictionary of the Efik Language*. Glasgow: Dunn & Wright, 1868.

Edisana Ñwed Abasi Ibom [The Holy Bible]. Trans. Esien Esien and Alexander Robb. Edinburgh: National Bible Society of Scotland, 1868.

Johnston, Geoffrey. *Of God and Maxim Guns: Presbyterianism in Nigeria, 1846–1966*. Waterloo, ON: Wilfrid Laurier University Press, 1988.

Kalu, Ogbu. *A Century and a Half of Presbyterian Witness in Nigeria, 1846–1996*. Lagos: Ida-Ivory Press, 1996.

Taylor, William H. *Mission to Educate: A History of the Educational Work of the Scottish Presbyterian Mission in East Nigeria, 1846–1960*. Leiden: Brill, 1996.

Waddell, Hope Masterton. *Twenty-Nine years in the West Indies and Central Africa*. London: Nelson and Sons, 1863.

---

50 https://www.oikoumene.org/member-churches/presbyterian-church-of-nigeria.

Bio Inset

Mary Slessor (1848–1915)

Todd Statham

Introduction

▲ Bank note with Mary Slessor

In 1997 the Clydesdale Bank in the United Kingdom featured Mary Slessor on its £10 note – a great and rare honour for a missionary! During her lifetime, Slessor came to be known around the world for her work with the UPCS/UFC mission in Calabar as an evangelist, educator and advocate for women and vulnerable children. The Efik and Ibibio people of southeastern Nigeria, among whom she laboured for almost forty years, admired her as *Eka Kpukpru Owo*: "everyone's mother." Slessor's legacy is enduring, and we should consider her a spiritual *Eka* of all Presbyterians in Nigeria.[51]

---

51 There are many books about Mary Slessor. This article draws primarily upon Jeanette Hardage, *Mary Slessor – Everybody's Mother: The Era and Impact of a Victorian Missionary* (Eugene, OR: Wipf and Stock, 2008), and Jeanette Hardage, "Mary Slessor," in *DACB* (2002): https://dacb.org/stories/nigeria/slessor-mary/.

Early Life

Slessor grew up poor in the Scottish city of Dundee. Her devout mother faithfully raised her children in a local UPCS congregation. But Slessor's father was often drunk and unemployed; he and several of her siblings died of tuberculosis. As a child Slessor had to support the family by working long hours in a jute mill. She studied the Bible while working her loom, attending school only after the long workday. Already in her youth she showed a heart for mission, sharing her faith in her rough neighbourhood and teaching Sunday school. Slessor was excited by David Livingstone's famous explorations in Africa to expose the slave trade as well as reports from her own church's missionaries around the world. And when she heard an UPCS missionary speak in Dundee about the work in Calabar, she was inspired to apply to this mission field. After brief training as a teacher, Slessor was commissioned and set sail from Scotland in 1876.

Clearly the hardships she experienced growing up prepared her for missionary work. She was resourceful, tireless, and tough; her faith was strong and she had a typically Presbyterian conviction of God's providence. And she knew well how uncertain and dangerous life could be, whether one was living in the slums of a Victorian city or the jungles of southeastern Nigeria.

Life and Work in Calabar and Beyond

Slessor began missionary work in 1876 in Duke Town. Over the next decades she moved further up the Calabar River and inland, exploring creeks by canoe or trekking through forest to make contact with new villages. There she would establish a preaching point or home for abandoned twins and their mothers and give out medicine. Always restless, in 1886 Slessor convinced her colleagues to let her venture further north to the Okoyong, a kingdom feared for its violence and even cannibalism. It was Slessor's work here from 1886 to 1904 that made her famous. Reports emerged in Britain and America about the "White Queen of the Okoyong" (as one visitor described her) who was labouring for the good and for the gospel in often dangerous settings. In time, she earned the trust of the chiefs and the people. "She is their trusted advisor and friend," wrote one of her colleagues. "They bring their palavers [disputes] to her to settle. They bring twins and orphans, who in former times would have met a speedy death either by murder or by neglect, for her to rear."[52] The British colonial administration would also come to respect her and value her knowledge of local customs. In fact, the colonial administration appointed Slessor vice-consul of the area when it was absorbed into the colony – what was unprecedented for a woman in that century.

---

52 Hugh Goldie, *Calabar and its Mission* (London: Oliphant, 1901), 343.

What made Slessor a great missionary? She did not make many converts among the Okoyong or anywhere else. But her evangelism, teaching, and her love for the downtrodden were preparing the soil for the church of the future to grow. And while she at first held many prejudices typical of her era – Africans were 'heathens' and their cultures 'backwards' – Slessor soon came to appreciate aspects of Efik and Ibibio culture. She spoke Efik fluently and learned their customs, religion, and laws so well that both British and African valued her judgement. She discarded her shoes and petticoats, cut her red hair short like an African woman, and allowed herself tea as her only 'western' food item. This gave her credibility when she was evangelising,

▲ Mary Slessor (centre – seated) with Arthur Wilkie (right). Wilkie conducted her funeral

confronting the power of the Ekpe, mediating between warring kingdoms, or preaching against customs contrary to God's truth like slavery, human sacrifice and infanticide. As an unmarried woman, Slessor was able to reach out to vulnerable women and children in ways impossible for male missionaries.[53] She rescued countless babies and adopted eight orphans as her own. She condemned the sexual abuse of female slaves, set up sanctuaries for runaways and the mothers of twins, and promoted what today is called 'maternal health'.

The last stage of Slessor's life and work saw her moving further inland to establish a new mission station among the defeated Aro. Once again, she combined busy missionary work with heavy administrative responsibilities from the colonial government. Slessor fell ill with malaria and dysentery and could not recover: she died on 13 January 1915 shortly after praying *"O Abasi, sana mi yok"* [O God, let me go]. Her coffin was floated down the river to Calabar. "All flags at Government Buildings and Offices were lowered to half mast ..." wrote her adopted son, Dan. "The band struck the National Anthem, officers with drawn swords formed an arch under which the distinguished coffin passed."[54]

---

53 For context see Dana Robert, "Women in World Mission: Purity, Motherhood, and Women's Well-Being," in *Christian Mission: How Christianity Became a World Religion* (West Sussex: Wiley-Blackwell, 2009), 114–141.
54 Cited in Hardage, *Mary Slessor – Everybody's Mother*, 280–81.

Slessor's Legacy

Her state funeral alerts us to the criticism that Slessor was a willing participant in Britain's growing imperial presence in Nigeria.[55] As we have seen, she served as vice-consul in several areas seized by the British and her advice was widely sought by officials. Slessor clearly believed that colonialism would create a more stable society where the gospel could flourish, and a Nigerian church take root. At the same time, she was critical of how the British used violence to create Nigeria, the economic exploitation of the colony and the often-racist attitudes of officials.

The legacy of this remarkable missionary should not be measured foremost by her part in the British Empire but rather her part in the kingdom of God. Slessor is an excellent example of the typically Presbyterian 'kingdom of God' approach to mission. By calling for personal conversion *and* cultural change and building churches *and* schools, she witnessed to God's redeeming love for the whole person and for all of life.[56] Further, Slessor believed the gospel was good news for men *and* women. Indeed, the first woman ordained (1982) in the Presbyterian Church in Nigeria, Mgbeke George Okore, credits Mary Slessor's legacy for empowering modern Nigerian Christian women in the church and also in Christian education, health, and home life.[57]

Select Bibliography

Hardage, Jeanette. *Mary Slessor – Everybody's Mother: The Era and Impact of a Victorian Missionary*. Eugene, OR: Wipf and Stock, 2008.

Hardage, Jeanette. "Mary Slessor," in DACB (2002): https://dacb.org/stories/nigeria/slessor-mary/

---

[55] This is argued by J. H. Proctor, "Serving God and the Empire: Mary Slessor in South-Eastern Nigeria, 1876–1915," *Journal of Religion in Africa*, 30 (2000): 45–61.

[56] See Andrew Walls, "The Scottish Missionary Diaspora," in *The Cross-Cultural Process in Christian History* (Edinburgh: T & T Clark, 2002), 259–78.

[57] Noted by Hardage, *Mary Slessor – Everybody's Mother*, 290.

Chapter 10

Equatorial West Africa and American Presbyterian Missions: Gaboon,[1] Corisco

J. C. Whytock

Chapter Outline
1. Introduction
2. The Gaboon Mission
3. The Corisco Island Mission
4. Merger
5. Handover
6. Postscript
7. Conclusion

Bio Inset: Robert Hamill Nassau

1. Introduction

The focus of this chapter is the beginnings and development of nineteenth century Presbyterian mission work in the modern-day countries of Gabon and Equatorial Guinea (an area often referred to by the regional name of Equatorial West Africa).[2] These beginnings were undertaken by two streams, the American Board of Commissioners for Foreign Missions and the Board of Foreign Missions of the Presbyterian Church in the United States of America and thus represent a combination of interdenominational, evangelical, Calvinist society missions and ecclesial missions.

This new field *was a development from the mission work in Liberia* and *a story of expansion into new territory along the west coast* and *a push into the interior*. It represents a complexity of beginnings, with both missionary society and Church involvement interacting within colonial conflicts and developments. The chapter

---

1 The Mission spelling was usually *Gaboon* at the time, hence *The Gaboon Mission*. Latterly *Gabon* became the favoured spelling yet in many instances so did *Gabun*.
2 Some will classify it also as basically *Western Africa* but not all will classify it as *West Africa*.

will provide a brief overview of this mission work from the beginning period of the 1840s of the ABCFM, and of the 1850s of the BFM PCUSA, through to the 1890s when the merged mission by that time was handed over to the Paris Missionary Society. The chapter also includes an insert on Robert Hamill Nassau, the longest serving missionary of the PCUSA in this mission. A separate chapter (that follows this chapter) is devoted to Ibia J'Ikenge, the first ordinand of this mission.

2. The Gaboon Mission

Beginnings

The Gaboon Mission was begun in 1842 by the ABCFM at Baraka, near Libreville, by the Gabon estuary of the Como River. This mission reached out chiefly to the Mpongwe tribe but was not limited to that tribe. The ABCFM had transferred its mission from Cape Palmas, Liberia to Gabon. There were several reasons for the change of mission of the ABCFM from Cape Palmas: financial constraints, forced military service of staff by the colonial government, rising tensions of colonial rebellion and control, and racial tensions overall between the three distinct entities in the area. The first preachers to begin ministry at the Libreville and Baraka mission station were Revs. John Leighton Wilson and Benjamin Griswold, and the assistant Josiah Dorsey with others following: Rev. and Mrs William Walker, Rev. and Mrs A. Bushnell. There were also Americo-Liberian *advanced students* and a *native worker* from Liberia who had come across from Liberia when it was decided to begin a new mission in Gabon: Robert Cross, Francis Allison, Packard Wilson, Sarah Holt, and more followed, Mary Clealand, John Edwards, James Bayard, and Wâsá Baker.[3] This long list would serve in the ABCFM schools in this new mission. The noted Cape Palmas printer, educator, and African American Benjamin Van Rensselaer James also came for one year to serve in Gabon before eventually returning to Monrovia and serving in the Presbyterian Church there[4]

The Wilsons had formerly been serving in Liberia with the PCUSA Synod of South Carolina and Georgia as auxiliaries to the ABCFM. They served ten years in Gabon, returning to America in 1852. The following year John Leighton Wilson[5] became a secretary for the Board of Foreign Missions, PCUSA and then executive secretary in 1861 for the Committee on Foreign Missions, PCUS. Wilson and Walker commenced the work of reducing the Mpongwe language to

---

3   Cloutier, *Bridging the Gap*, 17. Jane Cowper, an African American missionary of the ABCFM also served in the Gaboon Mission, 27.
4   Cloutier, *Bridging the Gap*, 18–21.
5   See chapter 3 written by Steve Curtis in this volume. Also, David Calhoun, *Swift and Beautiful: The Amazing Stories of Faithful Missionaries*. (Edinburgh: Banner of Truth, 2020), 37–54.

a written form in 1843, thus paving the way for the Mpongwe scriptures.[6] Wilson was the Presbyterian and Walker the Congregationalist, both serving with the ABCFM. Another noteworthy grammar was produced by this mission for the Akĕli tribe also of Gabon. It was prepared by ABCFM missionaries Preston and Best and was called *A Grammar of the Bakĕele with Vocabularies*.[7]

The Gaboon Mission also established two stations away from the coast, pressing on into the interior – one at a distance of 25 miles and the other a distance of 100 miles, plus numerous schools.[8] The problem was to have enough personnel to run this mission work. Reports reveal opening schools and then closing some schools due to a lack of personnel. For the Mission it was a hard road to advance churches and schools. The Mission also ran its own printing press so that books in Mpongwe could be produced to be used by the schools. Some of the students at the schools were orphaned receptives whom the Mission accepted. The presence of two Bible Women in this Mission should also be noted: Mbute, or Julia Green, and Bessie Good.[9]

As a mission the Gaboon Mission had good relations with the Corisco Mission when that mission commenced further north at Corisco Island (see next section). On occasion, Rev. Nassau would go to Baraka for the Gaboon Mission to preach and conduct communion services when he was at Benita. Rev. William Wilson, a congregationalist minister, would also travel to the Corisco Mission; he officiated at the Nassau's marriage and later also baptised their children.

Gaboon Mission of the ABCFM was a varied mission of establishing and planting churches, founding schools, undertaking translation, doing printing work, and engaging in women's ministry.

▶ Stamp of Gaboon Mission Church

---

6   *A Grammar of the Mpongwe Language with Vocabularies*. (New York: Snowden and Prall, 1847). Wilson was likely the main author of this grammar.
7   *A Grammar of the Bakĕle Language with Vocabularies*. (New York: J P Prall, 1854).
8   See John Leighton Wilson, *Western Africa*, and his brief history of the Gaboon mission, 492.
9   Cloutier, *Bridging the Gap*, 66–70 on the Bible Women.

3. The Corisco Island Mission

Beginnings

The Corisco Island Mission was established by the Board of Foreign Missions, PCUSA in 1850. Corisco Island was selected as a central location in the Bay of Corisco from which to engage in mission work to other islands, to the coastal mainland, and up the interior rivers pouring into the Gulf. All students of African church history should become familiar with some of the Islands on the West Coast of Africa as they are very significant for mission history and provide context, which is vital. Readers should know about São Tomé and Principe for earlier history related to the Portuguese and slavery, coffee, sugar, and cocoa as well as Catholic mission history. For early Presbyterian history in Equatorial West Africa, Corisco Island is very significant as it was the beach-head location for their mission work. Today Corisco Island belongs to Equatorial Guinea.

The early missionaries for this mission in 1850 were PCUSA missionaries Rev. and Mrs James Mackey and Rev. and Mrs George Simpson. Tragically Mrs Mackey died in Libreville (Gabon) before the mission station was established on Corisco Island. The Simpsons died one year later by drowning off Fernando Po. James Mackey carried on alone until other new missionaries came throughout the 1850s: McQueen's, Williams, Clemens, Ogdens, DeHeers, Loomis' and several single women missionaries: Jackson, Sweeny, Sneed, Kaufman, and Bliss.

Main Stations

The main station that was developed was at Evangasimba, where Rev. Mackey was the first pastor. Here a whole complex of buildings was built. The mission on the Island was centralised here for a period with out-stations developed across the Island and on adjacent smaller islands, such as Big Elobi – the station there being called McQueen. The Mission eventually spread to the mainland.

Rev. and Mrs C. De Heer began their work at Ugobi on Corisco Island with a boys' school for the Benga. This was the first station with a school and chapel. The mission faced trials due to traders on the Elobi Islands who often presented a very false and confusing impression of Christianity; these traders were notorious for immorality yet claiming to be members of the Churches of England and Scotland. The Ugobi work was assumed by a native evangelist after De Heer.

Evangasimba had a girls' school, central storehouses for payment by goods to teachers and workers (not by money), the first church building on Corisco Island, a rudimentary hospital, and a carpenter's shop or a rudimentary industrial training type school. At Evangasimba, candidates for the ministry were given instruction through an early Bible School-type ministry on the Island through missionary training and mentoring. Another school was established at Alongo to train boys from the mainland. This school was begun by Rev. William Clemens:

> That school was blessed by God. From its pupils arose almost all the young men who became assistants as Scripture-Readers among their own mainland natives. Its light shone. Light, if true light, cannot help shining. God blessed its former pupils' teaching among their own people, and saved many souls by their work, worth infinitely more than all the money that has been given for that school, or spent on the whole mission.[10]

The Corisco Mission had white and African American and Americo-Liberian missionaries/assistants coming from the Liberia mission to work in Corisco. In 1854 two African American women lost their lives in a fire of one of the mission buildings at Evangasimba. They had first managed to get the children out of the building. One noted African American missionary/assistant who came across from Liberia to Corisco Island in 1859 was Charity Sneed, together with her mother. Charity's work would grow in evangelism, educational work, linguistic, and vocational. The upliftment of girls and wives was a challenging ministry during this period. The support of the Liberian assistants to the Corisco mission has not always been appreciated nor fully recorded.[11]

In 1860 Mary Latta joined the Corisco Mission and in 1861 Dr Robert Nassau They were married in 1862 and lived at Maluku. In 1868 Miss Isabella Nassau, Robert's sister, joined the Corisco Mission. She would become known for her work in commencing the training of Bible women and also future ministers. Isabel was originally stationed on Corisco Island and then was transferred to the mainland.

On the mainland, a mission station at Aje was established and this mission was very successful in working with the Bapuku tribe. Native ministers such as Rev. Etiyani assumed this station. Other stations established on the mainland were: Mbini among the Kombe tribe, Meduma, Hanji and Etiyani, and the large station at Benita. In the American Presbyterian mission at Corisco, native evangelists were often referred to by the title *Scripture-Readers*. Without these Scripture-Readers, the mission could

▲ Miss Isabella Nassau

---

10 Nassau, *Corisco Days*, 9–10.
11 See Cloutier, *Bridging the Gap*.

not have advanced and been effective as they were key to providing preaching in many stations and out-stations. Many also served as teachers. In 1875 the white missionaries were all transferred to the mainland stations and the Corisco Island mission portion was placed under the labours of native Scripture-Readers and the minister Rev. Ibia J' Ikĕngĕ.

Mainland Station of Benita (in Rio Muni, Spanish Guinea)

Benita Station, Mbâbe, which had begun in 1865 with the first communion service, was constituted a separate church from Corisco Island. Some of the early members of the Benita congregation had been schooled at the missionary schools on Corisco Island. By 1875 it had become a thriving church of the Corisco Presbytery with its own mission works/daughter congregations at Bata, Evune, Myuma, Batanga, and Sĕnje. (The Batanga work was in Kamerun and will be picked up in the chapter on Kamerun.) In 1865 the Benita Session banned all members from owning slaves and then the presbytery likewise adopted the same position. The issue of slave owning was a problem for years in the Corisco mission.

The mission also had a lay-Presbyterian missionary, Peter Menkel, who was in charge of industrial work and also the missionary schooner for travel to the Island and also along the coast.

The first Bible woman, Matomba, began her work in 1871 in Corisco Presbytery. She had attended the mission's Girls' School on Corisco Island. Her ministry as a Bible woman was brief (due to death) but very effective. This, along with the deaths of several missionaries of the Benita Station in the early years, show the cost of missions: Rev. Paull after only a few months in 1865; Rev. Reutlinger again after only a few months in 1869 died of erysipelas; then Mary Nassau in 1870.

Presbytery of Corisco, 1860

The Presbytery of Corisco was established in May 1860 with Rev. James Mackey as the moderator and Rev. Clemens as the clerk *pro tem*. Rev. Ogden was also a member, and two others were made corresponding members. Three native elders also were present to constitute the first meeting. The presbytery, which met at the Evangasimba mission station on Corisco Island, connected itself with the Synod of New Jersey and was received by that Synod in October 1860. The boundaries of this presbytery were not limited to the Island but refer to the whole region. By 1888, the presbytery had ordained four native ministers: Ibia J'Ikĕngĕ (the first ordination, 1870), Ntâkâ Truman (1880), Frank Myongo (1886), and Etiyani ya Nyĕnyĕ (c.1888). Ibia's ordination made him the first indigenous African to be ordained and enrolled in a presbytery connected to the Synod of New Jersey, PCUSA.

The Corisco missionaries and local Scripture-Readers were heavily engaged *in linguistic work.* Several texts emerged from this mission. The most noted being the two editions of what became popularly known as Mackey's Grammar. James Mackey did the original edition in the 1850s and then Robert Nassau fully revised it. Here is a list of chief works done by the mission:

- Mackey's Grammar of the Benga-Bantu Language.
- The Benga Primer and Hymns.
- *Benga Old Testament, Part 1 & 2.*
- *Benga New Testament.*

The three dialects of Benga, Dikĕle, and Fanwe were transcribed to a written form with grammars and scripture translation work also done.

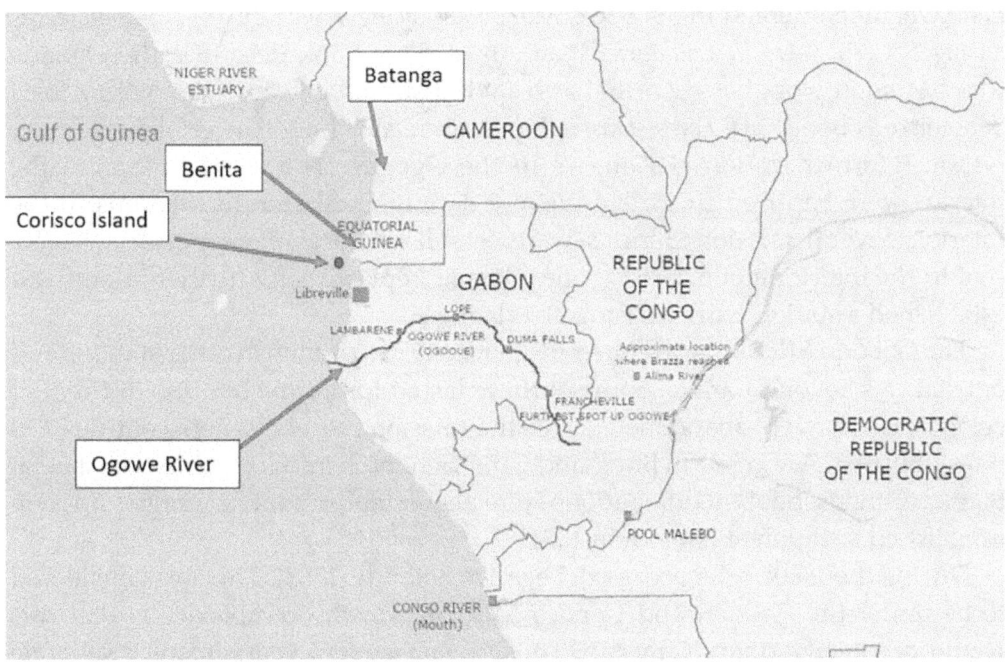

▲ Map of Equatorial West Africa

4. Merger

The ABCFM mission in Gabon was transferred over to the Board of Foreign Missions of the PCUSA in 1870/1 and thus the Corisco Mission and the Gaboon Mission merged and became known as the Gaboon and Corisco Mission. The ABCFM needed more personnel for this mission and a merger was viewed as the best solution. Both missions were in the Calvinist tradition, so they were basically compatible and were both paedobaptist. Teeuwissen wrote in his thesis that "Cordial relationships existed between the Corisco and Gabon Missions." The Congregationalist Church (established in 1843) in Libreville thus became a Presbyterian Church of the Corisco Presbytery in 1871 following the merger. By 1870, both missions, Gabon and Corisco, were in desperate need of personnel. "For several months, until the return of Dr. and Mrs Bushnell to Baraka in June 1871, Hamill and Isabella Nassau were the only protestant missionaries, where at one time there had been as many as ten residing on Corisco; as many as five stationed at Benita; and usually half a dozen assigned to Baraka."[12] This summation by Teeuwissen gives the real picture at the time of the "merger."

Expansion of the mission, both into the interior and north

Starting in 1874, the Gaboon and Corisco Mission expanded its work along both the Gabon and Ogooué rivers. Rev. Robert Nassau's work along the Ogooué has been well documented in his book, *My Ogowe; being a Narrative of Daily Incidents during Sixteen Years in Equatorial-West Africa*. This book describes the Ogooué River Mission work between 1874 and 1891; it should be compared with Albert Schweitzer's book, *The Forest Hospital of Lambaréné*, which was established near Nassau's former station at Kangwe in the Ogooué. The first converts in the interior were baptised in 1879, a historic date in Presbyterian missions in the interior. Several mission stations were established and more personnel were sent to the interior along the Ogooué. Nassau kept pressing further inland and established a station with the Fang at Talaguga.

The Gaboon Mission made attempts before 1870 to establish other stations and out-stations beyond Baraka. Some of these lasted for a time but due to tribal or colonial issues were abandoned. After the mission merger, others continued to be established. A successful Boys' and Girls' School/Seminary was established at Baraka. Other schools at out-stations were also established. The merged mission established a station at Angom in 1881.

During the 1880s, advance north began at Batanga (1885). This was considered to be under the Gaboon and Corisco Mission, yet the complexity is that this would become German Kamerun. Thus, in subsequent years it was a separate administrative region. Efulen was established inland from Batanga in 1893 as an interior station.

---

12 Teeuwissen, 25–26.

Colour

In reviewing missions' correspondence with the Board of Foreign Missions, one recurring theme of note is the controversy concerning having both white and African American missionaries in the Gaboon and Corisco Mission. There were a variety of opinions on this. Nassau appears to have been the most progressive in his thoughts on this, yet he was very realistic: he was not certain that the native population would see African Americans in a more favourable light than whites, but he was very much for their inclusion in the mission. He even stated to the secretary of the BFM that he would be willing to marry an African American. He also wanted them as full members of the Mission and Presbytery, whereas Rev. A. C. Good believed that African American missionaries should not be members of the Mission but have the same status as native workers or ministers.

Nassau did not necessarily believe that African Americans would fare much better health-wise in Equatorial West Africa than whites, so he did not see that as a valid argument (which some used). His attitude was that all should come to serve regardless of colour of skin.[13] Nassau maintained that there was "a colour line" in some ways in the BFM and in the Mission which he did not approve of (or as some may have viewed it "separate, but equal"). In a later BFM Report (1897), it states that recruitment of African American missionaries would continue to be sought for this field, but it does not seem to have continued.

5. Handover to the Paris Evangelical Missionary Society (PEMS)

In 1892 the Board of Foreign Missions PCUSA handed over its mission work and congregations on the Ogooué in Gabon to the Paris Evangelical Missionary Society (PEMS) or in full in French, *Société des Missions* Évangéliques *chez les peuples non-chrétiens à Paris* (SMEP). The reasons for this handover are rooted in the French colonial attitude to foreign missionaries at the time; in particular, there was an insistence on French instruction in education. France had claimed Gabon in 1885 in what is often referred to as "the scramble for Africa;" although administratively France had not consistently applied colonial rule, it was increasingly moving in this direction and fully did so in 1903. Prior to 1885, France (going back to 1838 and 1841) had protection treaties with local chiefs in the coastal areas, so there was a long-standing relationship going back to this "protectorate." The French had also freed the slaves of a captured ship in these waters in 1849 and had settled them in what became Libreville (French for "free-town").

---

13 Cloutier, *Bridging the Gap*, 172–173.

The Paris Society would have been viewed as theologically close and compatible to the Presbyterians and as the best option for the situation. Most of this Society was connected to the French Reformed Churches.[14] At the time of the 1892 handover, the Gaboon and Corisco Mission had twelve organised congregations with numerous out-stations and several schools. In the Ogooué there were at that time two stations, four churches, and several schools. The American Presbyterians needed French-speaking missionaries to work now in the mission. The Paris Society seemed like the best solution to this need.

The Presbyterian Mission was responsible for linguistic work also in the Gabon portion of their mission. The American Mission had prepared a *Mpongwe Gospels and Acts*, and then the whole *Mpongwe New Testament*. These works made a lasting contribution in Christian mission work in Gabon and remained the basic Bible text long after the Board of Foreign Missions did the handover to the Paris Society.

Although the PCUSA Board of Foreign Missions had handed over its mission on the Ogooué in the Gabon to the PEMS, this did not mean that American Presbyterian support or interest had completely vanished. The Presbytery of Corisco continued to be listed in 1897 in the statistical reports of the GA of the PCUSA and continued to be listed under the Synod of New Jersey. Also, missionaries continued to report back to the BFM, so the handover was a little more complex than often stated. Rev. Robert H. Milligan continued to work in Angom, Libreville, and Baraka, Gabon. In a letter back to his supporting church, Babylon Presbyterian, Long Island, New York, he discusses work in 1901–1902 at the boarding school and dispensary for boys in Libreville which was focusing upon Fang youth from outlying areas of the Estuary. Milligan wrote also about his evangelistic tours into towns and villages where Fang people lived that had not yet been evangelised. In addition, Milligan also wrote about his Saturday Sunday School training classes for teachers.[15] Milligan said that he could teach in French but with *an Irish accent*. Milligan is often referred to as a Canadian Presbyterian missionary yet was with the BFM, PCUSA and is generally associated with Rev. Adolphus Good in the Presbyterian mission in German Kamerun (Cameroon). Thus after 1892, it cannot be said that all PCUSA interest or support ceased in Gabon. The Presbyterians had also financed a steamer for Milligan to use, *Dorothy*, for visitations to villages on the waterways of the Estuary area.

---

14 Sometimes maps of the period (1890sff) will refer to Gaboon also by the name French Congo, Kongo-Français. Robert Nassau includes on the title page of his 1904 book, *Fetichism in West Africa* that he was "for forty years a missionary in the Gabun District of Kongo-Française." Readers need to be aware of the change of names constantly in this area.

15 Milligan, "Letter," *Assembly Herald*, 102–105. Milligan was born in 1868 and died in 1934. His mother was Irish.

Also, a mission to the dwarfs in the northern portion of the mission (Kamerun) was undertaken in the 1890s funded in part by a patroness (Miss Margaret MacLean) in Scotland to the BFM. However, by 1913 American Presbyterian interest was withdrawn in Gabon and the handover completed to the PEMS and the focus for the BFM was then on Cameroon. Later in the century, the PCUSA would become involved again but more on a partner basis to the PEMS.

6. Postscript

Readers will wonder what happened to this PEMS work after 1892 – does a Presbyterian Church or churches exist today in Equatorial Guinea and Gabon? The short answer is yes, a small body exists today by the name Reformed Presbyterian Church of Equatorial Guinea/ *Iglesia Reformada Presbiteriana de Guinea Ecuatorial* (IRPGE) which claims to be a direct descendent from the original mission of 1850 to Corisco Island and of the first Presbytery of Corisco, 1860. This nation experienced much oppression of the Protestant Churches and schools under Spanish rule. The Protestant Churches were forced to close in 1952, which included the Presbyterians. (The French had transferred the area of what is today Equatorial Guinea to the Spanish in 1900 by the terms of the Treaty of Paris).

In Gabon, after the handover to the Paris Missionary Society of the posts in the Ogooué, the Presbyterian mission became identified with the Confession of La Rochelle in 1892 and then in 1913 all the remaining churches/stations were merged into the PEMS. After a series of divisions and reunions, the descendent of the Gaboon and Corisco Mission today is known as the Evangelical Church of Gabon/*Eglise* évangélique *du Gabon (EEG).*

7. Conclusion

This chapter has demonstrated again that the beginnings of a Presbyterian mission was not always one track. Here we have seen both the ABCFM and the Board of Foreign Missions PCUSA involved in the beginning stage and the eventual merger of these two distinct yet co-operative missions. These missions were committed to an evangelical mission thrust of conversion, church planting, women's work, industrial development, basic medical ministry, and educational ministry. Mixed into this emerges strongly the theme of exploration and Christian mission. Also, this mission reveals the diverse mission personnel who laboured in these fields, white, African American, and Liberian, together with indigenous local Africans. Pragmatics does influence mission decisions, and this can be seen with both the merger and then the handover to the Paris Society – the latter which seemed to have been a slow process of handover and perhaps more a way to appease the

French Colonial administration. The issue of "colour line" in recent academic work about this mission has been a topic of research. It seems that there were many complexities of viewpoint – labouring as one is not always an easy matter.

Questions for study (fact type):

1 Name the first society mission organization as well as the first ecclesial mission that began work in Equatorial West Africa. Beside each mission, write the year and the location of where each began.
2 Reproduce the map of Equatorial West Africa in this chapter by drawing it yourself and placing the following locations on it: *Libreville, Baraka, Corisco Island, Benita, Ogooué River, Talaguga.*
3 From the chapter inset, write a one-paragraph summary of the life of Robert Hamill Nassau. Include any significant writing that may be of value today in understanding West Africa.

Questions for study (reflection type):

1 *"In the American Presbyterian mission at Corisco, native evangelists were often referred to by the title Scripture-Readers. Without these Scripture-Readers, the mission could not have advanced and been effective as they were key to providing preaching in many stations and out-stations."*

Reflect on the relationship between the gospel and culture. Consider the work of the Scripture-Readers in the Corisco mission. What advantages did the Scripture-Readers have as evangelists amongst their own people? What disadvantages did they have?

2 *"In reviewing missions' correspondence with the Board of Foreign Missions, one recurring theme of note is the controversy concerning having both white and African American missionaries in the Gaboon and Corisco Mission."*

Think of the time period of when these missions were being established. Why was it so controversial to send both white and African American missionaries to Gabon? What might Robert Nassau and others have said from Scripture to challenge any who opposed the sending of African American missionaries?

Select Bibliography

The 60th Annual Report of the Board of Foreign Missions, Presbyterian Church in the United States of America, 1897. New York: Presbyterian Mission House, 1897.

Campbell, Penelope. "Presbyterian West African Missions: Women as Converts and Agents of Social Change." *Journal of Presbyterian History* 56.2 (1978): 121–132.

Cloutier, Mary. *Bridging the Gap, Breaching the Barriers: The Presence and Contribution of (Foreign) Persons of African Descent to the Gaboon and Corisco Mission in Nineteenth Century Equatorial West Africa.* Eugene, OR: Pickwick, 2021.

Cogswell, James A. *No Turning Back: A History of American Presbyterian Involvement in Sub-Saharan Africa, 1833–2000.* Philadelphia: Xlibris, 2007.

Gardinier, David E. "The American Presbyterian Mission in Gabon: Male Mpongwe Converts and Agents, 1870-1888." *American Presbyterians* 69.1 (1991): 61–70

Milligan, R[obert]. H. "Letter." *Assembly Herald* 6:3 (March 1902): 102–105.

Milligan, Robert H. *Fetish Folk of West Africa.* New York: Fleming Revell, 1912.

Nassau, R. H. "Africa." In *Historical Sketches of the Missions Under the Care of the Board of Foreign Missions of the Presbyterian Church* [USA]. Philadelphia: Women's Foreign Missionary Society of the Presbyterian Church, 1886, 99–120.

Nassau, Robert Hamill. *Corisco Days: The First Thirty Years of the West Africa Mission.* Philadelphia: Allan, Lane & Scott, 1910.

Parsons, Ellen C., contrib. W. J. Holland & Adolphus Clemens Good. *A Life for Africa: Rev. Adolphus Clemens Good, Ph. D., American Missionary in Equatorial West Africa.* New York: Fleming H. Revell, 1897.

https://www.phcmontreat.org/bios/Bios-Missionaries-Africa.htm

Bio Inset

Robert Hamill Nassau (1835–1921)

J. C. Whytock

Introduction

Robert Hamill Nassau is one of the neglected and overshadowed names for American Presbyterian missionaries in Equatorial West Africa.[16] He spent over 45 years as a missionary of the PCUSA Board of Foreign Missions and was a most prolific author. He holds the record for the longest serving missionary in Africa of the PCUSA in the 19th century. Yet, no major biography has yet been published on him except curiously a short study in a medical journal done in 1963. The best study remains Teeuwissens' 1973 unpublished thesis. Curiously Albert Schweitzer saw himself as a successor of sorts to Nassau, medically, in Gabon: "I have always considered myself to be, somewhat, the successor to Dr. Nassau/ *"Toujours, je me sens un peu le successeur du Dr. Nassau."*[17] One of the complexities of Nassau's mission work is that it is all centred around Equatorial West Africa which is unifying but is spread over the three modern nations of Equatorial Guinea, Gabon, and Cameroon.

▲ Fetichism in West Africa

Nassau was born in Montgomery Square, Pennsylvania, near Philadelphia and was schooled partially at Lafayette College and at Lawrenceville, New Jersey and attended Princeton University (MA 1859) and concurrently at Princeton Theological Seminary. He did his medical training (MD) in Philadelphia at the University of Pennsylvania Medical School (graduating in a record two years, 1861[18]) chiefly to help him preserve his life as a future missionary. His seminary days were marked by decided interest in the Foreign Missionary Society and a Black Presbyterian congregation and summer work doing home missions. In 1861 he was sent by the Presbytery of New Jersey and the Board of Foreign Missions (PCUSA) as a missionary to Corisco

---

16 For an expanded paper on Nassau see my article in the 2022 *Haddington House Journal*, 24 (2022):134–156.
17 English translation by Raymond Teeuwissen from an original letter by Schweitzer, 1949.
18 Awarded the STD from this institution in 1891.

Island, West Africa which is today part of Equatorial Guinea. He quickly became fluent in Benga the dominant local language on Corisco Island and in parts of the nearby mainland which made him quickly received into a variety of ministries: superintendent of the girls' school at Evangasimba, preacher, trainer of candidates for the ministry, visiting the mainland out-stations, and regularly stated clerk of the Corisco Presbytery. He would remain four years living on Corisco Island. He and Rev. George Paull selected the first mainland permanent station for the Presbyterians, at Benita to settle a resident missionary. Nassau would assume the Benita station after Paull's death and establish the first Presbyterian congregation on the mainland in 1865. Benita was on the coast, but Nassau's vision was to go inland.

Nassau's first wife, Mary Cloyd Latta (1837–1870) translated several hymns into Benga at Benita. Mary died in 1870 and was buried in Benita, having served there from 1860–1870 a year before Robert had arrived. In 1868 Nassau's sister, Isabella joined the mission on the mainland from Corisco Island where she had gone in 1865.

Nassau's next work was at Baraka, near Libreville in Gaboon, now Gabon, moving there in 1871. The missions around Libreville were established by the American Board of Commissioners for Foreign Missions in 1842. In 1871 the ABCFM transferred this work over to the PCUSA Board of Foreign Missions.

Slowly from 1874 onwards Nassau pioneered stations inland on the Ogooue[19] River at Balimba, 200 miles inland, then at Kangwe and Talaguga, all in modern-day Gabon. The church at Kangwe was officially constituted in 1879 amongst the Mpongue. (Kangwe and Andende on the Ogooué River eventually became known as Lambaréné, where Schweitzer's famous hospital was located). This was a significant event as it was for the Presbyterians their first church in the interior with converts from the interior being baptised. From this often the epithet has been given to Nassau as the pioneer of Presbyterian missions in Gabon. He returned again to Baraka at Libreville from 1893–1903. His final work was in German Kamerun at Batanga, 1904–1906 and he retired from there in 1906.

Upon returning to America, he pastored a Presbyterian church in Florida and then moved to Ambler, Pennsylvania where he continued with writing projects and speaking engagements about West Africa. He died in 1921 and was buried in Lawrenceville Cemetery, New Jersey.

Nassau was conferred an honorary Doctor of Sacred Theology (STD) by the University of Pennsylvania. He always saw himself as a Christian preacher and evangelist and used his medical training as a supportive role. In contrast with Albert Schweitzer who saw himself as a medical missionary. Nassau was sent to Equatorial West Africa as a missionary not as a *medical* missionary, the missing adjective was a very important distinctive to Nassau.

---

19 Various spellings, one of the former, Ogowe.

He was esteemed by the English explorer Mary Kingsley (1862–1900) who introduced Nassau to a wider audience of explorers and readers – interesting in that Kingsley was not an evangelical like Nassau yet she references him in her noteworthy book, *Travels in West Africa* with acknowledgement that he was a walking-source of information.[20] It helped inspire him to compose his own book. His explorations in the interior on the Ogooué River were significant. He also met Savorgnan de Brazza (1852–1905) and developed a friendship with this naturalised French explorer of the Ogooué one year after Nassau had been doing his explorations of the Ogooué.

▲ Left: Anyentyuwe (governess) and her daughter, Right: Nassau and his daughter (Mary)

The controversial part of his life as a missionary was after his second wife Mary Brunette Foster (1849–1884) died in childbirth. Nassau made the avowed decision that his infant daughter, Mary, would remain by his side until at least aged seven, unlike two of his sons who were sent back to America to be raised.[21] He had Anyentyuwe serve as the governess for his daughter Mary at the Talaguga station. This was not well received by many fellow Presbyterian missionaries including Rev. Adolphus Good. It created many strains in his last years as a missionary. Nassau was also very much for inclusion of all races in mission work and at times also found himself in conflict.

Nassau has long been recognised for the contributions which he has made through his book, *Fetichism in West Africa*, or the modern print-on-demand edition *West African Shamanism*. Nassau was the premier missionary ethnologist in Equatorial West Africa in the 19th century. He has been marginalised by modern anthropologists, yet his works are extremely valuable and helpful. He served in what are today three African countries: Equatorial Guinea, Gabon, and Cameroon.

---

20 Robert H. Milligan viewed Kingsley with many reservations. See his, *Fetish Folk of West Africa*.
21 Baby Paull died at Benita Mission in 1867.

Select Bibliography

Mandeng, David J. "The Philosophy of Mission of Robert Hamill Nassau in the Contemporary World." PhD dissertation, Temple University, 1970.

Rogers, Fred B. "Robert Hamill Nassau (1835–1921): Apostle to Africa." *Transactions & Studies of the College of Physicians of Philadelphia* 30 (January 1963): 150–56.

Teeuwissen, Raymond W. "Robert Hamill Nassau, 1835–1921: Pioneer Missionary to Equatorial West Africa." ThM thesis, Louisville Presbyterian Theological Seminary, 1973.

"Robert Hamill Nassau Papers," Speer Memorial Library, Princeton Theological Seminary, New Jersey. Speer Library and Lincoln University Libraries have the complete published works of Nassau in their holdings. Speer has his MS autobiography and 33 volumes of his diaries.

"Robert Hamill Nassau Papers," Columbia University Libraries, New York.

"Robert Hamill Nassau Letters," Archives of the Paris Evangelical Missionary Society.

Nassau, Robert Hamill. *Corisco Days: The First Thirty Years of the West Africa Mission.* Philadelphia: Allan, Lane & Scott, 1910.

Nassau, Robert Hamill. *Fetichism in West Africa: Forty Years' Observation of Natives Customs and Superstitions.* New York: Charles Scribner's, 1904.

Wheeler, W. Reginald. *The Words of God in an African Forest.* New York: Fleming H. Revell, 1931.

Whytock, Jack C. "Reflections at the Centenary of Robert Hamill Nassau's death (1835–1921): An Overshadowed American Presbyterian Missionary to Equatorial West Africa." *Haddington House Journal* 24 (2022): 134–156.

Chapter 11

Ibia J'Ikenge: The First Ordinand in the Corisco Presbytery

Mary Cloutier

Chapter Outline
1. Introduction
2. Corisco Mission
3. Corisco Mission's First Convert
4. Ibia's Marriage
5. Licensed to Preach
6. Women converts
7. Demoralizing Influence of Trade
8. Ibia's Ordination
9. Women's Work
10. Schism
11. Pastor and Counselor
12. Installation
13. Kingsley Visit
14. Death & Legacy
15. Conclusion

1. Introduction

Mary Henrietta Kingsley listened intently as the aging pastor described his Benga ancestors: a powerful and proud nation occupying the coastal region of Equatorial West Africa. It was 1895, and the famed British traveler was visiting the island of Corisco, gathering scientific data on local fish species, and journaling her encounters with the indigenous people and the foreigners living among them. Pastor Ibia told Miss Kingsley how the Benga entered into trade with Europeans, exchanging ivory and slaves for European goods. Rum was destroying their culture, and men no longer valued hard work or the glories of war; their incentives were gone, and men had become idle. He regretted that the Benga had recently adopted the custom of infant marriage, a practice unknown forty years earlier; old men were now buying infant girls, future wives for themselves or for their infant sons.[1] Ibia

▲ Ibia J'Ikenge

---

1 Kingsley, *Travels in West Africa*, 402–403. (See also Boteler, 403–404, for an 1835 description of Benga marriage practices).

was glad that his people's former warlike, bloodthirsty spirit was now broken, but lamented that the ancient Benga values of *manhood* had been compromised by the influence of white men.

Throughout his forty-five years of Christian ministry, Ibia promoted a return to godly manhood through industry, education, and Christian values. He fought this war for Benga manhood on two fronts – standing against patriarchal Benga customs which held women in fear, subjection, and oppression, and standing against the mission patriarchy,[2] which kept ecclesial control in the hands of ordained missionaries, who were reticent to grant autonomy and authority to African church leaders. Ibia capitalized on the growing wave of women's work in the US and in West Africa, to bring social reform and spiritual renewal to his people. In many ways, it was his emphasis on women's ministry which brought transformation among the Benga men, and spiritual growth among the Benga people.

2. Corisco Mission[3]

The PCUSA Corisco Mission was established on the island of Corisco in July 1850, with the arrival of Rev. James Love Mackey and Rev. George and Eliza (Ross) Simpson. Within a year, the Simpsons were lost at sea in a powerful storm, leaving the widower, Rev. James L. Mackey, alone in the fledgling work.[4] Over the next decade, several other couples and single missionaries joined the Corisco Mission and were soon accompanied in their work by three local Christians who served as evangelists and schoolteachers. From the beginning, they established schools for local children, hoping to invest in the next generation of leaders who would be a blessing to their own people and eventually reach the many tribes in the region. The Presbyterian Board believed that these Equatorial Africans could best be reached and effectively influenced only by trained native Christian leaders. The missionaries also hoped that the education of girls and young women would transform the social conditions of their people, even as the first Christian marriages among them held promise for healthier family relationships.[5] The women of Corisco were otherwise treated by their husbands and fathers as *property*. One young Benga woman lamented to missionary Louise Reutlinger: "We are bought with bars of iron, and ruled with iron ..."[6]

---

2   Nassau, *Ibiya*, 442.
3   For an overview of the work of the Corisco Mission, see Chapter 10 of this volume.
4   Nassau, *History*, 5. Mrs Eliza Mackey died during their brief stay at the ABCFM Gaboon Mission, in March 1850.
5   Presbyterian Board, "*Corisco Mission Report*," 43, 41.
6   Reutlinger, Letter excerpt, 58.

3. Corisco Mission's First Convert

Ibia J'Ikenge was a young boy when the PCUSA Corisco Mission was established, and he became one of the earliest Benga converts. His first contact with Christians was as a young boy, employed on the distant island of Fernando Po. "Here... I first heard the gospel and the fear of hell got hold of me. Afterward I went home to Corisco and understood the word more perfectly from the missionaries there."[7] At the mission school, Ibia proved to be a bright student, well-behaved, and fully trustworthy.[8] Having completed his general education, he then prepared for ministry under the tutelage of Rev. William Clemens. As a growing Christian, Ibia was often in conflict with his community, confronting unjust and oppressive customs which held his people (particularly the women and children) in fear and bondage. He also faced the opposition of mission leaders as he pioneered Christian leadership among the local African peoples.[9]

4. Ibia's Marriage

In 1858, Corisco missionaries reported the loss of at least one missionary and the departure (due to sickness) of several others. These missionary absences would have ended the work of three mission stations had it not been for the faithful and efficient work of three native young men, Andeke (at Evangasimba), Sukonjo (at Ugovi), and Ibia (at Alongo). The missionary absences drew all three young men into *more active labor*, as a result. That same year, the mission reported the first native Christian marriage on the island of Corisco. Though their names are not given, the celebrated couple is Ibia and his bride Hika: "One of the older and more advanced pupils of the [girls'] school has recently been united in marriage to the native Christian man who has charge of the school at Alongo."[10] Hika was no more than sixteen years of age at the time of her marriage.[11]

Within a year, there were at least five more Christian marriages involving girls educated at the mission school. Missionaries saw this as an indication that the native Christians were turning from the practice of polygamy and conforming to "habits of civilization."[12] The marriage of Ibia and Hika seemed to be a stable and strong one. Forty-five years later, in an article on the ramifications of polygamy,

---

7   Ford, "Persecution," 531.
8   American Colonization Society, "IBIA," 120.
9   Nassau, "Rev. Ibia J'Ikenge," 106–107.
10 Presbyterian Board, "Corisco Mission Report [1858]," 39, 41.
11 Presbyterian Board, "Corisco Mission Report [1858]," 40. The girls' boarding school had sixteen girls, aged six to sixteen.
12 Presbyterian Board, "Corisco Mission Report [1859]," 42.

missionary Robert Hamill Nassau paid homage to Ibia, whose marriage to Hika was one of respect and equality, in contrast to the typical marriage: "It is man's idea here that woman is inferior, and must be in every way subservient. I know scarcely any of our male church-members who are thoroughly civilized on this matter."[13]

5. Licensed to Preach

Ibia is first mentioned by name in the Annual Report of the Board for 1858.[14] That year, he was listed as a *native teacher*. Subsequent annual reports list him as a *native assistant*,[15] a *native helper*;[16] and by early 1861, he was officially listed as a *licentiate preacher*.[17] Within six months of Ibia's placement as preacher at the Ilobi out-station, there were fifty persons attending services on the Sabbath, with seven expressing interest in salvation.[18] Despite the laudatory remarks on Ibia's ministry, and the responsibility given him when missionary leaders were absent, the 1863 mission report states that *"none of the native brethren, as yet, appear to be called to the pastoral office,* nor does the time seem to have come for organizing the native communicants into separate churches at the different stations." [19]

While the PCUSA prioritised the identification and training of indigenous church leaders, it should be noted that one of the greatest barriers to training local pastors at Corisco was the missionaries' own lack of organisation and availability in regard to theological instruction. In the early decades of the mission, according to Dr Robert Hamill Nassau, there was no formalised ministerial training program, no curriculum, no school, or designated instructor. Each missionary would find a protégé to mentor, often a mission employee or a school assistant. This informal theological training was irregular, as the missionaries had many other ministry responsibilities.[20] When absent missionaries returned to the field, or when new missionaries arrived, they were put in positions of authority over the native pastors. This is evident in the journal writings of a new missionary, Rev. George Paull, who worked with Ibia in 1864.[21]

---

13 Nassau, "Some ramifications," 238.
14 Presbyterian Board, "Corisco Mission Report [1858]," 37.
15 Presbyterian Board, "Corisco Mission Report [1859]," 36.
16 Presbyterian Board, "Corisco Mission Report [1860]," 34.
17 Presbyterian Board, "Corisco Mission Report [1861]," 30.
18 Presbyterian Board, "Corisco Mission Report [1861]," 38.
19 Presbyterian Board, "Corisco Mission Report [1863]," 19.
20 Nassau, "Ibiya: A West African Pastor," 442.
21 Wilson, *George Paull*, 114, 117.

6. Women converts

In the early 1860s, missionaries noted a positive trend in female attendance. Large numbers of adult women, who had not had the benefit of education and whose only instruction came from regular church services, were now professing faith and receiving communion. This was both unusual and encouraging and indicated that the mission work was prospering.[22] The same report also noted positive changes in the education of girls and women: "The habits, prejudices, and superstitious notions of the people were all opposed to the moral and intellectual elevation of the female sex. But this opposition is yielding to the influence of religious principle, and husbands and parents alike are becoming desirous of the education of their daughters and wives."[23]

Charity L. Sneed, an African American mission worker, lamented the plight of the Benga women whom she observed to be "very, very ignorant and miserable."[24] After thirteen years of ministry among the Benga women, Charity adapted her ministry to better suit their needs:

> It has been my custom for some time to visit the women in their different towns. I at first tried to get them to come every afternoon to the mission-house and let me teach them, but they did not continue this long, giving many excuses for not coming. I now go to them. Some are glad to see me and try to learn their letters, others will not try, as they say they cannot see. I also read to them from one of the Gospels and a hymn-book in the Benga language. Generally they are very quiet until I have finished, then they say, "You must come often, we like to hear, but are too tired to walk to you after we come from our gardens. We have so many things to do".[25]

Rev. Cornelius De Heer noted in his 1873 mission report that the work among the degraded Benga women had been the most promising and effective aspect of their ministry.[26]

---

22 Presbyterian Board, "Corisco Mission Report [1861]," 33.
23 Presbyterian Board, "Corisco Mission Report [1861]," 35.
24 Sneed, "Letter," 159–160. Charity Sneed was misrepresented in early mission reports as a *native helper*. She and her parents were African Americans, and had been emancipated in 1854 and emigrated to Liberia. In 1859, 16-year-old Charity was recruited to serve with the Presbyterian mission as a teacher's helper, though her role evolved over time to include evangelism, education, literacy, and vocational training.
25 Sneed, "Letter," 159–160.
26 De Heer, "Notices of the Corisco Station," 176.

7. Demoralisation Influence of Trade

During the mid-19th century, foreign traders had a corrupting influence on the men of Corisco, promoting greed, the excessive consumption of rum, and the temptation of easy credit which led to financial bondage. Various tribes in the region did what was right in their own eyes; artful and cunning men exerted control and power over people through the use of superstition and fetishes. Missionaries hoped to establish a trade school, to train men for artisan crafts, such as building furniture, which would enable them to earn a living independent of foreign trade and its destructive influences.[27]

By 1867, licentiate Ibia J'Ikenge had established a small industrial school for the purpose of teaching men woodworking skills; he welcomed a total of thirteen learners, including ten boys, two men, and one girl. Ibia also reported progress in the level of morality, industry, and marital equity in that some of the local men were choosing monogamy over polygamy and were now refusing to take trade goods on credit. Several men were now planting gardens of groundnuts (peanuts) and corn. One husband, in defiance of local customs, worked with his wife in making a garden and publicly carried cassava sticks (a woman's role) for the purpose of planting them. Ibia considered this to be a matter of "reason triumphing over pride."[28]

Missionary John Menaul described his visit to Ibia's place of ministry, noting vast improvements in the way people were now constructing their bamboo houses, erecting fences around them, and planting varied kinds of crops. While Ibia hoped that the industrial school would be self-sustaining, he asked the mission for help in procuring machinery to make boards of native lumber, a condenser to help in processing cane sugar, and a machine to grate a local tuber, called *mevonda*, into starch.[29]

8. Ibia's Ordination

Ibia J'Ikenge was ordained on 5 April 1870. Though this was the first ordination of a native pastor in the now combined Gaboon and Corisco missions, it was agreed upon by the missionaries *only to preserve the Presbytery*, which was otherwise reduced to one member.[30] Published reports of this historic event

---

27 Mackey, "Hindrances at Corisco," 275–276.
28 Nassau, "Mainland Work," 62.
29 Menaul, "A Visit to Ibia's Place," 215.
30 Nassau 1888, 12. The two missions, Gaboon (ABCFM) and Corisco (PCUSA) were joined in 1870–71, due to low missionary numbers. Ibia had been a licentiate for ten years when he was ordained. It would be another ten years before he was given a church, and three more before he was officially installed. Nassau notes that the 1880 ordination of the second native pastor, Ntâkâ Truman, was due to the same reason; all missionaries were absent, and only Ibia was left to represent the Presbytery.

indicate mission reticence in ordaining Ibia: "In the absence of any other missionaries, he has now sole charge of the work on the island of Corisco – a work altogether too great for him; indeed, one that heretofore required the services of two missionaries from this country."[31]

Shortly after Ibia's ordination, Dr Nassau visited the mission at Corisco and stayed one week at the home of the pastoral couple. Nassau was deeply impressed with Mrs Ibia's lady-like care and attentive hospitality. He also remarked that some local church women were now clothed with garments made by their own hands, in contrast to women who wore significantly *less* clothing in the public church gatherings.[32] This suggests that Ibia's congregation accepted women in either state, seemingly without reproach or shame.

9. Women's Work

Missionaries and travelers to Corisco witnessed the ill-treatment and oppression of women and girls by the men of their community through the customs of child marriage, polygamy, and *Ukuku*, a men's secret society which held women and girls in captivity to fear. Ibia J'Ikenge fought these traditions head-on. One could argue that Ibia merely appropriated and maintained the views of the white missionaries, which seems apparent in missionary reports of that time; yet, his own writings indicate a genuine pastoral attentiveness to the concerns of women and a belief that by improving the quality of life of the women of the community, he was bettering the quality of the community itself. Ibia's 1870 report to the Board describes the earliest women-initiated church ministries, notably a weekly prayer meeting. Ibia saw this as evidence of better things to come and was pleased to see the women "dropping foolish customs one by one, and reducing their knowledge to practice. It is true these things are not godliness, *but they help men to lead godly lives better.*" In the same report, Ibia noted an increase in attendance at Sunday services and Sabbath School; in fact, two of the Sabbath School teachers were women. Ibia concluded, "It appears at present on the island that the females take more interest in the things of God than the men."[33]

This increase in women's ministry in the local church coincided with the new emphasis on *Woman's Work* in the Presbyterian churches in the U.S. Women were now forming their own mission boards to promote ministries overseas which focused specifically on women. This was a great boon for Pastor Ibia,

---

31 American Colonization Society. "Ordination," 350.
32 Nassau, "Notices," 278.
33 J'Ikenge, "An African minister's report," 51.

who received empathy, encouragement, and support (prayer and financial) for the continued work at Corisco at a time when local unbelievers were fighting against the spread of the gospel and its transforming work among the women. Missionary Isabella Nassau drew reader attention to Ibia and his wife, Hika, by sharing two letters they had sent her regarding the progress of the women's ministry at Corisco. In the first letter to Miss Nassau, which was published in the November 1872 issue of *Woman's Work for Woman*,[34] Ibia wrote:

> The women receive much opposition from the men. The Bible woman got very ill treatment from one Nga-lo. This man Nga-lo thinks that the Bible woman is spoiling all women, and one of his own in particular. I do not believe that the men will accomplish much by their opposition. The Lord reigns. He will make their wrath to praise him, and restrain the remainder. Tell the Christian ladies to pray more and more for the women of Africa. We feel the influence of their prayers here. Among some of our wants here is a lady to teach the women. My wife salutes you, and hopes you are well. I am your friend in Christ, Ibia.[35]

Two months later, Ibia added the following report which indicates the continued tension between men and women:

> The women are making a good and hopeful progress both in religion and in civilization. If things continue progressing as they do now, there is much hope. We have now seven women in the inquirers' class, five having professed Christianity, for longer than sixteen months. There is much good news, but we have no time to say all that I like to say. The interest among the women is not confined to Corisco alone, but other places are not so fortunate as to have teachers. All polygamists are angry with what [it's] doing for women, but it is evident they cannot stop the course of events.[36]

---

34 *Woman's Work for Woman* was a missionary journal put out by the Woman's Foreign Missionary Society of the Presbyterian Church, describing mission work around the world that was both supported by women and focused on ministry to women. By early 1873, the magazine had a readership of 5,000.
35 J'Ikenge, "Letter from Rev. Ibia," 202.
36 J'Ikenge, "Letter of Ibia J'Ikenge," 272.

Ibia then added his wife's comments, reporting the progress of the sewing school and the women's prayer meetings on Corisco. The couple had moved to another mission outpost but made periodic visits to their former home and station. The letter is signed, "We are your friends,

*HIKA IBIA,
IBIA J'IKENGE".*[37]

The mere act of signing his name *below* hers is a silent tribute to Ibia's respect for, and deference to, his wife.

The 1873 Annual Report of the Gaboon and Corisco Mission noted the absence of the Corisco missionaries, which left the native minister, Mr Ibia, to do all preaching and other work "with good encouragement."[38] There was a significant increase in spiritual interest among the people, particularly among women. Ibia was pleased to add that they now had three candidates for the ministry; the local believers were building a chapel through their freewill offerings and were already worshiping in the incomplete structure; Ibia was gratified that the local Christians were now taking a stand "against that murderous imposture *Ukuku* and other superstitions."[39]

In his tribute to Ibia J'Ikenge, missionary Robert Hamill Nassau described this male secret society called *Ukuku*,[40] whose purpose was to control women and settle tribal disputes. As mere *men*, they knew that they would not be obeyed or feared. The members of the secret society took oaths and claimed that the society's decrees were given by the spirit, called Ukuku. Anyone who denied this belief or exposed the secrets of the Ukuku society, was instantly put to death.[41] Membership was required of all local men; while Christians would sever their membership with the society, they would not divulge its secrets. Women and children were terrified by the coming of Ukuku[42] and would hide or shield their eyes at its coming.

Ibia had once been a part of the Ukuku society and launched an effort to expose its deception. The incident nearly cost him his life, and he was spared only through the intervention of the missionaries and his own family. Though the society did not kill him, they put a curse on Ibia by concocting "fetich charms

---

37 J'Ikenge, "Letter of Ibia J'Ikenge," 272.
38 Presbyterian Board, "The Corisco Report," 34.
39 Presbyterian Board, "The Corisco Report," 35.
40 Nassau, *Crowned*, 101. Ukuku means 'departed spirit' in the Benga language.
41 Nassau, "Ibiya," 443.
42 The *Ukuku* was a man dressed up to impersonate the spirit. Runners would precede his arrival, warning women and children to flee or hide their eyes, lest they be killed.

which would destroy the life of his child, and ... would curse the ground on which he trod so that it should sicken his feet."[43] Ibia's infant son, in fact, died not long afterwards, and Ibia developed a painful ulcer on one foot, which lasted more than a year. While Nassau saw these as startling coincidences, "Ibia recognized his afflictions as a trial of his faith permitted by God."[44] *Ukuku* proved to be an ongoing threat to the missionaries and native ministers of the Corisco Presbytery. The Society could pressure whole communities to boycott their targeted *enemy*, refusing to sell them food, to give them access to water, or to interact with the community. *Ukuku* occasionally interrupted mission schools, church services, and other Christian activities.[45]

Another custom that Ibia challenged was the practice of polygamy and the "marriage-market."[46] Rich polygamists would buy up young girls for themselves or their infant sons. Marriage was necessary in this culture, and celibacy was virtually unheard of. The Christian young men were unable to find wives due to the *dowry* requirement. For a time, the mission paid the dowry of young Christian schoolgirls and would be considered their *guardian*. The young Christian men could choose a wife from these girls if she consented. Ibia had married Hika in this manner, but her parents demanded more money. Because of this, Ibia advised the mission to discontinue *giving away* wives and require the Christian young men to reimburse the mission, *from their own wages*, the price of the dowry. The system worked for several years but was eventually abandoned by the mission. By that time, the church had established a rule that Christian parents must not *sell* their daughter in marriage.[47]

Ibia wrote a treatise for his people, *Benga Customs*, which was published in his native Benga language in 1874, in the United States, under the direction of Rev. Robert Hamill Nassau. Many years after Ibia's death, his fellow pastor, Myongo, shared a translated copy of this book with missionary Jean Kenyon Mackenzie, who then featured it in an article submitted to *The Atlantic Monthly* magazine:

> The people do say, "A woman and a man are two different tribes." This is not so, woman and man are but of one nation ... Let the woman know everything, that which the man knows only; that which she herself does not want to learn; and let her eat that which the man eats, also except herself refuse. Let them not be kept in ignorance anymore, let them not be

---

43 Nassau, *Fetichism*, 144.
44 Nassau, *Fetichism*, 144.
45 De Heer, "Notices," 17.
46 Nassau, "Ibiya," 443.
47 Nassau, "Ibiya," 443.

deprived of good things ... I know and they shall ask me that I should shew them the nobility of a woman. I will also ask them that they should shew me of a man.[48]

10. Schism

With Ibia's ordination in 1870, he now had authority to communicate directly with the Presbyterian Board in New York. His private letters to the Corresponding Secretary reveal Ibia's frank assessment of the (male) mission hierarchy and its unwillingness to fully prepare and empower indigenous church leaders:

> I do not know whether it is the rule of the mission that black men [should] be in perpetual pupilage to white men. I know that it is the rule of some Missionaries and some have no sympathy in it. Some of you teach plainly that the training up of native laborers the aim should not be to govern them perpetually like children or let them be as dependent as children, but while governing them for a season to develop their manliness and self-dependence, teach them what and how they ought to do and then tell them to work in Jesus. Depending on him for every needed help and hold themselves responsible ... to him! This is sound and scriptural.[49]

Certain missionaries who had trained and praised Ibia during his licentiate years were uncomfortable with his now being equal or superior to them in the work. Their discrimination was evident to their missionary colleagues and community, and the matter appeared only in private correspondence with the Board Secretary.

By the late 1870s, there was a deep rift between Rev. Ibia J'Ikenge and those particular missionaries serving at Corisco. In early January 1878, Mrs Louise Reutlinger wrote to the Board Secretary, Dr Lowrie: "The mission has released us entirely from our work on Corisco committing it into Mr Ibia's hands, whom we trust will be faithful to his charge."[50] Rev. Cornelius De Heer, who had been

---

48 Mackenzie, "The Black Commandments," 796. Mackenzie also wrote of Ibia in her 1917 work, *An African Trail*.
49 J'Ikenge, Letter 382. Ibia's correspondence reveals his awareness of American race inequities, and the related controversies in the divided Presbyterian Church. He also understood Henry Venn's much-promoted "Three-Self" concept of preparing and empowering the indigenous church through self-governing, self-support and self-propagation. The mission did not follow this, in practice.
50 Reutlinger, Letter 307. Rev. John C. Lowrie was Corresponding Secretary for Mission Board from 1850 to 1891.

serving on Corisco Island for twenty-three years, had known Ibia since his youth. De Heer had buried his first wife and baby son on the island[51] and now served with his second wife, Reubina. Mrs Louise Reutlinger had come with her young husband eleven years earlier[52] and had also buried her spouse and a baby son.[53] The three missionaries had invested many years in the Corisco mission and church and were deeply wounded at their rejection by the native church members; they then asked to be released from that mission post.[54]

Ibia was then officially appointed to take charge of the mission, and one of the theological students was licensed to assist him in the work at nearby Benita station on the mainland.[55] Rev. Albert Bushnell, a longtime colleague and friend, lamented: "It is so sad, that they leave Corisco under circumstances so bad – no love or sympathy between them and the people, and no expectation of return there."[56] Rev. Bushnell squarely blamed Ibia for this schism and attributed it to Ibia's *ambition* to take full control over the Corisco mission stations.[57] That year, the mission sent no missionaries to either Corisco or the coastal Benita station but assigned them to Gaboon (Libreville) and other stations.[58]

Many years later, Dr Robert Hamill Nassau revealed the underlying tensions between Ibia and De Heer, which ultimately led to the schism:

> Mr De Heer had preached an earnest sermon, urging the Bengas to more active work, rebuking them for seeming to depend on white aid, and closing by saying, "What will you do if I should go away?" Just what he intended by that I do not know. But, Mr Ibiya in his prompt, bold, and somewhat curt manner, took it as "a dare" and replied: "Go away, and we Bengas will take care of ourselves!" Not long after, in 1877, Mr De Heer did remove to Benita, and Mr Ibiya was appointed in charge of the Corisco church and school, and carried them on successfully.[59]

---

51 Rankin, *Memorials*, 96–97.
52 Rankin, *Memorials*, 302.
53 Family information on both the De Heers and Mrs Reutlinger was provided by Mrs Holly Lemons, who is a descendant of Rev. De Heer and his first wife, and who has possession of the De Heer family archives.
54 The De Heers and Mrs Reutlinger served for many more years at the nearby coastal mission posts and remained as Ibia's colleagues for the duration of their ministry.
55 Bushnell, Letter 98.
56 Bushnell, Letter 102. Underlining in the original.
57 Bushnell, Letter 102.
58 Bushnell, Letter 98.
59 Nassau, "Ibiya," 442.

Nearly three years after the Corisco schism, Ibia wrote a frank letter to Dr Lowrie, describing the underlying causes from the perspective of the Benga people. The community and the church members were angry toward both Ibia and the foreign missionaries, seeking revenge by returning to what Ibia described as "heathenism and neglect of Christian duties."[60]

11. Pastor and Counselor

In 1879, Ibia kept a detailed journal of his ministry itineration to various towns on the mainland, including those that were asking for missionaries and schools. Among the common issues and questions posed to him were those related to the subject of marital relationships. On one occasion, during his visit to the Mbade church, the female members asked for a private interview with Ibia:

> They wished to know whether in the present condition of the country it was not a kind of necessity for them to marry polygamists after the death of their husbands, as they have no liberty to choose for themselves. I told them we must not yield to custom but fight against it, trusting in God for victory over custom. One of their number has yielded voluntarily to this: she can get free if she likes. Session took no action on her case hoping she might reflect and take a better course.[61]

Ibia's response is remarkably free of judgment or control and shows abundant grace towards women making these difficult decisions.

As the Corisco church progressed under Ibia's leadership, he noted continual improvement and promise among the women and consistent *apathy* on the part of the men. Ibia believed that the Corisco Church's greatest drawback was its want of male members. By 1881, they had only six male members, one of whom lived on Corisco and the rest on the mainland; most of the six were useless to the church.[62]

In a letter to Dr Lowrie in early 1883, Ibia shared some observations from his colleague, Mr Frank Myongo, who marveled at changes he had never seen before; when he visited towns for church meetings, female church members were the *crown* of the ministry activity and contributions were largely given by women. Of nine new church members received, eight were women.[63]

---

60 J'Ikenge, Letter 117.
61 J'Ikenge, "An African Minister's Journal," 314.
62 J'Ikenge, Letter 117.
63 J'Ikenge, Letter 264.

Ibia encouraged *self-reliance* by asking local families to contribute towards the costs of their children's education rather than depending on the mission to provide for them. Some fathers refused to provide for anything but clothing, arguing that they were not able to furnish food, as their wives had too much to do. Ibia noted that these same men, who had received a mission education and were now excommunicated, spent their time in drunkenness and idleness; yet, they always had money for "polygamous and heathenish purposes." [64] Ibia, likewise, discouraged the Presbyterian Board from supporting Corisco boys' educational expenses, as the local people would bury hundreds of dollars yearly with their dead, as part of their "heathenish institutions."[65] Ibia believed that the people were poor due to their indolence and poor practices. He worked to rid the church of "rotten members" [66] and felt that increased church activity and higher contributions were the positive result of this purge.

12. Installation

In early 1883, new missionaries Adolphus Good, William Gault, and Graham Campbell were sent by the *older missionaries* to address a problem with native elder Petiye, and to install Ibia as the pastor of the Elongo church at Corisco. Rev. Good was pleased with the installation, noting that it was the first such service of its kind on that field.[67] Rev. Campbell also commented on the momentous occasion, which seemed to heal and reconcile the church and mission,

> Mr Ibia's installation was a very interesting service as we remembered the labors of those who had formerly been on Corisco – some of them called Home to their reward, some still praying and indirectly working for the salvation of this people, it seemed to me that more than our little band were present but more than all we felt that we had the Spirit's presence and that not only our own hearts were strengthened and encouraged, but that this church and pastor were made stronger for the Lord's work through this union.[68]

Through 1883 and 1884, Ibia saw continued increase in female inquirers and church members, with a parallel increase in financial contributions. Many

---

64 J'Ikenge, Letter 264.
65 J'Ikenge, Letter 264.
66 J'Ikenge, Letter 264.
67 Good, Letter 278.
68 Campbell, Letter 280.

women suffered persecution from husbands who were either heathen or apostate.[69] Ibia continued to lament the lack of devoted men who could share in ministry leadership.[70] By late 1884, there were only eight male members in the Elongo church, the majority being poor models of Christian faith.[71] By contrast, most of the female members seemed to be mature in Christ and were drawing other women to the Saviour. Ibia knew that the church desperately needed Christian men, but he would not tolerate ungodliness in the church, preferring to discipline and excommunicate wayward members than increase the percentage of men through accommodation and compromise. He felt strongly that polygamy would "send more men to hell than any other iniquity, in this country."[72]

After decades of pastoring the church and overseeing the educational ministries, Ibia continued to express his intention to balance academic work with training in manual skills, for the purpose of increased productivity, industry, and division of labor in his community:

> I have not abandoned the idea, and I never will abandon it, of training boys and girls to be self-supporting, by teaching them something useful ... When any parent brings a boy to me they always say, 'I want you to make my boy a strong man.' Idle men are now despised by the women, and working men praised by them. No man that will turn to farming now will no more be laughed to scorn.[73]

13. Kingsley Visit

Perhaps one of the most remarkable descriptions of Ibia came from Mary Henrietta Kingsley, the British author and traveler, who gives a rare glimpse of Ibia and his wife, Hika, in her famed book, *Travels in West Africa*. Miss Kingsley had visited the Gaboon Mission, and was given a boat and crew, courtesy of Dr Robert H. Nassau; among the crew was a young man from Corisco, Eveke, son of Rev. Ibia, the sole clergyman of the Presbyterian Mission serving at Corisco.[74] Upon landing on the island, young Eveke introduced Kingsley to his mother, whom she describes as "a pretty, bright-looking lady who it is hard to

---

69 J'Ikenge, Letter 290.
70 J'Ikenge, Letter 62.
71 J'Ikenge, Letter 88.
72 J'Ikenge, Letter 88.
73 Presbyterian Board, 1891, 18.
74 Kingsley, *Travels*, 385.

believe old enough to be Eveke's mother."⁷⁵ Hika was likely in her mid-fifties by this time, and was surrounded by "a lot of strapping young women who came forward with her, and the grandmother of other strapping young women mixed up among them.⁷⁶ Mrs Ibea offered hospitality to Kingsley, insisting "in the kindliest way possible"⁷⁷ that Kingsley take her own room. Kingsley spent a great deal of time with the family, taking tea with Mrs Ibea and asking questions about the local people, their history, and their customs.⁷⁸

Days later, Kingsley finally met Ibia, who had returned from an evangelistic mission. She considered him to be "a splendidly built, square-shouldered man, a pure Benga, of the finest type, full of energy and enthusiasm."⁷⁹ When he disclosed his age, and that of his wife, Kingsley joked, "I still think he stuck a good ten years on."⁸⁰ Kingsley and Ibia conversed at length about the various local tribes, their migrations, and histories. He estimated that there were now two thousand of his Benga tribe left, "and that those that are now representing it are far inferior, physically, to those he remembers as having seen as old men, when he was a boy."⁸¹

14. Death and legacy

Ibia J'Ikenge died on 28 February 1901 and was estimated to be in his late sixties. When Dr Robert Hamill Nassau first met the young Ibia, in 1861, he was married with two children and already a licentiate in the Presbytery of Corisco. After forty years of serving with Ibia, Nassau recognised that his earlier conflicts with the mission arose from an appropriate desire to see his people independent and self-reliant, not dependent on the white man's trade (and its related immorality), and not subjugated to the perpetual

▲ Rev. Ibia J'Ikenge with presbyters

---

75 Kingsley, *Travels*, 386.
76 Kingsley, *Travels*, 387.
77 Kingsley, *Travels*, 387.
78 Kingsley, *Travels*, 393.
79 Kingsley, *Travels*, 399.
80 Kingsley, *Travels*, 399.
81 Kingsley, *Travels*, 402.

leadership of white missionaries. A committed follower of Christ, Ibia spoke out against the injustice and immorality of prevailing social and religious customs, drawing both opposition and vengeance from his own people. His book, *Benga Customs*, which denounced local customs and taught biblical truths and morals for daily living, seemed to have had a profound influence on later missionaries as well as his own people. Missionary Jean Kenyon Mackenzie, who arrived on the field several years after his death, immortalised his teachings on the Ten Commandments in *The Atlantic Monthly*, as well as in her book, *An African Trail*.

15. Conclusion

Dr Robert Hamill Nassau, in his 1902 obituary of Pastor Ibia, described him as "brave, outspoken, manly,"[82] yet Ibia showed a gentle and fervent concern for the women and children of his community, wanting them to know the Savior and to know freedom in Him. He affirmed women in their spiritual growth and in their leadership in the church, while respecting their difficult circumstances in polygamous marriages and the influences of heathen relatives. It was Nassau who recognized Ibia's true *manliness* and strength in standing up against the men in his community, in their oppression of women, and against the patriarchal rule of the missionaries who were reticent to relinquish power, authority, and autonomy to indigenous church leaders. Much was written about Ibia's godly character and gifted leadership for many years after his death. His legacy lived on in his son, Bodumba, who felt called into the ministry just following his father's death, in 1902.[83] In praising the son, missionary Melvin Fraser credited the father:

> Bodumba Ibia, of Sauline mien, modest and frank, still wearing the dews of youth and carrying seeds of promise, is ably holding the church at Corisco where he inherited the mantle of his sainted father, Rev. Ibia, who towered high among his fellows, and is cherished in memory as a man of marked ability and of weight in pulpit, parish, Presbytery.[84]

Ibia's story, only recently retrieved from mission archives, indicates that there is truly "nothing new under the sun" (Ecclesiastes 1:9) and that the church today is still trying to find balance in affirming culture, challenging unjust systems,

---

82 Nassau 1902, 106.
83 Nassau, "Ibiya," 442, 444.
84 Fraser, "What Missionaries are Doing," 24.

and standing firm in the faith. Pastor Ibia J'Ikenge models for us many of the traits mentioned in Romans 12 in his refusal to conform to the pattern of his contemporaries – whether of his own culture or even that of the missionaries serving among his people. His knowledge of Scripture and steadfast faith gave him the boldness to speak against hypocrisy as well as affirm the roles and giftedness of *all* members of the body of Christ, particularly women of faith, whose influence could transform their community for Christ. Ibia clearly welcomed a cooperative relationship with believers of other cultures but taught his people the value of independence, self-support, mutuality, and industry. Ibia and his wife offered hospitality and honor to Christians and unbelievers alike, little expecting that they would be immortalised in secular literature of their time. Though for many years he endured criticism and injury for his godly yet counter-cultural leadership, Ibia shows us that we can resist being *overcome by evil*, and truly *overcome evil with good* (Romans 12:21).

Questions for study (fact type):

1. Draw a timeline of Ibia's life that includes the following 7 key events: birth, conversion, marriage, licensing, ordination, installation, death.
2. What Presbyterian denomination founded the Corisco Mission?
3. Describe the social conditions for women and girls before the ministry of the Corisco Mission.
4. Explain the problem experienced by the Benga men with foreign traders. How did Ibia try to help the men to overcome this problem?
5. What is "Ukuku"?

Questions for study (reflection type):

1. Reflect on the schism between Rev. Ibia J'Ikenge and Rev. Cornelius De Heer. How could this schism have been avoided? Explain your solution using scripture to support your answer.
2. Explain the following statement: "Throughout his 45-year ministry, Ibia fought a war on two fronts – fighting against patriarchal Benga customs *and* against the mission patriarchy." Use examples to support your explanation.

Select Bibliography

American Colonization Society. "IBIA – The heathen boy of Corisco." *The African Repository* 37. 4 (April 1861): 120. http://books.google.com/books?id=iqooAAAAYAAJ&pg=PA120.

— — —. "Ordination of a Native African." *African Repository* 46. 11 (Nov. 1870): 350. http://books.google.com/books?id=qpAoAAAAYAAJ&pg=PA350.

Boteler, Capt. Thomas, R. N. *Narrative of a voyage of discovery of Africa and Arabia, performed by his majesty's ships Leven and Barracouta, from 1821 to 1826, under the command of Capt. F. W. Owen, R. N. in two volumes, Volume II.* London: Richard Bentley, 1835. http://books.google.com/books?id=TjlCAAAAcAAJ.

Ford, Edward A. "Persecution of a native pastor." *The Church at Home and Abroad* 10.12 (Dec. 1891): 530–531. https://www.google.com/books/edition/The_Church_at_Home_and_Abroad/P5IkAQAAIAAJ?

Fraser, Rev. Melvin. "What missionaries are doing in West Africa." *The Missionary Review of the World* 25.1 (1912): 22–29. http://books.google.com/books?id=cZ7NAAAAMAAJ&pg=PA24.

J'Ikenge, Ibia. "An African minister's report." *The Presbyterian Monthly Record* 22.2 (Feb. 1871): 51. http://books.google.com/books?id=5DYUAAAAYAAJ&pg=PA51

— — —. "An African Minister's Journal: April 16, 1879 [Part One]." *The Presbyterian Monthly Record* 30.10 (October 1879): 313–315. https://books.google.com/books?id=8kGPIGJubawC&pg=PA313

— — —. "An African Minister's Journal (Part Two)." *The Presbyterian Monthly Record* 30.11 (November 1879): 346–349. https://books.google.com/books?id=8kGPIGJubawC&pg=PA346

Kingsley, Mary Henrietta. *Travels in West Africa: Congo Français, Corisco and Cameroons.* London, MacMillan, 1897. http://books.google.com/books?id=sEcaAAAAYAAJ.

Mackenzie, Jean Kenyon. "The Black Commandments." *The Atlantic Monthly* 118 (Dec. 1916): 794–803. http://books.google.com/books?id=VIoRAAAAMAAJ&pg=PA794

— — —. *An African Trail.* West Medford, MA: The Central Committee on the United Study of Foreign Missions, 1917. https://www.google.com/books/edition/An_African_Trail/WS1lAAAAMAAJ?hl.

Mackey, Rev. J. L. "Hindrances at Corisco, West Africa." *The Home and Foreign Record of the Presbyterian Church in the United States of America* 15.7 (December 1864): 275–276.

Menaul, Rev. John. "A Visit to Ibia's Place." *The Record of the Presbyterian Church in the United States of America* 19.9 (Sept. 1868): 215. http://books.google.com/books?id=Cz4UAAAAYAAJ&pg=RA1-PA215.

Nassau, Robert Hamill. "Mainland work of the Corisco Mission." *Home and Foreign Record of the Presbyterian Church in the United States of America* 18.2 (March 1867): 61–63. http://books.google.com/books?id=Cz4UAAAAYAAJ&pg=PA61.

——. "Notices of Corisco and Benita work (letter dated July 27, 1870)." *The Presbyterian Monthly Record* 21.12 (December 1870): 278. http://books.google.com/books?id=weUqAAAAYAAJ&pg=PA278.

——. *Crowned in Palm-Land – A story of African mission life.* Philadelphia: Lippencott, 1874.

——. *A History of the Presbytery of Corisco.* Trenton, NJ: Brandt, 1888. http://books.google.com/books?id=C_8qAAAAYAAJ

——. "Rev. Ibia J'Ikenge." *The Assembly Herald* 6.3 (March 1902): 106–7. http://books.google.com/books?id=jpztAAAAMAAJ&pg=PA106.

——. "Some Ramifications of Polygamy." *The Assembly Herald* 8.6 (June 1903): 238–40. http://books.google.com/books?id=r2_UAAAAMAAJ&pg=PA238.

——. *Fetichism in West Africa.* London: Duckworth, 1904. http://books.google.com/books?id=-qUSAAAAYAAJ&pg=PA144.

——. "Ibiya: A West African Pastor." *The Missionary Review of the World* 27.6 (1914): 442–44. http://books.google.com/books?id=nnEJAQAAMAAJ&pg=PA442.

——. *My Ogowe: Being a narrative of daily incidents during sixteen years in Equatorial West Africa.* New York: Neake, 1914. http://books.google.com/books?id=WioUAAAAIAAJ&pg=PA237.

Presbyterian Board of Foreign Mission. "Corisco Mission Report [1858]." In *The Twenty-first Annual Report of the Board of Foreign Mission of the PCUSA*, 37–43. New York: Presbyterian Board Mission House, 1858. http://books.google.com/books?id=k7rNAAAAMAAJ.

——. "Corisco Mission Report [1859]." In *The Twenty-second Annual Report of the Board of Foreign Mission of the PCUSA*, 36–44. New York: Presbyterian Board Mission House, 1859.

——. "Corisco Mission Report [1860]." In *The Twenty-third Annual Report of the Board of Foreign Mission of the PCUSA*, 34–43. New York: Presbyterian Board Mission House, 1860.

——. "Corisco Mission Report [1861]." In *The Twenty-fourth Annual Report of the Board of Foreign Mission of the PCUSA*, 30–38. New York: Presbyterian Board Mission House, 1861.

——. "Corisco Mission Report [1863]." In *The Twenty-sixty Annual Report of the Board of Foreign Mission of the PCUSA*, 18–22. New York: Presbyterian Board Mission House, 1863. http://books.google.com/books?id=805AAQAAMAAJ.

— — —. "Gaboon and Corisco Mission [1873]." In *The Thirty-Sixth Annual Report of the Board of Foreign Mission of the PCUSA*, 31–37. New York: Presbyterian Board Mission House, 1873. http://books.google.com/books?id=dxtLAAAAMAAJ&pg=RA2-PA34.

— — —. "Gaboon and Corisco Mission [1891]." In *The Fifty-fourth Annual Report of the Board of Foreign Mission of the PCUSA*, 11–20. New York: Presbyterian Board Mission House, 1891. http://books.google.com/books?id=cnBJAAAAMAAJ&pg=RA1-PA18.

Rankin, William. *Memorials of Foreign Missionaries of the PCUSA*. Philadelphia: Presbyterian Board of Publication and Sabbath-School Work, 1895. http://books.google.com/books?id=9mzQAAAAMAAJ&pg=PA96.

Wilson, Samuel. *George Paull of Benita, West Africa – A Memoir*. Philadelphia: Presbyterian Board of Publication, 1872. http://books.google.com/books?id=XVAXAAAAYAAJ

Letters

Bushnell, Rev. Albert. Letter to Dr. Lowrie, dated 1 February 1878. Africa Letters: Vol. 12 Reel 74, Letter 98. Presbyterian Historical Society Archives (PHSA), Philadelphia.

— — —. Letter to Dr. Lowrie, dated 1 February 1878. Africa Letters: Vol. 12, Reel 74, Letter 102. PHSA.

Campbell, Graham. Letter to Dr. Lowrie, dated 6 March 1883. Africa Letters: Vol. 13, Reel 76, Letter 280. PHSA.

De Heer, Rev. Cornelius. "Notices of the Corisco Station – Letter of Rev. De Heer dated 18 Aug. 1873." *Presbyterian Monthly Record* 25.1 (January 1874): 176. http://books.google.com/books?id=_mvPAAAAMAAJ&pg=PA176.

— — —. "Notices of the Corisco Station." *The Presbyterian Monthly Record* 25.1 (Jan. 1874): 17. http://books.google.com/books?id=_mvPAAAAMAAJ&pg=PA17.

Good, Adolphus Clemens. Letter to Dr. Lowrie, dated 17 February 1883. Africa Letters: Vol. 13, Reel 76, Letter 278. PHSA.

J'Ikenge, Ibia. Letter to Dr. Lowrie, dated Sep. 1872. Africa Letters: Vol. 9, Reel 71, Letter 382. PHSA.

— — —. "Letter from Rev. Ibia, the Native Pastor at Corisco, to Miss Bella A. Nassau." *Woman's Work for Woman* 2.5 (Nov. 1872): 202. http://books.google.com/books?id=AhI3AAAAMAAJ&pg=PA202.

— — —. "Letter of Ibia J'Ikenge, to Miss B. A. Nassau, from Corisco, August 18, 1872." *Woman's Work for Woman* 2.6 (Jan. 1873): 272. http://books.google.com/books?id=ERI3AAAAMAAJ&pg=PA272.

— — —. Letter to Dr. Lowrie, dated Dec. 1881. Africa Letters: Vol. 13, Reel 75, Letter 117. PHSA.

.... Letter to Dr. Lowrie, dated 1 January 1883. Africa Letters: Vol. 13, Reel 76, Letter 264. PHSA.

.... Letter to Dr. Lowrie, dated 16 July 1884. Africa Letters: Vol. 13, Reel 76, Letter 62. PHSA.

.... Letter to Dr. Lowrie, dated 17 September 1883. Africa Letters: Vol. 13, Reel 76, Letter 290. PHSA.

.... Letter to Dr. Lowrie, dated 31 October 1884. Africa Letters: Vol. 13, Reel 76, Letter 88. PHSA.

Reutlinger, M. Louise. *Letter excerpt in Third Annual Report of the Woman's Presbyterian Board of Missions of the North-West*. Chicago: Blakeley, 1874. http://books.google.com/books?id=Zc1MAAAAMAAJ&pg=PA58.

.... Letter to Dr. Lowrie, dated 17 January 1878. Africa Letters: Vol 12, Reel 75, Letter 307. PHSA.

Sneed, Charity L. "Letter from Charity L. Sneed, a native Bible –reader, to the Martin Luther Mission Band, Wheeling, W. Virginia." *Woman's Work for Woman* 1.4 (January 1872): 159–160. http://books.google.com/books?id=vRE3AAAAMAAJ&pg=PA160 .

Chapter 12

The History of Presbyterian Missionary Work in Ghana & Togo before WW2 (In Two Parts)

Hans Blix Duodu

Chapter Outline
1. Introduction

Part One: The German Missionary Period 1828–1917
1. Biographical Survey of the Early Missionaries
2. The Socio-Spiritual Condition of the Gold Coast Before the Arrival of the Early Missionaries
3. The German Period Early Beginnings 1828–1840
4. The German Period Mission Revival, Conversions, and Expansion 1843–1917
5. The Bremen Mission of German Togoland 1847–1916

Part Two: The Adoptive Era of Scottish Presbyterian Take-Over 1918–Second World War
1. The Lingering Problem of Complete Attainment to Self-Church Government
2. The First World War
3. The Invitation to the Scottish Mission (United Free Church of Scotland)
4. The Journey to Full Independence and Presbyterianism
5. Conclusion

Inset: "The Mother of our Schools" – Akropong Seminary, est. 1848 – J. C. Whytock

1. Introduction

The late eighteenth and early nineteenth centuries saw a rise in foreign missionary activities, leading to gospel witness in distant corners of the world, with such notable examples as William Carey, 1793 in India, Adoniram Judson, 1812 in Burma and Livingstone, 1841 in Southern Africa.[1] The continent of Africa experienced its fair share of this resurgence in missionary activities, which will

---

1   *The Oxford Handbook of Presbyterianism,* 144.

see perhaps the first organised and sustained evangelical gospel witness taken to places like Ghana.

While early European settlers (although explorers and traders, originally) brought *some form* of the message of the gospel to Ghana (formerly the Gold Coast, owing to the vast gold deposits in areas bordering the coastal regions) as early as the 15th century,[2] it was not until the first half of the 19th century that the roots of what will later be a Presbyterian witness of the gospel reached the shores of Ghana in 1828 and later in 1847 in Togo, formerly German Togoland.

The earliest forebears of Presbyterian missionaries were the Basel group from Switzerland, who arrived in 1828, in a suburb of the present capital city, Accra. Suffering formidable early setbacks, they persevered in the Lord's blessings, and went on to achieve remarkable successes in the conversion of souls, establishing of a seminary, educational institutions, translation works and many more.

It will not be far-fetched to assert that some of these remarkable achievements re-galvanised interests in the mission field, which will later lead to the arrival of other missionaries – those joining the ranks of the established Basel mission, the Bremen missionaries who arrived in 1847 to work among the indigenes of the Ewe people in the erstwhile German Togoland and later the Scottish United Free Church (Presbyterians) towards the end of World War 1.

It is worth drawing attention to the use of the country name "Togo" as a reference to the area of missionary activity within what was formerly German Togoland, which was later split and partly absorbed into the present geographical Ghana.

This brief historical account of Presbyterian missionary work in Ghana and Togo will attempt to look at Presbyterian mission history from the beginnings through to circa the eve of the second World War. Efforts will be made to throw light on the dire spiritual needs of the indigenes prior to the arrival of the missionaries and the remarkable spiritual and practical blessings which later followed.

It must also be said that this survey is an unusual account of Presbyterian missionary history, as it really is the story of an originally non-presbyterian work being handed over to a Presbyterian mission group almost a century after its inception.

---

2   Harald Nielsen, "Ghana—The Gold Coast," 2. The first Catholic mass is believed to have taken place in January 1482 in the Gold Coast by the Portuguese, see, Cephas N. Omenyo, "Ghana, Liberia and Sierra Leone," in *Christianity in Sub-Saharan Africa*, eds. Kenneth R. Ross, J. Kwabena Asamoah-Gyadu and Todd M. Johnson. (Edinburgh: Edinburgh University Press, 2017), 203.

The chapter has two overarching parts:

- Part One will focus upon the German missionary period 1828–1917.
- Part Two will focus on the adoption period by the United Free Church of Scotland and through to the eve of WW2.

Part One: The German Missionary Period 1828–1917

1. Biographical Survey of the Early Missionaries

The German missionary period covers the period between 1828, being the year of arrival of the first missionaries, through to 1917/1918 near the end of the First World War.[3]

It is conveniently referred to as the German missionary period owing to the vast and varied contributions made by German Christian groups and individuals towards the mission cause in the Gold Coast and Togo. These contributions range from the formation of missionary societies in Switzerland and Northern Germany, a mission college in Basel to prepare missionaries, providing often very gifted and talented mission-field volunteers with training. These missionaries would eventually go on to change the course of the missionary work in the Gold Coast and Togo through their translation and other literary works.

The notable missionary societies of this period linked with the work in the Gold Coast and Togo are the Basel Mission, the Danish Mission, the Bremen Mission, the Moravian missionaries from the West Indies, and the Scottish Mission (UFCS). We shall consider each of these missionary groups to highlight their history and key individuals connected with their work in the Gold Coast and Togo.

The Basel Mission

The Basel Mission was formed in 1815 and was made up of people of diverse nationalities, mostly from Germany, Switzerland, and France.[4] Key missionaries associated with the mission who served in Ghana were: Johannes

▲ Andreas Riis

---

3   https://en.wikipedia.org/wiki/Presbyterian_Church_of_Ghana. Accessed 3 January 2023.
4   Babaloa, *Christianity in West Africa (An Historical Analysis)*, 78.

Phillip Henke, Gottlieb Holzwarth, Carl Friedrich Salbach, and Johannes Gottlieb Schmid, who were the first group of missionaries that arrived in the Gold Coast in 1828. Following eight months of arduous labour amongst the inhabitants of the Osu coast with some seed-sowing successes, they eventually succumbed to the harsh tropical weather and diseases. The Mission did not abandon the work, sending another group of missionaries in the persons of Andreas Riis, Peter Peterson Jäeger, and Christian Heinze, who arrived in 1832.

▲ J. G. Christaller

Two further notable missionaries linked with the Basel mission work in Ghana are Johann Gottlieb Christaller (19 November 1827–16 December 1895) and Johannes Zimmermann (2 March 1825–13 December 1876), both of German origin and renowned for their highly important translation works.

The Basel mission led the way in bringing the first organised evangelical gospel to the Gold Coast and continued the work for nearly a century until they left in 1917 during the First World War. Through the blessing of the Lord, their sacrifices, spiritual labours and achievements have earned them such a warm and enviable place in the hearts of the Ghanaian people.

▲ Mr & Mrs J. Zimmermann

The Danish Mission Society

Mainstream historical accounts of the Gold Coast gospel mission have not provided coverage for the contributions made by the Danish Mission Society (DMS), the reigning Danish monarch (King Frederick VI) and his relative (Prince Christian Frederik) at the time (in the year 1827) and other Danish contributors who played a key role in facilitating the execution of the Gold Coast mission cause. Among these ordinary Danish contributors was a well-connected 'nobleman' by the name Bone Falck Rønne, who was also the founder of the DMS (in 1821) and had tutored Prince Christian Frederik. The other worth mentioning is a Norwegian by the name Jørgen Cappelen who was sent by the DMS to study at the Basel Mission Society's (BMS) college. Cappelen, upon hearing the BMS's desire to establish a mission in the Gold Coast, passed on the idea to the DMS, doubtless with the firm hope that the Gold Coast being a Danish colony (at least a sizeable/strategic portion of the region) would meet the favour of the Danish ruling powers, which with historical hindsight was not unfounded. Thus, when we later read that the earliest missionaries were stationed in the

Danish's Gold Coast fort at Osu, called Christiansborg (translated Christian's castle), one will hardly wonder why it was so. Additionally, the DMS reports that "The first missionaries to the Gold Coast were sent jointly by DMS and the Basel Mission. This too goes for Andreas Riis, as mentioned the only survivor to continue the work."[5] If readers will pardon a slight digression, this same monarch King Frederik VI would have been the one who ultimately provided refuge to William Carey and his missionary entourage at Serampore in India,[6] when Carey was hounded out from the areas under the control of the East India Company. Praise be to God who raises such instruments (men [and women] of the hour) to advance His cause!

The West Indies Missionaries

"The work of the mission became stronger when Moravian missionaries from the West Indies arrived in the country in 1843." These are the words published in a web page in honour of the contribution of the West Indies missionaries to the spread of the gospel in the Gold Coast.[7]

The involvement of the missionaries from the West Indies arose chiefly from two main reasons: firstly, the frustration felt by the mission committee in Basel about the little, if not nil, progress made by the missionaries in the conversion of the natives despite the human cost and more than a decade of hard work on the mission field; and the second chief reason was the unfavourable tropical weather conditions which was claiming the lives of the European missionaries.

The committee took a decision to recall their missionary representative in the Gold Coast, Andreas Riis (who, it is reported, was suffering from ill-health) to Basel and effectively abandon the mission work. It is reported that it took a casual comment by a regional chief of Akropong-Akwapim (the area of mission activity) during a send-off durbar for the battered Riis to instil a challenge in Riis' mind to prove a point to the regional chief. The chief said "How can you expect so much from us? You have been staying among us all along for a short time only. When God created the world, He made the Book (Bible) for the European and animism (fetish) for the African, but if you could show us some Africans who could read the Bible, then we would surely follow you."[8] Certainly, at this period of world-wide missionary endeavours, Riis would have heard of African conversions in the West coast of Africa – Liberia, Sierra Leone,

---

5 Nielsen, "Ghana—The Gold Coast," 2.
6 https://en.wikipedia.org/wiki/Frederick_VI_of_Denmark, Accessed 11 February 2023. Schott, *Basel Mission on the Gold Coast: A Retrospect on Fifty Years of Mission Work*, 4–6.
7 https://en.wikipedia.org/wiki/Presbyterian_Church_of_Ghana. Accessed 3 January 2023.
8 https://en.wikipedia.org/wiki/Andreas_Riis. Accessed 3 January 2023.

and most certainly in the West Indies; thus the race to find Christian helpers in the African diaspora began, which will lead the Basel mission to Jamaica to find black African Christian converts to help in the work in the Gold Coast.[9]

In 1842, two years after Riis left the mission base in the Gold Coast, the Basel Mission sent a delegation, which included Riis, to the West Indies to find black missionaries. After careful examination of several candidates, they settled on a group of twenty-four people (all Jamaicans except one Antiguan). The group sailed from the Jamaican port of Kingston in February 1843 and arrived in the Gold Coast in April 1843. Among these volunteers were the names of A. W. Clerk, Greene, Hall, Horsford, Miller, Mullings, Robinson, Rochester, and Walker.

Alexander Worthy Clerk (4 March 1820–11 February 1906), was one of the Jamaican Moravian missionary pioneers who was elected the first deacon in the mission church at Akropong and later became a leader in education in the Gold Coast. He went on to become one of the inaugural faculty members of the Mission seminary at Akropong.[10]

▲ Alexander Worthy Clerk (centre)

The Moravian connection in recruiting and sending off helpers for the Gold Coast mission in 1843 is of historical interest. Their forebears in 1736, 1768 and 1809 made three unsuccessful attempts to establish missionary causes in the Gold Coast but had to abandon it due to high mortality among their missionaries and very little progress in the mission work.

---

9   https://en.wikipedia.org/wiki/Andreas_Riis. Accessed 3 January 2023.
10 https://en.wikipedia.org/wiki/Alexander_Worthy_Clerk Accessed 24 February 2022.

A Survey of Presbyterian Mission History in Africa

The Bremen Mission

The Bremen Mission Society was originally known as the North German Mission. It was formed by Reformed and Lutheran Christians in 1836 in Hamburg but later relocated to the German city of Bremen, hence its name the Bremen Mission.[11] The society established links with the Basel Mission which had been established in the Gold Coast two decades earlier; sending would-be missionaries to train at the Basel Mission College and later coordinating missionary activities together on the mission field in the Gold Coast and German Togoland.

In 1847 they arrived in the region east of the Gold Coast and settled amongst the Ewe people in a town called Peki, which was then part of the German Togoland.

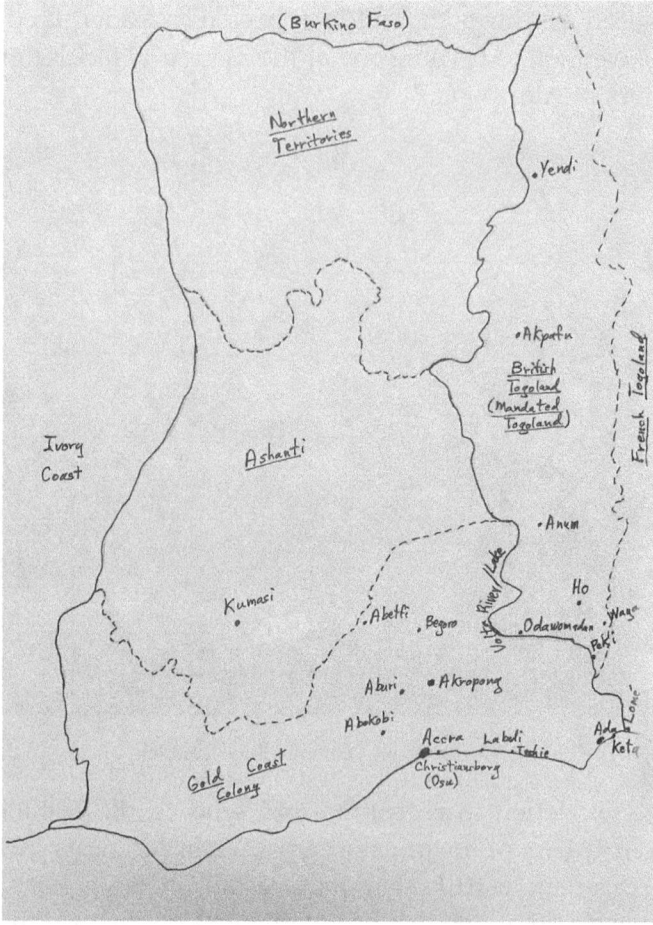

▲ Map of select Mission Stations of Basel & Bremen Societies in Gold Coast and British Togoland, c.1919

---

11 https://afribary.com/works/the-impact-of-the-bremen-mission-in-the-volta-region-of-ghana Accessed 24 February 2022.

Key missionaries associated with the Bremen missionary work are Johann Bernhard Schlegel (who translated the four gospels into the Ewe language), Weyhe, Merz, Jakob Spieth, and Gottlob Däuble. The areas of the Bremen missionary work among the Ewe people were: Peki, Keta, Waya, Anyako, Ho, and Amedzofe, all located in present day Volta region of Ghana.

The Scottish Mission

In December 1917, following the expulsion of the Basel missionaries of German descent from the Gold Coast and German Togoland (in 1916), the responsibility for overseeing and continuation of the missions' work fell on the United Free Church of Scotland (UFCS) who at the time had a station in Calabar, southeastern Nigeria. Such was the great and positive impact of the mission's work on the natives that the British colonial administration in their eagerness to preserve the mission work, apparently suggested the management of the mission be handed to the UFCS (doubtless influenced by men like J. H. Oldham of the UFCS, secretary of the International Missionary Council (IMC)), perhaps taking the view that they (UFCS) were much closely aligned to the Basel mission in theological convictions.[12]

The Scottish Mission thus took over from the Basel missionaries in 1917. They took responsibility until 1950, when the mission work was finally handed over to local church leaders. By all accounts, the Scottish Mission handled the takeover with the decorum needed in this unfortunate turn of events in the Basel Mission's work in the Gold Coast; striving not to overshadow the latter or take credit for the immense good which the latter had achieved in their close to hundred years of service in the Gold Coast. We see this propriety in the Scottish Mission's conduct, that they were resigned to the natives' desire to adopt a neutral name (as opposed to Basel or Scottish) for the Gold Coast mission (now a full-blown Church Denomination) who finally settled with the name *"The Presbyterian Church of the Gold Coast"*[13] during a Synod meeting in 1926, purposely timed to coincide with the return of the Basel missionaries in December 1925. Thus, a mission which previously started as a

▲ Crest of the Presbyterian Church of Ghana

---

12 https://www.ufcos.org.uk/about-us/history/ Accessed 24 February 2022.
13 Gyang-Duah, "The Scottish Mission factor in the Development of the Presbyterian Church of Ghana," 126, 343.

non-presbyterian – Lutheran/Reformed – had finally assumed a Presbyterian identity. Spiritual diplomacy in the Lord's goodness triumphed.

The man who led the Scottish Mission at this stage was Rev. Dr A. W. Wilkie, serving the 'orphaned' missions (Gold Coast and German Togoland) from 1918–1931. He is widely remembered for negotiating the return of the Basel and Bremen missionaries after the war, developing and nurturing the native churches to eventual independence.

Conclusion of Biographical Survey

This historical account of adopted Presbyterian missionary work in Ghana stands as a monument to what Christian unity can accomplish in leading souls to the Lord, promoting a Christian worldview through practical missions, etc. (without sacrificing core convictions) within the Protestant spiritual fraternity. It is therefore not surprising that the present Presbyterian churches in Ghana have for their motto *"that they all may be one"* and crown it all with an emblem which incorporates Swiss, Scottish, and Diaspora African/African symbols.

2. The Socio-Spiritual Condition of the Gold Coast Before the Arrival of the Early Missionaries

One is likely to fail to appreciate the vast accomplishments made by the Basel, Bremen, and Scottish Presbyterian missionaries, unless an awareness of the dire spiritual and social needs of the people before the arrival of the missionaries is understood.

Spiritual

The spiritual darkness that overshadows all societies cut off from the gospel light revealed in the Judeo-Christian faith was only too readily observable amongst the indigenes of the Gold Coast and surrounding regions prior to the arrival of the Basel missionaries. A very scholarly doctoral thesis by the learnt and former Moderator of the Presbyterian Church Ghana, Dr Sam Prempeh, provides an insight into the spiritual state of the land just before the First World War (1914):

> Professing Christians constituted about a third of the total population. In the North, however, the majority of the people were animists, but pockets of Muslim communities could be found.[14]

---

14 Prempeh, "The Basel and Bremen missions and their Successors in the Gold Coast and Togoland," 2.

If such a religious demographic observation could be made nearly a century after arduous missionary work, one could only imagine the spiritual state before missionary activities. Perhaps the following extracts of historical writings in the Gold Coast era, in chronological order, will help drive home the acute spiritual needs:

> i. [Prehistoric] Akan [which includes the Akwapim people among whom the Basel missionaries operated] believe in a supreme god who takes on various names depending upon the particular geographic region of worship. Akan mythology claims that at one time the god freely interacted with man, but after being continually struck by the pestle of an old woman pounding fufu, he moved far up into the sky. There are no priests that serve him directly, and people believe that they may make direct contact with him. There are also numerous *abosom* (gods), who receive their power from the supreme god and are most often connected to the natural world. These include ocean and riverine spirits and various local deities. Priests serve individual spirits and act as mediaries between the gods and mankind. Nearly everyone participates in daily prayer, which includes the pouring of libations as an offering to both the ancestors who are buried in the land and to the spirits who are everywhere. The earth is seen as a female deity and is directly connected to fertility and fecundity.[15]
>
> ii. In 1839, as already alluded to, the king of Akropong-Akwapim, mentioned to the stricken Basel missionary Riis, "How can you expect so much from us? You have been staying among us all along for a short time only. When God created the world, He made the Book (Bible) for the European and animism (fetish) for the African, but if you could show us some Africans who could read the Bible, then we would surely follow you."[16]
>
> iii. In 1874, at the signing of the Treaty of Fomena following the defeat of the Ashantis by the British, the following clause was made in the treaty: "The treaty also required an end to human sacrifice."[17]

---

15 http://www.101lasttribes.com/tribes/akuapem.html Accessed 24 February 2022.
16 https://en.wikipedia.org/wiki/Andreas_Riis Accessed 24 February 2022.
17 https://en.wikipedia.org/wiki/Anglo-Ashanti_wars Accessed 24 February 2022.

A quick glance through the above-mentioned extracts can only lead to the conclusion that animism and the Islam faith held sway amongst the people of the Gold Coast prior to the arrival of the missionaries. Islam, brought through the Saharan trade routes, and animist beliefs were religions in areas north of Akwapim, whereas centuries-old animism was the practice in the southern regions.

Social

On the subject of the social condition of the people of the Gold Coast and German Togoland the following: although the arrival of the European traders had already happened 350 years back, it will not be an exaggeration to say that the educational, economic and the general welfare of the indigenes were far from being their stated policy, at least not for the time being.[18] There would have been other preoccupations, for example the fierce struggle among the Europeans and some local dominant kingdoms for control of some of the lucrative trade in the region early in the nineteenth century. Thus, the natives remained destitute of the refinements that education and interactions with advanced cultures bring, to the extent that they lacked a written form of their language. The burden eventually fell on the missionaries, foremost of whom were Johann Gottlieb Christaller and Johannes Zimmermann, to develop Latinised scripts as a medium for the written forms of the native languages. Later in this survey, we shall see how the vehicle of written language led to the creation of educational institutions for training native converts for missionary work in addition to providing standard primary and advanced education to the natives.[19]

Conclusion

In this section, we have considered the spiritual and social needs of the natives of the Gold Coast and eastern bordering regions before the arrival of the missionaries as a way to prepare us to appreciate the enormous contributions made by the missionaries a century and a half later. We shall attempt to explore some of these achievements in greater detail in the ensuing sections of this survey.

---

18 https://en.wikipedia.org/wiki/Anglo-Ashanti_wars Accessed 24 February 2022.
19 Babaloa, *Christianity in West Africa (An Historical Analysis)*, 85.

3. The German Period Early Beginnings 1828–1840

Introduction

In the midst of all the mission advances in the late 18th and early 19th centuries, it pleased the Lord to lay it on the heart of Lutheran and Reformed Christians in Basel to consider a missionary venture in the Western coast of Africa, the Gold Coast, a place which, although well-known to Europeans, but as late as the early 19th century had very little to boast of in the form of organised gospel witness, let alone an evangelical form of witness.

"And there are also many other things which Jesus did, the which, if they should be written every one, I suppose that even the world itself could not contain the books that should be written …" (John 21.25 KJV). The vast activities, challenges and achievements of nearly a century's worth of missionary work present a formidable challenge for any historian to communicate in a book, let alone in a historical survey. Our earnest hope is that readers may find coverage of the location of missionary activities, mission entities and strategies, challenges, and achievements (in God's goodness seen in spiritual transformations and practical ways) as a helpful overview and basis for further research.

The German period is divided into two periods: *The Early Beginnings 1828–1840* and *The Mission Revival, Conversions, and Expansion 1843–1917*

The Early Beginnings 1828–1840

The key events of this period include the arrival of the Basel missionaries in 1828, early challenges, relocation to a more temperate region to escape the harsh tropical weather and diseases and the near closure of the mission in 1842.

> Wednesday, December 18th 1828 in the morning we got sight of Christiansborg. Fear and hope filled our hearts in perceiving the place of our destination. We saw crowds of Natives near the landing place, waiting for our arrival.
>
> At about 9 o'clock we landed at Christiansborg and were kindly received by a Danish officer, who brought us to the fort, where Governor Lind gave us a cordial welcome and promised to do all he could to assist us. He offered us lodgings in the fort, which we accepted etc.[20]

These are the words recorded in the diary of one of the first group of the missionaries who arrived in the Gold Coast in December 1828. They left

---

20 Schott, *Basel Mission on the Gold Coast: A Retrospect on Fifty Years of Mission Work*, 3–4.

▲ Christiansborg Fort

Denmark on 26 August 1828, travelling via Netherlands, England, and finally left England on the ship "The Hope" on 11 October 1828.

The location of the Christiansborg fort was to the east of the Gold Coast and to the west was the area of occupation by the English with their headquarters based in the Cape Coast Castle. It was the Danish Christiansborg that the missionaries will have their bases and carry out their spiritual work among the Danish settlers, the mixed-race affiliates known as the "mulattos" and doubtless the natives who availed themselves. A note by the Danish missionary patron Bone F. Rønne reads:

> Until now, they have preached in the fort (Christiansborg) every Sunday, and during the week, Holzwarth teaches school children the tunes they are going to sing in church on Sundays. The most able children can read but understand very little. Hencke is considering confirmation lessons and the two others would teach religion and understanding of reading materials. All teaching is in Danish, a language only few Negroes know, and that is why the missionaries to the best of their abilities are going to learn the local language.[21]

The men had not long been involved in their arduous mission engagements, when they were beset with illness. We read from the DMS records, "Schmid and Henke caught the climate-fever already in early 1829, reducing their work very much. Later that year Salbach caught the illness – and within the first year Holzwarth, Salbach and Schmid 'had gone home to their heavenly Father.' Henke held on a little longer. He did not die until 1831!"[22]

---

21 Nielsen, "Ghana—The Gold Coast," 4.
22 Nielsen, "Ghana—The Gold Coast," 4.

Was the Gold Coast mission embarked on by the BMS (with their DMS compatriots) going to suffer the same fate as the Moravians a century ago, when after three repeated attempts with great losses in human life they eventually bowed out from the mission field? Thanks be to God, a light had been set ablaze in a new breed of missionaries in that era of worldwide mission resurgence where young men and women were willing to avail themselves wherever the good Lord will send them. Thus, soon after news reached the mission societies back home, it pleased the Lord to raise up yet three men – two Southern Jutlanders, Peter Petersen Jaeger and Andreas Riis and the third one was a German doctor, C. F. Heinze.

The three young men arrived in the Gold Coast in March 1832. However, the season of rejoicing was to be brief, as just six weeks after arrival, the climate fever had overcome Dr Heinz. Jaeger soon followed Heinz to glory on the 18th July 1832. A brief pause for reflection at this point may cast our minds back into biblical and church histories, when the good Lord appears to use such 'dark' moments to teach us to look away from self and place our confidence in Him. The Lord was gracious to the mission societies and their praying supporters, in that it pleased the Lord to preserve the life of one of the three, Andreas Riis, who through much pain and sorrow would go on to lead the mission into a new era of steady growth.

Following the death of his missionary compatriots, Riis persevered in the mission work at the Christiansborg; as reported by the BMS in their 1879 reflections on the mission work,

> After the death of his brethren he preached and worked for some years among the Danish officers and Mulattos in the capacity of a Chaplain and Teacher to the Mulatto children. It was an arduous and thankless task, as Henke had experienced it before him. But patiently he waited for the direction of the Lord. In 1835 a Danish Chaplain took charge of the corrupted generation on the coast. Meanwhile Riis' interest was more and more drawn towards the Interior and especially to Akropong, the capital of Akuapim.[23]

The report provides a firsthand insight into the preserving grace of God over Riis life, the nature of his lonely mission work, misgivings with his mission base and desire to relocate to a more conducive place, evidently better suited for his health and mission work. Thus in 1835, Riis relocated to a region roughly 45 miles north of fort Christiansborg. The Christiansborg fort was located in the region called Accra, with Riis' new mission base directly 40–45 miles north from Accra.

---

23 Schott, *Basel Mission on the Gold Coast: A Retrospect on Fifty Years of Mission Work*, 6.

Conclusion of the First Phase

In 1835 following Riis's relocation to Akropong, he founded the first missionary church at the town, which continues to this day with the name Christ Presbyterian Church. Such was the warm welcome from the natives that Riis was moved to appeal to the mission society not to abandon the work. This appeal was followed by the sending of three new missionaries (J. Murdter and A. Stanger) among whom was the first lady missionary (Miss M. A. Wolter), who would go on to become Mrs Riis. It pleased the Lord to preserve the lives of Murdter and Stranger; but between the space of a year to fourteen months, they both departed to glory, leaving only Riis and his wife. This would have been a heartbreaking experience for Riis, eight missionary lives lost in the space of ten years, and they were yet to see one convert. Riis himself suffered recurring ill-health and returned to Basel in July 1840, having before embarked on a journey north-west of Akropong to visit Kumasi (or Kumase), the capital of the Ashanti people to explore possibilities of future mission work.

The achievements of this phase of the mission's work could be seen in terms of seed-sowing – establishing of a new mission base, preparation of the heart of the natives toward the gospel who will eventually embrace the faith.[24] The disengagement of the mission from the established European settlers in the coastal areas was particularly key for the mission's future success, owing to the latter's association with the slave trade, it was important for the mission to preserve an untarnished and distinct image to the natives. In Riis' own words, "a successful missionary work for the benefit of the tribes in the interior ought to take its starting point from a place, where European vices [Riis may be referring to other vices rather than slavery as the Danes had banned slavery in 1802] did not interfere with the propagation of the Gospel."[25]

4. The German Period Mission Revival, Conversions, and Expansion 1843–1917

The work of the mission was suspended in the intervening months and years during Riis' departure for medical rehabilitation in Europe from summer 1840 to April 1843. During this period of medical care, he advocated for the resumption of the mission work in spite of the serious setbacks which he and others had endured in the preceding ten to fifteen years of the work. The home Society in Basel were understandably resigned to the closure of the mission, but it pleased

---

24 Prempeh, "The Basel and Bremen missions and their Successors in the Gold Coast and Togoland," 2.
25 Schott, *Basel Mission on the Gold Coast: A Retrospect on Fifty Years of Mission Work*, 9, 20.

the Lord to raise a new Inspector of the Society in the person of Rev. W. Hoffmann, who urged the mission on to find new ways to get to the field.[26] Riis would have shared with Rev. Hoffmann and the entire society some of the positive developments on the field, examples being (a) the local chief's challenge to Riis to show him an African who reads the Bible, (b) the Church which he [Riis] had established in 1835, (c) the delight and warmth of the natives in the interior territories towards the mission cause and many more. The Society set up a committee to search for missionary volunteers of African descent to be sent to the mission field which led to the aforementioned twenty-four volunteers from the West Indies accepting the call to serve the Lord in the Gold Coast. Their arrival, together with Riis and a few others in April 1843, marked a key development in the mission's journey and set in motion a new chapter which saw an onward march to spiritual exploits. We read in the BMS's report of 1879 that by 1848 (five years after the 1840–1843 break and the arrival of the West Indian missionaries) there were 40 conversions among natives, 20 West Indian brethren still serving, 300 children received regular instruction, between 1838–48 only one missionary died (compared with eight deaths in a space of ten years a decade earlier), and regular prayers convened by new converts for the health of the missionaries. By 1858, regular church members had risen to 385, with a further 90 candidates for baptism. The year 1847 also saw the eastward expansion of the mission field to Peki in German Togoland through the arrival of the Bremen missionaries in that year. In no way exhaustive, yet the stellar growth of the mission at this stage may be seen in the following four (4) broad areas:

▲ David Asante

i) Spiritual Gains – if spiritual gains may be measured in a whole-hearted embrace of the unpopular truths of the "whole counsel of God" manifested in a sustained, transformed life of identifying with the Word and the people of God, then the Gold Coast mission was not behind in such attainment; for the mission could report that by the year 1879, there were 1,870 communicants, 288 non-communicants, 1,803 children and 178 catechumens all under the care of the mission. The mission had nine stations where the whole counsel of God was regularly taught and heralded to the natives to receive the heavenly truths. Children enrolled in the mission's various boarding schools were increasingly

---

26 Schott, *Basel Mission on the Gold Coast: A Retrospect on Fifty Years of Mission Work*, 8. Smith, *Presbyterian Church of Ghana*, 19–20.

won over to gospel ways, abandoning the unwholesome manners of their unregenerate upbringing which almost invariably were morally and spiritually harmful. The educational institutions were part of the mission's broader plan to produce literate natives who would be able to devote themselves to catechist and seminary studies to lead the work long after the European missionaries had stood aside or gone; thus achieving its aim in producing men like David Asante (23 December 1834–13 October 1892, first Akan native BMS's missionary, church planter, philologist, linguist and translator) and Theophilus Opoku (1842–July 1913, son of Akan royal linguist, gifted linguist, translator, philologist, educator and missionary) who made profound contributions in ministry and translation works.

ii) Education – The mission's attitude towards education may be captured in their own words:

> Our Schools, the most flourishing part of our African Mission, received every attention, because we must have a staff of well-educated Native assistants, before we reach our aim, the future independence of a Native Church. Boarding Schools were therefore opened in all our Districts for boys and girls, besides the Day Schools at each Station and Outstation. Our readers remember that, for a good while, a great number of the children under instruction were either orphans or belonged to heathenish families. In many cases also either the father or the mother were yet unconverted. It is clear that with children living with their ungodly relations the good influence of the school is apt to be weakened by the venomous influence of paganism. This is less the case with our Boarding Scholars, who live entirely with the Missionaries under strict discipline. It was no easy task to induce parents to give their children, especially their daughters, to the Missionaries for education. However all prejudices gradually disappeared by the enlightening influence of the Gospel.[27]

Although progress had been made towards education in the Gold Coast, almost exclusively by the missionaries, from as early as the days of the first BMS missionaries, nothing could be compared to the educational reforms from 1858–1861 in the mission schools embarked on by J. G. Auer, a German schoolmaster from Wurttemberg sent to the Gold Coast by the BMS. Smith reports that:

---

27 Schott, *Basel Mission on the Gold Coast: A Retrospect on Fifty Years of Mission Work*, 11.

> The proper organisation of the day schools had to wait for J. G. Auer, a Wurttemberg schoolmaster, who between 1858 and 1861 gave the Basel Mission school system a distinct pattern, one which was adopted by the [Gold Coast] Government, and which remains substantially the same to this day [Smith writing in the year 1966]. His [Auer's] problem was that of bridging the gap between the elementary schools and the Seminary, which he solved by the creation of Middle Schools [circa post-16 years education].[28]

Prempeh reports that by 1923, just a few years after the expulsion of the German missionaries, the mission's century-old education network could boast of 15,917 active pupils, 239 schools and 462 teachers (no doubt with teaching assistants supporting the teachers). On closer look, one can see that the mission's education system was all-encompassing for its standard, acknowledging that Gospel ministry should not be limited to the needs of the soul, but soul winners must seek to do good to men wherever possible. Thus, efforts were made to teach the natives how to read and write, equipping them to explore the beauties of the Creator's natural world, to innovate, engage in commerce and industry, interact with other cultures/civilisation, and for those gifted for the noble call to ecclesiastical service, seminary training was made available. Some of the subjects taught were reading, writing, grammar, the elements of arithmetic, the outlines of geography, Bible stories and Bible reading, the learning by heart of Scripture passages and of Hymns and singing. Others included English language, field and garden work (for boys), sewing, knitting and crochet work (for girls).

Those in the seminary were taken through the rigours of courses such as Introduction to the Old and New Testament, History of the Church, Exegesis and Reading of the Bible in the Original: Hebrew and Greek, Exercises and Grammar in these languages, Homiletical and Catechetical Exercises, Doctrines of Faith, Biblical Ethics and Comparison of Christian Churches (Knowledge of symbols). The seminarians were expected to do practical training, accompanying their teachers once or twice a week in open-air preaching in nearby villages or in preaching tours (limited to advanced seminarians).[29] Ghana today can boast of at least six prominent post-16 years institutions, among which are five Teacher Training colleges, at least two highly-rated boys and girls boarding schools, and a school for the Blind, all closely connected with the work of the Basel mission and its Scottish co-workers. The first university in Ghana established in 1948,

---

28 Smith, *Presbyterian Church of Ghana*, 43, 45.
29 Schott, *Basel Mission on the Gold Coast: A Retrospect on Fifty Years of Mission Work*, 30–32.

University of Ghana Legon, had almost all of its founding faculty come from Achimota College, formerly the Prince of Wales College. The leader of the Scottish Mission, Rev. Dr A. W. Wilkie was part of the committee that established the Achimota College.[30]

iii) Translation Works – If the steam engine could be said to be one of the catalysts behind the 18th century industrial revolution, then major advances in translation works from the 1850s to late 1860s in the Gold Coast mission may be said to be its equivalent. Attempts at translation of the Bible to the vernacular or learning the vernacular languages had been made by men like Andreas Riis, his nephew Hans Nicolaus Riis, but it became apparent that if the mission was to achieve its goal in evangelising the natives and to lead them to full independence, then major advances were required in the area of translation.

We have already heard the complex situation faced by the missionaries in a multilingual mission-field; the area where the mission had its original headquarters had in a twenty – thirty miles neighbourhood nearly five native languages. However, like Carey in India (who prioritised the Indian Sanskrit), the missionaries observed that the lingua franca of the region, and even beyond (owing to both the dispersion of the Akan people having the Twi as a root language and the preceding hegemony of the Akan Ashanti kingdom in all of the Gold Coast) were that of the Akan Twi and the Ga languages. They set out to work on these languages, aided by some of their fine seminary products in the persons of David Asante and Theophilus Opoku, who assisted translation luminaries like Johann Gottlieb Christaller (arriving in 1852) and Johannes Zimmermann (arrived in 1850). The former, Christaller, is renowned for his work on the Akuapim Twi language, with Zimmermann stationed at Odumase-Krobo, who worked on the Ga language.

By 1853, the oral form of the Akuapim dialect of the Twi language had assumed a written form, and in 1871, Christaller with his native assistants had completed the translation of the full Bible into Akuapim Twi. Other works by Christaller include his Scientific Grammar of the Twi language (1875) and the *Dictionary of the Asante and the Fante Language – called* Twi (1881). Zimmermann on the other hand focused on the Ga language of the Ga-Adangme region, which included the area of the Christiansborg. By 1865, he had translated the whole Bible into Ga. With the completion of the whole Bible into these two lingua franca languages, other works followed or were done concurrently, notably hymns, educational literature and in all probability theological works; we may discern this from the Home Committee's report in 1879:

---

30 Gyang-Duah, "The Scottish Mission factor in the Development of the Presbyterian Church of Ghana," 338, 349–350, xxii–xxiii.

> In travelling from Christiansborg to Odumase, we pass villages with five different languages: Ga or Akra, Tshi, Kyerepong, Ewe and Adangme. Which of these shall be adopted as the common medium of intercourse in church and school? Or shall we choose the easy and slothful way of preaching in English or in German and leave it to the Natives to understand what we mean to say? Nay! That would be against all common-sense! We deemed it therefore our duty to cultivate two of the chief vernacular tongues, the Ga or Akra and the Tshi [Twi], to become written languages. We succeeded so far as to have now a great number of useful Schoolbooks of every description and, above all, the translation of the whole Bible in both. The late Rev. J. Zimmermann finished the Ga translation in the Jubilee-year of our Society 1865, and Rev. Christaller issued his excellent Tshi Old and New Testament a few years later. The latter language is spoken by at least one million of Negroes on the Gold-Coast, far to the interior. We are greatly indebted to the British and Foreign Bible Society, who have generously paid the expenses of printing these translations.[31]

iv) Resourcefulness and Economic Self-Sufficiency – While the Home Board in Basel supported the missionaries in their practical needs, notwithstanding the ever-growing needs of the missionaries and the mission work would require other noble and complementary ways to cater for it. In 1843, there were 24 West Indians to feed and clothe, mission stations to staff with native assistants, mission schools to staff and equip, and much more. The economic situation in the Gold Coast in the nineteenth century was dire, sparing the coastal dwellings where the Europeans had made their mark, the nearby interiors lacked access roads, often thick jungle forests. Commerce was limited to the coastal dwellings and many products were imported into the Gold Coast. In such dire situations, the mission took steps which we refer to in their 1879 report:

> Another department in our work received its development between 1858 – 1868. Our friends are aware that our Missionary work is not limited to preaching and teaching alone. We think it not only right, but our bounden duty, to make our Christians from the Gentiles partakers of the social blessings, which we abundantly derive from Christianity. For this purpose,

---

31 Schott, *Basel Mission on the Gold Coast: A Retrospect on Fifty Years of Mission Work*, 13–14.

> Industrial Establishments were opened at Christiansborg for joiners, wheel wrights, lock-smiths, blacksmiths, shoemakers and book-binders. Our industrial brethren had to overcome many difficulties with their workshops. We are therefore thankful to state that, in this branch too, we have not laboured in vain. After many trials the different establishments became self-supporting, and all these different trades tended to promote Christian diligence, honesty and sobriety. These work shops have not only enabled the Europeans to build more salubrious and comfortable dwellings than those they first inhabited, but the natives too, following our example, have improved upon their former style of domestic architecture. All the social changes, which this branch of our work brought to the Gold-Coast, are uniformly appreciated and speak for themselves to everyone who has eyes to see and sense enough to observe past and present.[32]

Basel Mission Trading Company

Smith also reports:

> The commercial enterprise of the Mission, which became known as the Basel Mission Trading Factory, arose from the problem of obtaining supplies. So much of the time of the missionaries was consumed in this task that in 1854 the Committee sent out Hermann Ludwig Rottmann, aged twenty-two, to take control of the Mission imports and finances. He opened a store in Christiansborg, purchased the coffee grown in Akropong for export, stocked general goods and school materials, and despatched up country the requirements of the various stations. In 1859 the business had flourished so well that it was put under a special Trading Commission established by the Home Board on a share-holding basis. The Missionary Society itself held shares and prominent Basel laymen also subscribed; the profits accruing to the Mission being used in the development of its work. According to the registration notice of the Commission in Basel its aims were to fulfil the requirements of the Mission with European goods, to supply raw materials to the mission workshops and to Christian

---

32 Schott, *Basel Mission on the Gold Coast: A Retrospect on Fifty Years of Mission Work*, 13.

groups at the most advantageous terms, to promote the welfare of the people by giving an example of Christian industry in honest commerce. In a country where there was little organised commerce the Mission factory filled a great need.[33]

On the success of this avenue of ministry, Smith reports:

> To the non-Christians the followers of the new religion gave an example of steady industry. After morning prayers the Christians repaired to their plantations, perhaps to try out new crops and new methods of cultivation. The coffee which was head-loaded to the coast and there sold provided money for new needs, clothing, school fees, and imported household utensils and tools. Trained artisans returned from Christiansborg equipped with new skills in masonry, joinery and blacksmithing and set up their small workshops. This industriousness meant that there was no real poverty: parents were able to help with the cost of the education of their children in the boarding schools and to contribute in a small way to the work of the Mission.[34]

In concluding this inspiring period of the mission's work, the words of Schott truly capture the seemingly long journey they had travelled, the sacrifices, and the unmistakable hand of the Almighty in all this:

> And now looking back on half a century of patient toil and remembering the cares and troubles, the hundredfold obstacles of every description, the loss of valuable lives, and, for nearly thirty years, the slow and humble progress of this work, must we not exclaim that this corn of wheat too had to fall into the ground and die? And yet when the last twenty years pass review before our spiritual eyes, and we observe the joyous progress and flourishing present condition of this Mission field, are we not also bound to acknowledge, how gloriously the Lord fulfils His promise of making the corn of wheat to bring forth much fruit?[35]

---

33 Smith, *Presbyterian Church of Ghana*, 43, 45.
34 Smith, *Presbyterian Church of Ghana*, 99–100.
35 Schott, *Basel Mission on the Gold Coast: A Retrospect on Fifty Years of Mission Work*, 3–4.

Smith's account of the mission's progress in this era (which he describes partly as "The Period of Consolidation") is worthy of note:

> It is a period during which certain names stand out: David Asante, Alexander Clerk, Nicholas Clerk, Jonathan Palmer, Theophilus Opoku, Edward Samson, Joseph Mpere, Paul Mohenu (the evangelist and converted heathen fetish priest), John Hall, Peter Hall, Esau Ofori, Jonas Martinson and Carl Reindorf among the Africans, and J. G. Christaller, J. Zimmermann, Simon Suss, J. G. Widmann, J. A. Mador, J. G. Auer, J. D. Dieterle, E. Schrenk, A. L. Rottmann and A. Lang among the missionaries. By 1870 their endeavours had resulted in the firm establishment of a Christian mission which not only through its evangelical work but also through its educational, agricultural and commercial enterprises, had begun to make its presence strongly felt. The achievements during this period were remarkable: eight main stations were established, Christiansborg, Abokobi, Aburi, Akropong, Kibi, Odumase-Krobo, Anum and Ada; the Twi and Ga tongues were reduced to writing; there was the nucleus of a properly ordered educational system; a seminary for the training of African leaders of the new Christian groups was flourishing; many experiments had been made with cash crops, notably cotton, coffee and cocoa; the first road in the eastern province had been constructed from Christiansborg across the plain and along the Akwapim Ridge; artisans were being trained in well-equipped workshops; and organised commerce in local commodities and European goods had been begun.[36]

The frail mission which began in 1828 has now assumed a stature which was able to weather the storms to maintain its expanding course. Not only do we see hearts turned to the Lord among the natives, we also see congregations being established at various strategic locations in the country, educational institutions from primary, secondary, post-secondary and Training/Seminary being established, native languages now given literary forms acting as media to dispense heavenly truths and natural sciences, infrastructural projects to facilitate the mission's spiritual and practical projects being rolled out and commercial ventures to support missionary work wisely undertaken.

---

36 Smith, *Presbyterian Church of Ghana*, 31–32.

Strategy

In closing this section, it may be worthwhile highlighting some of the strategies adopted by the mission in their second attempt at the work in the Gold Coast. While the mission maintained its overriding goal to evangelise the Gold Coast, it was forced to adopt new strategies in this second attempt of the mission to the Gold Coast. In Smith's scholarly thesis on the Presbyterian Church of Ghana, he reports that the new and courageous Hoffmann who led the Society in 1843 realised that the earlier approach of sending a few missionaries who often succumbed to the harsh tropical climate would not work, and it was time to implement an approach where the mission base would be made up of second and third generation Africans working together with their European brethren. This may also be seen in the later Christian settlements called 'Salem' communities, where a mission station will encourage Christian converts to move into the mission's vicinity to form a closely-knit community. Smith reports that it was in response to the exacting burdens of the natives' pagan manners which pervaded almost all facets of the social fabric:

> But if the tenacity of traditional life and custom prevented the attainment of the highest ideals of Christian brotherhood, we must not underestimate the achievement and example of the new Christian groups in setting forth a new way of life. Every morning at dawn, in the Salems in many towns and villages, the church bell rang out calling men and women to praise the God and Father of the Lord Jesus Christ. Through the singing of a hymn, the reading of a Bible portion, a short exhortation and fervent prayer, the Christians offered themselves and their day to God. Again on Friday evenings at the prayer-meeting and on Sundays at worship, their faith and zeal were renewed. In the new Christian Asafo [Church or spiritual army] the ties of filial obligation were widened to include all men and the new ethic of love and forgiveness began to operate. Above all, the Bible and the new Twi hymns become the source and expression of the new-found faith; the Bible was much read and many converts learned passages by heart. The Twi hymns became the battle-cry of the Christian Asafo: "Let us sing a song to our Saviour, who makes us dwell in quietness and blesses us daily; let us praise and thank Him for He hears our prayer and watches over us. You people of the world, come and listen. He is your Saviour too, look at Him well! Abosom [idols] are worthless, idols are nothing. Serve Jesus Christ, He who Saves your life.[37]

---

37 Smith, *Presbyterian Church of Ghana*, 99–100.

We should not forget Josenhans, another courageous and visionary leader of the BMS in the 1850s who marshalled the mission's focus and energy to work on developing the main vernacular languages (Twi and Ga) of the natives into literary forms to speed up evangelistic efforts and facilitate the broader mission goals.

Yet, when all has been said and done, it is the Lord through his Spirit who blesses and grants the increase!

5. The Bremen Mission of German Togoland 1847–1916

In our introduction of missionary biographies, we established that the Bremen Mission Society originally started in 1836 as the North German Mission (Norddeutsche), in Hamburg, Germany. They were made up of mainly Reformed and Lutheran Christians and following the constitution of their Society, they established links with the Basel Mission Society, sending their missionary candidates for training in the latter's Mission College in Basel. By the eve of the First World War, historical accounts indicate that they had made missionary attempts in New Zealand, India and later the Gold Coast.

In May 1847, their missionaries Lorenz Wolf, Jens Graff, Luer Bultmann and Carl Flato arrived in the Gold Coast, in the coastal town called Cape Coast, (although originally meant to go to French Gabon, Bultmann attempted unsuccessfully to establish a Gospel witness there but faced fierce opposition from the French administration). The mission eventually settled in the south-eastern town of the Gold Coast called Peki, among the Ewe people, in November 1847 but lost three of their missionaries Bultmann, Flato and Graff to the harsh tropical conditions during this period. Due to threats of invasion by the Ashantis, they relocated southwards to the Coast in a place called Keta. According to historical sources, they had two main mission posts, Peki and Keta, but eventually their mission expanded to surrounding regions. For example, Smith reports that owing to practical difficulties in operating in two jurisdictions (British and German Togoland), the Basel Mission handed various of their outposts to the Bremen Mission, including Akpafu, Worawora, Ntsumuru, Kpandu, Vakpo and twelve village congregations making a total of 932 baptised Christians. By the end of the nineteenth century, they had firmly established their missions in Peki, Ho, Amedzofe, and Lome.[38]

In this brief survey of the work of the Bremen mission, efforts will be made to highlight the main missionaries associated with the work, the prevailing spiritual and practical difficulties faced, their achievements, the later connection

---

38 Smith, *Presbyterian Church of Ghana*, 136.

with Presbyterianism and the impact which the First World War had on their work.

Like all other southern people groups in the Gold Coast region, the Ewe were animist in their religious beliefs, believing that the creative order was possessed with spirit beings who had the power to impart good or inflict harm. They have been associated with the Vodun and Fon religious beliefs, claiming *mawu* to be the creator god and *trowo* as lesser deities. In a belief system held as Si, implying a spiritual marriage between the deity and the faithful (*Fofie-si* refers to faithful of the deity *Fofie*, *mawu-si* faithful of *mawu*), devotion to these gods is not uncommon. They also practiced ancestral worship.[39] Accusations of some of the most wicked acts against human lives emanating from such belief systems, as already highlighted in the case of the Akan tribes, have been associated with practices in the Ewe belief system, of which a quote (possibly in 1883) in an MPhil thesis by Asante, is apt:

> After Steven Kwami had criticised the fiaga (king) for sacrificing a human being …, the fiaga blocked the paths leading from Kpodzi to the other Peki towns and the direct way to the river. As a result, no inhabitants of the Peki towns could attend church services, and to fetch water the inhabitants of Kpodzi had to walk forty-five instead of fifteen minutes. The whole matter ended up in a scuffle …. The fiaga justifies his measures with the claim that 'the Governor of Accra gave him all these places to rule over it and do whatever he liked on it either good or bad, and nobody can accuse him of anything either a white man or black man.[40]

Additionally, the following account in the later experience of the Bremen missionaries being prevented from reaching the interior regions highlights the religious beliefs of the Ewes:

> However, they were prevented by the Anlo Chief because they claimed that the hinterland was reserved for the great Anlo deity (Troga) and the people living there should not be exposed to the gospel of the missionaries.[41]

---

39 https://en.wikipedia.org/wiki/Ewe_people, accessed 4 March 2023.
40 Asante, "Impact of The Bremen Mission in The Volta Region of Ghana," 55.
41 Asante, "Impact of The Bremen Mission in The Volta Region of Ghana," 51.

Besides the dire spiritual challenges in the mission-field faced by the missionaries, they had the practical difficulty of language to overcome in their efforts to bring the Gospel to the people of Ewe; although comparatively less daunting to that of the multi-lingual regions which their Basel missionary brethren faced.

Following the failed Gabon gospel expedition, Wolf and Graff moved to Christiansborg where they consulted with their Basel missionary acquaintances on possible areas for mission work in the Gold Coast. It was suggested to them to try the eastwards spiritually barren land of the Ewe people, and providence had it that an Ewe prince (Nyangamagu, son of Tutu, Togbui Dei, paramount King of *krepi*) studying at Christiansborg suggested Peki.[42] Following this recommendation, the missionaries travelled North-eastwards to Peki, from Christiansborg, and arrived in November 1847. An account on their arrival indicates they were accorded very warm reception. The missionaries set out to assure the natives that their mission was to bring the gospel of salvation to them, and not to buy slaves nor deprive them of their lands (in sharp contrast to the natives' previous experience with slave traders). Wolf and Graff set out to establish a mission base, and in January 1848, Wolf [Graff had gone home to glory in Nov 1847) had a mission house to operate from, which later became the nucleus and launching site of their later wider missionary activities. That the early gains in Christian witness achieved through the work of their missionary compatriots (Basel Missionaries) may be seen from the words of Wolf:

> Abutia [an area in Ewe], now we observed that we had reached Krepi country. We concluded this from the fertility of the land and from the cleanliness and diligence of the natives. November 14, 1847, in the morning at Anum. Thousands were assembled in the market place and welcomed me with music and shouts of joy. The Chief and his elders wanted to speak with us but as I was in a hurry, I asked them to meet me later at Peki. First day at Peki: Tutu, when being informed of my arrival, had ordered all people who were free from work to change the path leading from Anum to Peki about half an hour's walk into a broad road so that I might walk in comfort. When I was not far from Peki, the King's son whom I had seen at Accra with some of the confidants of the King met me on the way and said he had sent them to lead me home. I shook hands with him and greeted him. My reception and the welcome accorded to me by the people and the King at Peki was too glorious for a poor

---

42 Asante, "Impact of The Bremen Mission in The Volta Region of Ghana," 26.

missionary. The town consisted of three places. When I passed the first one (Dzake) it was the most beautiful African village I had ever seen, clean houses and a line of trees on both sides of the broad street – people shouted with joy and accompanied me by the hundreds. The same happened at the second place (Avetile). The people went with me to the house of the King's son at Blengo where I was to lodge. I hardly sat down when two volleys of gun-fire greeted me. It was said Tutu had done this in order to honour me.[43]

In 1849, Wolf was serving alone in Peki, and was later joined by Friedrich Groth, Friedrich H. Quinius (in 1849), and then in 1850 by Koroline Deist, who became Mrs Wolf. As a woman, Koroline was able to address certain aspects of the mission's work that were greatly needed at this time. However, the joys which the arrival of extra missionaries brought did not last long. The tropical diseases and the discouraging revolutionary chaos in Germany took their toll on the Wolfs and their colleagues, who all returned to Hamburg in 1851. Lorenz Wolf died shortly thereafter.

The Bremen Society Board were now on the verge of abandoning the Ewe mission, just like their Basel friends had resolved to on Andreas Riis's return to Basel in 1840. In their moment of despair and giving up, the thought came to their mind to consult their Basel missionary friends for advice. This consultation proved pivotal in the resumption of the mission to the Ewe people. The friends at Basel offered trained missionaries from their mission school to support the work in the land of Ewe.[44] These were Wilhelm Dauble and Johannes Menge, who arrived in 1852 to support the work which Wolf and others had begun, settling in Peki. They soon resolved to relocate the mission base to Keta at the southern Coast, east of Christiansborg, where they could hope for a favourable climate and also escape the constant threats of war between the Ashantis and other tribe groups.

In September 1853 they were temporarily housed in the Danish garrison fort in Keta, and set out to build their own mission house, which was completed that year, but their hope for an improved temperate/favourable climate was quashed when soon Dauble was taken ill and died in December 1853. By now another missionary, Plessing had joined. He was later joined by Brutschin (arriving January 1854). The missionaries pressed on with the work and in 1855, after

---

43 https://en.wikipedia.org/wiki/Peki_(Krepi), accessed 4 March 2023.
44 See the 1886 Report for the 50th Anniversary of the Bremen Mission [Norddeutsche] by Franz Michael Zahn. Accessible in the Bremen State Archive: St.AB NM-2417. An English translation is available. See Select Bibliography.

seven years of much toil mixed with 'blood,' they witnessed their first converts – seven converts in that year. One reports:

> The missionaries had laboured for seven years, buried seven of their members during this period and now had won seven souls for the Lord: Thus after many years of disappointments, the missionaries had the encouragement that their labour had begun to bear concrete fruits.[45]

Advances to Other Ewe Lands

Waya 1856

In 1856, the missionaries Wihm Brutschin, Hans J. Steinmann, Francis Djofoxe, Christian Hornberger and Wilh Lemgo were warmly received by the Ewe chief of Waya, Togbe Komla Asbeve, who gave them land to begin their missionary work. In 1886, it is reported that the work at Waya flourished, encouraging the missionaries to venture to other areas of Ewe.

Atakpame

Hornberger, a scientist, stayed at Waya but eventually pioneered a work in Atakpame.

Adaklu

Wilh Lemgo is reported to have begun a work in Adaklu.

Anyako 1857

Heinrich Knecht and his missionary colleagues arrived in Anyako in April 1857. In 1858, the mission was helped by Johann Mansfield, a master builder, to construct a mission house which became the meeting venue for the first synod meeting in 1858. The work at Anyako bore fruit; after ten years, they witnessed ten conversions, and also launched an additional mission station in Ho.

Ho 1858

The work here took off very well and appeared to have the backing of the rulers; we read that the chief of Keke, Morte Kofi, told his subjects to hear what the missionaries have to say, but for some unknown reasons he excluded himself from the reach of the good news. From Ho, the missionaries embarked on missionary tours with their mission students to other Ewe towns/villages.

---

45 Asante, "Impact of The Bremen Mission in The Volta Region of Ghana," 37.

Avatime, Amedzofe 1886

> In 1886, Mateo Seeger and Jacob Spieth came into contact with Jacob Anku and Dzoletsu, the first Avatime Christian converts, when the former were passing through Dzokpe to Nkonya. These two men had earlier on come into contact with the Basel missionaries at Mayera during the Ashanti war.[46]

That the Gold Coast in 1874 and 1886 had assumed an increasingly 'Christianised world' appears to be evident that, even the diaspora of Avatime were reaping the blessings of the labours of the Basel Missionaries when their subjects encountered the Basel missionaries in Mayera, and came to faith. In 1889, Seeger and his wife established a base in Amedzofe, and the following account underlies our earlier point of the abounding harvest which the Basel mission work had experienced:

> The missionaries were blessed to come into contact with Paul Ntumitse, an indigene of the town, who had his education and training as a catechist from the Basel school at Mayera. He was of immense help to the missionaries as an interpreter and a teacher. Their hard work and sacrifices began to produce fruits with the baptism of the first converts, five men and six children.[47]

In 1891 a mission building was completed following approval of funds by the mission board in 1890. Missionaries Johannes Schroeder, Deedrich Bavendum and Holsaphel in 1894 (Schroeder 1891) were posted to Amedzofe but died shortly, with Holsaphel dying in 1896. In 1895 the mission at Amedzofe established a dispensary clinic for dressing wounds, attending to other ailments and engaged in social welfare needs, including caring for orphans and widows.

Translation Work

The practical challenge of the language barrier hampered the mission work in the early stages 1847 onwards, with the missionaries relying on often poor translators/interpreters to convey their messages. A case in point which would have proven very uncomfortable if not perilous, may be seen in the following quote in Oduro Asante's thesis concerning Wolf's experience:

---

46 Asante, "Impact of The Bremen Mission in The Volta Region of Ghana," 51ff.
47 Asante, "Impact of The Bremen Mission in The Volta Region of Ghana," 32ff.

> During my first months, I had an interpreter. But his way of life was so immoral that I had to be ashamed of him; besides his interpretation was so bad that it was of little use. He had once to tell the king: 'in my country, there is no polygamy' but instead he interpreted my words to mean that the king was to give me one of his wives.[48]

In 1853 the Bremen missionary Benhard Schlegel arrived in the Gold Coast, settling in the Bremen mission station in Keta. He set out on his translation work and by 1857 he had completed the translation of the four Gospels into Ewe; later adding his "Key to the Ewe Language," which contains Ewe grammar, proverbs and fables. Schlegel's translation engagement was brief, as he suffered from ill-health and eventually died in 1859.

The work of translation continued after Schlegel; the missionaries Weyhe and Merz worked on the book of Acts, the epistles of Paul, Peter, and James. We read that under the leadership of the Bremen Society's head, Zahn, a school for the study of Ewe language was established in Wurttemberg, Germany, in 1884 offering a three-year study programme;[49] indicating that during the intervening period of Schlegel's death and the establishment of the school, much progress had been made on the mastery of the Ewe language.

Successes and The Impact of the First World War

By 1914, the two Bremen mission stations in the Gold Coast, Keta and Peki, recorded four serving missionaries (most likely with European and native assistants), 2,000 converts, and 3,600 pupils in their various schools. The stations in Togoland reported nine mission stations, 21 missionaries, 7,780 converts and 5,250 pupils.[50] These were no mean gospel successes after 70 years of the mission's work. We are yet to mention the success achieved in practical ways, such as translation and mastery of the Ewe language, the many natives educated and nurtured to hold key positions in the mission's work or engaged in civil services and other social initiatives the mission had established. In 1864, the missionaries Johann Conrad Hauser and Johann Gottlieb established the Ho Seminary. Notable students who passed through the seminary are the Quist brothers – Isaac, Solomon, Peter and Emmanuel from Dzelukofe; others were Heinrich Theodore and Solomon Gudeti. We read that fruits from the seminary work became evident when the first batch started serving alongside their European missionaries in stations like Keta and

---

48 Asante, "Impact of The Bremen Mission in The Volta Region of Ghana," 32ff.
49 Asante, "Impact of The Bremen Mission in The Volta Region of Ghana," 32ff.
50 Prempeh, "Basel and Bremen missions and their Successors in the Gold Coast and Togoland," 332, appendix A.

Anyako. The Seminary folded up during the Ashanti wars in the late 1860s but re-established in Amedzofe through the work of Mateo Seeger and Ernest Burgi, with assistance from native seminarian graduates Samuel Quist and Theodore Sedode.[51]

On the issue of the impact of WW1, in June 1916, nearly two years after the start of the war in July 1914, the Bremen missionaries stationed in the Gold Coast region Karl Freyburger and his wife Lina Freyburger, Reinke, and three other mission workers Elizabeth Meir, Conradine Schmidt and E. Theyn were interned and deported in late June 1916 (Reinke earlier in March 1916). The supervision of the two stations and remaining stations in occupied Togoland fell on Ernst Burgi, who was of Swiss origin and serving with the Bremen missionaries.

Prempeh reports that during the war, by late 1918, the 'orphaned' Basel mission was under the Scottish Mission, whereas supervision for the Bremen mission did not happen until August 1923. Supervision for the French region of the Bremen mission's work happened even later in 1926. The Togoland regions under the control of the British had more favourable dealings than those in the French Togoland; an edict issued by the French administration in March 1922 speaks volumes:

> No congregation, or religious association, Church, Chapel or oratoire, or any establishment destined to public worship can be established without the authorisation of the administration. No religious (cultuelle) service can be held outside the authorised establishments. The French language, Latin or the native language of the Colony in question are alone authorised to be used in the exercise of worship. No journeys of propaganda involving the appeals for money among the adherents (fideles) can be undertaken except by administrative authorisation given to individuals, and only in those parts.[52]

Assumption of Presbyterian Polity

The expulsion of the German missionaries from the Bremen and Basel mission stations in the Gold Coast and Togoland in the period of the war was arguably the one most single major event or shake-up in Gold Coast/Togoland missionary history for close to a hundred years. Almost overnight churches and mission stations lost spiritual shepherds; educational institutions were rid of human resources; seminaries lost their faculties and perhaps for some most painfully spiritual ties appear to have been severed:

---

51 Asante, "Impact of The Bremen Mission in The Volta Region of Ghana," 34ff.
52 Prempeh, "Basel and Bremen missions and their Successors in the Gold Coast and Togoland," 332, appendix A.

> The congregations were equally affected by the unstable conditions of the war time. With the approval of the boundary division the Bremen Mission field was divided. On the Gold Coast was the Keta and Peki districts. Ho, Amedzofe, Kpando and Akpafu districts came under British Togoland while Lome, Palime, Agu and Atakpame came under French Togoland. This political arrangement divided the Bremen Mission for good.[53]

The Bremen congregations/stations falling under British Gold Coast/Togoland territory were Keta and Peki districts, Ho, Amedzofe, Kpando and Akpafu, whereas Lome, Palime, Agu and Atakpame went to French Togoland. Ernst Burgi who assumed supervision of the Bremen churches retired to Germany from ill-health in September 1921 and the responsibility fell on trained native mission workers, in all likelihood from the pool that Burgi had trained and ordained between January 1915 and February 1918: Samuel Quist, Simon Peter Quist, Albert Binder, Robert Baeta, Solomon Mallet, Nehemiah Akude, and Robert Boadozo.[54]

In 1923, the six Bremen mission stations finally came under the supervision of the United Free Church of Scotland (Scottish Mission) and assumed the name "The Presbyterian Church of the Gold Coast:"

> A visit by Wilkie to the Bremen Mission stations in British Togoland and a few other stations in French Togoland disclosed the extent of the work not covered by Ashcroft's report and especially the tragic consequences of the years of neglect; and also the deep-seated affection of the converts for their missionaries to have them back. Even more encouraging was the determination of converts to suffer temporary hardships if that would ultimately secure the unity of the divided Church; and the wish to have the Amedzofe seminary for leadership training re-opened. It could not have come as a surprise when after clearing some minor difficulties with the Government, which had demonstrated more than ordinary interest in the whole negotiations, the Scottish Mission eventually agreed to supervise the Bremen Mission stations in British Togoland in August 1923.[55]

---

53 Prempeh, "Basel and Bremen missions and their Successors in the Gold Coast and Togoland," 319.
54 Prempeh, "Basel and Bremen missions and their Successors in the Gold Coast and Togoland," 323.
55 Prempeh, "Basel and Bremen missions and their Successors in the Gold Coast and Togoland," 331.

The remaining four stations Lome, Palime, Agu and Atakpame went to the Paris Mission.

The current Evangelical Presbyterian Church of Ghana, the successor of the Bremen mission group of churches reported that in 1922,[56] prior to the Scottish Mission's takeover, the Bremen Church held a synod and assumed the name The Ewe Church with a church polity along the lines of the Bremen Mission. The takeover may have undone the naming as the following reports indicated:

> In May 1922 the first synod of the mission at Kpalime declared itself the supreme governing body of the Ewe Church and elected the first moderator. The Congregational order of the North German Mission became the church order. In 1923 Scottish missionaries began to work in British Togo and in 1929 the Paris Mission took over in French Togo. For practical reasons, separate synods had to be set up in the two territories which led to separate development. To this day however, the two churches share the same constitution and hold a joint synod meeting every three years. In 1926 the name Ewe Hame (Ewe Church) was changed to Ewe Presbyterian Church. In 1954 the Ghana part of the church adopted the name Evangelical Presbyterian (EP) Church as a result of the expansion of the church beyond Eweland.[57]
>
> Wilkie's comment perhaps was a true reflection of the general attitude of the Scottish Mission to the new status of the Church. But for the Bremen Mission [Home Board] the reaction was less favourable. The simple exercise of choosing a name could evoke doctrinal issues the practical applications of which could ultimately affect the co-operation. In late 1926 Wilkie informed Schlunk of the adoption of the name 'Presbyterian' and expressed the hope that the mission would follow suit.

Schlunk had some reservations:

> I do not see if there is any possibility to accept this name for the Ewe Church. You know we have friends ... of the Lutheran and the Reformed Church in Germany and with us the name Presbyterian Church involves the idea of a reformed Church

---

56 https://en.wikipedia.org/wiki/Evangelical_Presbyterian_Church,_Ghana, accessed 09/08/2023.
57 https://www.oikoumene.org/member-churches/evangelical-presbyterian-church-ghana, accessed 04/04/23

and this is intolerable for our Lutheran friends. I know that Presbyterian Church derives its name not from faith but from order. But this again brings a little difficulty. We prefer to give the right idea or the faith of the Church in its name and not to underline a word of second importance.[58]

Though Schlunk was expressing a personal opinion here, his intentions were clear. Convinced as he was that 'God will give the right word at the right time' he refused to have the issue opened for discussion.[59]

The Breakthrough to Ashanti and Northern Territories

A brief account of the final capitulation of Ashanti and Northern territories to the Gospel is worthy of note. The former, a powerful kingdom whose military campaigns influenced daily lives in the Gold Coast in the eighteenth–nineteenth centuries proved impenetrable to the Gospel. The best the Basel mission could do was to establish frontier outposts in Abetifi and Begoro (both in 1875) as launch posts into the territory. The missionary Ramseyer and his wife were captured during an Ashanti raid and imprisoned in Kumasi. Following his release, he resolved to take the Gospel to the people of Ashanti and the door was opened in 1896 when the Ashantis' military might was suppressed by the established British colonial forces. The gospel achievements in the territory may be seen in Prempeh's account, writing about the dilemma of the Scottish-led mission on priorities of evangelistic efforts, whether Northern Territories or the Ashanti:

> But the future of the work depended largely on the development and opening of new stations in Ashanti and not in the north. Unlike the Colony, Ashanti was still a mission field. Kumasi, the major centre of activity, offered a stepping-stone to the interior where the bulk of the work lay. The early 1920s witnessed the evangelistic campaigns of Samson Oppong (c.1884–c.1960 or 1965, the eccentric Akan preacher/evangelist) in Ashanti. Within four months over 5,000 converts had been won, in some cases whole villages, including the chiefs, submitted their names for baptism. The work of Oppong continued unabated, bringing into the Methodist Church thousands of converts. Although

---

58 Prempeh, "Basel and Bremen missions and their Successors in the Gold Coast and Togoland," 319-497.
59 Prempeh, "Basel and Bremen missions and their Successors in the Gold Coast and Togoland," 497.

the outcome of the campaign in 1920/21 was 10,000 converts and the destruction of many fetish cults, the Methodist Church was caught unawares with inadequate staff to meet the challenge. The little available staff were mainly untrained men and the Church was thereby compelled to make serious efforts to train adequate African workers. The Ashanti district was therefore ripe for harvesting provided the Basel missionaries discerned the signs of the time and responded positively to the demand for the Gospel in Ashanti.[60]

Smith created a full chart on the growth of the work in the Ashanti Presbytery from 1918 to 1959. A key extract is that in 1918 there was one minister's station and 16 village congregations, then in 1959, there were 18 minister's stations and 222 village congregations.[61]

The Northern Territories proved difficult to reach, perhaps owing to the long distance to the established mission stations/outstations in the south. However, Smith reports that by 1914, there was a mission station/outstation in Yendi. Additionally, Smith states that the Northern Presbytery in 1959 had 5 ministerial stations and 28 congregations.[62] This indicates that by 1959, the Gospel had reached the northern territory but in no way comparable in terms of progress to those of their southern neighbours.

The words of the Psalmist capture the story of the Basel Missionaries, "He that goeth forth and weepeth, bearing precious seed, shall doubtless come again with rejoicing, bringing his sheaves with him" (Psalm 126:6 KJV). The Moravians' futile attempts (in human judgement) in the 18th Century were not all lost. The arduous labours, toils, tears and blood of the early BMS's missionaries were all an unbroken link of divine mercies that would culminate in what would be described in Smith's account at the close of the year 1917:

> whatever lay in the future the sacrificial endeavours of the Basel missionaries had borne great fruit: in 1918, when the statistics were read at Synod, the results of their labours, from Christiansborg of the Coast to Yendi [a town] in the North [of modern-day Ghana], were evident to all. On eleven central stations and in almost two hundred towns and villages were Christian congregations shepherded by thirty African

---

60 Prempeh, "Basel and Bremen missions and their Successors in the Gold Coast and Togoland," 488–489.
61 Smith, *Presbyterian Church of Ghana*, 231.
62 Smith, *Presbyterian Church of Ghana*, 312.

pastors and a host of catechists and teachers, a total Christian community of thirty thousand. Apart from the religious change, the Basel Mission had been one of the most significant factors in social change in the south-east of the country. The example of the Salems or Christian villages influenced the style of building of dwelling houses (with an increased use of stone and shingles) laid out alongside wide and straight streets. "Everywhere (sc. in Akwapim), one sees churches, schools and, most of all, private houses, which clearly show the Swiss and German influence? In education and in agriculture, in artisan-training and in the development of commerce, in medical services and in concern for the social welfare of the people, the name Basel by the time of the expulsion of the Mission from the country, had become a treasured word in the minds of the people.[63]

Part Two:
The Adoptive Era of Scottish Presbyterian Take-Over 1918–Second World War

It has been our aim to trace Basel and Bremen missionary history in the Gold Coast and Togoland to get us to the point where they assumed a Presbyterian character. In this journey, it was needful to appreciate the input of the various missions who had some involvement one way or the other in this soul-moving exploration. The Moravians who led the way in the eighteenth century, the Basel and Danish Mission Societies who answered the heavenly call, the array of divinely-appointed human instruments, among whom of royal blood who decreed favourably towards the mission cause, the noble army of missionaries (men and women) who were burdened for souls and launched to often unknown hostile territories to rescue dying souls, and the praying faithful who not only prayed but supported the cause with their hard-won widow's mite; all these have featured in this great retrace of missionary achievements.

In 1918, when the mission was transferred from the BMS to the Scottish UFCS mission (Bremen to Scottish later in 1923), many a thousand souls, towns,

---

63 Smith, *Presbyterian Church of Ghana*, 153–154.

villages, first-and second-generation families in the nearly hundred years of evangelical gospel witness in the Gold Coast and Togoland had witnessed the light of the Gospel and experienced it inwardly or the outward benefits of it. That, on the eve of the First World War, there were over 196 large and small church congregations, over ten thousand pupils in 176 schools (making up one-third of the total educational system of the Gold Coast) marks a remarkable missionary feat.

▲ Synod of Gold Coast after Scottish Mission involvement

Additionally, noticeable progress had been made towards the long-term goal of equipping the natives to take over the mission work. This was evident in the case of the Basel mission, as clearly observable in Smith's helpful overview of key stages in the mission's development:

> We may distinguish four main stages in the whole process of development: the 'mission' period to 1880; the period between 1880 and 1918 marked by the gradual assumption by Africans of local congregational responsibility and the achievement of financial self-support in the Twi and Ga districts; the process by which, beginning with the Synod of 1913 and ending with the adoption of the Revised Constitution in 1950, the Church became fully autonomous; and the final phase of complete integration of the Basel and Scottish missionaries within the Church.[64]

The process of native assumption of mission offices was accelerated by the conscious programme of training (foremost seminary) implemented by the missions to achieve their original goal of handing over the reins to their native brethren. That the Inspector of the BMS advocated this long before the prospect of a world war, is evident:

---

64 Smith, *Presbyterian Church of Ghana*, 155–156, 163.

The initiative in accelerating progress towards a greater devolution of responsibility came from Inspector Schott in Basel in 1879, whose main concern was to build up an indigenous Church so that missionaries would be freed for pioneer work elsewhere. As a result of his overtures to the missionaries the first African Twi District Synod was convened a year later which discussed the installation of presbyters, Church discipline and problems connected with the growth of the Christian community. The missionaries met after the synod to try to formulate a programme by which Schott's plan might be put into effect.[65]

1. The Lingering Problem of Complete Attainment to Self-Church Government

We read that notwithstanding the significant progress made in preparing native church/mission leaders in the mission period up to 1880, the overall direction of the mission still rested with the European missionaries, which usually happened in their Missionaries' Conference of which the natives did not take part.[66] Schott's reiteration of the mission's vision to hand over the reins to their African brethren led to renewed efforts to see through that vision; especially a general conference of missionaries was held in 1881 to which their first African participant David Asante took part. The outcome of this conference led to natives being allowed to take charge of large and small congregations in the main and outstations.

The missionaries were also concerned that, although much progress had been made in breaking the yoke of pagan practices off their native converts, yet at the turn of the 20th century, African societies were still steeped in superstition and pagan ways which were interwoven in everyday living (funeral rites, childbirth, marriage etc.); and allowing natives to lead the mission or church would lead to compromising situations. Thus, the process had to be gradual, as society becomes more centrally governed. The punitive repercussions for Christians accused of violations of customs became centralised in the Civil administration, who would adjudicate and offer a fairer trial than what may be experienced in a customary/tribal setting. The traditional rulers by and large had more respect and restraint when dealing with the Europeans than with the native converts.

---

65 Smith, *Presbyterian Church of Ghana*, 155–156, 163.
66 Smith, *Presbyterian Church of Ghana*, 155–156, 163.

2. The First World War

The impact of the war was not immediately felt in the missions' work, barring the obvious security measures which would have been implemented. The British Colonial administration saw the spiritual and social good of the work of the missionaries and was at pains to preserve it. This was evident in post-expulsion negotiations to find a caretaker for the mission's work where they accommodated the spiritual/emotional sensitivities of the natives and mission societies.

> Notwithstanding these precautionary measures, the attitude to the situation was not characterised by overreaction and panic. The Government did not consider it necessary to proclaim martial law, though a draft Bill was made in readiness to empower the Governor to take control of the situation should any British or alien subjects be suspected of acting in the interest of the enemy. The attitude to the missionaries in particular was very favourable. Addressing a proclamation to the chiefs and their subjects on the defence of the Colony Robertson [Acting Governor] was at pains to warn them of the consequences of assisting the German cause, and encouraged them to grow more foodstuffs to avert any future famine. But more significant was his stern warning to the chiefs that maltreatment of any German subjects whose services and kindness the local population had freely enjoyed for years would be met with punitive measures.

He observed:

> They are entitled to more than our charity; they are entitled to our chivalry. Let therefore the chiefs make it known that they will lay a very heavy hand on any of their people who seek an occasion to insult or molest those who for many years have been amongst us as our good friends and guests. Robertson's warning was indeed a genuine testimony and a reflection on the cordial relationship between the Government and the German institutions in the Colony.[67]

---

67 Prempeh, "Basel and Bremen missions and their Successors in the Gold Coast and Togoland," 2–3, 108, 155, 234.

Two years after the war started (in the case of Basel three years), the missions' works experienced its first major interruption since the days of Andreas Riis in 1840 (when he took a three-year break for recuperation). The Bremen mission work, as already alluded to, was curtailed overnight when their mostly German missionaries were interned and later deported. Among the Basel Missionaries in the Gold Coast, this happened in December 1917, when the German subjects serving in the mission were rounded up and deported in a matter of a few days. Mission stations, outstations, churches, schools, institutions, and seminaries became empty overnight of some of their most able staff. Their non-German fellow-missionaries (Swiss, an American, Australian) were subsequently deported in January 1918.

> The whole exercise was carried out expeditiously with no incidents. This account of the arrest of the missionaries at Akropong is illustrative:
> On 7th December 1917 the usual teachers' Examination was going on. The Swiss missionary Stricker, who was head of the Teacher Training Department, was helping with the examination late one afternoon. Some of the African teachers were conversing together in the calm and pleasant sunlight when they saw the District Commissioner, with a single escort policeman come down the College lane. The D.C. entered the quadrangle and asked to see Mr Stricker. He asked Stricker to tell the German missionaries that the Government had decided to deport them, and that they were to be taken down to Accra that very evening. They were given one hour to collect their belongings together. These were placed on an open lorry. Those who were arrested included Principal Jehle, Nothwang, Monninger and Grau. Grau had to leave his wife behind for she was about to give birth to their first child. Fortunately, he was allowed to return to her next day, and he was thus the only one who had the chance to dispose of his personal effects before he and his family left.
> The evacuation generally was characterised by humanitarian principles for those unfit to travel were left behind, and record of protest letters received from the internees made no mention of physical threats.[68]

---

68 Prempeh, "Basel and Bremen missions and their Successors in the Gold Coast and Togoland," 108. Prempeh is quoting from G. G. Gunn, *A Hundred Years 1848–1948: The Story of the Presbyterian Training College Akropong* (Edinburgh, 1848), 41–44.

Given the sudden nature of the departure, we are told that one of the last acts of the European missionaries was to put the African Pastors in charge of the districts and set up a standing Church authority composed of pastors and elders. This was the arrangement which the Scottish Mission came to meet and build upon into a Presbyterian character.[69]

3. The Invitation to the Scottish Mission (United Free Church of Scotland)

Into this vacuum came missionary support from the United Free Church of Scotland's mission in Calabar (Nigeria).[70] Rev. Arthur West Wilkie (1878–1958) arrived at the Gold Coast in January/February 1918 to lead the Basel Mission's work and eventually also the Bremen's in 1923. At the time of Dr Wilkie's arrival, all the areas of the mission's (Basel) work were fully functional with the exception of the Girls' school in Aburi, which lacked qualified female staff. Wilkie holds a most unique position in Scottish mission history as he served in three African fields during his missionary years: Calabar (1901–1918), Gold Coast (1918–1930), and Lovedale in South Africa (1931–1941) and became noted as a missionary educationalist. Andrew Walls described him as one who skillfully promoted harmony in assimilating the legacies of the Basel and Bremen Mission Societies.[71]

At the first Synod convened in August 1918 at Akropong Akuapem, Gold Coast it was encouraging to see the sacrificial labours and fruit of the labours of the Basel Mission when the statistics were reported: eleven central stations (districts) with almost 200 congregations meeting in towns and villages, 30 African pastors, and a large body of catechists and teachers, numbering as a Christian community 30,000.

A transition in July 1922 occurred at the Synod meeting in Kyebi where the districts were formalised within five Presbyteries: *Ga and Adangme; Akuapim and Anum; Agona and Kotoku; Akyem and Okwawu;* and *Asante and Asante Akyem.* Thus a classical three-court Presbyterian system of session, presbytery, and synod was implemented in 1922/3.[72]

---

69 Prempeh, "Basel and Bremen missions and their Successors in the Gold Coast and Togoland," 155.
70 See chapter 9 in this volume on this Calabar mission dating back first to the SMS work in Jamaica. The first offer was to the CoS but they were not in a position to accept this invitation to the Gold Coast, hence the invitation was extended to the UFCS. *DSCHT*, 576.
71 *DSCHT*, 871. See also chapter 8 in this volume for Wilkie's role at Lovedale.
72 A. A. Beeko, "From Synod to General Assembly," https://asantepresbytery.org/from-synod-to-general-assembly/ accessed 6 September 2023.

- The early list of Scottish missionaries[73] includes:

Arthur W. Wilkie	to Accra January/February 1918 to 1930
George Douglas Reith	to Abetifi 1918 and left within one year
William Gray Murray	to Akropong 1919 to 1926
Thomas Lorimer Beveridge	to Gold Coast 1920 to 1938
William Ferguson[74]	to Akropong 1920 to 1938
Robert Russell Davidson	to Akropong 1921 to 1933
Robert Ritchie Watt	to Gold Coast 1922 to 1931
John Alexander Robson Watt	to Gold Coast 1929 to 1935
F. D. Harker[75]	to Gold Coast as an educator 1930s
Douglas Benzies	to Akropong 1937 to 1947
Mrs J. Moffat	to Gold Coast 1918 …
Miss Gladys Muriel Wallace[76]	to Aburi, Gold Coast 1918 (died there in 1921)
Mrs Martha Howie	to Aburi, Gold Coast 9 June 1920 (died there 13 November 1920)

It is worth noting that Wilkie played a pivotal role in arguing for the return of the Basel Missionaries. They returned in late 1925 and participated in a meeting that saw the adoption of a new name for the increasingly self-conscious Gold Coast Mission Church. The name adopted was *"Presbyterian Church of the Gold Coast."*

---

73 *Fasti United Free Church of Scotland 1900–1929*, ed. J. A. Lamb (Edinburgh: Oliver & Boyd, 1956), 560–561. *Fasti Ecclesiae Scoticanae*, ed. J. A. Lamb, volume 9 (Edinburgh: Oliver & Boyd, 1961), 727–755. It appears that there were also more that came at least temporarily from Calabar for periods of time to serve. There was much transfer between Calabar and the Gold Coast in this UFCS period. Many wives of the men also came and made valuable contributions but are not always included with their husbands in *Fasti* as to their labours.
74 Was ordained by the Presbytery of the Gold Coast in 1920.
75 Harker started at first an informal school for the blind in 1932 and this then became a formal school for the blind in 1943/5, the first such school in West Africa.
76 Both Miss Wallace and Mrs Howie are buried in Christiansborg.

4. The Journey to Full Independence and Presbyterianism

The road to ecclesiastical self-rule for the maturing mission church in the case of the Basel Mission of the Gold Coast started with the synod meeting in August 1918:

> As a first step towards a re-organization of the Church the Synod of 1918 approved a number of constitutional measures. Wilkie nominated twelve of the ministers of which the Synod delegates elected eight as the Executive of the Church. They were Messrs. Peter Hall (Moderator); Nicholas Clerk (Synod Clerk); Nathan Asare, William Quartey, W. Odjidja, Christian Martinson, and Ludwig L. Richter (members). The Synod Executive were responsible for matters of general policy in consultation with the Mission Council. Wilkie reserved the right of veto so as to exercise some sort of moderating influence on the young and inexperienced Committee. Even so for the sake of eventual independence of the Church it was necessary that the Committee had responsibility for decision making and matters affecting the Church. Wilkie, therefore, conceded that "merely nominal power would certainly not bring out the very highest possible in the African Church". Desirous of maintaining the essential unity of the Church and its continuity in the past, Wilkie ensured that very little re-organization was effected. All the same some fundamental changes were necessary if progress towards self-government and self-support was to be achieved. Locally, three main courts were instituted. (1) The Session, (2) The Presbytery and (3) The Synod.[77]

▲ Dr Arthur W. Wilkie

Smith reports that slowly the church moved towards independence, in 1929 a complete review of its regulations, practice and procedure was undertaken leading to the Synod Committee assuming responsibility for the legal trustees

---

77 Prempeh, "Basel and Bremen missions and their Successors in the Gold Coast and Togoland," 2–3, 108, 155, 234.

for all properties. Twenty years later in 1950 the posts of Manager of Schools and Treasurer were taken over by Africans.[78]

We conclude the journey to complete independence with a quote from Gyang-Duah:

> We have noted that one of the first things that the Scottish Mission did as soon as they arrived in Ghana was to constitute the Synod and appoint Ghanaians as Moderator and Synod Clerk. By 1950 these two positions had been well established. After the integration, Ghanaians were appointed to positions previously held by missionary personnel. Furthermore, committees were set up to plan and supervise aspects of the church's life such as finance, education, evangelism, literature, youth work and women's work. The presbyteries were reconstituted and for the first time vested with executive power and also provided with permanent officers. The Synod Committee had also been reconstituted with some of its work devolved to the presbyteries and the representation of the Missions on the committee reduced. These measures put the church's administration and the decision-making process firmly in the hands of Ghanaians. This completed the process which was started in 1918 by the Scottish Mission.[79]

5. Conclusion

In our survey of the Basel, Bremen and Scottish missionary works, we see some great ideals or qualities which characterised their labours and outlook in the mission work, those qualities of faith in the revealed Word as sufficient for Faith and Christian living, a lifelong missionary outlook to Christian service, hard work as opposed to ease and presumption, self-sacrifice, love for souls, humility-helpfulness-love towards the wider evangelical cause and to crown it all a child-like faith in their Triune God. Like their apostolic forebears in the first century AD, the Roman expansionism while in discord with the moral values of their faith, they seized the opportunities which the Greco-Roman cultural refinements in Greek language, civic order, infrastructural advances left on its trail as the

---

78 Smith, *Presbyterian Church of Ghana*, 155–156, 163.
79 Gyang-Duah, "Scottish Mission factor in the Development of the Presbyterian Church of Ghana," 304–305. Note, the UFCS technically was the Scottish mission involved from 1917 to 1929 a period of twelve years and then from 1929 the mission became CoS as the majority UFCS merged with the CoS, this making the last ten years to the eve of WW2 CoS.

wheel of expansionist campaigns of imperial Rome marched forth. The colonial transport routes, practical provisions of castles and forts as conscience allowed, the civic magistrate maintaining law and order, infrastructural advances and much more were the equivalent for our nineteenth century missionary heroes and heroines, who though believing in the Sovereignty of God to save HIS elect in sub-Saharan Africa, yet concurrently acknowledged the biblical truth of human responsibility in soul winning.

> And blessèd be his glorious name
> to all eternity:
> The whole earth let his glory fill.
> Amen, so let it be.
> *Scottish Psalter, Psalm 72:19*

Questions for study (fact type):
1. Name the three continental European mission societies involved in the Gold Coast in the 19th century. Name the mission grouping from the West Indies in the 19th century. Name the Scottish denominational mission which began work in the Gold Coast early in the 20th century.
2. Identify by name two of the leading missionary translators in the 19th century in the Gold Coast.
3. Describe why the mission underwent a major change in 1917/1918?
4. Make a timeline of the mission from 1828 to 1925.

Questions for study (reflection type):
1. Discuss the nature of the adoption of the Basal and Bremen Mission into the UFCS mission in terms of theology, noting that all bodies were paedobaptists for similarities. And any other similarities? Also note differences.
2. The role of translation work was critical for both Basal and Bremen mission work. Discuss from the chapter this topic and its relevance for mission strategy.

Select Bibliography

Ansre, Gilbert, ed. *The Evangelical Presbyterian Church, 150 Years of Evangelisation and Development 1847–1997*. Ho, Ghana: EPCG, 1997.

Asante, Leticia Oduro. "The Impact of The Bremen Mission in The Volta Region of Ghana." MPhil thesis, University of Ghana, Legon, 2018.

Babaloa, E. O. *Christianity in West Africa (An Historical Analysis)*. Ibadan, Nigeria: Book Representation and Publishing Company, 1988.

Beeko, A. Anthony. *The Trail of Blazers: Fruits of 175 Years of the Presbyterian Church of Ghana (1828–2003)*. Accra: Afram Publications Ltd, 2004.

Gyang-Duah, Charles. "The Scottish Mission factor in the Development of the Presbyterian Church of Ghana, 1917–1957." PhD thesis, University of Edinburgh, 1996.

Hewat, Elizabeth G. K. *Vision and Achievement 1796–1956: A History of the Foreign missions of the Churches united in the Church of Scotland*. London: Thomas Nelson, 1960, 243–250.

Nielsen, Harald, "Ghana – The Gold Coast," *Danmission Historie* (2018). https://danmission.dk/photoarchive/area/ghana-the-gold-coast/?lang=en

Okyerefo, Michael Parry Kweku. "Scottish Missionaries in Ghana: The Forgotten Tribe," in Afe Adogame & Andrew Lawrence, eds. *Africa in Scotland, Scotland in Africa: Historical Legacies and Contemporary Hybridities*. Leiden: Brill, 2014, 251–262. doi: https://doi.org/10.1163/9789004276901_013

Prempeh, Samuel. "The Basel and Bremen Missions and their Successors in the Gold Coast and Togoland, 1914–1926; a study in Protestant Missions and the first World War." PhD thesis, University of Aberdeen, 1977.

Schott, O. *The Basel Mission on the Gold Coast: A Retrospect on Fifty Years of Mission Work*. Basel: Felix Schneider Press, 1879.

Smith, Noel. *The Presbyterian Church of Ghana, 1835–1960*. Accra: Ghana Universities Press, 1966.

Wilkie, A. W. "An Attempt to Conserve the World of the Basel Mission to the Gold Coast." *International Review of Missions* 9 (January 1920): 86–94.

Zahn, Franz Michael. "Festschrift for the 50 Year Jubilee Celebration of the North German Missionary Society," trans. Sabine Bajahr, from the original German of 1886. *Haddington House Journal*, 26 (2024), forthcoming.

Inset

"The Mother of our Schools" – Akropong Seminary, est. 1848

J. C. Whytock

This inset highlights an institution which was established in 1848 as the Akropong Seminary, Akropong, Gold Coast (Ghana). "Seminary" here again must be taken in a very inclusive educational sense and not be defined exclusively to modern theological education (but also is inclusive of such). Its formal name has changed or has had popular names in parlance: Akropong Seminary, Basel Mission Seminary, Catechetical Institute, Scottish Mission Seminary, Scottish Mission Teacher Training College, Presbyterian Training College, and now Presbyterian College of Education. It was established by the Basel Evangelical Missionary Society and was modeled in many regards upon that society's seminary in Basel, Switzerland: "for the training of men to become teachers and preachers of the Gospel among the heathens in different lands."[80] The college is declared to be the second oldest higher educational institution in West Africa, after Fourah College in Sierra Leone.

As an institution, it came about following the early Basel mission work in Akropong, which had begun in January 1835 with a short visit by Andreas Riis, followed in March 1835 by his return and settlement there. He remained until 1840, when he returned to Basel, Switzerland and then subsequently went back to Akopong in 1843. However, the 1843 return was to place the mission station on a new footing as this time Riis brought a party of 25 Afro-Caribbean Christians from Jamaica and Antigua who were associated with the United Brethren (Moravians) together with Johann Wildmann and George Peter.[81] It was this June 1843 arrival of an expanded mission group that would be the catalyst for the mission's advance at Christiansborg (Osu), Akropong, etc., and be the critical factor for the establishment of the Basel Seminary.[82]

---

80 *A History of the Presbyterian Training College, Akropong*, 1.
81 *A History of the Presbyterian Training College, Akropong*, 4–8.
82 These Afro-Caribbean Christians helped establish a school at Christiansborg in 1843 and also were instrumental in the development of the town, church, and seminary at Akropong. See, Odamtten, *The Missionary Factor in Ghana's Development (1820–1880)*, 104, 109. A suggestion had been put forward that the Seminary be established in the Caribbean to train teacher-catechists and then send them to the Gold Coast. This idea was rejected for several reasons.

In 1847 it was decided to proceed with a teacher-catechist seminary to advance the schools and preaching work of the mission. The Seminary was opened in 1848. At first the Seminary had to offer further transitional educational training due to the inferior levels (at this pioneering stage) in the schools of the area. This was achieved by using a three-year course of studies followed then by the proper teacher-catechetic training. By 1852/3 more advanced courses were added to formalise the curriculum and in 1863 courses in theology were offered including Greek. In order to be admitted to the seminary, one had to be baptised and also be willing to be trained not only to teach but also to preach and to do practical work.[83] Both English language studies were included as well as Twi, the vernacular of the area.

Besides the academic programme of studies, industrial training was included: gardening, carpentry, blacksmithing, bookbinding, shoemaking, locksmithing, and masonry. Teachers and preachers were to be competent also in trades. The students (under the supervision of the missionary agriculturalist Joseph Mohr and also the first principal Rev. Dieterle) built a chapel as well as stone houses for the compound. Spiritual exercises were held morning and evening with prayer meetings and hymn singing times. Students took turns for two hours each morning serving as monitors in the local primary schools as part of their field work and training.[84] The Seminary students also assisted the missionary preachers and accompanied the missionaries to serve either as translators into Twi or else preach themselves on occasion. Today this would be called interning or practice teaching and preaching, but it all shows a vital component to establishing a seminary which was academic, spiritual, and practical. It very much continued the tradition of pietism in the Lutheran and Reformed background of the Basel Evangelical Mission Society.

It seems the course of study at first was about five years and then settled upon a four-year course of studies after 1863. Students came from both the Twi and then also from the Ga-speaking communities with whom the Basel Mission was focusing on. Also, Afro-Caribbean descended students were enrolled, and without these the success of the Seminary would have been greatly hampered. The Afro-Caribbean community at Akropong also introduced new plants to the station: mangos, pears, cocoa, and coffee, which all created a practical emphasis for work and study to be combined.[85]

A second seminary for Ga-speaking students was established in 1850 at Osu. In 1853, this seminary came under the leadership of Rev. J. Zimmerman

---

83 *A History of the Presbyterian Training College, Akropong*, 9–10.
84 *A History of the Presbyterian Training College, Akropong*, 10–11.
85 Odamtten, *The Missionary Factor in Ghana's Development (1820–1880)*, 128

who was to become the noted Ga linguist. Zimmerman advocated merging the Osu seminary with that of Akropong and the plan was supported by Rev. J. G. Christaller. Eventually the Osu seminary was merged into the Seminary at Akropong. Zimmerman recognised a lack of resources to run two seminaries and to have sufficient tutors for two institutions at this time.

As the Seminary matured, the course became fixed and remained so through to the end of the 1920s: "a three-year academic and teacher training period followed by one-year catechist course for training in theology and homiletics." With improvements in primary schools and the addition of middle schools, the seminary did not have to spend as much time on the "three R's."[86] Thus, a standard of four years developed.

The training of evangelists was perceived as limited at the seminary and so refresher courses were implemented starting in the 1860s. Also, in 1857 selected students were sent from Akropong to the seminary in Basel, Switzerland for further training. One of these students was David Asante who had been adopted by Rev. Wildmann after his father was killed. David became the personal assistant to Rev. Dieterle. David Asante was the first from the Gold Coast to be ordained in Basel in 1862. He returned and served as a missionary and helped to extend the mission's work to Akyen, beyond the Volta, and north to Salaga, which helped prepare for further missions for the Okwawu, Asante and Northern missions. Likewise, others from the Seminary at Akropong helped to take the gospel to many of these locations mentioned above and to the towns of the Akuapem.[87] The work of this teacher-catechist training seminary established at Akropong was of absolute importance for the advancement of the Basel Societies' gospel work on the Gold Coast.

The Seminary and its associates must also be recognised as providing a place from which vernacular language work was promoted. Zimmermann concentrated on Ga and Christaller focused upon Twi.[88] Zimmerman started in 1854 with a translation of the four Gospels, then in 1857 a Ga grammar and dictionary, and in 1866 a Ga Bible and a Ga hymnal. Christoller worked with Seminary-taught teacher-catechists Jonathan Bekoe, Paul Keteku and David Asante to translate the four Gospels into Twi (1857), the entire Bible into Twi (1871), produce a Twi grammar (1875), and compile a dictionary (1888). Other alumni of the Seminary made valuable contributions to vernacular work, such as through *Kristofo Senkekafo* (Christian Messenger).[89] As Noel Smith wrote: "This

---

86 *A History of the Presbyterian Training College, Akropong*, 13.
87 *A History of the Presbyterian Training College, Akropong*, 13–15.
88 Twi is a form of Ashanti or Fante.
89 *A History of the Presbyterian Training College, Akropong*, 24; Odamtten, *The Missionary Factor in Ghana's Development (1820–1880)*, 121–123.

emphasis on vernacular languages became and remained a marked feature of the work of the Basel Mission."[90]

The history of the Seminary falls into three eras. The first we have surveyed here, being the Basel Era (1848–1918). With the forced withdrawal of the Basel Missionaries in 1917, the seminary would then have mission leadership first from the United Free Church of Scotland mission and after the union of 1929, the Church of Scotland – thus the second era (1918/20–1962). It was also after the Scottish mission became involved that the name eventually became Presbyterian Training College. In 1963, the Seminary had its first indigenous African become the principal, Erasmus Awuku Asamoa,[91] an alumnus of Presbyterian Training College – thus its third era (post-1962).

Space does not allow us a full historical survey here, but one incident during the Scottish era needs to be highlighted.[92] This concerns one of the tutors, Ephraim Amu, who started as a tutor in 1925 at Akropong and served there until 1933 when he was dismissed. Amu's ideas were deemed as too progressive, and it was thought they could lead to compromise. He promoted wearing traditional African clothing as well as the inclusion of African instruments and music.[93]

In 1924 a second union occurred when the Basel Seminary at Abetifi (which was founded in 1898) was merged into the Seminary at Akropong.[94] The curriculum at Akropong from 1928 through to 1952 remained basically the same, a three-year teachers' course followed by a one-year catechist course. Linguistics in the vernacular remained a constant theme, also during those years.[95]

The model of this seminary should be compared to the work of Scottish missions at Lovedale Institution/Seminary,[96] South Africa and similar institutions which developed in Malawi, Calabar, and Kenya. They are not all identical, but there are many parallels for comparison.

Below is a chart of the principals during the first two eras which are predominantly the dates of this book on historic missions.[97]

---

90 Smith, *Presbyterian Church in Ghana*, 56.
91 Served 1963–1965 (died Feb 1965)
92 Many topics could be pursued such as a desire by many to have the Seminary affiliated with a Scottish University to offer degrees which was not pursued.
93 *A History of the Presbyterian Training College, Akropong,* 33–34. Also, see chapter 27 in this volume where Amu receives focus.
94 Smith, *Presbyterian Church in Ghana*, 178–179.
95 Smith, *Presbyterian Church in Ghana*, 179.
96 See chapter 8 in this volume which is devoted to a study of the Lovedale Institution.
97 *A History of the Presbyterian Training College, Akropong,* 56–86.

"The Mother of our Schools" – Akropong Seminary, est. 1848

▼ The Principals of the Seminary during the Basel Mission Era 1848–1918

Rev. John Christian Dieterle	1848–1851
Rev. Johann Georg Widmann	1852–1867
Rev. Johann Adam Mader	1868–1877
Rev. Johannes Mueller	1878–1888
Rev. David Eisenschmidt	1889–1890
Rev. Bahasar Groh	1891–1905
Rev. Wilhelm Jacob Rottmann	1906–1909
Rev. Immanuel Bellon	1909–1911
Rev. Dr Gustav Jehle	1912–1917

▼ The Principals of the Seminary during the Scottish Mission Era through to 1962

Rev. William G. Murray	1920–1926
Rev. William Ferguson	1926–1937
Mr Douglas Benzies	1937–1947
Rev. John Strachan Malloch	1949–1957
Rev. Dr J. Noel Smith	1958–1962

Statistics 1917 for the Basel Mission of the Gold Coast:[98]

- 196 congregations in the Gold Coast spread throughout the South-Eastern, Central and Asante regions
- 176 schools
- Two Seminaries: Akropong f. 1848 and Abetifi f. 1898
- 28 indigenous ministers
- Over 2,000 alumni teacher-catechists had been trained
- The Central Fund was operating to pay all ministers, seminary tutors, and teachers-catechists and build all houses for workers
- agricultural undertakings
- translation and linguistic efforts

---

98 *A History of the Presbyterian Training College, Akropong*, 26.

The Akopong Seminary truly was the mother of the Basel mission schools, primary and middle and of the schools of the faith or Christian churches established as mission stations and out-stations. It can also be argued that Akropong was also a mother towards much community enrichment and development in practical skill development, agricultural diversity, and literary and linguistic work.

In the first line of the college anthem set to music by Ephraim Amu, and words by Mrs Ferguson, "For this our Training College the mother of our schools ..."[99] is correct. From Akropong went forth leaders who birthed schools and churches and nurtured scholars and disciples of Jesus Christ. Its achievements and its place in mission history must be fully recognised together with the sacrificial labours of all its staff, missionary and native.

Select Bibliography

Christaller, J. G. *A Dictionary of the Asante and Fante Language, called Tshi* [Twi]. First Edition 1881. New Edition, Basel: Basel Evangelical Society, 1933.

Odamtten, S. K. *The Missionary Factor in Ghana's Development (1820–1880)*. Accra: Waterville Publishing House, 1978.

Owusu-Agyakwa, Gladys, Samuel K. Ackah and Micheal Kwamena-Poh. *The Mother of our Schools: A History of the Presbyterian Training College, Akropong, Akuapem and Biography of the Principals 1848–1993*. Accra: Presbyterian Training College, 1994.

Smith, Noel. *The Presbyterian Church of Ghana, 1835–1960*. Accra: Ghana Universities Press, 1966.

Zimmermann, J. *The Four Gospels in the Ga Language*. London, 1855.

Zimmermann, J. *A Grammatical Sketch of the Akra-or Ga-Language and some Specimen of it from the mouth of the Natives*. Stuttgart: J. F. Steinkopf, 1858.

---

99 *A History of the Presbyterian Training College, Akropong*, 106.

Chapter 13

Beginnings of Presbyterian Work in German Kamerun, c.1879–c.1940

Mary Cloutier

Chapter Outline
1. Introduction
2. Beginnings in German Kamerun
3. Pioneering into the Interior
4. Bulu Apostles to the Bene
5. Eastward Push
6. Missionary Writings of Kamerun
7. Frank James Industrial School
8. Theological Education
9. European war interruption
10. French Occupation
11. Sakbayeme Station
12. Church Organisation Develops (c.1920–c.1940)
13. Summary Conclusion

Bio Inset: Lydia Walker Good

1. Introduction

The Presbyterian Cameroon mission[1] work was born out of the Gaboon and Corisco Mission in late 1879, as a natural outward movement of Benga Christians from Corisco Island and nearby Benita, sharing the Gospel with the unreached tribes to the north. While the foreign missionaries planned and pioneered the growth of the mission, they were devastated by disease and death, insufficient personnel, colonial interference, and the European war. It was the African Christians, with their zeal for evangelism and education, who helped the Kamerun field to grow by hundreds, and then thousands, to become the largest Presbytery in the world for a time.

---

1 Spelling here will be the German form *Kamerun*, the French form *Cameroun*, and the English form *Cameroon*.

2. Beginnings in German Kamerun

Batanga Station

The earliest Presbyterian work in what would be known as German Kamerun was inaugurated by Equatorial African church leaders from the Benita region, in April 1879. A travel itinerary of Rev. Ibia J'Ikenge related the great emotion of the Benita people as they bid goodbye to their own Elder Itongolo, who was leaving them for his new post further north among the Banâkâ people.[2] Dr Robert Hamill Nassau's *History of the Corisco Presbytery* notes the date as April 16 1879, when the Batanga Church was established by Itongolo and two newly-elected elders (possibly Myongo and Petiye) along with thirty-eight of the Benita church members located north of Evune.[3]

One of the first known women of the Batanga church was *Bekalidi*, who visited the Ogowe Kangwe mission in late 1879.[4] The Batanga church and parsonage buildings were built by indigenous believers, through their own resources.[5] This early Batanga Presbyterian Church was, thus, wholly an indigenous congregation, and remained so for a full decade. The Presbyterian Board missionaries considered Batanga a *mission outpost* at the time and were sending their new missionaries deep into the Ogowe River region of Gabon, hundreds of miles further south. The missionary clergy and the indigenous church leaders worked cooperatively, however, through the Corisco Presbytery.

Batanga Christians Invite Missionaries

By January 1883, the Batanga Christians expressed their desire for a missionary and offered property to Miss Isabella Nassau, should she be willing to locate among them. Miss Nassau had spent years at the Bolondo Mission, some 50 miles to the south, and was fluent in the Benga language. She was just returning to the field from furlough and had travelled with a newly-appointed African American missionary, Miss Mary Lucy Harding. Miss Nassau provided Miss Harding with Benga language materials so that she could study them while on the long voyage to Africa. By the time they landed, Miss Harding was reading it fluently.[6] Both women visited the Batanga site and anticipated that the mission would confirm their appointment to that location. Instead, the mission voted to expand further into the Gabon interior and appointed both women to that growing work on the Ogowe River. The two missionary women were greatly disappointed, but joined the work at Kangwe Mission, near what is now Lambarene, Gabon.

---

2 J'Ikenge, 314.
3 Nassau, *History*, 10.
4 Nassau, *My Ogowe*, 320.
5 BFM-PCUSA 1881, 32.
6 WFMS, "Dark Continent," 182.

First Missionaries at Batanga

In 1889, a newly arrived missionary couple, Rev. Burgess B. Brier, and his wife, were appointed as the first Presbyterian Board missionaries to serve in Batanga. Dr Nassau objected to this move, as the mission had long opposed sending new missionaries alone to a given field. Dr Nassau learned later that missionary Joseph Hankinson Reading had encouraged the new missionary couple to consider serving at Batanga rather than on the Ogowe River.[7] Mr Reading and the Briers travelled north to Batanga, with building materials and needed supplies, and established the first missionary dwelling at Bongaheli, near the Luma Creek.[8] Rev. Brier was soon conducting multiple Sunday services, weekday services, prayer meetings, and Sunday school, while Mrs Leda Brier discipled the women, led prayer meetings, met with new inquirers, formed a church choir, and taught sewing.[9] Within nine months of their arrival, Rev. Brier died of fever at Batanga, and Mrs Brier returned to the US.

Rev. George Albert Godduhn and his wife, Emma, were appointed to Batanga in 1891. Mrs Godduhn taught sewing and led large groups of women's prayer meetings. Rev. Godduhn preached to crowds of 500 or more on Sundays.[10] The Godduhns served with Rev. William C. Gault and his wife, Lizzie, who had spent ten years at the Benita Mission further south.

▲ Missionaries c.1893

---

7 Nassau, *My Ogowe*, 624.
8 Nassau, *My Ogowe*, 635.
9 BFM-PCUSA 1890, 21
10 WFMS, "Letters."

3. Pioneering into the Interior

The Gaboon and Corisco Mission now occupied a vast region of Equatorial Africa governed by three different European colonial governments – the Gaboon stations at Libreville, Angom and Ogowe River were thwarted by the French, who favoured the French Catholic missions; the Corisco mission on Corisco Island and Benita were limited by the Spanish government; the German colonial territory of Kamerun proved to be friendly toward Protestant missionaries and the use of indigenous languages. The Presbyterian Board and its missionaries determined that the best strategy would be to transfer the Gaboon work to the Paris Evangelical Mission Society, and to build upon the work begun at Batanga, with a view toward the vast interior.[11]

Rev. Adolphus C. Good (1856–1894), who had been serving for many years in the Ogowe region, was zealous to begin a pioneering work among the unreached peoples to the north. He visited the Kamerun interior and determined that it was densely populated with large villages of people who were likely to respond to the Gospel. Rev. Good obtained permission from the German Governor of Kamerun to begin a work in that region, but with the stipulation that the missionaries be permitted to carry on their work using the indigenous languages.[12]

Transfers and New Missionaries to Kamerun

Missionaries who had long been serving in the French territory gradually moved to the northern stations, turning their mission properties and work over to French Protestant missionaries, as the Kamerun field became the centre of the Presbyterian West Africa field. Rev. Adolphus and Lydia Good, with their son Bertie, came from Kangwe, on the Ogowe River; Dr Robert Hamill Nassau and Miss Isabella Nassau both transferred from their Ogowe River mission stations. New missionaries, Mr Edward Albert Ford and Miss Louisa Babe also joined the Kamerun mission in 1891. A year later, Dr Charles James Laffin and his wife, Mary, arrived on the field. In 1893–94, several single men and young couples arrived, including Mr Matthew Henry Kerr, Rev. Melvin Fraser, Rev. Herman Schnatz, Mr Oscar and Dr Florence Roberts, and Dr Silas F. and Mrs Mary Johnson.

Though published annual reports offer a glowing account of the ongoing work at Kamerun, private missionary letters of the time reveal tensions between missionaries, particularly regarding Rev. A. C. Good, whose zeal and impatience to expand the mission into the interior compromised the health and safety of the group. Because of the complications of health and pregnancy, Rev. Good

---

11 BFM-PCUSA 1890, 12.
12 BFM-PCUSA 1890, 20.

recommended that single men be sent to Kamerun, so that they could live simply, travel extensively, and work unencumbered by family cares. Instead, young couples arrived on the field, who would eventually produce families.

Missionary deaths

As the new missionaries continued to explore, preach, teach, and build the Kamerun mission, they also cared for one another in illness and death. A dangerously ill Mrs Lydia Good[13] returned with her son to the US in mid-1894. Her husband, Rev. A. C. Good, remained on the field, to ensure that the new missionaries were fully trained and well-situated.

Mrs Laffin died at Batanga in November 1894, shortly after welcoming and orienting the new missionary women. She was buried in the Batanga mission cemetery next to her infant daughter.[14] In December 1894, Rev. Good returned from his fourth exploration journey into the interior and fell ill for many days. He died of hematuric fever, at Efulen, at the age of 38.[15]

More missionaries arrived in 1895, including Rev. William C. and Emily Johnston, and two bachelors, Rev. Frank Hickman and Mr Charles McCleary, and Miss Ida Engels, who later married Mr Schnatz. With the increased missionary presence, the indigenous church in Kamerun grew exponentially. Families of the Banâkâ, Bapuku, Mabea and Bulu tribes sent their children to mission schools throughout the region.[16]

By 1896, the Batanga Mission extended along 80 miles of coastline, from Little Batanga (Lukonje River) 30 miles north of Batanga, to the southern tip of German territory at the Campo River and extending deep into the interior. That year, Dr Herman and Louisa Cox arrived on the field. The mission annual report lists numerous Presbyterian missionaries and Rev. Itongolo ja Ivina serving at Batanga. There were now churches at Mbenji, Batanga and Kribi. Roman Catholic missionaries in the region turned people's hearts away from the Protestant work, though several local tribes had constructed church buildings in hopes that they would have someone to teach them God's Word.

Dr Florence Roberts was a trained physician and provided high-quality medical care for a time. Her husband trekked for days in the interior (Ngumba region) once visiting nearly a hundred Mabeya villages in eight days. Likewise, Miss Louisa Babe made long journeys into the interior, evangelising, visiting believers and offering medical care to the sick. Rev. William Gault was giving

---

13 See inset with this chapter.
14 McNeill, 25.
15 Parsons, 285.
16 Ford 1903, 98.

theological training to a select group of young men, while Mrs Gault provided more general education courses. The Presbyterian mission favoured the indigenous languages in their schools and churches, but many of the tribes sought to learn the German language and were drawn toward the Catholic schools which gave instruction in the colonial language.[17]

Efulen Station

The Efulen mission, originally called *Ekonemekak*, was established in 1893, and situated among the Bulu people, who showed eagerness to learn God's Word.

Dr Silas Franklin Johnson and his wife, Mary, were assigned to Efulen in early 1895. Details of their life in Kamerun are given in the book, *The Great Ngee*, written by their daughter, Lois Johnson McNeill. Dr Johnson notes that missionaries recruited boarding school students by offering their fathers 4-yard lengths of calico cloth. The amount of cloth varied, depending on enrolment numbers, and sometimes the fathers argued over the amount. It was difficult for the missionaries to convince them of the value of sending their children to school in the early years.[18]

The Amazing story of Obam Mve

One day, Dr Johnson approached the men of Ekowoñ, to ask them to send a boy to the mission school. The men hesitated, then one smiled and said, "Give him Obam!"[19] They produced a pitiful and neglected boy of about seven years of age and offered him to the mission. The child was malnourished and dirty; the men of the village waited to see the missionary's response to their prank. He took Obam with him to the mission. Weeks later, these same men of Ekowoñ were astonished to see the boy in church, clothed, healed, clean and happy. Forty years later, Obam Mve was a respected church leader and excellent preacher, a strong and highly honoured pastor who accomplished much for Christ among his people.[20]

The Johnsons offered education and medical care, while they learned the Bulu language and customs at Efulen. Doctor Johnson built a small hospital, seeing patients and performing surgeries. He won the hearts of the Bulu people when he challenged the local witchdoctor and exposed his deceits. The people gave him the nickname "Dokita Nnom Ngee" (Doctor Great Witchdoctor), which endured

---

17 BFM-PCUSA *Annual Report* 1896.
18 McNeill, 41.
19 McNeill, 42.
20 McNeill, 43.

his forty years among them.[21] After a year of serving alone at the Efulen Mission, the Johnsons welcomed a new couple – Rev. William and Mrs Emily Johnston, just weeks before Mrs Mary Johnson was to give birth to her first child.

The schoolboys of the Efulen Mission helped to build the first church building in nearby Nyabitandi, in 1896. Dr Silas Johnson later encouraged them to participate in the evangelism of more distant regions of Bululand through supporting and sending their own Gospel-bearers. They took up the first offering ever taken among the Bulu, which amounted to about $1.58. With that, they sent out two young men, who went out for six days, preaching the Gospel in unreached areas. Dr Johnston credits these Bulu schoolboys with the "remarkable and fruitful movement for the evangelization of the Bulu,"[22] which resulted in the spectacular growth of Christianity in Kamerun.

The first known convert from Efulen was a tiny, elderly woman named Minkoé mi Ntem, though she was called "Nane" (mother). After receiving Christ as Saviour, Nane immediately set out in the night to travel thirty miles to share the Good News with her sister, Zamo, who subsequently put her trust in Jesus Christ. Nane, her daughter Abômô, and her sister Zamo were all faithful Christians, hard workers, and evangelists among the Bulu. It was Nane Minkoé who welcomed Mary Johnson on her arrival to Efulen and became her Bulu mother.[23]

Elat (Ebolewo'e) Station

From Efulen Mission, the work expanded to Ebolewo'e (meaning *rotten chimpanzee*), a site selected by Dr Good in his 1894 travels. This mission, later renamed "Elat" ("uniting" – indicating a meeting place for friendship and understanding), was established in January 1895, with the arrival of three unmarried missionaries, Mr Kerr, Mr Fraser and Mr McCleary and some fifty-four carriers and catechists from Efulen. The group purchased three native dwellings and began to construct mission buildings. The two missions were about four days' journey through the forest, with dangers of robbery and intertribal aggression.[24] Mrs Johnson grieved for the unmarried missionary men at Elat, knowing that their loneliness, hard work and poor diet made them vulnerable to deadly illnesses. She believed that missionary women should be allowed to share in the hard work and sacrifice of the pioneering work in the Kamerun interior.[25] The first missionary woman would not come to Elat until the arrival of Dr Alfred Lippert and his wife, Eliza, in 1898.

---

21 McNeill, 58.
22 McNeill, 68.
23 McNeill, 70.
24 BFM-PCUSA 1897, 31.
25 McNeill, 69.

Mrs Roberts, the medical missionary, died of fever at Batanga in May 1896.[26] While missionaries tended to attribute deaths to overwork and physical stress, many of their constituents at home believed that homesickness and isolation contributed to their mental and emotional breakdown, which weakened their ability to fight off the effects of fever. Yet, missionary deaths were fewer, due to healthful diets, well-constructed homes and the increased supply of mail and encouragement from supporters at home.[27]

Lolodorf (MacLean) Station[28]

Two single men, the newly widowed Mr Roberts and Mr Kerr, were sent to establish another station in the Kamerun interior. The MacLean Mission station, at Lolodorf, opened in 1897, and was originally established to reach the Bakweya, or dwarf tribes, and adopted the Bulu language. This mission also reached the Ngumba people.[29] Through 1897 the churches in the Kamerun region had attendances between 200 and 300. The mission schools were thriving and now had Rev. Good's translation of the Gospels in the Bulu language.[30] The German colonials were building roads between the major towns, thereby easing and shortening missionary travel considerably. In 1898, the Annual Report announced the new MacLean Memorial Station, at Lolodorf, 90 miles northeast of Batanga.[31]

The missionaries received regular mail and supplies due to regular steamer ships coming from England and Germany. As there was no harbour, the steamers would anchor two miles out and transport people and supplies by small boats in the rough surf. Missionary Charles McCleary wrote to a group of youth at home, asking for prayer as missionaries worked in a vast field, full of people seeking more of those who would *talk God's words*.[32] In a letter to his parents, McCleary lamented the small missionary force in such a broad field, "extending even to the center of this great continent, with millions dying without the Gospel, and there are but three of us weak men to tell them the life giving news."[33]

---

26 BFM-PCUSA 1897, 21.
27 WFMS *Historical Sketches*, 29.
28 This station went by three different names: Lolodorf, MacLean, or Bibia.
29 Ford, 100.
30 BFM-PCUSA 1897, 29.
31 BFM-PCUSA 1898, 19.
32 McCleary 26 May 1898, in *The Beloved*, 160–162.
33 McCleary 28 May 1898, in *The Beloved*, 162–164.

The missionaries had a *man of peace*[34] in the person of the Mvonde, the great chief of Ebolowo'e, and another in a lesser chief named Ntoze – Mvonde being the greater because he had the most wives, numbering eighty at the time.[35] McCleary noted the occupations of the people, "the women make gardens and prepare food for the men. The men talk, eat, sleep, and fight."[36] Mvonde was mighty but never came to faith in Christ. He was a fierce and brutal husband. At his death, in July 1899, many of his wives were shut up in a hut. Missionaries attempted to intervene, but the Bulu believed that even natural deaths were the work of witchcraft and sought to punish the culprit(s) – often the wives or slaves of the dead man. Ultimately it is a scramble for the goods and property of the deceased.[37] Two weeks later, in August 1899, Rev. William Gault died at Batanga. His colleague, Mr McCleary described him as an "elephant" – quiet, strong, steady, always working – a pillar of the mission.[38] Rev. Gault had served with the mission for almost two decades, at various stations. His widow, Lizzie Gault, would continue to serve in Kamerun for six more years, at Batanga.

Bulu Life and Ministry

German colonial powers eventually occupied the original hilltop site of Elat, and the mission relocated to a nearby lower area. In 1899, various tribal leaders rose up to rebel against the German colonial powers. While the American missionaries were not targeted, this brought great tension and danger in the region.[39]

Local Christians at Efulen raised an offering of $10.50 for the carrying of the Gospel to the region of Ntum. One woman removed her ankle bracelets and added them to the offering, giving all that she had.[40]

The Presbyterian Church of Efulen was organised in 1900. The first Bulu baptisms took place on May 13, 1900, and the Lord's Supper was shared for the first time. Ndongo was ordained as the first Bulu church elder.[41] The charter members of the Efulen church included one man (Elder Ndongo), a young man of seventeen, named Nlate, and four women: Mese, Abia Ngon, Biso and Minkoe (called Nane), who was well-known for her skill in leading others to Christ.

---

34 A modern missiological term rooted in Luke 10:5–7, where in missions a providential person may be encountered amongst the people group being evangelised who is an aid to seeing more doors open.
35 McCleary, "Bule People," 147.
36 McCleary, "Bule People," 148.
37 Hinkhouse, 207.
38 Hinkhouse, 211.
39 McNeill, 84.
40 McNeill, 85.
41 McNeill, 86. See also, Cogswell, *No Turning Back*, 9 referencing Mary Johnson.

Nlate would eventually become the first ordained Bulu pastor, some eighteen years later.[42]

The Elat Presbyterian Church was organised in October 1902. By this time, the whole Bible was available in the Benga language, and the Gospels and Book of Acts were translated into Bulu.[43] The first service of the First Presbyterian Church at Elat, on 26 October 1902, had an attendance of 855. Their offerings included native food, live animals, ivory, knives, articles of clothing, and other trade goods, totalling an estimated $35. The Elat Church charter members included four women, one man and one boy, whose names were Osom, Biwola, Evindi, Osela, Avoto and the boy, Ngane.[44]

Missionary Deaths

The Kamerun Christians lost many of their missionaries in 1902–03. Miss Hulda Christensen, who had served ten years among them, died in her homeland of Norway. Rev. Itongolo ja Ivina, the first missionary and pillar of the church,[45] died in 1902, after more than twenty years' ministry. Itongolo had been a fisherman in the Benita region when he met Dr Nassau, who shared the Gospel with him. Itongolo became a follower of Jesus Christ, and a disciple of the mission; soon, he was a teacher and preacher among his own Benga people, and eventually a cross-cultural missionary to the Banâkâ people. Itongolo was licensed in early 1889.[46] Dr Nassau described him as faithful, earnest, and true to his calling, a man above reproach.[47]

While new missionaries continued to arrive in Kamerun, many soon returned to America for their health. Mr David H. Devor died in 1902, having served one year, and Mr Charles McCleary died of fever in 1903, months after bringing his new bride, Myrtie, to the field. Mrs Mary Johnson's terminal illness required the family to return to the US. After her death, in 1903, Dr Johnson left their two small daughters with Lydia (Mrs A. C.) Good, in Ohio, and returned to Kamerun alone. A year later, his fiancée Laura Moser arrived on the field, and the two were married. Dr Johnson and his new wife were two of seven missionaries now serving at Efulen station.

Despite missionary attrition and death at the turn of the century, several missionary couples arrived (or married) on the field and remained for many years, including Dr Alfred B. T. Lippert and his wife, Eliza, Rev. William Moore

---

42 McNeill, 87.
43 Ford, 100.
44 Dager, 104.
45 DeHeer, 13.
46 Nassau, 1914, 401.
47 Nassau, 1916, 507.

Dager and his wife, Sarah, Dr Wilmer S. Lehman and his wife, Anna, Dr Hyman Weber and his wife, Ethelbert, and Mrs Myrtie McCleary.

4. Bulu Apostles to the Bene

The Unique commencement of the Metet Station

Twenty-eight days after leaving Lolodorf, a missionary caravan left the forest and entered a clearing, finding a town comprised of sixty-three bark huts in a long row. The missionaries would recommend this site to the Mission Board for the next mission outpost; however, the Mission did not have enough funds or personnel at the time. They revisited the area in 1908, selecting a site two miles east of Metet, and the missionaries contributed the needed funds to purchase the land. Though there were no available missionaries at the time, the native Elat church sent several of their fine leaders and supported them through offerings. These *apostles* included elder Ako'o Ze ("Rock Leopard") and his wife, Ajap Evina. For two months, this Bulu couple visited the Bene people living along the Nlong River and held fifty-four meetings to share with them the Gospel. One meeting grew to 900 listeners, and the couple estimated that they had shared the message with 3,000 Bene tribesmen.

Two more men from Elat Church, whose people had been enemies at one time, went hand in hand to preach the Gospel among the Bene people near Metet. It was Osom, however, who served the longest among them. He had been the first elder of the Elat Church, ordained in 1902. It was Elder Osom who spent two years clearing the hilltop that would be the Metet Mission. He built himself a dwelling, and then gathered Bene children, teaching them to read and write, to sing praise songs and to memorise scripture. Elder Osom walked along the trails, playing his accordion and singing to the Bene people, who were great lovers of music.[48] Oscom's nickname was "The Bulu John the Baptist" as he truly went ahead and prepared the way for the station and also several outposts all in this region amongst the Bene.[49] The Bene people were familiar with German colonials, who were harsh. Elder Osom told them of the missionaries who desired to serve and teach them but would not exploit them. In this way, he prepared the way for the American Presbyterian missionaries who would soon settle at Metet.[50]

Dr Silas Johnson, who had been serving for several years at Angom Mission (Gaboon), was reassigned to the newest station of Metet, in the vast unreached

---

48 McNeill, 113.
49 Cogswell, *No Turning Back*, 10.
50 McNeill, 114.

Bene region. In the four years that Dr Johnson had been absent, Kamerun had changed considerably. The Germans had built roads which connected all four of the mission stations to the larger cities of Yaounde and Kribi. They had also begun work on a railroad. The mission schools taught in both German and the vernacular language, and the German government was supportive of the schools. Hundreds of young boys sought education at the mission schools and found teaching opportunities with the mission.[51] Dr Johnson planted 4,000 plantains, twelve hundred pineapples, a hundred pawpaw trees, sixty avocado trees, and imported chickens and ducks. He planted two flamboyant trees anticipating that they would give much shade to those listening to the Gospel message.

Mrs Myrtle McCleary, who had arrived as a bride in 1902, and was widowed in 1903, remained on the Kamerun field for nearly four decades; she was known as "Mama McCleary" to hundreds of Kamerun schoolboys educated at Elat over the years. In 1910, Mrs McCleary was eager to visit the new Metet site, and rode her bicycle there, stopping at villages to share the Gospel. She referred to these as *women's meetings*, but the village men also crowded in to hear her message. The people would ask Mrs McCleary to let down her hair, which they considered beautiful, like a horse's tail.[52]

Elder missionaries

While Kamerun welcomed countless young missionaries and their families in the early years, there were also a number of elder missionaries who had served at Corisco and Gaboon since the 1860s and 70s and were finishing their long years of service in this new field. Dr Robert Hamill Nassau served at all the Gaboon and Corisco Mission stations over four decades and ended his service at Kamerun in 1906. Three missionary widows also finished their missionary careers at Kamerun. They were Reubina (Mrs C.) DeHeer and Louise (Mrs Solomon) Reutlinger, who both retired in 1906, and Phebe (Mrs T. S.) Ogden, who retired in 1909. Another widow who served for many years was Lydia Belle (Mrs A. C.) Good, who remained in the US for fifteen years after the death of her husband, but returned with her grown son, Rev. Albert I. Good, in 1909. Mrs Good retired in 1921.

---

51 McNeill, 115.
52 McNeill, 118.

5. Eastward Push

By 1910, there were fifteen self-supporting churches in Kamerun, who were building their own chapels and supporting their own catechists and evangelists. The church in Kamerun now had seminary graduates, licensed and ordained young men, with a vision for preaching the Gospel to the regions beyond them.[53] Dr Silas Johnson and Mr Gayle Beanland hoped to further the work ninety miles east of Metet, in the region of the powerful Yebekolo and Mekae tribes. Both tribes were known to be hostile and cannibalistic. The German colonial government warned foreigners from travelling in that area. One brave Bene Christian from Metet was willing to *spy out the land* but was met with hostility; he was soon reinforced when missionary Gayle Beanland and a large group of Bene schoolboys arrived to preach the gospel to this yet unreached people. One powerful chief, Biwole Beti, allowed the group to stay a night and speak, but he refused to allow them to establish a church or school in his town; another chief, Zenge Bilunga, agreed to receive two Bene men, an evangelist and a teacher, but the two fled the hostile villagers shortly thereafter.[54]

Efufup Station

The Metet church was organised in March 1911 with an attendance of one thousand persons. Ten were baptised, and were the charter members, and 300 more signed up for inquirer classes.[55] Following this important ceremony, missionaries Johnson and Beanland and the Bene evangelists once again trekked to the region of the Yebekolo people, ending up in the town of a one-eyed chief named Olinga. Dr Johnson set up a makeshift clinic and treated physical maladies, while the rest were communicating the Gospel message. The visiting Christians proposed to buy a portion of land, on which they would build a school. It was 200 square metres, and the purchase price was twenty German marks. Within a few weeks, there was a school and forty schoolboys, while Sunday services drew crowds of 350. This site at Olinga's town was now called *Efufup*, meaning "light," by its first converts.[56] Their first teacher, Owono, would teach at the school each day, and then visit the people in the nearby villages, to invite them to Sunday services. Soon, the other villages wanted their own school, pastor, and teacher. Another Bulu teacher from Efulen, a pioneer missionary among the people of Metet and Yebekolo, was Mvondo Ngbwa. Having already served for thirteen years in ministry, Mvondo relocated, with his wife and children, to this strange and

---

53 McNeill, 115.
54 McNeill, 127.
55 McNeill, 128.
56 McNeill, 133.

hostile place. After two years there, Mvondo became ill with sleeping sickness and died in 1917. This untimely death inspired a flood of Efulen believers to join in the evangelistic work, which became the Great Awakening in that region.[57]

6. Missionary Writings of Kamerun

One notable missionary was Miss Jean Kenyon McKenzie, who served in Kamerun from 1904 to 1914. Miss McKenzie wrote numerous articles and books about her years in Africa, giving a richly detailed account of missionaries and indigenous church members, local culture, and daily life. Miss McKenzie's writings reveal the personalities and relationships of the various people in and around the mission, adding depth and colour not found in the factual information of mission annual reports.

Miss McKenzie recounted the day, in early 1906, when a small group of missionary men trekked north-eastward, beyond Yaounde, to find a suitable site for the next mission. The group consisted of Wilmer Lehman, M.D., Silas F. Johnson, M.D., and Mr Francis Guthrie, who travelled by bicycle, by canoe and on foot, for more than six weeks. They covered more than 800 miles, meeting tribes who had never heard the Gospel of Jesus Christ. The local languages varied, but most understood the Bulu language used by the missionaries. The eighteen young carrier boys who accompanied the missionaries gave their testimonies to the many villagers.[58] The group crossed the Nlong River into the territory of the Bene people, and made friends with a powerful chief, Mbita Menge. Dr Johnson subsequently extracted the chief's painful tooth, relieving him of great pain. Mbita then sent his drummer to beat a summons for the people to come and hear the foreigners' message. A crowd of 570 Bene assembled and listened to Dr Johnson's message of the Gospel.[59]

7. Frank James Industrial School

The Frank James Industrial School was named after an American man who had died while hunting elephants in Kamerun in 1893. His sister honoured his memory and name by providing the funding for the mission school. The funds were available as early as 1902, but the mission lacked a qualified missionary to run it.[60] Missionary Fred H. Hope arrived with his wife at Elat in January 1908. They began teaching tailoring in February, but Mrs Hope died at Elat in May.

---

57 McNeill, 134.
58 McNeill, 100.
59 McNeill, 101.
60 BFM-PCUSA 1902, 32.

Mr Hope taught his students the value of quality materials and skilled workmanship. In time, the students learned carpentry, and constructed many of the mission buildings. They built quality furniture, and developed skills in caning, hat-making, shoemaking, mechanic arts, auto repair, blacksmithing, ivory, and metal crafts. The school attracted hundreds of young men, and was soon self-supporting, and even profitable. As the trained Christian craftsmen earned admiration and respect with their quality work, they also served as teachers and evangelists. The school expanded and offered more varied training and skills.[61] Mr Hope married again in 1911, and his five daughters were born at Elat Mission. The Hopes remained at Elat for four decades of ministry, retiring in 1945.

8. Theological Education

Miss Isabella Nassau was the earliest and oldest theological educator of the mission,[62] having served for more than forty years with the Gaboon and Corisco mission, beginning at Corisco in 1869, then Bolondo-Benita, then Ogowe River (Gaboon), and finally at Kamerun. She was an educator and itinerating evangelist, training African men and women for Christian ministry and evangelism. As a woman, she had no power or authority in the mission, but she was a tremendous influence on the earliest church leaders in Equatorial Africa. For many years, the ordained missionary men planned and attempted to offer theological training, but illness, interruptions and competing needs kept them from offering consistent, quality theological education. The young Benga men of Benita gathered around Miss Nassau, asking for training, and she gave it. She prepared these African men for licensing and ordination, while the ordained missionary men examined and ultimately ordained them. The Presbyterian Board considered Miss Nassau's cottage to be the theological seminary of the West Africa Mission.[63] Miss Nassau continued to train young men for ministry in Kamerun, well into her old age. She died and was buried at Batanga Mission cemetery in June 1906.

The William Dager Theological Seminary (named after the noted missionary evangelist William Dager) was established circa 1909 in a building that cost $15. It provided theological training to young men from the various churches. The one instructor was missionary Melvin Fraser, who taught Church History, Acts

---

61 BFM-PCUSA 1918, 79.
62 "Obituary – The Death of Miss Nassau in Africa." The mission made many attempts at formal theological education, but all failed. Miss Nassau was the only dedicated and consistent theological educator in the Gaboon and Corisco Mission between 1870 and 1905.
63 Halsey, 39.

of the Apostles, Life of Christ, and Theology of the Shorter Catechism to six Bulu students. This number grew to eleven students by 1914, when Kamerun Christians were at their highest numbers in church attendance: 8,000 at Elat, 1,000 at Metet, and 5,000 at Foulasi. The Elat church baptised 1,079 adults and 200 infants in a single service.[64]

By early 1917, there were 61 candidates for ministry receiving theological training.[65] In 1917, Nlata Bikam was the first Bulu to be ordained as pastor. Nlata served at the Zingi outpost of the Efulen Mission.[66]

The missionaries prioritised training and sending the mission schoolboys to both preach and teach at the many communities seeking leadership. At this time, there were considerably fewer girls educated in the schools, due to early marriage customs. Women's ministry, however, gave both teaching and opportunity to churchwomen, who fully participated in the many evangelistic efforts.

9. European war interruption

The Fulasi Church, some 70 miles east of Elat, was organised on Easter Sunday 1914, with a charter membership of 354, with 251 being from the mother church at Elat.

In early 1914, the mission identified a new site 250 miles east of Elat, near Lomié, where they hoped to establish a new outpost. However, as the European war loomed, [67] these plans would be delayed for years. For twenty years they had been convincing Africans to believe in Christ and lay down their weapons. Now, the Christian European countries were at war, and it spilled into various parts of German Kamerun. Missionaries of opposing nations maintained their mutual kindness and respect, even sheltered one another, but many were evacuated or taken as war prisoners. French forces evacuated hundreds of Africans from active war zones to safer places, far from home. Pastors Ndenga and Eduma were among the exiles and shepherded their fellow refugees during that difficult time. Later in life, Ndenga contracted leprosy, and finished out his ministry years pastoring his fellow lepers.[68]

---

64 McNeill, 139.
65 "African Churches Grow," 319.
66 BFM-PCUSA 1918, 77.
67 McNeill, 139.
68 McNeill, 145.

10. French Occupation

The Germans evacuated Kamerun by February 1916, and French forces took control of the territory, changing its name to the French Cameroun. At this point, the mission opened another outpost further east at Lomié. While the war interrupted missionary mail, travel, and meetings, the Kamerun churches were growing and multiplying. Three churches were organised in December 1916: the Biba church (sixteen miles southwest of Elat) was organised on December 10, with 234 charter members; the Ngomedan church (seven miles southeast of Elat) was organised on December 17, with 803 charter members; the Endam church (24 miles east of Elat) was organised on December 31, with 600 charter members. Each of these ceremonies had attendance of two to three thousand.

In the years immediately after the war, missionaries established cordial relations with the French colonial officials and were now required to give all instruction in French. At the time, only one missionary, Miss Marie Gocker, was knowledgeable in French, and she began to give language training to male teachers at Batanga. The mission now needed to print materials in French and required new missionaries to gain French language proficiency before coming to the field. The war had interrupted the flourishing trade and industry in the region, which created a shortage of supplies and smaller wages for church and mission workers. Yet, their commitment to the Gospel was even stronger and they maintained their tithing pledges despite these losses.[69]

In 1919, a great flu epidemic swept through Bululand, which the natives called *mbu ôkon*, meaning, "the year of sickness." The mission sent typed instructions to the village headmen on how to isolate, take precautions, and how to care for the sick. Dr Johnson rode his motorcycle to the villages, giving counsel from a distance. There were 200 influenza patients within two miles of Metet, but these many precautions and medical care kept the mortality rate low.[70]

11. Sakbayeme Station

In 1920, the Presbyterian Mission established Sakbayeme Mission, in Basa Country, some 90 miles northwest of Elat. It had formerly been part of the Basel Mission with German missionaries. The Basel Mission territory was divided in 1920 between the Paris Missionary Society taking the coastal area around Douala and the American Presbyterian Mission taking the territory further north at Edea and Sakbayeme in 1920 and also further to Bafia in 1921. This was a critical mission as it began the Presbyterian mission working for the first time

---

69 McNeill, 150.
70 McNeill, 152.

with the Bassa peoples and also brought them for the first time into territory where Islam was advancing in various villages in this region.[71] Cogswell notes that the Basel Mission "continued its work in the British Cameroons, work which later produced the English-speaking Presbyterian Church of Cameroon."[72]

Printing Press

The Mission opened a printing press, named in honour of the former Secretary of the Board of Foreign Missions, Dr Abram W. Halsey, who had made a prolonged visit to the field in 1905. Missionary John H. Bradford, a printing specialist, gave oversight and training for the printing press at Elat. The mission press was considered one of the most significant press operations on the foreign field at the time, printing schoolbooks, Bibles, periodicals, and various types of literature in seven dialects. The press machinery was installed in 1925 and had been highly productive for a year when Mr Bradford suddenly died. There was no other missionary skilled in printing at that time.[73]

Long-term missionaries to Cameroon

High numbers of new missionaries arrived in Kamerun prior to 1920, and many remained for ten years or more on the field, including:

Name[74]	Years of Service
Rev. James and Mrs Minnie Cunningham	1903–1913
Rev. John A. and Mrs Una Wright	1906–1920
Mr L. D. and Edna Heminger	L. D. 1903–1920, Edna 1903–1941
Mr George and Mrs Jewel Schwab	1905–1941
Dr Oliver and Mrs Lida Pinney	1907–1920
Rev. Frank and Mrs Alta Emerson	Frank 1906–1947, Alta 1906–1929
Miss Verna Eick	1911–1946
Rev. Jacob and Mrs Eleanor Reis	1908–1945
Rev. Albert and Mrs Mary Good	Albert 1909–1949, Mary 1918–1949
Mr Herbert and Mrs Christina Grieg	1909–1931

---

71 Cogswell, *No Turning Back*, 29.
72 Cogswell, *No Turning Back*, 353.
73 "In Memoriam," 360.
74 A number of these rest in the mission cemeteries in Cameroon.

Name	Years of Service
Rev. Herbert and Mrs Eunice Hoisington	Herbert 1910–1943, Eunice 1910–1950
Mr Alexander and Mrs Maria Patterson	1912–1937
Rev Frederick and Mrs Mildred Neal	1911–1951
Mr Alvin and Mrs Effie Carr	1912–22
Rev. Gayle and Mrs Lillian Beanland	Gayle 1910-1948, Lillian 1919–1948
Rev. Danvers and Mrs Mary Love	1911–1953
Rev. Peter and Mrs Beatrice Kapteyn	1912–1923
Rev. Roland and Mrs Bertha Evans	Roland 1909–1932, Bertha 1914–1932
Rev. Edward and Mrs Lucia Cozzens	Edward 1914–1959, Lucia 1919–1949
Miss Marie Gocker	1914–1936
Rev. Joseph and Mrs Lois McNeill	1918–1959

12. Church Organisation Develops (c.1920–c.1940)

Throughout the 1920s, 1930s, and to 1940 more mission stations were developed deeper into the interior: 1922 at Yaounde, 1928 at Nkol Mvolan, 1933 at Momjepom, and 1940 at Ilanga. Thus, by 1940 the American Presbyterians had twelve stations and many evangelistic outposts (numbering over 100) and these outposts were led by indigenous leaders under the zeal of missionary Frank Emerson. By 1940 the Mission had 178 organised congregations with over 1,000 other groups meeting, such that there were over 800 ordained ministers and over 1,500 evangelists.[75] Until 1936 all of this was still organised under the Presbytery of Corisco and attached to the Synod of New Jersey. In 1936 the Synod of Cameroun was established by the GA of the PCUSA with now three presbyteries: the Presbytery of Corisco, the Presbytery of Metet, and the Presbytery of Sanaga.[76]

13. Summary Conclusion

This survey chapter has clearly revealed the incredible extent of the mission work of the Presbyterian Church in the United States of America in Cameroon. In effect it became its largest concentrated mission in West Africa; a vast number of mission personnel and indigenous leaders were used in this mission. For

---

75 Cogswell, *No Turning Back*, 29–30.
76 Cogswell, *No Turning Back*, 30.

example, in 1914 the PCUSA had 62 missionaries serving in Kamerun, an incredible commitment to this field. The mission was wholistic or integrated, as evidenced by the educational endeavours which included industrial training and artisan work, medical missions, and women's mission work. The constant theme was one of incredible sacrifice for the sake of the Evangel and the spread of the Word of the Lord to see many come to salvation and become followers of the Lord Jesus Christ. The backdrop of the colonial struggles between Germany, France, and Britain are clearly woven into this mission story of Cameroon and are very complex. There is also a reminder here that often we build upon the labours of others and a hint is found at that from the work inherited by the American Presbyterian Mission from the Basel Mission.

Questions for study (fact type):
1. Name the elder that was first sent by the Benita people to take the gospel to the German Kameron. Also, name the first mission station there. What year was this?
2. After ten years, what mission board began to send missionaries to this work?
3. What year was the Synod of Cameroun established?
4. Reproduce the map in this chapter and place the following mission stations on the map: Batanga (the first), Elat (Ebolewo'e), Lolodorf, Metet, Efufup. Many other mission stations were also established. Include two others on your map that are of interest to you.

Questions for study (reflection type):
1. The events of the First World War greatly affected German Kameron as it now came under French control. *"For twenty years they had been convincing Africans to believe in Christ and lay down their weapons. Now, the Christian European countries were at war, and it spilled into various parts of German Kamerun. Missionaries of opposing nations maintained their mutual kindness and respect, even sheltered one another"*. Explain the tensions that came into the mission because of the war in Europe. How did the missionaries respond? Use the Romans 12:18 to explain your answer.
2. *"The young Benga men of Benita gathered around Miss Nassau, asking for training, and she gave it. She prepared these African men for licensing and ordination, while the ordained missionary men examined and ultimately ordained them. The Presbyterian Board considered Miss Nassau's cottage to be the theological seminary of the West Africa Mission.[77] Miss Nassau continued to train young men for ministry in Kamerun, well into her old age. She died and was buried at Batanga Mission cemetery in June 1906."*

---

77 Halsey, 39.

Miss Isabella Nassau made a significant contribution to theological education. Consider her informal method of training in her home. What would you think were the strengths of it? What were the possible weaknesses? Contrast this method to your own theological education and discuss.

Select Bibliography

"African Churches Grow Despite War." *The Continent* 48.11 (15 March 1917): 319.

Board of Foreign Missions of the PCUSA. "Gaboon and Corisco Mission." *The Forty-third Annual Report of the Board*. NY: Mission House, 1880: 26–28.

.... "Gaboon and Corisco Mission." *The Forty-fourth Annual Report of the Board*. NY: Mission House. 1881: 31–34.

.... "Gaboon and Corisco Mission." *The Forty-fifth Annual Report of the Board*. NY: Mission House. 1882: 32–38.

.... "Gaboon and Corisco Mission." *The Fifty-third Annual Report of the Board*. NY: Mission House. 1890: 13–21.

.... "Gaboon and Corisco Mission." *The Fifty-fourth Annual Report of the Board*. NY: Mission House. 1891: 11–20.

.... "Gaboon and Corisco Mission." *The Fifty-fifth Annual Report of the Board*. NY: Mission House. 1892: 17–25.

.... "Gaboon and Corisco Mission." *The Fifty-ninth Annual Report of the Board*. NY: Mission House: 1896. 21–31.

.... "Gaboon and Corisco Mission." *The Sixtieth Annual Report of the Board*. NY: Mission House. 1897: 21–32.

.... "Gaboon and Corisco Mission." *The Sixty-first Annual Report of the Board*. NY: Mission House. 1898: 19–30.

.... "West African Mission." The Sixty-Fifth Annual Report of the Board. NY: Mission House, 1902: 27–39.

.... "West Africa Mission." *The Seventieth Annual Report of the Board*. NY: Presbyterian House, 1907: 27–42.

.... "West Africa Mission." *The Eighty-First Annual Report of the Board*. NY: Presbyterian House, 1918: 73–84.

Cogswell, James A. *No Turning Back: A History of American Presbyterian Involvement in Sub-Saharan Africa, 1833–2000*. Philadelphia: Xlibris, 2007.

Dager, William M. "The First Presbyterian Church at Elat," "The West African Mission." *The Assembly Herald* 8.3 (March 1903): 104.

DeHeer, Reubina Hope. "Amid Losses in Africa, Hoping Still." *Woman's Work for Woman* 15.1 (Jan. 1903): 13.

General Assembly of the Presbyterian Church. "Foreign Mission Notes." *The Church at Home and Abroad* 7 (Sept. 1890): 203–204.

Ford, Edward A. "The West African Mission." *The Assembly Herald* 8.3 (March 1903): 98–100.

Halsey, Abram W. *A Visit to the West Africa Mission of the Presbyterian Church in the U.S.A.* New York: Board of Commissioners for Foreign Missions, 1905.

Hinkhouse, John Frederick, ed. *The Beloved: An Iowa Boy in the Jungles of Africa*. Iowa: Privately published by friends, 1909.

"In Memoriam." *Women and Missions* 3.9 (Dec. 1926): 360.

J'Ikenge, Ibia. "An African Minister's Journal." *The Presbyterian Monthly Record* 30.10 (Oct. 1879): 313–315.

McCleary, Charles W. "Bule People Around the New Station [Ebolobo'e]" *Woman's Work for Woman* 11.6 (June 1896): 147–148.

… . Letter dated May 26, 1898. In *The Beloved*, 160–162.

… . Letter dated May 28, 1898. In *The Beloved*, 162–164.

McNeill, Lois Johnson. *The Great Ngee: The Story of a Jungle Doctor*. Commission on Ecumenical Mission and Relations of the United Presbyterian Church in the USA, 1959.

Nassau, Robert Hamill. *My Ogowe: Being a Narrative of Daily Incidents During Sixteen Years in Equatorial West Africa*. NY: Neale, 1914.

Nassau, Robert Hamill. *A History of the Presbytery of Corisco*. Trenton, NJ: Albert Brandt, Jr., 1888.

Nassau, Robert Hamill. "Itongolo: The Black Fisherman." *The Missionary Review of the World*, 39.7 (July 1916): 507–508.

"Obituary – the Death of Miss Nassau in Africa." *The Assembly Herald* 12.8 (Aug 1906): 409–410.

Parsons, Ellen C. *A Life for Africa: Rev. Adolphus Clemens Good, Ph.D.*, Second Edition. New York: Fleming H. Revell, 1898.

Wheeler, W. Reginald. *The Words of God in an African Forest.* New York: Fleming H. Revell, 1931.

Woman's Foreign Missionary Society of the Presbyterian Church. "Africa: Woman's Work on the Dark Continent." *Woman's Work for Woman* 13.6 (June 1883): 181–183.

——. "Letters from the Front." *Woman's Work for Woman* 6 (June 1891): 164.

——. *Historical Sketches of the Missions Under the Care of the Board of Foreign Missions of the PCUSA*, Fourth Edition. 1897.

Bio Inset

Lydia Walker Good: Native American Missionary to Gabon & Cameroon

Mary Cloutier

Introduction

Lydia Belle Walker Good was a Native American Presbyterian missionary who served in Equatorial Africa in the late 19th century. Though overshadowed by her famous missionary husband and son, Lydia's story, as an indigenous American missionary to indigenous people of Africa, is perhaps more fascinating to our present generation.

Early Life

Lydia Belle Burnham was born March 1856 and adopted into the family of Peter and Eliza Walker, an elderly white couple who lived in Wilson, New York. Lydia's origins are unknown, but the Walkers believed she was born in Canada.[78]

Lydia graduated from Union High School (Wilson, NY) in 1871 and Cooper Seminary for Young Ladies (Dayton, Ohio), in 1873. That same year, she was appointed as a missionary through the Presbyterian Board of Missions.[79]

Ministry among Native Americans

Lydia first served as a mission schoolteacher among the Ojibwa people at Odanah, Wisconsin. The community numbered 600, and the mission school had around 65 pupils. Mission reports indicate that Lydia was *of Indian parentage*,[80] perhaps to reflect the Presbyterian Board's commitment to training and appointing indigenous workers for ministry among their people.

---

78 Lydia Burnham first appears in the 1860 census, living with the Walkers in Wilson, NY. By the 1870 census, she is listed as Lydia Walker, their adopted daughter. Census reports suggest she was born either in New York or Canada, but Lydia's 1919 passport application indicates that she did not have a birth certificate, and believed she was born in Syracuse, NY.
79 Presbyterian Historical Society, Guide to Lydia Belle Walker Good Papers.
80 Presbyterian Board, "Lake Superior Indian Mission," 6.

After serving at Odanah for four years, Lydia requested a transfer to the PCUSA West Africa Mission, located in present-day Gabon. She sailed in November 1877 with two returning missionaries. Their arrival at the mission was a time of celebration and warm welcome.[81]

Ministry in Africa

Lydia Walker served as teacher and caregiver for the mission schoolgirls, who affectionately called her *Ngiaingango* (little mother).[82] Lydia found joy in her ministry and friendships. She remained strong for the demanding work and climate, but after three years, she took a health furlough.

In America, Lydia reunited with friends and family in a whirlwind of activity which left little time for rest and recuperation. That year, she met a missionary appointee, Rev. Adolphus Good. She perceived that he would be a valuable worker and advised him to find a helpmeet to bring with him.[83]

Rev. Good arrived in Gabon in November 1882. He was deeply interested in pioneering work in the interior but requested placement at the Baraka Mission, a choice his colleagues attributed to his keen interest in Miss Walker.[84] When Lydia Walker arrived in February 1883, she was again assigned to the Baraka Girls' School. She and Rev. Good were married in June 1883. To avoid French colonial laws, they sailed four miles out to sea, aboard the American vessel *Quinnebaug*, where Rev. William Gault performed the marriage ceremony under the American flag.[85] In April 1884, the Goods welcomed a son, Albert (Bertie) Irwin Good.

Through marriage and motherhood, Lydia Good continued her ministries, including a weekly women's prayer meeting. Many came to her door seeking aid and comfort; she shared with them the good news of Jesus Christ and offered practical help, inwardly grieving over their ongoing struggles with alcohol, tobacco, and other vices.[86]

In early 1885, the Goods moved to the Kangwe Mission, deep in the interior. The missionary force had dwindled due to constant sickness and death; added to this was the ongoing stress of inter-tribal wars and increasing opposition by French priests and colonial authorities.

Lydia and little Bertie sailed for America in June 1886 for a year's rest in Wilson, New York, while Rev. Good remained in Africa. He joined his returning

---

81 Nassau, *My Ogowe*, 240.
82 Lydia Walker, "Miss Walker," 334.
83 Walker, Letter 140.
84 Nassau, *My Ogowe*, 418.
85 Parsons, *A Life for Africa*, 44–45.
86 Lydia Good, Letter 94.

family in Europe, where he met with the Paris Evangelical Mission Society to recruit French missionary teachers.[87]

Upon their return to the mission, Rev. Good resumed his travels and was often absent for long periods. Lydia assumed the role of station head and liaison between the inexperienced French teachers and the natives.[88] During this period, Rev. Good was weak from overwork, and nearly died from fever. The family returned to the US for his health.[89]

Returning to the Ogowe River mission in late 1890, the Goods co-laboured with European missionaries, the Jacots, until their relocation to Kamerun, to the north, in early 1893. Through the early 1890s, missionary illnesses and deaths devastated the mission, though Rev. Good was relentless in his zeal to expand the work.[90]

New missionaries arrived in 1893, including medical personnel. As Rev. Good redoubled his speed and efforts to reach the interior, Lydia suffered from nervousness and dyspepsia, agonising over his safety.[91] Finally, in fragile health, Lydia and her son, Bertie, left for the US, while Rev. Good stayed in Kamerun to oversee the new missionaries and expanding work.[92]

Lydia and Bertie spent the summer of 1894 at a sanatorium in upstate New York, where Lydia regained her health.[93] They then relocated to Wooster, Ohio, expecting Rev. Good to join them.[94] However, in December 1894, they received word that he had died of hematuric fever in Kamerun. Lydia mourned her husband deeply. After twenty-one years as a missionary, she resigned from the mission, and committed to raising her son in Wooster.[95]

Nearly five years after her husband's death, Lydia Good received an invitation from the Presbyterian Board to return to Kamerun. She was a gifted linguist and experienced in preparing manuscripts for printing; she was also a valued and trusted co-labourer among both missionaries and indigenous peoples. Lydia declined, however, citing her health.

In October 1903, Lydia informally adopted two motherless missionary girls, Mary and Lois Johnson, whose widowed father, Dr Silas Franklin Johnson, was returning to Kamerun. The girls were then seven and five years of age.

---

87 Parsons, *A Life for Africa*, 82;113.
88 Nassau, *My Ogowe*, 550.
89 Nassau, *My Ogowe*, 619.
90 Ford, Letter 188.
91 A. C. Good, Letter 223.
92 A. C. Good, Letter 1.
93 Lydia Good, Letter 61.
94 Lydia Good, Letter 130.
95 Presbyterian Historical Society, Guide to Lydia Belle Walker Good Papers.

For the next five years, Lydia Good provided them with a loving home and a mother's care, nursing them through the measles, mumps, chicken pox and other childhood pains. She skilfully managed with a limited budget and saw to it that they wrote monthly letters to their papa in Africa. Dr Johnson returned for his daughters in 1908. By then, Lydia's son, Albert Good, had graduated from Wooster college and was now at Western Seminary.[96]

In January 1909, Lydia received an invitation to serve again in Kamerun; this time, she accepted. Friends celebrated with her until her departure on February 27, 1909. Albert Good was also appointed to the Kamerun mission but would sail months later.

▲ Lydia Good c.1910

▲ Lydia at Baraka Women's Meeting, 1909

Lydia Good arrived in Gaboon in April 1909. Many of her former Baraka Mission schoolgirls were now mothers and grandmothers. They were amazed that she could still speak Mpongwe after twenty-five years.[97]

When Albert Good arrived in late 1909, he and his mother relocated to Kamerun. At their arrival, they were welcomed by more than a thousand Bulu people, many of whom had known Rev. A. C. Good. Albert Good, like his father, was a pioneering missionary and was away for long periods of time. These separations were stressful for his mother, who was keenly aware of the dangers he faced as he trekked the Kamerun forests.[98] Lydia Good was thankful to God that she could serve in Kamerun, but she suffered malarial fevers, abdominal pain, anxiousness over her work, and insomnia. The frequent rains brought sadness; visitors and mail from home lifted her spirits.

---

96 McNeill, *The Great Ngee*, 90–91.
97 Mackenzie, *Black Sheep*, 188.
98 LBG diary, entries dated 10–25 Feb.1910.

Lydia formed close friendships with the Bulu people, including Abesula, a young mission worker who was her cultural informant and like a son to her; and Nana, one of the first Bulu Christians, who told Lydia of the early years of the mission, and gave her the Bulu name *Nzam-Ntem*.[99] She considered her service a *silent* one,[100] yet her presence and kindnesses gave comfort to her missionary colleagues and African friends. She visited and prayed with them, celebrated the births, weddings, and holidays; she prepared meals, cared for the sick, doted on the children, and mourned with those who mourned. In her diary, she remembered private celebrations and losses.

Both Lydia and Albert Good left Kamerun in July 1912 for a furlough year. They gave missionary talks and visited their Walker relatives in New York as well as the Goods in Pennsylvania.[101] Mother and son returned to Kamerun in mid-1913, where Lydia resumed her work, teaching sewing to women and discipling young boys.[102]

The Goods took another furlough in late 1916, during World War I. Albert married in Jan. 1918 and left for Africa with his new bride. Lydia's return to Kamerun was delayed until 1919 due to the flu epidemic.

Lydia's last term in Kamerun was less than two years. She worked closely with her daughter-in-law, Mary, and enjoyed her infant grandson, but her health was fragile. Lydia left Kamerun in early 1921, accompanied by her family. She settled in Wooster, Ohio, where she died on 11 March 1924.[103]

Select Bibliography

Good, Lydia. "Personal Diary, 1909–1915." Lydia Walker Good Papers, 1909–1920. Presbyterian Historical Society Archives (PHSA), Philadelphia, PA.

Ancestry.com.

Ford, Edward A. Letter to the Board Secretary, dated 24 June 1893. Africa Letters, Reel 80, Letter 188. PHSA.

Good, Adolphus C. Letter to the Board Secretary, dated 21 November 1893. Africa Letters, Reel 81, Letter 223. PHSA.

—— . Letter to the Board Secretary, dated 1 January 1894. Africa Letters, Reel 81, Letter 1. PHSA.

---

99 LBG diary, entries dated 20–6, Nov.–Dec. 1910.
100 LBG diary, entries dated 27, 28 May 1911.
101 LBG Diary, entries dated Aug 14, 1912 to March 12, 1913.
102 LBG diary, entries dated Oct 19 to Dec 31, 1913.
103 PCUSA, "Death of Mrs Good," 10.

Good, Lydia B. Letter to the Board Secretary, dated 2 Dec. 1884. Africa Letters, Reel 76, Letter 94. PHSA.

——. Letter to the Board Secretary, dated 20 June 1894. Africa Letters, Reel 81, Letter 61. PHSA.

——. Letter to the Board Secretary, dated 9 November 1894. Africa Letters, Reel 81, Letter 130. PHSA.

Ploeger, Pamela I. Email dated 15 Apr 2020. Pam Ploeger is a direct descendant of Silas Franklin Johnson and confirmed details on the Johnson family mentioned in this article.

Mackenzie, Jean Kenyon. *Black Sheep: Adventures in West Africa*. New York: Houghton Mifflin, 1915.

McNeill, Lois Johnson. *The Great Ngee: The Story of a Jungle Doctor*. University of California, 1959.

Nassau. Robert Hamill. *My Ogowe: Being a narrative of daily incidents during sixteen years in Equatorial West Africa*. New York: Neale, 1914. http://books.google.com/books?id=WioUAAAAIAAJ&pg=PA237.

Parsons, Ellen C. *A Life for Africa: Rev. Adolphus Clemens Good, Ph.D., American Missionary in Equatorial West Africa*. New York: Fleming H. Revell, 1897. https://www.google.com/books/edition/A_Life_for_Africa/FwMNAAAAIAAJ?hl=en&gbpv=1

Presbyterian Board of Foreign Mission of the PCUSA. "Lake Superior Indian Mission." In *Minutes of the General Assembly of the PCUSA*, 6. New York: Presbyterian Board of Publication, 1874.

Presbyterian Church of the USA. "Death of Mrs Good." *Herald and Presbyter* 45.26 (25 June 1921): 10.

Presbyterian Historical Society. *Biographical Note*. Guide to Lydia Belle Walker Good Papers, RG 214. https://www.history.pcusa.org/collections/research-tools/guides-archival-collections/rg-214.

Walker, Lydia B. "Miss Walker, Gaboon, Africa." *Woman's Work for Woman* 9.10 (Oct 1879): 333–334.

——. Letter to the Board Secretary, dated 4 March 1882. Africa Letters, Reel 75, Letter 140. PHSA.

United States Federal Census. 1860, Niagara, New York; Roll: M653_822; Page: 317; Family History Library Film: 803822. https://www.ancestry.com/imageviewer/collections/7667/images/4236758_00326?pId=47489920

——. 1870, Wilson, Niagara, New York; Roll: M593_1055; Page: 641B; Family History Library Film: 552554. https://www.ancestry.com/imageviewer/collections/7163/images/4276910_00675?pId=31554215

Part Two:
Eastern & Central Africa: Historic Beginnings & Developments

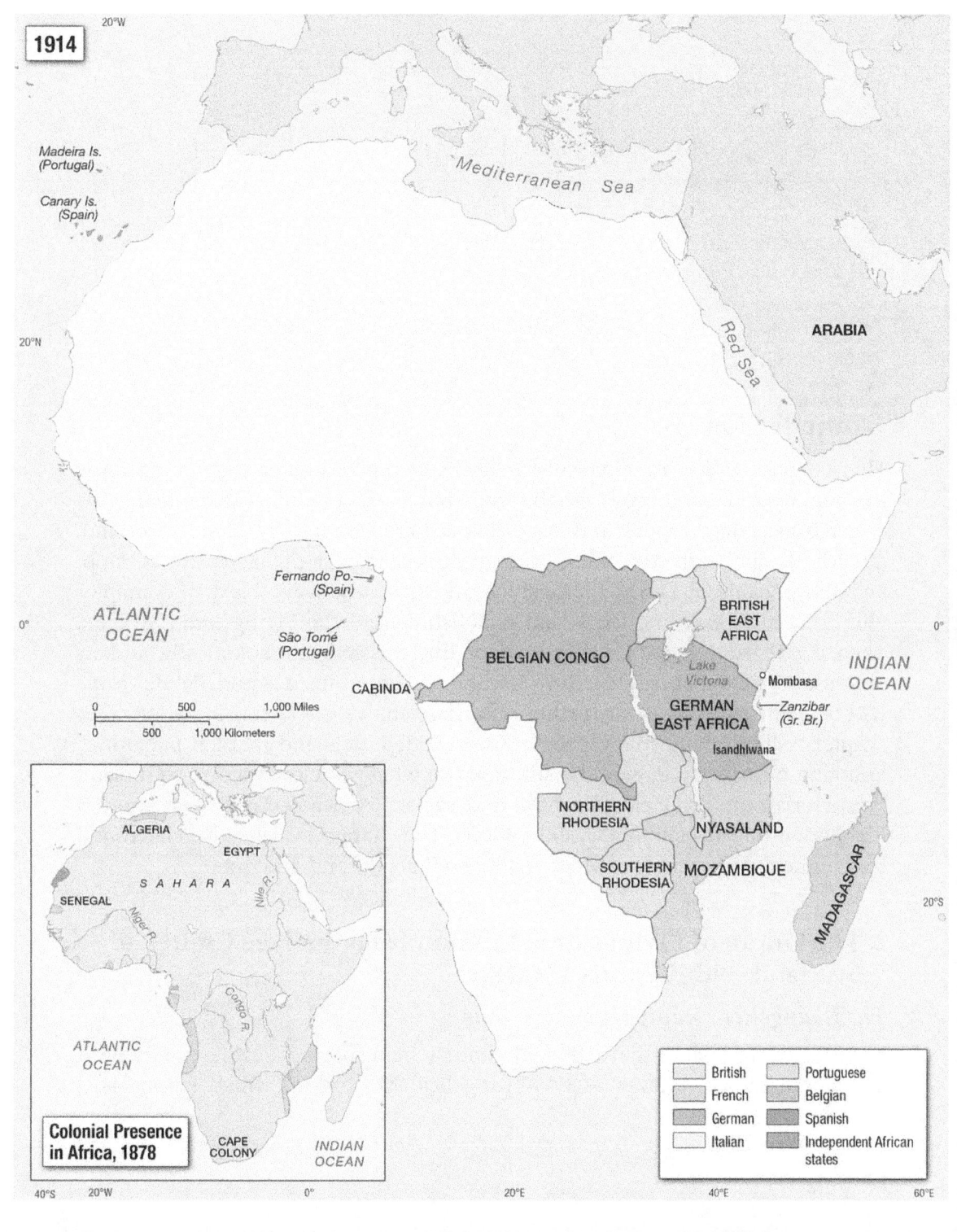

Chapter 14

The Livingstonia Mission and Synod

Humphreys Frackson Zgambo

Chapter Outline
1. Introduction
2. The Origin of Livingstonia Mission from the Free Church of Scotland: 19th-Century Context
3. The Establishment of the Livingstonia Mission and Subsequent Synod
4. Ecumenical unity and the relevant developments for the Livingstonia Mission
5. Reflections for further consideration and research
6. Summary conclusion

1. Introduction

This chapter will chronologically investigate the origin of the Livingstonia Mission, which commenced with the Free Church of Scotland. The chapter begins with a brief context review of this mission as to religious revivalism in Scotland, nineteenth and early twentieth-century ecclesiological divisions in Scotland, and the persons of David Livingstone and James Stewart. Next, the chapter will proceed to examine the actual establishment of the Livingstonia Mission. Then it will survey the development of this mission chronologically and its organisation into mature structures leading to it becoming a synod. Finally, hints will be made as to areas for further reflection, analysis, and consideration. This chapter will highlight many people – both indigenous and mission personnel, locations, mission stations, and institutions for what was clearly a very significant Presbyterian mission field in central and eastern Africa centred today around Malawi with reaches into adjacent nations. The chapter is critically related and intertwined to the chapters which follow on Blantyre and Nkhoma.

2. The Origin of Livingstonia Mission from the Free Church of Scotland: 19th-Century Context

The Evangelical Revivals & Missions

Historical records show that in the 19th century, many parts of Europe experienced a spiritual revival known as the Evangelical Movement, which emphasised preaching and prayer. The movement brought many young people to experience personal faith in Jesus Christ. This spiritual reformation shaped young men and women in the Highlands in Scotland, which had far-reaching consequences for missionary work, yet this revival was also significant for Lowland Scotland and the rising missionary movement. The Evangelical Revival Movement experience conditioned mission-minded Scots, such as David Livingstone, to prepare for long-period missionary endeavours.[1]

Free Church of Scotland and unions and mergers

The origin of the Livingstonia Mission comes from the Free Church of Scotland, a church in continuity from the 16th century Reformation, which was built on Calvinistic theology and Reformed principles. The Free Church emerged from the Church of Scotland in 1843 in an event popularly known as the Disruption – a protest primarily over patronage within the Church of Scotland. The Livingstonia Mission traces its origin back to this body, the Free Church of Scotland. However, in 1900 the Free Church of Scotland and the United Presbyterian Church of Scotland, a denomination which was formed by 18th century Scottish Seceders in 1847, united to form the United Free Church of Scotland, and thus after 1900 the Livingstonia Mission have been identified with the United Free Church through to 1929 when the United Free Church united with the Church of Scotland. It should be noted that the minority *continuing* the United Free Church did not exercise mission work post-1929 in Malawi, nor did the minority *continuing* Free Church after 1900 exercise mission work in Malawi. Rather, those minority continuing bodies would labour elsewhere in Africa post-1929 and post-1900 respectively (see other chapters in these two volumes).

David Livingstone and Missions

David Livingstone was born in 1813 and brought up at a small town called "Blantyre" in Scotland; his father's family originally came from a rural area in the Highlands and then moved to the Lowlands to industrial Lanarkshire. Having come to faith in Christ as a young man through the influence of the Evangelical Revival, he trained as a medical doctor and enlisted with the London Missionary Society (LMS). Prevented from serving in China, then regarded as the pre-eminent mission field, he went to South Africa. He soon adopted a pro-African approach to *missio Dei*, a missionary enterprise which characterised the early involvement of the London Missionary Society (LMS). This chimed with the determination to eradicate slavery that had been imbibed from the Evangelical Revival leaders

---

1 Ross & Fiedler, *A Malawi Church History*, 27; Kenneth Ross, *Mission as God's Spiral of Renewal*, 253.

such as William Wilberforce and Thomas Buxton. Through their influence Livingstone had come to Africa convinced that the introduction of Christianity and commerce held the key to the elimination of slave trade. Livingstone was a Christian deeply motivated with a vision for the future of the African continent that included the growth of an indigenous church.[2]

During his early years in Africa, Livingstone learned the Sechuana (Tswana) language, which honed his skills as a linguist and gave him a lasting appreciation of the richness and subtlety of the Bantu languages. Initially based at Kuruman in the Northern Cape, where Robert and Mary Moffatt had established a famous mission station, his thoughts were soon occupied by the unexplored territory to the north. Having married the Moffatt's daughter Mary in 1845, he set up home in Kolobeng, not far from Gaborone in Botswana. From here Livingstone made contact with the Makololo, a Zulu splinter group who had settled on the Upper Zambezi due to the *Mfecane*.[3] Both in the trans-African trek which took him and his Makololo companions to Luanda on the west coast (and back) and in his final journeys searching for the source of the Nile in Tanzania and Zambia, Livingstone spent many months entirely in African company. Andrew C. Ross writes about David Livingstone:

> It is striking that Livingstone's relationships with fellow Europeans were often stormy while his friendships with Africans were marked by a remarkable degree of affection and loyalty.[4]

This gave him closeness to African community life and an appreciation of its qualities, which would become rarer in the later colonial era in Africa. It reinforced the anti-racism which he had developed in his early days in South Africa. Livingstone related to Africans with sympathy and fellow feelings which were distinct at the time and set a tone that would be influential in Malawi for generations to come. Above all, his approach to missionary work was marked by confidence in the integrity and strength of African life and culture, not least when it came to the reception of the Christian faith. His early missionary experience amongst the Tswana led him to the conviction that they were not bereft of the knowledge of God, a concept of the afterlife, or a moral conscience. Livingstone also became deeply interested in traditional African methods of healing.[5]

---

2   Ross & Fiedler, *A Malawi Church History*, 23–24.
3   Ross & Fiedler, *A Malawi Church History*, 24. *Mfecane* was a disrupting time of war and migration during the early 1800s in Southern Africa.
4   Andrew C. Ross, "Livingstone, David," 736.
5   Ross & Fiedler, *A Malawi Church History*, 24–25.

Mapala holds that the history of Christianity in Malawi, Zambia, Tanzania and elsewhere in Africa, cannot be complete without referring to David Livingstone, the great Scottish explorer.[6] Before 1861, James Stewart, as a theological student at the University of Edinburgh, is quoted by W. P. Livingstone as having urged the Free Church of Scotland to send missionaries to the Lake region. James Stewart said: "We are willing to go out and begin a mission somewhere in the countries opened by Dr Livingstone. We ask you to send us."

Later, David Livingstone, while in company with Stewart to Africa, is quoted in W. P. Livingstone to have said to him, "I am glad you have come, come up and see the country for yourself." Upon his arrival in Malawi, however, Stewart was not impressed with what he found and decided not to continue with his ambition to start a mission.[7]

Consequently, Bishop Charles Mackenzie and companions from England followed Livingstone to establish the Universities' Mission to Central Africa (UMCA), the Anglican Church at Magomero in Chiradzulu, Malawi in 1861. Upon arrival, they soon experienced tragic losses of the leader, Bishop Mackenzie, and others who died due to the inhospitable conditions of malaria. The rest of the missionaries left the area and headed for a safer place in Zanzibar. However, David Livingstone, as not only the first symbol of British power but also a pathfinder for the British missionaries to this part of Africa, continued with missionary endeavours. After becoming famous for his exploratory journeys in Africa, Livingstone persuaded the British Government to sponsor an expedition that would aim to introduce "commerce, civilization, and Christianity" to the Zambezi region. Livingstone's guiding concept was to use the great rivers and lakes of Southern Africa to develop trade and introduce modern infrastructure. This he believed could unlock the potential of Southern Africa to prosper in the global economy and break the stranglehold of the slave trade. His consular appointment from the British Government led to him being criticized for having apparently abandoned his missionary vocation. However, in his mind he was always a missionary, personally devout and ever ready to speak of his faith, preparing the path for Christianity to reach the interior of Africa. Livingstone once wrote:

> God had an only Son, and he was a missionary and a physician.
> A poor, poor imitation of Him I am. Or wish to be … In this
> service I hope to live; in it I wish to die.[8]

---

6 Mapala, "A historical study of the border dispute between the Livingstonia and Nkhoma Synods," 44.
7 McCracken, *Politics and Christianity in Malawi*, 54–57.
8 Ross & Fiedler, *A Malawi Church History*, 27.

Later in 1862, Dr James Stewart accompanied David Livingstone in search of the place in Central Africa where the Free Church of Scotland could start mission work along the Lake Malawi region. In 1879, the Universities Mission to Central Africa (UMCA – the Anglican Church) returned to work among the Yao at Malindi and Mponda in Mangochi in the Southern Region of Malawi. Later, they established their headquarters at Likoma at Lake Malawi in the Northern Region.[9]

James Stewart and Missions

Rev. Dr James Stewart was the person who initiated missionary work that developed into the establishment of the Livingstonia Mission. He originally came from Scotland and settled at Lovedale Mission in the Eastern Cape, South Africa. Under the influence of James Stewart, the Principal of the Lovedale Institution in South Africa, the Livingstonia Mission was established by the Free Church of Scotland. It all began in 1873, at the funeral of David Livingstone, where Stewart's previous ambition was reinvigorated. After attending the funeral of Livingstone in Westminster Abbey, Stewart felt strongly that launching a mission in Central Africa in memory of Livingstone was imperative and on 18 April 1874, the indelible impression fired up his enthusiasm. Financial backing was offered mainly by Glasgow-based industrialists and businessmen who provided a committed support base for Livingstonia during its early decades, to the extent that they formed the effective governing body with the Free Church Foreign Mission Committee invariably ratifying their decisions.[10] Just as the Universities Mission to Central Africa (UMCA), later called Anglican, traces its origin from the speech made by Dr David Livingstone, the Livingstonia Mission also traced its origin from the speech made by Dr James Stewart to the General Assembly of the Free Church of Scotland in 1874, after the burial of the great Scottish explorer David Livingstone at Westminster Abbey. James Stewart was deeply moved by the death of Livingstone. He then asked the General Assembly of the Free Church of Scotland to reconsider sending missionaries to Malawi's lake region.[11]

---

9   Sundkler & Steed, *History of the Church in Africa*, 469–470.
10 Ross & Fiedler, *A Malawi Church History*, 38–39. Though primarily a Free Church Mission, the Scottish Reformed Presbyterian Church was also involved, as was the Scottish United Presbyterian Church. The salary of Rev. Dr Laws was provided by the United Presbyterian Church. See, Robert Laws, "The Dark Continent," in *Alliance of the Reformed Churches Holding The Presbyterian System: Proceedings of the Fifth General Council Toronto, 1892*, ed. G. D. Matthews (London: Publication Committee of the Presbyterian Church of England, 1892), 136.
11 McCracken, *Politics and Christianity in Malawi*, 54–57.

The Livingstonia Mission and Synod

▲ Two stamps: Zambia & Livingstone's death (left) and Malawi and Livingstone

From the onset, Livingstonia Mission, unlike any other mission, demonstrated that it was geared to fulfil Livingstone's vision and aspiration. Livingstone's vision was to introduce commerce to replace the horrible trade in human beings in slavery, with civilisation, and Christianity, what often is called the Three Cs: *Commerce, Civilisation and Christianity*.[12] The first crew of the Livingstonia Mission comprised well-trained personnel ranging from the clergy, medical doctors, a carpenter, engineer and blacksmith, agriculturalists, marine specialists, and businessmen. The Livingstonia Central African Company, which was later called the "African Lakes Company," (ALC) was to champion commerce while the Mission was for civilization and Christianity.[13]

According to Sundkler & Steed, the life, work and death of David Livingstone in 1873 inspired at least three Missions to begin their work in Malawi namely: the Free Church of Scotland, the Universities' Mission to Central Africa (UMCA), and the Church of Scotland.[14] James Stewart was deeply moved by the death of Livingstone. However, Stewart was greatly motivated by both the permanent withdrawal of the Universities Mission to Central Africa (UMCA) in 1863 from the area David Livingstone dedicated his life to and the lack of interest shown at home by fellow Scots to pursue David Livingstone's dream. Stewart felt the UMCA's withdrawal was a betrayal to the efforts of the patriotic Scot who served the people of God outside Europe.

He appealed to the General Assembly of the Free Church of Scotland to support the noble cause. Dr James Stewart passionately concluded his speech with the following words:

---

12 McCracken, *Politics and Christianity in Malawi*, 25–27.
13 Pachai, *Malawi*, 88.
14 Sundkler & Steed, *History of the Church in Africa*, 467–480, 795.

I would humbly suggest, as the truest memorial of Livingstone, the establishment by this church, or several churches together of an institution at once industrial and educational, to teach the truths of the gospel and the arts of civilized life to the natives of the country. Moreover, it shall be placed in a carefully selected and commanding spot in Central Africa, where from its position and capabilities it might grow into a town, and afterwards into a city, and become a great Centre of commerce, civilization and Christianity, and this I would call Livingstonia.[15]

3. The Establishment of the Livingstonia Mission and Subsequent Synod

Robert Laws and Missions

A young ordained medical doctor read the report of Stewart's speech in the newspaper and exclaimed, "There is the very thing I have been preparing for all my life!" When Rev. Dr Stewart met him later, he thought, "There is the man for us!" His name was Rev. Dr Robert Laws of the United Presbyterian Church in Scotland, who was to spend over fifty years in Africa. By 21 May 1875, a pioneering party under the leadership of Edward D. Young, a Warrant Officer in the Royal Navy and veteran sailor, with experience of travelling with David Livingstone, left for Africa. Other members were Rev. Dr Robert Laws, a medical officer, John McFadyen, Allan Simpson, (engineers), George Johnston, (a carpenter) and William Baker, (a seaman). Henry Henderson who was sent by the General Assembly of the Church of Scotland to find a suitable site for establishing a mission station also accompanied them.[16]

On arrival in Cape Town, the party was joined by four men who originated in the Malawi area and had been previously freed by David Livingstone and Bishop Mackenzie in 1861, namely Lorenzo Johnston, Thomas Bokwito,

▲ Robert Laws

---

15 Selfridge, *The Church's First Thirty Years in Nyasaland*, 19–20.
16 Selfridge, *The Church's First Thirty Years in Nyasaland*, 20; Ross & Fiedler, *A Malawi Church History*, 38; McCracken, *Politics and Christianity in Malawi*, 47–64.

Samuel Sambani and Frederick Zarakuti. By this time, they had been educated at Lovedale Mission and were able to serve the fledgling mission as advisers, interpreters, and managers. Other Africans were recruited by the Mission to assist with their journeys from the coast such as Joseph Bismarck, the son of an African planter from Quelimane, who later became an influential farmer and church leader in the Blantyre area. The party entered Malawi on a small steamer called the *Ilala*, named after the village in Zambia where David Livingstone had died. In the Lower Shire, they met the Makololo, Livingstone's old friends, who promised that they would send their children to the mission school.[17] After some difficulty travelling up the Zambezi River and over land, they reached the Shire River in Malawi, the country of their destination, and on 12 October 1875, they sailed onto Lake Malawi itself. Young called for the Old Hundredth (Psalm 100 Scottish Metrical version) to be sung in praise to the Lord their God. They eventually came to drop anchor at Cape Maclear: "Livingstonia is begun," wrote Laws, "though at present a piece of canvas stretched between two trees is all that stands for the future city of that name."[18]

Livingstonia Mission to the Yaoland

On 12th October 1875, the Livingstonia Mission landed at its final destination in the area belonging to Chief Mponda, a Yao chief, which Dr Livingstone named as Cape Maclear after his friend Dr Maclear. Besides being a magnet for immigrants, the Livingstonia Mission also began to make its first tentative contacts with the Yao, Mang'anja, Ngoni and Chewa people who were living nearby. When they arrived at the Lake, they were joined by people like Albert Namalambe and James Brown Mvula who later played significant roles in the early development of the Livingstonia Mission.[19]

In the following year (1876), the Mission opened the first school. Despite the Livingstonia Mission starting mission activities in this area, the Yao chiefs, who were predominantly Muslims, did not allow their children to attend classes because they were suspicious that their children could be converted to Christianity. Instead, it was the redeemed slaves of the Mang'anja and the Makololo, former porters of Livingstone, who began attending classes. At that time Cape Maclear had been lightly populated, but the presence of the mission attracted growing numbers of people, rising to 590 after five years. The medium of instruction opted for by the missionaries possibly was Chinyanja, alongside English because the teachers were English speakers. Mr E. D. Young stayed for a

---

17 Ross & Fiedler, *A Malawi Church History*, 39.
18 McCracken, *Politics and Christianity in Malawi*, 66.
19 Ross & Fiedler, *A Malawi Church History*, 39.

short time as a leader for the Mission. Then he was succeeded by James Stewart in 1876. At the end of 1877, Stewart resigned as the leader for the Livingstonia Mission, and handed over the leadership to Dr Laws at Cape Maclear in Mangochi.[20]

The second group of missionaries led by Dr James Stewart of Lovedale arrived in 1876. This included four Xhosa Africans from the Eastern Cape namely: Shadrach Mnqunana, Isaac Williams Wauchope, Mapasa Ntintili and William Koyi, all Lovedale graduates with a significant role to play in Livingstonia's early years. This allowed the mission to get fully into gear, working on the four tasks they had assigned themselves: evangelistic, educational, medical, and industrial (which included agriculture). The medical work of Dr Laws quickly created a big impression. He was soon performing surgical operations with the use of chloroform, which caused much amazement.[21]

▲ Xhosa Missionaries from Lovedale to Livingstonia, L. to R. William Koyi, Mapassa Ntintili, Shadrach Mngunana, Isaac Wauchope

Laws enjoyed a working partnership with his wife Margaret, who did much of the work on the first translation of the New Testament into Chinyanja, which Dr Laws published in 1884.[22] The industrial side of the work got well underway, but things were slower with the educational dimension with regard to issues of discipline. Shadrach Mngunana, one of the Lovedale missionaries, did good work as a teacher, which sadly ended with his death in 1877. However, the work continued and by 1881 there were 59 boys and 39 girls in the school. The most difficult aspect of the work was the evangelistic side. At first, there was no response to the gospel, until 1881 when the first baptism took place. The baptismal candidate was Albert Namalambe, originally a slave who had been brought from the Lower Shire by the Makololo. He later became an inspiring teacher and was for many years head of station at Cape Maclear.[23]

---

20 Ross & Fiedler, *A Malawi Church History*, 40; Shepherd, *Lovedale South Africa 1824–1955*, 19–20.
21 Shepherd, *Lovedale South Africa 1824–1955*, 20; Ross & Fiedler, *A Malawi Church History*, 41.
22 Ross & Fiedler, *A Malawi Church History*, 41; See also for more discussion on linguistics, Kenneth R. Ross, "Language of the Heart," in *Malawi and Scotland: Together at the Talking Place Since 1859* (Luwinga, Mzuzu: Mzuni Press, 2013), 115–117.
23 Ross & Fiedler, *A Malawi Church History*, 41–42.

Poor health, deaths of missionaries such as Mngunana and William Black, a Scottish doctor, and political difficulties caused Stewart and Laws to question whether Cape Maclear was the best base for their work. The Cape was surrounded by the waters of the Lake and on the landward side the Yao communities were radically turning to Islam and were heavily involved in violence and slave trade.[24]

However, Stewart returned to Lovedale in Eastern Cape, South Africa at the end of 1877. Laws was then placed in charge of the Livingstonia Mission, a position he held until his retirement fifty years later in 1927. It was Laws who in 1880 decided that the Livingstonia Mission should transfer its headquarters to Bandawe, a lakeshore centre near Nkhata Bay. Since 1878, the Livingstonia Mission had developed outposts at Bandawe and at Kaning'ina (where the city of Mzuzu later developed) and thus became aware of the potential for missionary work in Northern Malawi, Zambia, Tanzania, South Africa and elsewhere.[25]

Consequently, Cape Maclear Mission Station was left in the hands of the first convert, Albert Namalambe, a Makololo by ethnicity. Namalambe was in charge of Cape Maclear Station until it was later handed over to the Dutch Reformed Church (DRC) missionaries. It was Dr Laws who became instrumental for the growth of the Mission, and to the formation and development of the CCAP. Dr Laws remained the leader of the Livingstonia Mission until 1926 when he was forced to retire because of old age.[26]

▲ Advert for published works by Dr and Mrs Robert Laws

---

24 Ross & Fiedler, *A Malawi Church History*, 41–42.
25 Ross & Fiedler, *A Malawi Church History*, 42.
26 Ross & Fiedler, *A Malawi Church History*, 42.

However, ninety years after its handover, the Nkhoma Synod still considered Cape Maclear to be a co-owned place with the Synod of Livingstonia, even though Cape Maclear was within the bounds of the Nkhoma Synod. One occasion the General Synod resolved to build the great historic monument around the missionary graves at Cape Maclear with the responsibility shared among the four synods of the CCAP. The Dutch Reformed Church Mission (DRCM) later surrendered it to the General Assembly of the Church of Central Africa Presbyterian (CCAP). Unfortunately, Cape Maclear Mission Station's historic place has been abandoned for a long time now.

Livingstonia Mission to Tongaland

In search for a new place, the Livingstonia missionaries came into contact with many ethnic groups in Kasungu and other districts in Northern Malawi as early as 1877. This led to the establishment of stations such as Kaning'ina, close to the Moyale Barracks in Mzuzu City and Bandawe Mission in 1878. Kaning'ina station bordered the Tonga areas of Lakeshore and the M'mbelwa Ngoni areas especially under Chiputula Nhlane, although it was later abandoned.[27]

However, the evangelisation mission to Tongaland proved successful. There was an overwhelming response from the lakeside Tonga, which resulted in opening many congregations. The earlier "Christian village" evangelism approach at Bandawe had been abandoned but was later replaced by an approach of establishing schools in the Tonga villages. The Tonga schools enrolled more than 1,000 students in the 1880s. Missionaries moved again from Bandawe to Kondowe in 1884, and Robert Laws named the new mission site "Livingstonia." The hold of the traditional Tonga religion was very strong, and the first converts did not appear until 1889. Chief Mankhambira governed Tongaland. He was opposed to the establishment of churches in his area but when the Ngoni who had come from Mzimba invaded the land, Chief Mankhambira asked for military help from the missionaries, "an effective medicine" to defeat the Ngoni and to acquire new economic outlets: in return he would allow Christian churches in the Atonga land. The Atonga then welcomed the mission's employment on a "wages basis," and the opening of new vistas. It is generally accepted that the Tonga were spared extermination at the hands of the Ngoni by the arrival of the Livingstonia Mission and especially by Robert Laws's personal influence on the Ngoni Chief Mbelwa of Mzimba.[28]

---

27 Sundkler & Steed, *History of the Church in Africa*, 472ff.
28 Sundkler & Steed, *History of the Church in Africa*, 472ff.

The Livingstonia Mission and Synod

Livingstonia Mission to the Ngoniland

Dr Laws made a first visit to the Ngoni very early in September 1876. He first spoke to a village headman, but he never conceded to grant him an audience to meet Chief Mbelwa. Three months later the Mission sent William Koyi, the Xhosa evangelist from Lovedale, who managed to meet with the real paramount ruler Mbelwa. Here was an African leader from the Eastern Cape of Ngoni background, speaking the language of the Ngoni Chief. William Koyi moved warily and did not even begin emphasising the impending arrival of the white missionaries but suggested that the king might need a school for the children. A fortnight later Koyi returned to Chief Mbelwa, accompanied by Rev. Alexander Riddle who showed him the Bible and explained: "It was this that made our nation rich and powerful." The school was opened and Koyi was placed in charge of the school. The children liked their teacher and Chief Mbelwa appreciated the advantage of having schools and missionaries in his kingdom, but only on condition that the Ngoni's would have a monopoly.[29]

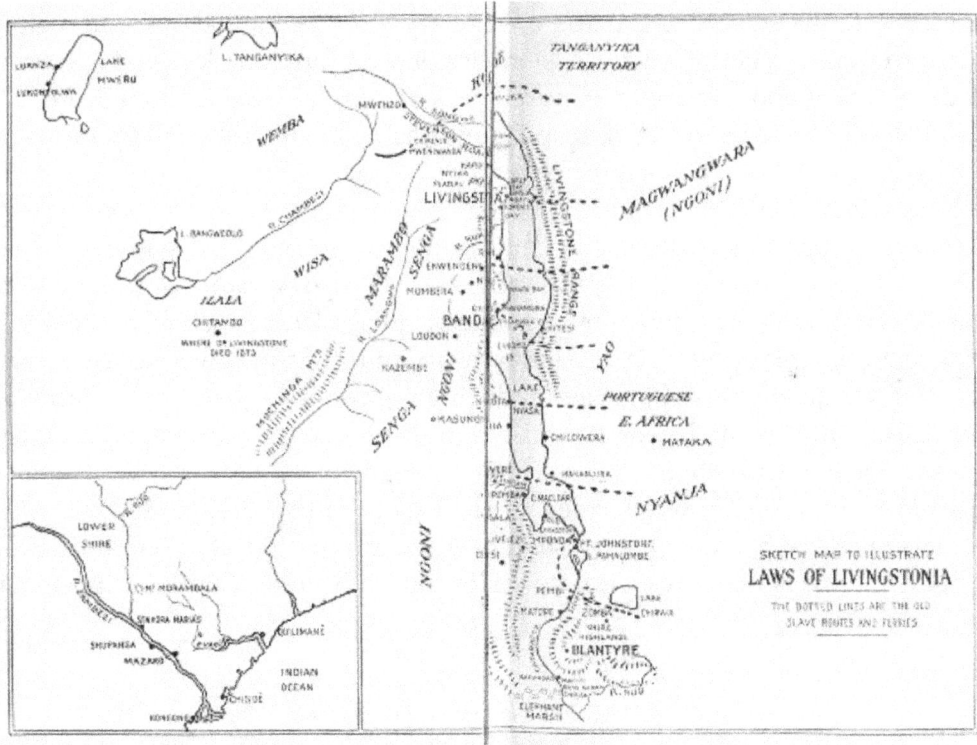

▲ Map of the Livingstonia Mission

---

29 Sundkler & Steed, *History of the Church in Africa*, 473–474.

In 1890, there were only 53 communicants in the whole mission, including the Cape Maclear outpost and Ngoniland. The outstanding pioneer missionaries in northern Malawi were Dr Laws, head of "Livingstonia Mission" and one of the great strategists of the centre who led the Mission for fifty years, his fellow Scottish partner was Rev. Dr W. A. Elmslie (1856–1935), missionary to the Ngoni, and the dynamic Rev. Donald Fraser (1870–1933) who influenced both the Tonga and the Ngoni.[30] Frequent mission expansions were also soon made among the Ngoni in Mzimba, Chewa in Kasungu, Tumbuka in Loudon and Ekwendeni. The Livingstonia Presbytery met for the first time as an annual general conference in 1899, marking the first step the church was taking towards self-sufficiency.[31]

The Livingstonia Presbytery 1899

The Livingstonia Mission propagated Christianity and civilisation through evangelisation, education, and industrial training. It is this arrangement that led to its successful history in its mission enterprise. According to Alexander Hetherwick, the subject of starting missionary work in the Lake Nyasa region was introduced to both General Assemblies of the Church of Scotland and Free Church of Scotland. Unlike the Church of Scotland, the Free Church Scotland, which was missionary-minded, responded quickly to Stewart's call by forming a mission named after the Scottish explorer Livingstone.[32]

This Livingstonia Mission came to the Lake Nyasa (Malawi) region to start the work Livingstone wanted his countrymen to do after the withdrawal of the Universities' Mission to Central Africa (UMCA). The name of the mission was linked to Dr Livingstone for symbolic purposes. This is one of the reasons for Chitambo area, where Livingstone's heart and intestines were buried, was reserved for the Livingstonia Mission during the comity agreement in Zambia, to retain Livingstonia's legacy and vision of the Three Cs, namely: Commerce, Civilization and Christianity.[33]

In 1899, a presbytery was formed by the Livingstonia Mission known as the Livingstonia Presbytery. This presbytery was for a period also referred to as the North Livingstonia Presbytery to distinguish it from the South Livingstonia

---

30 See, Walter Angus Elmslie, *Among the Wild Ngoni: Being some chapters in the History of the Livingstonia Mission in British Central Africa.* (London/Edinburgh: Oliphant Anderson & Ferrier, 1899) [note: several reprint editions]; R. A. Fraser, *Donald Fraser of Livingstonia.* (London: Hodder & Stoughton, 1934); T. Jack Thompson, *Christianity in Northern Malaŵi: Donald Fraser's Missionary Methods and Ngoni Culture.* Studies in Christian Mission, 15 (Leiden: Brill, 1995).
31 Thompson, *Livingstonia Centenary*, 7.
32 Munyenyembe, "Lofty but not powerful," 20ff.
33 Ross & Fiedler, *A Malawi Church History*, 26–27.

▲ *Ilala*, first steamship on Lake Nyasa, Livingstonia Mission 1875

Presbytery, which comprised its southern stations including those that had recently opened and occupied by the Dutch Reformed Church missionaries. The name reverted to the Livingstonia Presbytery.[34]

In 1878, the following were some of the congregations opened by the Livingstonia Mission: Kaning'ina 1878 and Bandawe in 1878. Kaning'ina was under the leadership of Alexander Riddell. Kaning'ina station was located to the south of the Matete River in the city of Mzuzu. It was estimated at a distance of six to seven hours walking to Chiputula Nhlane village, built between Mzuzu and Ekwendeni, and about 14 hours walking to Bandawe. Kaning'ina was later abandoned because of the raids the Ngoni and the Tonga waged on each other, and that the weather was hotter than Bandawe.[35]

Dr Laws and his wife transferred to Bandawe in 1881 as the head of the Mission, Bandawe became the new headquarters for the Livingstonia Mission, Njuyu in 1882 among the Ngoni of M'mbelwa, Ekwendeni in 1889, Ncherenje opened in 1883, Ncherenje was close to Mwenibanda village at Kapoka, Livingstonia in

---

34 Sundkler & Steed, *History of the Church in Africa*, 471ff; Chilenje, "(CCAP) in Zambia, 1882–2004," 244.
35 Ross & Fiedler, *A Malawi Church History*, 37, 43–44.

1894. It was situated to the east of Chitipa District headquarters, to serve the Lambya, Sukwa, Ndale, Nyiha, Nyika and Tumbuka people and Karonga Station was opened among the Nkhonde, Karonga Mission Station for the Nakyusa and Henga-Tumbuka people in 1885, in order to prevent the Roman Catholic missionaries from encroaching into the area. The Livingstonia Mission opened congregations at Hora in 1902, and Loudon in 1902. The Livingstonia Mission opened congregations at Tamanda 1894, which were later handed over to Dutch Reformed Church in 1926, Kasungu 1897 handed over to Dutch Reformed Church in 1923, Livulezi Station in 1887 handed over to Dutch Reformed Church in 1896 among the Ngoni of Chief Chikuse, in Ntcheu District in the Central Region bordering with Blantyre Mission in the Southern Region, latterly as the South Livingstonia Presbytery while Kasungu District northward was referred to as the North Livingstonia Presbytery. In Zambia, the Livingstonia Mission opened congregations at Mwenzo in 1894, Chitheba, Chitambo in 1894, Lubwa in 1904, and Chisefu.[36]

▲ Loudon Church c.1910 (with permission of the National Library, Scotland)

First Ordinations in Livingstonia Presbytery

The first ordinations for ministers in the Livingstonia Presbytery occurred in May 1914 at Ekwendeni when Yesaya Zerenji Mwasi, Hezekiah Tweya, and Jonathan Chirwa were ordained.

The opening of the Overtoun Institute

The result of the exceptional educational response from Tonga, Tumbuka and Ngoni, the Overtoun Institution was opened in the Livingstonia Mission in 1894

---

36 Ross & Fiedler, *A Malawi Church History*, 37–51.

at Kondowe.[37] This school ensured "the continued pre-eminence of northern Nyasaland in the field of education." Overtoun Institute had an unashamedly British syllabus with three years of English language and literature, British and European history, philosophy, psychology, mathematics, ethics and sociology; students from this institution made prominence as African intellectuals in Southern Africa.[38]

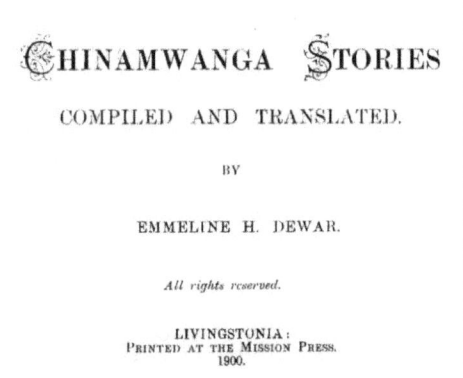

▲ *Emmeline Dewar book title pages*

In 1906, the number of pupils at Overtoun had increased overwhelmingly from 107 to over 3,000 pupils.[39] According to Velsen[40] Tongaland along the shores of Lake Malawi in Nkhata Bay was the scene of extraordinary educational enthusiasm, influencing a whole generation to accept modernisation and development. Initial results in terms of church baptism and statistics were not impressive, though. McCracken[41] contends that their education prepared them for the time when Africans would run their own affairs in the church and state as political leaders. This Protestant Livingstonia Mission sent their best men to Bemba in Zambia. In 1895, John Afwenge Mphonongo Banda, Chewa evangelist (father of Dr Hastings Banda, the first President of Malawi) began work at

---

37 It was primarily driven by the vision of Robert Laws and the finance came initially from Lord Overtoun and James Stevenson. McCracken wrote, "The founding of a central institution in November 1894 rivals the move to Bandawe, thirteen years earlier, as the most significant event in the history of the Livingstonia Mission" in *Politics and Christianity in Malawi*, 171 (in the 2000 edition, Zomba). Chapter six "The Overtoun Institution" in McCracken is a helpful overview.
38 Weller & Linden, *Mainstream Christianity*, 114ff.
39 Pachai, *Malawi*, 21.
40 In Sundkler & Steed, *History of the Church in Africa*, 472.
41 McCracken, *Politics and Christianity in Malawi*, 75ff.

Mwenzo. Having stayed there for many years during the First World War, he carried virtually all responsibility for mission work there. A decade later, a Tonga evangelist, David Kaunda (the father of Dr Kenneth Kaunda, the first President of Zambia), followed, building up the Chinsali station and guiding its rapid expansion. The Livingstonia Mission also sent African agents to other missions in the region: the South African General Mission (SAGM), the Dutch Reformed Church (DRC), and the London Missionary Society (LMS).[42]

According to the *World Atlas of Christian Missions*,[43] Southern Tanzania also received its share from Overtoun, with six teachers going to Moravian Rungwe and another six to the Berlin Lutherans at Ilembula. The "seeds" sown at the Overtoun Institution were blown all over East and Central Africa. In 1910, the Livingstonia Mission, with 12 ordained missionaries and 1,260 un-ordained African preachers, teachers, and Bible women, had a Christian community of 13,000.[44]

4. Ecumenical unity and relevant developments for the Livingstonia Mission

David Clement Scott had suggested to Robert Laws that there should be one ecumenically united church for British Central Africa and by the early 1890s the two Scottish Missionaries were beginning to explore the possibility of a *United* Presbyterian Church. In 1903, the Blantyre Presbytery again approached Livingstonia Presbytery with the same suggestion of church unity and proposed that the Creed, Constitution and Canons could be based on those of the Presbyterian Church in India.[45] The discussions on name, constitution, aims and objectives of the ecumenical unity of the Blantyre and Livingstonia Presbyteries continued in 1904. In the following years, further discussions were held before the United Missionary Conference at Mvera Mission in Nkhoma Presbytery. In 1914, the two "mother" churches in Scotland were to give permission, and plans were made for the union of Livingstonia and Blantyre Presbyteries, but because of the outbreak of the First World War, all advances for unity were postponed since most of the ministers were busy with Army chaplaincy.

---

42 Weller & Linden, *Mainstream Christianity*, 114ff.
43 *World Atlas of Christian Missions*, eds. J. D. Dennis, H. P. Beach, C. H. Fahs. (New York: SVMFM,1911), 95.
44 Sundkler & Steed, *History of the Church in Africa*, 471ff.
45 Weller & Linden, *Mainstream Christianity*, 114ff.

The formation of the General Synod 1924

When the war ended in 1918, the Missionary Conference was re-arranged for 1924 and it was decided that the new church would come into being then. The Conference met in September 1924 at Livingstonia and formally constituted the Church of Central Africa, Presbyterian (CCAP) General Synod and Rev. Dr Robert Laws was elected as its first Moderator. The General Synod of the Church of Central Africa Presbyterian (CCAP) became the highest court in the federation, although by that time the church had not yet received its autonomy from the United Free Church of Scotland and the Church of Scotland.[46] Two years later (1926) the DRC Mission was admitted as the Nkhoma Presbytery into this new General Synod. They agreed that each presbytery would remain unique and autonomous in its organization, decision-making and missionary enterprise in line with the practices and traditions of the "mother" church. This made the position of the General Synod in the CCAP questionable, bringing disputes in the following decades. The General Synod became a federation of the Presbyterian Churches in Central Africa.[47]

The development the Livingstonia Mission and subsequent synod

The Livingstonia Mission and subsequent synod development was made possible by strong and visionary leadership from both Scotland and Malawi. The development of the leadership of the mission included the following:

Outstanding and visionary leadership from Scotland

The Livingstonia Mission developed by strong and visionary leadership from Scotland. The first crew for the development of the Livingstonia Mission and subsequent synod was comprised of the following: Lieutenant E. D. Young, the leader of the expedition, George Johnston, the carpenter, Allan Simpson, the blacksmith, John Macfadyen, the engineer, Alexander Riddle, the agriculturalist, William Baker, the seaman, Robert Laws, the only clergy whom the Free Church Scotland (FCS) had on loan from the United Presbyterian Church (UPC), and Henry Henderson, a member of the Church Scotland (CoS), whose primary task was to find a place where the CoS could start mission work in Malawi.[48] Therefore, the Livingstonia Mission was established by strong and visionary leadership from Scotland for socio-economic development in line with the principles of the Scriptures and Reformed church polity.

---

46 Weller & Linden, *Mainstream Christianity*, 114ff.
47 Munyenyembe, "Lofty but not powerful," 6, 20.
48 Weller & Linden, *Mainstream Christianity*, 114ff.

Development of the African leadership

The Livingstonia Mission championed the development of the African leadership for the future of the church and society. The early people to join the mission station were William Koyi, Albert Namalambe, baptized in 1881, and James Brown Mvula, baptized in 1882 at Cape Maclear, respectively. Among other children who came to the early schools in the Bandawe area became leaders within the Livingstonia Mission, included Yuraya Chatonda Chirwa, Edward Boti Manda, outstanding teacher and minister. David Kaunda opened Lubwa congregation in Zambia and Yesaya Zerenji Mwasi became an influential church minister and social activist.[49]

In 1890, Mawelera Tembo became the first Ngoni to be baptized. He became a significant Christian leader and hymn writer.[50] The Livingstonia Mission produced many outstanding, well-educated leaders who made their mark in Malawi and beyond, such as the trade unionist Clements Kadalie in South Africa, the civil servant Ernest Alexander Muwamba, the politician and first President of the Nyasaland African Congress Levi Mumba and the critical thinker and church leader Charles Domingo. These men's outstanding competence in English, high level of education and determination equipped them to take leading roles in shaping the future of the country.[51]

The Women's Guild called *Umanyano, Chikondi cha Wanakazi* or *Chovwirani cha Wanakazi* was first organized at Bandawe in 1939.[52] There had been groups in Karonga, Livingstonia, Ekwendeni, Bandawe, Loudon, and Chasefu. In 1940, Miss Alice Boyce submitted a report on the operations of the groups to the Livingstonia Presbytery. The Moderator, then Rev. Dr W. Y. Turner received the report wholeheartedly and recommended that it should be adopted. The Livingstonia Presbytery meeting of 1941 decided that the *Umanyano* be organised in all congregations of the presbytery.

In 1956, Rev. Patrick Chaweya Mzembe became the first African Senior Clerk (now General Secretary) who served until 1978.[53] In 1978, Rev. Wedson Chibambo was appointed as the Livingstonia Synod's second General Secretary, followed by the recent past younger generation Moderators and General Secretaries such as Revs. Mazunda, Matiya Nkhoma, Chivwati Gondwe, William Manda, Henry Mvula, W. Mwale, Timothy Nyasulu, Levi Nyondo, J. P. V. Mwale, and William Tembo and many more church ministers.

---

49 Ross & Fiedler, *A Malawi Church History*, 45–49.
50 See chapter 27 in this book.
51 Ross & Fiedler, *A Malawi Church History*, 45–49.
52 Mlenga, "Post-Missionary Leadership," 6–18.
53 Ross & Fiedler, *A Malawi Church History*, 276.

The subsequent Synod of Livingstonia 1956 & Postscript

In 1956, the Livingstonia Presbytery attained the status of synod, it was known as the CCAP Synod of Livingstonia.[54] In 2022, the Livingstonia Synod had 32 Presbyteries: Bandawe, Champhira, Chitipa, Dwangwa, Ekwendeni, Engalaweni, Euthini, Henga, Johannesburg, Cape Town, Western Cape, Durban, Jombo, Kanyenjere, Karonga, Lilongwe, Limphasa, Livingstonia, Loudon, Luwerezi, Milala, Misuku, Mapazi, Mzalangwe, Mzuzu, Ngerenge, Njuyu, Nkhamenya, Nkhata Bay, Nyika, Rumphi, and Wenya. The Livingstonia Synod consists of over 180 congregations, 1000 prayer houses with 300,000 members in Central and Northern regions of Malawi, Tanzania, and South Africa. The Synod has over the century built numerous primary and secondary schools, mission hospitals, technical colleges, the University of Livingstonia, the Voice of Livingstonia Radio, as well as the following vibrant departments: youth, education, development, lay training centre, health, early childhood development, Church and Society, Mission and Evangelism, Men's, and Women's Guild Ministries. The Livingstonia Synod Office is located in Mzuzu. The Moderator (2022) was Rev. Isaac M. Malongo and the General Secretary was Rev. William Tembo.

5. Reflections for further consideration and research

I offer here to the reader five select areas for serious reflection, analysis, and further investigation which I think arise from the history contained in this survey chapter. There are more areas but here are five key areas:

Calvinism from the mother church

This chapter has been stressing the historical development of the Livingstonia Mission from its Scottish mother. One area where reflection could be given beyond this chapter would be to analyse the nature of the Calvinistic and Evangelical theology which was introduced into this Mission primarily through the Scottish missionaries and how this has impacted the mission through the years. This would move the subject now clearly into the theological.

James Stewart and the Livingstonia Mission

The persona of James Stewart of Lovedale to distinguish him from the other James Stewart, the civil engineer, was a key person in the instigation of the Livingstonia Mission. There are many areas here for reflection: his missiological strategy, the theology of this leader, limitations of his role, etc.

---

54 Zeze, "Christ the Head of the Church," 175ff.

Highly hierarchical and clerical system of church government

I would assert that church polity for the Livingstonia Mission was characterized by tendencies of "hierarchy" and "clericalism." Ecclesiastical power in the church was expressed in the establishment of the all-white "Mission Council" influenced by the mother church in Scotland, the "first governing assembly." The powerful ecclesiastical "Mission Council" was responsible to the Home Committee in Scotland. McCracken holds:

> It is one of the ironies of Livingstonia Mission that a Presbyterian Free Church Mission should be organized on highly centralized autocratic lines. The Free Church of Scotland was a decentralized body with semi-autonomous parishes controlled by a minister supported and to some degree supervised, by a committee of lay elders.[55]

However, the Livingstonia Synod harboured strong tendencies toward hierarchy and clericalism, providing ministers with exclusive authority like the administration of an archbishop or bishop in prelacy church government. The matter of parity among ministers, elders and deacon did not receive any consideration. Thompson quotes the remarks made by Rev. W. A. Elmslie in Livingstonia Synod who noted sharply about his African colleague:

> He is an assistant to me, working under my supervision. He has no congregation of his own. He lives on the station with me and takes his work according to my guiding.[56]

Reflection should be done here about the nature of the polity of this Mission and its subsequent development and determine if the above statements are substantive and what type of Presbyterian polity was practised and developed?

The Livingstonia Mission and socio-economic development

I would argue that there had been a strong partnership in socio-economic development between the Livingstonia Mission and the Malawi Government. Consequently, the Livingstonia Mission runs various enterprises in education, health, and food security and relief development in all districts of Northern Malawi. The establishment of churches, schools and hospitals in rural areas has also greatly contributed to the growth of trading centres and industrialisation in

---

55 McCracken, *Politics and Christianity in Malawi*, 224.
56 Thompson, *Livingstonia Centenary*, 178.

Malawi. In the Reformed church perspective, the Kingdom of God includes all forms of authority and governance: the differences in the government of different institutions are all under the authority of Christ given to Him in heaven and on earth. Christ's Sovereign authority encompasses the office, gift or *charismata* as service, the church and the state. Everything belongs to God. God governs in Christ over the entire cosmos. Therefore, the Livingstonia Mission was characterised by a strong partnership with the Malawi Government. It could be considered historically by a comparison of the Mission in its early years with the colonial administration and then secondly in its later years post-independence. Also, a critical analysis should be undertaken here to consider if the Church is prophetic then in its role to the state.

Ecumenical unity and formation of the General Synod

The question as to the real nature of ecumenicity could be analysed concerning the three presbyteries which over time formed the CCAP. Is ecumenicity here defined as limited to Presbyterian ecumenicity? A comparison to background here could be made to Ross and Fiedler.[57]

6. Summary Conclusion

This chapter began with a brief reference to the spiritual context in Scotland from which the sending of missionaries to Livingstonia would come. This spiritual context is important for us to understand the impetus and type of mission which would emerge. This context must also be coupled with understanding the aspirations of the Christian missionary explorer David Livingstone. It is important to understand his aspirations for this region of Africa as well as the relationship back to Scotland and the Christian evangelical community there.

In this chapter, we have also examined key leadership figures. The vision and leadership of James Stewart to this mission and its funding, undertaking, and relationship to the Free Church of Scotland was critical. The theme of perseverance emerged with the early mission parties who strove to find the best locations from which to operate mission stations and to conduct out-stations. A diversity of missionary personnel was involved in this mission – ordained, medical, artisan, Scottish, Xhosa, and emerging indigenous evangelists and leaders. The establishment of organised churches, schools and centres of learning were critical for the development of a wholistic, integrated missional approach and institutional names emerge in this chapter which have had abiding significance. The Livingstonia Mission impacted areas beyond its initial geographic target

---

57 Ross & Fiedler, *A Malawi Church History*, 167–171.

and also through training for other missions. Today the synod ministers in three African countries.

The chapter has also shown us that ecclesiastical alignments in the mother country (or sending nation) impact the mission field also. Therefore, from the Free Church, to United Free, and finally to Church of Scotland, we can trace that story in Malawi with the Livingstonia Mission. The chapter also shows us tensions that were there in this Mission – tensions over leadership, between missionaries and indigenous leaders, and within churches.

Finally, there are many more matters which need continuing research and discussion. Further discussion about theological issues that arose in the Livingstonia Mission, Livingstonia Presbytery, and subsequent Synod await further investigation from this survey of mission history of the Livingstonia Mission.

Questions for study (fact type):
1. State a) the year the Livingstonia Mission began, b) by which Church body and, c) who provided the finances.
2. Name the key leaders of the early development of the Livingstonia Mission.
3. Name the four Xhosa missionaries who were sent from Lovedale.
4. What year was the Livingstonia Presbytery formed?
5. Who were the first ministers to be ordained in the Livingstonia Mission?
6. What led to the creation of the Church of Central Africa Presbyterian?

Questions for study (reflection type):
1. Discuss the merits of the two persons of David Livingstone and James Stewart as critical to the rise of the Livingstonia Mission.
2. Summarise the mission strategy of the Livingstonia Mission in the first twenty years of its existence.
3. Discuss the issue of a two-tiered approach to polity in the Livingstonia Mission between Presbytery and Mission Council.
4. Research (on the internet or elsewhere) Donald Fraser (missionary to Livingstonia) and write a one-page overview of his missionary life. Evaluate.

Select Bibliography

Chilenje, Victor. "The Origin and Development of the Church of Central Africa Presbyterian (CCAP) in Zambia, 1882–2004." PhD thesis, University of Stellenbosch, 2007.

Fraser, Donald. *Livingstonia: The Story of our Mission*. Edinburgh: FMCUFCS, 1915.

Hokkanen, Markku. *Quests for Health in Colonial Society: Scottish Missionaries and Medical Culture in the Northern Malawi Region, 1875–1930*. Eds. Petri Karonen & Pekka Olsbo. Jyväskylä, Finland: Publishing Unit, University Library of Jyväskylä University, 2006.

Johnston, James. *Robert Laws of Livingstonia*. Second edition. Glasgow: Pickering & Inglis, [1910].

Laws, Robert. *Reminiscences of Livingstonia*. Edinburgh: Oliver & Boyd, 1934.

Livingstone, W. P. *Laws of Livingstonia*. London: Hodder & Stoughton, nd.

Mapala, C. W. "A historical study of the border dispute between the Livingstonia and Nkhoma Synods of the Church of Central Africa Presbyterian (CCAP 1956–2015)." PhD thesis, University of KwaZulu-Natal, 2016.

McCracken, J. C. *Politics and Christianity in Malawi 1875–1940: the Impact of the Livingstonia Mission in the Northern Province*. Original. Cambridge: Cambridge University, 1977. Second edition imprint, Zomba, Kachere Series, 2000.

McIntosh, Hamish. *Robert Laws: Servant of Africa*. Carberry, Scotland: Handsel Press, 1993.

Mlenga, M. "Fifty Years of Post-Missionary Leadership in Livingstonia Synod, 1958 to 2008." PhD module, University of Mzuzu, 2009.

Munyenyembe, R. "Lofty but not powerful: a critical analysis of the position of the General Assembly in the union of the Church of Central Africa Presbyterian (CCAP) Malawi." *Studia historiae ecclesiasticae* 42.3 (2016):1–21. https:upjournals.co.za.

Pachai, B. *Malawi: The History of a Nation*. London: Mackintosh, 1973.

Ross, A. C. "Livingstone, David." In Daniel Patte, *Cambridge Dictionary of Christianity*. Cambridge: Cambridge University Press, 2010, 736.

Ross, A. C. *Blantyre Mission and the Making of Modern Malawi*. Blantyre: Christian Literature Association in Malawi (CLAIM), 1996.

Ross, K. R. *Mission as God's Spiral of Renewal*. Mzuzu-Luwinga: Mzuni Press, 2019.

Ross, K. R. & Fiedler, K. *A Malawi Church History 1860–2020*. Mzuzu-Luwinga: Mzuni Press, 2020.

Selfridge, J. *The Church's First Thirty Years in Nyasaland (Malawi) 1861–1891*. Lilongwe: Nkhoma Press, 1976.

Shepherd, R. H. W. *Lovedale South Africa: The Story of a Century 1841–1941*. Alice: Lovedale Press, 1940.

Shepherd, R. H. W. *Lovedale South Africa 1824–1955*. Alice: Lovedale Press, 1971.

Stone, W. V. "The Livingstonia Mission and the Bemba." *Bulletin of the Society for African Church History* 2 (1968): 211–322.

Sundkler, B. & Steed, C. *History of the Church in Africa*. Cambridge: Cambridge University, 2000.

Thompson, T. Jack. *Livingstonia Centenary 1875–1975*. Nkhoma: CLAIM, 1975.

Thompson, T. Jack. *Ngoni, Xhosa and Scot: Religious and Cultural Integration in Malawi*. Zomba: Kachere Series, 2007.

Thompson, T. Jack. "The Legacy of Donald Fraser." *International Bulletin of Missionary Research* 18.1 (1994): 32–35.

Thompson, T. Jack. *Touching the Heart: Xhosa Missionaries to Malawi 1876–1888*. Pretoria: University of South Africa, 2000.

Weller, J. & Linden J. *Mainstream Christianity to 1980 in Malawi, Zambia and Zimbabwe: From Mission to Church*. Gweru: Mambo Press, 1984.

Zeze, W. "Christ, the Head of the Church: Authority, Leadership and Organizational Structure within the CCAP – Nkhoma Synod in Malawi." *Protestant Church Polity in Changing Contexts II, Case Studies*. Berlin: Verlag, 2014. [Paper presented at the International Conference, Utrecht, The Netherlands 7–10 November 2011]: 35–44.

Zgambo, H. F. "Ethnicity in the church and church structures: An assessment of the CCAP Livingstonia and Nkhoma Synods in Malawi." PhD thesis, North-West University, Potchefstroom: 2018.

Chapter 15

The Blantyre Mission and Synod

Humphreys Frackson Zgambo

Chapter Outline
1. Introduction
2. The Context for the Establishment of Presbyterian Missions in Malawi
3. The Initial Efforts for the Blantyre Mission, c.1876–1878
4. Scandal and Recovery for the Blantyre Mission, 1878–1898
5. Growth and Development in Blantyre Mission from 1898 to 1956
6. Postscript: Blantyre Presbytery/Synod from 1956 to 2020
7. Reflections for further consideration and research
8. Conclusion

1. Introduction

This chapter will survey the history of the Blantyre Synod of the Church of Central Africa Presbyterian (CCAP) in Malawi from the early years in mid-1870s to the early 2020s in Malawi. The history of Blantyre Synod will be incomplete without the Scottish base, as Ross writes:

> [It] is a study of the Scottish Missionaries who served the Blantyre Mission, their beliefs and ideas that are implied in their actual policy as well as those that they expressed when reflecting on their task. However, just as these must not be seen apart from African society, neither can they be properly understood without some reference to Scotland and the Church of Scotland from which these men and women came.[1]

The aim of this chapter will be to chronologically put a proper historical record on how both the European missionaries and African workers contributed to the life, work, development, and growth of the Blantyre Mission over the past decades in Malawi.

---

1 Andrew Ross, *Blantyre Mission*, 17.

The opening question of this chapter will be: what is the context that led to the establishment of the Church of Central Africa Presbyterian Missions in Malawi? The following structure will be used: the context for the establishment of the CCAP Missions in Malawi; then the history and development of the Blantyre Mission from 1875 to 2020 with an overview of the life, work and activities of the European missionaries and African workers in Malawi and a conclusion.

2. The Context for the Establishment of Presbyterian Missions in Malawi

As with the last chapter on the Livingstonia Mission, the context for the Blantyre Mission can be summarized as follows. One of the major ideologies that provoked Dr David Livingstone to think of mission work in Africa was to reach new peoples in the interior of Africa, introduce Christianity, and end slavery and its evils. Local traditional chiefs and Arabs were highly involved in tribalism, conflict, and the slave trade. Livingstone faced a lot of difficulties on his mission to stop tribalism, conflict, and the slave trade without giving the people an alternative economic enterprise. He pleaded to Christian Mission agencies in Europe to send missionary enterprises composed of different professionals to Africa to engage African natives in "Christianity, Commerce and Civilisation," (popularly known as three Cs), the "Gospel and Modern Culture" which would also have deep respect for African culture.[2]

The first outstanding person after David Livingstone was the Rev. Dr James Stewart. Stewart initiated and championed Christian missionary work which developed into the establishment of the Livingstonia and Blantyre Synods. Stewart originally came from Scotland but permanently settled at Lovedale Mission in the Eastern Cape, South Africa. According to Sundkler & Steed, the life, work, and death of David Livingstone inspired at least three Missions to begin their work in Malawi: the Free Church of Scotland, the Church of Scotland, and the Universities Mission to Central Africa (UMCA), later called the Anglican Church from England.[3] After attending the funeral of Livingstone in Westminster Abbey, James Stewart felt strongly that launching a mission in Central Africa in memory of Livingstone was imperative and on 18 April 1874 the indelible impression caught fire in his mind. He appealed to the General Assembly of the Free Church of Scotland to support the noble cause. James Stewart passionately concluded his speech by the following words:

2　Gama, *Role of the Church in Politics*, 49. For a fuller and more detailed summary of the beginnings of the Livingstonia Mission see my chapter 14 here in volume one.

3　Sundkler & Steed, *History*, 467–480, 795ff.

> I would humbly suggest, as the truest memorial of Livingstone, the establishment by this church, or several churches together of an institution at once industrial and educational, to teach the truths of the Gospel and the arts of civilized life to the natives of the country, and which shall be placed in a carefully selected and commanding spot in Central Africa, where from its position and capabilities it might grow into a town, and afterwards into a city, and become a great Centre of commerce, civilization and Christianity, and this I would call Livingstonia.[4]

A young ordained medical doctor read the report of Stewart's speech in the newspaper and exclaimed: "That is the very thing I have been preparing for all my life!" When Stewart met him later, he thought, "There is the man for us!" His name was Rev. Dr Robert Laws, who was to spend over fifty years in Africa.

In May 1875, a pioneer party under Edward D. Young, veteran sailor, left Scotland for Africa. Other members of the group were Rev. Dr Robert Laws, a medical officer, John McFadyen, Allan Simpson, engineers, George Johnston, a carpenter, and William Baker, a seaman. Henry Henderson, a lay Christian, who was sent by the General Assembly of the established Church of Scotland to find a suitable site for planting a mission station also accompanied them. In South Africa, Stewart recruited four Xhosa African missionaries namely: Shadrach Mnqunana, William Koyi, Isaac Wauchope and Mapassa Ntintili to serve as teachers and evangelists. After some difficulty travelling up the Zambezi River and on land they reached the Shire River in Malawi, the country of their destination, and on 12 October 1875 they sailed onto Lake Malawi itself. Young called for the Old Hundredth (Psalm) to be sung in praise to the Lord their God. They eventually came to drop anchor at Cape Maclear: "Livingstonia is begun," wrote Laws, "though at present a piece of canvas stretched between two trees is all that stands for the future city of that name."[5] Now we turn to the story of the second Scottish Church mission, that of Blantyre, of the Church of Scotland which began on its own field a year later.

---

4   Selfridge, *Church's First Thirty Years*, 19–20.
5   McCracken, *Politics and Christianity*, 66.

3. The Initial Efforts for the Blantyre Mission, c.1876–1878

This early period for the Blantyre Mission was during the pre-colonial period when Malawi characterised itself by numerous problems such as tribal migration, scramble for land, chieftainship conflicts, and slavery between 1876 to 1891.[6] It was an incredibly challenging time for the establishment of a new mission. *The key leader of the initial phase of the Blantyre Mission was Henry Henderson and this phase is of short duration, about two years.*

Henry Henderson

Henry Henderson (1843–1891) made a trip from Cape Maclear around Lake Nyasa (modern Lake Malawi) on the steam ship *Ilala*, as instructed by the Foreign Mission Committee (FMC) of the Church of Scotland to find a suitable site on the shores of the lake, but he could not find a place that he considered suitable.[7] He returned to Cape Maclear, from where he considered the possibility of settling the mission in the Shire Highlands which he had passed through on the journey up the Shire. On his mission to identify the site for the Church of Scotland, the Livingstonia Mission engaged an African interpreter for Henderson – Tom Bokwito (1846–c.1900s). Bokwito was to be an important person in communicating with the local chiefs in the area.[8] The Church of Scotland group travelled through Machinga and Zomba until they reached Mount Nyambadwe in the land of Chief Kapeni.[9]

This location and vicinity were chosen for the new mission station around Ndirande Mountain in Chief Kapeni's area along the Shire Highlands. Henry Henderson settled a site for their mission station among the Yao tribe that would become the centre for Christian mission, commerce, education, and agriculture in the Southern Region of Malawi. On 23rd October 1876, the mission site was identified and named "Blantyre" after the birthplace of David Livingstone, a small town in Scotland. Selfridge holds that Chief Kapeni gave the European missionaries this place because he wanted them nearby to provide security as he feared the Makololo and Maseko Ngoni who settled west of the Shire River.[10] In this ethnic Yao dominated area, refugee slaves would turn up running away from Arab slave traders and seek shelter at the missionary's house in the Blantyre Mission. Small communities were established, a motley group of refugees and individuals from varied backgrounds, including the educated Makololo.[11]

---

6 Gama, *Role of the Church in Politics*, 49.
7 Selfridge, *Church's First Thirty Years*, 30.
8 Tom Bokwito was a slave freed by David Livingstone and Bishop Mackenzie at the age of 15 in 1861, who later studied at Lovedale College in Eastern Cape in South Africa. He accompanied Dr Livingstone and the Scottish Missions as guide and interpreter in Northern Malawi and Zambia.
9 Phiri, *Malawi*, 134.
10 Selfridge, *Church's First Thirty Years*, 32.
11 Gama, *Role of the Church in Politics*, 123–124.

Leadership fluctuations

By April 1877, Henry Henderson felt that his work of finding a site for the mission and seeing that it was established had ended, so he prepared to go back to Scotland. Selfridge holds that before leaving the post as head he had a strong conviction that the time had come for an ordained minister to take control of the mission station.[12] Since no minister seemed to be available from Scotland, Henderson wrote to ask Rev. Dr Robert Laws from Livingstonia Mission to temporarily come and take charge of the mission until the arrival of Rev. Duff Macdonald.[13] Having agreed to Henderson's pleas, Laws and Stewart agreed to jointly take care of the Blantyre Mission until a leader was identified. In that regard both Laws and Stewart took periods away from Livingstonia to supervise the work at Blantyre mission until July 1878 when Duff Macdonald arrived in Malawi to take charge. Therefore, the beginnings at Blantyre Mission faced a lot of difficulties – chief of which was inadequate leadership.

4. Scandal and Recovery for the Blantyre Mission, 1878–1898

The Blantyre Mission Scandal, 1878–1881

As stated above, during the initial years the Blantyre Mission faced a lot of difficulties and challenges, because the Mission did not have the leadership of a clergyman and other suitable personnel.[14] The mission did not commence on a positive note due to repeated attacks of malaria, fever, deaths, a lack of spiritual direction, and the inexperience of the young white missionaries who could not understand the traditions of local Africans. While Henderson had succeeded in finding a suitable place for the Blantyre mission station, Dr Macrae, Chairman for the Foreign Missions Committee (CoS, FMC) and the Committee back in Scotland, had failed to find an ordained minister to go and start work at the Blantyre Mission in the Shire Highlands.[15] Instead, laymen volunteered to come to Africa because they were promised to be paid good salaries. Some volunteers were mere Christians with limited technical skills who had no spiritual calling to work as missionaries in Africa.

The mission staff, white European lay artisans, came to exercise virtual chiefly authority, taking over the authoritarian role of magistrate and civil governor in the settlement of refugees and tribal people occupying the area after Henderson's departure. In 1878–79, in what has popularly been referred to as the Blantyre

---

12 Selfridge, *Church's First Thirty Years*, 34.
13 Andrew Ross, *Blantyre Mission*, 44.
14 Gama, *Role of the Church in Politics*, 124.
15 Phiri, *Malawi*, 135.

Atrocities, severe disciplinary action led to the death of two African natives. Some see this as possibly rooted in the injurious effects of "Social Darwinism" that had led to an estrangement between white and black missionaries. That may be one of the reasons why the Blantyre Mission artisans John Buchanan, John Walker, and George Fenwick did what they did, but there are other factors, spiritual, and contextual. They flogged and executed Africans without proper legal mandate and procedures being followed yet had seen flogging under the lay worker Mr. James Stewart who had come over from Livingstonia to help (not to be confused with Dr James Stewart), some therefore claimed precedence and no alternative, given the vacuum of civil control. Ross and Fielder summarise it this way:

> In the unsettled conditions created by the slave trade, numerous freed slaves and other refugees gravitated to the Blantyre Mission which quickly became a numerous community. Whether they liked it or not, the missionaries found that they were expected to settle disputes and, in effect, provide government for their small settlement. Under pressure of this expectation they set up a rudimentary judicial system which could try cases and administer punishments, including flogging and imprisonment. Unfortunately, this was taken to extremes ... In one case the flogging was so severe that the victim died ...[16]

Therefore, the involvement of some white Missionaries in scandalous activities created a lot of problems leading to the administrative dysfunction of mission work at the Blantyre Mission.[17] The scandals were widely publicised and the Blantyre Mission defended its position with difficulty, both in Malawi and in Scotland. The General Assembly CoS of 1877, the Foreign Mission Committee (FMC) was compelled to report that:

> It is with pain and regret that the committee has to report that, notwithstanding many and sustained efforts, they have not succeeded in obtaining an ordained minister to the mission

---

16 Ross and Fiedler, *A Malawi Church History*, 56. Jane Waterston makes references to the Blantyre Atrocities in her letters. See, *The Letters of Jane Elizabeth Waterston, 1865–1905*. Second Series No. 14 (Cape Town: Van Riebeeck Society, 1983), 143–156. A good summation is found in Englund, *Visions for Racial Equality*, 43–45, 49–50.

17 Weller & Linden, *Mainstream Christianity*, 45; Phiri, *Malawi*, 136. A short book by Andrew Chirnside, *The Blantyre Missionaries: Discreditable Disclosures*. (London: Ridgeway, 1880) would highlight many of these to the reading Scottish public.

> ... It was scarcely dreamed of, that a year would pass, and yet, notwithstanding many calls, see the mission without its spiritual leader. The want, indeed, is temporarily supplied by the charity of the sister mission but it is now a matter of humiliation that no one has come forth from the ordained ranks of the church to go to Blantyre.[18]

Context: Arabs and Portuguese territorial ambitions in 1880s to 1890s

Further complications of the 1880s included that the Arabs and Portuguese had strong political and socio-economic ambitions of taking over the territories of the Southern part of Malawi to the Indian Ocean. The Scottish missionaries became more concerned with the Arabs and Portuguese territorial and socio-political interests.[19] With the Calvinistic background of involvement in social issues, the Blantyre Missionaries initiated and campaigned vigorously to get thousands of signatures to persuade the Scottish Parliament to pass a Bill that could make the British Government withdraw from its initial willingness to cede the area to Portugal and establish a formal "British Protectorate."[20]

One of the missionaries in Malawi made a statement to the Foreign Mission Committee in Scotland against the slave trade for the committee to urgently respond as follows:

> That this great sore of the world may be healed is certain. The commencement will be made as soon as the mission is planted at Lake Nyassa. No Arab gang will come near an Englishman, if they can help it. With them the English name is synonymous with destroyer of slavery ... [sic]. We are assured that a mission once established, they [the Africans] will settle around it, receive our instruction and our help, place themselves under our authority, and rise by order and Christian observance into the state of civilized communities.[21]

Consequently, to protect its interests including settlers, farmers and missionaries, the British Government declared Nyasaland a "Protectorate" over the whole of

---

18 General Assembly of the Church of Scotland 1877, FMC report, in Andrew Ross, *Blantyre Mission*, 134.
19 Andrew Ross, *Blantyre Mission*, 77–78.
20 Gama, *Role of the Church in Politics*, 124.
21 Andrew Ross, *Blantyre Mission*, 50–51.

Malawi in May 1891.²² In 1891, the British Government finally declared Malawi a British Protectorate with Harry Johnston appointed as the first Commissioner and Consul-General to govern the protectorate. As a British Protectorate, the administration, church missionaries, and tea and coffee planters joined hands to run the country. The church, with recommendation from the Foreign Mission Committee (FMC), cooperated with the government to be an industrial as well as an evangelistic enterprise.²³

In the formation of a Christian settlement called the "mission village," it was necessary for the Blantyre Mission to teach the African natives some of the colonial industries and skills such as general education, gardening, ploughing, and joinery work. The government undertook responsibility for maintaining law and order sustained by the collection of hut taxes from the population. The role of African traditional chiefs was to collect hut taxes for the government. The socio-economic development was mainly in the hands of European settlers, tea and coffee planters and traders, while education, agriculture and health services were generally done by Blantyre missionaries. However, the policies of labour, land and political economy were formulated with the interest of the white Europeans in mind and most of the needs of African natives were largely ignored. Consequently, the educated African native elite began to question some of the bad policies and encouraged people to resist the unjust policies, particularly the increases in hut taxes and the punitive labour laws that benefited estate owners. It eventually led to Rev. John Chilembwe's uprising in 1915.²⁴

Duff MacDonald

In November 1877, Rev. Duff MacDonald (1850–1929) was approached and accepted to take charge of the Blantyre Mission as the first ordained minister from the Church of Scotland. In terms of the administration of the mission station, it had numerous problems. Ross notes that the outstanding and disappointing activity was the poor behaviour of some of the first team of missionaries who were involved in the most unholy activities against the locals.²⁵ This was called the "Blantyre Mission Scandal" because the missionaries who came to preach God's Word were involved in the mistreating of the same people to whom they came to minister; it was hardly a good imitation of the humility of Christ.

Consequently, the Foreign Office in Scotland instituted a commission of inquiry led by Dr Rankin and Mr Pringle to investigate the reports that came

---

22 Gama, *Role of the Church in Politics*, 124ff.
23 Muluzi, *Democracy with a Price*, 4ff; Gama, *Role of the Church in Politics*, 117.
24 Andrew Ross, *Blantyre Mission*, 50; Gama, *Role of the Church in Politics*, 118.
25 Andrew Ross, *Blantyre Mission*, 64.

from Malawi about the behaviour of the missionaries at Blantyre Mission. This misconduct led to Duff MacDonald's resignation[26] and the dismissal of the artisans; it also led to the appointment of new church leaders to take over the Blantyre Mission work.[27] However, the Blantyre missionaries, who came from the Church of Scotland, felt the need to remain in the Southern Region of Malawi and minister among the Yao and Lhomwe.[28] Informed by their Reformed church polity, the white Missionaries at Blantyre would take an early bold step to train African church workers. After almost collapsing in its early years under pressures of scandals and maladministration, the Blantyre mission became well established in the 1880s under the inspirational leadership of Rev. David Clement Scott.

Recovery or Re-establishment

In December 1881, after the difficult time of five scandalous years, the Blantyre Mission was fortunate that it received a new leader, by the name of Rev. David Clement Scott – one of the outstanding missionaries in this mission. Rev. David Clement Scott joined Henry Henderson and Jonathan Duncan, both retained from the original mission party.[29] He also gathered around him a very able group of people such as Dr Bowie, Rev. W. A. Scott, and Rev. Henry Scott, Rev. Robert Cleland, Rev. Alexander Hetherwick, John McIlwain, Miss Janet Beck, and Miss Margaret Christie.[30]

David Clement Scott, from 1881 to 1898

Rev. David Clement Scott (1853–1907) managed to save the mission by giving it a new direction like that of the Livingstonia Mission. Scott came to champion evangelism by which he believed in spreading the gospel of Christ in an African

---

26 MacDonald was only a scapegoat for the scandals. Andrew Ross thought so and that the problem was deflecting from the original recruitment problems, Andrew Ross, "MacDonald, Duff," *DSCHT*, 509. Also, Todd Statham, "Macdonald, Duff" *DACB*, https://dacb.org/stories/malawi/macdonald-duff/ Duff MacDonald had obviously good qualities (reference could also be made to MacDonald's two volume *Africana*, a most significant work for the time). but in the context the question remains was he passive given these artisan missionaries and their pursuits of justice? MacDonald thought the mission should not be involved in civil justice issues. Regardless, matters were occurring around him to the contrary.
27 Andrew Ross, *Blantyre Mission*, 63.
28 Selfridge, *Church's First Thirty Years*, 32.
29 Henderson under Scott helped establish new stations at Zomba, Domasi, and Mulanje. A steamer was named in Henderson's honour as was the stations' central educational endeavour at Blantyre. Owen J. M. Kalinga. *Historical Dictionary of Malawi*. Fourth Edition. (Lanham, MD: Scarecrow Press, 2012), 191–192.
30 Gama, *Role of the Church in Politics*, 45; Andrew Ross, *Blantyre Mission*, 24.

culture. Rev. David Scott's main goal was to promote education, which was to be given in an African context. Most outstanding was that Scott empowered Africans to develop Christianity for local people and help them become members of the true universal church. Rev. Scott firmly believed that Africans were part of the same humanity and that they would contribute to the Christian Church as well as benefit from it like the rest of advanced societies globally.[31] He insisted on the David Livingstone heritage, combining "Christianity, Civilization and Commerce," (popularly known as three CCC), a formula which Scott translated as the "Gospel and Modern Culture" which also meant deep respect for African culture. He and his successor, Alexander Hetherwick, insisted on generous opportunities for the African co-workers. Africans as co-inheritors of world culture in African forms was his educational formula; to make the African a conscious member of the catholic church of Christ was his ecclesiastical programme.[32]

In the spirit of the historic Reformed/Presbyterian tradition which advocated for the priesthood of all believers and distribution of specific offices of minister, elder, and deacon according to gifting, Rev. David Scott felt the need to take the challenge and put his ministry on risk. However, many white European missionaries opposed the ordination of natives because it implied a kind of "equality" which they saw as wrong.[33] However, the discussion is complex and nuanced. Some issues also related to the limitations of office in the Scottish Presbyterian system of the day.[34]

▲ St. Michael's and All Angels' Church

▲ First church of the Blantyre Mission

---

31 Andrew Ross, Blantyre Mission, 24ff; Pachai, *Malawi*, 206.
32 Andrew Ross, *Blantyre Mission*, 118–119.
33 Gama, *Know Your Synod*, 6.
34 For a fuller discussion on the breadth of transitional ministry positions during the early days of the Scottish Reformation, see *The First Book of Discipline* (1560).

In 1888, the church building at Blantyre Mission, which eventually became known as St Michael's and All Angels,' was begun with the leadership of Rev. David Scott and cooperation of African workers.[35] Within three years on 10 May 1891, the church building was officially inaugurated by Scott himself. It stands to this day as a work of inspiring architecture combining Western and Eastern traditions in a beautiful style of its own, not Scottish, nor English but supposedly African.

The school system was well developed with mission stations founded in the districts. Some key mission stations that were opened in the Southern part of Malawi in his tenure included Domasi, Chiradzulu, and Mulanje. Rev. David Scott had a gift of encouraging his African co-workers. He promoted the training of the local people, some of whom were sent to Scotland, one of them was Mungo Chisuse who was sent to Scotland to study printing.[36]

Deacons

In November 1893, Rev. Scott ordained some of his African colleagues as deacons: Joseph Bismark, Kambwiri Matecheta, Mungo Murray Chisuse, Harry Mtuwa, Rondau Kaferanjira, Donald Malota and John Gray Kufa.[37] Rev. Scott gave them all tasks to do in which they had responsibility and virtual autonomy, apart from infrequent supervisory visits from missionaries. However, Scott found little support for his "radical views" among white European settlers.

However, many other British missionaries of the day thought Scott's views on African race and culture were progressive. He opposed certain elements of traditional culture as incompatible with Christianity (e.g., initiation rituals, polygamy, but he did not condemn African customs wholesale). Scott held that:

> People will not believe how much the Africans are capable until they have tried. Our aim is always to teach responsibility, and at the proper time to lay it on those who have to bear it. In many ways the time has now come. It is a fatal mistake to keep the African in leading strings. We cannot too soon teach him to realise he has a part to play in the education and life of Christ's church and kingdom.[38]

---

35 Editor's note: there appears to be slight variations on this name in terms of possessive marks in books and reports.
36 Phiri, *Malawi*, 136–137; Andrew Ross, *Blantyre Mission*, 82.
37 Phiri, *Malawi*, 139.
38 Andrew Ross in Gama, *Know Your Synod*, 6.

Dictionary, Scriptures, and Pilgrim's Progress

Scott produced a dictionary of the Chinyanja language that evidenced not only considerable linguistic abilities but also a deep and sympathetic grasp of African culture.[39] Scott's other major contribution was his translation of the four Gospels in 1893 and then the whole New Testament in 1896 into Chinyanja.[40] David Clement Scott's brother, William Affleck Scott (1862–1895), was also a missionary in Blantyre and he made a contribution in linguistic work as well and translated John Bunyan's *Pilgrim's Progress* into Mang'anja (1892). There is a common theme which emerged across missions in nineteenth-century Africa and that is the use of Bunyan's *Pilgrim's Progress* and its translation into the vernacular languages of Africa. As in the Eastern Cape with Tiyo Soga, so also at Blantyre, Bunyan's work was a popular text next to the Bible, hymns, and catechisms to translate and adapt for use. Other significant works of the mission included *Kalata wa Ku punsitsira sintu sa Mulungu* and *Kalata wa Ku punsitsira wa chimang'anÿa* a catechism and reading book.[41]

In 1898, Rev. David Scott was forced to resign his post perhaps in part for health reasons and Alexander Hetherwick (1860–1939), his assistant, assumed leadership. After his furlough in Scotland, Scott proceeded to Kenya where he became superintendent of the CSM Kikuyu Mission in 1901, now the Presbyterian Church in East Africa. Rev. Scott died after he succumbed to thrombosis of the legs in 1907.[42]

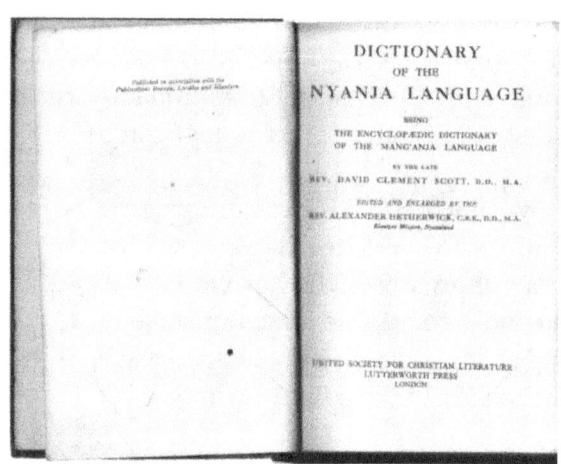

▲ Dictionary of the Nyanja Language

▲ Drs. Hetherwick and Laws

---

39 David Clement Scott, *A Cyclopaedic Dictionary of the Nyanja Language* (Edinburgh: FMCCoS, 1892). Hetherwick edited and revised Scott's work and it was reissued in 1929. Alexander Hetherwick, *Dictionary of the Nyanja Language*. Original 1929. (London: Lutterworth Press for the United Society for Christian Literature, 1951).
40 Ernst R. Wendland, "Bible Translation – a Lighthouse and a Library for the Promotion and Preservation of Language and 'Literature' in Africa: The example of Chinyanja," 85.
41 Both Blantyre/Edinburgh, 1891.
42 Sundkler & Steed, *History*, 799–800.

Summary

The Blantyre Mission from 1878 to 1881 was in a very perilous position when Duff MacDonald was appointed as the ordained minister to lead this mission. Interpretation of MacDonald's ministry during those four scandalous years remains a divided issue, from scapegoat to complicit. Evidence seems to point to the reality that preceding issues were at work already when he was appointed to this position, and these continued to develop. Under David Clement Scott's leadership, 1881 to 1898, *recovery and advance* were the themes.

5. Growth and Development in Blantyre Mission from 1898 to 1956

The third period for the Blantyre Mission was when the mission stations faced many challenges: rapid growth, financial difficulties, the socio-political context of 1898, the First World War in 1914 to 1918, the Second World War in 1939 to 1945, and the move toward Blantyre Mission autonomy in 1956.

Major challenges in 1898 to 1914

Gama argues that in this period (1898 to 1914) of the Blantyre Mission the church faced two challenges: rapid growth and development of the African leadership of the church and poor financial income partly due to advances of the First and Second World Wars in 1914–1918 and 1939–1945.[43]

Rapid growth and the African leadership in 1898 to 1956

Harry Kambwiri Matecheta (1870–1962), a Yao, first heard about Jesus Christ at the age of six during Henderson's and Bokwitos' trip to Nguludi in Chiradzulu and surrounding areas in 1876. In 1884, Matecheta went to school at Blantyre Mission up to grade four before becoming a teacher at the same school. He was later trained in printing. He was baptised on 29 December 1889. He would be one of the members of the famous deacons' class already mentioned above.

Ross describes the *first stage* in the training which started in 1893 for the seven candidates as deacons. The class met at seven o'clock each morning. These seven were ordained as deacons on the 4th of November 1894.[44] In 1894, the seven ordained African deacons were given responsibility together with Rev. David Clement Scott to exercise church discipline, be involved in the work and life of the mission and be sent to establish churches in villages around Blantyre. However, the Malawian office of the "deacon" was not properly familiar to the

---

43 Gama, *Know Your Synod*, 45.
44 Andrew Ross, *Blantyre Mission*, 112. For fuller details about Harry Kambwiri Matecheta see chapter 17 in this first volume.

traditional Presbyterian Churches in general. Scott's view of the deacon was closer to Anglicanism than historic Presbyterianism in a quest for contextualisation of the African church. It was the innovative creation of Rev. David Scott who wanted to use the knowledge and wisdom of the Africans, especially in the area of native evangelisation, care for the vulnerable, and church discipline.

In January 1895, in the *Life, and Work of Blantyre Mission*, Rev. David Clement Scott was quoted saying:

> Africa for the Africans has been our policy from the first, and we believe that God has given us this country into our hands that we may train the peoples how to develop its marvellous resources for themselves.[45]

But later, in bits the Africans began to get more powers and responsibilities. In 1900, the Scottish Presbyterian and Dutch Reformed Missions in British Central Africa made a resolution to ordain African natives to the ministry despite strong opposition from some staff members at the Blantyre Mission, such as R. S. Hynde who argued:

> It is utterly wrong to teach any native he is as good as a white man because he is not. If he were, he would be on the level with the white man, but it is because he is inferior that he is under the white man.[46]

All the ministers in the Blantyre Mission remained European Missionaries only until 1911. In 1911, on 9 March, Harry Kambwiri Matecheta was the first indigenous minister to be ordained at a service held at St Michael's and All Angels' Church in Blantyre, and three days later 12 March 1911, Stephen Kundecha was ordained as second minister at a service held at Zomba Church. The two had been trained for four years prior to their ordination. Rev. Harry Matecheta had been a leading Evangelist in the history of the church who fully connected to the Presbyterian Mission in loyalty and served, among other places, at Mulanje Mission, Chikwawa, Blantyre, in the Southern Region and Nthumbi, Bemvu and many surrounding places among the Ngoni in Ntcheu for forty-six years. In 1933, he was elected Moderator of his church. He was ably assisted by his wife. Her last words on her deathbed sum up the faith and aspiration of a whole generation of forgotten women in the church with simple eloquence:

---

45 Gama, *Know Your Synod*, 6, quoting from page 216 of *Life, and Work of the Blantyre Mission*.
46 Gama, *Know Your Synod*, 6–7.

> My way is open. I am glad my children are all educated, married, and settled. I am not worried. I have done my duty.[47]

In the Blantyre Mission, therefore, the ordination of an African church minister was a sign of giving more powers and responsibility to an African. Consequently, in all local congregations, the African pastors, elders, and evangelists went about doing their evangelism tasks.[48] Therefore, the church and government complemented each other in sharing responsibilities in their cause and interest to serve the people in Malawi.

Heatherwick continued to promote Translation work etc.

Heatherwick was actively involved in linguistic work in the Blantyre Mission. He continued this on from David Clement Scott and as already mentioned revised Scott's noted dictionary. Related publications of Hetherwick were *Manuel of Nyanja Language* (1901); *A Handbook of the Yao Language* (1902); and *Translation of New Testament into Yao Language* (1907). Besides these, he was a promoter of the missions through such publications as *Robert Hellier Napier in Nyasaland* (Edinburgh, 1925); and *The Building of Blantyre Church, Nyasaland* (Edinburgh, 1926).

Rapid growth and financial challenges

Due to pressures from the rapid growth of the Blantyre Mission, the church experienced serious financial problems. The mission frequently failed to manage its resources to meet the needs of the missionaries, institutions, and workers. The Advance Movement Sub-committee was formed for raising funds for Mission work in Scotland and could not meet targets because the needs were too many. However, the Advance Movement Sub-committee, at last with difficulties, managed to clear some debts that had burdened the Foreign Mission Committee until 1914.[49]

In 1909, the Blantyre Mission opened the Henry Henderson Institute,[50] which became an important facility, training Africans in the same manner as the Overtoun Institute of Livingstonia Mission. The Boarding school for both girls and boys at Blantyre Mission was as prim and proper as any on the continent where emphasis was on English language, mathematics, higher learning, and African culture.

---

47 Sundkler & Steed, *History*, 799–800.
48 Gama, *Know Your Synod*, 6; Sundkler & Steed, 799–800.
49 Gama, *Role of the Church in Politics*, 45; Andrew Ross, *Blantyre Mission*, 33.
50 See, Kalinga, *Historical Dictionary of Malawi*, 192 for an overview summary of this institute.

However, on the management of the Blantyre Mission, the church and institutions, Alexander Hetherwick recommended that the highly "hierarchical" system of government for the church resemble the civil government where the chief and headman ruled over his council of elders. The system, according to Hetherwick, represented the "true rule" of the church, like that of the bishop in his synod of presbyters, of the minister in his Kirk session, and Moderator in the Church of Scotland. Ecclesiastical power in the Blantyre Synod was the establishment of the all-white "Mission Council" of the Blantyre Mission as the "first governing assembly," This was followed by the founding of a Kirk Session around 1900 at the St Michael's and All Angels' Church, and the Blantyre Presbytery in 1904. The powerful ecclesiastical "Mission Council" was responsible to the "Home Committee" in Scotland. Ross observed that although in some areas indigenous structures were set up, the "Mission Council" was always the real source of both ecclesiastical power and authority in the hierarchy of Blantyre Synod.[51] It controlled the larger resources including land, all buildings, schools, hospital, churches, and funds.

The local session and presbytery had little or no control over major elements in the staff and property of the churches in their area. The "Mission Council," in effect a white oligarchy, controlled all the major financial resources in the field, paying African ministers, teachers and evangelists (for most full-time staff), and controlling their posting and work. Neither the Kirk Sessions formed in 1900 nor the Blantyre Presbytery founded in 1904 had any authority over these vital matters. Matters pertaining to vision, mission and directions in which the church should expand appeared on the agenda of the "Mission Council."[52] Between 1904 and 1924, the Blantyre Presbytery was officially the highest ecclesiastical court for Europeans and Africans in all church matters, but in reality, the "Mission Council" was responsible for everything.

The long road to the formation of the General Synod from 1890 to 1924

In the early 1890s, Rev. David Clement Scott had suggested to Dr Robert Laws that there should be one united church for British Central Africa. The two Scottish Missionaries began to explore the possibility of a *united* Presbyterian Church. In 1903, the Blantyre Presbytery again approached Livingstonia Presbytery with the same suggestion of church unity and proposed that the Creed, Constitution and Church order could be based on those of the Presbyterian Church in India.

In the following year, further discussions were held during the United Missionary Conference at Mvera Mission in Nkhoma Presbytery. In 1914, the

---

51 Ross, *Blantyre Mission*, 172, 177.
52 Ross, *Blantyre Mission*, 172, 177.

two "mother" churches in Scotland were to give permission and plans were made for the union of Livingstonia and Blantyre Presbyteries, but because of the outbreak of the First World War, all advances for unity were postponed since most of the ministers were busy with Army chaplaincy.[53]

Constitution of the General Synod

When the war ended in 1918, the Missionary Conference was re-arranged for 1924 and it was decided that the new church would come into being then. The Conference met at Livingstonia and formally constituted the Church of Central Africa, Presbyterian (CCAP) General Synod and Rev. Dr Robert Laws was elected as its first moderator in September 1924. The General Synod of the Church of Central Africa Presbyterian (CCAP) became the highest ecclesiastical court of this federation, although by that time the church had not yet received its autonomy from both the United Free and Church of Scotland. They agreed that the two Presbyterian Missions (Livingstonia and Blantyre) would remain unique and autonomous in their organization, decision-making, and missionary enterprise in line with the practices and traditions of the "mother" church. This made the position of the General Synod in the CCAP unstable over the decades.

Developments

The General Synod was committed to the historic ecumenical creeds: Apostles' Creed and the Nicene; the Westminster Confession of Faith and Shorter and Larger Catechisms, and in time also added the Heidelberg Catechism. Areas of cooperation in church work included theological education, worship, and Bible translation; the Blantyre and Nkhoma Synods opted to use ethnic Chichewa as lingua franca, while the Livingstonia Synod chose ethnic Tumbuka/Tonga. They also agreed on a joint hymnbook. Other Synods that joined the CCAP General Synod are Lundazi (Zambia) and Harare (Zimbabwe).[54] The office headquarters have been in Lilongwe, the Capital City of Malawi.

In January 1946, in Blantyre Presbytery, Rev. Andrew Doig, the Senior Clerk, pleaded with the former Moderators of Blantyre Presbytery to meet quickly and elect the next Moderator after retired Moderator Rev. Duncan Msaka. On 15th January 1948, the Blantyre Presbytery unanimously elected Kenneth Mackenzie as Moderator of Blantyre Presbytery.[55] On 13th January 1949, Rev. Stephen Green was elected the Moderator, while Rev. James Alexander was appointed as

---

53 Munyenyembe, "Lofty but not powerful," 4–6, 20; Weller & Linden, *Mainstream Christianity*, 114ff.
54 Weller & Linden, *Mainstream Christianity*, 114ff; Munyenyembe, "Lofty but not powerful," 20ff.
55 Gama, *Know Your Synod*, 5

Senior Clerk. In 1950, Rev. Augustine Ndalama was elected unanimously as the Moderator of Blantyre Presbytery. Other moderators nominated in the following years were Revs. Allan Thipa in 1951, Jonathan Sande in 1952, Stainer Mambiya in 1953, William Pembereka in 1954, S. F. Chintali in 1955.[56]

6. Postscript: Blantyre Presbytery/Synod from 1956 to 2020

The fourth period for the Blantyre Presbytery dawned when the church adopted a new constitution, attained autonomy as the Blantyre Synod, and recruited more African ministers in the leadership of the church from 1956 to 2020.

In 1956, the Blantyre Presbytery approved a new constitution which led the Presbytery to attain the status of Blantyre Synod and Rev. C. J. Watt was elected Blantyre Synod Moderator in 1956. In 1958, the Blantyre Synod received autonomy from the Church of Scotland and Rev. D. Kunyenga was elected Synod Moderator in 1959. Up to 1960, the Malawi government was run by white people at the same time the church was also under the white people. In the socio-political, economic, and spiritual life in Malawi, many Africans felt regarded as incapable and inferior.[57]

More African ministers taking over leadership

However, the Rev. Baxter was elected Moderator of Blantyre Synod in 1961, while the Rev. Jonathan Sangaya became the first African to take the position of General Secretary in 1962.[58] Others who were appointed as Moderators of the Blantyre Synod were Revs. L.W. Makwalo in 1964, J. B. Lamya in 1966, Cedric B. Simuja in 1968–69, J. L. Kapolo in 1969, B. E. Malikebu in 1970. In 1967, Rev. Sangaya in partnership with Rev. Canon Aiden, Bishop of the Anglican Church championed the establishment of the Chilema Ecumenical Lay Training Centre in Zomba for the joint training courses of elders, deacons, youth, and women leaders from both churches.[59]

Eventually in the late 1960s, Rev. Sangaya was also instrumental in the formation of the Ecumenical Christian Organizations, Malawi Council of Churches (MCC), Christian Service Committee (CSC) and the Christian Students Organization (SCO) in Blantyre.

---

56 Gama, *Know Your Synod*, 5.
57 Gama, *Know Your Synod*, 5.
58 Zeze, "Christ the Head," 175ff.
59 Gama, *Know Your Synod*, 5.

In 1977, the CCAP Blantyre Synod with support from the General Synod opened the Zomba Theological College for the training of its ministers. Later, the other four Presbyteries of the CCAP and the Anglican Church joined the Zomba Theological College for the ministerial formation training of their ministers and priests. Therefore, during Rev. Sangaya's tenure of office, Blantyre Synod experienced tremendous growth in its membership, training of young ministers, financial development, and partnership with overseas churches. In 1979, Rev. Sangaya died mysteriously (allegedly in the hands of police), and then Rev. Dr Saindi Chiphangwi was elected General Secretary of Blantyre Synod in 1980–1985. In the 1980s the following were elected Moderators of Blantyre Synod: Revs. B. G. Kuntembwe, R. H. Makonyola, J. J. Mphatso, B. G. Kuntembwe, R. H. Makonyola, and in the 1990s Revs. G. Chimowa, L. D. Chingadza, and G. Bona. In the 2010s, R. Mangisa, M. Chilapula, Chimkwezule and M. L. Mbolembole were elected Moderators of the Blantyre Synod.[60]

The Blantyre Synod recent achievements and developments

In 1992, after the Roman Catholic Church's pastoral letter critical of Malawi Government: "Living our faith," the Blantyre Synod in partnership with other religious bodies and political pressure groups in Malawi such as the United Democratic Front (UDF), the Alliance for Democracy (AFORD), Malawi Democratic Party (MDP), Malawi Law Society and others formed the Public Affairs Committee (PAC). The purpose of the PAC was to offer a platform for serious dialogue for political transition to democratic change with the Life President Dr Hastings Kamuzu Banda and the Malawi Congress Party. The Public Affairs Committee (PAC) was instrumental in translating a popular desire for political freedom and change into reality.[61]

Nevertheless, in Blantyre Synod, other outstanding ministers who were elected to the office of the General Secretary included Revs. Silas Ncozana in 1985–1995, Misanjo Kansilanga in 1995–1999, Daniel Gunya in 1999–2009, Alex Maulana in 2009–2019 and the incumbent Rev. Dr Billy Gama in 2019–2020.

In the year 2020, Blantyre Synod has a historic record of 210 ordained ministers in charge of 600 congregations and 300 prayer houses with 1.8 million members across Ntcheu District in the Central and Southern Regions of Malawi.[62] The Blantyre Synod runs numerous primary and Secondary Schools, the University of Blantyre Synod, Mulanje Mission Hospital, Zomba Theological College, Chigodi Women's Centre, and Likhubula Youth Centre, Blantyre Synod

---

60 Gama, *Know Your Synod*, 71.
61 D. Kaspin, "The Politics of Ethnicity in Malawi's Democratic Transition," 10, 595–620.
62 2019 Blantyre Synod Conference Minutes 29:12. See also footnote 65 in this chapter.

Development Commission (BSDC), Domasi Likuni Phala Company, Blantyre Synod Radio and many other institutions of social development. Consequently, Blantyre town has grown up around the Mission station and in the year 2020 it is a city of 2.5 million residents. It still proudly bears the name of "Blantyre City" in memory of the birthplace of David Livingstone (southeast of Glasgow in Scotland).[63]

7. Reflections for further consideration and research

As in chapter fourteen on the Livingstonia Mission, I include also a section on reflections and areas for further consideration and research.

Governance

In light of the discussion above, this survey raises the question that the Church of Scotland from the very beginning based itself on the compromised principles of Scriptures, Calvinistic tradition, and church polity in Reformed church perspective. The Reformed views claim that the legitimate church government and its operations must be rooted in the principles of Holy Scriptures and that the confessions regarding church provide the normative guidelines for the church. However, to evaluate the life, work, and activities of the Blantyre Mission, I further argue the Church of Scotland made a lot of compromises in the sense of principles of Scripture and Reformed church polity. For example, the Blantyre Mission was characterised and bound by decisions made at the Foreign Mission Committee (FMC) of the Church of Scotland. The powerful ecclesiastical "Mission Council" at Blantyre in Malawi, was responsible to the "Home Committee" in Scotland. The "Mission Council" was always the real source of ecclesiastical power and authority in the hierarchy of Blantyre Synod. It controlled the larger resources including land, all buildings, schools, hospital, churches, and funds contrary to the principles of Scriptures and reformed church polity.[64]

This is clearly an area for ongoing reflection and discussion: how, for instance, to become a self-governing body within the three-self paradigm?

Missionary workers' scandals and unspiritual behaviour

The Blantyre Mission was characterized by scandals and unspiritual behaviour amongst its officers and workers compromising the principles of the Scriptures and Reformed church polity. Some workers and volunteers had technical skills

---

63 Selfridge, *Church's First Thirty Years*, 31–32.
64 Ross, *Blantyre Mission*, 172, 177.

with no spiritual calling to work as missionaries in Africa. There was evidence that they committed "Blantyre Atrocities" in 1878/79, where severe disciplinary action on Africans led to death. Ongoing discussion on this needs to continue to understand this controversial aspect of the Mission's early history and recruitment policies, pre-colonialism, authority vacuums, and the tribal context.

Scottish Missionaries' political and territorial concerns

In the 1880s, the Blantyre Missionaries were characterised by a strong campaign against Arabs and Portuguese territorial and socio-political ambitions for taking over the whole of Southern Malawi compromising the principles of Scripture. In the Reformed church perspective, the relationship of church and state distinguishes clearly between the task and territory of the church and state respectively. Both the church and the state are servants of God and each in its own way serves the kingdom of God (Isa 49:23). This is one aspect here to discuss as a case study in mission history and related to this is the missiological principle of integrated or wholistic mission, another aspect for discussion.

The formation of the General Synod

In the 1890s and 1924, the Blantyre Mission championed for unity and the establishment of the CCAP General Synod in advancing the principles of Scripture and Reformed church polity. Ongoing discussion of both the federative nature of this Synod and also the extent of such a federative expression could be explored. Perhaps comparative case studies could be done with the structures of the Presbyterian Church of Australia and its state assemblies.

The growth of African leadership in the church

In a positive note, from 1956 to 2020, Blantyre Synod had been characterised by the development and rapid growth of the African leadership in line with the principles of Scripture and reformed traditional polity. In 1911, Harry Kambwiri Matecheta and Stephen Kundecha were the first two Africans to be ordained as ministers and in 1962 the Rev. Jonathan Sangaya became the first African to take the position of General Secretary. Again, this all relates well to discussions about the three-self principle.

Socio-economic development

There had been a strong partnership in socio-economic development between the Blantyre Synod and the Malawi Government. Consequently, the Blantyre Synod runs various enterprises in education, health, and food security and relief development in all districts of Southern Malawi. The establishment of churches, schools and hospitals in rural areas has also greatly contributed to the growth of trading centres and industrialization in Malawi. Perhaps a critical analysis of this relationship between church and state in these areas would reveal a diverse range of conclusions.

8. Conclusion

The context for the establishment of Presbyterian Missions in Malawi (and the Blantyre Mission in particular) was very much related to the anti-slavery efforts of David Livingstone and the desired presence of British missionaries in fighting this evil. Likewise, Chief Kapeni also initially welcomed the establishment of the Blantyre Mission, partly motivated no doubt by a desire for protection from the brutality of nearby enemy tribes. Sadly, the early years of the mission saw brutality from some British (including some associated with Blantyre Mission) that was equally grievous. The arrival of Rev. David Clement Scott marked a new and very positive beginning, yet the controversies of the past continued to re-visit the mission at various developmental stages. The growth toward self-governance, self-support and self-propagation was not an easy path and the factors that hindered it along the way were complex. Despite these hindrances, the Mission went on to mature into a Synod of the CCAP. As of 2022, this particular synod alone has over 1.2 million members, 600 churches and 700 prayer houses.[65] The history of the Blantyre Mission, both positive and negative, is instructive for all who desire to take the gospel to another continent and culture.

Questions for study (fact type):
1. a) Missionary Henry Henderson from the Church of Scotland established the Blantyre Mission amongst what tribe?
   b) Why was it named Blantyre Mission?
   c) What year was it established?
2. Write one paragraph describing the Blantyre Atrocities using the information question: Who, What, When, Where, Why, and How?
3. Who was Rev. David Clement Scott?
4. Make a list of significant works that were translated into vernacular languages in the early days of the Blantyre Mission.
5. Who was the first African ordained minister of the Blantyre Mission?

---

65 http://www.ccapblantyresynod.org/ accessed 29 July, 2022. These statistics should be viewed as approximations as there are other statistics also to be found at the WCC website for 1.8 million members (oikoumene.org accessed 16 August 2023).

Questions for study (reflection type):
1. *"Rev. David Scott's main goal was to promote education which was to be given in an African context. Most outstanding was that Scott empowered Africans to develop Christianity for local people and help them become members of the true universal church."*
Why is education vital for the development of Christianity within any culture? Consider Christ's words in Luke 10:27 in your answer. Also consider Romans 12:2.
2. *"Due to pressures of rapid growth of the Blantyre Mission, the church experienced serious financial problems. The mission frequently failed to manage its resources to meet the needs of the missionaries, institutions, and workers. The Advance Movement Sub-committee was formed for raising funds for Mission work in Scotland and could not meet targets because the needs were too many."* The issue of finances for a mission can be very challenging. Discuss this one aspect of the three-self principle – "self-supporting". Is it possible? What practical steps can be taken toward this goal?

Select Bibliography

Blantyre Synod. 2020. Minutes for the Blantyre Synod Bi-Annual Conference 29:12. Blantyre. With permission from the General Secretary. Blantyre: July 2020.

Duncan, G. A. "Historiography and ideology in the (Mission) history of Christianity in Africa." Paper was given at a post-graduate seminar in the Dept. of Church History, University of South Africa on 10 September 2004.

Englund, Harri. *Visions for Racial Equality: David Clement Scott and the Struggle for Justice in Nineteenth-Century Malawi.* Cambridge: Cambridge University Press, 2022.

Gama, B. *The Role of the Church in Politics in Malawi.* Edleen: Acadsa Publishing, 2010.

Gama, B. *Know Your Synod: History, Leadership and Ordained Ministers from 1911 to 2015, CCAP Blantyre Synod.* Blantyre: University of Blantyre Synod, 2017.

Foreign Mission Committee Report, 1877. General Assembly Reports (21:134) in Andrew C. Ross, *Blantyre Mission and the making of modern Malawi.* Blantyre: CLAIM, 1996.

Haynes, Roderick Sutherland. *Before the Scramble: A Scottish Missionary's Story: The Journal of James Sutherland, Agriculturalist Livingstonia Mission British Central Africa 1880–1885.* Renton, WA: Highlander Press, 2015.

Hetherwick, Alexander. *The Romance of Blantyre: How Livingstone's Dream Came True.* London: James Clarke, nd.

Kaspin, D. "The Politics of Ethnicity in Malawi's Democratic Transition." *Journal of Modern African Studies* 33.4 (1995): 595–620.

Kalinga, Owen J. M. *Historical Dictionary of Malawi.* Fourth Edition. Lanham, MD: Scarecrow Press, 2012.

Life and Work in British East Africa/Nyasaland. 1888–1919.

Maluleke, T. S. "'A morula tree between two fields': The commentary of selected Tsonga writings on mission Christianity." DTh thesis, UNISA Pretoria, 1995.

McCracken, John. "Class, Violence and Gender in Early Colonial Malawi: The Curious Case of Elizabeth

Pithie." *The Society of Malawi Journal* 64.2 (2011):1–16. http://www.jstor.org/stable/41289177.

McCracken, J. C. *Politics and Christianity in Malawi 1875–1940: the Impact of the Livingstonia Mission in the Northern Province.* Cambridge: Cambridge University, 1977.

Munyenyembe, R. "Lofty but not powerful: a critical analysis of the position of the General Assembly in the union of the Church of Central Africa Presbyterian (CCAP) Malawi." *Studia historiae ecclesiasticae* 42.3 (2016):1–21. https:upjournals.co.za.

Muluzi, B. E. et al. *Democracy with a price: the history of Malawi since 1900.* London: Heinemann,1999.

Pachai, B. *Early History of Malawi.* London: Longman, 1972.

Phiri, D. D. *History of Malawi: From earliest times to the year 1915.* Blantyre: Claim, 2004.

Ross, Andrew C. *Blantyre Mission and the Making of Modern Malawi.* Blantyre: CLAIM,1996.

Ross, Andrew C. "The Origins and Development of The Church of Scotland Mission, Blantyre, Nyasaland, 1875–1926." PhD thesis, University of Edinburgh, 1968.

Ross, Kenneth R. and Klaus Fiedler, *A Malawi Church History 1860–2020.* Mzuzu-Luwinga: Mzuni Press, 2020.

Selfridge, J. *The Church's First Thirty Years in Nyasaland (Now Malawi) 1861–1891.* Nkhoma, Lilongwe: Nkhoma Press, 1976.

Shin, J. H. "An Evaluation of the Presbyterian Church in Korea's use of assistant pastors: A reformed church polity perspective." MTh. mini-dissertation, North-West University, 2015.

Sundkler, B. & C. Steed. *History of the Church in Africa.* Cambridge: Cambridge University, 2000.

Weller, J. & Linden J. *Mainstream Christianity to 1980 in Malawi, Zambia, and Zimbabwe: From Mission to Church.* Gweru: Mambo Press, 1984.

Wendland, Ernst R. "Bible Translation – a Lighthouse and a Library for the Promotion and Preservation of Language and 'Literature' in Africa: The example of Chinyanja." *Scriptura* 85 (2004): 81–96.

Zeze, W. "Christ, the Head of the Church: Authority, Leadership and Organizational Structure within the CCAP – Nkhoma Synod in Malawi." *Protestant Church Polity in Changing Contexts II, Case Studies.* Berlin: Verlag, 2014. [Paper presented at the International Conference, Utrecht, The Netherlands 7–10 November 2011]: 35–44.

Chapter 16

The Nkhoma Mission and Synod

David Kawanga

Chapter Outline
1. Introduction: The Macedonian Call
2. The Early years of the DRC Mission Church: 1889–1914
3. The Growth of the DRC Church from 1914 to 1950s
4. Growth Towards Autonomy: 1956 to 1962
5. Approaches and Major Achievements of the DRCM
6. Areas for Further Reflection
7. Conclusion & Postscript

1. Introduction: The Macedonian Call

The Nkhoma Mission (later to develop into a Synod) was the third mission to be established in the modern-day country of Malawi, which would eventually form the CCAP. While the first two, Livingstonia Mission to the north and Blantyre Mission[1] to the south, were established through the work of Scottish ecclesial missionaries, this third mission was developed through the Dutch Reformed Church of South Africa by a Macedonian call. It should be recalled that the Murray family in South Africa, though from Scotland, were labouring in the DRC in South Africa;[2] the ties between Scotland, Malawi (present-day), and South Africa were strong. "The Free Church of Scotland Mission at Bandawe had been established and now made an appeal for help in their enormous field. The DRC responded."[3]

---

1 The Nkhoma Synod was originally bounded by the Livingstonia Mission in the North at the 13th degree latitude and alongside Dwangwa River, the Blantyre Mission in Southern part of the districts of Ntcheu and Mangochi, Lake Malawi in the East, and Mozambique and Zambia in the West. Also, a note on the spelling for *Nkhoma*, which historically was also *Mkhoma*, but also on occasion *Mkoma*, hence the variety of spellings.
2 See Retief Müller's chapter (26) in this volume: "Scots Presbyterians and the NGK/DRC of South Africa."
3 Parsons, "Scots and Afrikaners in Central Africa: Andrew Charles Murray and The Dutch Reformed Church Mission in Malawi," 24.

▲ Mvera Church (with permission of the DRC Archives)

The DRC sent Rev. Andrew Charles Murray[4] (1862–1936) in 1888 to work and observe with the Livingstonia Mission. The next year he was joined by Rev. Theunis Botha Vlok[5] (1866–1936) who arrived in Malawi on 8 July 1889 and together they set up the first administrative mission station at Mvera in Dowa District in the Central Region of Malawi on 28 November 1889. From this eventually emerged a separate mission, fully under the auspices of the DRCM but having been mentored first through the Livingstonia Mission.

---

4 "Which members of this remarkable [Murray] family developed in Andrew Charles Murray a zeal for mission? His Uncle John (1826–1882) and Uncle Andrew (1828–1917) had studied in Scotland in the mid-1840's and then proceeded to Holland to study Dutch and theology. There, they had joined a small evangelical group. The two brilliant scholars had taken a stand in favour of vital, transforming faith and returned to South Africa to become prime movers in the Dutch Reformed Church." Parsons, 23–24. A. C. Murray had been corresponding with James Stewart at Lovedale about a possible mission field and Stewart sent his brother-in-law John Stephen to meet Murray at Stellenbosch. A. C. Murray then proceeded to Edinburgh for further studies and then after that to Bandawe to meet Dr Laws who extended a welcome hand to the DRC. Murray studied the mission strategy of the Livingstonia Mission to use this for the DRCM. Clearly the Macedonian call was being made to the DRC. John Selfridge, *The Church's First Thirty Years in Nyasaland (Now Malawi) 1861–1891* (Nkhoma: Nkhoma Press, 1976), 60–61.

5 Rev. Theunis Christoffel Botha Vlok was born in Sutherland in the Northern Cape on 18 January 1866 and passed away on 2 September 1936 in Wellington.

2. The Early Years of The DRC Mission Church: 1889–1914

When Rev. Andrew Charles Murray and Rev. Theunis Botha Vlok arrived in Mvera in 1889, they were preoccupied with the establishment of the mission church structures. They made treaties with the local chiefs, and it was successfully done. The most outstanding work which they did was to establish a school[6] through which they evangelised the people and after three years, in February 1892, three men registered as catechumens and the first two, Moses Kamadia and Paulos Maodze, were baptised. At the same time mission work was expanding to other areas beyond Mvera station.

▲ Rev. Andrew Charles Murray (with permission of the DRC archives)

Apart from Mvera station (1889), the Dutch Reformed Church (DRC) founded ten more stations in the historic period before WW2, with Kongwe (1894) and Nkhoma (1896) following after Mvera in the 19th century, while the stations of Livlezi (1886, received 1894) and Malembo (1895, received 1907) were taken over from the Livingstonia Mission because they were located south of the 13th degree latitude. (For a full list of mission stations in the historic period see the chart at the end of this chapter.) The missionaries were assisted by indigenous evangelists, elders, and deacons whom they appointed in all congregations. The work was also expanded using enterprises such as education, medical services, industrial work, and literature. The whole work was under the supervision of the Mission Council, which was established in 1897 by the DRC in South Africa to oversee the mission work abroad.

▲ Rev. Theunis Botha Vlok right (with permission of the DRC archives)

---

6   It was the first school which was known as the Mission School, or the Murray School, by the indigenous people around the Mission Centre.

The founding of Nkhoma station as Headquarters—1896

In the year 1896, a new site was identified by Vlok at the foot of Nkhoma Mountain, about 56 km south of Mvera. Four years earlier Vlok had met the Chewa chief Mazengera who was living with his people on Nkhoma Mountain, driven by continuous Ngoni and Yao raids. The chief was desirous to have a mission near him, more for political and protective reasons. Hence the missionaries were received with enthusiasm. On Sunday 31st May 1896, they conducted the first ever church service which attracted 600 indigenous people.

Despite this encouraging attendance, the mission work met some problems. The British colonial administrators took advantage of the coming of the DRCM to be collecting hut tax and forced labour from the people that were being evangelised and also the Ngoni and Yao raids who wanted men for the slave trade. Another challenge was the deaths of some missionaries due to black-water fever, malaria, and attacks from wild animals. However, the first two converts were baptised on 19 September 1897, two months after the death of one of the missionaries, Rev. J. F. du Toit. Three years later, in 1900, there were twenty-one baptised members with fifty-nine attending catechumen class. Over 1,300 children were being taught on the station and in thirteen village schools.

A Church Council had also by then formed to lead and organise the young mission church. This council had decided and recommended the transfer of the headquarters from Mvera to Nkhoma mission station. There were several reasons that necessitated this decision. The first was insufficient water supply at Mvera and limited agricultural prospects for gardens for the increasing number of teachers, evangelists and others being trained at the head station, better climatic conditions at the higher altitude of Nkhoma and the fact that the route to the South (where the water highway connected Malawi from the outside through Zambezi and Shire rivers) was now going overland via Dedza and no longer via the Lake. All this made Nkhoma a better prospect. Another crucial reason was the advance of an epidemic of sleeping sickness from the lakeshore. Therefore, Nkhoma officially became the Head Station of the DRCM in 1913 and in the course of years was built up to become the biggest station of all the Dutch Reformed Church's Mission operations in different parts of Africa. All mission operations were consequently moved to Nkhoma to facilitate the evangelisation endeavours.

3. The Growth of the Church from 1914 to 1950s

When the DRCM headquarters had moved from Mvera to Nkhoma during the years 1911 to 1912, the missionaries were preoccupied with the work of promoting education which was the key and strategic area for the success of mission work. This was led by the new DRCM leader Rev. W. H. Murray who had taken over the leadership mantle from A. C. Murray. A. C. Murray had gone back to South Africa due to poor health to recuperate. From the time of their arrival till this time, the DRCM relied much on the Livingstonia Mission when training their workers. Livingstonia had a very famous institute known as Overtoun Institution at Livingstonia station. Therefore, the first DRCM teachers and evangelists were trained there. It was expensive to send students to Livingstonia from Nkhoma and the DRCM quickly developed their own policy of education and opened a lot of schools from 1910 to 1919 (which was based on the Village School concept) in order to reach out to many learners. This philosophy of the mission school had as its primary object to lead the pupils to an intelligent grasp of the Bible truth and through that under the Holy Spirit's guidance to a saving knowledge of the way of salvation. The DRCM also opened a school to train leaders, teachers, evangelists, and ministers at Nkhoma.[7] The qualification for members of the Mission Church to apply for training as teachers was simply commitment to teaching in the mission. However, in 1919 the Mission Council (which was formed soon after the move to Nkhoma from Mvera) decided in principle also to accept candidates for training at higher level who did not intend to become Mission teachers. Therefore, the policy made in 1912 of not teaching English was cancelled and it was now introduced to students.

In the following years, many mission stations along with schools were opened, a move that facilitated the growth of the Mission church. This was made possible by the funds provided by the General Mission Council in South Africa. The DRCM was so privileged because A. C. Murray who was the founder of DRCM work in Malawi had become the Secretary of the GMC in South Africa. In 1922 the DRCM obtained the services of a well-qualified educationist, J. G. Steytler, who was appointed Head of the Normal School which was a high school for the Mission at Nkhoma. His arrival ushered in positive developments in as far as the mission work was concerned through opening schools and mission stations all over the Central Region of Malawi.

Nkhoma Presbytery and the formation of the CCAP

In this section there is a survey about the relationship which was there between the Presbytery of Nkhoma and the CCAP as a whole. At the time of conception there were three presbyteries which constituted The Federated Mission Council

---

7   The DRCM opened a school in 1901 to train leaders, teachers, evangelists, and ministers at Nkhoma known as Normal School or Nolomala by the indigenous people because they could not pronounce the English term (normal) properly. This school survived till 1941 when the colonial government took over the management of Mission schools and made them grant-aided institutions.

(FMC). These were: Blantyre, Livingstonia and Nkhoma Presbyteries. Each did the training of ministers, licensing, and ordination separately. However, in the year 1914, both the United Free Church of Scotland General Assembly and the Church of Scotland General Assembly approved the formation of a Synod of the CCAP in Malawi and this decision was communicated to the Federated Mission Council (FMC) of which the DRC mission church was a member.

The proposed Union could not be consummated until ten years later due to the war. But in 1924 all preparations had been made and on the evening of 17 September 1924, the two Presbyteries held a united session in the Church at Livingstonia and the motion to unite *"in One common Synod ... was unanimously and with acclamation, agreed to."* Dr Robert Laws, the leader of Livingstonia Mission, was unanimously elected as first Moderator of the new Synod. In other words, this was the genesis of a united, indigenous African Church. At this point in time the Nkhoma Presbytery had not yet joined the CCAP. A committee by the DRCM was appointed to negotiate without delay with the Presbyteries of Blantyre and Livingstonia and with the General Mission Committee (GMC) in Cape Town. The resolutions of the GMC supported the idea unreservedly! After considerable negotiations and discussions concerning the Statement of Faith for the CCAP, all Presbyteries agreed to form the CCAP and the Nkhoma Presbytery was accepted and welcomed into the Synod of the CCAP in 1926.[8]

▲ Evangelists of Nkhoma Mission, 1928
(with permission of the DRC archives)

▲ Evangelist Albert Namalambe
(with permission of the DRC archives)

---

8   Both prior to and after it joined the CCAP the Nkhoma synod used three confessional documents for its church polity and these are the Belgic Confession of Faith, the Heidelberg Catechism and the Canons of Dordt. In 1892 A. C. Murray developed a small catechism called *Nsonga* printed at Bandawe. Then in 1898 A. C. Murray produced a new catechism based upon three works: the Heidelberg Catechism, the abridgement *Kortbegrip*, and the Westminster Shorter Catechism, and this work was also printed at Bandawe. This was revised and eventually took the form of a teacher's handbook and also a catechism, the latter popularly known as *Buku la Katekisima*, a unique catechetical work with a distinctive history and source background.

The years from 1926 were characterised by tremendous church growth by the DRCM during which many mission stations were opened along with village schools and secondary schools. The reason was that the Mission Church had trained a lot of teacher-evangelists who were doing commendable work in the mission front. The newly formed Union in the CCAP played a big role in the social and political development of the church in the face of British imperialism. The church for the first time had made concerted efforts regarding the socio-political and economical challenges which were exerted on the church by the colonial masters. This in due course created a conducive environment for mission work in Malawi. However, the three presbyteries which constituted the CCAP at the time of inception were still so independent that the Synod could even have been regarded as being more of a "Federated Church" than a "United Church." Each presbytery retained its own constitution, liturgy and standing orders.

Although the Synod was the supreme Court of the united church, its functions only included matters pertaining to the general welfare of the Church, for example public worship, Christian life, and conduct. In other words, the Synod had no legislative powers over the respective member Presbyteries. For example, Nkhoma Presbytery was finding itself in a very difficult position in its relationship with the CCAP Synod because of paternalistic tendencies by the mother DRC in Cape Town, South Africa. They had a tighter hold on the DRC mission church in Malawi. The GMC in Cape Town had the right of decision in almost every ecclesial action by the Mission Church in Malawi.

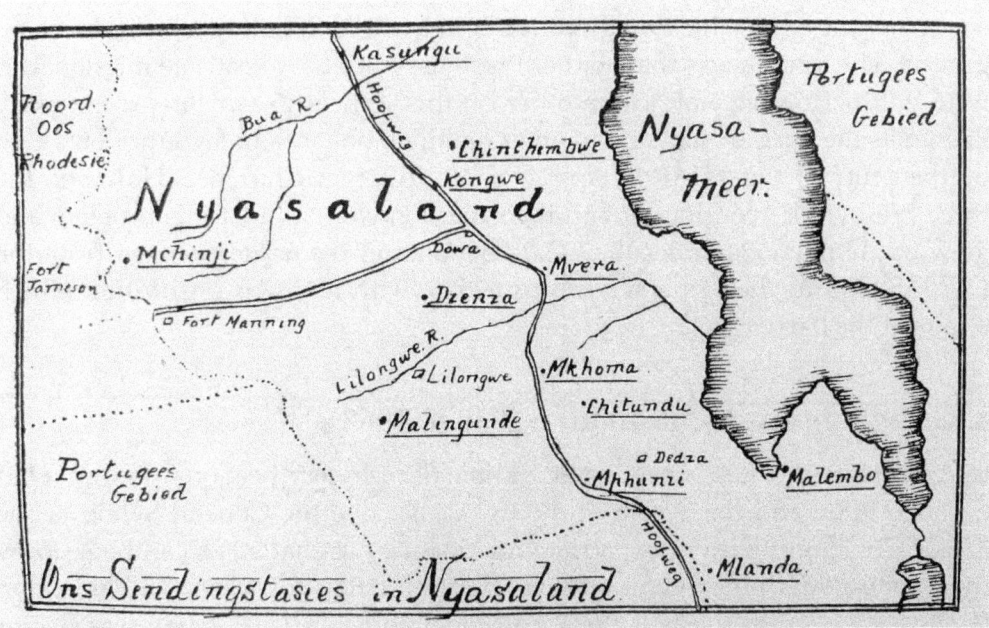

▲ Map of Nkhoma Mission (with permission of the DRC archives)

Despite this precarious position of the Nkhoma Presbytery in the CCAP Synod, mission work continued to grow, and all the three Presbyteries had harmonised their respective constitutions to formulate the Constitution of the CCAP Synod by which they would organise their mission work in Malawi as One Church. Hence the new constitution drafting work was launched in 1945 to iron out some articles which formed differences. It was crafted in a very important Article which the DRCM wanted to be corrected. The two Presbyteries wrote that "the Bible contains the Word of God" in their constitutions whilst the Nkhoma Presbytery's article about the Bible stated that, "the Scripture of the Old and New Testaments are the Word of God" not that they merely contain the Word of God. Therefore, in 1949, the GMC in South Africa approved the New Constitution and waved a go ahead for the Nkhoma Presbytery to remain in the CCAP Synod.

In 1951 the New Constitution was not approved, and the Synodical Committee postponed the Synod meeting because there was still a problem with Article 15 of the Constitution which was a bone of contention. The problem was about the position of the expatriate missionaries in the Church in respect of two matters: Full voting powers for missionaries in the young Church and integrated membership of the Mission personnel in the young Church, coupled with the right of the CCAP to exercise oversight and discipline. With the paternalistic philosophy by the expatriate missionaries in dealing with the indigenous people, this attitude was obvious. On the other hand, there were feelings for autonomy by the indigenous leaders in the young Church. This therefore became a very serious issue which required wisdom to avoid derailing mission work on ground. The trouble was that neither Presbytery nor the expatriate missionaries were willing to give way to the other on this Article 15 which was famously known as the Barrier Act. On the other hand, no one was in favour of breaking up the unity of the CCAP by splitting into different Churches. However, the three Presbyteries continued with their mission work amidst this problem and grew up into Synods under the CCAP Synod and the name changed from the CCAP Synod to the General Synod in 1956, with a New Constitution which removed the Barrier Act.

4. Growth towards Autonomy: 1956 to 1962

In April 1956 the CCAP, meeting at Nkhoma Presbytery headquarters, adopted a Constitution and the Synod of the CCAP became the General Synod of the CCAP. The dominance of expatriate missionaries at that stage can be seen by the composition of the Synod officers. There was Rev. J. J. Watt, the Moderator; Rev. A. S. Labuschagne was the Vice Moderator; Rev. G. F. Hugo was Senior Clerk and Rev. F. S. Chintali was a Junior Clerk. In August 1956 the Presbytery of

Nkhoma became the Synod of Nkhoma. Rev. Labuschagne was the first and last white Moderator. In 1958 Rev. J. S. Mwale became the first Malawian Moderator.

With Rev. J. S. Mwale leading the Synod, indigenous members had confidence to push for autonomous leadership for the young Synod. This was a very commendable step to achieving autonomy by the indigenous church. In 1959 the Synod assumed the right to appoint members of other committees which had been the prerogative of the Mission Council. In 1960 the Nkhoma Synod Teachers' Association (NSTA) was formed and issued an ultimatum to the Chairman of the General Mission Council of the DRC in South Africa. They were to agitate for the acceleration of the dissolution of the Mission and the autonomy of the indigenous church.

The GAC coordinated the governance issues of the Synod and liaised with the General Missions Committee of the DRC Synod in South Africa who were tasked to draft the Deed of Agreement. Nkhoma mission teachers clearly warned the GMC and resisted any restrictions such as a need to consult the DRC on any important decision such as disposal of property. Therefore, in April 1962, the DRC Mission Council and Nkhoma Synod unanimously approved the Deed of Agreement with few amendments and the Deed of Transfer was read at which thirteen DRC missionaries were received into the ministry of the Nkhoma Synod. Hence on 23rd April 1962 the leadership of the CCAP Nkhoma Synod was officially handed over to the indigenous leadership by the DRC missionaries.

5. Approaches and Major Achievements of the DRCM

The growth of the Church from 1914 to 1950s is attributed to the type of approaches and methods of evangelisation which the DRCM employed when doing mission work. Missionary work to Malawi was part of a greater missionary project to the whole Africa by the Western Missionary Societies in the revival and evangelical spirit to reach the whole world with the Gospel. More importantly Dr David Livingstone features highly since he is the one who made efforts to appeal to the British and Scottish Church leaders, scholars, and government officers to consider sending missionaries to the land of the Lake as Malawi was known during the colonial era.

Much as Dr David Livingstone planned to start commerce so that the slave trade is stopped; there were different approaches which they employed to spread Christianity to this part of the dark continent of Africa. That is why the early missionaries who came to Malawi came from the United Kingdom of Great Britain. They all came from different Christian backgrounds with varying approaches and methods to Missions. They also differed in their social background, hence different approaches in socialising with the indigenous people. However, the DRCM used the principle of Multiple Approach in the work of Mission and Church based on the DRC mission policy.

The Concept of Comprehensive Approach

In this approach, the DRCM understood that the Church in the world cannot be limited to a mere verbal proclamation of the Gospel. Taking its incentive from the work and teaching of Jesus Christ, the Church should approach a human being not as an isolated individual, but as a person who is rooted in a particular and complete life situation. This situation cannot be ignored when proclaiming the Gospel to him or her. Hence, the DRC missionaries popularised the terminology, *"comprehensive approach"* after the International Missionary Conference in Jerusalem, 1928. They aimed at balancing the proclamation of the Gospel with other three "elements" of so-called *Comprehensive Approach*, i.e., education, medical services, and socio-economic assistance.

Education

After arriving in 1889, one of the first things done at Mvera was to open a school, followed by schools at various other mission centres in due course. A boarding school for girls was begun in 1893, the same year that A. C. Murray and Robert Blake married and brought their brides to the country. By 1899 there were 30 girls, while youth groups and children's groups were started, as well as classes for older women. The first attempts at providing literature for the people learning to read resulted in several booklets by A. C. Murray. These booklets, which were written by the first missionaries, were used to impart religious lessons. For purposes of education to the indigenous people, a small catechism[9] was written, based on Reformed catechisms. Two additional and important books for Church history and a translation on the Old Testament were written to facilitate religious education. The DRC Mission also decided to compile a hymn book to replace the one in Nyanja (Chewa) compiled by Robert Laws of the Livingstonia Mission.[10]

The DRCM valued the close relationship between the school and evangelism, which remained one of the basic principles in the work of the mission. The mission never saw its task as providing a purely secular education, but to provide an education permeated with and serving the interests of Christianity. Likewise, the training of leaders, teachers, evangelists, and pastors was seen as a thoroughgoing process in which the mission sought to provide for the needs

---

9 The Small Catechism was known as *Katekisima Wa Mng'ono* by the indigenous people. Up to now it is in use because it is the summary of the main doctrines. It is used to teach the elderly and illiterate converts because they easily memorise it.

10 The two Books are *Mbeu za Moyo* (Religious lessons) and *Mkhweri* (Beginners' reader Book). The Old Testament Book was named *Mbiri Yakale* (Old History), Pauw, 150; CCA P3 3/2: Copy A. C. Murray to Lavis, 3/2/1899; CCA V9 1/1: MMU minute 5, entry for 15/8/1902; Council Minutes, 17/1909, 107.

of the Church above all. For long the policy was such that people were accepted for further education and training as teachers only if it was evident that they would be suitable and committed to teaching in the mission. This philosophy of education met the general educational needs of the country and that is why the DRC Mission concentrated on two main tasks: the training of evangelists, pastors and medical assistants, and the training of teachers for village schools. To implement and fulfil this philosophy of mission education, all prayer points were opened along with school blocks where evangelists/teacher personnel were appointed to teach how to read and write and above all else to teach Sunday school and catechism to learners. Boarding primary schools for boys and girls were also opened in strategic mission centres to facilitate education to learners.

Agricultural Development and Training

The DRCM work in Malawi is distinguished from most other missions. Apart from the obvious, that the early arrivals of the DRCM had no choice but to provide their own vegetables and build their own buildings with whatever simple tools and crafts they had available, training helpers as they went along, there was the fact of the background of these missionaries. Most came from rural farm stock, men who were born and bred in Africa and made their living from its soil, becoming experts at improvising where more sophisticated tools or machinery was not available. This explains why the DRCM concentrated on developing a form of industrial training which would fit in with the needs and potentials of rural Malawi of half a century and more ago.

What further prompted the DRC Mission was the fact that they found it necessary to teach people such skills and crafts in agriculture and manufacturing as would enable them to pay their taxes, provide for their daily needs and financially support the church through giving without necessarily having to leave their homes to work as migrants. The problem of labour migration remained a strong motivation for agricultural and industrial work in this mission for a long time. In the process the mission engaged itself in the fighting and overcoming indolence, preventing great numbers of people from going to the mines in the South rather than working in their own country, civilising people, while also assisting the general development of the individual and preventing the negative influence migrants brought back with them which tended to unsettle and uproot. Therefore, the overall effect would be the economic uplifting of the people in general by avoiding the system of apprenticeship to provide artisans for employment in the European sector. The aim was that a person who entered the service of one of the mission departments, and received a certain amount of instruction, could then choose to stay on for some years or go to work for another employer or set up for himself in a village. This was particularly the case with carpentry.

One further important motivation should be sought in the theological background of the DRC missionaries. The Reformed doctrine concerning the *Ethics of Work*, including any form of manual work as an honourable and God-honouring activity based upon the divine command, was bound to influence their views on encouraging manual and other forms of industrial activity. This was part of the reason why pupils as well as trained teachers and evangelists were taught to work with their hands *"so that they should not get the impression that manual work is something degrading."*

The further aim in teaching industrial skills to teachers was that they would in turn be able to demonstrate to others how to improve their agriculture and in this way help the country to develop. That is why the DRC Mission embarked on vigorous agricultural activities in almost all the mission stations. They sent agriculturalists to all the stations to instruct members of the church to plant crops like coffee, cotton, fruit trees like peaches, apples, plums, oranges, guavas, and paw paws. They also introduced livestock like high breed cows from South Africa to improve the local breeds for the supply of meat and milk, transport, and ploughing.

Industrial Development and Training

The basket and cane chairs industry at Mvera, the first mission station, was one of the most successful enterprise and village industries by the DRCM. Many hundreds of persons were trained to make a variety of wicker and cane chairs and other furniture, as well as all sorts of smaller articles from palm leaves. Women were also taught earthenware pot making, used for cooking, decorations and flower growing. Apart from those directly employed, many more benefited from supplying the raw materials required, thus creating an economic chain reaction. By 1925, many people were in private business while by 1928 the workshop of Mvera still received orders for as many as 300 chairs a year from many parts of Central Africa. The mission began to run out of business – because of local competition, which was exactly what the aim was.

Another important industrial development was the running of shops in mission stations. These were the small mission stores mainly because they could make goods available to both missionaries and Africans at a reasonable price and particularly because it was a way of protecting people against exploitation by unscrupulous traders coming into the country. It also had educational value as it could give people an idea of modern trading methods and they could learn the value of cash payments and honest business dealing. To facilitate industrial education to reach every corner of the DRCM's catchment area, model villages existed at most stations where teachers came to stay with their families. In connection with such a village, agricultural and industrial work was conducted while the wives and girls received instruction in hygiene, soap making, sewing, and laundry and child welfare.

From a general point of view the diversity and intensity of training in agriculture and village industries reached a peak during the 1920s. Ploughing demonstrations were being given; six ploughs were imported from America while a special plough had been invented by one of the DRC missionaries in Zambia, which was locally available for only eight shillings. Demonstration farms were opened! Oxen were being trained, as well as the men to handle them, for Chiefs and others to use for ploughing cotton and wheat fields. Others were sending their cows to the mission for breaking in for milking while an agricultural missionary paid visits to villages to advise people on breeding and selecting, while at the same time castrating inferior cattle. People were also taught brick laying, tiled roofing, and improved methods of thatching. At Nkhoma, the second mission station which later became the mission headquarters, men were trained in carpentry and building. Lime making was another associated industry attached to the building department. People were taught how to burn and produce lime. This was being taught at Mlanda where there was another carpentry shop with nine men in training and two at the motor garage of the mission's transport department. Men were also trained as ox wagon drivers who in turn worked as instructors in villages.

Spinning and weaving was a tailored training earmarked for the disabled persons, including the blind, the crippled and deaf-mutes. The mission worked together with the chiefs and village headmen in different districts. Cloth was made which was used to manufacture shirts. In addition, knitting, yarn spinning as well as making door mats and passage runners was taking place. Tailoring training was hence provided to compliment this industry. Teachers and evangelists and others were being taught to make soap to extract oil from castor oil seeds and groundnuts. Cakes of soap were made. A hand press oil plant was acquired for this purpose at Nkhoma mission headquarters. Printing and bookbinding was taught as early as 1930, which formed the embryo of the present printing press at Nkhoma. Men were taught the techniques of printing and bookbinding. A very famous magazine called *Mthenga* (messenger) was printed at Nkhoma Press. It circulated from the Cape to Cairo and up to India, especially during the two world wars and facilitated communication and evangelisation.

Medical work

The first medical work upon their arrival in 1889 at Mvera station was undertaken by ordained men who had followed a short course in medicine, either in Edinburgh or at Livingstone College, London in addition to their theological studies. These included A. C. Murray, W. H. Murray, A. L. Hofmeyr, A. G. Murray, J. S. Murray, J. A. Retief, and P. A. Rens. A. G. Murray laid the foundations of obstetrics at Mlanda. That is why from the 1930s up to 1960s, Mlanda medical clinic centre was the most famous and popular clinic where almost all white missionary women gave birth and used to get medication for their children.

The first qualified medical doctor to arrive in 1900, was Dr W. A. Murray, brother of Rev. A. C. Murray. He stayed for twelve years and laid the foundation of the medical work. A hospital was built at Mvera in 1903 and various men and women trained as nurses, including Mrs. Sara Lingodzi Nabanda, who began training in 1909 and served for 34 years. Sara Lingodzi Nabanda was the most outstanding of all indigenous midwives trained by the DRC missionaries. There are stories about how this wonderful midwife conducted herself when carrying out her duties. When an expectant woman was about to deliver, she would first go into a closet and cover her head with a white piece of cloth and pray. By the time she came back to attend to the woman, she would find her already given birth and simply cared for the newly born baby. Small clinics were also operated in mission stations manned by nurses and medical assistants. When the sleeping sickness epidemic swept the Lakeshore in 1910–1912, Dr Murray collaborated with the government and supervised a quarantine camp near Mvera, where a sort of roadblock was mounted. In 1915 the hospital was moved to Nkhoma and expanded in 1919. Work with lepers was started at Nkhoma for which a small government grant of £100 was obtained for building. A camp was set up on the Katete stream near Madetsa and in 1929 there were 110 patients. Numbers later declined and after ten years in 1939 the Leprosarium was closed!

An important development, the fruit of Dr Retief's interest in eye surgery, was the building of an ophthalmic ward in 1955. The hospital at Nkhoma has gained repute all over Central Africa for its eye surgery and today there is a fully fledged eye hospital manned by both qualified expatriates and Malawian doctors. Although this aspect of Mission work is of less direct significance for the growth and life of the church, it was a factor in the general development of the people who were reached by the DRC missionaries. As a means by which people could be brought into contact with the gospel it served the additional function of an evangelising agent. Not only the Christian atmosphere in a mission or church hospital, but also the personal contact between a patient and the Christian message to a patient made the medical work part of the evangelising endeavours of the mission. Moreover, as a method of showing Christian concern and service to people in need, it served as a means to convey to people the message of Christ's compassion. Ultimately the highest reason for this work lay in the example of Christ himself and in his command to heal the sick, Luke 9:2. As such, it was seen as an essential part of the Christian message and mission to show compassion and care for the sick and suffering.

Literature work

This was one of the auxiliary services through which the DRCM did its mission work. It was a very important supporting ministry in the three main areas where the work of the DRCM concentrated. The three approaches which they launched after 1904: the development of widespread education and mass literacy through the village school concept, the concentration on teaching rural agriculture and village industries and the work amongst women and girls could all be conducted with much greater effectiveness because of the availability of a variety of literature in the vernacular. Therefore, the DRCM's small printing press at Mvera was started in 1907. The press was bought in Scotland with a gift from a person in Stellenbosch and the first publication to come off was the Bible reading almanac for 1908. One of the most notable indigenous people trained for this work was Mr Anderson Kadzichi who was a rescued slave and converted into Christianity while at Mvera. He was trained to type by Mrs. W. H. Murray and later in the years became the first printer of the Press and rose to become the head African printer in the Lusaka Government Printing Works in Zambia.

After the headquarters were moved to Nkhoma in 1913, the Press continued at Mvera for some years. When new machines became necessary, new premises were built at Nkhoma in 1917. Under the management of Mr Petrus van Wyk, who came in 1915, the printing department grew into one of the largest and most successful departments of the mission. The Nkhoma Press supplied all the needs of the DRCM and the Nkhoma Presbytery and had become so widely known that it also handled printing orders from practically all the Protestant missions in Malawi. During the difficult years of the Second World War, many books and tracts were sent to the front, including 800 copies of each edition of *Mthenga* (Messenger) magazine. This literature was appreciated by the chaplains.

▲ Union Bible title page

The work continued to grow and in 1952, it was reorganised into two departments, the bookshop and publishing department and the printing department. Books for Bible exposition, Scripture biographies, theology, booklets explaining the way of salvation and Christian living and doctrines were printed. The most famous publications of all were the Bible reading daily guide called *Mlozo* and *Mthenga,* which was later known as *Kuunika* (light) in the language of the people were printed and distributed to all mission stations. However, the greatest literacy and literary contribution of the DRCM was its share in providing the country with a translation of the Bible in, as it was then called, *Union Nyanja* (1922).[11] The DRCM appointed W. H. Murray to continue with the work of translating the remaining Old Testament section. Therefore, Murray resigned as head of the DRCM and settled at the guest house of the mission on the mountain of Kaso, which overlooked the first station of Mvera. Murray was assisted by the three indigenous Malawian linguistic advisers, for the Old Testament section: Jonathan Sande from Blantyre Mission of the Church of Scotland, Ismael Mwale from Mlanda, and Wilbes Chikuse from Nkhoma. The two indigenous assistants on the New Testament were Thomas Maseya (Blantyre) and Samson Bogaozi (Nkhoma). Other missionaries who helped with the Union Bible were A. Hetherwick, James Murray, W. A. Murray, Louis Hofmeyr, Robert Napier and Mrs W. H. Murray who was a faithful second reader.

Additional names of the Malawians who were collaborators in this work were a Jacob from Mvera, a Benjamin from Mlanda and a Filemon. The typist who typed the entire manuscript was Gersom Chipwaira who joined the DRCM press in 1911 and continued until 1965 by which time he had become manager of the Press at Nkhoma. After his retirement, he settled away from the mission head office but within the boundaries of the mission about 4 km to the east. The role of local native assistants is wonderfully summarised by Katsulukuta and Pretorius:

> What these advisors lacked in formal education they made up for with their wide knowledge of the Chinyanja dialects. When translations were doubtful, they would go out into the villages to ascertain what the people, particularly the older people, said. Their contribution towards producing a Bible understood throughout Southern and Central Malawi and the Eastern Province of Zambia cannot be overemphasised.[12]

Mission work beyond borders

As early as 1899, mission work into other areas became an extension of the work of the DRCM. The work beyond the borders started by the request from Ngoni chief Mpezeni in Eastern Zambia. Although the DRC synod of the Orange Free

---

11 The *Union Nyanja* was a Bible translation which was named *Union* for two reasons. First it was jointly published by the Federated Missions of Nyasaland (Malawi) and second, the Nyanja language was widely accepted and understood by countries which were under the British Colonial Federation of Southern and Northern Rhodesia (Zimbabwe and Zambia) and Nyasaland (Malawi). Pauw, 1980, 220. See R. Kilgour, "The Bible for a million Africans," in W. J. W. Roome, *A Great Emancipation*, (London: World Dominion Press, 1926), 57–60. See Select Bibliography at end of chapter for details on this Bible.
12 C. M. Pauw, "Mission and Church in Malawi: The History of the Nkhoma Synod of the Church of Central Africa, Presbyterian 1889–1962," (Unpublished DTh thesis, University of Stellenbosch, 1980), 214–215.

The Nkhoma Mission and Synod

State began working in Zambia, there was an overwhelming need for the DRCM in Malawi to team up with their brothers and sisters who were already working in Zambia. Therefore in 1916, a separate council of congregations was formed for this church in Zambia. This mission work developed so much that two flourishing and autonomous churches developed: the Church of Central Africa Presbyterian and the Reformed Church in Zambia.

The DRCM also started work from 1909 to 1922 in Mozambique, the area lying between Malawi, Eastern Zambia, and the Zambezi River. However, the DRCM experienced a lot of problems when they encountered stiff opposition by the Portuguese colonial masters who opted for the Roman Catholic Church and not Protestant mission work. Work proceeded through the perseverance by Rev. A. G. Murray, who referred the case to the General Mission Committee of the DRC in Cape Town. The General Mission Secretary and the Moderator of the DRC subsequently appealed to the Prime Minister of the Cape Colony to obtain permission from the Governor-General of Mozambique for the DRC to start a Mission in Portuguese Angonia. Eventually permission was granted by the Governor-General in Maputo in 1908. This mission work in Mozambique went on very well despite the political problems experienced by Rev. A. G. Murray, who left in 1922. After Murray had left, the church was left without anybody from the DRCM in Malawi to take care of it. However, as time passed around 1932, the DRCM married the Mozambique congregations with those from Malawi along the border of Malawi and Mozambique. Such congregations were Mlanda and Chilobwe in Ntcheu; Mphuzi, and Dedza mission stations who intermittently sent their evangelists and elders to pastor the Mozambique congregations. The first indigenous evangelists who were sent there by the Nkhoma Presbytery were Zefania Malikebu and Paulo Milota Mumba. Unfortunately, their history has not been kept by the missionaries. After fifty years, in 1973, the Mozambique Reformed Church (*Igreja Reformada em Moçambique*) grew into a Synod which is named the Mphatso Synod.[13]

Soon after countries in this region were declared British Protectorates, all the British colonies were open to each other in terms of migration. This political situation proved to be difficult for the DRCM work. From the year 1903 men who were converts and members of the young mission church began migrating to other areas. The imposition of hut tax forced large numbers to go abroad to seek work in Salisbury (Harare) and Johannesburg. This prompted the DRCM to open mission work in Harare for the spiritual and moral lives of the people who went there annually. In 1905, a delegation of Malawians working in Zimbabwe walked on foot to Mvera to ask for a missionary and four years later the request was tabled during the Mission Council meeting and resolved to send a minister to Harare. In 1912, Rev. T. C. B. Vlok was assigned to Harare and started working

---

13 This church is in Mozambique and it is not part of the Nkhoma Synod although it is the fruit of the mission work by Nkhoma.

in the area. Although he was sent by the DRC Mission Council in Malawi, Rev. Vlok served all mission bodies in Malawi under the Federated Missions representing all the Protestant mission bodies in Malawi, because these migrant workers in Zimbabwe and South Africa came from the whole country of Malawi. Currently, there is a self-governing CCAP Synod (Harare Synod) which has been nurtured by the Nkhoma Synod for many years.[14]

Mission work to Muslims

In 1923 the work amongst the Muslim Yao people started in chief Tambala's land where Chitundu mission station was later opened by the DRCM. This was a response to the upsurge of Muslim activities which were experienced in the early 1920s. In 1929, after nine years of launching evangelistic campaigns in this area, the DRCM set aside Rev. A. C. van Wyk to minister amongst Muslims and shortly after that he went to Cairo in Egypt for Islamic Studies. He worked at Chitundu for about nine years until in 1940, when he departured back to South Africa. By 1929, Nkhoma Presbytery began to budget for supporting an indigenous evangelist working amongst the Yao. A congregation was established at Chitundu in 1939. By 1945, a growing interest in Christianity by the Yao people was reported and two years later the presbytery resolved to accept the Yao work as its field of mission work and place an evangelist at Chitundu.

In 1951, James Kathumba completed his theological training. Being himself a Yao and having formerly worked with some success as a mission teacher-evangelist at Chitundu, the presbytery agreed to appoint him as minister working full-time amongst Muslims and stationed at Chitundu. In other words, he was the first indigenous missionary of Nkhoma Presbytery. Since work progressed very well in chief Tambala's area the DRCM decided to beef up the strength of labour and sent Rev. J. S. Minnaar, the first expatriate to go there since 1940. He was to concentrate on the Chewa people while Kathumba would continue amongst the Yao. However, a short while after Minnaar had arrived at Chitundu, there were disagreements between Minnaar and Kathumba possibly due to racial supremacy issues. Eventually, Rev. James Kathumba left Chitundu station and in the process stalled all the work of evangelisation amongst the Yao. This can be taken as the first reason that contributed to failure by the Nkhoma Presbytery to reach out to Muslims and by the time the Mission Church was being handed over to the indigenous leadership in 1962, the zeal to evangelise the Muslim Yaos had drastically waned.

---

14 As a result of Vlok's work, the CCAP was established in Zimbabwe which was a member of the Federated Mission Council. Currently there is a self-governing CCAP Harare Synod which has been nurtured by the Nkhoma Synod for many years and continues to be a member of the CCAP General Assembly up to now.

Regardless of this problem at Chitundu station, the work grew so much along the Lakeshore areas where there was considerable population of the Yaos that the Nkhoma Press produced a lot of literature about how to evangelise the Muslims. However, after the handover of the leadership of the church in 1962 to the indigenous leaders, very little work or nothing significant can be pointed out about deliberate efforts to evangelise Muslims by the Nkhoma Synod due to the lack of continuity.

6. Areas for Further Reflection

There are three areas that merit further reflection. The first concerns educational philosophy between the three missions – Livingstonia, Blantyre and Nkhoma. Here comparisons and contrasts could be studied. Also related but more generally with education would be the matter concerning education and the Nyau cult (a secret society amongst the Chewa people used for initiation ceremonies for boys and girls) which was still very strong in many parts of the country. A growing tension was developing between church and mission on the one hand and the Nyau cult and its supporters on the other hand. More than one flourishing school disappeared once the Nyau succeeded in establishing its influence in a particular community.

Second, would be the matter of Ethiopianism as relates to the Nkhoma Mission. As much as Ethiopianism affected the DRCM, no single secession of any significance had taken place from within its ranks. However, complexities can be studied here as it relates to church discipline cases and the movement over to Ethiopian churches.

Third, there is the matter of ecclesial discontinuity which emerged between the first generation of missionaries and the second generation of missionaries. This also occurred with the shift in the socio-political context due to the presence of the British colonial administrators that exerted a lot of pressure on the frontier of mission work. It raises the question: "Was the DRCM good at orthodoxy but poor in respect of orthopraxis of love and justice?" This needs to be studied in light of mission policy and ecclesial policy.

7. Conclusion & Postscript

Despite many failures and weaknesses, the Nkhoma Synod had by 1962, after almost three-quarters of a century, grown into a strong and virile church counting 80,000 communicant members, with 34,000 catechumens undergoing instructions while 200,000 souls were estimated to be in the care of 52 congregations under the leadership of 37 ordained ministers and 1,236 elders.

In comparison to other fields of the DRCM work, Nkhoma Synod had been the most fruitful of all, with an average five percent annual growth rate in membership over half a century, thereby outstripping even its sister Synods in the CCAP. By 1962, it had developed a high degree of self-sufficiency and was finally totally independent at congregational and presbytery levels, paying the salaries of all national workers, namely ministers, evangelists, and certain categories of teachers. That is why it is an undeniable fact that the church made a manifold contribution towards the development of the nation of the new state of Malawi by 1962.

Today (2021), the Nkhoma Synod is one of the five synods of the Church of Central Africa Presbyterian (CCAP) in Central Africa. The others are the Blantyre, Harare, Livingstonia, and Zambia Synods. The Nkhoma Synod currently (2021) covers 15 of the 23 Malawian administrative districts; thus, the whole of Central and Northern Regions and one district in the South. The Synod has 219 congregations divided into 27 presbyteries (Synod Records, August 2021). Its administrative offices are at Nkhoma, a mission station fifty kilometres south of Lilongwe City.

▼ 1939 List of Stations in the Historic Period[15]

Name of Station	Year established
Mvera	1889
Kongwe	1894
Livlezi	est. 1886, received 1894
Mkhoma	1896
Mlanda	1901
Mphunzi	1903
Malingunde	1907
Malembo	est. 1895 received 1907
Cinthembwe	1909
Mcinji	1914
Dzenza	1921
Kasunga	1923
Chitundu	1924

---

15 A pamphlet produced by the DRC, *Ons Nyasa-Sending* (DRC, 1937), 4–5, compared to the pamphlet, *The DRC Mission in Nyasaland 1889–1939* (Nkhoma: DRC Mission Press, 1939), 1, shows 12 stations. Whereas, in 1944 the central mission stations were listed as follows: Mvera, Kongwe, Mkhoma [Nkhoma], Mcinji, Mlanda, Malembo, Cinthembwe, Dzenza, and Malingunde (9) in"Notule Van die 61ste Vergadering van die Uitvoerende Raad van die Sending van die N. G. Kerk na Midde-Afrika, gehou te Mkhoma vanaf 8 tot 13 April, 1940," 563–564. The correct number was 13 for the historic period prior to WW2.

The Nkhoma Mission and Synod

Questions for study (fact type):
1. Why and how did the DRC become involved in the Nkhoma Mission? Where was the first mission station established?
2. Name at least two other mission stations that were established by the DRC for the Nkhoma Mission.
3. List two reasons why the Nkhoma Mission headquarters was moved from Mvera to Nkhoma.
4. Name the first two ordained ministers to work amongst the Muslim Yao people (one was from South Africa and the other was a Yao convert to Christianity).
5. What is a "hut tax"?

Questions for study (reflection type):
1. "The greatest literacy and literary contribution of the DRCM was its share in providing the country with a translation of the Bible in, as it was then called, *Union Nyanja.*" "W. H. Murray [DRC missionary] was assisted by the three indigenous Malawian linguistic advisers for the Old Testament section, Jonathan Sande from Blantyre Mission of the Church of Scotland, Ismael Mwale from Mlanda, and Wilbes Chikuse."
   a) Explain why Bible translation is vital to evangelisation and discipleship.
   b) Discuss the importance of involving native speakers in the translation of the Scriptures into a particular language.
2. "After the handover of the leadership of the church in 1962 to the indigenous leaders, very little work or nothing significant can be pointed out about deliberate efforts to evangelise Muslims by the Nkhoma Synod due to lack of continuity." Consider this quote and provide possible reasons for the decline in evangelisation efforts amongst the Yao Muslim people following 1962.

Select Bibliography

Brown, Walter Lawrence. "The Development in Self-understanding of the CCAP Nkhoma Synod as Church during the First Forty years of Autonomy: An Ecclesiological study." DTh thesis, University of Stellenbosch, 2005.

Bolink, Peter. *Towards Church Union in Zambia*. Franeker, Netherlands: T. Wever, 1967.

Buku Lo Patulika Ndilo Mau A Mulungu Chipangano. [The Holy Bible in the Union Nyanja Version] Edinburgh: NBSS/BFBS, 1921.

Du Plessis, J. *The Evangelisation of Pagan Africa: A History of Christian Missions to the Pagan Tribes of Central Africa*. Cape Town: J. C. Juta, 1929.

Nkhoma Synod Archives Records, Mthenga and Kuunika Magazines, 1912 to 1962.

Labuschaigne, A. *The Messengers of Christ Following in the Footsteps of the Missionaries in Central Africa 1849–1999*. Bloemfontein: Fichardtpack, 2003.

Lamba, Isaac C. "The Cape Dutch Reformed Church Mission in Malawi: A Preliminary Historical Examination of Its Educational Philosophy and Application, 1889–1931." *Transafrican Journal of History* 24 (1983): 51–74.

Mitchell, M. "'Living our faith': The Lenten Pastoral Letter of the Bishops of Malawi and the Shift to Multiparty Democracy, 1992–1993." *Journal for the Scientific Study of Religion* 41.1 (2002): 5–18. https://doi.org/10.1111/1468-5906.00096

Murray, A. C. *Nyasaland en Mijne Ondervindingen aldaar*. Amsterdam/Kaapstad:Hollandsch-Afrikaansche Uitgevers-Maatschappij, 1897.

Murray, A. C. *Ons Nyasa-Akker: Geskiedenis van die Nyasa Sending van die Nederd. Geref. Kerk in Suid-Afrika*. Stellenbosch: Uitgegee op versoek van die Sendingraad in Nyasaland, 1931.

Murray, C. and O'Regan, C. "No place to rest: Forced removals and the Law in South Africa." *Journal of South African Studies* 19.3 (1986): 539–541.

Parsons, Janet Wagner. "Scots and Afrikaners in Central Africa: Andrew Charles Murray and The Dutch Reformed Church Mission in Malawi." *The Society of Malawi Journal* 51.1 (1998): 21–40.

Pauw, C. M. *Mission and Church in Malawi: The history of the Nkhoma Synod of the Church of Central Africa, Presbyterian 1889–1962*. Wellington, SA: CLF, 2016.

Pretorius, Johan L. "The Story of The Dutch Reformed Church Mission Nyasaland." MS PPV 348/1/3 DRCSA Church Archives, Stellenbosch.

Pretorius, P. "An Introduction to the history of the Dutch Reformed Church Mission in Malawi: 1889–1910." In *The Early History of Malawi*, ed. B. Pachai. London: Longman, 1972.

Retief, W. *William Murray of Nyasaland*. [Alice]: Lovedale Press, 1958.

Ross, Kenneth R. and Klaus Fiedler, *A Malawi Church History 1860–2020*. Mzuzu-Luwinga: Mzuni Press, 2020.

Rotberg, R. *The Rise of Nationalism in Central Africa: The Making of Malawi and Zambia, 1873–1964*. Cambridge, MA: Harvard University Press, 1965.

Selfridge, John. *The Church's First Thirty Years in Nyasaland (Now Malawi) 1861–1891*. Nkhoma: Nkhoma Press, 1976.

Shepperson, G. and T. Price, *Independent African: John Chilembwe and the origins, setting and significance of the Nyasaland native rising of 1915*. Edinburgh: Edinburgh University Press, 1958.

Van der Merwe, W. J. *The Development of Missionary Attitudes in the Dutch Reformed Church in South Africa*. Cape Town: Nasionale Pers, 1936.

Van Donk, M. *Land and the Church: The Case of the Dutch Reformed Churches*. Cape Town: Western Province Council of Churches, 1994.

Worden, G. *The Making of Modern South Africa*. Western Sussex: Southern Gate, 2012.

Zeze, W. "Christianity: A state-sponsored religion in Malawi? A critical evaluation of the relationship between the CCAP Nkhoma Synod and the MCP-led Government (1964–1994)." Paper presented at the Conference on Law and Religion in Africa, University of Ghana, 14–15 January 2013, accessed 20 May 2020 from https://www.iclrs.org/content/events.28/751pdf

Timeline for the Livingstonia, Blantyre, and Nkhoma Missions (Chapters, 14, 15, & 16)[16]

1859	David Livingstone reaches Lake Nyasa/Lake Malawi
1861	Universities' Mission to Central Africa (UMCA) opens a work in Nyasaland
1864	UMCA abandons work in Nyasaland and goes to Zanzibar
1873	David Livingstone died at Ilala
1874	David Livingstone buried at Westminster Abbey James Stewart of Lovedale suggest setting up a Memorial Mission for Livingstone FCS approves of the Stewart proposal
1875	Livingstonia Mission founded at Cape Maclear
1876	CoS founds Blantyre Mission Four Xhosa from Lovedale join the Livingstonia Mission
1877	First missionary deaths at Cape Maclear
1878	Africa Lakes Company formed
1881	Livingstonia Mission moved to Bandawe First convert of Livingstonia Mission baptised Mark's Gospel translated into Chichewa
1882	UMCA sent Johnson and Janson to lake country
1883	First British Council appointed
1886	Death of William Koyi First complete NT translation in Nyanja (Robert Laws)
1888	Commencement of *Life and Work in British Central Africa*
1889	DRCM begin station at Mvera First Tonga convert
1890	First Ngoni converts
1891	British Central Africa Declared a Protectorate (Nyasaland)

---

16 This timeline uses as a starting point that of John (Jack) Selfridge's short timeline in *The Church's First Thirty Years in Nyasaland (Now Malawi) 1861–1891*, 63–64. I have expanded it to be more encompassing for the historic period of missions. *–The Editor*

The Nkhoma Mission and Synod

1894	Overtoun Institution founded
1898	Blantyre Mission completes NT in Yao, revision completed by Hetherwick and published 1907
1899	Presbytery of North Livingstonia
1901	Normal School, Nkhoma founded
1902	Presbytery of Blantyre
1903	Council of Congregations (later renamed Presbytery of Nkhoma)
1908	Henry Henderson Institute founded
1911	First ordination of ministers in Blantyre
1914	First ordination of ministers in Livingstonia
1922	Printing of Union Nyanja Bible [Chichewa]
1924	Synod Church of Central Africa Presbyterian formed with two presbyteries, Livingstonia and Blantyre
1925	First ordinations of ministers in Nkhoma
1926	Nkhoma Presbytery joins Synod of the CCAP
1936	New edition of Union Nyanja Bible with paragraph headers, etc.

Chapter 17

Presbyterian Mission through Education of Indigenous Clergy, including a Case Study of Blantyre Mission's Harry Kambwiri Matecheta

Thokozani M. Chilembwe

Chapter Outline
1. Introduction: The Presbyterian Historic Commitment to Education within the Missionary Context of Malawi
2. The Goal of Education Offered in Early Mission Schools
3. The Presbyterian Historic Commitment to Raising up An Educated Indigenous Clergy
4. Harry Kambwiri Matecheta (1870–1962): An African Pioneer of the "Presbyterian Pastors"
5. Conclusion

1. Introduction: The Presbyterian Historic Commitment to Education within the Missionary Context of Malawi

Towards the end of the nineteenth century and the dawn of the twentieth century, Malawi, as it is known today, experienced an educational explosion spearheaded by Christian missionaries under the banner of the UMCA, the Presbyterian and Reformed missionaries, and Roman Catholics. This chapter focuses on the efforts by the Scottish Presbyterian and Dutch Reformed missionaries who had established Livingstonia mission in the North, Blantyre mission in the South, and the Dutch Reformed Church Mission (DRCM) in the central parts of Malawi. These three missions grew up to form, what is known as the Church of Central Africa Presbyterian in 1926. In 1875 the Synod of Livingstonia was the first to be established by missionaries from the Free Church of Scotland, while its sister synod of Blantyre was established a year later by missionaries from the Church of Scotland, and finally, in 1889, the Dutch Reformed Church missionaries from

South Africa established the Nkhoma Mission work.[1] This period, alongside the coming of the Gospel, saw an increase in the number of mission schools which also served as churches, while its teachers also served as evangelists.

As John McCracken noted, the Livingstonia mission had already established important diplomatic and educational contacts with a variety of people in the northern region of Malawi almost fifteen years before the colonial occupation.[2] For instance, at its mission meeting in 1906, it was reported that the number of schools within the North Tribe of Tongas had rapidly increased from eighteen in 1895 to a hundred and seven, while the enrolment moved from 1000 to 3000 within the same period.[3]

But this should not come as a surprise as in October 1876, Dr James Stewart (on his way to take over the leadership from E. D. Young) brought along four teacher-evangelists from Lovedale in South Africa: Shadrach Ngunana, William Koyi, Mapas Nthintiri and Isaac Wauchope.[4] This was a strong statement on the mission's commitment to educate the natives. While these four were foreigners on the land, Malawi's first Christian, Albert Namalambe (who was baptised by Laws on the eve of 27th March 1881) raised the flag of education in Malawi even higher under the guidance of both the Livingstonia mission and later the DRCM. Pauw noted that by 1899, Namalambe was looking after a network of fourteen schools with forty-eight teachers and one thousand three hundred learners.[5] However, the big landmark contribution in the education sector for the Livingstonia mission was the establishment of the Overtoun Institute at Khondowe in November 1894.[6] Fifteen years later, this institution was followed by the Henry Henderson Institute at Blantyre and the Kafue Training Institute in Northern Rhodesia.[7] Overtoun Institute was created in part to address the demand for trained African labour and skilled labourers – demand created from the influx of Europeans coming into the country as a result of the establishment of the British protectorate. This saw Africans being trained in a variety of skills, such as building, carpentry, telegraphy, book-keeping, typing, printing, and engineering.

---

1   See chapters 14, 15, & 16 in this volume for further details.
2   McCracken, *Politics and Christianity in Malawi*, 19.
3   McCracken, *Politics and Christianity in Malawi*, 156.
4   Groves, *The Planting of Christianity in Africa*, 308.
5   Pauw, *Mission and Church in Malawi: The History of the Nkhoma Synod of the Church of Central Africa, Presbyterian*, 72.
6   See, H. W. K. Nyambose, "The Establishment and Contribution of the Overtoun Institute in Northern Malawi and Beyond (1895–2010)," (Unpublished MA thesis, Mzuzu University, 2015).
7   McCracken, *Politics and Christianity in Malawi*, 171.

When the Blantyre Mission opened its doors to educating Africans in 1884, children of the Magololo and the Yao Africans who were seeking refuge and working at the mission were the first groups to enrol for school. Matecheta is quick to point out that, apart from the European missionaries who were teaching at the school, there were also Africans like Kagaso Sazuze, Joseph Bismark from Chinde and Quelimane (Mozambique), Kolombo Chinkolimbo, evangelist Sawelenjera, Henry Cowan, Donald Malota, Rondau Kaferanjira, and a female teacher, Rosie Majonanga. At one point the school had eight African teachers and one European.[8] This shows that establishing schools was not only the role of European missionaries but an African initiative as well.

The coming of Rev. David Clement Scott in 1881 defined the mission's objective of "building [an] African church – not Scottish nor English – but African."[9] D. C. Scott very much believed in the conviction of David Livingstone that "Africa would best be evangelized by Africans."[10] This conviction led him to open the doors of both spiritual training and formal education to a number of Africans. Among such Africans were Mungo Murray Chisuse, who went as far as Scotland for his training in printing and photography; many others went to South Africa or Scotland for further studies. In addition to the Henry Henderson Institute, the Blantyre Mission went further to establish several other mission schools at the Domasi Mission, Zomba Mission, Mulanje Mission, and Nthumbi Mission in Ntcheu. Statistics show that from 1891 to 1914 the number of African teachers at the Blantyre Mission increased from 46 to 447 and the number of schools increased from seven to 220, while the student enrolment rose from 971 to 11, 630.[11] On behalf of the church, in 1894, Scott trained seven men for one full year and ordained them as deacons, which was meant to be a step towards ordination for word and sacrament. Those ordained as deacons included John Macrae Chipuliko, Mungo Murray Chisuse, Thomas Mpeni, James

▲ "An outschool"

---

8 Matecheta, *Blantyre Mission: Stories of Its Beginning*, 47–48.
9 W. H. Murray, *Mbiri ya Misyoni ya DRC*, 154.
10 Ross and Fiedler, *A Malawi Church History*, 171.
11 Ross and Fiedler, *A Malawi Church History*, 68. Citation from, *Reports of the schemes of the Church of Scotland 1892*, (Edinburgh: William Blackwood, 1892), 163–64; *Reports of the schemes of the Church of Scotland 1915*, (Edinburgh: William Blackwood, 1915), 297–298.

Gray Kamlinje, James Auldearn Mwembe, John Gray Kufa and Harry Kabwiri Matecheta.[12]

Barely a year after their arrival at Mvera in 1890, the DRC missionaries Andrew Charles Murray and Theunis Vlok started a school whose first teacher was Davis Tomani, a young man from Cape Maclear and a former student of Rev. James A. Bain. At first, this work met with resistance due to the fear and suspicion on the part of many natives that their children might be captured and sold into slavery if they went to school. These fears and suspicions did not last long, because by 20th November 1890 boarding facilities for boys were provided and later in 1893 boarding facilities extended to girls at the Mvera mission station. By and by mission schools spread like fire in the surrounding villages, such that by 1897 there were thirteen schools around Mvera while the number of learners increased to one thousand three hundred.[13] Eventually, by the end of the first decade, schools spread alongside the new stations such as Kongwe, Nkhoma, and Livulezi. Just like in the northern and southern regions, the DRCM in the central region also opened education opportunities into medical, educational, and industrial sectors. Even today, the CCAP family remains one of the main partners of the government in the education sector, providing both basic and tertiary education. The Synod of Livingstonia has continued to spearhead this endeavour by being the first to establish a university while the Nkhoma and Blantyre synods have followed suit.

2. The Goal of Education Offered in Early Mission Schools

It is important to point out that the primary objective of education that was offered in mission schools was the conversion of people to Christianity. Beyond this, different missions held contrasting views which even led to a decision by the Dutch Reformed Church Mission to withdraw from the Livingstonia Mission's scheme of education. Robert Laws' dream of the Overtoun Institution at Livingstonia seemed to agree with D. C. Scott of the Blantyre mission. Their position was to apply all efforts on a few selected Africans in order to give them the highest and best education in preparation even for life careers beyond making them just converts of Christianity. Therefore, it became clear that a secondary objective had emerged within the mission schools to educate Africans for different vocations in life, such as agricultural work, carpentry, printing, teaching, and nursing. On the other hand, such a move to provide Africans with classical education met some resistance from their counterparts in the DRCM with people like A. C. Murray who clearly stated his position like this:

---

12 Ross & Fiedler, *A Malawi Church History*, 58.
13 Pauw, *Mission and Church in Malawi: The History of the Nkhoma Synod of the Church of Central Africa, Presbyterian*, 67–69.

> We are not sent out, I think, to civilize peoples, but to convert them. Not to give them a high secular education, but to "teach them to keep all things" which our Lord and Master has commanded. Let those who will be our helpers as evangelists, catechists or teachers, learn what is necessary for their work, but as far as the people in general are concerned, let us impress the Word of God upon them in all possible ways, and furthermore teach them to read the Bible for themselves in their own language.[14]

A number of reasons could account for the position taken by Murray and his allies. Firstly, implementing this secondary objective would require a lot of resources. Secondly, they feared that the pre-eminent place of the Bible in the mission schools would be undermined. Thirdly, there was a danger of self-destruction as highly qualified people were likely to seek greener pastures in other commercial firms other than the church and mission,[15] although at that time many government agents and settlers still shared a prejudice against African Christians who had attained some education. For example, J. Wordsworth Poole once quoted his father saying in 1895, "Whatever you do, don't have boys from the mission"[16] referring to African Christians who were learning at mission schools. The only reason that educated Africans were allowed to be employed in skilled labour such as building, railway construction, ship making, administration, and engineering was because they were regarded as cheap labour. Of course, one would also say the DRCM took the matter to extremes when you consider the fact that they even rejected the teaching of English in mission schools until in 1902 when only two of their schools were permitted and the rest only got a similar nod in 1912.[17] Perhaps this too was meant to "walk the talk" as they wanted to offer education that would not cause an individual to rise beyond his social class.[18] One would also not be at fault to conclude that the Nkhoma Synod, for some years, struggled with the racist attitudes of Dutch Reformed missionaries owing to their South African background. This also explains their preference for vocational training over 'classical' education that the Scottish missions fostered.

---

14 Pauw, *Mission and Church in Malawi*, 67–69.
15 Pauw, *Mission and Church in Malawi*, 153.
16 W. H. Murray, *Mbiri ya Misyoni ya DRC*, 154.
17 Council minutes of 23/1912, 152; also quoted in a letter dated 15/6/2/15 from W. H. Murray to A. C. Murray.
18 W. H. Murray, *Mbiri ya Misyoni ya DRC*, 223–224.

3. The Presbyterian Historic Commitment to Raising up An Educated Indigenous Clergy

Thus far it is clear that nearly all the Scottish Presbyterian and Dutch Reformed missionaries who came to Malawi at the end of the nineteenth century had used schools as a tool for evangelism. The teachers in these mission schools also served as evangelists for the church while some went further to become ordained ministers. The Scottish Presbyterian missionaries should be commended for opening theological education to Africans at an early stage, but they too should be critiqued for failing to treat these educated Africans with due respect and the recognition they deserved. As Ross and Fiedler observed, there was a sharp "contradiction between the policy of educating Africans to a higher level and giving them significant responsibilities."[19]

As we will see in this chapter, a number of Africans studied theology and were ordained at the dawn of the 20th century despite Christianity being in its infant stage on the land. By 1907, the Livingstonia Presbytery, led by Robert Laws, had passed a policy regarding the licensing and ordination of native ministers. Although this policy had a discriminating clause that stipulated that an African pastor should stay under the care and supervision of European missionaries for a longer probation period, it still achieved its main purpose of incorporating the natives into ordained ministry. By the time of its golden jubilee (fiftieth anniversary) in October 1925, the Synod of Livingstonia had ten ordained indigenous ministers. Consequent to this policy, the Livingstonia Mission had Yesaya Zerenji Mwase, a former student of Arts at the Overtoun Institute, given permission to study theology, licensed in 1906, and ordained on 17th May 1914 alongside two other Africans.[20]

Eventually Matecheta caught the attention of David Clement Scott who had an agenda of grooming Africans to take up leadership positions in the church. Harry Kabwiri Matecheta and his ally Steven Kundecha studied theology and were eventually ordained into ministry on 9th and 11th March

---

19 Ross and Fiedler, *A Malawi Church History*, 171–174.
    There was reluctance among both the Scottish and Dutch missionaries to ordain those Africans who had been trained for ministry. Secondly, ordination of Africans in all Synods took a slow pace as from 1911 to 1945 there were a total of 71 ordained African ministers in the CCAP: 34 in Livingstonia, 23 in Blantyre and 14 in Nkhoma synods. Thirdly, educated Africans were not accorded the same status with missionaries. Such treatment contributed to the breakaways from CCAP of such people like Charles Domingo, Charles Chinula and Yesaya Zerenji Mwasi of the Blackman's Church. See chapter 29 in this volume.
20 Kenneth R. Ross, "Introduction," in Y. Z. Mwasi, *Essential and Paramount Reasons for Working Independently*, 7. The other two African ministers who were ordained alongside Mwase were Hezekiya Tweya and Jonathan Chirwa.

1911 respectively in the Blantyre Mission.[21] This is a clear testimony to James Amanze's claim that theological education in Southern Africa is as old as the Church itself and that it is the very reason for the continued existence and growth of the church in this part of the continent.[22] The racist attitude of most of the Dutch Reformed missionaries also affected their view of ordination for Africans into holy ministry. Despite training the natives as catechists and evangelists from the very beginning, Nkhoma Synod did not receive approval from the DRC to ordain natives until 1925. The same year, 1925, saw the ordination of Rev. Andreya Namkumba and Rev. Namon Katengeza.[23] Just a few months later the DRCM ordained the Livingstonia-trained Lameck Kasuzi Manda at Kasungu on 20th December 1925 as their third African minister. By the time the Mission celebrated its fiftieth anniversary in 1939, the number of ordained Malawian ministers had risen to just eight.[24] Perhaps this too speaks volumes of how the work of raising indigenous leaders was affected by the racist attitude among the Dutch missionaries.

4. Harry Kambwiri Matecheta (1870–1962): An African Pioneer of the "Presbyterian Pastors"

Harry Kambwiri Matecheta, born in 1870, was a son to a Yao family from Lopsa village in Chiradzulu district of Malawi. He first heard about the name of Jesus Christ in 1876 when Henry Henderson and Tom Bokwito passed by his home village on their way to identify a site for the Blantyre Mission. Later on, when his family moved from Mpemba to stay close to the mission, Kambwiri found an opportunity to enrol in school between July and August 1884. Kambwiri was a brilliant student, both in class and worship services, and his abilities caught the attention of Dr Hetherwick, until Kambwiri convinced his father to allow him to move to Maganga House at the mission.[25] Later, in 1887, Kambwiri moved even closer to the missionaries when he was elected as a table boy for the Henderson family. This position gave Kambwiri more opportunity to learn from a number of missionaries who were coming to visit but also those that were being visited by the Henderson family.

Due to a shortage of teachers on the mission, Kambwiri and his classmates who had completed standard 4 were enlisted as teachers. Kambwiri received

---

21 Matecheta, *Blantyre Mission: Stories of Its Beginning*, 15.
22 Isabel Apawo Phiri and Dietrich Werner, eds, *Theological Education in Africa* (Oxford: Regnum Books International, 2013).
23 Ross and Fiedler, *A Malawi Church History*, 166–167.
24 Pauw, *Mission and Church in Malawi*, 98.
25 Matecheta, *Blantyre Mission: Stories of Its Beginning*, 39, 44–45.

his first Bible through the partnership that existed between African students and partner mission schools in Europe. For instance, Kambwiri used to receive annual support of about £5 from St Columba's in London. Apart from serving as a table boy, Kambwiri was also enrolled for a course in printing and bible classes (under Miss Beck as the Bible class teacher). He was baptised together with seven other men and two women on 29th December 1889.

For Harry Kambwiri Matecheta, a step into full time ministry came in 1893 when he was assigned to accompany the two white ladies Miss Bell and Miss Alice Werner to plant a station in the Ngoniland at Nthumbi. He went there as a teacher and evangelist. Matecheta says in his book that "in 1884 the Ngoni had brought their warring to our village. In 1893 we brought the Gospel to their villages."[26] The two ladies did not stay long at Nthumbi because of malarial problems and threats of wars in the Ngoniland. Therefore, they returned to Blantyre leaving the mission in the hands of Matecheta alone. Malaria did not only affect the Europeans; Matecheta also lost his wife Jeanie and four children in Blantyre during the time he was at the Nthumbi Mission, but that did not make him to change his mind about the mission. Here was a Yao missionary in the Ngoniland. When problems arose at Mulanje Mission (where all the Europeans had to flee the station), Matecheta was called in 1895 to 1897 to act as leader in the absence of Scottish missionaries. A comment in the July 1896 edition of the *Life and Work in British Central Africa* was that Matecheta's work among the Ngoni in Nthumbi has been very successful: "the Angoni reckon him, boy as he is, a sort of Atate or Father among them ..."[27] From this comment we learn that the way Matecheta conducted himself among the Ngoni earned him a lot of respect regardless of his age.

Robert Napier argues in his letters that Matecheta's ordination was necessitated by the evidence of the work he was doing in the Nthumbi Mission. In 1910 Napier visited Nthumbi to examine candidates for baptism or catechumen.

▲ Harry Kambwiri Matecheta

---

26 Matecheta, *Blantyre Mission: Stories of Its Beginning*, 68–69.
27 Matecheta, *Blantyre Mission: Stories of Its Beginning*, 65. Citation from *Life and Work in British Central Africa*, (July 1896), 4.

The first alarming phenomenon was that he found over a hundred candidates. The second surprise was that over half the candidates passed the examination process.[28] Suffice it to say, Matecheta was doing a good job in planting the church and winning new souls for Christ. In 1907, Matecheta was part of a committee that was tasked to produce a catechism for the African Church followed by another committee which was appointed to pursue the union of the Blantyre, Livingstonia, and Nkhoma Missions into the CCAP. He thus worked far beyond his parish. Outside the CCAP, he was at the centre of organising native conferences that assembled indigenous pastors, evangelists, and catechists to discuss issues pertinent to the Christian faith in the African context, such as polygamy, alcohol, labour, and migration.

In 1907, Harry Kambwiri Matecheta and Steven Kundecha were chosen to undergo theological training in preparation for ordination. The two went through a four-year theological training under Dr A Hetherwick and Rev. R. H. Napier. The curriculum for their study was approved by a council in Britain and was taught and examined in English. This too should not come as a surprise because at the time he was teaching, Matecheta's essay on "Useful Trees of British Central Africa" won a writing competition set by Sir H. H. Johnston. Upon successfully passing examination, Harry Kambwiri Matecheta was ordained on 9th March 1911 at St. Michael's and All Angels' church while Steven Kundecha was ordained two days later at Zomba CCAP.[29] In 1933 Rev. Harry Kambwiri Matecheta was elected Moderator of his Blantyre Presbytery after serving, among other places, at Mulanje Mission, Chikwawa, Blantyre, Nthumbi, Bemvu and many surrounding areas.

5. Conclusion

On 6 July 1964, Malawi received its independence from Britain, barely two years after the death of Matecheta – crowned "a grand old man of Christianity in Malawi."[30] Harry Matecheta represents a generation of the first beneficiaries of Scottish Presbyterian commitment to educating indigenous clergy. By the time of his death in 1962, Matecheta's contribution to his nation was far beyond the confines of his church. For instance, on 24th May 1933 the British Governor and commander-in-chief Sir Herbert Young awarded Matecheta a certificate of recognition for rendering valuable social services for thirty-eight years as a councillor and a member of Ntcheu district school committee.[31] With

---

28   *Robert Hellier Napier in Nyasaland; Being his Letters to His Home Circle*, 46.
29   Matecheta, *Blantyre Mission: Stories of Its Beginning*, 65.
30   Sundkler & Steed, *History of the Church in Africa*, 9.
31   Sundkler & Steed, *History of the Church in Africa*, 89.

such awards, it was no longer just D. C. Scott seeing Africans as people and individual Africans as capable.[32] Even Herbert Young, who was the eyes of King George the fifth in Nyasaland, was able to appreciate Matecheta's outstanding contribution. This award did not come on a silver platter; Scott himself confessed of Matecheta's character that "he was a splendid fellow, brave and wise, true as steel, and [a man of] a very fine influence."[33] It was such a personality plus the educational empowerment that made Harry Kambwiri Matecheta, a Yao by tribe, to be a great missionary in the Angoniland. He lived to prove that if an African is given a chance, he is capable of delivering.

Questions for study (fact type):
1 Name the four teachers/evangelists who came to the Livingstonia Mission with Dr James Stewart to support the development of education in what is now Malawi.
2 When, where, and why was the Overtoun Institute established?
3 Draw a timeline of Henry Kambwiri Matecheta's life that includes the following 9 key events: birth, first hears of Jesus, enrolled in mission school, baptised, enters full-time ministry, beginning of theological education, ordination, moderator of Blantyre Mission, death.
4 Draw an outline map of Malawi. Use this map to identify and label places where Matecheta ministered from Section 4 of this chapter. You should identify at least five places that are significant to his life and ministry.

Questions for study (reflection type):
1 Nearly all the Scottish Presbyterian and Dutch Reformed missionaries who came to Malawi at the end of the nineteenth century had used schools as a tool for evangelism. Do you agree with this evangelism strategy? Why or why not?
2 The closing sentence of this chapter reads: "He lived to prove that if an African is given a chance, he is capable of delivering." Explain at least three *particular* opportunities that Matecheta was given and how they contributed to his success.

---

32 A. C. Ross, *Blantyre mission and the making of modern Malawi*, 118.
33 Matecheta, *Blantyre Mission: Stories of Its Beginning*, 12.

Select Bibliography

DRCM Council minutes of 23/1912, p.152; also quoted in a letter dated 15/6/2/15 from W. H. Murray to A. C. Murray.

Groves, C. P. *The Planting of Christianity in Africa. Vol.II. 1840–1878.* London: Lutterworth, 1954.

Matecheta, H. K. *Blantyre Mission: Stories of Its Beginning.* A translation, introduction, and annotation by Thokozani Chilembwe and Todd Statham. Berlin 2016. Reprint, Mzuzu: Luviri Press, 2020.

McCracken, J. *Politics and Christianity in Malawi, 1875–1940.* Cambridge: Cambridge University Press, 1977.

Murray, W. H. *Mbiri ya Misyoni ya DRC.* Blantyre: CLAIM, 1996. (A translation of the History for the DRC Mission).

Napier, R. H. *Robert Hellier Napier in Nyasaland; Being his Letters to His Home Circle*, ed. Alexander Hetherwick. Edinburgh: W. Blackwood and Sons, 1925

Pauw, C. M. *Mission and Church in Malawi: The History of the Nkhoma Synod of the Church of Central Africa, Presbyterian 1889–1962.* Wellington, SA: CLF, 2016.

Phiri I. A. & Dietrich Werner, eds, *Theological Education in Africa.* Oxford: Regnum Books International, 2013.

Ross, A. C. *Blantyre mission and the making of modern Malawi.* Blantyre: CLAIM, 1996.

Ross, Kenneth R. "Introduction." In Y. Z Mwasi, *Essential and Paramount Reasons for Working Independently,* Original 1933. Blantyre: CLAIM. 1999, 7–14.

Ross, K. R. & K. Fiedler. *A Malawi Church History 1860–2020.* Mzuzu: Mzuni Press, 2020.

Sundkler, B. & C. Steed. *History of the Church in Africa.* Cambridge: Cambridge University, 2000.

Chapter 18

Mauritius: Two Missions and an Historic Joining and Receiving, c.1810–c.1900

J. C. Whytock

Chapter Outline
1. Introduction
2. The London Missionary Society, 1814, Jean Le Brun – "Apostle of Mauritius"
3. The Church of Scotland,1851, John Anderson the lay preacher, Patrick Beaton the ordained missionary
4. An Historic Joining and Receiving, 1876/77
5. Postscript
6. Conclusion

1. Introduction

Mauritius is often overlooked when doing survey church histories of Africa, yet it has an interesting history for historic Presbyterian missions. This chapter will highlight the two different streams – Congregational through the LMS *and* Church of Scotland – which eventually "merged" to become a unified Presbyterian mission history on this island. Mauritius had been under French control until 1810 when it came under British governance.[1] The roots of (what will become) Presbyterian churches go back to the early 1810s, and that is where the story will begin. This chapter highlights early missionaries, strategies, struggles, and books (authored by early missionaries) which continue to have important relevance for the history of missions in Africa.

---

1 For a helpful overview of the Dutch period, the French period, and the British periods, see, Alessandra Miklavcic, "The Mauritians in Canada: Between Globalization and Nation-State Building" (unpublished MA thesis, York University, 1999), 57–66.

2. The London Missionary Society, 1814, *Jean Le Brun – "Apostle of Mauritius"*

The London Missionary Society sent its first missionary, Jean Le Brun, to the newly controlled British island of Mauritius in 1814. Jean Joseph Le Brun, or John Le Brun (1789–1865), was born on Jersey in the Channel Islands and came from a Huguenot family from France.[2] He studied in England at the Gosport Academy under David Bogue and also had training in the Monitorial or Lancastrian system of education,[3] which would become vitally important to his future mission work in Mauritius.

One of the key texts that Le Brun committed to memory while at Gosport, was Watts' Catechism – a catechism based upon the Westminster Shorter Catechism. (This work became a cornerstone to his work in Mauritius when it was translated into French.) Since Le Brun was conversant in French and showed excellent ability in languages, it was only logical that the LMS would assign him to a place such as Mauritius; they had been approached in 1813 to send a missionary to Mauritius to aid the coloured population there. Le Brun accepted this call and, before leaving, prepared to take a large quantity of Bibles and texts for teaching and ministry purposes.

Le Brun's arrival in Mauritius in May 1814 ushered him into a society with whites, free coloured, and slaves, as this was before emancipation.[4] He soon noted that the large, coloured population or *gens de couleur* in and around Port Louis were largely unschooled. Education was to become his entry into missions, together with chapel ministry. He started a school with four students in September that same year, 1814, and by the end of 1814 it had grown to 30, and by the end of

▲ Rev. Jean Le Brun

---

2   Le Brun has not left much by way of publications or diaries other than reports and letters and translation publications. There is a short journal, in French, Jean Le Brun, "Journal, 2 July to 19 December 1816," CWM/LMS/13/05/01 file 1, SOAS.
3   The Monitorial, also called Lancasterian system, was a teaching method, practiced most extensively in the 19th century, in which the older or better scholars taught the younger or weaker pupils.
4   Miklavcic, "The Mauritians in Canada," 66–83. Mauritius today has four main people groups, The Franco-Mauritians, the Creoles, the Indians, and the Chinese. When Le Brun first went there it was chiefly the first two and with various divisions within these.

1815, 100,[5] and by the end of the 1820s about 300 coloured students were in a system of schools of the LMS mission. The figure then reaches 414 for all schools associated with the LMS mission by the mid-1840s.[6] School mission work was intimately connected to chapel ministry. Le Brun was able to constitute a chapel membership role in 1818 with 14 (native) members and in 1829 it had 59 members.[7] The chapel was a dissenting chapel or what would be termed a Congregational church.

The adoption of the Lancastrian system of schooling aided the development of indigenous leaders within the schools. These schools were devoted to both free coloured and (increasingly also) to slave children. Most of these slave children were from parents of slaves who were originally from Madagascar. Those whom he schooled *and* became monitors in his schools *and* became members of the chapel often became preachers and thus more chapels and schools were added across the island. For example, in 1825 Le Brun developed two schools, a chapel, and a lodge in Rivière du Rempart, a rural area to the northeast of Port Louis.[8] Le Brun's wife Coralie served as schoolmistress for the girls' schools.

One of the earliest catechists that Le Brun trained was Jean Lebon, a former slave who assisted Le Brun in the translation work of Watts' Catechism.[9] Le Brun was also an early advocate for the rights of the coloured community and helped to draft a famous landmark petition to have legal disadvantages removed for this community. Scholars here see parallels with Dr John Philip, the LMS missionary in the Cape Colony at the same period. Le Brun was a missionary who practised wholistic missions as an evangelical; his work illustrates the David Bebbington thesis on the evangelical quadrilateral.[10] Le Brun often spoke out openly against abiding fetish practices and the ongoing use of amulets. Those who joined his chapels were to make a clear break with such practices at conversion.

---

5 Anonymous, "Chronological Review of the LMS Mission in Mauritius 1833," CWM/LMS 13/02/01/003, folder 4, file C, SOAS.

6 Jean Le Brun, Port Louis, Mauritius to [LMS Secretary] 3 October 1848, CWM/LMS/13/02/01/032, folder 4, file B where it seems the schools of Port Louis are not included in the tabulation, so the number could be much higher than the 414 tabulation.

7 "Names of the members of the church 1818–1829", compiled by J. Le Brun. CWM/LMS/13/02/01/003, folder 3, file D, SOAS. It seems there were 17 but three died almost immediately after joining so it was really 14.

8 Yank, "Women, Slavery, and British Imperial Interventions in Mauritius," 156–157.

9 Anderson, *Esquisse de l'Histoire du Protestantisme à l' île Maurice*, 34. Baker would be the printer for this.

10 The four qualities are conversionism, activism, biblicism, and crucicentrism. For more information on this concept, https://biblicalstudies.org.uk/pdf/churchman/122-03_201.pdf

▲ Port Louis Harbour, Mauritius 1889

Since slavery and government apprenticing was still practiced in his early years on Mauritius, Le Brun and his assistants made a concerted effort to provide Sabbath Schools for slaves and apprentices. These were held on Sundays from 10:00 am to noon and were for both men and women. The purpose was "moral evangelism," and they were referred to this school by their master or mistress to attend. Both oral instruction and books were used, and each class was limited to twelve and there could be multiple classes. Singing, Bible reading, church history, catechism, and prayer were part of each school session. Records of attendance were also kept.[11]

Jean Le Brun occasionally had relief and the assistance of some short term LMS missionaries and also long term LMS workers such as: William Ellis, Thomas Bevan, David Jones, David Griffiths, John Jeffreys, John Canham, William Crow, David Johns, Charles Hovenden, John Joseph Freeman, Theophilus Atkinson, T. S. Kelsey, and Edward Baker and many of their wives during the years 1816 through 1846.[12] Often these missionaries would stay for a few weeks or months in connection with opening and developing the LMS mission in Madagascar or other areas. In essence, the LMS mission to Madagascar grew out of the LMS Mauritius Mission and was formally recognized in 1818. In Port Louis the LMS missionaries took turns when passing through of providing Sunday services there in Malagasy, the latter preachers in Malagasy being Jones, John, and Baker.[13]

---

11 "Regulations of the School for the Instruction of the Slaves instituted by Mr Le Brun under the auspices of the Earl, 1825/1826." These regulations are written in French. CWM/LMS/13/02/01/003, folder 3, file C, SOAS.
12 *Register of the LMS*, 11–30.
13 *The Report of the Directors to the 44th General Meeting of the LMS*, (London: William Tyler, 1838), 107.

Often these assistant LMS missionaries specialised in a particular mission, such as in instructing slaves, or, in the case of the LMS artisan-missionary Mr Edward Baker (1805–1885), a printer, running a printing press. Baker worked to produce small books for the schools on Mauritius and also books for Madagascar at Port Louis, from 1836–1846 before going to pastor in Australia. His contribution must be considered significant as it greatly aided Le Brun's expansion of the mission's work on the Island. It seems Baker was the longest serving LMS missionary on Mauritius outside of the Le Brun extended family.[14] While in Port Louis, Baker also authored and printed an *Outline of a Grammar of the Malagasy Language* (1845) and gave instruction in schools. Some of the works which he printed can be verified; like a French Hymnal, French primers, English primers, and Watts' First Catechism with Prayers in French. Baker was the first printer to produce school books on the Island.[15] LMS workers also assisted Jean Le Brun with his heavy preaching schedule each week in French/Creole and English.

Ministry by the LMS on Mauritius endeavoured to reach as many as possible for Christ. This included ministry to seamen. Revs. Le Brun and Johns and Mr Baker worked together to obtain a ship to be fitted upon which to hold church services to minister to seamen. This was known as the Seaman's Chapel or Bethel. An unused vessel, the John Marsh, was equipped for this purpose in the harbour of Port Louis. Here services were held, literature distributed, and a small lending library housed.[16]

Le Brun was seen as a strong supporter of the Anti-Slavery Act. It seems this stressed his body immensely, and he had to leave the Island for a short time and go to the Cape

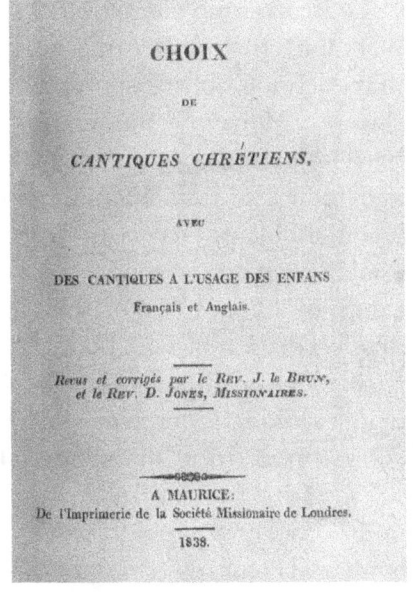

▲ Hymnal prepared and printed on Mauritius in 1838

---

14 Baker was technically with the LMS until 1842 and the last three years was independent of the LMS yet working with them. Insufficient funds appear to have been the issue as in 1846 a strong appeal was made for better funding for the mission on Mauritius. "Appeal for Help" January 1846, J. Le Brun et al, Mauritius to the LMS, Secretary, London, CWM/LMS/13/02/01/032, folder 3, file C.

15 Edward Baker, Mauritius to Rev. W. Ellis, LMS, London, 8 March 1838, CMW/LMS 13/02/01/002, folder 3, file A, SOAS.

16 [Edward Baker], "Brief account of the Appropriation of the Hulk 'John Marsh' lying in the Harbour of Port Louis, Mauritius for a Seamen's Chapel, or Bethel" (Port Louis,1842), CWM/LMS/13/02/01/032, folder 1, file B.

Colony to recover. When he returned in 1834, he was appointed superintendent of education and established more schools. These schools especially targeted the now freed slave population as per the Negro Education Act. At first Le Brun used texts which he brought from England, but over time he authored several of his own texts and produced a noted translation into French of Watts' Catechism. All of these were printed by the LMS mission on the island.

The black and coloured people whom Le Brun was ministering to spoke what was known as Creole. It was an Island language which was based upon French, yet with a linguistic mixture within it mainly from the slaves from Africa, chiefly Madagascar. It cannot be universally said that Creole is the same in the Caribbean, Sierra Leone, and Mauritius, hence the term *Mauritian Creole*. There are distinctions with each. It is best to see it as a close family of siblings who do not necessarily all look alike in height etc. Creole is a hybridisation linguistically.[17]

Le Brun's two sons, John Joseph and Peter, also served in the LMS mission work with their father in Mauritius in the Evangelical Independent Church and in the schools. John Joseph served amongst Malagasy refugees and emancipated slaves in Moka and the "camps" (a term for villages outside of Port Louis), and his wife served at a Malagasy school for these refugees and emancipated slaves and their children. In his letter dated 10 April 1843, he speaks of baptising 47 emancipated slaves, performing several marriages within a few months, establishing a new school, and establishing new preaching stations in the new camps or villages.[18] Later, John Joseph served as assistant to his father in the main mission station at Port Louis. Here John Joseph helped train native evangelists in theology for Madagascar.[19] John Joseph Le Brun also spent about six months undertaking mission work on Madagascar in 1861. After the "merger" of the two entities in 1876 (the Independent Evangelical Church and the Church of Scotland) he was admitted a minister by the General Assembly of the Church of Scotland in 1877 and continued to serve nine churches and four preaching stations in the black and coloured communities. John Joseph died in 1909.[20] Peter Le Brun was a pastor for the Independent Evangelical Churches at Moka and Plaine Wilhelms from 1851 to his death in 1865.[21]

---

17 Miklavcic, "The Mauritians in Canada," 85–87. In Mauritius some scholars think there are four varieties of Creole in use. Also, Piers Larson, *Ocean of Letters: Language and Creolization in an Indian Ocean Diaspora* (Cambridge: Cambridge University Press, 2009).

18 John Joseph Le Brun, Mauritius to Rev. J. J. Freeman, LMS Secretary, London, 10 April 1843, CWM/LMS/13/02/01/032, folder 2, file A.

19 *Register of the LMS*, 58 entry # 463. Newcomb, *Cyclopedia*, 538.

20 *Fasti*, volume 7, 559.

21 *Register of the LMS*, 63–64 entry # 503.

Jean Le Brun senior served with the LMS from 1814 to 1833 and from 1841 to his death in 1865. The period from 1833 to 1841 was when the LMS "closed" their mission in Mauritius but reappointed Le Brun in 1841 as their agent (his death announcement by the LMS states that Jean Le Brun had served with the LMS's Mission at Mauritius for fifty years).[22] Again, finances were an issue. When LMS missionaries had to flee Madagascar to Mauritius the mission in Mauritius then started to come back into the LMS Reports. During the six years without LMS support, Le Brun supported himself primarily through educational work.[23] Mauritius changed dramatically in the 1840s and 50s with many Indians or "Coolies" coming as indentured workers and then later the Chinese. The Le Bruns' ministry did not focus upon these next waves of peoples who came; their ministry remained very much centred upon the Creole peoples (black and coloured) or slaves, emancipated slaves, and free coloured peoples.[24] The main stations of the Independent Evangelical Church were Port Louis and Moka and out-stations at Plaines Wilhemes, Grande Rivière, Riche Terre, Pointe-aux-Piments and Nouvelle Decouverte. Basically, at this time most Protestants amongst the black and coloured population were with this mission Church.

▲ Evangelical Protestant Chapel, Port Louis

---

22 *The Missionary Chronicle New Series* 29.7 (1865), 216.
23 *Register of the LMS*, 10, entry # 135.
24 Beaton, *Creoles and Coolies*, spoke with glowing words of Jean Le Brun's ministry in Mauritius and that he was "an Israelite indeed in whom there is no guile," 277.

3. The Church of Scotland, 1851, John Anderson the lay-preacher and Patrick Beaton the ordained missionary

The 1850s saw dramatic changes in Mauritius (as we have hinted above). This is clear from the primary source text written by Patrick Beaton, the first Church of Scotland minister/missionary to Mauritius. Patrick Beaton (1825–1904) was appointed to Port Louis and set about to establish the congregation of St. Andrew's, Church of Scotland in 1851 (the name is also sometimes listed as St. Andrew's Scots Church). Many of these congregants had been adherents at the local Anglican Church but desired a Presbyterian Church. The key lay-leader was John Anderson, whom we will introduce further in the next sub-point.

There was an earlier brief visit to Mauritius by Rev. Nesbit, a Free Church of Scotland missionary to India. He preached on the Island for Rev. Le Brun and was well received by some of those who eventually formed St. Andrew's congregation. St. Andrew's was a predominately white English-speaking congregation of Scottish colonists, merchants, military, and civil servants at this time but also included a few Indian immigrants who had been influenced in India by Rev. John Anderson's (no relation to the above lay-person of that same name) school there and were latterly baptised by Beaton in Mauritius; it seems that Beaton received the fruit of seeds that were planted in India by Scottish Presbyterian missionaries there.[25] Beaton is a fascinating figure; he was from Scotland but served most of his life outside of Scotland – in Mauritius, Reunion, New Zealand, and Paris. He was also a chaplain in the army and a prolific author and translator of books from German and Italian. Two of his works that are significant for this chapter are *Creoles and Coolies* (1859) and *Six Months on Reunion* (1860).[26] Patrick Beaton was also instrumental in reviving the British and Foreign Bible Society on the Island and furthering its work to distribute scripture there. He served as its secretary and was very active for this auxiliary branch in Mauritius.

The chief concern that Beaton attempted to raise for all who read his *Creoles and Coolies*, as openly stated in the preface, was to arouse missionary interest in the arrival of the Indian indentured workers who had been coming in the 1850s to Mauritius.[27] The 1850s were the zenith of economic labour changes on Mauritius. Beaton identified these indentured workers as a neglected field of mission.[28] The word *coolie* today is generally seen as a negative use of language. It

---

25 Beaton, *Creoles and Coolies*, 280.
26 *Fasti*, volume 7, 536.
27 For further context see, Ashutosh Kumar, *Coolies of the Empire: Indentured Indians in the Sugar Colonies* (Cambridge: Cambridge University Press, 2017).
28 Beaton, *Creoles and Coolies*, v–vi.

likely comes from the Hindi and means *hard labourer*. It is generally replaced with the words indentured worker, or simply, Indian, in the context of this chapter. Beaton argued that since many would serve their time on the Island and then return to India, it was critical to reach out to these Indians before they returned; he believed this could be a mission strategy to also advance the Gospel in India. Beaton was supportive of a separate Tamil-speaking congregation being formed; and it is uncertain if this congregation was included under St. Andrew's or if it was separate and independent. This congregation appears to have been connected also with Anglicans, but Beaton was very supportive of it as the worker who founded it, a Mr Taylor, served with the British and Foreign Bible Society. It seems that Beaton was very evangelically and ecumenically minded. He was pleased personally to have "Coolies" (some who had been trained at the Free Church Institution in Madras, India) attend his own Bible Class at St Andrew's, and he baptised some of these attendees and they joined the St Andrew's congregation. As some Tamil speakers did attend St. Andrew's, the lines here are not exact as to the relationship also to the separate Tamil congregation. Since it was a constantly changing demographic with the Indians, hard conclusions are not in order here.[29] Beaton was instrumental in founding a school connected with St. Andrew's that was for Indian children. It seems that the "board" of the school, if we can call it such, was comprised of members of St. Andrew's: Hay, Stein, and Campbell, and Beaton. The school had 90 Indian children attending it in Port Louis.[30]

Thus, the Church of Scotland mission in Mauritius was reaching out in very different ways than the mission work of the Le Bruns. Mauritius has a very complex ethnic mix, and this is very much reflected in these two distinct missions, yet both evangelical and Reformed. It makes sense then that as time passed the two missions would "merge" together.

4. An Historic Joining and Receiving, 1876/77

What does one call it when two missions/churches join forces yet retain the name and structures of the one entity? Is it a *merger* of two missions or a *union* of two missions or is it a *joining and receiving*? One example from the late twentieth century is a good place to start: in 1982 the Reformed Presbyterian Church Evangelical Synod joined with and was received by the Presbyterian Church in America. This process was popularly called by the term "joining and receiving." It is not clear exactly where this language came from; it was a type of merger and union, yet the name of just one was retained. Others have done similar things in mission work. In Chapter Ten of this book, we noted it there with the two

---

29 Beaton, *Creoles and Coolies*, 240.
30 Beaton, *Creoles and Coolies*, 248; Anderson, *Mauritius*, 128.

missions of the Corisco Mission (ABCFM) and the Gaboon Mission (PCUSA) coming together basically in a "joining and receiving" manner and all becoming known as Presbyterian after this. This appears to be what happened in Mauritius.

The Anderson Family

The Anderson family were a predominant family involved in Presbyterian missions in Mauritius, but this family also had very close ties to the other mission. The father, John Anderson (1814–1890), Church of Scotland, was sent out to Mauritius in 1839 as the principal of the Mico Normal School for the Lady Mico Trust and thus worked closely with Jean Le Brun of the LMS for Creole education. John Anderson was also instrumental in helping to organise the first Presbyterian (Church of Scotland) Church on the Island with English services for the Scottish colonists, it appears, in the late 1840s. There were some Highland Scots on Mauritius, e.g., from Lewis, who spoke Gaelic but a minority, so English was to be the medium of worship. John was a lay preacher and preached often throughout the Island. He married a French wife of Huguenot background whose family had immigrated to Mauritius during the French period, and he had three sons who became ministers.

It will be noted that John Anderson, though a Scottish Presbyterian, worked with the LMS missionary Jean Le Brun whom he held in the deepest respect and this respect carried onto the next generation of sons both Le Brun and Anderson. Separate congregations emerged due to linguistic and cultural realities – the black and coloured of Le Brun in Creole and the Scottish Presbyterians originally in English. The two missions were theologically virtually the same in essential Evangelical and Reformed theology and on the sacraments. The origins of this merger can really be traced back to the harmonious relations between Jean Le Brun and John Anderson. Patrick Beaton was succeeded in 1856 by Rev. George McIrvine who was the minister at St. Andrew's Church of Scotland, Port Louis from 1856 to 1899, also an encourager of this merger.

Also, like the Le Brun family, the Anderson family had two sons who were to serve in Christian work in Mauritius; these were the brothers, James Forrester Anderson, and Samuel Honeyman Anderson, who both made significant contributions to the development of the mission in Mauritius. Both were born in Mauritius of this Scottish merchant class. James Forrester Anderson (1852–1926) had his Bachelor of Theology thesis published in Paris in 1903, which remains today a significant source of information. The dedication was to his father and mother and to Jean Le Brun. It is entitled *Esquisse de l'Histoire du Protestantisme à L'île Maurice et aux îles Mascarègnes 1502 à 1902*, or in English, *Sketch of the History of Protestantism on Mauritius and Mascarene Islands 1502–1902*.[31] James was fluent

---

31 Published in Paris in 1903.

in French and so studied at the University of Paris and was ordained at Passy Reformed Church in Paris in 1903. He became the minister at St. John's Church of Scotland in Port Louis, Mauritius and served there for over twenty years. His older brother Samuel Honeyman Anderson (1845–1923) studied at Cheshunt College, England and in Paris. He was ordained in Paris in 1870 and served nineteen chapels and out-stations across the island of Mauritius in the missions connected with the LMS or the Independent Evangelical Church.

In 1877, with the merger of the two missions, Samuel was admitted by the General Assembly of the Church of Scotland as a minister on her roles serving in Mauritius. In 1883, after thirteen years of serving these chapels, he accepted a call to the English Congregational Church in Paris, France and remained there until his death. To aid his congregants and mission work in Mauritius, Samuel translated the Gospel of Matthew into Creole for teaching purposes.[32] It was also used on other Islands, including the Seychelles, not just Mauritius. He also translated the Psalms into Creole and other portions of the New Testament. It seems by going to Paris he was able to ensure the publication of the above and their shipment to Mauritius, so his interest in Mauritius did not wane after leaving for Paris.

Fusion

The merger of the two missions was harmonious and very much facilitated by these two chief leading families of Le Brun and Anderson. It was more like a *joining and receiving arrangement* into the Church of Scotland and the two families overlapped in both missions and churches. In French it was described as *"et la fusion de l'Église indépendante avec l'Église Presbytérienne d' Écosse en novembre 1876."*[33] *Fusion* is also a good way to describe this union. The Independent Church was no longer receiving financial assistance from the LMS and no doubt this was another factor pushing forward the need to merge together after the deaths of Jean and Peter Le Brun in 1865 and the need to strengthen leadership in the Evangelical Independent Church.[34] No doubt the prospect of adding more leaders to a united cause was a factor. The union occurred on 30 November 1876 and then in May 1877 two ministers (Revs. Samuel Anderson and John Joseph Le Brun) were added to the roles of the CoS when they were accepted from the former Independent Evangelical Church by the GA. The Independent Church brought eleven chapels into the union and an extensive ministry to the black and coloured Creole population of Mauritius.

---

32 *Fasti*, volume 7, 558–559.
33 Anderson, *Esquisse de l'Histoire du Protestantisme à l' île Maurice*, 47.
34 Anderson, *Esquisse de l'Histoire du Protestantisme à l' île Maurice*, 66.

5. Postscript

Post early-1900s, it does not seem that the momentum for expansion, evangelism, and church planting continued at the same pace as in the first two generations. Mauritius became an independent nation in 1968. This also was a factor for the Church of Scotland in Mauritius to become an independent entity, known after 1979 as the Presbyterian Church in Mauritius (PCM)/*Eglise Presbyterienne de Maurice*. In 2022 it describes itself as a plurilingual church with Creole, French, English, and Malagasy languages being used in ministry and currently is centred in six distinct parishes inclusive of the Malagasy chaplaincy: Saint-Columba, Phoenix; Saint-André, Rose Hill; Saint-Jean, Port Louis; Saint-Joseph, Grand Gaube; Saint-Pierre, Pointe-aux-Piments; and the Malagasy Chaplaincy.[35] The revived Malagasy work, due to an influx of people from Madagascar to Mauritius from the 1990s onwards, is reminiscent of the early mission period on Mauritius and the printing of a Malagasy grammar at Port Louis in 1845. The mission has come in one sense full circle to this people group.

6. Conclusion

Mauritius was an important mission field for the LMS and is often overshadowed by larger LMS mission fields of the early 19th century. It exhibits many strategic signs of mission activity under Jean Le Brun and his wife and by his two sons. Mauritius was important for the development of the LMS Madagascar mission field; this should not be ignored as in many ways it served as a launching station or as Lovett described it "preparatory also to the opening of the Madagascar Mission."[36] Many LMS missionaries did what today may be termed short-term mission work in Mauritius, especially in the first 30 years of the Mauritian mission. The name of the printer Edward Baker must not be ignored as the development of literacy in the mission was a critical strategy. The development of the Church of Scotland and local mission shows the complexity of a diaspora/immigrant church and its foray into mission work in its context. The Church of Scotland on Mauritius did not really fall within the purview of the Foreign Missions Committee for the long-term, rather we should view the word "missions" here more in the sense of the local CoS doing mission work rather than a GA directed committee work.[37] Patrick Beaton's book is of value here to understand the wider scope of missions. The "joining and receiving" of the LMS Evangelical

---

35 See, https://www.presbyterian.mu/en/about-us/our-history.html
36 Richard Lovett, *The History of the London Missionary Society 1795–1895*. Vol.1 (London: Henry Frowde, 1899), 105.
37 A. F. Walls, section on, "Mauritius," *DSCHT*, 578 for a nuanced understanding on this aspect.

Independent Church connects to a wider theme of LMS missions merging or seeking cooperation with other missions as time passes. There remains much scope for more history to be written from post-1900 and further explorations on Mauritian workers.

Questions for study (fact type):
1. Name the first LMS missionary to Mauritius and state where he was born.
2. Define Creole in the context of Mauritius.
3. List the main reasons for the merger of 1876/77.
4. What catechism was used on Mauritius by the LMS?

Questions for study (reflection type):
1. Discuss the challenges of a plurilingual mission and church. Also discuss the positive side to such plurilingual ministry.
2. Discuss the unique missionary family dynasties which emerged in Mauritius and discuss this considering Psalm 133:1.
3. Discuss the missionary strategy which was espoused by Patrick Beaton in *Creoles and Coolies*.

Select Bibliography

Anderson, James F. *Esquisse de l'Histoire du Protestantisme à l' île Maurice et aux îles Mascarègnes 1502 à 1902*. Paris: Société Française d' Imprimerie et de Librairie, 1903.

Anderson, John. *Descriptive Account of Mauritius ...* Port Louis, Mauritius: L. A. Denny, 1858.

Anderson, Samuel Honeyman, trans. *L'Évangile Selon S. Matthié: Dan Langaz Créol Maurice*. [The Gospel According to St Matthew: in Mauritian Creole]. London: British and Foreign Bible Society, 1885.

Anderson, Samuel Honeyman, trans. *L'Evangile Sélon S. Marc: Dan Langaz Créol Maurice*. [The Gospel according to St. Mark in Mauritian Creole]. London: British and Foreign Bible Society, 1888.

Anderson, Samuel Honeyman, trans. *Les Evangiles selon saint Matthieu, saint Marc, saint Luc, saint Jean et les Actes des Apôtres dans le patois créole*. London: British and Foreign Bible Society, 1900.

Baker, Edward. *Outline of a Grammar of the Malagasy Language*. Port Louis: [Edward Baker printer], 1845.

Edward Baker, Mauritius to Rev. W. Ellis, LMS secretary, London, 8 March 1838, CMW/LMS 13/02/01/002, Folder 3, File A, SOAS.

Beaton, Patrick. *Creoles and Coolies, or Five Years in Mauritius*. London: James Nesbitt, 1859.

Beaton, Patrick. *Six months in Reunion: A Clergyman's Holiday, and How He Passed It*. 2 vols. London: Hurst & Blackett, 1860.

Kalla, Abdool Cader. "Jean Le Brun Missionary Education and the Fashioning of Coloreds in Colonial Mauritius." *Week-End*, 18 January, 2017.

Le Brun, Jean. "Fourth Report of the Schools in Port Louis connected with the London Missionary Society, for the year 1840, Port Louis, 1840." CWM/LMS/13/02/01/002/ folder 4, file D, SOAS.

Le Brun, Jean. "Fifth Report of the Schools in Port Louis connected with the London Missionary Society, for the year 1841, Port Louis, 1841." CWM/LMS/13/02/01/002/ folder 4, file D, SOAS.

LeBrun, Jean, "Journal, 2 July to 19 December 1816," CWM/LMS/13/05/01 file 1, SOAS.

Le Brun, Jean, "Names of the members of the church 1818–1829," CWM/LMS/13/02/01/003, folder 3, file D, SOAS.

London Missionary Society: A Register of Missionaries, Deputations, etc. From 1796 to 1923. Compiled by James Sibree. London: LMS, 1923.

MacDonald, Jim. "Jim MacDonald's, 'Memories,' c.1995," https://www.theymetinmauritius.com/jim-macdonalds-memories Contains aspects of life in the Church of Scotland congregations in Mauritius.

Miklavcic, Alessandra. "The Mauritians in Canada: Between Globalization and Nation-State Building." MA thesis, York University, 1999.

Newcomb, Harvey. *Cyclopedia of Missions Containing a Comprehensive View of Missionary Operations Throughout the World*. Second Edition. New York: Charles Scribner, 1856.

Quenette, Rivaltz L. *L'Oeuvre du Révérend Jean Le Brun à l'ile Maurice*. Moka: Institut Mahatma Gandhi, [1982] 2014.

Scott, Hew, comp. *Fasti Ecclesiae Scoticanae*. Vol. 7. Original 1866. New Edition, Edinburgh: Oliver & Boyd, 1928.

Yank, Tyler. "Women, Slavery, and British Imperial Interventions in Mauritius, 1810–1845." PhD thesis, McGill University, 2019.

Chapter 19

The American Presbyterian Congo Mission (APCM) c.1890–c.1945

J. C. Whytock

Chapter Outline
1. Introduction
2. Preparing the Way
3. Pioneer Work of the APCM
4. Developments, 1892–1911
5. Expansion,1912–c.1945
6. Postscript
7. Conclusion
Bio Inset: William Sheppard
Bio Inset: Joseph Phipps

1. Introduction

The Congo Free State, or what is today the Democratic Republic of the Congo (DRC),[1] was a very significant field for American Presbyterian mission work in Africa. For one branch in particular, the old Southern Presbyterian Church or PCUS, the DRC was one of their chief mission fields and the largest in terms of personnel, finances, and inclusive of active participation of children in home Sunday Schools, something often ignored in mission studies. This mission took the name, the American Presbyterian Congo Mission (APCM). It brought together both white and African American missionaries. Its context was rooted in the world of King Leopold II of Belgium and the complexities of this time period.

Two rare books today, which serve as helpful texts to understand the beginnings and early development of this mission, are Ethel Taylor Wharton's *Led in Triumph: Sixty Years of Southern Presbyterian Missions in the Belgian Congo* and William Sheppard's *Presbyterian Pioneers of the Congo*. (Wharton relied heavily upon Sheppard for the opening sections in her work and also updated her work

---

1 Named Congo Free State from 1884 to 1908, when changed to Belgian Congo. Latterly Zaire, and then Democratic Republic of the Congo today.

to a later period from Bedinger's earlier work up to 1920). These two books were used in part for this survey history chapter and have been supplemented as needed through annual reports and other works. Two additional insets have been included in this chapter to help to round out our understanding of this mission story by way of biographical emphasis. We begin this mission story with a John-the-Baptist-like figure.

2. Preparing the Way

As with most new missions, there is a backstory to the main story. Such is the case here: Why were the Southern Presbyterians in America interested in the interior of the Belgian Congo? There are two parts to the answer. First, John Leighton Wilson, the noted missionary of Liberia and Gabon, had been agitating for many years for an African interior mission by the PCUS to move beyond the coastal areas of West Africa. He boldly made such a statement in 1881 to the Executive Committee of Foreign Missions PCUS and gave his reasons as to why such a mission should be undertaken in God's providence by the PCUS. He died in 1886 with his vision unrealized. Second, there was one missionary to the interior of the Congo, a Methodist Episcopal medical missionary, whose story had become known. He was Dr William R. Summers (1855–1888), born in the Channel Island of Guernsey, who spent three years in Angola and the Congo Free State (1885–1888) serving for the illustrious Bishop Taylor.[2] Summers had a vision to establish mission stations deep in the interior of the Congo centred around the Kasai (Kassai) River, sometimes also referred to as the Congo Valley of Africa.[3] There were mission stations along the Congo River but not deep into the heart of the Congo. Summers' desire was to see stations move past the Congo River and enter through the Kasai River.

This "John-the-Baptist" type figure made his way to Luluabourg deep in the centre of the Congo, witnessed to the Bena Lulua peoples, and established a mission station there with three houses. Perhaps this was planting seeds and preparing the way for those who would follow after Summers and share his vision. Summers' mission lasted two years at Luluabourg before he died there.[4] He was not alone with this vision – others, including the English Baptist

---

2 Taylor University in Indiana bears his name.
3 See the subtitle for Lapsley's collected writings ... *Missionary to the Congo Valley*.
4 Buried near Luluabourg, the grave was seen by Sheppard who testified of those who were blessed by Summers' ministry there. Also, James Reid, *Missions & Missionary Society of the Methodist Episcopal Church*, vol. 1, (New York: Eaton & Mains, 1895), 268–272 and Douglas D. Tzan. *William Taylor and the Mapping of the Methodist Missionary Tradition: The World His Parish* (Lanham, MD: Lexington Books, 2019), 201.

missionary George Grenville, shared this vision of seeing a new mission begun away from the Congo River and centring upon one of the other major interior rivers. The Belgian Congo was a vast area and populated with many peoples. The reality was that the mission societies needed to realise that they needed to engage others for this great undertaking.

Thus, between Wilson's agitating and Summers' attempt to establish a mission deep in the Congo Valley, the time for the PCUS to take up this mission was ripe. At the same time, the "scramble of the 1880's" for central Africa by European powers brought the interior into focus in this decade. This latter point does not seem to be central to the PCUS starting a mission in the interior; the other two reasons above appear to be predominant. Who then in particular took up this gospel call into the interior?

3. Pioneer Work of the APCM

The PCUS had one candidate who had offered himself for Africa – the African American William H. Sheppard (1865–1927) (For Sheppard's background see the inset in this chapter). The Executive Committee of Foreign Missions PCUS wanted to send two missionaries to a new mission endeavour in Africa. A second person was secured with Samuel N. Lapsley (1866–1892) coming forward. Lapsley was a graduate of the University of Alabama and of McCormick Theological Seminary, Chicago. He was from Selma, Alabama and had served briefly with the Washertown Mission in Anniston, Alabama.

The mandate of the Executive Committee of Foreign Missions in 1889 was:

- To find a site, preferably in the Congo Free State, far enough from other missions to enable us to open a wholly independent work.

- To find a healthful location in the highlands but not too distant from a base of supplies.

- To work among a population large enough to constitute a good mission field and use a language which is widely current.

- To present to the Committee an estimate of the needed missionary force, an estimate of expenses to be incurred in opening the work and of the cost of maintenance.[5]

---

5 Quoted by Wharton, 12–13.

Providences

Before leaving America, Lapsley had the opportunity to read all the manuscript material of Dr Summers' diary and letters with particular attention on the Kasai River. There is no doubt that this was extremely valuable in the years to come. On the boat trip from New York to Liverpool in February 1890, the two missionaries met a Presbyterian elder who was to link them in London with the exporting firm of Whyte, Ridsdale & Co. For the next thirty years this firm significantly helped the mission with necessary supplies. Once in London, they were introduced to Dr Henry (Harry) Grattan Guinness, they resided at Harley House, and were exposed to the East London Training Institute (Bible School). While at Harley House, they became acquainted with several missionaries who were enroute to the Congo.[6] These contacts proved to be immensely important in the development of the APCM and helped to furnish valuable information and connections.

While in England, Lapsley had the opportunity to visit Brussels and had a meeting with King Leopold II where the young missionary announced the new mission of the American Presbyterian Congo Mission (APCM).[7] He no doubt was able to reference this meeting in the Congo when interacting with Belgian State officials there. Supposedly, King Leopold also recommended they establish their mission station at Luebo. Providentially, more missionaries heading for service in the Congo were on the ship from Rotterdam to the Congo – an excellent opportunity for exchange and connecting.

Once in the Congo (May 1890), Lapsley and Sheppard went to Boma and had a meeting with the Governor there who welcomed them and allowed them to study his maps of the interior and especially of the Kasai River. They also visited the English Baptists for six weeks at their station at Tunduwa; this provided an opportunity to learn and become initiated into what to expect in the interior. Next, they visited the American Baptists at their station at Lukunga to study what they did particularly in terms of preaching and running a school for boys and young men. Lapsley was very impressed with this visit and recorded the advice he received from the missionary, Mr Hoste, in his journal:

> Expect men to be converted; trust the power of the Gospel and the coming of the Holy Spirit; then stick to your place and preach always whenever they will listen. Teach each convert

---

6 Guinness's mission, Congo-Balolo Mission, later known as Regions Beyond Missionary Union, was founded in 1889 and grew out of the earlier Livingstone Inland Mission, founded in 1877. Sheppard, *Pioneers*, 20

7 The mission would be called such until 1970.

to testify ... Be patient with the errors and ignorance of new converts and the endless 'palavers' arising in church work.[8]

Finally, an important meeting took place at Bolobo with the English Baptist missionary there, George Grenfell. He helped them to study the maps of the interior and discussed both the Kwango and Kasai Rivers with them.

All of these providential meetings with various missions and missionaries and others were a time of learning context and becoming prepared for a new mission work. Wharton said it this way: "Without this interest and without the help of these older missions, their task of opening a work so far inland would have been almost an impossible one."[9] They had visited virtually every Protestant mission station in the Lower Congo.

Exploration was also key during these first ten months in the Lower Congo. Skills were developed, language acquisition begun, knowledge was gained of the various tribes, and in particular of the various kingdoms of the interior. When the travel time out to Africa, the meetings along the way, and the engagements and explorations in the Lower Congo are put together, there was over thirteen months of informal mission preparation.

Luebo Missionary Station

In the end, it was deep along on the Kasai River that the first APCM station was established at Luebo when they pitched their tents there on 22 April 1891 – 1,200 miles from the Congo coast. Not that long before, Luebo had been opened up for trade by the *Societe Anonyme Belge* and further trading posts were being planned on the Kasai River. Luebo was well situated as it sat between the Kasai and Sankuru Rivers and beside the Luebo and the Lulua Rivers. The main Kasai tribes in the region were the Bakuba, Bashilange/Bena Lulua and Baluba. Before journeying on the Kasai, Lapsley and Sheppard had also recruited George Adamson from the Free Church of Scotland for the mission (he had trained with Guinness at the East London Training Institute). He was working to restore a steamer for the Congo Bololo Mission. When finished that project, he joined with Lapsley and Sheppard in October 1890. Adamson remained with the APCM until 1894 and was of great service in this pioneering period. His wife, Maggie, died at Luebo and was the first missionary to be buried at that station.[10]

---

8 From *Life and Letters of Samuel N. Lapsley*, as quoted by Wharton, 18.
9 Wharton, 27.
10 Maggie, nee Waugh, had also trained at the East London Missionary Training Institute, London where she had met her future husband.

The mission began virtually immediately. On 3 May 1891 the first Communion service was held at Luebo, so the gospel was proclaimed in Word and sacrament. In June, a Sunday School commenced with basic studies on the book of Genesis. Lapsley continued with language study (Bukete) and began writing down some vocabulary and grammar. By October of 1891, there was evidence of the "Spirit of God working in the hearts of the people."[11]

Lapsley's death in March 1892 was a great loss to the fragile mission.[12] He had served slightly less than two years in the Congo but had helped lay the foundation which was indispensable for the future work of the APCM. Sheppard greatly felt the loss of his brother missionary. He and Adamson soldiered on. Sheppard did what no foreigner had ever done before: he went further and entered the capital city of the Bakuba at Mushenga and met with the Bakuba King in 1892.[13]

4. Developments, 1892–1911

The first baptisms took place at Luebo on 10 March 1895 and in April 1895.[14] Three adults and four station youth were baptised. By the end of 1895, there were 48 converts at the station. By 1901, there was a membership of 550. The mission's philosophy was that the Sunday evening and Wednesday evening prayer meetings were to be led by local converts. Also, the local converts were to go out two-by-two into the villages to testify and evangelise. Gospel work was at the centre of the mission: to see people won to Christ and incorporated into the visible church.

New stations were opened at Ibanche and Ndambi, but both experienced conflict with the State who insisted that they be closed. Ibanche was destroyed by the Bakuba king's men in 1904. In 1905 the mission commenced rebuilding this station. The famous picture often seen of the Lapsley Memorial Church in Ibanche is that of the rebuilt church.

More missionaries arrived to help with the work. These did not all come from the ranks of the PCUS. Joining the Adamsons were Rev. and Mrs Arthur Rowbotham (1892)[15] from England and from the PCUS in the 1890s Rev. and Mrs DeWitt Snyder (1892), Miss Maria Fearing (1894)[16] and Rev. William M. Morrison

---

11 Wharton, 33.
12 Lapsley was buried at Underhill in Matidi.
13 Sheppard, *Pioneers*, 105ff. Bakuba today is Kuba.
14 Sheppard, *Pioneers*, 150.
15 Dworkin, *Congo Love Song*, 53.
16 Miss Fearing was one of the most remarkable missionaries in the Congo. She and others developed a home for girls which was a wholistic missions ministry.

(1896) and many others.[17] Sheppard was a recruiter of several African Americans to the APCM.[18]

The missionaries quickly realised the need to rely upon indigenous workers to spread the gospel and meet the spiritual needs of converts. The State imposed a quota of a maximum of 15 days for any missionary to remain in an African village. Thus, having local converts ministering was crucial to the development of village work. The training of local evangelists for the villages thus became an important task of the mission.

The APCM tried to establish new stations, but these were generally refused by the government. By 1911 Luebo had a population of between 10 to 20 thousand with large shed-type churches to accommodate the great crowds of people. The same was true at Ibanche. The main people who responded were from the Baluba and Bena Lulua peoples, not the Bakuba or Bena Kasenga. By 1911 the mission had a membership of 7,000, had begun to ordain elders and deacons, and had many evangelists and teachers. Several testimonies speak of burning piles of fetishes in the villages when the Christian faith was embraced.[19]

Pantops Girls' Home was one of many such Boys' and Girls' Homes where redeemed slave children and orphans were brought. Often these homes had to refuse many children as they just could not take care of all those who were brought. From 1894 to 1917 Maria Fearing devoted herself to this type of mission work with children at Pantops.

In addition to the Girls' Home, day schools were also a critical work of the mission with the goal of developing literacy and Bible reading. Luebo was the centre for these schools and there were some in other villages. In reality, the mission could not meet all the needs for such schools in the surrounding villages.[20]

Linguistic work engaged much attention of the mission throughout the 1890s. Lapsley began the work on the Bukete language (now called Tshikete) and others took up this work. Dr Snyder developed a full dictionary and grammar and a First Reader, and did some preliminary work on some hymns and the opening chapters of Matthew, all in Bukete. In 1897 Rev. William Morrison then

---

17 Wharton includes a list of all missionaries for each chronicled period. It is an invaluable list of information. See, 39, 58, 84, 115–116, 144–146, 158–159, 185–187.
18 Phipps, *William Sheppard*, lists what appears to be a majority or perhaps all of the African American missionaries and their years of service, 123. He lists William Sheppard, Lucy Gant (Sheppard), Henry Hawkins, Maria Fearing, Lilian Thomas (De Yampert), Joseph Phipps, Althea Brown (Edmiston), Lucias De Yampert, Alonzo Edmiston, Adolphus Rochester, Annie Taylor (Rochester), and Edna Atkinson (Rochester). See Chapter 31 of this volume.
19 For a photo image of one of these burning piles of fetishes see, Bedinger, 78.
20 Bedinger, 60–61.

switched to the Baluba and Bukua Lulua dialects (sensing that they were more universal) and gained full approval of Dr Snyder to do so.[21] Morrison's grammar of the Buluba-Lulua (now called Tshiluba) was to become a standard grammar for generations. Morrison produced a full dictionary of 417 pages, a catechism, texts on the parables, etc. and also a translation of the letters to the Romans and the Corinthians. In 1911/3 *Malesona, Lessons from the Bible* was completed and printed, which contained 150 Bible stories/lessons. His well-used catechism was based upon the Shorter Catechism and the Child's Catechism and another Catechism from England. This catechism was to become a hallmark of the APCM. Rev. Snyder ran the first press and later Lillian Thomas. In time a new press was dedicated and called the J. Leighton Wilson Press. In 1898 the first hymnal in Buluba-Lulua (Tshiluba) was compiled by Lucy Sheppard, William's wife, a trained vocalist and expert on Negro Spirituals.[22]

Formal medical mission work began in 1906 when Dr Coppedge came to Luebo with the APCM. Medical ministry had been done by almost all the missionaries starting with Lapsley and Sheppard and also at the two stations of Luebo and Ibanche, but with Coppedge formalised medical mission work began. For many years, he was literally the only medical doctor for hundreds of miles in the Congo interior.

Transport by steamer for many African interior missions was a common theme during this time. A most fascinating and engaging story occurred to make the mission's first Presbyterian mission steamer a reality. Following Samuel Lapsley's death, children from First Presbyterian Church Selma, Alabama began collecting money for a steamer in his memory. This project spread throughout the PCUS congregations and also to Sao Paulo, Brazil where many donations were received for this APCM steamer. A steamer, the *Samuel. N. Lapsley,* was built in Richmond, Virginia and then disassembled and shipped to the Congo in 1900. It was reassembled under the guidance and direction of one of the missionaries, Rev. Vass, who was not an engineer! The new steamer arrived at Luebo in May of 1901 and a crowd of over 1,000 gathered to give thanks to God and 5,000 greeted its arrival.[23] For eighteen months, the steamer plied the waters of the Kasai River and tributaries before it was destroyed in a whirlpool.

---

21 Buluba-Lulua "is the mother tongue of the two largest tribes and is readily understood by the other tribes," Bedinger, 33.
22 Lucy Sheppard had this hymnal printed in Richmond. *Musambu ws Nzambi* [Songs of God]. (Richmond, VA: Curtiss Press, 1898). A second expanded edition came forth in 1902 as *Mukanda wa Mismbu* [Book of Hymns]. (Luebo, Congo: APCM, 1902).
23 L. C. Vass, "Steamer Notes," *The Kassai Herald*, 1.2 (1 July 1901), 23.

▲ Lapsley Steamer

A second steamer was built with funds which were quickly gathered from the mission stations in the Congo, congregations in the USA and in Brazil, China, and Mexico. The replacement steamer was built in Glasgow and dedicated there under the watchful hand of Robert Whyte of Whyte and Ridsdale. Once again, it was torn down and then reassembled in the Congo also under Rev. Vass's direction along with a Scottish industrial missionary who came to take charge of the steamer. This steamer was to serve for 25 years as the main vehicle of transport for the mission and its expansion around the Kasai and its tributaries: "To the people of the Congo she was a beloved Steamer of God bringing the gospel to many who knew it not, and strength and encouragement to Christians scattered in the settlements along the river."[24]

Human abuses in the Congo Free State grew to a point where the call for reform was taken up by many within the APCM, perhaps somewhat reluctantly for some as there was an undercurrent that the church was to do spiritual work and not involve itself politically. 1903 was the turning year. William Morrison went on furlough that year and stopped in Belgium seeking an interview with King Leopold II and was denied such. He went next to England and with the help of Robert Whyte gained access to many at Whitehall and also in the Houses of Parliament concerning Congo Reform. The result was the formation of the Congo Reform Association in England in 1903 and 1904 in America.

---

24 Wharton, 67.

In 1906 Morrison returned to the Congo and continued his writing in the *Kassai Herald* pointing out factual cruelties and injustices in the Congo.[25] The British government ordered their Consul in the Congo to investigate reports of abuse across the Congo. The report was issued in 1909 and appeared to prompt a response of libel charges brought against Morrison and Sheppard by the Kasai Company. Robert Whyte secured a Belgian lawyer who was a supporter of reform, Emil Vanderveld, to defend the two American missionaries. He did not accept any payment for his services but rather was delighted to help see that justice be done in the Congo. The missionaries were vindicated and acquitted.

While this was all happening, in 1908 King Leopold II acquiesced to the Belgian Parliament who forced the Congo Free State to be handed over by the King and become a colony, the Belgian Congo, 1909. There were many besides the King who were complicit with the abuses and cruelties which occurred. His name has popularly been at the centre of this, but the story is much more involved than that of one person.[26]

The APCM was a costly mission for the PCUS. It was a very noted mission work having received much global attention through the trial of the two missionaries. By 1911 some in the PCUS were desirous that only one mission station be maintained and that Ibanche be closed and the work consolidated to Luebo. The reality was the needs were overwhelming and the size of the territory so vast. Things looked very precarious for this mission work. The Lord had other plans!

▲ APCM missionaries, 1909

---

25 Benedetto comments that Morrison "was the only Protestant missionary who developed a procedure for dealing with violations of human injustice," *Presbyterian Reformers in Central Africa*, 10.
26 See the popular book by Adam Hochschild, *King Leopold's Ghost: A Story of Greed, Terror and Heroism in Colonial Africa*. Original. (Mariner Books, 1998) and the 2006 documentary. A new movie is being made by Ben Affleck but not released yet.

5. Expansion, 1912–c.1945

1912 would turn out to be a pivotal year for the APCM's advancement and growth. Rather than retrenchment and retreat, advance occurred. In February 1912 in Chattanooga, Tennessee at the Laymen's Missionary Convention, the PCUS, despite the debt, stories were told of the great needs in the APCM. These inspiring stories included accounts of tribes 300 miles deeper in the interior from the main mission station which needed missionaries. At this convention, 28 candidates came forward for the Congo. Chattanooga marked a new era for the APCM.

Four new stations were opened between 1912 and 1920: Mutoto, Lusambo, Bulape and Bibanga. Bulape focused once again on the Bakuba peoples amongst whom the Sheppards had clearly focused before this time. In one letter, William Sheppard is even described as the apostle to the Bakuba.[27] In the 1910s many turned to Christ and many evangelists emerged amongst the Bakuba. Eventually 53 out-stations were formed. Conversion was a key emphasis and desire of the mission. The APCM Annual Report of 1914 commented that

> to look at the number of additions which we have had this year 1204 makes our hearts glad. This is not as many conversions as last year. The new station Bulape among the Bakuba has not yet begun to baptize as the work is all new. It was thought best that those seeking baptism should be instructed for some time longer before being baptized. They report 720 though in the Inquirers' class ...[28]

Co-operative arrangements were also made to include missionaries from other missions into the APCM: workers came from the Belgian Evangelical Church and also Scandinavian missionaries. The years 1912 to 1920 were days in which the APCM saw a mass movement of men and women and boys and girls turning to Christ. The early 1920s were a difficult period after this time of incredible growth.[29] Membership declined in both the church and the day schools but increased again in the late 1920s. The 1920s was a period of much change in the Belgian Congo. Perhaps also there was a growing tension with the developing indigenous leaders and the expansion of mission institutions.[30]

---

27 See the APCM acceptance letter of the Sheppard's, 2 December 1909, MS, RG 457, Box 1, Folder 3, Presbyterian Historical Society, Philadelphia, PA.
28 Annual Letter from the APCM to the Executive Committee of Foreign Missions, PCUS, 1914. RG432, Box 40, Folder 3, page 1. Presbyterian Historical Society, Philadelphia, PA.
29 See, Annual Letter from the APCM to the Executive Committee of Foreign Missions, PCUS, 1923. RG32, Box 40, Folder 9, page 1. Presbyterian Historical Society, Philadelphia, PA.
30 See, Cogswell, *No Turning Back*, who sees this tension and growth of mission institutions as taking away the spiritual vitality of the earlier period, 38–39. Cogswell makes reference to Kiantandu and Crane for this thesis as well.

New mission ventures began during the 1910s which were to bear much fruit. Four new ventures were formalised: the Carson Industrial School, McKowen Hospital, the Agricultural School, and the opening of a Bible School. The Carson Industrial School was opened in 1915 under C. R. Stegall's leadership and had to close in 1930 due to the Depression. It trained 750 students in carpentry, brickmaking and masonry, tailoring, tanning, shoemaking, blacksmithing and ivory carving. This is very comparable to what other Presbyterian missions were doing (such as at Lovedale in South Africa).

McKowen Hospital was started in Luebo in 1914 and opened in 1916 with 56 beds. It had a unique operating room with huge windows for people to stand outside and watch the operations. It was a hub of activity during the epidemics which swept through the Congo during the 1910s, including the Spanish Influenza.

Other medical mission work developed focusing upon the sleeping sickness and leprosy. Dr Eugene Kellesberger directed Leprosy Camps which were like villages where lepers lived and worked together. Assistance came from the American Mission to Lepers for some of Kellesberger's work.

The Agricultural School was located on a 250-acre farm near Luebo missionary station. It paralleled what the PCUS were doing at their agricultural farm at Lavras, Brazil. The Agricultural School produced vegetables for the Pantops Girls' Home and for the Luebo Station.

In 1913 a Bible School was formalised, first in Luebo, to train evangelists to reach the Bakuba and Buluba-Lulua speaking peoples. In 1918 the Bible School was moved to Mutoto and named the Morrison Bible School in memory of the missionary William Morrison.[31] In addition to the formal courses at the Bible School, annual conferences were conducted to train evangelists. The Bible School functioned at two levels: a preparatory level for those with less schooling and a theology course for those with more schooling. It started with 12 students in 1913 and by 1920 had grown to 300 students. Training and work in manual labour for vegetable production was included for all students. The Bible School helped to supply the mission stations and out-stations with the growing need for leaders. A Woman's Bible School for the training of the wives of the evangelists was also conducted in connection with the Morrison Bible School.

---

31 Morrison was a conservative evangelical Presbyterian who was not involved in the rising tide of modernism. Benedetto summarized his views of inspiration, the atonement, and his commitment to the Westminster Standards as all very orthodox yet he was willing to engage in the injustice of the political landscape as he saw it in the Congo Free State. "Presbyterian Mission Press," 63.

Central School

Issues surrounding the children of the missionaries has been a perennial concern in Protestant missions. Initially, many missionary children died in the Congo. Consequently, many missionary families began to leave their children in England or America. For many, missionary parents felt that they were choosing separation over death. Some thought perhaps one parent should remain "at home" to help to raise the children and others wondered about home schooling but felt this often took them from their calling as missionaries. One solution that developed was that of residential schools for missionary children, although this too had many issues attached to it. Today the issue of residential schools is very much a topic of discussion. The unique history below cannot be ignored or quickly passed over, nor can the rationale above.

In 1926/7 an experimental residential missionary children's school was opened at Mutoto; it was modelled upon similar work in China. Then in 1927/8, the Executive Committee of Foreign Missions PCUS established the Central School for Missionary Children. It was located at the Lubondai Missionary Station with Miss Virginia Holladay as the first teacher. The school grew to also receive children from many other Protestant mission societies or agencies whose parents were labouring in the Belgian Congo. The Walter Sheppards served at this school; Walter was the principal from 1947–1960. In recent years, Central School has received much scrutiny. This scrutiny is mainly in the time period beyond the limitations of this chapter.[32] For purposes here, the issue of the rationale (as outlined above) in the APCM for such a school is critical to understand.

Expanded Linguistic and Print Work

From the 1910s to 1945, linguistic work and print work continued to expand in the APCM. By 1916 William Morrison had completed the translation of the four Gospels and Acts and this was printed by the John Leighton Wilson Press. By 1926 the whole Buluba-Lulua Bible was completed and published by the American Bible Society. This work was finished by Rev. T. C. Vinson, who continued on the mammoth task of the remainder of the translation project after Morrison's death. The hymnal begun by Lucy Sheppard was expanded by Morrison who added another fifty hymns to it. Although Buluba-Lulua was the prominent language which became the APCM linguistic focus, work was not confined to this dialect only. Mrs A. L. Edmiston translated a series of readers and the Parables of Jesus into Bukuba and she also produced a dictionary and a

---

32 Howard Beardlee, et al. *Final Report of the Independent Committee of Enquiry, Presbyterian Church (USA)* (Louisville, KY: Presbyterian Church (USA), 2002).

▲ Mission printing press at Luebo Station

grammar for the Bukuba dialect.[33] Ethel Wharton also translated the catechism and the Apostles' Creed into Bukuba and others helped produce a Bukuba hymnal. The John Leighton Wilson Press was printing Bible commentaries in Baluba-Lulua and Wharton wrote that "by 1935 the Baluba-Lulua speaking peoples were said to be provided with a literature in the vernacular unequalled by that of any other tribes in Africa."[34] The press was also filling mail orders for other protestant missions in the Belgian Congo.

Developing Church Structures

By the mid-1940s, ten mission stations had been established as smaller stations had been developed alongside the five full stations. In the 1930s, these smaller stations were primarily for evangelism and were referred to as "Gospel Centers;" they were devoted solely to evangelism and did not initially centre upon education and medical missions. However, as these smaller stations progressed, they too basically took the form of the older main stations by adding dispensaries, day schools, homes for boys and girls, and evangelism training centres. In 1944 there were 81 missionaries present in the APCM with a church membership of 50,000 in 1945.

The mid-1940s would begin another transitional phase as demographics were shifting; there was the need for a normal school; accreditation of the mission schools became an issue; and state subsidies, which started in 1948, were put in place. Thus, the post-World War Two period created much transition in the APCM.

The *stations* and *out-stations* were well structured into *districts* with so many villages arranged into out-stations with a *superintendent* appointed for each district who was responsible to help teachers, evangelists, and missionaries when they came to a district. Annual conferences of elders, teachers, and evangelists met at the various stations to discuss the respective ministries and also for inspiration. In essence, during the 1910s these conferences were like *"proto-presbytery"* meetings and in 1919 discussion took place in the Executive Committee of Foreign Missions PCUS about the formation of an African Presbytery in the Congo. In

---

33 Althea Edmiston, *Grammar and Dictionary of the Bushonga or Bukuba Language As Spoken by the Bushonga or Bukuba Tribe Who Dwell in Upper Kasai District, Belgian Congo, Central Africa*, (1932). A work of 619 pages.

34 Wharton, 141. See also Benedetto, "Presbyterian Mission Press in Central Africa," 61ff for discussion on Bukuba linguistic work.

1920 a Book of Church Order was printed by the John Leighton Wilson Press. By 1944, there were five *provisional* presbyteries basically arranged around the main stations. The post-WW2 years would see tension and development to move from "provisional" to "fully indigenous" and from "Mission" to "Church".

Three indigenous pastors were ordained in 1916: Kubeya Lukengu, a redeemed slave of the mission, who had first become a deacon, then an elder (one of the first five ordained in the mission) and teacher in Luebo, an evangelist and a superintendent, and then a pastor at Luboudai; Musonguela, a superintendent beyond Mutoto and pastor at Lusambo; and Kachunga, a redeemed slave and a translation helper for William Morrison, who became a pastor and then returned to the office of evangelist at Mutombo Katshi.[35] Other prominent indigenous leaders included the evangelists Tshisungu Daniel and Lumbala. Mabuluke/Tatu Mako became the agricultural director at the Morrison Bible School/Institut Morrison.

6. Postscript

In the Democratic Republic of the Congo post-1945, the APCM was integrated into the Presbyterian Church of Congo/Eglise Presbyterienne au Congo (EPC) in 1970 when all property was now owned by the indigenous Church, which was known as the Presbyterian Community in Congo (*Communauté Presbytérienne de Congo*, CPC) and the Presbyterian Community in Kinshasa (*Communauté Presbytérienne de Kinshasa*, CPK), within the Protestant umbrella organisation, the Church of Christ in Congo, CCC (*Eglise du Christ Au Congo*). This explains the unique use of the word *"communaute"* or "community" since each denomination is a community within the federated CCC. Today the main branches are the Presbyterian Community in Eastern Kasai, the Presbyterian Community in Western Kasai, and latterly the Reformed Community of Presbyterians all of which trace themselves back to the APCM.[36] There is also the Sheppard and Lapsley Presbyterian University of Congo, in Kananga (*Université Presbyterienne Sheppard et Lapsley du Congo*, UPRECO).[37] The roots of the university go back to

---

35 Bedinger, 124–127.
36 See, https://www.presbyterianmission.org/ministries/global/democratic-republic-congo/ accessed 9 August 2021 and https://en.wikipedia.org/wiki/Presbyterian_Community_in_Congo. James McGoldrick, *Presbyterian and Reformed Churches*. (Grand Rapids: Reformation Heritage, 2012), 421–423. Cogswell, 145–171, 229–235. Monique Misenga Ngoie Mukuna with Elsie Tshimunyi McKee, *Cradling Abundance* (Downers Grove, IL: IVP Academic, 2021), 79 for a most helpful explanation here of this idea of communities in the CCC, 79. For further details see, Isabel Apawo Phiri, "Presbyterian Churches in Africa," in *Anthology of African Christianity*, eds. Isabel Apawo Phiri & Dietrich Werner (Oxford: Regnum, 2016), 303.
37 http://media.jmcameron.net/media/docs/UPRECO_Brochure.pdf

the Bible School and in 1998 it became a university with two faculties, theology and law.

7. Conclusion

The APCM c.1890–c.1945 was a large mission work by one of the American Presbyterian branches, the Southern Presbyterian Church or PCUS. This was a unique mission as it combined both white and African American missionaries in this period of study. There are many references of a cordial working relationship between the two ethnically diverse American groups, yet there are also references that there were tensions and, over time, a lessening of the inclusion of African Americans. This is not surprising given the context in America and also from the Belgian government perspective.

Much sacrifice went into this mission with many dying while in service in the Congo and this must not be ignored; it is the price of Kingdom mission work. The mission clearly centred upon evangelistic work for the conversion of the native peoples to the Christian faith and also conducted itself upon the lines of a wholistic mission with education, literacy work, medical work and sounding the alarm against colonial abuses and injustices. Today the debate continues in missiology as to how to describe such a mission of evangelism and wholism or an integrated missional approach of evangelism, discipleship and service. Many would see the APCM as an example of integrated missions. It should be noted that although the APCM was clearly predominated by American personnel (most who were from the Southern States), there is more diversity than is often recognized. The APCM needed to recruit beyond its bounds. Thus Scots, English, Belgians, (including one Belgian who defected from the Catholic priesthood to the APCM),[38] Scandinavians, West Indians from St Kitts and Jamaica at various times were also serving in the APCM. This shows more complexity, including Moody Bible Institute, Chicago as a recruiting base for the APCM on occasion.

The APCM as an American mission needs to be studied comparatively next to the mission in South Africa initiated by the Scottish Societies and then carried on by the Free Church of Scotland, then the United Free Church of Scotland, and then the Church of Scotland. This would be a worthy study to compare the mission strategy and developments of these two tributaries, one Scottish and the other Southern American and the issue of integrated mission.

The development in linguistics for Tshikete, Bukuba, but, particularly for

---

38 Joseph Savels, a Belgian Roman Catholic priest, joined the APCM in 1918 and served until 1936. Some native evangelists also came over to the APCM from Roman Catholicism when Father Savels converted. See, Bedinger, 180–181. Savels married and his wife also served as a missionary in the APCM and died in the Congo.

Tshiluba, by the APCM was a very strong contribution by this mission in Central Africa. Many were involved with this work, both indigenous and missionary. The outstanding contribution of William Morrison for the Tshiluba language is most significant.

▲ Lapsley Memorial Church

Clearly the development of the APCM went hand-in-hand with the indigenous evangelists and teachers and pastors who were raised-up. This is a strong aspect of this mission's growth and enlargement from the main stations to so many out-stations and villages. By WW2 tensions between Mission and Church were clearly there and the post-WW2 years would see this mission undergo many changes.

Questions for study (fact type):
1. Name the first two missionaries sent out by the PCUS to serve in the American Presbyterian Congo Mission (APCM).
2. Where was the first mission station of the APCM and when was it established?
3. Various boys' and girls' homes were developed as part of the mission. What was the purpose of these homes?
4. Concerning printing:
   a) Who translated the Four Gospels and Acts into the Buluba-Lulua language? What year was this completed?
   b) What year was the entire translation of the Bible completed?
   c) Who produced the first hymnal in Buluba-Lulua? What year was this published?

Questions for study (reflection type):
1. "When the travel time out to Africa, the meetings along the way, and the engagements and explorations in the Lower Congo are put together, there was over thirteen months of informal mission preparation."
   From Section Three, sub-section "Providences" from this chapter, make a list of at least 7 providential meetings that were used to prepare and assist Sheppard and Lapsley for their part in the work in the Congo. Read 1 Corinthians 3:1-9. Explain how you can use the example of Sheppard and Lapsley as you serve in any leadership role in the church.
2. "The State imposed a quota of a maximum of 15 days for any missionary to remain in an African village." How was this state law used to develop indigenous leadership? Consider Paul's missionary methods in The Book of Acts. Read Acts 18:18-23. In what ways was his approach similar to the methods used in The Congo?

Select Bibliography

"Congo Miscellaneous Missionary Documents," One Box, 21 folders, plus books. Presbyterian Heritage Center, Montreat, NC.

"Guide to the American Presbyterian Congo Mission Records," RG432. Presbyterian Historical Society, Philadelphia, PA. A very helpful guide to the 91 boxes of archival material related to the APCM.

"William Sheppard Papers, Location 20.1 and Artifacts (Kuba Art Collection)." Hampton University Museum and Archives, Hampton, VA.

Bedinger, Robert Dabney. *Triumphs of the Gospel in the Belgian Congo.* Richmond, VA: Presbyterian Committee on Publications, 1920.

Benedetto, Robert, ed. *Presbyterian Reformers in Central Africa: A Documentary Account of the American Presbyterian Congo Mission and the Human Rights Struggle in the Congo, 1890–1918.* Studies in Christian Mission. Leiden: Brill, 1997.

Benedetto, Robert. "The Presbyterian Mission Press in Central Africa, 1890-1922." *American Presbyterians* 68:1 (1990), 55–69.

Cogswell, James A. *No Turning Back: A History of American Presbyterian Involvement in Sub-Saharan Africa,* 1833–2000. Xlibris, 2007.

Crane, William H. "Presbyterian Work in the Congo: a Historical Study of the Development of Mission and Church in the Kasai (1891–1959)." ThM thesis, Union Theological Seminary, Richmond, Virginia, 1960.

Dworkin, Ira. *Congo Love Song: African American Culture and the Crisis of the Colonial State.* Chapel Hill, NC: University of North Carolina Press, 2017.

Kiantandu, Mavumi-sa Makumunwa, "A Study of the Contribution of American Presbyterians to the Formation of the Church of Christ in Zaire with Special Reference to Indigenization, 1891-1960." ThD thesis, Union Theological Seminary in Virginia, 1978.

Lapsley, Samuel N. *Life and Letters of Samuel Norvell Lapsley, Missionary to the Congo Valley, West Africa, 1866–1892.* eds. R. A. Lapsley and James W. Lapsley. Richmond, VA: Whittet and Shepperson, 1893.

Sheppard, William H. *Presbyterian Pioneers in the Congo.* Richmond, VA: Presbyterian Committee of Publication, 1917.

Wharton, Ethel Taylor. *Led in Triumph: Sixty Years of Southern Presbyterian missions in the Belgian Congo.* Nashville: Board of World Missions, Presbyterian Church, 1952.

Bio Inset

William Henry Sheppard (1865–1927)

Barry Waugh

William Henry was born to William and Fannie Sheppard just west of the scenic Blue-Ridge Mountains in Waynesboro, Virginia, 8 March 1865. The Civil War would end in April leaving all the enslaved free from bondage but living in a racially segregated society. William described his parents as Presbyterians who emphasized the importance of prayer. Education was not easy for blacks to acquire in post-war Virginia, but William was tutored by sympathetic individuals who recognized his potential and prepared him for the Hampton Normal and Industrial Institute in 1880. Hampton was started to provide an education that combined academics with vocational training, and it included among its graduates Booker T. Washington. During the Hampton years William became interested in Africa as a mission field, and his seeds of gospel propagation were cultivated when the Hampton chaplain enlisted him to establish a Sunday school for poor children in a nearby village.

After graduation, William returned to Waynesboro and began the process for ordination to the ministry. His denomination, the Presbyterian Church in the United States (PCUS), sent him to the Tuscaloosa Theological Institute which had been established in 1875 to prepare black men for the ministry. While pursuing academics, he participated in worship leadership, local evangelism, and home visitation, but he was especially active praying for the infirm and homebound. After a time supplying a church in Montgomery, he was ordained pastor of the Harrison Street Presbyterian Church in Atlanta, 1887. The thought of missions was ever on his mind but despite persistent communications with the Foreign Missions Committee of the PCUS, its members would not send him to Africa without a white missionary. In 1890, a judge's son, Samuel N. Lapsley from Anniston, Alabama, was appointed with Sheppard to open a mission station in the Congo Free State. After all his preparation and experience, Sheppard was bound for Africa.

Sheppard and Lapsley embarked for England where they secured supplies in London and told people about their missionary plans. Ever since accounts of the explorations of missionary David Livingstone were published, Africa was a subject of great interest in Britain. Pith helmets and light-weight tropical attire packed for the voyage, they headed for the port of Banana in the Congo Free State arriving early in 1890. As their ship approached the docks, the missionaries marvelled at the great brown Congo River diffusing into the rich blue Pacific Ocean. The team journeyed hundreds of miles into the Kasai region to establish a mission station. As their work progressed, the two sent reports home for publication in their denomination's *The Missionary*. Their work generated considerable interest in the PCUS and among others sensitive to the need for African missions. Sheppard and Lapsley became good friends, but their association was short-lived. The climate, African diseases, and insects were especially difficult for Lapsley. Young, enthusiastic, and devoted to Christ, Samuel Lapsley died of fever in 1892.

In 1893 Sheppard left for furlough in the United States. While enroute he laid over in London and attended in June a meeting of the Royal Geographical Society where he became a fellow (a subscribing member). He continued to America to tour, lecture about his ministry, and more importantly for him personally, marry Lucy Gantt. Lucy was born in Tuscaloosa, February 21, 1867, to Eliza Gantt, whose husband had deserted her. Lucy entered Talladega College, which was a school for black Americans where she remained until graduation in 1886. She taught in a Birmingham school for six years. During a visit to Tuscaloosa she met William Sheppard while he was studying for the ministry. They soon were engaged but at the time William was ready to leave for Africa, so they delayed marriage until his furlough. The two were married in Jacksonville, 21 February 1894 and then set sail for Africa.

After an arduous journey the African American mission team (recruited by Sheppard while on furlough) which included not only the Sheppards but also Henry Hawkins, Lillian Thomas, and fifty-six-year-old Maria Fearing arrived at Luebo in the Kasai region. Lucy's teaching experience equipped her for operating a school. There was neither a building nor supplies, so she arranged for a facility and fabricated her own supplies. Because of dire medical needs among the people, she became a nurse and operated a make-shift hospital. The Sheppard's gospel work bore fruit in 1895 when an adolescent boy professed faith in Christ and became the first member of the Luebo Presbyterian Church. Then in quick succession six more boys joined him. As the Sheppards worked they struggled to have children. Their first baby, Miriam, lived only a few weeks, and their second child, Lucille, lived but eight months. Seven months after Lucille's death, on the anniversary of Miriam's birth, a third daughter, Wilhelmina, was born. Because of Lucy's exhaustion from work and the many dangers for young children, her colleagues suggested that she escort her daughter to America. Lucy returned to the States and was away nearly two years. Wilhelmina was entrusted to the care of some of William's relatives before Lucy returned to Africa.

In 1897 thirty-year-old William Morrison, a white man, joined Sheppard and the mission team. He arrived in Luebo sick with fever and was carried to the Sheppards' home to be nursed back to health. Together, the two missionaries toured the region, preaching, teaching, and caring for the sick. Shortly after

Morrison arrived, the Sheppards were blessed with their only son, William Lapsley Sheppard, who was also given an African name, Maxamalinge, for the Bakuba king. The mission team worked hard and saw the Lord harvest his own from the Congo people. In Ibanje, a village near Luebo, Lapsley Chapel had been built to seat 250, but it had to be replaced with a facility that seated 400. David Calhoun notes that as the Congo mission grew, the largest congregation of the PCUS was not in the United States but central Africa.

By the turn of the century soldiers under orders of King Leopold II of Belgium were plundering the Congo Free State for rubber. Rubber sap was processed for its elastomeric and sealing properties to waterproof materials and manufacture tires. The soldiers recruited the Zappo-Zap tribe to enforce Leopold's policies. The Zappo-Zaps enslaved other tribes and kept them in submission with brutality. Morrison and Sheppard decided to do something about the situation, so Sheppard took his Kodak camera (recently invented) and documented atrocities against the Congo people. One grizzly image shows eighty-one hands severed from the arms of the oppressed whose quotas of rubber were not met. Morrison and Sheppard made known the evils of Belgian oppression through their publication, *The Kassai Herald*, which was distributed by the PCUS. The General Assembly of the PCUS issued statements condemning Belgian abuses. Leopold's Kassai Rubber Company brought charges against the two missionaries contending that their campaign against it was fabricated and built on lies. The missionaries were tried in Leopoldville (currently Kinshasa) in September 1909. Two envoys were sent by President William H. Taft to represent the interests of the United States and support the missionaries. Because of a technicality, the charges against Morrison were dropped leaving Sheppard standing alone before the court. Having heard the case, the judge dismissed all charges and ordered the Kasai Rubber Company to pay court costs. It was a victory for the abused and enslaved people of Kassai that was achieved through investigation and exposure by Sheppard and Morrison. Unfortunately, the joy of the great victory would be quickly diminished for Sheppard.

▲ William & Lucy Sheppard and family

In 1910 the Sheppards returned to the States because they were concerned about the continued challenges of life in Africa, their health, and reuniting their family. But this was not the whole story. It was not made public, but the PCUS

Foreign Missions Committee met with Sheppard to investigate the charge that he committed adultery with a Congo woman. William was tearfully repentant but after a one-year suspension from the ministry, he confessed to relations with other women which in one case had resulted in a son named Shepete. The suspension was extended beyond a year until his presbytery was satisfied that his repentance was genuine. Lucy's considerable work with and love for William included a healthy portion of forgiveness.

During the time of William's suspension, the Sheppards resided in Virginia, but once he was restored in 1912, Rev. John Little recruited him to work with the black community in Louisville, Kentucky. Little began working as the superintendent of Grace and Hope Colored Mission in 1898 and would continue until his death in 1948. The mission had been in operation fourteen years when the congregation was organized 15 September 1912 with Sheppard becoming the pastor of Grace Presbyterian Church in the Smoketown district. In addition to Sheppard's pastoral work, he spoke to groups of children (his favourite audience) about Africa. He also wrote some Sunday School literature in a series titled, "True African Stories," which included stories such as *An African Daniel* and *A Little Robber Who Found a Great Treasure*. William continued ministry with Grace Church until he suffered a stroke and passed away 25 November 1927. The funeral was held in Second Presbyterian Church, Louisville, with a great crowd of both black and white mourners gathered to remember Sheppard. Lucy continued to serve at Grace Church and spoke to congregations about foreign and home mission work. She was also a government social worker for a number of years. In 1955, Lucy Gantt Sheppard passed away and was buried with William in Louisville Cemetery.

What is the missionary legacy of William Henry Sheppard? His book, *Presbyterian Pioneers in Congo*, recounts his work with Lapsley and then his continued ministry in the Congo Free State. When the Sheppards left Africa in 1910 the two mission stations in Luebo and Ibanje reported 6,847 communicant members gathering in 74 places for worship under the leadership of 15 ordained and non-ordained missionaries joined by 90 non-ordained nationals. Average attendance at services including adherents and communicant members was 23,200. It is really a remarkable legacy for the mission team and Sheppard as their faith and fortitude reached the Congo people with Christ's gospel. Great distances were involved as preaching stations were established and the challenges of witch doctors, superstitions, climate, cannibals, colonialism, disease, insects, and wildlife were overcome, as well as Sheppard's adultery, but in the end, he had enjoyed a fruitful life with Lucy among Congolese Africans and in Louisville with African Americans.

Select Bibliography

Archival material including photographs, correspondence, African art, and publications are available at Stillman College, Hampton University, and the Presbyterian Historical Society, Philadelphia, Pennsylvania.

Calhoun, David B. "William Henry Sheppard (1865–1927) and Lucy Gant Sheppard (1867–1940): Shepherd and shepherdess of his sheep." In *Swift and Beautiful: The Amazing Stories of Faithful Missionaries*. 109–128. Carlisle, PA: Banner of Truth, 2020.

Cater, Sarah, Mrs Roy M. Williams, and Mrs E. Guice Potter, Jr. eds. Introduction by J. Phillips Noble. *Four Presbyterian Pioneers in Congo: Samuel N. Lapsley, William H. Sheppard, Maria Fearing, and Lucy Gantt Sheppard*. Anniston: First Presbyterian Church, 1965.

Hendrick, John R., and Winifred K. Vass. "Sheppard, William H. and Lucy (Gantt)." In *BDCM*, ed. Gerald H. Anderson. Grand Rapids: William B. Eerdmans Publishing Company, 1998.

Lapsley, James W. *Life and Letters of Samuel Norvell Lapsley: Missionary to the Congo Valley, West Africa, 1866–1892*. Richmond: Whittet & Shepperson, 1893.

"Meetings of the Royal Geographical Society, Session 1892–93." *The Geographical Journal* 2 (August 1893): 182–183. Sheppard was a fellow 1893 to 1909.

Phipps, William E. *William Sheppard: Congo's African American Livingstone*. Louisville, KY: Geneva Press, 2002.

Sheppard, William H. *Presbyterian Pioneers in Congo*. With an introduction by S. H. Chester. Richmond: Presbyterian Committee of Publication, 1917.

Thompson, Ernest T. "When Black Missionaries Opened Africa." *Presbyterian Survey*, (June 1978): 24–25, 44–45; (July 1978): 26–27, 40–41.

Bio Insct

Joseph E. Phipps – Missionary to the Belgian Congo (1895–1908)

Mary Cloutier

Joseph E. Phipps stumbled drunkenly into a rescue mission in Scranton, Pennsylvania, one July night in 1892, and came to a saving knowledge of Jesus Christ. The mission offered meals, shelter and biblical counsel to men who were struggling with addiction and poverty. Until that night, "Joe Caffir" had been touring the United States with a traveling museum, performing African dances, and walking over broken glass and hot irons. After his conversion, Joe remained at the mission; he joined other converts in ministering among the needy and the fallen and visiting the sick in the poor neighbourhoods of Scranton.[39] He joined the Second Presbyterian Church of Scranton, whose pastor was impressed by his earnestness, humility and devotion to Bible study. Men in the church took a deep interest in his spiritual development. Early on, Joe communicated to them his fervent hope "of going to Africa to tell his people about Jesus."[40]

Joseph Phipps was born circa 1862 on the island of St. Kitts. He believed his grandfather was born in Central Africa and had been brought to the West Indies as a captive.[41] The family and community retained some memory of their ancestral languages and cultural distinctions, which likely drew Joe's heart toward the Belgian Congo.

Joe Phipps spent a full two years at Moody Bible Institute and was likely their first black student. After completing his course of study in summer 1894, he returned to St. Kitts. In a letter to Moody friends, he wrote:

> I am about to learn the carpenter's trade, which they told me is requisite in Africa to win the affections of the heathen … Meanwhile I am having open air services Sunday afternoons. The first meeting I had the Lord wonderfully blessed us; a good many raised their hands for prayer and determined by the help of God to live a Christian life. Please bear me

---

39 Biederwolf, Scrapbook, n.p.
40 Robinson, "An African Returned," 6.
41 Williams, *Black Americans*, 27, 96.

up in prayer daily for the outpouring of the Holy Spirit ... I am expecting to remain here for six or seven months before starting for Africa.⁴²

Joe Phipps was ordained by the Lackawanna Presbytery, and appointed by the Southern Presbyterian Board to serve in the Belgian Congo.⁴³ He was assigned to travel and work with Samuel Verner, a white man who had volunteered to go as a business manager.⁴⁴ Their ship docked in England, where the pair purchased clothing, cooking utensils, tools, food, camping gear and items for barter.⁴⁵ They set sail from Liverpool on 27 November 1895. Verner noted that the passengers, black and white, dined at the same table and enjoyed learning from one another. There were friendly boxing matches between African warriors and European men, and Verner had wished that Phipps would compete in these matches, as his impressive physical strength would have won respect for both Africa and the mission cause.

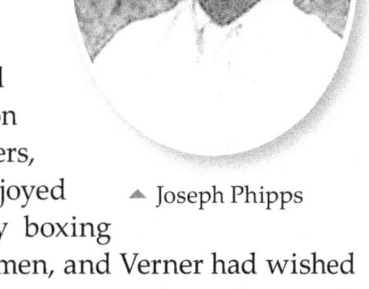

▲ Joseph Phipps

On Christmas night 1895, the captain, crew and passengers sang songs of their respective countries. For his turn, Joe sang in a sonorous bass voice, which rang out over the sea, some of the circus songs from his earlier days, followed by his favourite hymns.⁴⁶ During a stop in Batanga, Cameroon, Verner and Phipps met Presbyterian missionaries, including Dr Robert Hamill Nassau who had served thirty-five years in Africa. Nassau offered them wisdom and encouragement and expressed his approval that the Southern Presbyterian Mission was including black missionaries in their work.⁴⁷ Nassau had been disappointed when his own mission (Northern Presbyterian) had recently refused to appoint a young African American, Miss Mary McLeod, despite her superior training and preparation.⁴⁸

Verner and Phipps arrived at their destination 7 January 1896, joining a multi-mission community comprised of British, Dutch, Africans, and Americans, both black and white.⁴⁹ William Sheppard had recently returned with a wife, and two

---

42 "Notes," *Record*, 322.
43 Robinson, 6.
44 Verner, 7.
45 Phipps, 8.
46 Verner, 32.
47 Verner, 34.
48 Nassau, Letter dated 25 Dec 1895.
49 Verner, 103.

other African American women, Miss Thomas and Miss Fearing. They were joined by an African American named Henry Hawkins. All eventually located at the interior Luebo Mission.

The missionaries suffered through malarial fevers, each caring for the others, in turn.[50] Verner and Phipps witnessed murders, warfare, kidnapping and enslavement as they lived among the various tribes. Their own mission workers were either redeemed from slave-trafficking or in danger of capture at any given moment.[51] When Verner nearly died after falling into a game pit, his thigh pierced by a poisoned stake, Phipps and Hawkins nursed him through his pain and delirium, feeding him, weeping and praying for him. This caused the white missionary to renew his desire to serve the African people. As Verner was preparing to leave the Luebo mission, he noted Phipps' progress in learning the local language and winning the hearts of the people.[52]

Phipps, whom the people called *Fikisha*,[53] proved courageous and strong. He walked with difficulty, his leg disabled from malaria, yet he visited many towns and faced imminent dangers, and lived among the people. Verner was impressed with Joe's patient industry. He was often alone in the mission, and despite the many wars and dangers around him, he remained steady, without murmur or complaint. Joe was a man of simple faith. He prayed and expected answers to his prayers. He had a remarkable memory, was gifted in music and in drawing, and knowledgeable in tropical agriculture, which proved valuable. Phipps was a man of self-control, and even temper. He was consistently the same person, in all circumstances.[54]

In early 1901, Joe described his evangelistic work to friends at Moody:

> My co-laborer and I had a week's camp-meeting over here. When my turn came to speak, the Holy Spirit took hold of me, and the words went home to the hearts of the hearers. I also played on my little organ several hymns I had practiced by notes. The music lessons I took while at the B.I. [Moody Bible Institute] became a great help to me ... As a result of these meetings we baptized thirteen men and women. I have at present seventy in my catechumen class, learning the way of life."[55]

---

50 Verner, 189.
51 Verner, 233, 244.
52 Verner, 246, 249.
53 Benedetto, *Presbyterian Reformers*, 110.
54 Robinson, 6 (quoting Verner at length).
55 MBI, "From Foreign Fields," 174.

Joe Phipps would spend thirteen years in the Belgian Congo,[56] and was one of several black missionaries who helped translate hymns into the local language, a body of work later published.[57]

By 1906, there had been twenty-five missionaries serving with the Southern Presbyterian Mission in the Congo. Death and illness claimed nearly half of their number in the first fifteen years.[58]

Joe served during a time when the Belgian colonial powers increasingly displaced and blocked missionary presence in the Congo. Local kings and their villages sometimes sought protection and friendship with the foreign missionaries,[59] who spoke out against the oppression and atrocities committed by the Belgian authorities.

Joe Phipps was forty-four years of age when he resigned in 1908, following allegations of misconduct.[60] Colonial powers in Africa were tightening their restrictions on foreign black missionaries, fearing their influence on the local people. Joe Phipps sought re-appointment to Africa in several letters written during the 1920s but was not reappointed.[61]

In January 1914, Joe married a West Indian woman, Olivia Semper, in New York City. He served as a Presbyterian pastor and mission speaker for many years, notably at Saint James Presbyterian Church in Harlem. He died on 10 September 1935, at the age of 73, in New York City.

Bibliography

Benedetto, Robert, ed. *Presbyterian Reformers in Central Africa: A Documentary Account of the American Presbyterian Congo Mission and the Human Rights Struggle in the Congo, 1890–1918*. Leiden, Netherlands: Brill, 1997.

Biederwolf, W. E. Collection 195: Papers of William Biederwolf, Folder 1–7, Scrapbook. Billy Graham Center, Wheaton, IL.

Dworkin, Ira. *Congo Love Song: African American Culture and the Crisis of the Colonial State*. Chapel Hill: University of North Carolina Press, 2017.

Moody Bible Institute, "From Foreign Fields." *The Institute Tie* 1.6: 174.

---

56 Williams, 190.
57 Dworkin, *Congo Love Song*, 112.
58 Morrison, "The Story," 58.
59 Morrison, 133.
60 Morrison, 423.
61 Benedetto, 33.

Morrison, William. "The Story of Our Congo Mission" in *Presbyterian Reformers in Central Africa: A Documentary Account of the American Presbyterian Congo Mission and the Human Rights Struggle in the Congo, 1890–1918*, ed. Robert Benedetto. Leiden, Netherlands: Brill, 1997, 56–70.

N. A., "Notes for September." *Record of Christian Work* 13 (October 1894): 322.

Nassau, Robert Hamill. Letter to Dr. Gillespie, Board Secretary, dated 25 Dec. 1895. Africa Letters, Vol. 21, Reel 82, Microfilm Collection, Letter 321. Presbyterian Historical Society, Philadelphia.

Phipps, William E. *William Sheppard: Congo's African American Livingstone*. Louisville, KY: Geneva Press, 2002.

Robinson, Charles E. "An African Returned to Africa." *The Evangelist* 70.8 (1899):6.

Verner, Samuel Phillips. *Pioneering in Central Africa*. United States, Presbyterian Committee of Publication, 1903.

Williams, Walter M. *Black Americans and the Evangelization of Africa, 1877–1900*. Madison: University of Wisconsin Press, 1982.

Chapter 20

Part One: The Roots of The Presbyterian Church of East Africa: The East Africa Scottish Mission 1889–1901

Watson A. O. Omulokoli[1]

Chapter Outline: Part One
1. Introduction: Formation of The East Africa Scottish Mission
2. Initial Efforts at Kibwezi
3. Transfer of the Mission to Kikuyu
4. Progress Under Hardships
5. Handing Over to The Church of Scotland Mission

Chapter Outline: Part Two
1. Introduction: From the EASM to a Church Mission
2. David Clement Ruffelle Scott, a transitional phase: 1901–1907
3. Growth, Development, & Crisis: The Henry Scott and John William Arthur Years, 1907–1937
4. The Second Stream: The GMS and Union
5. Summary Conclusion
Bio Inset: Minnie Cumming Watson

1. Introduction: Formation of The East Africa Scottish Mission

The Presbyterian Church was not introduced to East Africa by the official church itself, but rather by a group of committed lay Christians who formed a private Christian body known as the East Africa Scottish Mission (EASM). In 1888, the Imperial British East Africa Company (IBEAC) was formed and given a Royal Charter by the British government to conduct trade and commerce in

---

[1] Reprinted with permission by the author from, "The Roots of the Presbyterian Church of East Africa," *Africa Journal of Evangelical Theology* 16.1 (1997), 59–66.

▲ Sir William Mackinnon monument (photo N. Whytock)

East Africa.² As the Company took control over the territory under its jurisdiction, some of its directors felt that they should also turn their attention to the spiritual and moral well-being of the people in the region. Among these were, Sir William Mackinnon, who was the chairman of the Company, Mr Alexander Low Bruce, who was a son-in-law of Dr David Livingstone, and Sir T. Fowell Buxton, from a renowned philanthropic family.³ With this in mind they formed a private Christian body in 1889 known as the East African Scottish Mission.⁴

The Mission was to work along comprehensive lines, combining evangelistic or spiritual, education, medical, and industrial elements. This was in tune with the thinking of Livingstone and others who believed that the best way of evangelising Africa was on the broad basis of Christianity, commerce, and civilization. The implementation of this kind of philosophy had proved successful at Lovedale and Blythswood in South Africa, as well as at Blantyre and Livingstonia in Malawi.⁵ It was in this connection that, when the Mission was looking for a suitable leader, its directors asked the Free Church of Scotland to release to them Dr James Stewart, the Principal of Lovedale, for one year to enable him to start the Mission's work in East Africa.

As the task of recruiting the missionary party went on, apart from Stewart, there was another person from the South African front. This was Dr Robert Unwin Moffat, a grandson and a namesake of the famed missionary to the Batswana in South Africa, Robert Moffat. Together with these two, there was also a group of four people from Britain. These were, Thomas Watson as evangelist, John Linton as carpenter, John Grieg as engineer, and Cornelius Rahman as storekeeper. The two groups converged at Mombasa, and, together with George Wilson,

---

2   C. P. Groves, *The planting of Christianity in Africa. Volume Three, 1878–1914* (London: Lutterworth Press, 1964), 26.
3   Roland Oliver, *The Missionary Factor in East Africa*, 170. Mrs Henry E. Scott, *A Saint in Kenya: A Life of Marion Scott Stevenson*, 58, includes the name of Peter Mackinnon.
4   Robert Macpherson, *The Presbyterian Church in Kenya,* 21. Note: For much of the work, I have relied heavily, but not exclusively, on Macpherson.
5   C. P. Groves, 88. Mackay refers to this as the approach which takes care of the hand, head, and heart.

an employee of the Company as guide, they eventually left for the interior on 19th September 1891. Their instructions then were that they should establish the first mission station at Dagoretti, a place where the Company had set up an outpost which George Wilson had evacuated in early 1891, after about one year of existence.

▲ Original Expedition at Mombasa, September 1891

2. Initial Efforts at Kibwezi

Contrary to the wishes and instructions of the directors of the Mission, Stewart seemed to have decided early against Dagoretti[6] and instead opted for an alternate site among the Kamba. Eventually, because of adverse reports at that time about the situation at Dagoretti, and since, on the surface, Kibwezi seemed to be the most suitable option, after the missionary party had stopped there for some time, Stewart decided to establish the first mission station at Kibwezi. Located on the Maasai-Kamba border, and about 200 miles from the coast, Kibwezi looked attractive when the group arrived there and made the decision on it in December 1891. Soon, an agreement was reached in which the Mission purchased 300 acres of land there from Kilungu, the chief of the area.

Once the group had settled on Kibwezi as the right choice, the process of opening up the mission station began in earnest with the construction of the required buildings. These facilities included houses, stores, cowsheds, a dispensary, and a church. One of the highlights of this early period was the completion of the construction of a church, which was duly opened in a special service on 10th March 1892. It was after this first crucial landmark that Stewart went to Scotland on leave that month, leaving behind Dr Moffat to be in charge of the work of the Mission.

While the work of establishing the Mission station at Kibwezi was going on, the Mission began to experience losses in the personnel sphere. First, in the very

---

6   Horace R. A. Philip, A *New Day In Kenya* (London: World Dominion Press, 1936), 15.

initial days, John Grieg died of dysentery on 18th December 1891. Then in March 1892, Stewart went on furlough, and from there, relocated to his base in South Africa. This bad situation changed drastically for the worse in that after the personnel losses of the period of June 1892 to January 1893, Thomas Watson was the only person left in the work of the Mission. We learn that

> In June, Rebman seems to have had some sort of breakdown and had to be repatriated. John Linton fell ill and remained ailing for the rest of the year. George Wilson, having completed his assignment as guide, took charge of work on the Mombasa-Kibwezi road. In December, Dr Moffat resigned to join Sir Gerald Portal's expedition to Uganda. In January,1893, Linton died. Watson was now, after only 13 months, the sole survivor at Kibwezi of the original missionary party [7]

At the end of January 1893, Watson was the lone missionary at Kibwezi. This state of affairs changed when three new people arrived within the next twelve months. First, on 15th March 1893, a medical man, Dr David Charters, and a gardener, Mr John Paterson arrived as new recruits. Then on 12th January 1894, a teacher, Victor Hill, and his wife joined the missionary team.

At the mission station, progress picked up in a number of directions. After some experiments in brick making, a brick dormitory was erected. With time, brick making became an established feature of the station's development, and in turn, this facilitated the building of many more permanent houses. In the agricultural sphere, Paterson's skills and competence were soon demonstrated as Kibwezi increasingly took on the picture of a thriving garden. With experiments in farming grapes and coffee, by 1896, the Mission was able to supply coffee seed for planting to two European farmers around Nairobi.[8] All the while evangelistic activities were being promoted as well.

When the personnel situation appeared to be stable and the work at Kibwezi running smoothly, Watson traveled to the upper areas of Ukambani where he opened a new station at Nzoi in 1894. In this same year, however, two setbacks were experienced. To begin with, Dr Charters, together with a guest, went on a hunting trip near Kibwezi but never came back, possibly killed by the Maasai or wild animals. [9] Next, in December 1894, the Hills resigned on account of ill-health and returned home. When Charters disappeared, Watson was forced to

---

7 Robert Macpherson, 25.
8 C. P. Groves, 223. Paterson introduced the growing of the coffee crop in Kenya.
9 H. R. A. Philip, 16.

abandon the new station at Nzoi and return to Kibwezi to take charge of the work there.

With the reduction in the missionary task force, which had been experienced in 1894, it was truly encouraging when a medical person, Dr Matthew Wilson, and a carpenter, Mr James Lundie, arrived as new reinforcements in April 1895. This restored the stability which was needed in the personnel level at Kibwezi. This same year, 1895, Watson and Dr Wilson made an exploratory visit to Dagoretti with a view to gauging its suitability as the central station of the Mission. Their assessment was positive, and after discussion with the rest of the missionary team at Kibwezi, it was agreed upon that it was important and urgent that the field headquarters of the Mission should be relocated from Kibwezi to Dagoretti. It was resolved, however, that implementation should wait until Watson was able to go home on furlough, during which period he would present to the Mission directors in Edinburgh the case for moving the main station from Kibwezi to Dagoretti.

Watson was not able to leave for Britain until June 1896, and remained there for about fifteen months, arriving back at Kibwezi on 24th October 1897. While in Scotland, he had been involved in a number of significant developments on behalf of the Mission. First, he had been ordained as a minister in the Free Church of Scotland. Secondly, he had assisted in inspiring the Mission's directing committee at home to capture a fresh vision for the work in East Africa. Since the death in 1893 of two key directors of the Mission, Mackinnon and Bruce, the Mission had suffered from lack of effective leadership. In the reorganisation which ensued, the committee received a new lease of life. Through this rejuvenation, for the first time, a code of regulations was issued, and 40,000 pounds was raised in the form of an endowment trust. Thirdly, and lastly, Watson was given permission by the committee to transfer the central station of the Mission from Kibwezi to Kikuyu, upon his return to Kenya.

3. Transfer of The Mission to Kikuyu

Watson returned from his furlough in Britain on 24th October 1897 and joined Paterson, Lundie, and Dr Wilson at Kibwezi. Three days later, on 27th October, he began making arrangements aimed at setting up the central station of the Mission at Kikuyu. First, he went to see the Commissioner-General of the Protectorate at Machakos, where the latter was then on a visit from his base in Mombasa. Next, he went to Kikuyu to hammer out some agreements with the local leaders. Although Watson had preferred a particular site near the Company's former fort at Dagoretti, the leader of the local clan, Munyua, a son of Waiyaki, offered him land at neighbouring Baraniki instead. It was on 2nd December 1897, when Watson left Kikuyu, returned to Kibwezi, and from there proceeded to Mombasa to secure final authority from the government to acquire the site at Baraniki as offered by Munyua.

Getting approval from the government took long. When it had been finally granted, Watson left Kibwezi on 29th February 1898, to open a station at Baraniki.[10] He was joined there by Dr Wilson on 30th March. In the meantime, the piece of land purchased from Munyua, and the necessary stamp duty requirements from the government were fulfilled. As they cleared the land, they also began the construction of buildings. Then on Sunday, 10th April, they began holding English services in Fort Smith.

In December 1897, Paterson had gone on leave. On the very day on which English services commenced at Fort Smith, news had come to Baraniki that Lundie, at Kibwezi, was sick from black water fever. Dr Wilson went to attend to him at Kibwezi before proceeding to Mombasa to recruit some Swahili workers for various tasks. As it turned out, on his way back from Mombasa, Dr Wilson himself died at Mtito Andei on 8th June 1898, of black water fever. Watson was forced back to Kibwezi in June and when Lundie's health continued to deteriorate he repatriated him to Britain on 11th July. This meant that as had happened in January 1893, Watson was alone again in July 1898, but now, with two stations to take care of. In the midst of this predicament, he evacuated the Kibwezi station on 27th August 1898, and returned to Kikuyu.

Following his closure of Kibwezi on 28th August 1898, Watson settled at Baraniki where he began making progress in his work. It was here that he was joined on 7th January 1899 by two missionaries, Paterson, who was returning from leave, and Alexander Walker, a carpenter who accompanied Paterson. An additional missionary, arrived on 27th February, in the person of a medical man, Dr Homer. It was not long after his arrival that Dr Homer disapproved of Baraniki as being an unhealthy location not suitable for the main station of the Mission. This eventually resulted in the relocation to the present site at Thogoto where thirty acres of land was purchased on 20th July 1899, with a further ten acres bought in the following year. With this done, the construction of permanent mission buildings was embarked upon, facilitated by the availability of strong quarry stone on one hand, and the success in endeavours in brick-making on the other. When Thogoto was opened, however, Baraniki was not closed as Paterson remained there, continuing with his agricultural projects.

---

10 Robert Macpherson, 27. This marks the actual moving to the Kikuyu area and not August when Watson merely returned there after evacuating Kibwezi. See, H. R. A. Philip, 17.

4. Progress Under Hardships

There was wide-spread drought in the entire region in the last three years of the 1890's. In the case of Kikuyu and its vicinity, this was accompanied by famine, rinderpest, and smallpox. These caused much havoc among the population and drove the mission to devising ways and means of dealing with this crisis. Because of the complications which smallpox had contributed to the combined difficulties, it was estimated that by April 1900, about 50% of the population at Kikuyu had died. An appeal for famine relief was made to the directors of the Mission in Scotland. When the financial assistance for this purpose was released towards the end of 1899, those on the actual scene set up a famine relief camp at Thogoto on 8th January 1900, under Watson, with another one at Baraniki, operated by Paterson and Walker.

▲ Thomas Watson

The tragedies of drought, famine, rinderpest and smallpox not only issued in famine relief on the part of the Mission, but also provided opportunities for assisting the surrounding community in other ways. At one level, in May 1900, Mrs Watson started a day school for refugee children, and in another direction, an evening school was set up to serve the young men who were workers in the mission in the daytime.[11] This laid the foundation for the educational work of the Church, which was to prove to be a very significant facet of its endeavours in later years. While all this was going on, the English Sunday services which Watson had started in 1898 at Fort Smith were maintained. Then, when normalcy returned after the years of struggle under drought, famine, and disease, Sunday services in Kiswahili were started at Thogoto on 19th August 1900. With the confidence of the local Kikuyu people having been gained, the Mission seemed to be set on a path of progress and prosperity.

These bright prospects were, however, jolted by crucial occurrences on the personnel scene in 1900. Earlier, Watson had travelled to Mombasa where he had married Minnie Cumming on 18th December 1899, at the Church Missionary Society (CMS) church at the Freretown mission station. In the latter part of 1900, Dr Homer resigned in September, then Walker had to be repatriated home, and finally, a tired and worn-out Watson succumbed to an attack of pneumonia, dying on 4th December 1900 almost a year after his wedding. This signified the end of an era.

---

11 Mrs Henry E. Scott, 59.

Watson's death in December 1900 left two people in the work of the Mission. One of these was John Paterson who continued with his agricultural activities at Baraniki, where he had remained and retained when Thogoto was opened as the main station. The other one was Watson's wife, Minnie, widowed after only one year of marriage. She took overall charge of Thogoto, running the two schools, one for refugee children during the day and the other one in the evenings for the young men working in the mission station. She even went on to ensure that the quarrying of stones continued, convinced that they would be needed for building in the near future.

With the death of Watson, the Mission had reached a crucial turning point in its life. In the past, even when the missionary force decreased, Watson was always there as the constant factor from the inception of the Mission. With the disappearance of that main chain of continuity, very significant steps needed to be taken to propel the Mission beyond that moment of loss and deprivation.

5. Handing Over to The Church of Scotland Mission

The East Africa Scottish Mission had been founded in 1889 as a private venture by a group of concerned Christians. Although it had experienced a slump after two of its key directors died in 1893, it had sprung up to new vigour following Watson's encouragement during his furlough in 1896–1897. It was providential that even before his death towards the end of 1900, negotiations had been underway for the directors of the Mission to hand it over to the Church of Scotland to administer its work. With his death, the tempo for this take-over was accelerated.

Indeed, on 15th December 1900, less than two weeks after his death, the directors formally approached the Foreign Mission Committee (FMC) of the Church of Scotland on this matter. Although there was a long transitional period in which the details were being worked out, the basic framework of the agreement between the two parties had been reached by 21st April 1901. It was understood that the Mission would hand over all assets and endowments, and that the Church in turn, would fully take over the work of the Mission in East Africa. When these steps were taken and the changes effected, the Church of Scotland Mission (CSM) took over from the East Africa Scottish Mission (EASM) in 1901.[12]

---

12 (Mrs) Henry E. Scott, 60. Although the handing over was agreed upon in 1901, the process was not actually completed until 1907.

Questions for study (fact type):
1. a) What was the first station of the EASM? b) Why was this station transferred and to where was it transferred?
2. Who was the longest serving missionary with the EASM?

Questions for study (reflection type):
1. Discuss the difficulties experienced from sub-section four above. Also relate this to the Christian life and struggles and challenges that the believer faces in light of some forms of modern Christianity which emphasize health and wealth.
2. Discuss and evaluate where EASM fits in the spectrum of Christian missions as an entity.

Select Bibliography

East Africa Scottish Mission Reports, Reports I–V. Glasgow, 1892–1901.

Kikuyu: 1898–1923: Semi-Jubilee Book of the Church of Scotland Mission, Kenya Colony. Edinburgh: William Blackwood/FMCCoS 1923.

Macpherson, Robert. *The Presbyterian Church in Kenya.* Nairobi: Presbyterian Church of East Africa, 1970.

McIntosh, Brian G. "The Scottish Mission in Kenya, 1891–1923." PhD thesis, University of Edinburgh, 1969.

Oliver, Roland. *The Missionary Factor in East Africa.* London: Longmans Green & Co., 1952.

Scott, Mrs Henry E. *A Saint in Kenya: A Life of Marion Scott Stevenson.* London: Hodder and Stoughton, 1932.

Wells, James. *Stewart of Lovedale: The Life of James Stewart.* Second Edition. London: Hodder & Stoughton, 1909. See chapter 23, "The Pioneer of the East African Mission, 1891–1892," 231–241.

Part Two: Presbyterian Developments in Kenya, c.1901 to 1946

J. C. Whytock

1. Introduction: From the EASM to a Church Mission

The EASM did not align with either the FCS prior to 1900 or with the UFCS in 1901 but rather aligned itself with the CoS as Watson Omulokoli stated at the end of Part One. The EASM as originally constituted was an *evangelical, "undenominational," Westminster Confession of Faith, Presbyterian Mission* and reaffirmed such as it revived its efforts in the mid-1890s.[13] It thus made for a most unique mission undertaking in Africa. James Stewart, the key pioneer leader, was FCS as was Thomas Watson, the sole missionary, who really kept continuity for this mission during its term under the EASM.[14] Today it seems puzzling why the EASM did not align with either the FCS or the UFCS and the answer seems chiefly to be due to Sir William Mackinnon's vision and also his growing dissatisfaction with ecclesiastical trajectories in the FCS in the 1890s.[15] There is a debate as to whether the EASM ever really offered itself to the UFCS as there is no evidence in board minutes to this effect.[16] Following Mackinnon's death in 1893, Mackinnon's vision was maintained by the EASM trustees that the EASM remain an independent mission.

However, with Thomas Watson's death in December 1900, a personnel crisis faced the EASM. Since the CoS mission in Blantyre was well known, it was the CoS to whom the EASM turned and not the UFCS (even though the UFCS had noted missions at Livingstonia, Calabar, and South Africa and James Stewart had been their pioneering leader who was now UFCS). After 1894, Stewart had abandoned his connection with the EASM when it did not come under the FCS.[17] Yet curiously, in 1897 the Committee of the EASM organised a set of rules for

---

13 McIntosh, 54, 141.
14 Watson was ordained by the FCS for mission work with the EASM, and Stewart in April 1891 was endorsed by the FMC of the FCS to proceed to work temporarily with the EASM. McIntosh, 57. The *Annals*, Volume 1, omit Thomas Watson.
15 McIntosh, 19. Mackinnon cancelled by a codicil his bequests just a few months before he died to the FCS. Macpherson, *Presbyterian Church in Kenya*, does not discuss this question, 32–33.
16 McIntosh, 153, and Wells, 239.
17 McIntosh, 136.

its mission modelled after the FCS Livingstonia Mission.[18] So it is a somewhat puzzling question about how the EASM joined with the CoS.

There is perhaps another factor, and this was the CoS had a missionary, David Clement Scott, from Blantyre whom they needed to place somewhere immediately. He had been home in Scotland on furlough since 1898. The issues here were over the Scoto-Catholic liturgical practices of Scott and mounting dissatisfaction with David Scott's autocratic leadership where some saw him more as a bishop.[19] Thus he was not allowed to return to the Blantyre field. The EASM presented a field upon which to the CoS they could place Scott immediately and resolve their dilemma in this matter. They accepted the new field offered by the EASM and were pleased because there was also no obligation of finances by the CoS. That of course within a short time would be far from the case but all initially looked like a way which was a solution for all parties.

2. David Clement Ruffelle Scott, a transitional phase: 1901–1907

David Clement Ruffelle Scott[20] (1853–1907) was appointed the superintendent of the CoS's newly acquired EASM field in 1901. His main focus would be agricultural missions during his superintendency rather than direct evangelism or education, both of which of course still continued to be done more indirectly.[21] By the time of his death, he had 3,000 acres under cultivation with a native workforce at Thogoto (Kikuyu[22]). His vision was to see the development of a self-sustaining commercial station and the workers in this mission would then reach the local people with the Gospel and continue to develop ten more self-sustaining stations northward to Abyssinia. His approach was punctuated with financial woes not necessarily all of his own doing, whereby more land was acquired and

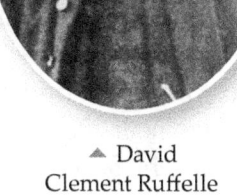

▲ David Clement Ruffelle Scott

---

18 McIntosh, 143.
19 McIntosh, 132, 156, 171.
20 See chapter 15, section 4, in this volume on D. C. Scott and Blantyre. Also, Todd Statham, "Scott, David Clement," *DACB*, https://dacb.org/stories/malawi/scott-davidc/
21 See, Macpherson, *Presbyterian Church in Kenya*, 34 "Scott's conception of a Christian mission in Africa coincided with that of the trust laid down by the original East Africa Scottish Mission and, from the day of his arrival in Kikuyu, he set about translating the vision into fact on a grand scale."
22 English generally uses the spelling as Kikuyu. Today some also use the non-Anglicised form, Gĩkũyũ. Unless quoted the period form will generally be used.

placed under cultivation to make profit by growing potatoes which would be shipped to markets in South Africa.[23] This way he could help *extend the missions work* since the Endowment Fund from the EASM only paid salaries of missionaries and there was little money left over to actually extend mission work. Thus, Scott's effort at acquiring land and growing potatoes was his attempt to find a creative solution to this problem as the CoS did not at that time give any additional funds to the mission.

After Scott's death, the CSM was determined to focus the mission's course directly to that of evangelism and education rather than the land/agricultural focus which was paralleled by the growing settler migration to East Africa.

The missionary personnel in 1901 and 1902 were Mrs Minnie Cumming Watson and John Paterson who continued on from the EASM and were augmented with new CSM missionaries Mr and Mrs William Fraser and Dr Karl Uffmann during the beginning of Scott's superintendency. It was under Scott's superintendency that transitional matters were accomplished from the EASM to the CSM especially on resolving endowment matters.

The CSM was facing criticism that the mission in Kikuyu was not advancing spiritually or materially during these initial years under David Clement Scott. Two CoS clergy missionaries visited the Kikuyu Mission from the Blantyre Mission and each gave reports to the FMC back in Scotland. These reports were critical of Scott and his vision. With Scott's death in October 1907, the mission commenced the next phase of the Kikuyu mission work when Rev. Henry Scott was appointed superintendent.

Yet before leaving David Clement Scott, there is one fact which must be stated. Shortly before he died, he baptised the first Kikuyu convert of the CMS, Filipo Karunja. The baptism took place from Scott's bed. Karanja was to become the first catechist in the mission.[24] This was followed only a few weeks later by the second baptism of chief Muleu, who was baptised by Dr Arthur in the absence of any ordained minister at the time since Dr Scott had just died. Muleu died on 16 November 1907 and was the second baptised convert of the mission.[25]

Clement Scott's leadership of six years of the CSM has many challenging aspects when we attempt an evaluation. His efforts to deal with the difficult financial constraints imposed at that time through his scheme for self-sustainable mission extension work will not be the only time this will be attempted. He must be viewed from a longer-range lens.

---

23 McIntosh, 169–170, 175.
24 Minnie Cumming Watson. https://www.europeansineastafrica.co.uk/ Accessed 31 January 2023.
25 *Kikuyu:1898–1923*, 37.

3. Growth, Development & Crisis: The Henry Scott and John William Arthur Years, 1907–1937

Mission Focus "Redirected"

From 1907 to 1937 under the superintendencies of Henry Scott and John Arthur the CSM was, in the words of Brain McIntosh, "redirected in its objective."[26] The emphasis was to establish a key missionary training institution at the central Kikuyu station and then the development of out-stations and to focus on evangelism and education, schools being the effective agency of evangelism.[27] Henry Scott saw the need to establish a boarding school at the main station as one of the most effective ways of training youth rather than having them working on the agricultural estate and going to school part of the day, as had been the practice under Clement Scott.

▲ Henry E. Scott

Overall, the period under Henry Scott and John Arthur was a period of growth and development for the CSM in education, evangelism, medical mission work, linguistics, church and mission ecumenism or co-operation, church planting, indigenous leadership, and organisation. It was also a period of many challenges and controversies. Two in particular need to be highlighted: circumcision and also the best way forward to develop church governance in the CSM, intertwined in part with the settler community and a separate church structure, something which would continue to be a matter for resolution after the second world war.

Kikuyu Mission Council

Under Clement Scott local mission governance was a very informal conference and really centred power in the superintendent. This was to change in 1907 when a monthly missionary staff *conference* was to be held. This evolved into a *Mission Council* eventually taking the formal name *Kikuyu Mission Council*. However, this Council was not open to all as implemented by Henry Scott. Artisan missionaries were not members of the Council unless they had served for many years. It was an unusual arrangement, and the Council was technically appointed by the FMC of the CoS. Criticisms of being undemocratic were often

---

26 McIntosh, i.
27 McIntosh, 196; Henry Scott's vision was, "Kikuyu should be to East Africa what Lovedale is to South Africa, and what Blantyre and Livingstonia are to British Central Africa." Quoted in J. Du Plessis, *The Evangelisation of Pagan Africa* (Cape Town: J. C. Juta, 1929), 329.

levelled at the Council. It was not until after 1932 that the Council arrangement in the CSM was changed to be in parallel with the Councils on the other now-merged CoS mission fields following the 1929 union with the UFCS when all missionaries were then made members of the Council.[28]

Kikuyu Sub-Committee in Scotland

Administratively from 1907 to 1936 the CSM was under the FMC but in an unequal way as the CoS did not directly fund this mission during these years. A special sub-committee, the *Kikuyu Sub-Committee*, of subscribers and members selected from the FMC existed to raise funds for this mission field and for administration.[29] In addition there was a *Glasgow Auxiliary Committee* which also raised funds for the CSM which was convened by John Arthur's father, a noted Glasgow merchant. The Kikuyu Sub-Committee was abolished in 1936. Finally post-1936, the CoS assumed the same financial responsibility for this field as its other foreign fields.

Kikuyu News

To increase awareness of the CSM Henry Scott devised a periodical in 1908 called *Kikuyu News*. The periodical was highly successful in finding subscribers, new donors and bringing in funds for mission projects in British East Africa back in Scotland. Students were sponsored for schooling, beds were sponsored for the mission hospital, church buildings were subscribed, and boys' brigade units sponsored.[30] This periodical was of great value especially through to 1936 when the above-mentioned financial arrangements were changed for this mission.

Medical Mission Advances

The EASM had begun with the inclusion of one medical missionary, Dr Robert U. Moffat, in its original party and then was followed by others: David Charters, Matthew Wilson and Thomas Homer. When it became CSM, Dr Karl Ulmann joined the team. In January 1907 Dr John William Arthur (1881–1952) came to be the new CSM medical missionary. Arthur had studied medicine at the University of Glasgow and had gained valuable medical experience on a shipping vessel with voyages to Calcutta. Just shortly before Clement Scott died, he laid the foundation stone on 8 January 1908 for the new Hunter Memorial Hospital in Kikuyu of which Dr Arthur would be in charge.[31]

---

28 McIntosh, 209–211.
29 McIntosh, 201.
30 McIntosh, 203–205.
31 *Fasti Eccelesiae Scoticanae*, vol. 7, 705; *Kikuyu: 1898–1923*, 39.

Arthur would be a key Church of Scotland missionary and eventual superintendent in 1912 after Henry Scott's death in 1911. Initially appointed as a medical missionary, Arthur was then ordained a CoS minister in 1915 and would transition into more administration and church work.

Arthur planned and supervised the development of the first hospital in 1907 in Kikuyu and was both rigorous in medical work and in evangelistic work and education. Arthur held the position of missionary chair/superintendent until 1937 when he returned to Scotland.

Tumutumu Station, 1908

Starting in 1908, two African teacher-catechists, Peter Mugo and Daniel Wachira, were sent to Tumutumu to start a second central mission station. They developed a school which when Arthur Barlow arrived the next year had 25 boys.[32] This work was expanded in 1912 with the addition of a girls' school when Marian Stevenson (1871–1930) who had been serving with the CSM at Thoguto since 1907 was transferred in 1912 to Tumutumu in the Mt. Kenya area. This school grew into the Tumutumu Girls' High School. Stevenson's work brought her into direct contact with young girls and the issue of female circumcision (now referred to as FGM). In 1929 she coined the nomenclature of "sexual mutilation of women" for FGM. This issue was to be one of the key controversies during the leadership period under Dr John Arthur and the CSM.

Chogoria Station 1922

The CSM desired a station at Chogoria but it was a long time in coming. Part of this was the comity agreements which were made by the various Protestant Missions in British East Africa (BEA). This was a time of working through comity agreements by the various Protestant missions working in British East Africa. Much spade work had been done prior to 1922 in nearby Chuka and Gaitungi where at the latter location in 1915 Daudi Makumi a teacher-evangelist and a medical assistant, Samsoni Njoroge were sent and established a school. This spade work was for one year and with periodic visits afterwards between 1916 and 1921.[33]

The Chogoria station was advanced in 1922 when Dr Clive Irvine (1893–1974) was appointed the CMS missionary there. Irvine was pledged funding for five years from his father-in-law, Ernest Carr of *Carr's Biscuits*. A central school was built, and several out-schools established staffed by native assistants. A hospital

---

32 McIntosh, 255.
33 *Kikuyu: 1898–1923*, 45.

was established which eventually had several wards and an operating theatre. Dr Irvine was much more than a medical missionary; he was a noted evangelist and minister and also a supporter of the East Africa Revival Movement (EARM). This led to extensive growth in the church around Chogoria in the 1940s.[34]

In 1932 the first elders were ordained at Chogoria: Gerishom Mukaugu, Jonathan Muriithi, Musa M'Muga and Willie Kanini. Elders usually taught at out-schools and served as evangelists in the out station or would be appointed elsewhere.[35]

United Missionary Conferences and early ecumenism

In 1909 Henry Scott organised and chaired the first united missions conference with representatives from eight missionary bodies participating: CSM, AIM, CMS, GSM, United Methodist Mission, Friends African Industrial Mission, English Friends Industrial Mission, and the Seventh Day Adventist Mission. As was predictable, church union would be slowed down over the issue of the historic episcopate. However, it was a time for sharing common missionary problems and working towards united areas of action or activity.[36] A possible federation of the missions was discussed and was less offensive than union yet still really a hill too high to climb for most. Henry Scott was really the chief leader of this early ecumenical venture and its visionary. He drafted papers about a United Native Church and also a *Federation of Missions*. Discussions carried on after Henry's death, but it ended in controversy and no federation or union. There were also hints of underlying differing views of Scripture.[37]

The next stage of these early ecumenical mission ventures was the formation in 1918 of the *Alliance of Protestant Missions* which was a way for the Protestant missions to work cooperatively on specific projects or areas of common ministry.[38] This would gain ground in the 1920s with the Alliance High School (see below).

---

34 Alison Wilkinson, "The Heritage of Chogoria," *Life and Work* (October 2022), 32–33.
35 Elders of the Church at Chogoria,
   https://calisphere.org/item/3d49540bd2197912c985095da815ffda/;
   Chuka Outschool 1929. https://calisphere.org/item/699eb391cac03c23a7626f283bf165ea/
36 McIntosh, 280–281.
37 McIntosh, 292. No doubt a reference in some way to the merging modernist-fundamentalist controversy.
38 For a helpful overview see, Kevin Ward, "The Kenyan Alliance of Protestant Missions 1919–1963: Ecumenism Adrift in a Colonial Society," in *Costly Communion* (Leiden: Brill, 2019), 260–280; and Du Plessis, *Evangelisation of Pagan Africa*, 347–349.

Organisational Development 1920

In 1920 a key stage in organisational development occurred with the CSM in East Africa as authorised by the GA of the CoS in 1918. This was the establishment of the Presbytery of Kenya Colony, also sometimes referred to as the Presbytery of British East Africa, in September 1920 by the newly ordained elders of Kikuyu and the session of St. Andrew's. The first native elders were ordained in September 1920 for Kikuyu and Tumutumu (see chart). The first three parish sessions were at Kikuyu, at Tumutumu, and at St. Andrew's, Nairobi. The establishment of the *Presbytery of Kenya Colony* was constituted the same year Kenya officially became a colony of Britain on 23 July 1920 and no longer a protectorate.

In 1943 the name Presbyterian Church in East Africa was adopted when a second presbytery was added. Then in 1946 a third presbytery would be added through the GMS (see section 4).

Some early publications of which the CSM was involved:

Ũhoro *Mwega wa Mũathani Wita Yesu Kristo ta ũrĩa watemiruo marũa nĩ Marko* (Mark in Kikuyu, tentative edition). Trans. A. R. Barlow. Edinburgh: NBSS,1909.

Ũyũ nĩ Ũhoro *Mwega ũrĩa WaandĩKirũo nĩ Marko* [St. Mark's Gospel in Kikuyu]. Revised by A. R. Barlow. Revised Edition. London: NBSS/BFBS, 1917.

Haro ya Maundu ma Ngai. Nairobi: Church of Scotland British East Africa Mission, 1908.

Kabuku ya kuurania. Thogoto: CSM British East Africa Mission, 1919.

A. R. Barlow, *Tentative Studies in Kikuyu grammar and idiom*. Edinburgh: W. Blackwood, 1914. This work was revised over the years:

Tentative Studies in Kikuyu grammar and idiom. Revised edition. Edinburgh: Blackwood, 1931,

Studies in Kikuyu grammar and idiom. Revised edition. Edinburgh: FMC CoS, 1951,

Studies in Kikuyu grammar and idiom. Revised edition. Edinburgh: FMC CoS, 1960.

Ũyũ nĩ Ũhoro *mwega ũrĩa waandĩKirũo nĩ Johana* [St. John's Gospel in Kikuyu]. Trans. A. R. Barlow. London: NBSS/BFBS, 1919.

Kĩkĩkanĩro kĩrĩa kĩerũ kĩa Jesu Kristo: ũrĩa wĩ mwathani witũ o na mũhonokia witũ [The New Testament in Kikuyu, Trans. H. Leakey, A. R. Barlow, assisted by J. Henderson (GSM), H. L. Downing (AIM), Marion S. Stevenson (CSM), Stefano Kinuthia, and Mathayo Njoroge]. London: BFBS/NBSS, 1926.

Thaburi [Kikuyu Psalms]. Trans. A. R. Barlow. London: NBSS/BFBS, 1936.

Thaburi [Revised version]. Trans. A. R. Barlow. London: NBSS/BFBS, 1948.

Mbuku ya Mahoya ma Kũhoithia [Prayers for Public Worship]. Edinburgh: Blackwoods/CSM Kenya Colony, 1926.

Schools, Linguistic Work, Worship and Evangelism

The CSM was involved in significant language work which intersects with education, evangelism and worship.[39] It can be helpful to see this from an interdisciplinary perspective and see these together as all complimenting each other in mission activity. Literacy needs linguistic tools and texts as does evangelism and discipleship, preaching and worship, and literacy needs education. There is a circle here.

The CSM's main linguist was Arthur Ruffelle Barlow (1888–1965). He had been David Clement Ruffle Scott's assistant secretary coming out to assist David Scott (his uncle) when he was 17 years old in 1903 and quickly learnt Kikuyu. He started teaching in 1906 and made the decision that Kikuyu should be the language used at the mission and not Kiswahili. This necessitated him to develop an early Kikuyu primer/grammar starting in 1906 together with the help of two indigenous workers, Mugo and Wachica. He also very early on began to translate portions of Scripture into Kikuyu with the assistance of two native workers, Mwenja and Kabengo. The earliest published Scripture portion was Mark's Gospel released in 1909. Barlow was 21 years old at the time. The work was a *tentative edition* and subsequently revised. The two Gospels which were foundational for use in the mission appear to have been Mark and John. Later Barlow completed the Psalms into Kikuyu.

▲ Watson-Scott Memorial Church

Barlow was also involved in working with at first an informally appointed united translation committee in the lands of the Kikuyu. This committee of members from the CSM, AIM and CMS produced liturgical works on The Lord's Prayer, The Apostles' Creed and the Ten Commandments. These were then used for the joint dedication service of the Watson-Scott Memorial Church (CSM) in January 1909.[40]

---

39 Vicky Khasandi-Telewa, "'She Worships at the Kikuyu Church:' The Influence of Scottish Missionaries in Worship and Education among African Christians," in *Africa in Scotland, Scotland in Africa* (Leiden: Brill, 2014), 287–306.
40 McIntosh, 304.

Next this committee was formalised as the *United Gikuyu Translation Committee*. It was not an easy committee to manage as it faced difficulties over the appointment of members with variable linguistic abilities. It was this United Translation Committee that worked upon an early Kikuyu hymnal which was published in London in 1911 by the Society for the Propagation of Christian Knowledge (SPCK).[41] The Committee was reorganised again in 1913 as the *United Translation Language Committee* with four missions now represented in the Committee: CSM, CMS, AIM and also now the Gospel Missionary Society (GMS). Unity in such projects was not an easy matter.

In 1907 Barlow together with John Arthur and Mrs Watson all had the vision to establish the mission's first boys' boarding school at Kikuyu which opened in April 1909 and in 1909 Barlow was appointed to teach at a boys' school at the new station of Tumutumu. It was at Tumutumu that Barlow also acquired knowledge of other related dialects and languages around Mount Kenya.

Barlow began a teachers' class and one of the first members of that class was Stefano Waitito who had been one of the students taught by Mrs Minnie Watson.

Later Barlow was involved in assisting two Church Missionary Society missionaries helping create an *English-Kikuyu Dictionary*[42] and was a key member of the translation team for the first edition of the whole Kikuyu New Testament published in 1926, but which had begun formally in 1913. Barlow was responsible for translating the Gospel of John, the three epistles of John, and the book of Revelation.

Educational mission work was really laid in the pioneer stage by Mrs Minnie Watson with her day school and evening school for the agricultural workers. This foundation of educational missions was developed by Barlow and then Marion Stevenson and others in this post-1907 phase of the mission's history. Between 1920 and 1945 literacy and education was a key emphasis in the Kikuyu mission and has often been called *Kusoma* Christianity.

---

41 McIntosh, 305. It seems this hymnal was: *Nyīmbo cia Kūinīra Ngai* [A Book of Hymns in the Kikuyu Language] (London: SPCK, 1911). There is some confusion about this hymnal and who were the specific compilers, and actual translators. Rev. A. W. McGregor, CMS, seemed upset with the work that he had not been consulted sufficiently. It seems that Barlow was one worker on it from the CSM. See Eugene Stock, *The History of the Church Missionary Society*, vol.4 (London: CMS, 1916), 82 for confirmation that this was a joint translation project. Later editions of the hymnal can be found for 1955 and 1956. Also, Macpherson asserts that Barlow worked on Kikuyu hymns, *Presbyterian Church in Kenya*, 39 and clearly had ability and knowledge of hymnody and singing: "And so with our Gikuyu friends, we bring them songs with strange semi-tones and an outlandish sound...It is one of our infirmities that we cannot yet adapt ourselves to their mode of scale and tonal values as to give them their own gospel songs, into which they could put their heart." Macpherson, 46, quoting Barlow in *Kikuyu News*, (35), 8.

42 The 1975 Oxford edition states that A. Ruffelle Barlow was the compiler of this dictionary, and that T. G. Benson was the editor (Oxford: OUP/Clarendon Press, 1975).

Higher Education

A significant step forward in education took place in 1926 when George A. Grieve (1888–1965) who had been working in teacher training in Kikuyu became the first headmaster of the Alliance High School. There was a tension between the settlers/colonists who saw only a need for basic primary level education for the native people and industrial training and the missionaries who wanted to see higher education for all. The CSM along with others pushed for secondary level education for all. There were several steps in this process. One initial step was when Dr John Arthur organised a conference in 1913 for the Protestant missions and one of the issues discussed was higher education for the native community. Next in 1918 the *Alliance of Protestant Missions* was formally organised by the CSM, the Anglican Church of the Province of Kenya, AIM, Quakers, GMS, and Methodists. This body worked towards the goal of higher education. Following the Devonshire Paper of 1923, the Alliance began the Alliance High School for Boys in Kikuyu in 1926 of which the CSM missionary George Grieves was the first headmaster. In 1948 its sister institution was founded by the Alliance, the Alliance Girls' Secondary School, the first such institution in Kenya for girls.

Settler Congregations

The theme of settler migration into East Africa meant that an English-speaking white congregational ministry would develop. This parallels the story of settler congregations likewise developing in Southern Africa alongside native mission work. Thus in 1908, with the growing European settler migration to Kenya and the spiritual needs of this community, St. Andrew's Presbyterian Church[43] was formed in Nairobi. (Both Thomas Watson and Clement Scott had ministered to settlers on Sundays in Nairobi, so the roots of this congregation actually go back about nine years previous.) St. Andrew's was eventually placed within a separate Overseas Presbytery in 1936 and under the GA of the CoS, and its Colonial and Continental Committee rather than remaining under the CSM and its Presbytery of Kenya Colony.[44] A second congregation called St. Columba's was established at Nyeri, 100 miles from Nairobi.[45] St Andrew's congregation remained in this Overseas Presbytery until 1956 when it was amalgamated within the PCEA. St. Andrew's had its own building in 1910. The original building has since been relocated but still can be seen today in Nairobi.

This story of how to relate settler congregations with indigenous mission churches is not unique here in Kenya or British East Africa. As has been already

---

43 Also sometimes called St. Andrew's Scots Presbyterian Church, Nairobi. *Kikuyu: 1898–1923*, 39.
44 Macpherson, *Presbyterian Church in Kenya*, 116, comments that this in essence amounted to "a form of ecclesiastical apartheid."
45 *Fasti Ecclesiae Scoticanae*, vol. 7, 558.

stated above this parallels very much Southern Africa and all the challenges that this means to create unity and good working relations between the settler congregations and the indigenous Church. There is a difference in that the settler congregations never attained the numerical size with multiple organised congregations as was the case in Southern Africa. St. Andrew's Nairobi in essence had a parish boundary covering all of British East Africa – Kenya, Uganda, and Tanzania.

More attempts at Land used for Mission Extension Funding

During Henry Scott and John Arthur's tenures the issue of land and self-sustainable projects did not go away. There may appear to be ambivalence by Henry Scott yet at the same time it is not that easy. The CSM had acquired much land and much of it was left fallow. The land both at Kibusi and at Kikuyu was not being very productive. Schemes were entertained for lease arrangements as a way to enlarge funds for mission extension work. Most of these lease arrangements proved to be highly ineffective for the purposes intended and fraught with numerous challenges. In some ways it was a quiet vindication of Clement Scott's earlier efforts.[46] In part the fund raising through the *Kikuyu News* for various projects was the solution similar to much modern project-based fund-raising in the latter twentieth-century and early twenty-first century.

Female Circumcision Controversy

The issue of female circumcision was a matter which from almost the beginning of the CSM was a topic of discussion with converts. Many missionaries encouraged parents to drop the custom and tried to show that girls could be viewed as women in different ways from this custom. As the CSM developed its medical work, the hospitals voiced concerns about the serious consequences for some women who were subject to this procedure. With the language which was used by Marion Stevenson about "sexual mutilation" lines were hardening about this custom amongst the Kikuyu. Also, some of the Kikuyu Christians in Kiambu were also opposing the custom: "We find it our duty to take up our stand on the matter and show that it is not the Europeans that make the law against circumcision of women but we Kikuyu ourselves."[47]

The CSM in 1920 ruled that no member should practice this custom and any who did would face discipline. The GMS in 1920 made the same ruling. Then in 1929 the United Mission Conference declared that the custom of FGM must be abandoned. This led to a direct confrontation in March 1929 with the Kikuyu

---

46 For a summation of the many lease arrangements see, McIntosh, 223–228.
47 Park, 174. Source not identified in Park.

Central Association who saw the issue as much wider than this actual act – it was a destruction of a tribal culture and was viewed as imposition from Europeans. It is interesting that Arthur of the CSM and Knapp of the GMS are both linked together by the Kikuyu Central Association as leaders against this custom.[48] Tied to this was also land tenure. Next the missions requested their members sign a petition to the government for protection of their women and girls from forcible circumcision. The GMS had by far the largest number of signatures and the CSM the second and then the AIM the third. One result was as Park summaries: "The importance of this episode was that it led to the start of many Kikuyu separatist churches and independent schools' organisations away from mission Christianity."[49] The other direct result connected to this of course led to a loss of members and adherents to the CSM. The GMS lost the least, but some estimates say the CSM lost up to 90% of its members and adherents initially, yet many did return.[50]

The government approach was education not confrontation. The three missions in particular GMS, CSM and AIM were seen by the government as provoking the female crisis of 1929 and 1930, and the government was not sympathetic towards their approach. The CSM slowly through the 1930s began to recover by adding new members after this loss but it was a difficult decade especially with the Depression of the 1930s.

First Native Ministers

The first indigenous ministers were ordained by the CSM on 7 March 1926 when three were ordained at the Kikuyu station:
>   Musa Gitau,
>   Benjamin Githieya, and
>   Joshua Matenjwa,

then one week later, 14 March 1926 at the Tumutumu station five more were ordained:
>   Simeon Karechu
>   Joshua Riunga
>   Paulo Kahuho
>   Jeremiah Waita
>   Solomon Ndambi

---

48 Wamagatta, "The Presbyterian Church of East Africa: An Account of Its Gospel Missionary Society Origins, 1895–1946," 224.
49 Park, 177.
50 Wamagatta, "The Presbyterian Church of East Africa: An Account of Its Gospel Missionary Society Origins, 1895–1946," 226. This figure may be on the high side or need qualification by the word "initially."

making the number a total of eight ordained in 1926 by the Presbytery of Kenya Colony.[51]

▲ First eight ordinands in the CSM, BEA mission
(with permission of the National Library, Scotland)

Then in 1935 another six were ordained so that by 1946 the CSM had 24 ordained ministers as it approached the union with the GMS.

4. The Second Stream: The GMS and Union

"Two streams of missionary enterprise converged to produce the Presbyterian Church in East Africa – one Scottish Presbyterian in origin, the other American Baptist [Gospel Missionary Society]."[52] So we read in a recent doctoral thesis about spirituality and the PCEA. The quotation highlights an often-forgotten reality that there was a second mission stream to the makeup of the PCEA. Now we will briefly look at this second stream.

---

51 Macpherson, *Presbyterian Church in Kenya*, 78.
52 Park, Sung Kyu. "Spirituality of Kenyan Pastors: A Practical Theological Study of Kikuyu PCEA Pastors in Nairobi," (Unpublished PhD thesis, University of Pretoria, 2008), 172. Park is asserting basically what Robert Macpherson had also stated about the two streams. It is correct but a nuance on the American Baptists must be made. Macpherson, *Presbyterian Church in Kenya*, 21.

Background

The writer above calls this second stream, "American Baptist" which is a popular statement that many have made but not exactly historically accurate. The Gospel Missionary Society was rooted in the revival atmosphere of Dwight Moody and Ira Sankey in the United States of America at the end of the nineteenth century and as a mission it emerged out of an independent and interdenominational congregation, The People's Church of Christ in New Britain, Connecticut and so the story of what in time became the GMS is intertwined with this congregation. This congregation was not aligned with any of the Baptist denominations in America but belonged very much to the independent and evangelical interdenominational family of churches which were developing in many places in America at the time of the noted revivalists. The People's Church practiced believers' baptism by immersion. There were other local independent or nondenominational churches in North America which took the name The People's Church and many of these were likewise known to be rooted in revivalism, holiness, the fundamentalist-modernist controversy, opposed to theological liberalism, often premillennial, and consciously strong on foreign missions and evangelism. One thinks of a somewhat later congregation, The People's Church in Toronto founded by Oswald J. Smith. This is a stream in North American evangelicalism which is distinctive from organised associations of Baptists and Pentecostals.

First Station

As a Society it was closely aligned with Peter Scott and the Africa Inland Mission (AIM) and in fact both came to British East Africa at the same time in 1895. The first missionary of The People's Church, Connecticut was Rev. Frederick Krieger who came to investigate a possible mission work and spent two years in this initial AIM alliance situation before going solo in 1897 with The People's Church and their overseas mission Association. Krieger's background was that of a German immigrant to America who had been converted at The People's Church in Connecticut and then trained at the Christian Missionary Alliance Bible School in Nyack, New York before being ordained and sent to Kenya. Krieger founded the first station at Thembigwa in Kikuyuland in 1898 and this is really the formal commencement of the real work of the GMS as a separate mission in Kikuyuland.[53] However, three years later the GMS and AIM entered into a formal alliance to work together once again, yet this second alliance would cease in 1912 when AIM wanted to subsume the GMS field into its field.

---

53 Krieger left the GMS in 1906 and remained in the Highlands as a farmer.

The first GMS baptism service was held by Krieger in Kikuyuland in 1903 with a native worker of Krieger's, Mabruki, a Girama who was baptised. Then, "The first six GMS Kikuyu adherents to go through the inquirers' class were baptized in December 1906. The six were Wanyoike wa Kamawe, Gicuhi wa Kamau, Ndaguri wa Kinuthia and his wife Wanjiku, and Mutwanjeru wa Muciri and his wife Nyambura."[54]

GMS Missionaries and Teacher-evangelists and Native Ministers

More missionaries were sent out under the Association/GMS from New Britain, Connecticut mission: Rev. William and Myrtle Knapp, Miss Gertrude Wheeler, Charles and Eva Atwood in the early years. The Knapps were to be the longest couple of this mission and key to its advancement. Other missionaries of the GMS followed: Mary Gamertsfelder who served for thirsty years, the Bodas, Margaret Gough and Stella Ross and others. Dr John Henderson was the GMS/AIM medical missionary and established hospitals at Kambai and Ng'enda, the Central Stations and was also involved in translation projects. Native teachers/evangelists were trained at these Central Stations and from there they went forth to establish out-stations. Wamagatta summarised this well:

> The GMS had many outstanding teacher-evangelists who served it faithfully for many years. They included Kihurani wa Gatundu from the Mitahato out-school; Wanyoike wa Kamawe from Komothai; Watatua from Githiga; Mutaru wa Njoga from Kihumbuini; Kabui wa Magu from Ng'enda; Kimani wa Mugekenyi and Kirika from Kambui; Ngomane wa Kiarie from Gatamaiyu; Ngumba wa Gakibe from Thiririka; and Ngaii wa Kimama from the Kanjai out-school.[55]

Some of the GMS teacher-evangelists did studies at the Kijabe Bible School so that they could obtain their evangelist certificates. The GMS did not conduct its own formal Bible School unlike most missions of the time but ran informal Bible Schools as needs arose to train evangelists.

▲ William & Myrtle Knapp

---

54 Wamagatta, "The Presbyterian Church of East Africa: An Account of Its Gospel Missionary Society Origins, 1895–1946," 189 and Wanyoike, *An African Pastor*, 64.
55 Wamagatta, "The Presbyterian Church of East Africa: An Account of Its Gospel Missionary Society Origins, 1895–1946," 131. Native nursing assistants for the GMS included Toro wa Kung'u and Kamau, 150.

In 1930 the GMS ordained its first ministers: Wanyoike wa Kamawe and Mutaru wa Njoga.

Union Rationale

Union discussions between the CSM and the GMS had begun in 1934. It was a very slow process and culminated in 1946 when the GMS united or merged into the CSM/PCEA and formed the Presbytery of Chania. There are several reasons for this union. We could start with the growing relations through the Federation of Missions and then the Alliance of Missions but also a common people group was shared by the two missions, CSM and GMS, namely the Kikuyu. Perhaps though the more significant reasons are the following: financial problems were dogging the GMS Kikuyu mission and it just could not keep up with the needs educationally to keep advancing; the GMS was having recruitment problems in finding more missionary personnel in the 1930s and 1940s and this appears to have been a critical reason for the merger; and a general reason may well have been the GMS was overextending itself as a mission in too many foreign fields.[56] Likewise there was a strong link for many years between Robert Macpherson of the CSM and his first wife, who was the daughter of GMS missionaries (the Knapps). Macpherson was seconded to help at the GMS Kambui station where he married Alta Knapp.[57] He returned to be principal at Kambui for the GMS and supervisor of their out-schools in December 1942 when he was seconded by the CSM to the GMS. No doubt this human Macpherson-Knapp factor must be considered as a key reason for this union at this time. All of the above are valid reasons why this union/merger took place. The GMS may have very well looked at the growing church structures of the CSM and seen that it would benefit its own converts and national workers in the GMS Kikuyu field by uniting. In reality the reasons are likely several. One noted PCEA minister who spoke of his roots in the GMS stream of the PCEA was Dr John Gatu.

The GMS though practicing immersion of its converts was not completely dogmatic on this and so could adapt to working with the baptismal customs of the CSM over time. This would be different from most Baptist denominations and missions. The GMS saw elders as important in local church government so in many ways they could easily adapt to presbyterian governance practices. It

---

56 Wamagatta, "The Presbyterian Church of East Africa: An Account of Its Gospel Missionary Society Origins, 1895–1946," 243–285.
57 Robert Macpherson (1904–1984). Went to BEA in the mid-1920s first serving as an educational missionary in Kikuyu (CSM) and at Kambui station for the GMS, then at Chogoria. He knew well the GMS field and the CMS. He married Alta Knapp at Kambui in 1930, so personal ties to the GMS for Macpherson were longstanding.

may seem that it would have been logical for the GMS to unite with the AIM but there were two underlying factors here at play. One, was clearly the education trajectory of the GMS and how they perceived the CSM as much stronger on this than AIM in terms of the push towards offering higher education and second the human factor of acquaintance with MacPherson and the marriage connection here must be considered as forming a close bond between two missions.

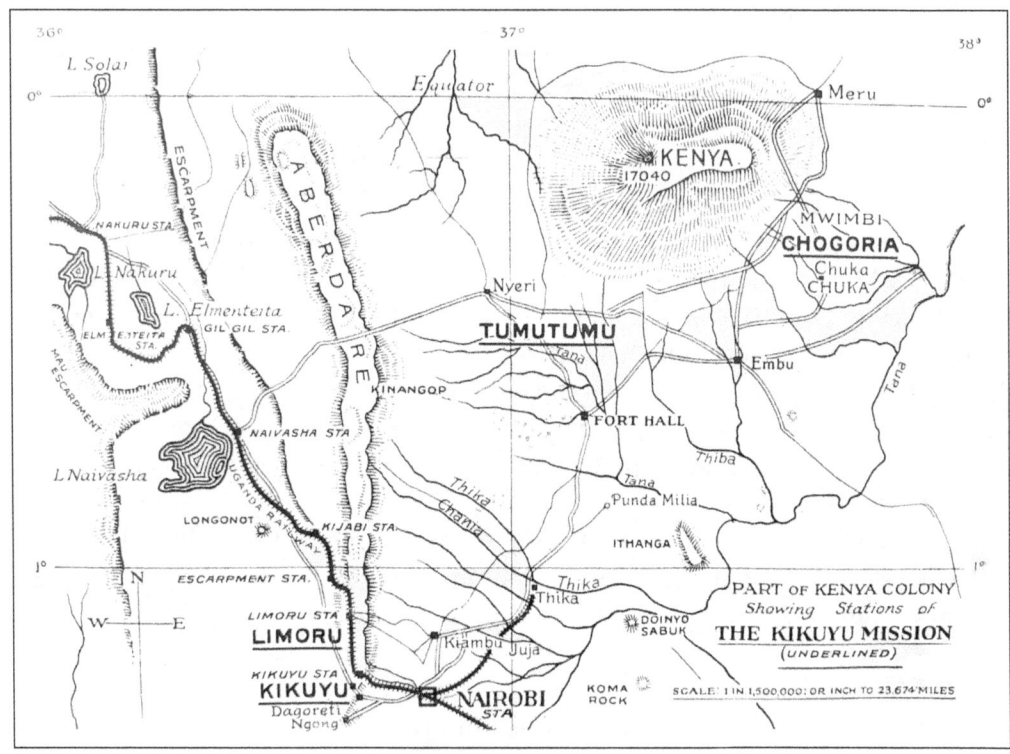

▲ Map of Kikuyu Mission

The GMS brought to the CSM in 1946 a crucial enlargement of territory in Kikuyland which immediately expanded the territorial base of the CSM mission. Likewise, it brought to the CSM what immediately formed a third presbytery with three central stations (Kambui, Ngenda, and Kihumbuini[58]) and several out-stations and out-schools, and 2,000 church members, two native ordained pastors and many native teacher-evangelists. The missionary contributions of the Knapps and Dr Henderson present exemplary service for the Kingdom and models of mission labours worthy for reflection.[59]

---

58 Wanyoike, *An African Pastor*, 141.
59 Macpherson, *Presbyterian Church in Kenya*, 88–89.

5. Summary Conclusion

This second part began with the transition from the EASM to the CSM and attempting to answer the question as to the affiliation to the Church of Scotland. In this handover from an independent Presbyterian mission we see a move to an ecclesial mission. This transition brought in David Clement Ruffelle Scott as the first superintendent of the CSM in British East Africa and his focus on an agricultural model for this mission in his effort to fund the mission given the ecclesial lack of funding to extend the mission work. After six years and amidst much criticism the CMS then under the superintendency of Henry Scott redirected the mission to education and evangelism yet the issue of land and development could never be far from the surface. Mission and settler communities become themes which in many ways are complex and intertwined so are not always easy to separate out in mission history and East Africa is no exception.

The CSM from the time of Henry Scott to the eve of the Second World War experienced many changes and developments and also faced crises as section 3 shows. There was clearly much happening in the CSM work during this period. Though full attention has not been given to the changes taking place politically and developmentally with railway and settlement to colony status the CSM mission these have been in the background as we tried to grasp some of the key facts in this survey of the growth of the CSM to becoming the Presbytery of Kenya Colony 1920 and then the Presbyterian Church in East Africa 1943. The 1943 name is significant as it does not limit its name by the word Kenya and yet in so many ways this mission was tied to the Kikuyu peoples although not chiefly as mission work was done with other tribes or related tribes.

The story of the union of the CSM with the GMS is often eclipsed by mission historians. The variety of reasons for this union are worth reflecting upon. It also highlights the reality that mission streams often flow together to make church history more complicated than we often see at first glance.

Questions for study (fact type):
1. a) Locate Kikuyu on a map and then Tumuturu, and finally Chogoria.
   b) Explain what is meant by "central stations" and "out-stations" and "out-schools" for a mission strategy development.
2. Create a skeleton timeline of the EASM, CSM and PCEA from 1891 to 1946.

Questions for study (reflection type):
1. Explain why an interdisciplinary approach is helpful to understand linguistic work in missions as related to education, evangelism, worship, and church leadership.
2. Discuss the circumcision crisis of 1929 and give your personal evaluation. Provide scriptural reference for input in your answer.

Select Bibliography

Githii, D. "The East African Revival Movement and the Presbyterian Church of East Africa." ThM thesis, Fuller Theological Seminary, 1992.

Kikuyu: 1898–1923 Semi-Jubilee Book of the Church of Scotland Mission Kenya Colony. Edinburgh: William Blackwood/FMCCoS, 1923.

Kikuyu: 1898–1948. The Jubilee Book of the Church of Scotland Mission, Kenya Colony. Eds. R. G. M. Calderwood, A. C. Irvine, Robert Macpherson. Edinburgh: FMCCoS, 1948.

McIntosh, Brian G. "The Scottish Mission in Kenya, 1891–1923." PhD thesis, University of Edinburgh, 1969.

Macpherson, Robert. *The Presbyterian Church in Kenya: An account of the origins and growth of the Presbyterian Church of East Africa.* Nairobi: Presbyterian Church of East Africa, 1970.

Park, Sung Kyu. "Spirituality of Kenyan Pastors: A Practical Theological Study of Kikuyu PCEA Pastors in Nairobi." PhD thesis, University of Pretoria, 2008.

Wamagatta, Evanson N. "The Presbyterian Church of East Africa: An Account of Its Gospel Missionary Society Origins, 1895–1946." PhD thesis, University of West Virginia, 2001. *Subsequently published as:*

Wamagatta, Evanson N. *The Presbyterian Church of East Africa: An Account of Its Gospel Missionary Society Origins, 1895–1946.* New York: Peter Lang, 2009.

Wanyoike, E. N. *An African Pastor.* Nairobi: East African Publishing House, 1974.

A Survey of Presbyterian Mission History in Africa

List of Elders ordained at Thogoto (Kikuyu)[60] on 19 September 1920

Ishmael Wango	Samuel Gitau	Daudi Makumi	Benjamin Githiaya
Filipu Karanja	Andrea Wainaina	Samson Njoroge	Ibrahim Njuguna
Zakaria Wambura	Yusuf Ngwaci	Daudi Makumi	James Muriu
Musa Ngururia	William Njoroge	Tomaso Wanyoike	Shadraka Mbirua
George Njoroge	Joshua Matenjwa	Musa Gitau	Daudi Ndatha
Shadraraka Kang'u	Ayub Nguyai	Douglas Itotia	Joseph Ngure
Musa Ndirangu	Elijah Kibacia		

List of Elders ordained at Tumutumu on 26 September 1920

Solomon Ndambi	Gideon Gatere	Jonathan Ng'ang'a	Joshua Riunga
Musa Matu	Daudi Kamau	Maina Maina	Zakayo Kagotho
Luka Macaria	Samson Maingi	Zakaria Mutahi	Asa Muhuga
William Mwema	Jeremia Waita	Lazaro Theuri	Paulo Kahuho Simeon Karecu

---

60 PCEA Nairobi East Presbytery, accessed 4 February 2023. pceanairobiastpresbytery.org/background. Two dates are given for the ordination of elders at Kikuyu in this website narrative, but it would seem the correct date was 19 September 1920 and then on the 21st the Presbytery was constituted. See also, Macpherson, *Presbyterian Church in Kenya*, 77. I have read three different dates for the exact day in September when the Presbytery was constituted and one date for October 1920.

Bio Inset

Minnie Cumming Watson

Nancy J. Whytock

Minnie Cumming Watson was a pioneer educator, evangelist, and promoter of the education and welfare of Kikuyu girls in Kenya colony. She was born in Dundee, Scotland on 3 June 1867, the daughter of William Cumming, a ship captain, and Janet Lawson Cumming.[61] From a young age she had a desire to serve in foreign missions, so she gladly left for Kenya in late 1899 to become the wife of the Rev. Thomas Watson, already serving as a missionary for the East Africa Scottish Mission. Thomas Watson, also from Dundee, was one of the original six missionaries sent to Kenya in 1891 by the EASM.

The first mission was established at Kibwezi but was eventually found to be unsuitable, so the mission was then re-established at Kikuyu on the 11th September 1898. The railway reached Kikuyu in December 1899, the very month that Minnie Watson arrived in Mombasa to marry Thomas. Miss Minnie Cumming had been engaged to the Rev. Thomas Watson for eight years; and, until the Mission Committee considered it advisable and possible for her to join him in his work under the East Africa Scottish Mission, she patiently continued her work of teaching in one of the schools near her home in Dundee.[62]

She and Thomas were married near Mombasa[63] and then took the train inland. Just weeks after their marriage, on 8 January 1900, they began a relief camp as locust invasions, drought, and rinderpest[64] had left the Kikuyu people in a state of starvation. The next month, a smallpox epidemic broke out and Thomas and Minnie found themselves looking after over 80 very ill people while trying to feed hundreds of others.

Finally, by May 1900, the worst of the epidemic and the drought were over. Minnie was then able to commence her life's work in establishing schools for the Kikuyu people. She began by teaching the children during the day[65] and the

---

61 Also known as Jessie Cumming. See Charles Kasaja – From Uganda to Dundee. – The Dundee City Archives Blog (wordpress.com) Accessed 17 February 2023.
62 *Kikuyu News*, No. 117 (September 1931), 2.
63 There were two ceremonies – the church one took place at the CMS church Freretown, Mombasa and the civil one at Nairobi.
64 Also known as cattle plague.
65 She used the verandah of their home – a house built by her husband – as her classroom and the window shutter was her blackboard. *Kikuyu News*, No. 117 (September 1931), 3.

young men in the evenings. Then on 4 December 1900, Thomas, her husband of just less than one year, died of pneumonia. Minnie resolved to stay and carry on the work that she and her husband had begun.

> The natives had so profited by his [Rev. Thomas Watson's] example and friendliness, that when Mrs Watson was alone she had the offer of more labour than needed, and was able to make **perfect attendance at school** the condition on which alone employment could be obtained. By this means she was able to keep a regular day – and Sunday school of twenty pupils – besides an evening-school of over forty lads who worked during the day at stone-quarrying, for that future building of whose accomplishment she was assured by faith. These also formed a Sunday evening class.
> The foundations of the Kikuyu Mission, then, were laid in sacrifices, rare and costly, of lives laid down, and lives spent. Glory to God for these; and not least for His strength vouchsafed to the brave widowed lady, living alone; rarely enjoying European intercourse, and doing single-handed the work of a Mission Staff![66]

That same year (1900), the board of the EASM had come to the realization that they did not have the resources to continue to support the Kikuyu Mission Station on their own. An agreement was reached with the Church of Scotland in 1901, and the transfer process was begun. The biggest benefit for Minnie was that the new Church of Scotland Mission (CSM) was better able to support educational initiatives. In April 1907, the first boarding school began with seven boys who were already wards of the mission. The programme was highly successful (mostly between fourteen and twenty years old), and student numbers rapidly increased. Eventually, the mission schools and the colonial government formed a partnership in education. One lasting effect of this partnership was that the principles of education that Minnie laid down continued to have influence even after her years of service.

The number of school pupils had risen to almost 3000 by 1920. Minnie Watson was the headmistress of the mission school system. Her duties included training the best students to be teachers, teaching and supervising in the day and boarding schools, and teaching the mission workers in the evenings. Village schools were established in the surrounding area and even in more remote locations (if a chief

---

66 *Kikuyu News*, No. 3 (May 1908), 13.

▲ Minnie Watson and her nursery school

or plantation owner would allow Minnie to send one of her trained teachers). The teachers were also trained in evangelism and, as a result, the 1920s saw a huge growth in church membership. Jomo Kenyatta, the first president of Kenya, began his education at the Kikuyu Mission in one of Minnie Watson's classes.

Mrs Watson became well known for her love for children. In the early days, when schooling was a problem, some settlers' children lived with her and were taught by her. There was also a young boy, Charles Kasaja Stokes, who was brought to her from Uganda at age six.[67] She took him to her home in Dundee, where he lived with her mother and attended school at the Morgan Academy, enrolling

---

67 As well as adopting Charles Kasaja Stokes from the Scottish Mission Station, she also adopted John McQueen (born in British East Africa) and brought them both back to Dundee in 1907. Accessed 16 February 2023.
History records that Charles never knew his father. Charles Henry Stokes was arrested in January 1895 by the Belgians, for trading arms with their colonial enemies – Britain and Germany. In a botched trial, Charles Snr was convicted and sentenced to death by hanging – just a few months before Charles Kasaja Stokes was born
https://www.thecourier.co.uk/fp/news/dundee/1704835/feature-family-trace-legacy-of-late-grandfather-charles-adopted-by-dundee-missionary-minnie-watson-in-africa/ published 14 November 2020 – author Michael Alexander.

about 1908[68] for four and half years. He eventually became a valued bacteriologist in the Kikuyu Hospital following training at the Nairobi Laboratory.[69] He died in the mid-1990s of cancer.

Minnie Watson insisted that girls be included in education. Three of the seven students that began education on her veranda in 1900 were girls.[70] The first boarding school for girls was opened in 1908.[71] Besides learning reading, writing and arithmetic, classes eventually included sewing, needlework, laundry, cleaning, gardening, and other practical domestic skills.[72] By 1923, Mrs Watson reported that the sewing and knitting classes for women and girls had 300 in regular attendance. That year they were asked to submit samples of their work to the Exhibition of Native Industries under the Government Agricultural Department and were successful in gaining three first prizes.[73]

Initially, many Kikuyu could not see any value in educating girls and were afraid that schooling would make the young ladies unmarriageable. The root of the issue was economic. A girl who could not be married did not bring a bride price to the family. The meetings that Mrs Watson held in the villages to encourage families to send their children to the mission schools were often disrupted by such tactics as throwing bags of ants into the gathering.

Mrs Watson also taught against the practice of female circumcision from the earliest days of her work. She was supported in this opposition by Rev. Dr John Arthur, a Glasgow-born medical missionary who established Kikuyu Hospital in 1908. Many Kikuyu believed that female circumcision was an essential part of their culture and was necessary to bring a girl into full womanhood. Mrs Watson's teaching against the practice made it even harder to recruit female students for her schools.

The establishment of The Kikuyu Central Association (KCA) in 1924, a group of activists who wanted to take political power from the colonial administration, brought the female circumcision issue to a boiling point. The KCA asserted that teaching against this custom was depriving the Kikuyu of their culture. Great debate arose and there was anger on both sides. Eventually the CSM missionaries decided that it was necessary to determine whether or not church

---

68 For more information on Charles Henry Stokes, see https://dundeecityarchives.wordpress.com/2019/10/17/charles-kasaja/ accessed 16 February 2023.
69 *Kikuyu News*, No. 117 (September 1931), 4.
70 *Kikuyu News*, No. 107 (March 1929), 1.
71 *Kikuyu News*, No. 117 (September 1931), 3.
72 *Kikuyu News*, No. 107 (March 1929), 2. For a fuller description of the training offered to the girls, see *Kikuyu: 1898–1923 Semi-Jubilee Book of the Church of Scotland Kenya Colony*, 76–82.
73 Extracts from the minutes of the Foreign Mission Committee, Church of Scotland Mission Committee, Edinburgh, 1903–1926, 244–245.

members would support the church law that forbade this practice. In October and November 1929, the Kirk Session and then the full congregation were asked to make a public declaration that they fully supported church laws against female circumcision. The immediate result was that the CSM Kikuyu Mission lost nine tenths of its membership in the first month. Many members left under severe pressure from their tribal leaders. "By the end of 1929, many of the out-schools had been closed, and as a whole, they had lost over 85% of their students."[74]

An article by the Editor of the *Kikuyu News*, December 1929, clearly explains the weight of the issue:

> Fomented by a native political organisation which is agitating for the preservation of tribal customs, there has been a recrudescence of antagonism to the Christian Evangel so far as it has come into conflict with certain heathen rites of a revolting character. To the European these rites are degrading as well as repulsive. They react upon the moral as well as the physical stamina of the women of Africa, and stand in the way of their emancipation. But native resentment is not against these rites: it is against those opposed to them.[75]

▲ Minnie Watson leaving Kikuyu on retirement, 1931, pictured here with two of her first students

By mid-1930, some of the church leaders and teachers who had left the Church of Scotland had founded new independent churches and schools. Others had returned to the CMS congregations and the strife was subsiding. Mrs Watson was deeply affected by the damage done to the work she had dedicated her life to, but before retiring and leaving Kenya in 1931, she saw that progress had been made "towards a cleaner and purer womanhood in the Kikuyu land and in the African Church."[76]

She returned to Dundee, where

---

74 DACB, Spencer I. Radnich, "Watson, Minnie Cumming," accessed 17 February 2023.
75 *Kikuyu News*, No.110 (December 1929), 1.
76 *Kikuyu News*, No. 117 (September 1931), 3.

she died 13 February 1949. It was at the request and expense of her African friends that her "remains" were flown out to Kenya and given reverent burial beside those of her husband[77] – almost exactly fifty years after their wedding. The inscription on the headstone reads, "Aria marehire utheri wa Ngai Kikuyu" (they brought the light of God to the Kikuyu people).

At the time of her death, Mrs Watson was described by her former students and mission staff colleagues as an outstanding Christian role model. She is especially remembered for her work amongst the women and children. She was a fervent champion of girls' education, and her fearless defence of the girls who fought to be free from the cruel custom of mutilation can never be forgotten.

When she was leaving Kikuyu in 1931, it was said of her:

> Everyone here and elsewhere who knows her will miss 'dear Granny.' She has led a lovely life, and God has richly used and blessed her. The Africans will never forget her service for them; her name is a very fragrant one in their memory. [78]

Select Bibliography

Extracts from the minutes of the Foreign Mission Committee, Church of Scotland Mission Committee, Edinburgh, 1903–1926.

Kikuyu News, Church of Scotland Mission, Kenya Colony, East Africa. 1908–1951.

Kikuyu: 1898–1923 Semi-Jubilee Book of the Church of Scotland Kenya Colony, Printed for The Foreign Mission Committee of the Church of Scotland. William Blackwood and Sons, Edinburgh, 1923.

---

77 *Kikuyu News*, No. 198 (December 1951), 1204.
78 *Kikuyu News*, No. 117 (September 1931), 5.

Chapter 21

Foundations of the Free Presbyterian Mission in Zimbabwe

J. Cameron Fraser

Chapter Outline: Part One
1. Introduction
2. An Auspicious Start
3. A Challenging Transition
4. Expansion to Shangani
5. Troubles at Ingwenya
6. Further Developments in Shangani
7. A Remarkable Provision
8. Conclusion with Postscript: Ongoing Expansion

1. Introduction

It is both a privilege and a challenge for me to write about the history of the Free Presbyterian Church of Scotland's mission in what is now Zimbabwe. I was born there, back when it was Southern Rhodesia. Not only my parents but other members of my family as well as friends have played an integral role in the mission's history. It seems strange for me to refer to them objectively and formally, but this I have tried to do. I have been helped by several published resources, including biographies of key leaders. As much as possible, I have told the story in my own words but have also paraphrased and quoted liberally from other sources on occasion. One of these was my own short account of my missionary father, and in places I have shamelessly plagiarized my own words, to which I hold the copyright!

2. An Auspicious Start

John Boyana Radasi (c.1876–1923)

The way in which the Free Presbyterians' African mission began was quite remarkable and auspicious, clearly indicating divine guidance and provision. John Boyana Radasi was born sometime around 1876 and grew up in a Christian home in Seymour, Transkei, an area in what was then Britain's Cape Colony of

South Africa. As part of the celebrations for Queen Victoria's Diamond Jubilee in 1897, John Radasi had joined a choir that travelled to the United States the previous year. There he became friends with another young African, James Saki. Having apparently heard that "Scotland was a very religious country where there were good preachers,"[1] the two men decided to visit Scotland on their way home. They made their way to Edinburgh, where they found themselves standing at the side of a street across the road from the house of a Free Presbyterian member, Mrs Sinclair. Her son was looking out the window and was interested to see two African men, as he had lived in South Africa himself for some years. He went outside to speak to the men, then invited them in for a meal. Conversation ensued, indicating the Africans' spiritual interest. "Mrs Sinclair knew that the Rev. Neil Cameron, then a Free Presbyterian minister in Glasgow, was prayerfully interested in beginning foreign mission work. She sent him a telegram which read, 'I have your missionary'. Mr Cameron replied, 'Send him along'."[2]

This was just three years after the founding of the Free Presbyterian Church of Scotland (FPCS).[3] Both men began studying for the ministry in the new denomination, with a view to returning to Africa as missionaries. In 1900 Saki left to join the Plymouth Brethren, but Radasi continued his studies as both a teacher and a minister, was ordained in 1904 by the FPCS, and set sail for Cape Town in his native South Africa.

Radasi belonged to the Fingo tribe and had heard that some of his people had settled among the Ndebele near Bulawayo in Matabeleland, part of what was then known as Southern Rhodesia. As the languages of the Fingo and Ndebele were similar, in that both tribes were offshoots of the Zulu race, which in turn traced its roots to the Bantu of the Congo, he decided to take the train north to Bulawayo and begin his missionary work there. He arrived at the train station not knowing anyone but was glad to see someone wearing clerical attire (as was he). This turned out to be an African Wesleyan minister, "who introduced himself and offered the newcomer accommodation for as long as he would require it – a wonderful provision for a stranger in a strange land."[4] There was also a young

▲ John B. Radasi

---

1 Nicolson, *John Boyana Radasi: Missionary to Zimbabwe*, 10.
2 Nicolson, *Radasi*, 11.
3 The Free Presbyterian Church of Scotland was formed in 1893, in response to a Declaratory Act passed the previous year by what was then the Free Church of Scotland. This act modified the Free Church's adherence to the Westminster Confession of Faith.
4 Catherine Tallach, *Mfundisi Tallach: a man with a burden for souls*, 38.

porter by the name of Stephen Hlazo who came from a Fingo location thirty-eight miles from Bulawayo. He overheard the conversation between the two ministers and some days later, while visiting his father, Chief John Hlazo, told him about this newcomer.

Chief Hlazo and a few friends set off for Bulawayo to meet John Radasi and discovered that they knew some of his relatives in Cape Colony. As their present location was situated next to the Ndebele, they helped arrange for the newcomer to settle on a ten-acre piece of land (for a pound a year) that came to be named Ingwenya Mission, in the Ntabazinduna Reserve (now "Area"). Ingwenya, meaning "crocodile," was named after a nearby river.

It is interesting to note some of the historical background that led John Radasi to choose Matabeleland as his mission field. Matabeleland had been settled by a noted warrior Mzilikazi, who had defied the fearsome Zulu chief Shaka and then fled north with a small group of his followers. Mzilikazi met the Scottish pioneer missionary Robert Moffat who was father-in-law to missionary-explorer David Livingstone. A friendship developed between the two men. In 1859, Moffat and his son received permission to begin a mission in what became known as Matabeleland, under the auspices of the London Missionary Society.

Southern Rhodesia was formed in 1898, named in honour of Cecil Rhodes of the British South Africa Company, comprising Matabeleland to the south and Mashonaland to the north. Rhodes invited the Fingos from Cape Colony to settle in Matabeleland, as they had been loyal to the British. Thus, it seemed natural for Radasi, a Fingo, to make this area his mission field.

Something of the challenges native Africans faced under colonial rule can be gauged from a letter John Radasi wrote to Rev. Neil Cameron in Scotland:

> Rhodesia is under the British Chartered Company, and it seems as if I am in a foreign country. Its laws are quite different from the Cape Colony. As soon as I arrived in Rhodesia, I had to go to the police and report my arrival. All natives without a pass are arrested. The Matabeles have to carry a pass for being in Bulawayo, and another special pass if they want to go out after nine in the evening, and another pass if they are going to the country. They have to report themselves to the police in every place they go to, and ask permission to stay. If they wish to visit friends, they have to get a special pass. I had to go to the magistrate and ask for an exemption pass for Bulawayo and district. The Matabeles are just living in terror of being arrested, as there are so many kinds of passes wanted.[5]

---

5 *The Life and Labours of a Native African Missionary*, compiled by M. Macpherson, 11. Letter to Rev. Neil Cameron, December 29th, 1904.

Such indignities would eventually be a factor leading to armed rebellion and the establishment of African rule in Zimbabwe as well as in other African nations, but there was no indication of this as of yet in Radasi's time.

In the new mission field at Ingwenya, a church building, a school and a home were constructed. In addition to evangelistic work among the animistic people of the region, Radasi began primary school teaching and also some medical work, with the help of a textbook. He later extended his teaching to young adults. Whenever people learned to read, they were rewarded with a Bible, a policy that continued for some time. The new missionary "found that polygamy and superstition were the main hindrances, and lack of

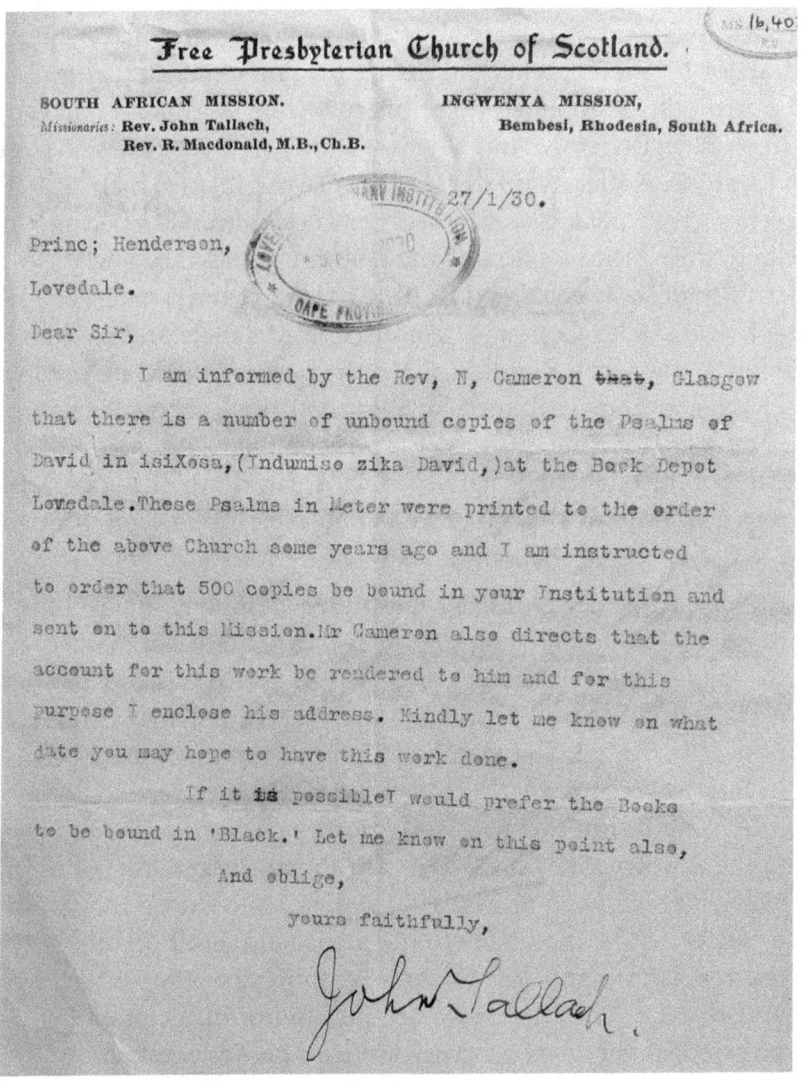

▲ FPCS, South African Mission, Ingwenya, Letter 27 January, 1930 from John Tallach to Principal Henderson, Lovedale

European clothing was often given as the reason for not attending the services." With the help of some Fingo Christians, services were arranged at two outstations and "in May 1908 Mr Radasi's fourth year of labour saw the first fruits of that in two adult and eight infant baptisms, and a Communion service for the few Fingo members of the Church."[6] A number of metrical Psalms in Xhosa (the language of the Fingo) were found in the Wesleyan hymn-book and used, and references to the translation and printing of Psalms continued through the twenty years of John Radasi's ministry. The entire Psalter was printed in 1922 in Xhosa. It would be forty years later before a translation of the Psalms into Ndebele was completed (1962).

Radasi's wife (a daughter of Chief Hlazo) died in 1910, after only four years of marriage, leaving a baby girl. He married another chief's daughter five years later and was to have four sons and a daughter with her. The year 1915 was otherwise

> a bad year for sickness, mainly malaria. A sufferer's first resort was usually to a witch-doctor, because the prevalent belief was that an enemy had had him bewitched, and only a witch-doctor could undo that … Mr Radasi had to be continually visiting the sick, seeking to inform them of the spiritual cause underlying all the ills that afflict men, and praying with them and for them. Many died that year.[7]

The Spanish flu also caused many deaths. In August 1923, Radasi became unwell from diabetes and arrangements were made for him to receive treatment in Johannesburg, South Africa. There was initial improvement, but a relapse the following year.

John Tallach (1890–1955)

Meanwhile, arrangements were being made in Scotland for John Tallach, a ministerial student, to join the work at Ingwenya. With Radasi's deteriorating health, it was felt advisable to speed up Tallach's ordination and induction to the work. He arrived in Bulawayo on the 6th of November 1923, expecting to be met by Radasi. Instead, he

▲ John Tallach

---

6 Alexander McPherson, "Missionary Endeavour in Africa Part I: 1904–1959," in *One Hundred Years of Witness*, 168–69.

7 McPherson, "Missionary Endeavour I," 169–170.

received the news that his intended missionary colleague had been run over and killed by the train he had intended to board for Bulawayo at nearby Bembesi Halt. Thus, Tallach's first official act of ministry at Ingwenya was to conduct Radasi's funeral. He observed that "The whole service bespoke (the people's) love for their pastor and his influence over them."[8]

A number of tributes were received from government offices in Salisbury (now Harare) and other parts of the country. Among them, the Director of Education wrote:

> Although it is now a good many years since I last saw Mr Radasi, I have always followed his work with much interest, and have known him to be steadfast, loyal and devoted, without any trace of arrogance though living in surroundings which might easily have made even an upright and God-fearing man somewhat arrogant ... I know that his example was a pure one and am persuaded that his influence will remain among the people whom he served so long and faithfully.[9]

3. A Challenging Transition

It is difficult to imagine a more challenging introduction to missionary work than the one faced by John Tallach, a challenge "that only Divine grace, coupled with the natural qualities of cheerfulness, adaptability and energy of body and mind could meet."[10] His situation was greatly helped after a few months by the arrival of his fiancé, Ann Sinclair, to become his wife. Together, they were to have five children, two sons and three daughters. Two of the three daughters, Catherine and Margaret, and the elder son, James, were to play important roles in the mission's future. Catherine also wrote a biography of her father, *Mfundisi Tallach: a man with a burden for souls* (*mfundisi* meaning "teacher" or "minister") – a long awaited and fitting tribute to an outstanding and much-loved father and missionary pioneer. The book also provides useful information on the mission's background and several other key leaders.

Medical Mission Work

In 1928, the Tallachs were joined by Dr Roderick MacDonald as an ordained medical missionary.

---

8 Nicolson, *Radasi*, 106.
9 Nicolson, *Radasi*, 107.
10 McPherson, "Missionary Endeavour I," 172.

To begin with, Dr. MacDonald had to use as a dispensary a small iron-roofed hut which had been Mr Radasi's study. In the summer it became like an oven, and was almost intolerable for doctor and patients alike. Along with many minor ailments, there were cases of pneumonia, dysentery, malaria and venereal disease. Sick visiting was done on horseback, and 2,000 cases were treated in the first year.[11]

After almost nine years of hard but productive work, John Tallach was overdue furlough, so with his wife and family he returned to Scotland in June 1932. He "spent a good deal of his time giving lectures, which did much to increase the Church people's interest in their Foreign Mission work. In his absence, Dr. MacDonald took responsibility for the oversight of the work."[12] When the Tallachs returned in 1933, they were accompanied by Jean Nicolson, a remarkable and courageous woman who had been born in the Arizona desert to Scottish parents. Following her father's death when she was just one year old, she moved (after a brief stay in San Francisco) to Scotland with her mother and older brother and grew up there. She was to devote her life to mission work in the FPCS, beginning as head teacher at Ingwenya, and later as an administrator. Her widowed mother also made the trip and proved to be of assistance to the mission in a number of ways. Jean Nicolson never married but was in later years to be known as "Auntie Jean" to the children of other missionaries.

Boarding School

John Tallach observed "It is owing to (Jean Nicolson) that we have a boarding school. It is owing to Mr Radasi that we have a mission."[13] In one of his annual reports to Synod, he noted that the local people "whether adults or children, require some understanding and 'Misi' (Jean Nicolson) seems to have understood them immediately. To us it was a wonder to see the trust they immediately placed in her; there seemed to be no suspicion. This I take it is owing to her large sympathy. The school is now run on systematic lines and a new life has entered into all parts of it."[14] Miss Nicolson's leadership in the school freed up Tallach's time to visit the surrounding kraals (traditional African villages consisting of a number of mud huts), "which he did every weekday except Saturday."[15]

---

11 McPherson, "Missionary Endeavour I," 173.
12 McPherson, "Missionary Endeavour I," 174–75.
13 MacCuish, *A Heart for Africa: The story of Jean Nicolson–Missionary in Zimbabwe*, 70.
14 MacCuish, *A Heart for Africa*, 72.
15 MacCuish, *A Heart for Africa*, 72.

Jean Nicolson's biographer, Dolina MacCuish, explains:

> By the time Mr Tallach had arrived in 1924[16] about 360 pupils were being taught under the aegis of Ingwenya Mission, 120 at Ingwenya School, the rest in four Kraal Schools. The policy was that when there were converts in a village and a preaching station had been established, only then would a school be opened. These schools were at first taught by persons who had simply learned to read and their function was chiefly to teach Bible knowledge and reading. Writing and simple arithmetic were also taught according to the teacher's ability, and cleanliness and order were promoted. The schools were thus an extension of the Mission work of spreading the gospel. Such schools came to be called officially Kraal Schools – that is, elementary schools taught by an unqualified teacher ...[17]

Mr Tallach carried on the work, supervising the schools, and teaching as necessary just as Mr Radasi had done. The education offered was a great advance over no education, but it had its limitations. For one thing, Kraal Schools attracted minimum grants, so scope for improvement was limited. It was desirable that Ingwenya should take its pupils beyond the elementary stage of education.

This is what Mr Tallach decided to do. Thus, the school was in 1927 upgraded from a Kraal to a Central School with four teachers – three African and one European. It attracted about three times the former grant with the great bonus of being able to train its own teachers for the side schools instead of sending them to other institutions for training.

Throughout the years there had been girls in the school, but they were greatly outnumbered by the boys. The prevailing view was that girls did not matter. Mr Tallach had other ideas. He was something of a pioneer in his attitude to the education of girls; they were the mothers of the future, he argued, and the well-being of a family was largely in their hands. Girls did matter.[18]

As an experiment, John Tallach decided to accept up to 20 girls from outstations as boarders. In fact, 24 girls from the outstations attended.

> In addition another 40 or 50 youngsters attended as day pupils for domestic and industrial instruction ... The new venture

---

16 This date is incorrect. It should be 1923.
17 MacCuish, *A Heart for Africa*, 61.
18 MacCuish, *A Heart for Africa*, 61–63.

> was a great success and numbers increased steadily … The boys were not neglected. It was proposed to start agricultural work with them. The Government was approached for an extension of the grounds allocated to the Mission and they were enlarged from 20 to 60 acres. The boys were encouraged to plant vegetables and were allowed to take their produce home … their families' appreciation nurturing their enthusiasm.[19]

A government requirement that one member of the staff should be appointed mission superintendent for administrative purposes led to John Tallach occupying that position. Meanwhile, "Dr. MacDonald was now giving 3,000 treatments in the year and had around one hundred in-patients in the same period. His wife, along with Mrs Nicolson, was helping by teaching practical subjects to children and adults. The MacDonalds went on leave [furlough] in 1936 and the Nicolsons two years later."[20] At that time, and for many years later, the standard period of service was seven years for men and five for women.

During the eighteen months that Miss Nicolson was away, her place at Ingwenya was taken by James Fraser who had recently begun a teaching career in the Scottish Highlands. "Ingwenya Primary School was now regarded as second to none in the colony, and continued to hold that place."[21] Many new members were accepted into the church, particularly at Ingwenya from among the girl boarders.

It was April 1940 before Jean Nicolson was able to return to her post, and another six months before her mother managed to join her, after being a German detainee – a dramatic story of suspense and bravery vividly told in Jean's words in her biography *A Heart for Africa*. James Fraser then left to take over teacher-training at Hope Fountain, a mission station of the London Missionary Society. (This was one of the missions originally founded by Robert Moffat.) It was there that he received the nickname *Thandabantu* ("the man who loves the people") and earned a reputation as a trainer of teachers perhaps without an equal in the country. In years to come, the teacher training centres in both government and missionary schools were to be run on principles developed by him.

During his time at Ingwenya, Fraser had developed what was to be a lifelong friendship with James Stewart, a fellow Scot who was the government inspector of native schools. Once Stewart made a surprise visit to announce that pupils at Ingwenya had taken five out of eleven prizes for essays on "veld fires,"[22] in

---

19 MacCuish, *A Heart for Africa*, 63.
20 McPherson, "Missionary Endeavour I," 175.
21 McPherson, "Missionary Endeavour I," 175.
22 Also known as "bush fires" or "wildfires." "Veld" is "open, uncultivated grassland in southern Africa."

some cases competing against students two grades higher in other schools. As a result, there was a flood of applications to the school, but Tallach as mission superintendent had already been forced, due to space limitations, to reject quite a few.

▲ James Fraser & members of class at Ingwenya, 1939

It was as a result of James Stewart's recommendation that James Fraser went to Hope Fountain, originally intending to stay for a year before resigning and returning home to help in the war effort. However, appeals originating from the mission superintendent resulted in a letter from the prime minister's office requesting him to stay at his post, as it was "of the greatest national importance." Thus, it was not until September of 1945 that he returned to Scotland, after what had been a seven-year absence from his homeland. Before he left, he offered himself as a full-time Free Presbyterian missionary (despite having received attractive offers from other mission agencies) and while at home studied for the ministry, as well as taking a dentistry course in London. He also married his childhood sweetheart Christina (Chris) Finlayson, a nurse. Their first child, Elizabeth, was born in 1946 and the following year the young family set out for Africa. (A second daughter, Isobel, and the present writer were born on the mission field. A second son was stillborn in 1956.)

Meanwhile, the church work at Ingwenya continued to expand, and the ordaining of a number of elders and deacons meant that outstations which had depended on visiting preachers now had their own regular services. There were fourteen elders, the same number of deacons, and twenty-six African teachers with 1,200 pupils. Ingwenya itself had four hundred pupils and eight African teachers.

By 1945 education at Ingwenya was being handicapped by a severe shortage of accommodation. Nearly five hundred pupils in thirteen classes were being taught in only eight classrooms, so the Director of Education suggested that a large H-shaped block of classrooms be erected at a rate of two or three rooms annually. A low interest loan would be available. It was also stated that Jean Nicolson needed an assistant. She received one in January 1946 in the person of Jane Mackay.

The new school buildings for Ingwenya were approved. An advertisement in the *Free Presbyterian Magazine* for a builder was answered by Alexander MacPherson, then a deacon in the Glasgow congregation. He was accepted and the condition made that he should also help with services and teaching "as opportunity offered." In April 1947 he arrived at Ingwenya and "taking up the work which under Dr. MacDonald's supervision had made an impressive beginning, tried, as soon as materials became available, to prepare the first classrooms for use."[23]

John Tallach's health had deteriorated to the point that in 1946 he tendered his resignation. After seven years of ministry in the Oban congregation back in Scotland, he died there in 1955 at the age of 65. Although he was known to be an effective and much appreciated preacher, it was the example of his life as a whole that one African friend recalled in commenting, "It can be said of Mr Tallach that he preached more by deed than by word. His life was a powerful sermon to many souls in Rhodesia'."[24]

It is fitting that when a secondary school was built at Ingwenya in 1957, it was named "The John Tallach Secondary School." It was built under the supervision of John Tallach's son James who, having trained as a carpenter and joiner (finishing carpenter) in Scotland, had returned to work in Rhodesia and had been recruited by the mission to replace MacPherson who had returned to Scotland by this time.

4. Expansion to Shangani

In 1923, due to government resettlement policies, a local chief and his people were moved about eighty miles northwards, to the Nkayi District in the Shangani Reserve. Despite being approached by two other missions, the chief indicated his preference for the FPs and asked for a preacher, so John Mpofu, a lay preacher from Ingwenya, and his son Alexander, a teacher, went there. The scope of the work increased greatly over the years. John Tallach, on his arrival at Ingwenya, became concerned to offer as much support and encouragement as possible. First, he sent an elder and Stephen Hlazo to visit. Then towards the end

---

23 McPherson, "Missionary Endeavour I," 178.
24 MacCuish, *A Heart for Africa*, 150.

of 1925 he used money received as wedding gifts to buy a car in Bulawayo, had a half-hour driving lesson, and drove it back to Ingwenya, accompanied by his wife. By the time they arrived, the fuel gauge registered empty, and they had to await a further gift before they could buy enough petrol to drive to Shangani. This was the first of several trips.

In his 1940 report to Synod, John Tallach pointed out that the Shangani area might well become of greater importance than the Ntabazinduna Reserve, where Ingwenya Mission was situated. The latter was a small reserve where already five different missionary bodies were operating. Shangani, on the other hand, was about one third the size of Scotland, and people were moving into it all the time.

Before he left for Scotland, James Fraser had made two visits to Shangani with James Stewart. He also accompanied Tallach on occasion. It was after visiting Shangani with Tallach that Fraser wrote to the convener of the Foreign Missions Committee offering his services as a full-time missionary. On that trip, he and Tallach had been accompanied by an African convert, Paul Magaya. Fraser noted that Magaya seemed very happy and asked why. Magaya replied,

> Well, it is not so long ago that the Reserve was in total darkness and, even now, there is only a little light but the Word of God is in this Reserve and the Holy Spirit is at work here too – and there is no hope for the power of darkness. Christ must prevail. The whole Reserve will yet be lit up with the glory of the gospel of the Lord Jesus Christ."[25]

While at home in Scotland, James Fraser presented the challenge of Shangani to the annual Synod meeting in 1946. After explaining the situation and its needs, he continued,

> There is a cry from Africa going out to us here tonight, and the cry – a cry for help – is none the less urgent because it is not articulate. I have stood on one of the hills of the Shangani Reserve and have looked forth on, I believe, hundreds of square miles of forest and grassland, with the smoke of African villages rising in the evening air here and there among the trees, and I have felt almost overpowered by a realization of the enormity of our task as a missionary body, and yet when

---

25 Alexander McPherson, *James Fraser: A Record of Missionary Endeavour in Rhodesia in the Twentieth Century*, 128.

we think of the almighty power of God and the prayers of a sympathetic Church at home, we feel that we can go on in the strength of God the Lord, and we feel too that our Church may yet be used more and more in the conversion of the heathen.[26]

Edwin Radasi (c.1913–c.1980), a son of the mission's founder, had gone to Scotland in 1932 at age eighteen to be trained "for future usefulness in the Mission."[27] This included preparation for the ministry, and he was ordained in Scotland in 1944. After a delay caused by the war, he returned in 1946 and began work at Zenka in the Shangani Reserve.

He was joined by the Frasers in January 1948. By now there were twenty-two kraal schools. The Native Education Department regulations required that a certain proportion of trained teachers be employed. To this the FP Mission added the further requirement that such teachers be brought up in the church, or at least have attended a mission school. Fraser determined, with synodical approval, that the mission would have to do its own teacher training. He began this in Shangani in addition to his other work, and an advertisement back home was made for an assistant in that work. Chris Fraser was also running a busy clinic at Zenka, with dentistry assistance from her husband.

Meanwhile, Dr MacDonald and family left for home in 1948 after twenty years as a doctor, minister and (after Mr Tallach's departure), mission superintendent. "He had some time before predicted that government provision of medical facilities for Africans would obviate the need for missions near cities and towns to provide clinics."[28] He saw this as applying to Ingwenya and was proved to be correct.

During his furlough he resigned and spent the rest of his life as pastor of the FP's Vancouver, Canada congregation. Jean Nicolson was then appointed mission superintendent and a further building project was begun at Ingwenya with the help of a government grant. Four dormitories, a dining hall and a matron's house were built, "creating a great improvement in the living conditions of the boarders."[29]

▲ Petros Mzamo

Edwin Radasi was appointed to take Dr MacDonald's place as minister at Ingwenya and its outstations on a temporary basis, as it was thought by the

---

26 McPherson, *James Fraser*, 127.
27 McPherson, "Missionary Endeavour I," 175.
28 McPherson, "Missionary Endeavour I," 179.
29 McPherson, "Missionary Endeavour I," 180.

Synod in Scotland that a white missionary was really needed at Ingwenya. At the same Synod, the Zenka Kirk Session was authorized to examine Petros Mzamo (1918–2012) as a candidate for the ministry. He was accepted and a course of studies set by the Synod was to be carried out under James Fraser's supervision. Petros was a son of Patrick Mzamo, a noted elder at Ingwenya "who into old age had given the mission good service by example and preaching."[30] Petros was at this time head teacher at Zenka.

5. Troubles at Ingwenya

The years 1951–55 were difficult ones specifically for Ingwenya. The period following the end of World War II saw the beginning of African nationalism. Trade unions were formed, and a general strike took place briefly in Bulawayo in 1947. These developments affected mission work as well. It came to light that Edwin Radasi had been holding secret meetings with office-bearers in Ingwenya who believed African ministers should replace white missionaries. When challenged to produce minutes of these meetings, Radasi admitted that there were none. A minister was sent out from Scotland, but he sided with the disaffected Africans, and so was withdrawn after eighteen months. Charges of malpractice were made against James Fraser, who had come from Mbuma to deal with the situation, but Jean Nicolson and her mother were the main focus of mistrust and resentment[31]
At the same time, Radasi confided to Miss Nicolson that he was finding the office-bearers a hindrance more than a help. The missionaries took the view that he was being used by his fellow-Africans, rather than being an instigator of trouble himself. However, he abruptly resigned from the mission and started his own independent church – known as the African Free Presbyterian Church of Zimbabwe.[32] Over time, some of those who left with him returned, but the damage was done.

It is difficult at this distance in time, with all the main players deceased, to assess the situation and how it was handled. It has become fashionable among academics to portray missionaries as agents of colonialism. This is a gross misrepresentation that fails to take into account the motives of missionaries and the sacrifices they often made as compared to those who profited by exploiting Africa and Africans.[33] Frequently, missionaries sought to intervene when they

---

30 McPherson, "Missionary Endeavour I," 180.
31 To his credit, the Scottish minister in question visited Jean Nicolson in her Edinburgh retirement to apologize for his treatment of her.
32 See chapter 29 "Presbyterian Ethiopianism in South Africa and Malawi" in this volume for wider discussions on such secessions.
33 See Thorsten Prill, "Ambassadors Of Christ Or Agents Of Colonialism? Protestant Missionaries In Africa And Their Critics," 81–99.

saw Africans being mistreated. On the other hand, with few exceptions, they were content to operate under the benefits of colonial rule and showed no interest in challenging the *status quo*. In the case of the FP Church of Scotland, although a Southern Rhodesian (now Zimbabwean) Presbytery was later formed in 1962, it continues to function as a branch of the Scottish church, and while at the present time, all ministers and most teachers and nurses, as well as administrators, are in fact African, there is no thought of forming an indigenous Free Presbyterian Church of Zimbabwe.

On a visit to the mission in 1974, I was privileged to meet Edwin Radasi at the Ingwenya home of Jean Nicolson. He came specifically to meet me and demonstrated obvious respect for my father's legacy. He impressed me as a gracious Christian gentleman. Certainly, there was no hint of any ill-will between himself and Miss Nicolson.

6. Further Developments in Shangani

As a head station, Zenka had some disadvantages, so after some further exploration the decision was made in May 1952 to move to Mbuma, further into the Reserve. African families were beginning to move into the area, and more were expected. After five years of building projects at Ingwenya, Alexander McPherson moved to Zenka with his wife and son, Dugald, in September 1952. A classroom and large church building were the first jobs, both to be done at the least possible cost. Norman Miller, an English businessman, arrived with his family in February 1953. After two weeks of intensive briefings on the tasks facing the new arrival, James Fraser and family departed for a much-needed furlough. They returned in early December and the family moved to their new home at Mbuma on the 16 January 1954. Three days later Fraser began a one-year course of teacher training with fourteen students and the following month decided to switch to the more useful standard two-year course. Less than two weeks after the beginning of classes he had to take over the supervision of the building operations. McPherson had suffered a serious breakdown in health and had to go back to Scotland in June. Providentially, John Tallach's son James was now in the country, and he accepted the vacant position of builder on a temporary basis. Under him the work went on well, and later he became a permanent member of the staff. He continued to serve the mission until 1972 when, with his wife, Helena (Ello), and their four children, he returned to Scotland. James' place as builder was then capably taken over by an African, David Ndlovu. (James' sisters, Catherine and Margaret, were also to serve in the mission hospital that was set up at Mbuma in the Shangani Reserve.)

Going back to 1955, James Fraser was greatly relieved to obtain an assistant in the teacher training work in March of that year. Katie Mary Macaulay from the

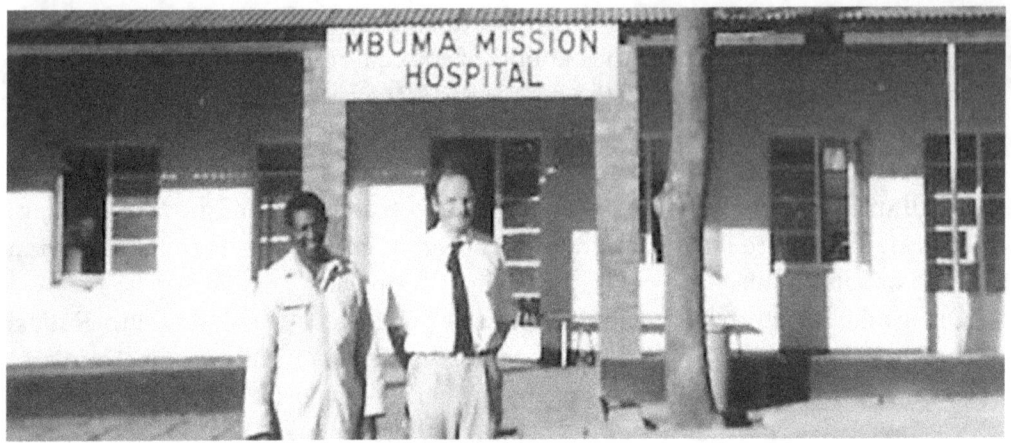

▲ David Ndlovu & Dr James Tallach (nephew of Rev. John Tallach),
the first doctor at Mbuma Mission Hospital

Scottish Island of Lewis proved to be an excellent colleague in every way. She was a cheerful helper, with a ready smile. Just before her arrival, Norman Miller had to return to Scotland to attend to business there, so that for the next five months the kraal schools and Zenka itself became James Fraser's responsibility. Zenka's need for a missionary became especially pressing when Norman Miller, soon after his return to work, was posted to Ingwenya to oversee the schools in that area. Fraser, who now had the spiritual oversight of Ingwenya on top of his other responsibilities, managed to visit Zenka each month and was glad to find the congregation there "holding together well under their godly elders."[34]

Petros Mzamo went to Scotland in 1957 and was ordained in May. Returning home in June, he became superintendent of the Shangani kraal schools, did pastoral visitations and assisted at communions.[35] Another addition to the staff at this time was Jan van Woerden, originally from Zeist in the Netherlands, who had been converted under the preaching of an FP minister in Scotland and became a member of the London (England) congregation while working there. He was a male nurse and motor mechanic with bookkeeping experience, all of which had prepared him for missionary service of a practical nature. He was initially designated for Zenka and also accompanied Mzamo in his trips to the Mbuma area. Nearly 9000 treatments were given at Mbuma in 1957 and

---

34 McPherson, "Missionary Endeavour I," 183.

35 Later in 1963, Petros Mzamo (since deceased), then minister at Mbuma became the first African to become Moderator of the supreme court (synod) of any denomination in Scotland and most likely in the entire United Kingdom. This led F. F. Bruce, then editor of the *Evangelical Quarterly*, to comment that the Free Presbyterian Church, which seldom received a "good press … showed itself to be well ahead of the current climate of opinion." A similar honour was subsequently conferred on the late Aaron Ndebele, formerly of Ingwenya.

Jan van Woerden, once he experienced the work involved, spoke of the need for a doctor and a hospital. Meanwhile, a teacher was required to begin the secondary work in Ingwenya and this post was filled by Ishbel MacCuish who began teaching in January 1958.

As the Frasers were expected to go on furlough in January 1959, it was decided to transfer the second year of the current teacher training course to Ingwenya under Miss Macaulay. Then in December, James Fraser took ill and had to be taken to hospital in Bulawayo. He was treated for a virus of uncertain origin. Drugs were sent from the UK and USA, but to no avail and after three months of suffering he died. In retrospect, we wonder if he had not contracted some sort of acquired immunodeficiency from a monkey bite while retrieving a small boy's ball from a tree at Victoria Falls.[36] He was buried in Ingwenya next to his infant son and the elder Radasi. Some 2000 people, mostly Africans, attended his funeral. Chris and the three children continued on to Scotland. She had been in poor health for some time and passed away in 1961.

In the words of the Convener of the Foreign Missions Committee, James Fraser's death was a "crushing blow", but it soon became apparent that the Lord's work is dependent on no one person, as others rose to the challenge.

7. A Remarkable Provision

Back in 1956 when Chris Fraser was suffering from ill health, she wrote to her sister Margaret Finlayson, asking her to come out from Scotland to give her some support. Margaret went for three years, for some of this time working as a nurse in Bulawayo. She returned to Scotland in 1959 with her sister and the three children, following James Fraser's death.

In 1961, Jan van Woerden appealed to the Foreign Mission Committee to send someone out to help him develop the medical work based at Mbuma. The committee approached Margaret Finlayson and she agreed to return to Rhodesia where she not only assisted van Woerden but married him in 1961! The van Woerdens had four children, all now settled in Scotland.

Mbuma Mission Hospital

As noted above, van Woerden saw the need to develop the medical work into a hospital with a fully trained doctor. This presented a considerable challenge

---

36 According to The AIDS Institute and other sources, the HIV infection mutated from a similar virus in a type of chimpanzee in west Africa. The earliest known case in humans was detected in a 1959 blood sample from a man in the Democratic Republic of Congo. The virus spread slowly across Africa and other parts of the world. (https://www.theaidsinstitute.org/education/aids-101/where-didhiv-come-0).

in terms of fund raising. For this, van Woerden turned to a cousin in the Netherlands, M. A. Meijnders-van Woerden, a journalist married to a wealthy businessman and always referred to as Mrs Meijnders. She wrote about the need in a church publication, which sparked an outpouring of Dutch interest in this Scottish mission. A missionary organization, *Mbuma Zending* was set up. "By 1965 over seventy congregations in Holland were supporting the hospital. Initially the money went directly to the hospital, but by 1968 the support from Holland was going into the General Missions Fund and all areas of the work were benefiting."[37]

Thembiso Children's Home and a Bookroom

Jan van Woerden worked mainly at Mbuma from 1957 to 1968. He and his family moved to Scotland in 1977. He died there in 2019. Rev. John Tallach (a nephew of his missionary namesake) conducted the funeral and subsequently published a short tribute in article form. Describing van Woerden as a visionary, he summarized his work post-1968 as follows:

> As time passed ... differences arose between Jan and the leadership of the FP Mission ... In the end, Jan felt led to explore new areas of work. This involved the setting up of a new organisation—the 'Ebenezer Scripture Mission'. This provided literature evangelism, adult literacy, and Scripture correspondence courses. It also led, in 1976, to the opening of a home for destitute children. Called **Thembiso**, this was the only such home at the time in the whole of Matabeleland.[38]

A new support organization, initially called *Rhodesia Zending*, was set up in the Netherlands.

Despite his differences with denominational leaders, Jan van Woerden remained a member of the church and served as an elder in a congregation that was developed in Bulawayo.[39] Later, when, for family and other reasons, the van

---

37 James R. Tallach, "Missionary Endeavour in Africa Part II: 1960–1993," in *One Hundred Years of Witness*, 191.

38 John Tallach, "Jan van Woerden," in *The Door* (Associated Presbyterian Churches), 18. The vision for Thembiso Children's Home was initially Margaret van Woerden's.

39 In Scotland, Jan van Woerden served the FP Church as a home missionary before joining others in forming the Associated Presbyterian Churches in 1989. In a 2013 article in *The APC News* (later renamed *The Door*), he indicated that as early as 1963 he and Margaret "were developing an interest in tribes in more remote parts of the country and visited the Tonga people in the Zambesi valley" ("Memories of Zimbabwe," May/June 2013). This outward looking vision, rather than one of building on the mission work already begun no doubt contributed to the "differences" mentioned above.

Woerdens left for Scotland, Thembiso Children's Home and a Bookroom they had started were taken over by the FP mission. Eventually, *Zimbabwe Zending* (as the new support organization became) merged with *Mbuma Zending*.

One significant result of the financial help from the Netherlands was that when the Prime Minister of Rhodesia Ian Smith declared a Unilateral Declaration of Independence from Britain in 1965, in an attempt to stave off the inevitability of majority rule, and Rhodesia became subject to British sanctions, there was no restriction on money received from the Netherlands. "This meant that, while other missions had to cut back on buildings and sometimes staff, (the FP mission was) able to expand and grow."[40]

8. Conclusion and Postscript: Ongoing Expansion

Expansion and growth have in fact continued in subsequent decades, with considerable financial help from Mbuma Zending. Other chapters in volume two detail relatively short-lived expansions into Kenya and Malawi (as well as Mozambique). Mission stations were also opened east of Bulawayo in Zimbabwe, among the Shona people. By 2022 there were six stations, now called charges (Bulawayo, Mbuma, New Canaan, Ingwenya, Zenka, and Nkayi), and 40 preaching stations forming the Presbytery of Zimbabwe, FPCS.

European staff have come and gone. By the early 2020s, there were two Dutch doctors at Mbuma Missions Hospital and out clinics, plus a Dutch nurse; all other staff being African. The headmaster at Ingwenya primary was an African with a Scottish deputy head, as well as a Canadian teacher. All other teaching staff were African, as were those in various (five) primary schools and in administration etc. The John Tallach High School continues its work at Ingwenya. Bible Knowledge teachers remain a vital part of the ministry. All ministers and evangelists are African. The staff at Thembiso Orphanage are all African. Boards have been set up to help run the different institutions with the majority of the board members being local people. Thus, although still ultimately governed by the Foreign Missions Committee in Scotland (FPCS), the work that, under God, was begun by an African, John Radasi, continues as he no doubt would have wished and for which he would have fervently prayed.

---

40 James R. Tallach, "Missionary Endeavour II," 193.

Questions for study (fact type):
1 Who was the first missionary in the Free Presbyterian Mission in Zimbabwe? Write one paragraph about his life, especially the story of how he came to serve as a missionary.
2 What is a kraal school?
3 Name the first mission station for the FP Mission. Name the second mission station.
4 What is *Mbuma Zending*?

Questions for study (reflection type):
1 "*European staff have come and gone.*" Throughout this chapter, many names of Europeans have been highlighted as well as names of Africans. Why is it vitally important for local, indigenous leaders and workers to be trained in any gospel work? Use the account of Paul's missionary methods in the book of Acts. Also, use examples from historical events discussed in this chapter to illustrate and support your answer.
2 "*The prevailing view was that girls did not matter. Mr Tallach had other ideas. He was something of a pioneer in his attitude to the education of girls; they were the mothers of the future, he argued, and the well-being of a family was largely in their hands. Girls did matter.*" Consider this quote. Do you agree or disagree? Use relevant scripture to support your answer.

Select Bibliography

Fraser, J. Cameron. Thandabantu: *The Man Who Loved the People*. Belleville, ON: Guardian books, 2010, 2016.

MacCuish, Dolina. *A Heart for Africa: The story of Jean Nicolson—Missionary in Zimbabwe*. Glasgow: Free Presbyterian Publications, 2008.

McPherson, Alexander. "Missionary Endeavour in Africa Part I:1904–1959." In *One Hundred Years of Witness*. Glasgow: Free Presbyterian Publications, 1993, 167–185.

..... *James Fraser: A Record of Missionary Endeavour in Rhodesia in the Twentieth Century*. London: Banner of Truth, 1967, 1968.

Macpherson, M. (compiler). *The Life and Labours of a Native African Missionary*. Gisborne, NZ: The Gisborne Herald Co. Ltd., 1966.

Nicolson, Jean. *John Boyana Radasi: Missionary to Zimbabwe*. Glasgow: Free Presbyterian Publications, 1996.

Prill, Thorsten, "Ambassadors Of Christ Or Agents Of Colonialism? Protestant Missionaries In Africa And Their Critics." *Scottish Bulletin of Evangelical Theology* 37.1 (Spring 2019): 81–99.

Tallach, Catherine J. N. *Mfundisi Tallach: a man with a burden for souls* imprintdigital.com, 2012.

Tallach, James R. "Missionary Endeavour in Africa Part II: 1960–1993." In *One Hundred Years of Witness*. Glasgow: Free Presbyterian Publications, 1993, 186–208.

Tallach, John. "Jan van Woerden." *The Door* (Associated Presbyterian Churches) (Autumn/Winter, 2019).

Van Woerden, Jan. "Memories of Zimbabwe." *APC News* Issue 159 (May/June 2013): 30–32.

Chapter 22

History of Presbyterians in Rwanda

Ezra E. Kwizera

Chapter Outline
1. Introduction
2. Brief History of the Church in Rwanda
3. German East Africans: The Mission Context
4. Ernst Johannsen and the Bethel Mission and German East Africa
5. The Takeover by the Belgian Society of Protestant Missions
6. Autonomy of the Church in 1959 and Official Adoption of being Presbyterian
7. Postscript: The Presbyterian Church in Rwanda in 2021
8. Summary Conclusion

1. Introduction

Christianity did not break through the African interiors until sometime in the middle of the 19th century and at the beginning of the 20th century. For instance, Rwanda, located inland in Africa, did not receive Christianity until the beginning of the 20th century. This saw Rwanda as one of the last African countries to accept Christianity.

In this chapter, we trace the history of Presbyterianism in Rwanda back to Ernest Johannsen and his team. Johannsen and his team entered the country around 1907. The history of Presbyterianism in Rwanda is unique from many other African countries as it did not begin with Presbyterian missionaries; there is, thus, more complexity here. We start with a brief history of the arrival of Catholic Christianity in Rwanda and its development – including the massive conversion that took place in the 1930s after King Mutara IV Rudahigwa complied with the Belgians. The king dedicated the whole country to Christ, the supreme King, making Christianity the state religion. Following this context, we proceed to the stages of development of what would eventually lead to and become known as the Église Presbyteriénne au Rwanda (EPR or Presbyterian Church in Rwanda).

2. Brief History of the Church in Rwanda

Under King Kigeli IV Rwabugiri, king of Rwanda, who ruled for over four decades, from 1853 to 1895, Rwanda became a feared regional power. This prevented Rwanda, unlike Uganda and Tanzania, from getting involved in the East African trading system, through Port Zanzibar, in the mid and later 19th centuries. Christianity in Uganda and Tanzania, thus, predated by almost three decades that of Rwanda, making Rwanda one of the last African countries to receive Christianity.

In the year 1900, during the reign of King Yuhi IV Musinga, Christianity emerged in Rwanda. French White Fathers, led by bishop Jean Joseph Hirth from Uganda and Tanzania in Bukumbi and Nyegezi, saw Rwanda as a perfect place to minister. White Fathers were the most influential Europeans to arrive in Rwanda during the early twentieth century; and were arguably the most significant missionary congregation in twentieth-century Africa.[1] Their arrival saw the dawn of Christianity on the Land of a Thousand Hills. This arrival followed Gustav Adolf von Götzen and his team, who marched to Rwanda through Rusumo Falls in 1897. Their arrival in the country came at the peak of the thirty-year scramble for Africa inaugurated by Otto von Bismarck's Congress of Berlin in 1884–1885. Otto von Bismarck was the head of the German government, which colonised the kingdom of Rwanda.

The king received Bishop Hirth and his team, and they started the ministry in the central area. Hirth thrived as the first five years saw numerous converts and more stations created. The church grew in numbers such that by 1919, there were 16 mission stations and crowned with the ordination of five priests.[2] And in 1912, the White Fathers set up the first vicariate called the apostolic vicariate of Kivu, which served the area until 1922.[3] Things changed a little, however, as the First World War brought changes in administration. Rwanda became a Belgian colony that saw a Belgian Protestant missionary society, namely the Belgian Society of Protestant Missions in the Congo, taking over the leadership of the former German mission stations.

In the 1930s, King Mutara IV Rudahigwa, son of King Yuhi IV Musinga, embraced Roman Catholicism. This became a significant shift in Rwandan Christianity because around the 1930s to 1950s, Rwanda experienced enormous conversions that led to the establishment of Rwanda as a Christian kingdom in the heart of Africa.[4] As a result, King Rudahugwa could address himself to the

---

1 Carney, *Rwanda Before the Genocide*, 17.
2 Baur, *2000 Years of Christianity in Africa*, 317.
3 Sousa, *World Atlas*.
4 Carney, *Rwanda Before the Genocide*, 2.

Lord Jesus by saying: "You had given our country a long line of kings to govern it in your stead even when they did not know you."[5] Following this event, many were baptised due to their genuine faith. In contrast, others were baptised without this faith; because Christianity was accepted as a new cult rather than a religious challenge that demanded a total conversion of mind and will.[6]

During this time, Anglican missionaries were also working in Rwanda. It was amongst them that we trace the story of the beginnings of what became known as the East African Revival that started "from Rwanda, and then spread to Uganda and Kenya."[7] So here we raise this essential question of whether, during the 1930s and beyond, the East African Revival directly impacted the work of the missions we are talking about in this chapter. Thus, Rwanda, in the first forty years of the twentieth century, was a Roman Catholic mission field and the context for the start of the East Africa Revival even though Protestant mission work was very much the minority in the region. So now we are ready to see the story of the first Protestant missions that began in Rwanda.

3. German East Africa: The Mission Context

During the Congo Conference[8] from 15 November 1884 to 26 February 1885 in Berlin, Germany, Africa was divided among the European powers. The Germans received large parts of East Africa. But even before the final declaration was signed, Carl Peters, the Pioneer of German East Africa, had already obtained a territory comprising 140,000 square kilometres by fraud."[9] German East Africa (covering Rwanda, Burundi, and mainland Tanzania) was officially given to the Germans in April 1885. This would open the door to German missionaries in these lands.

Bodelschwingh, the backstory of Bethel Mission

Here is where we must begin our survey story. It starts with Friedrich von Bodelschwingh (1831–1910), nicknamed "the apostle of love," a conservative Lutheran pietist pastor, a German nationalist, and the founder of the Bethel institutions for charities and home missions. This mission approach was integrated and comprehensive in Word and deeds missiological principles. Bodelschwingh's influence in Africa would come directly through his disciple

---

5   Baur, *2000 Years of Christianity in Africa*, 318.
6   Carney, *Rwanda Before the Genocide*, 318.
7   Harper, *Christianity Today*.
8   Also known as the Berlin Conference or West Africa Conference. Popularly known as the Scramble for Africa conference.
9   Stumer, *The Media History of Tanzania*, 31.

Johannsen; who, coupled with others, would play a vital role in planting what would, one day after a very unusual route, emerge as the Presbyterian Church in Rwanda. But that is a story yet to be told in this chapter. Bodelschwingh must be studied as a conservative pietist and not just through the eyes of secular social welfare reformers for home and foreign mission work. There are many complexities here, but he developed and impacted home and foreign mission work through German evangelicals. He did this by directly and indirectly relating to his pietism and his views of wholistic Christian ministry in the late nineteenth and early twentieth centuries.

Therefore, a thorough understanding of Bodelschwingh is needed as we approach German East Africa. Scholars today speak of Bodelschwingh's distinctive, *Arbeitserziehung*:[10] "Rather than providing individuals with charity, effective poor relief should focus on reintegrating them into society by stressing spiritual reform."[11] As Snyder helps us understand, Friedrich had developed a philosophy of poor relief that stressed a strong work ethic – asserting that only after physical labour would one receive material assistance. Bodelschwingh developed workers' colonies/estates in Germany that became noted models for poor Christian relief in the late nineteenth century. Bodelschwingh is part of a broader mission movement within the Inner Mission, or Home Mission German movement (Johann H. Wichern). It often crossed over into city rescue missions that emerged across nineteenth-century Europe, and deaconesses and their ministries were revived through leaders like Theodore Fliedner.

Conservative German leaders accepted Bodelschwingh's ideas and supported him in initiating his plans in East Africa. He was named a leader of the *Evangelical Mission Society for German East Africa* (EMDOA) to train their workers (which had just been disorganised after the failure and resignation of Carl Peters, the leader). The EMDOA was technically separate from the Bethel work, but in reality, with Bodelschwingh at the head of both, they were one and thus combined both home and foreign missions work. They were hoping, however, that through the mission, unemployed workers would be forced to go to German colonies and rejoin German society later after being trained. But Bodelschwingh's philosophy was more about transforming working-class men into conservative Protestants than providing material assistance."[12] At this time, German colonial authorities in East Africa had difficulty engaging Africans to work on colonial labour projects, particularly on their cotton plantations. Hence, mission societies started sending more trained missionaries to German East Africa. This way, Ernst Johannsen,

---

10 A German term for one's philosophy of labour education.
11 Synder, *"Work not Alms: The Bethel Mission to East Africa,"* 150.
12 Synder, "Work not Alms: The Bethel Mission to East Africa," 150.

who would become the founder of sorts for the adoptive Presbyterians in Rwanda, enters the picture.

4. Ernst Johannsen and the Bethel Mission, German East Africa

Ernst Johannsen[13] (1864–1934) studied theology and strongly desired to become a missionary. His knowledge would enable him to formulate and develop his ideas concerning religion in Rwanda and at Shamballa and Bukoba in Tanzania. While German Mission societies were sending Missionaries to Africa, Johannsen, who wanted nothing but to be a Missionary, contacted the Basel Mission Society to help him. But while waiting for an answer, Bodelschwingh saw his potential and zeal and approached him. He convinced him to join the Bethel mission.[14] Having been persuaded, Ernst Johannsen said, "This first encounter would be of decided importance of my life … the more I got to know him [Bodelschwingh], the more this synthesis of nature and virtue, of spirit and humility, of a worldview of love and grounded in work, of passion and perseverance won me."[15] Thus, Johannsen trained with the Bethel institutions before going to East Africa.

The Bethel mission (via the EMDOA) first began work in Africa in 1887 in Dar es Salaam, German East Africa. African children from German East Africa were also sent to Bethel in Germany to further their education and training to return to East Africa to work in the mission. In 1891, Johannsen came to German East Africa together with Paul Wuhlrab. They arrived in Tanzania and started working and genuinely befriending the indigenous people. From 1897 to 1904, he worked at Mlalo Mission station in German East Africa.

On 23 July 1907, a group including Ernst Johannsen, Wilhelm Ruccius, and some indigenous Washamba Tanzanians, Abel Mtungudja, Filippo Shemweta, Shemlondwa, and probably many others, came to Rwanda, being the first Protestant mission in Rwanda. They came to Rwanda to bring the light of the gospel and forestall Muslim advances.[16]

---

13 Gensichen, "Johannsen, Ernst," in *BDCM*, 333.
14 The Bethel Mission was centred in Bielefeld in East Westphalia. Friedrich von Bodelschwingh went there in 1871 to oversee a house for epileptics and also a deaconesses' house (Sarepta). Later a male brotherhood (deacons') house (Nazareth) would also be added, and a church called Zion. The whole of Bethel was a very noted work by the end of the nineteenth century in Protestant mission circles in Germany and many believe it was the largest Protestant centre for evangelical comprehensive relief work in Europe. Bodelschwingh is little known outside of German circles and remains virtually unknown to English-speaking Christians. One hundred years later in 1971, The Bethel Mission merged with the Rhenish Mission Society in 1971 and the new name is the United Evangelical Mission yet the name Bethel is still used.
15 Synder, "Work not Alms: The Bethel Mission to East Africa," 150.
16 Scholz, "Hutu, Tutsi, and the Germans: Racial Cognition in Rwanda under German Colonial Rule," 39.

The Shambala people are one of the Tanzanian Tribes who live in the mountains of Kilimanjaro in the Usambara area. The Usambara area was one of the earliest colonial control centres for German East Africa. Thus, Washamba became one of the earliest people to receive the gospel in the East African region. King Yuhi IV Musinga received Ernst Johannsen and his team. Some say that Johannsen's speaking skills and good character saw him find favour in the eyes of the king, and that's how he managed to survive in the country dominated by the Catholic White Fathers who preceded him. Johannsen said we try hard to avoid conflict with the ruling class as far as possible.[17] The White Fathers were obsessed with potential religious rivals and as they became conversant with local language and customs, they used their influence to stop the development of other missions.

Upon his arrival, Johannsen and King Yuhi IV Musinga decided on the site for the first protestant mission on the hill of Zinga in the Munyaga province. So, Johannsen and his team were stationed at Zinga. This place would become very significant in the history of Presbyterians in Rwanda. The first Presbyterian Church in Rwanda was built here. Now it has turned into "what is known today as Zinga Presbytery"[18] with over 17 Parishes. In August of the same year, Pastor Otto Johannes Mörchen and deacon Heinrich Herbst (1884–1915) joined the group at Zinga. The same month, the second station was built in Kirinda, and in 1909, yet another station was built in Rubengera under the supervision of pastor Karl Röhl (1879–1951). The last station established before the First World War was in Remera/ Kigali City in 1912. Before that, however, another station on the Island Idjwi, the most oversized Island in Lake Kivu, was established but only ran for a short time. This was because, in 1910, the Island was considered part of the Republic of Democratic Congo under Belgium's colonial rule. Therefore, the German missionaries retreated.

On the eve of World War One, the Bethel Mission was present in Rwanda with four Missionaries [Ernst Johannsen, Wilhelm Ruccius, Otto Johannes Mörchen, and Heinrich Herbst], five deacons, and six local assistants, whose achievements comprised 13 baptised Christians and 38 contenders.[19] Pastor Otto Johannes Mörchen assumed management of the Zinga station from Johannsen and directed it from 1907 to 1915. In 1916, however, the Belgians expelled them from the country and only allowed them to return in 1921. As a result, their mission work stopped, and the Belgians took over the stations. The number of

---

17 Scholz, "Hutu, Tutsi, and the Germans: Racial Cognition in Rwanda under German Colonial Rule," 43.
18 Mwizerwa, *The Outreach Foundation*.
19 Scholz, "Hutu, Tutsi, and the Germans: Racial Cognition in Rwanda under German Colonial Rule," 40.

converts increased during the massive conversions through the East African Revival around the 1930s and 1940s.

We have to understand, however, that Johannsen did not start a Presbyterian church immediately, but he and his colleagues faithfully preached the Word of God. But being Lutheran, most of his teachings would be either Lutheran or Presbyterian. In the various German territories [in East Africa] the Reformation had been extended in a Lutheran or in a Presbyterian form. Nevertheless, it is difficult to trace and exactly confirm what the converts believed; were they Presbyterians, Lutherans, or, being young in the faith, they did not care much about denominations, which they might have perceived as divisions? All these are questions that are a bit hard to answer with certainty. Nonetheless, we see the church having "Evangelical Presbyterian Church in Rwanda" as its official name back in 1959.

Being a Lutheran,[20] it would have been difficult for Johannsen to preach the gospel different from his own convictions. Thus, along this line, we would expect the converts to be more Lutheran than Presbyterian. But Lutherans in Rwanda do not trace their history back to Ernst Johannsen; in fact, Lutherans were not operating on Rwandan soil until less than three decades ago. Instead, they trace their history to Rwandan refugees returning from Tanzania after the 1994 genocide.[21] As a result, it is one of the youngest denominations in Rwanda, having up to 7000 members, 37 pastors, and 28 parishes with 50 congregations.

In contrast, Presbyterianism is one of the oldest denominations in Rwanda. They trace their history back to Ernst Johannsen; both the officials and all the members believe the church started in 1907. In the book *Faith-Based Organizations in Development Discourses and Practice*, edited by Jens Koehrsen and Andreas Heuser, we read that the EPR's beginnings date back to 1907, when German missionaries from the Bethel Mission came to Rwanda.[22] Therefore, it would not be too farfetched if one say that Johannsen's converts were more Presbyterian in doctrines than Lutheran. If indeed, they did care about denominations.

5. The Takeover by the Belgian Society of Protestant Missions

In 1916, during the First World War, the Germans lost all their territories. The Belgians took over, with Rwanda becoming a Belgian Protectorate. Johannsen did not leave Rwanda, but the Belgian troops captured and expelled him from the former German East Africa in 1916. After the First World War, Belgian and

---

20 Ernst Johannsen, Wikipedia.
21 The Lutheran World Federation, Lutherans in Rwanda celebrate Silver Jubilee.
22 Andreas Heuser and Jens Koehrsen, *Faith-Based Organizations in Development Discourses and Practices*. (London: Routledge, 2000), 143

Swiss missionaries came to Rwanda. In later years also, Dutch missionaries came. Jean Pirotte tells us that the Belgian Society of Protestant Missions in the Congo managed to take over in 1921 the three stations of Remera, Kirinda, and Rubengera, which the German missionaries had been forced to abandon during the war.[23] The Belgian Society of Protestant Missions thus controlled all the former Bethel Mission Society stations, and eventually, they managed and formally organised what would become the Presbyterian Church in Rwanda. The missionary work concentrated on three different areas: Kirinda, Rubengera, and Remera, located in Kigali city. As a result, the Presbyterian Church grew stronger under Belgian rule.

6. Autonomy of the Church in 1959 and Official Adoption of being Presbyterian

Little is known about when and how the church fully became Presbyterian in doctrines. But it is clear that before the church's autonomy in 1959, it had the official name of *Evangelical Presbyterian Church in Rwanda*. The church later changed its name to become the *Presbyterian Church in Rwanda*.

In the 1950s, political tensions rose in the country, and many political parties emerged as the revolution continued. The pressure was so high that it touched every corner of the country and reached the major Seminary of Nyakibanda. As a result, some extremist Rwandan students forced Burundian and Congolese students and the White Fathers out of the Seminary. Not only did the chaos change church structure, but it also left changes even in political settings. It was around this period, therefore, that Rwandan indigenous people took over the control of the Presbyterian Church. As a result, the church changed from the *Evangelical Presbyterian church in Rwanda* to *Presbyterian Church in Rwanda*.

Like many other institutions in Rwanda, the 1994 genocide affected the Presbyterian Church in Rwanda; the church lost 16 of its pastors and many other members. Following the genocide, much emphasis has been placed on preparing the younger generation for peace-building and reconciliation. At the same time, the church also faces the challenge of caring for the many orphans and widows, most of whom still suffer from trauma.

---

23 Pirotte, CAIRN INFO.

A Survey of Presbyterian Mission History in Africa

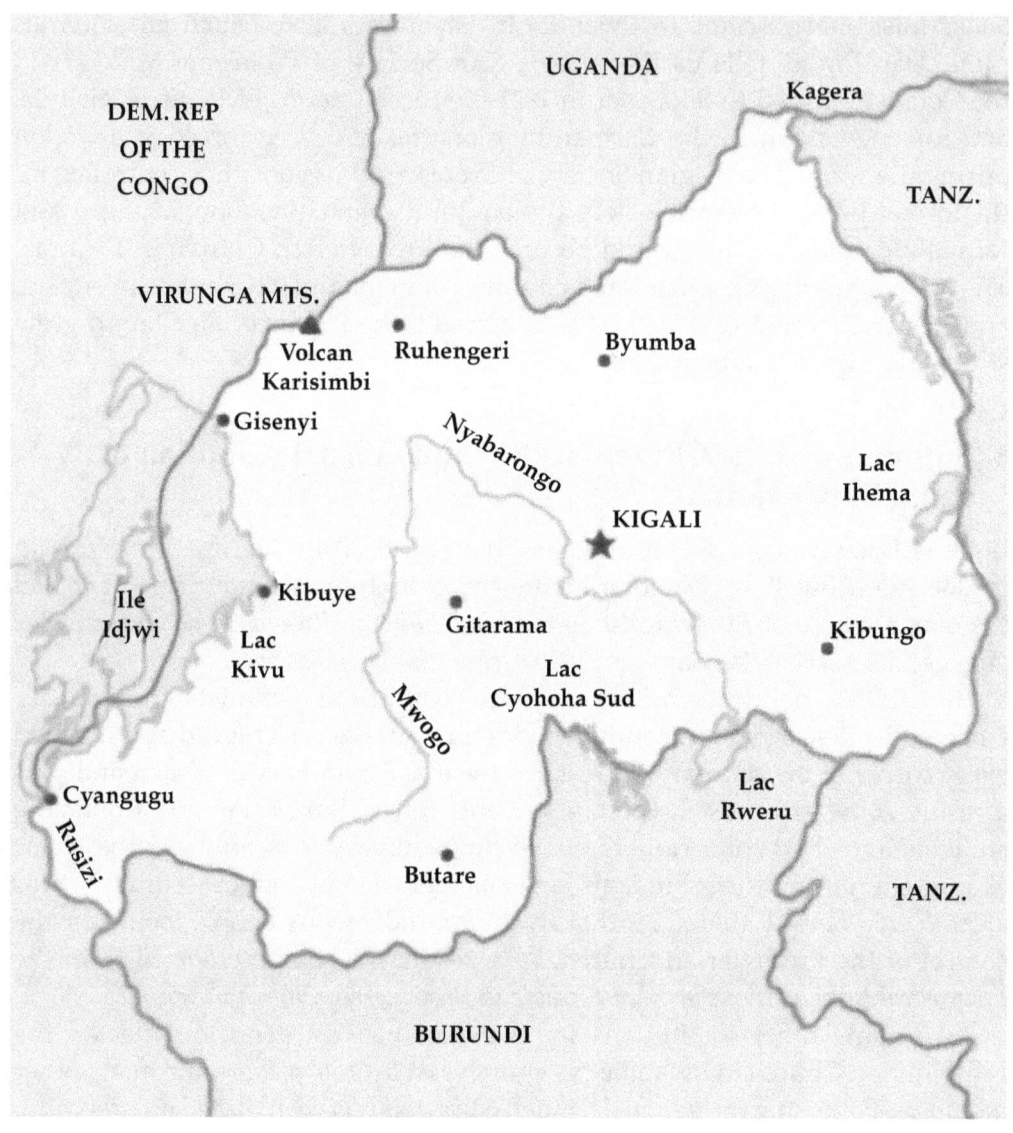

▲ Map of Rwanda

7. Postscript: The Presbyterian Church in Rwanda in 2022

Under the leadership of Naasson Hitimana, who served as the first president of the Presbyterian Church in Rwanda from 1959 to 1977, the church expanded its boundaries throughout the country. They built many schools and established many other stations throughout the country. After Naasson Hitimana came Michel Twagirayezu from 1977 to 1994, and then Andre Karamaga, the current president of the Synod. Now the church has seven Presbyteries: Kigali Presbytery with 33 parishes, Rubengera Presbytery with 34 parishes, Remera Presbytery with 14 parishes, Kirinda Presbytery with 12 parishes, Gisenyi Presbytery with

20 parishes, Gitarama Presbytery with 16 parishes, and Zinga Presbytery with 17 parishes; it has 117 schools, 163 stations, and eight healthcare companies including two hospitals and about 300,000 members.

Although the church claims to have been reformed within itself in 2014 and claims to hold to the Apostles' Creed and Westminster Confession, it is still too hard to know which kind of doctrines it has. It appears to be more of a mixture of Charismatic and Pentecostalism than it is Reformed. The authority of the scripture is not emphasised, women are ordained as ministers, Church governance is more Episcopal than Presbyterian, etc.

The EPR belongs to the World Council of Churches and has pursued a more ecumenical approach in the last few decades. Its leading partnership overseas is with the PC(USA), which has provided aid for church buildings and training programs for women. The EPR vision is to build a solid foundation for the church in which her children will be spiritually mature and able to testify to God's Kingdom by spreading the gospel in love to the whole world.

8. Summary Conclusion

Though Africa was among the earliest societies to receive Christianity, it did not penetrate the interiors of Africa until sometime later, at the end of the 19th and the beginning of the 20th century. Rwanda was amongst the last African countries to receive Christianity. The establishment of a Presbyterian Church in Rwanda can be traced through three distinct stages in Rwanda:

- First through the labours of the Bethel Mission, in 1907, through Johannsen and his Tanzanian team of brothers,
- next, through the efforts of the Belgian Society of Protestant Missions, when the indigenous church expanded, post-1920
- finally, the name Presbyterian came into use at the time the church became autonomous in 1959

The first stage ended with the defeat of German control of East Africa during World War One, which resulted in the involvement of the Belgians having Rwanda as a mandate and the forced withdrawal of the German Bethel missionaries from Rwanda. The Belgian period saw a diversity of Swiss, French, and Dutch missionaries working in the former Bethel fields and beyond and lessening German pietism's background. Now the background was more Reformed in orientation and polity. The indigenous church uniquely in Africa adopted a Presbyterian name in 1959. It was only after that, that involvement directly with foreign Presbyterians can be found starting much later with the PC(USA) as a partner in the mission model late in the twentieth century and into the twenty-first century.

Questions for study (fact type):
1. Why was Rwanda one of the last African countries to receive Christianity?
2. Who was Bishop Hirth, and why is he important to the history of Christianity in Uganda?
3. What was the Berlin Conference? When and where was it held? What European country was given control of Rwanda at this conference?
4. Who was the leader of the first Protestant missionary group to evangelise in Rwanda? What mission society did this group serve?
5. "In 1916, the Germans lost all their territories during World War I, and the Belgians took over." What was the name of this Belgian Mission Society? What was their primary contribution to establishing Presbyterian churches?
6. When did the indigenous Rwandan people take over control of the Presbyterian Church in Rwanda? Why was this necessary at that time? (Scholz, 2015)

Questions for study (reflection type):
1. "Some say that Johannsen's speaking skills and good character saw him find favour in the eyes of the king, and that's how he managed to survive in the country dominated by the Catholic White Fathers who preceded him." Discuss the importance of Christian character in evangelism. Use Matthew 5:1–15 to support your answer.

Select Bibliography

Baur, John. *2000 Years of Christianity in Africa*. Nairobi: Paulines Publications Africa, 2009.

Carney, J. J. *Rwanda Before the Genocide*. Oxford: Oxford University Press, 2014.

EPR. EPR-Eglise Presbytérienne au Rwanda. 5 March 2020. http://www.epr.rw/spip.php?article7 (accessed 5 May 2020).

Ernst Johannsen, Wikipedia. June 4, 2018. https://de.wikipedia.org/wiki/Ernst_Johanssen. (accessed on 24 August 2022).

Fiedler, Klaus. *Christianity and African Culture: Conservative German Protestant Missionaries in Tanzania 1900–1940*. New York: Brill, 1996.

Gensichen, Hans-Werner. "Bodelschwingh, Friedrich von," "Johannsen, Ernst." In *BDCM*, 72, 333.

Harper, Michael. *Christianity Today*. 2020. https://www.christianitytoday.com/history/issues/issue-9/new-dawn-in-east-africa-east-african-revival.htm (accessed 14 May 2020).

Jenkins, Philip. *The New Faces of Christianity*. Oxford: Oxford University Press, 2006.

Langbehn, Volker & Mohammad Salam. *German Colonialism: Race, The Holocaust, and Postwar German*. New York: Columbia University Press, 2011.

The Lutheran World Federation. Lutherans in Rwanda celebrate Silver Jubilee. 1 November 2019. https://www.lutheranworld.org/news/lutherans-rwanda-celebrate-silver-jubilee (accessed, 24 August 2022).

Murangi, Manuel & Patrick Mbaasa, eds. *The East African Revival Through 80 Years 1935–2015*. Kampala: Mwesigwa Mugabi Publications, 2018.

Mwizerwa, Ebralie. *The Outreach Foundation*. 25 October 2016.

https://www.theoutreachfoundation.org/updates/2016/10/25/rwanda-church-construction (accessed 29 November 2019).

Pirotte, Jean. CAIRN. INFO. January 2013. https://www.cairn.info/revue-histoire-monde-et-cultures-religieuses-2013-1-page-107.htm (accessed 5 May 2020).

Scholz, Anton. "Hutu, Tutsi, and the Germans: Racial Cognition in Rwanda under German Colonial Rule." MA thesis, Leiden University, 2015.

Snyder, Edward N. "Work not Alms: The Bethel Mission to East Africa and German Protestant debates over Eugenics, 1880–1933." PhD thesis University of Minnesota, 2013.

Sousa, Gregory. World Atlas. 25 April 2017. https:// www.worldatlas.com/Article/religious-beliefs-in-rwanda.hml (accessed 27 November 2019).

Stumer, Martin. *The Media History of Tanzania*. Original edition. [Tanzania]: Ndanda Mission Press, 1998. Revised edition 2008.

Part Three:
The Nile Corridor: Historic Beginnings & Developments

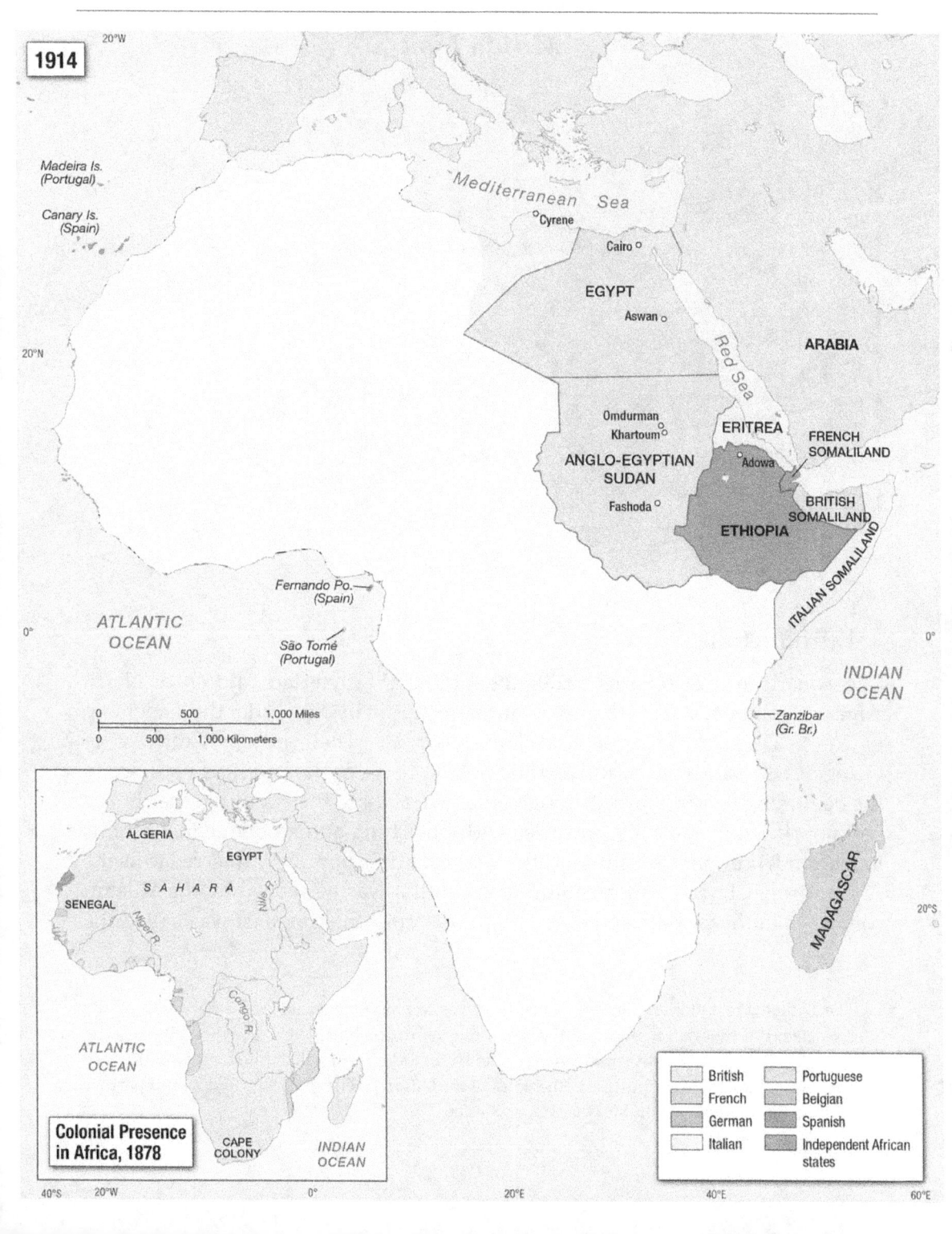

Chapter 23

The American United Presbyterian Church and its Mission in Egypt: Pioneering Efforts

Milton Lipa

Chapter Outline
1. Introduction
2. The Religious Condition of Egypt at the Commencement of the American Mission in 1854
3. The Establishment of the American Mission in Egypt
4. Sketches of history from the beginning of the Mission up to 1863
5. John Hogg
6. Development
7. Conclusion

Bio Inset: Tadros Yusif
Bio Inset: Mary Galloway Giffen
Inset: Hope Waddell Hogg

1. Introduction

The American missionaries under the United Presbyterian Church of North America[1] mission, started their work in Cairo, Egypt in 1854 under the leadership of Revs. Thomas McCague and James Barnett. Their primary interest to evangelise Muslims, Jews, and Orthodox Egyptian Coptics had little progress in the beginning before a breakthrough emerged. Prior to their coming, the church had flourished in the early centuries with preaching and academic institutions in Alexandria under the Church Fathers. The church, popularly referred to as the Alexandrian Church, had great influence until it was weakened by the Muslim conquests in the seventh century. The church after the conquest was called the

---

1 The United Presbyterian Church of North America was formed in 1858 as a union of the Associate Presbyterian Synod and the Associate Reformed Presbyterian General Synod. The Associate Reformed Presbyterian Synod of the South did not enter this union but would, as we see in this chapter, be supportive of the work of the UPs in foreign missions and would partner with them. See the inset on Mary Galloway Giffen.

Coptic Church, named after the Christians who endured the oppression and persecution of the Muslims. After the coming of the Evangelical missionaries, the church which emerged has been known as the Evangelical Church of Egypt.[2] It is this Evangelical Church in Egypt that is the discussion of this chapter.

At the request of the UPCNA General Assembly, the Rev. Andrew Watson wrote the history of this Egyptian mission. He accomplished writing this history with the help of sources from missionary diaries, mission reports, and letters of his colleagues: Barnett, McCague, Hogg, and Lansing. Watson's history will be relied upon for much of this chapter and will be supplemented by other materials.[3]

Dr Andrew Watson is considered as the Nestor of the American Mission in Egypt. On 9 December 1916 he died at his home in Cairo, being 83 years of age. He had been ill less than two weeks. On Sunday evening, November 26, he had conducted the English service in the mission church, including preaching and communion. On November 30, he was present at the American thanksgiving celebrations of the American community.

> Dr Watson was a Scottish man by birth, he was born at Cliverburn, Perthshire, 15 February 1834. While yet a boy, he emigrated with his parents to America. He was educated in the schools and a college in his adopted state, and at Princeton and Pittsburgh theological seminaries. Having been appointed a missionary in Egypt, in order to prepare himself for a wider service, he took a partial course in medicine, at Jefferson medical college, Philadelphia. In 1861, he arrived in Egypt, and after spending a few years in Alexandria and Mansura, he was assigned to the work at Cairo. At the time of his death, he was one of the oldest foreign residents in Egypt, and it is believed he was the oldest Protestant missionary in active service in all Africa. During the 55 years which he spent in this country, he witnessed many wonderful changes that have taken place economically, socially, administratively – in education, justice, and order. He came while Said Pasha Wali was the leader of Egypt. He lived through the Khediviates of Ismail, Tewfik, and Abbas. He saw the withdrawal of the French and the occupation of the English. He witnessed the enthronement of the first Sultan and establishment of the British Protectorate.[4]

Dr Watson was always among the leaders for the first six decades of the American UP Mission in Egypt.

---

2 Lois Farag, "Egyptian Christianity," 802–806.
3 Andrew Watson, *The American Mission in Egypt, 1854–1896*, 1–3.
4 J. R. Alexander, "Andrew Watson of Egypt," *The Muslim World* 7.2 (April 1917), 196.

2. The religious condition of Egypt at the commencement of the American Mission in 1854

The pioneer American missionaries began their mission by first identifying the main religious groups, and their core beliefs. This helped them in the sharing of the gospel and responding to the questions with the members of each religion. These religious groups were: The Muslims, The Coptic Orthodox, the Greek Orthodox, the Roman Catholic, the Coptic Catholics, and a few historic Christian Armenian communities, and the Jews. This chapter will briefly describe two of the above, that is, the Muslims and the Coptic Orthodox:

The Muslims

The most important duties required of the Muslims are summed up in their five pillars viz:

1. *The recital of the creed.* "There is no God but God, and Muhammad is the Apostle or prophet of God."
2. *The observance of the five stated seasons of prayer every day.*
3. *The fast of thirty days* – during the month of Ramadan.
4. *The giving of the legal alms* – one-fortieth part of the person's income.
5. *The pilgrimage to Mecca.*

The American missionaries found many points of contact with the Muslims. These were:

1. *The conception of the unity and attributes of God.*
2. The utter *formalism* and evident want of spirituality in the Muslim worship of a *spiritual God*.

But the first missionaries could not help seeing, also, two conspicuous omissions in the Muslim teaching:

1. There is no mention of *the fall of humans and the corruption of human nature through sin, and no mention of any atonement.*
2. The doctrine of the *Incarnation* is missing, and indeed with *the denial of the Trinity* there is no possibility for its existence.[5]

---

5 Watson, *The American Mission in Egypt, 1854–1896*, 45–51.

The Copts

How some American Missionaries described the spiritual state of the Coptics falls harshly on modern ears:

> Christian in name, Christian in form, it was well typified by the mummied human body taken out of the tombs. Externally a perfect body, but no intelligence in the head, no motion in the limbs, no life in the heart, wound up in memories of fathers and councils, waiting for the Lord to say to some earnest souls, "Prophesy upon these bones, and say unto them, O! ye dry bones, hear the Word of the Lord ... Come, O breath, and breathe upon these slain, that they may live."[6]

3. The Establishment of the American Mission in Egypt

At the time of their arrival, the Americans were not the only missionaries in the country; there were British and European Protestant missionaries as well as Jesuit missionaries ever since the 18th century. However, as the following account will show, the Lord's providence led the American Presbyterians to join the missionary efforts in this ancient land.

The population of Egypt in the mid-nineteenth century was around eight million. Of these about 7-10% were members of the Coptic Orthodox Church, most of whom were located in Upper or Southern Egypt (also known as the "Said"). Demographics were important in determining the mission's early methods and strategies, because from the onset of their mission the Americans concentrated their efforts on the Copts.[7]

In 1853, Dr J. G. Paulding, of the Associate Reformed Presbyterian Church mission in Damascus, wrote a letter to the General Synod of the West in which he described his time in Cairo in 1851–1852. He had gone down to Egypt for health reasons but during his time there became convinced of the need to establish a mission in that ancient country. This letter went on to basically outline four reasons for seeking the permission of the Synod to establish a new work in Cairo: 1. Dr Paulding's health was such that he was required to relocate from Damascus to a more moderate climate. This meant either returning to America or finding a suitable climate abroad from which to continue to serve, 2. There were now too many workers in Damascus and they needed to spread out, 3. It was generally agreed that a place of refuge was needed as there was at that time much unrest in Turkey, 4. It was noted that the field in Egypt was open and

---

6   Watson, *The American Mission in Egypt, 1854–1896*, 58.
7   Nelson, 4.

needy and that "the state of Egypt was favourable for missionary operations."[8] Therefore, in June 1853, permission was granted to open up this new field in Cairo. Instructions were also given to the Board of Foreign Missions to recruit a new man and send him to this field as well as those who would transfer from Damascus.

In the providence of the Lord, the original personnel for Cairo arrived first from America and then from Damascus within twenty days of each other. Upon the decision to open a station in Cairo, the ARPC General Synod sent the Rev. Thomas McCague and his wife Henrietta McCague, whose arrival in Egypt on 15 November 1854 marked the beginning of the American Mission in Egypt, soon to become the largest missionary enterprise in the country. On 5 December 1854, Rev. James Barnett arrived from the Damascus Mission to join the work in Cairo. He was already fluent in Arabic, having ten years' experience in his previous post, and became the tutor and mentor to the newly commissioned McCagues.[9]

The McCagues

Thomas McCague was born in Ripley, Brown County, Ohio, on 25 December 1825 and died in Nebraska in 1914 at the age of 88. As a young man, he pursued college studies before going on to seminary. While he was still studying at Oxford Theological Seminary, his dormitory don informed the UP Board of Foreign Missions that he would probably accept an appointment to the foreign field if it were offered to him. Soon after he received a communication from the Board on the subject, and after careful consideration, he answered favourably. The Board then formally appointed him in 1854 to a new field, Egypt. Mr McCague was accompanied by his wife, Henrietta, of Warren County, Ohio.

Rev. Dr James Barnett

Dr Barnett was a missionary in Beirut, Damascus, and Cairo from 1845–1875. He was born in Pennsylvania but was raised in Ohio. Dr Barnett studied theology at the Associate Reformed Seminary at Oxford, under the Rev. Joseph Claybaugh, DD. He was chosen missionary to Syria by the General Synod of the Associate Reformed Church in 1844, was ordained by his presbytery that year, and sailed from America in 1845, landing in Beirut, Syria, in February 1845. He studied the language and travelled in the country before settling down for mission work in Damascus in 1846. In 1854 he founded the American Mission in Cairo, Egypt with Rev. Thomas McCague, DD. Dr Barnett returned to America in 1861 for four

---

8 Watson, *The American Mission in Egypt, 1854–1896*, 64.
9 Watson, *The American Mission in Egypt, 1854–1896*, 70–71.

years. He received the degree of Doctor of Divinity from Monmouth College in 1863 and was married in 1865. In 1866 he returned to Egypt where he spent the rest of his missionary life until 1875.[10]

4. Sketches of history from the beginning of the Mission up to 1863

Cairo

Rev. McCague spent his first year in Cairo conducting English services, which were infrequently attended by other people. He also committed himself to learning the Arabic language. The McCagues also visited various denominational schools and sold scriptures and other Christian books written in Arabic and other languages. They continued with their daily visits even amidst a cholera outbreak. God used this outbreak to stir up spiritual interest, but as soon as the pestilence was over, this interest seemed to diminish. McCague, in writing at the time of the cholera outbreak, says: "But what effect does it have upon the morals of the people? We perceive no change. They will lie, blaspheme, steal, dissipate, just as before."

However, some of the people did come and show an interest, but then for some reason (not known to the missionaries) would suddenly stop coming to the mission house and would avoid any contact.

At the close of the year 1855, they reported to the Mission Board:

> We have now laid before you a specimen of our labors, prospects, and wants. Immediate and extensive success must not be the index of our duty. Especially this is true in this field, where there are so many retarding circumstances attending the work; but while the field is large and we have room to work, while it is open and we can enter in, we must listen to the command, 'Go forward, occupy till I come.' 'Go, go, go into all the world and preach the gospel to every creature.'[11]

First Mission School Established

A school for boys was opened in Cairo on 29 November 1855 with Mr Awad Hanna as teacher.[12] The initial enrolment was five boys, but this soon increased to twenty. The main studies were reading and writing in Arabic and English,

---

10 https://archiveswest.orbiscascade.org/ark:80444/xv58602
11 Watson, *The American Mission in Egypt, 1854–1896*, 84–85.
12 A school for girls was opened in Cairo in 1860 by Mrs McCague, see Watson, *The American Mission in Egypt, 1854–1896*, 442.

Arabic grammar, arithmetic, and Brown's Catechism. There were devotional exercises in the morning, consisting of a lesson in the Scriptures, a few remarks on the passage, and prayer. Many people ended up attending Sabbath services through their children's connection with the school. McCague taught several classes in the school and also remained busy studying Arabic. On 1 February 1857, McCague conducted his first service in Arabic. He was soon able to take a regular turn in leading the Arabic services, as he had been doing in the English.[13]

The McCagues' second child (who had not yet received the smallpox vaccination due to a lack of supply) died of that disease on 2 May 1857. He was laid to rest in the English cemetery. Shortly after this time, Mr McCague had a severe attack of ophthalmia (inflammation of the eye), and his oldest son was also unwell. The doctor ordered them to seek a change of climate in Syria. Mr Barnett remained at his post in Cairo all summer. The McCague family returned to Egypt early in October, much to the relief and joy of Mr Barnett, whose health had been weakened by the heat of the summer, together with the extra work that had fallen on him. [14]

Rev. G. Lansing

The work of the mission in Egypt was to be further strengthened by the arrival of Rev. Gulian Lansing (1826–1892) in Cairo in November 1856. Lansing was only intending this as a stopover to spend the winter with his former colleague Mr Barnett before returning to Syria, but the Lord redirected Lansing's call for the mission work in Egypt.

Rev. Lansing was ordained as a minister in the Associate Reformed Church in 1850, he served six years in Syria, and then from 1857 (when he officially joined the work in Egypt) to his death in 1896 he laboured for the kingdom of God in Egypt, originally in Alexandria, and then based in Cairo, from 1858 under the auspices of the United Presbyterian Church of North America. Lansing recounted the early experiences of his travels and labours in *Egypt's Princes: A Narrative of Missionary Labor in the Valley of the Nile* (1864, 1865).[15]

Itineration to Asyut and Inquiry into Further Stations

In early 1857, Barnett was laid aside with fever, from which he did not recover for some weeks, and then he was weak and unable for duty. It was, therefore, thought best that he should have a change. In order to unite means of recuperation with

---

13 Watson, *The American Mission in Egypt, 1854–1896*, 80–81, 87.
14 Watson, *The American Mission in Egypt, 1854–1896*, 91.
15 See also the lasting legacy of Rev. Lansing, noted in Chapter XXIII, Watson, *The American Mission in Egypt, 1854–1896*.

mission work, Lansing and Barnett hired a boat for a month and made a trip up as far as Asyut, taking every opportunity to interact with the people. Due to health problems and the death of the McCagues' second child (as noted above), the McCagues left Cairo in June 1857 to spend the summer in Damascus. Lansing accompanied them as he was about to pack up in Damascus and prepare to move to Alexandria to expand the Egyptian mission there.

Alexandria: The Lansings

Lansing arrived at Alexandria on 17 October 1857 and was joined by his family (who had been in America for about eighteen months) on the 6th of the following month. He wrote from Alexandria, saying: "I sit here this evening in what I hope will be my future home. The sea, which comes up to within twenty paces of the house, is roaring beneath my window, and I sit with my gloomy light in one end of a room, nearly eighty feet in length, in which I expect on the next Sabbath to commence declaring the truth as it is in Jesus. May it be said, when the Lord counts and writes the people, that this man and that man were born here." On November 19, he wrote, saying:

> The week after coming here we gave notice that on the following Sabbath we would hold Arabic services if any wished to attend. None came, however, and so I had a Sabbath of rest. The next Sabbath two natives attended, and we could claim the fulfilment of the promise given to two or three, and I trust it was fulfilled. The following Sabbath seven were present, and last Sabbath ten. This is very encouraging.[16]

The attendance remained about ten during the month of December.

Scottish Jewish & UP Mission merged into the American UP Mission in Alexandria

Lansing was not the only worker in Alexandria at that time. The first recorded attempts made in Alexandria to spread the light of the Gospel in that ancient city in modern times were through the efforts of Rev. Dr Hermann Philip and the Rev. R. Grant Brown, who came out under the auspices of a Scottish Society for the Conversion of Israel.[17] Further to develop this field Philip and Grant had suggested to their Society that the best strategy for reaching more people

---

16 Watson, *The American Mission in Egypt, 1854–1896*, 92.
17 See chapter 30 in this volume, section 3 for further background. Also, *The Friend of Israel*, 3 (1855–1857), 46, 52, 157, 194, 277, 300–302.

might be to establish a college in Alexandria. They had already established a school on 10 June 1854 with many Jewish and Muslim children attending. As a result, committees were formed in Alexandria, Edinburgh, and Glasgow, for the purpose of collecting the necessary funds for a college.

Sadly, they failed to raise sufficient funds to carry out this college project, but John Hogg, the teacher they had recruited to initiate this college, was willing to begin a school on a smaller scale. Therefore, the committee decided to continue a school of "humbler pretentions" than that which was originally proposed as a college. Consequently, Mr John Hogg (afterwards Dr John Hogg of the American Mission), a graduate of Edinburgh, who had already taken three years in the Divinity Hall in that city, came to Alexandria under engagement for three years. He reached Alexandria on 6 December 1856 and opened the new school on December 15 of the same year. The school was located on the ground floor of Dr Philip's house. While conducting the school, he also studied Italian and Arabic, and in a few months was able to speak the former reasonably well.

During 1857 the school moved to an old palace in the Abu Abbas quarter. Dr Philip went to Malta during the summer and returned to Alexandria for only a short time; Rev. R. Grant Brown had already left. Therefore, Hogg was left in full charge of the school, under the nominal direction of the local committee. The school did not improve in the new location, because it was too far away from where the pupils would be expected to come.

This was the state of this effort at mission education when Lansing arrived. Efforts had been made, as already intimated, to affect a union with Dr Philip in the educational and other departments of mission work in Alexandria, but nothing had been accomplished. On the arrival of Lansing, Hogg gave up his house to him and his family and became their guest.

The Scottish Mission to the Jews gave up that year (1857) all its work to the United Presbyterian Church of Scotland, and the Board of Foreign Missions of that Church proposed at first to concentrate its missionary efforts in Alexandria, but on Dr Philip asking a sum of 1,600 Pounds for the work there, which they considered more than they could collect, they therefore refused to give their consent. Dr Philip then withdrew, and the mission, as far as the United Presbyterian Church of Scotland was concerned, was abandoned. Negotiations were still carried on by the local committee in Alexandria, with this one result, that a promise of aid to the amount of a year was secured towards the support of the boys' school.

In addition to the boys' school under the direction of Mr Hogg, there was also a girls' school in Alexandria when Lansing took up his residence there. The origin of this school was in consequence of Dr Philip and Rev. R. Grant Brown's visit to Scotland after they had been some years in Alexandria. In their efforts to stir up the people of Scotland to take an interest and share in female education in the East, they succeeded in having a Ladies' Association formed in Paisley, Scotland for the promotion of the Christian education of girls in Alexandria.

A young woman with exceptional linguistic qualifications, Miss Pringle from Scotland, was found and a school was opened in December 1856. The school grew so rapidly that within a year there were between eighty to ninety female students from various religious backgrounds – predominantly Jewish. "Her very success, however, threatened the effort with early failure, for having no efficient assistant, she was tempted, as most of our missionaries frequently are, to overtask her strength, and in the autumn of 1857, she was constrained to return to Scotland. The local committee carried on the school for a short time by means of such teachers as could be obtained in the country." [18]

The year 1857 closed with Lansing and Hogg occupying the same house in Alexandria and assisting each other in the mission work. Hogg, for the most part, engaged in the educational department. This Scottish Society continued to send its annual liberal contribution for the school long after it was transferred to the UP mission; while Lansing spent the most of his time and strength in the evangelistic department, both in English and Arabic. There was yet no formal agreement, but negotiations had already been opened looking to a united mission between the United Presbyterian Church of Scotland and the Associate Reformed Church of North America, for the commencement of mission work in the maritime city of Alexandria, Egypt.

Further advance and trial

The year 1857 ended in Cairo with Barnett and McCague both on the ground. McCague was just beginning to improve following a severe attack of fever, and Barnett was struggling having been on the field for so long without any change. The attendance at Arabic service had increased, and the school continued to grow in numbers and efficiency. Through the book department, the Scriptures and other religious books were being put into the hands of the people. Thus, the seed was being sown for a future harvest.[19]

In late 1861, Andrew Watson concluded the missionary labours in this year as follows: "This ends the record of the year 1861, during which much good seed had been sown along the Nile valley in many places, and there was much evidence that the Gospel of Jesus Christ, in the nineteenth century as in the first, is the power of God and the wisdom of God unto salvation."[20]

---

18 Watson, *The American Mission in Egypt, 1854–1896*, 95.
19 Watson, *The American Mission in Egypt, 1854–1896*, 92–96.
20 Watson, *The American Mission in Egypt, 1854–1896*, 136.

In 1862, Rev. A. Watson, his wife, and Miss McKown[21] spent the year in Alexandria; Rev. J. Hogg and his wife spent the months of January and February in Alexandria. Then in March, April, and part of May they travelled along the Nile as far as Aswan. They returned to Alexandria May 10 and remained there until August to serve in the place of Mr Lansing in Cairo who was very ill.[22] During that year, the missionaries sold scripture and Christian books in the villages and towns they travelled to. The development of the work meant that more time was needed for preaching, directing, and encouraging the many workers at the numerous stations occupied, and giving spiritual counsel and encouragement to professed Christians.[23]

1863 witnessed severe sickness, trial, and persecution among the missionaries. Towards the beginning of the year, Mrs Watson was seriously unwell for two months and then Andrew Watson was seized with a severe attack of ophthalmia, which lasted for seven months. He had to remain in a dark room and wear a thick bandage over his eyes because of extreme sensitivity to the light. He left for Syria with his family about the end of June and returned early in October, and his eyes greatly improved, though he was still obliged, from fear of a return of the disease, to use them with great care and precaution. They had only been home two months when their only child, George Andrew, was taken from them, at the age of eleven and one-half months. In March of the same year, Mrs Hogg was attacked with smallpox. Mr Lansing was also experiencing health issues and left Cairo for America with his family about the beginning of June, while Mr Hogg's health was in an uncertain state.

During this period, the missionaries lived in fear of Muslim uprising. Opposition to the missionary work through persecution of converts from the Coptic religion to true Christianity arose as a new patriarch in the Coptic Church took over leadership. There was also reduced pay of the missionaries due to the civil war in America (to one-fourth). God providentially responded through timely aid from English friends.[24] "Notwithstanding the terrible civil war in America, and the demands made on the Church at home, the Lord had interposed for His work in Egypt and made the outlook for the coming year a bright one."[25]

---

21 For a short account of the life and work of Miss Martha J. McKown, see, https://archive.org/details/blindmissionaryo00port/mode/2up, also mentioned in section 6 of this chapter.
22 Watson, *The American Mission in Egypt, 1854–1896*, 137.
23 Watson, *The American Mission in Egypt, 1854–1896*, 148.
24 Watson, *The American Mission in Egypt, 1854–1896*, 149–150.
25 Watson, *The American Mission in Egypt, 1854–1896*, 174.

5. John Hogg

John Hogg (1833–1886), was one of the pioneer Presbyterian missionaries in Egypt. He was born in Penston, Scotland. In 1856 he accepted a call to Alexandria, Egypt in connection with the Scottish Society for Conversion for the Jews. Four years later in 1860, the work passed on to the American (United Presbyterian) mission due to failure by the Scottish UP Church to continue financial support. This could be one of the reasons why some history books describe Hogg as American, because he spent more years in Egypt working under the American mission than he did under the Scottish mission. He was a firm believer in the establishment of independent, self-sustaining, and self-propagating churches. He was a fine Arabic scholar, a notable personality, and tireless preacher, teacher, translator, and administrator.

In 1862 Hogg went to Cairo to take the place of Lansing (who was sick). While there, he worked to improve the school there. From March up to May, Hogg made his first missionary tour of southern Egypt. He sailed for 1,160 miles, visited 63 villages, sold books in 40 villages, walked, or rode donkeys 200 miles, had conversation with 62 priests, 45 monks, 2 bishops and over 600 common people. The principal conversations and discussions with nominal Christians were centred on: the one sacrifice, the one Intercessor, the perfect atonement, the true nature of fasting and prayer, the reasonable service, the fullness of the Gospel revelation, innovations of fathers and councils, confessions to priests, baptism and the Lord's Supper, the true nature and design of church discipline, spiritual worship, picture worship, praying and talking in unknown tongues, the nature and design of the ministerial office and the necessity of the new birth.

In 1865, Hogg, his family and in the company of Miss McKown accepted to pioneer a mission in Asyut. They soon started a school which was later to be temporarily stopped by the outbreak of cholera; this was after the death of Hogg's daughter. The mission rapidly developed by the power of God. A desire to study scripture was created among the Coptics and their reverence for the word of God caused them to overlook the warning of their leaders not to read the word. However, their leaders continued to rebuke them openly when they found them reading the translated Bibles.

In 1866, Hogg and his family served in Cairo before leaving for Scotland for a vacation. Hogg returned from the vacation after campaigning among the British churches concerning the need to establish a theological institution (seminary) for the training of kingdom ministers. Through his sacrificial campaign, he raised $2,500, and obtained promises for annual contributions for the same.

Hogg is remembered for his pioneering work in education, leadership development, evangelism, and church-planting. He assisted in this mission work and is celebrated for his work in the Church in Egypt. Much of the Evangelical Church's strength and reputation has grown from the schools and hospitals founded by the early church workers in Egypt. These institutions continue today and have been joined by the world-renowned development work of the Coptic Evangelical Organisation for Social Services (CEOSS).

▲ *Pioneer missionaries 1854–1864*

6. Development

A Presbytery of Egypt was formed in 1860 which was connected to the UPCNA. Then in the early 1870s, when the work had grown and the number of local workers and churches increased, the board of missions requested the presbytery to form a separate body from the presbytery in Egypt which would oversee business which was not presbyterial in nature. An association was formed to incorporate Christian servants who were not part of the presbytery to have a mechanism to operate as they served the church. This helped local congregations to set up their leadership and appoint ministers.

Miss Martha McKown and Advances in Education

Miss Martha McKown was born in Elizabeth, Pennsylvania in 1834. She began teaching school at the age of sixteen. Later she graduated from Monmouth College, Illinois, and then became principal of a Ladies' Seminary in Oskaloosa, Iowa until she was called by the Foreign Mission Board of the United Presbyterian Church as a missionary to Egypt.

She sailed from America on 6 October 1860. For the first five years, she taught girls from many nationalities in Alexandria. She was then assigned to Asyut and travelled up the Nile about 250 miles to this new location in upper Egypt. Here she opened a school (later to be known as Pressly Memorial Institute), beginning with 3 pupils, and soon had 30 students. The school and its founder, McKown, were also involved in rescuing girls who had been taken into slavery. As Baron notes,

> Missionary schools had also given shelter to freed slaves before. The Pressly Memorial Institute in Asyut had taken in three Sudanese girls from Darfur – Keltuma, Assa, and Fanna – who had been "rescued by the pluck of some Soudaneese boys", according to Margaret McKown, founder of the school. The girls were placed in the boarding school, which gathered girls from area villages to train them in "common school education" and domestic work, and sent them back to their villages to minister to their own communities. At the school, the freed slaves received "the same training as the Egyptian girls" and were baptized three years after their arrival.[26]

In 1884, Miss McKown began losing her sight and by 1890 she was totally blind. Despite this difficult providence, she remained on the field until 1894, when she sent in her resignation and in April of that year sailed home to America. She died on 30 January 1897.

McKown's efforts and those of many co-labourers were multiplied beyond expectation. By 1901 the American Mission had 14,000 children studying under their schools in Egypt. There were both Coptic and Muslim children and about 3,000 of these were from Muslim families. The number of converts up to 1915 from a Muslim Egyptian background appears to have been very low. One estimate is about 200 Muslims were converted and were connected to this Mission out

---

26 Beth Baron, "Liberated Bodies and Saved Souls: Freed African Slave Girls and Missionaries in Egypt," in *Christian Missions and Humanitarianism in The Middle East, 1850–1950*, Inger Marie Okkenhaug and Karène Sanchez Summerer, eds., Leiden Studies in Islam and Society, Volume 11 (Leiden: Brill, 2020), 52.

of the 15,000 connected to this Mission.²⁷ The majority of those attached to the Mission came from a Coptic background.

▲ *Jubilee Anniversary of the American Mission, missionaries and national workers*

7. Conclusion

The American Mission in Egypt which began by God's providence in Cairo, was sustained by the same providence. Like Paul in Corinth, who had been intimidated to run away, but was encouraged by the Lord to remain in Corinth, because God had his own people, God had his elect in the mission field of Egypt (see Acts 18:1–11, especially verse 10). This is a story of God's faithfulness to encourage all He calls to serve in mission and ministry. The chart below shows the significant size of the American mission in Egypt by 1898, both geographically and in terms of personnel. It is a story similar to all missions in the New Testament church. It has successes amidst challenges, so that God alone receives the glory for seeking and saving His people.

The ethos of the American Mission very much reflected the tributaries of the American and Scottish Secession stream of Presbyterianism and hence the Alexandria merger was a logical development. From this Egyptian American Mission, the work extended further south and southeast into Sudan and Ethiopia. The second chart highlights this corridor of missions which developed.

---

27 Shaymaa Zantout, "'Living Under Different Skies:' Misrepresenting Egyptian Education during the British Occupation in the North American Press," (Unpublished MA thesis, University of Windsor, 2012), 21–22. This thesis takes a very negative view of Christian missionary work.

American United Presbyterian Missionaries in Egypt 1898[28]

Station Location	Missionaries
Cairo	Rev. & Mrs S. C. Ewing Rev. & Mrs W. Harvey Rev. & Mrs Andrew Watson Rev. & Mrs John Giffen Rev. & Mrs J. Krudenier Rev. & Mrs J. G. Hunt Miss Anna Thompson Miss Margaret Smith Miss Ella Kyle Miss Grace Brown
Alexandria	Rev. & Mrs Thomas Finney Rev. & Mrs Geo. A. Sowash Miss Leonora McDowell Miss Adele McMillan
Asyut (Assiut, Assioot)	Rev. & Mrs J. R. Alexander Rev. & Mrs E. M. Giffen Rev. & Mrs S. G. Hart Professor & Mrs R. M'Clenahan Dr & Mrs L. M. Henry Miss Jessie Hogg Miss Carrie Buchanan Miss L. Teas Miss Cora Dickey
Monsurah (Mansura)	Rev. & Mrs J. P. White Miss Minnehaha Finney
Benha	Rev. & Mrs C. Murch
Zagazig	Rev. & Mrs K. W. Macfarland
Tanta	Rev. & Mrs J. Kelly Giffen Dr Anna Watson Dr Caroline Lawrence
Luxor	Rev. & Mrs W. M. Nichol
Semaloot	Rev. & Mrs W. H. Reed
Maghagha	Rev. David Strang

---

28 W. J. W. Roome, ed. *Blessed be Egypt: A Missionary Story*, (London: Marshall Brothers, 1898), 101–102.

The United Presbyterian Mission Stations along the Nile Corridor

Egypt Mission Stations	Year Established
Cairo	1854
Alexandria	1856/7
Asyut (Assiut, Assioot)	1865
Monsurah (Mansura)	1865
Fayoum	1866
Luxor	1883
Middle Egypt	1891
Tanta	1892
Benha	1894
Zagazig	1894
Sudan Mission Stations	
Khartoum area – including Omdurman	1900
Doleib Hill	1902
Nasir	1912
Akobo	1937/8
Wad	1938
Ethiopia Mission Stations	
Sayo	1919/20
Gore	1922
Addis Ababa	1923

Questions for study (fact type):

1. Name the first three missionary personnel to serve in Egypt under the American Presbyterian Mission (one married couple and one single missionary).
2. What year did the American Presbyterian Mission begin in Cairo? In Alexandria?
3. Who did the American Presbyterian Mission in Egypt unite with to form a merger and work together in Alexandria?
4. Using the internet, draw a map of Egypt and on it place the mission stations listed in Chart Two. Beside each place name, write the year it was established (see information from the chart)
5. Write one paragraph on the first Presbyterian Egyptian ordinand – Tadros Yusif. Give facts – who, what, when, where, how, why?

Questions for study (reflection type):
1 "A school for boys was opened in Cairo on 29 November 1855 with Mr Awad Hanna as teacher … The main studies were reading and writing in Arabic and English, Arabic grammar, arithmetic, and Brown's Catechism." Explain the importance of educating children in their mother tongue – especially as it relates to the gospel. Consider the following scripture passages: Acts 2:5–11 and Rev. 5:9–10 as you answer.
2 In this chapter, it was noted of the mission work in Asyut: "The mission rapidly developed by the power of God. A desire to study scripture was created among the Coptics and their reverence for the word of God caused them to overlook the warning of their leaders not to read the word. However, their leaders continued to rebuke them openly when they found them reading the translated Bibles."
   a) Why were the Coptic leaders against their people reading the Word of God? Consider the following scripture passages: Acts 17:10–12 and Psalm 119: 105–112.
   b) How would you respond to someone who says that the Bible is "irrelevant" for our culture or for our period in history?

Select Bibliography

Burke, Jeffrey. "The Establishment of the American Presbyterian Mission in Egypt, 1854–1940: An Overview." Unpublished PhD thesis, McGill University, 2000.

Elder, Earl Edgar. *Vindicating a Vision; the Story of the American Mission in Egypt, 1854–1954*. Philadelphia: Board of Foreign Missions of the United Presbyterian Church of N.A., 1958.

"Egypt." Presbyterian Mission. Mar 27, 2018. https://www.presbyterianmission.org/ministries/global/egypt/

Farag, Lois. "Egyptian Christianity." In *Encyclopedia of Christian Civilization*, ed. George Kurian, vol. II. Oxford: Wiley-Blackwell, 2011: 802–807.

Finnie, David. *Pioneers East, The early American Experience in the Middle East*. Cambridge, MA: Harvard University Press, 1967.

Hunter, Jane. *The Gospel of Gentility: American Women Missionaries in Turn-of-the-Century*. New Haven & London: Yale University Press. 1984.

Kamil, Jill. *Christianity in the Land of the Pharaohs*. London & New York: Routledge Taylor & Francis Group. 2002

Lansing, Gulian. *Egypt's Prince: A Narrative of Missionary Labor in the Valley of the Nile*. Philadelphia: William S. Rentoul, 1864.

Lipa, Milton. "The Life and Impact of Dr John Hogg as a Missionary in Egypt." *Haddington House Journal*, 18 (2016): 11–24.

Nelson, Samuel. "The American mission in Egypt: The Reshaping of Modern Egyptian Christianity" (nd).

Richter, Julius. *A History of Protestant Missions in the Near East*. New York: Fleming H. Revell Company, 1910.

Sedra Paul. "John Lieder and His Mission in Egypt: The Evangelical Ethos at Work Among Nineteenth-Century Copts." *The Journal of Religious History* 28. 3 (October 2004): 219–220.

Sharkey, Heather. *American Evangelicals in Egypt*. Princeton: Princeton University Press, 2013.

Stanley H. "The American Presbyterian Mission in Egypt: Significant Factors to its Establishment." *American Presbyterians: Journal of Presbyterian History* 64 (Summer, 1986): 83–95.

Watson, Andrew. *The American Mission in Egypt, 1854–1896*. Second Edition. Pittsburgh: United Presbyterian Board of Publication, 1904.

Watson, Charles. *Egypt and the Christian Crusade*. Philadelphia: The Board of Foreign Missions of the United Presbyterian Church of North America, 1907.

Watson, Charles. *In the Valley of the Nile; A Survey of the Missionary Movement in Egypt*. New York & Chicago: F.H. Revell Company, 1908.

Watson, John. *Among the Copts*. Brighton/Portland: Sussex Academic Press. 2000.

Bio Inset

Tadros Yusif: The First Ordained Egyptian Presbyterian Pastor

Sherif A. Fahim

Introduction

On 31st of October 1517, the Augustinian monk Martin Luther nailed his 95 theses on the door of the church in Wittenberg. 354 years later, on the same day 1871, Tadros Yusif was ordained as the first Egyptian Presbyterian pastor in Nakheilah, Asyut. Yusif was the first indigenous ordained Reformed minister in Egypt as a fruit of the labour of the American Presbyterian mission.

Background

The Protestant mission began in Egypt with the Moravians who sent Dr Fredrick William Hocker in 1752, then John Henry Danke in 1768. This mission did not last for long and was ended in 1782 without establishing any local ecclesiastical organisation.[29] Then, from 1825, the Anglican Church, and through the Church Mission Society (CMS), started another mission work in Egypt. This endeavour had two main goals: "To propagate the knowledge of the gospel among the Heathen, and to reform the existing Oriental churches."[30] Generally speaking, the Anglican mission was more involved in the distribution of Bibles in Arabic and in the establishing of schools with the hope of reforming the Coptic Church so that they could witness with the gospel to the Muslims. The Coptic patriarch gave permission to this mission to start two schools in Cairo, one for boys and one for girls. In 1842 the boys' school became a theological seminary for training Coptic clergy under the leadership of J. R. T. Leider,[31] who was one of the first five pastors to serve in Egypt through CMS. He stayed in Egypt till his death in 1865. One of the students in that school was Tadros Yusif.

---

29 Emil Zaki & Venise Nicola, *Al Kenissa El Ingeleya Al Mashekheya be Masr* [The Presbyterian Evangelical Church in Egypt: The Beginnings, the Interaction and the Development] (Cairo: Dar El-thaqafa, 2015), 43.
30 Tharwat Wahba, *The Practice of Mission in Egypt* (Carlisle: Langham Monographs, 2016), 37.
31 Wahba, *The Practice of Mission*, 37.

A Chosen Vessel

Yusif was born in Cairo in 1842 and he joined Rev. Leider's school when he was 10 years old.[32] But due to opposition from the Coptic Church, this school was closed. Then Yusif joined for three years a small school that was established by one of the teachers from his former school; then he joined the Great School of the Copts. After graduating, he worked in another Coptic school for some years. In God's providence, He was preparing Yusif for ministerial roles for many years under the teaching of protestant teachers, from his early years.

As Tadros Yusif was being prepared by the Lord, the American Presbyterian Mission started its work in Egypt in 1854. By making the Scripture more available to the Copts, the number of those who started to follow the Protestant teachings increased. In 1860, the first official presbytery was formed in Egypt with James Barnett, one of the first missionaries to arrive in Egypt, as its moderator.[33] The first official act for this presbytery was the ordination of the Scottish missionary Mr John Hogg in May 1860.[34] Hogg would play a major role in the Presbyterian mission in Egypt and in the life of Tadros Yusif!

In 1862, Yusif was assigned to manage the boys' school in Cairo under the supervision of Rev. John Hogg.[35] Four years later, he was transferred to manage the school of the American Mission in Fayum and started a protestant ministry there, which was the beginning of the Presbyterian Church in that area.[36] Meanwhile, Yusif joined the first class in the Theological Seminary that was formally instituted in 1863.[37] Tadrus Yusif and his brother Ebrahim became the first graduates of the seminary in 1871. Of course, this was a special year for Yusif, but became even more special as it was the year for his ordination as the first Egyptian Presbyterian pastor.

First Ordained Egyptian Presbyterian Pastor

By the end of 1870, the members of the mission in Egypt, in coordination with the Board of Foreign Missions and the Church at home, started what is called the Mission Association. This was a huge step towards self-government and self-

---

32 Adib Naguib Salama, *Tareekh Al Kaneesa El Ingeleya*, 168.
33 Andrew Watson, *The American Mission in Egypt* (Pittsburgh: United Presbyterian Board of Publication, 1898), 113.
34 Watson, *The American Mission*, 113.
35 Salama, *Tareekh*, 168.
36 Salama, *Tareekh*, 74.
37 Stanley H. Skreslet, "The American Presbyterian Mission in Egypt: Significant Factors in Its Establishment," *American Presbyterians* 64. 2 (1986), 92.

support within the Egyptian church. One of the reasons for the establishment of this Mission Association as stated by the missionaries was the following:

> The blessing of the great Head of the Church upon our labors has brought us to begin ordaining native pastors and elders. These have full right to the official exercise of their functions, not only in reference to the churches over which they have been ordained, but also in the higher courts of the Lord's house, and we recognize their full official equality with ourselves and consequent right to a seat with us in all church courts.[38]

This strategy reflected the mindset of the American missionaries at that time. John Hogg wrote these words in one of his draft resolutions to be presented to the Association: "Whereas, we believe that the great ultimate of the missionary enterprise is not merely the conversion of individual souls, nor the culture and enlightenment of the body of the people, but the planting in their midst of an independent, self-sustaining, self-propagating, Christian Church."[39]

Accordingly, on October 31, 1871, the first presbytery took place in Nakheliah, which was a village near Assiut, at which native members took part, and in which the business was transacted in the Arabic language. At this occasion, Tadros Yusif was ordained as the first Presbyterian pastor and was installed over the congregation of that town.[40] Moreover, in the same meeting, Yusif was elected to be the presbytery's secretary, and since then it became a rule that the secretary of the presbytery should be an Egyptian.[41]

Yusif's Ministry

In the summer of 1870, Tadros Yusif did his internship training in Nekheliah.[42] Then on 22 April 1871, the congregation was organised in Nekheliah and a call was extended for Mr Yusif to become their pastor; that call was accepted. On the anniversary of the reformation, October 31st, 1871, "Tadros Yusif was solemnly set apart to the ministry of the Word and installed as pastor over the Lord's people in Nekheliah."[43]

Yusif's ministry was not limited to Nekheliah but extended to many villages

---

38 Watson, *The American Mission*, 282.
39 Rena L. Hogg, *A Master-Builder on the Nile: Being a Record of the Life and Aims of John Hogg, Christian Missionary* (New York: Fleming H. Revell Company, 1914), 197.
40 Watson, *The American Mission*, 284.
41 Wahba, *The Practice of Mission*, 56.
42 Salama, *Tareekh*, 168.
43 Watson, *The American Mission*, 294–295.

▲ Tadros Yusif

and cities around it. He served in Mutiah, Bakur, and Abu Tig. He also involved members of his congregation in the ministry in the surrounding villages such as El Badary, El Dweir, Mashta, Tima, Deir El Gandala, El Zaraby, Sidfa, and El Masoudi. Two elders from his church were helping him in all his endeavours and ministry in all these places, elder Greiss and elder Abadeer.[44] All these labours were not without opposition. The evangelical church was just in its childhood and Yusif's ordination and ministry in that antagonistic context, whether from Muslims or from the Coptic Church meant renouncing the love of honour and endorsing the shame that resulted from joining this despised evangelical party.

Starting from 1886, Yusif started to have health issues with his sight, and he lost his vision completely in 1890.[45] Yet, this inability did not stop him from continuing his ministry for 10 more years until his health became very poor. Yusif had to go back to Fayum in 1903 after serving in Nekheliah for more than 30 years, during which time 246 members joined the church. The missionary Andrew Watson described Tadros Yusif and his ministry in the following words:

> Few Egyptians have a better head and better heart than Rev. Tadros Yusif. The amount of hard work he has done, with no grumbling, with no mercenary spirit, with no seeking after glory, is only known to the Master Himself. The growth of the evangelical church in the neighborhood is largely due to his energy and perseverance, tact, and unselfish labor.[46]

---

44 Salama, *Tareekh*, 168.
45 Salama, *Tareekh*, 168.
46 Watson, *The American Mission*, 295.

Bio Inset

Mary Galloway Giffen (1842–1881): The First Missionary of the ARP Synod of the South

Alex Pettett

In the 1860s, more than 50 years after the establishment of the ARP Synod of the South, Mary Galloway petitioned the ARPs to send her as their first missionary. Shortly before this request, Rev. W. A. Wilson had offered to give himself to the UP mission field in Egypt (1873). Family troubles though had prevented Rev. Wilson from being sent. In the book, *Life and Letters of Mary Galloway Giffen*, her relative, Rev. J. C. Galloway comments, "The whole church hailed this step with unfeigned rejoicing as the omen of a better and brighter day for our Zion, feeling that our reproach among the thousands of Israel was now taken away."[47]

United Presbyterians, well aware of Mary's desire to be a missionary, had long encouraged the ARP Synod of the South to send a missionary to the point of exhorting them in this letter, "You have a young lady [Mary Galloway] who is spoiling for a mission."[48] Mary had been running a school in Due West for emancipated slaves and had also established schools in the frontier in Texas.

The UPs formally petitioned the ARPs to join them in sending a missionary to Egypt. Dr Bonner, then the president of the Due West Female College and the secretary of the Board of Foreign Mission, urged her to join the UPs in this work. Mary answered, if "it was the concurrent wish of the Board," she would willingly go. She was unanimously appointed. Most in the denomination were excited about this, though a few remarked, "Why all this excitement and enthusiasm; it is *only a woman*. Why send her; she can't preach the Gospel?"

▲ Mary Galloway Giffen

---

47 J. C. Galloway, *The Life and Letters of Mrs Mary Galloway Giffen*, (Louisville, KY: Myers, Shinkle and Co., 1882), 31.

48 Galloway, *Mary Galloway*, 31.

On hearing this Dr James P. Pressly instantly responded, "Indeed she will."[49] She left for Egypt from New York city accompanied by two UP missionaries in February 1875.

Eighteen months after arriving in Cairo she married a fellow missionary Rev. John Giffen whom she had met on the ship going out to Egypt and bore three children. She spent her time starting schools, helping to grow churches, and evangelising many in Alexandria, Ramleh, Cairo, Mansoura, and chiefly Asiut. Mary's time in Africa was limited to seven years as she died in Cairo of an unknown disease shortly after the birth of her third child. Her tomb is located in Cairo.

A question may well be asked of the good of such a short-lived missionary career of seven years in such a hostile environment. On this side of history however, there is a peek of just what God did through her. First, at her farewell meeting in Due West, Rev. N. E. Pressly was so moved by her being sent out that he devoted his own life to missionary service in the country of Mexico. His work would lead to the birth of the ARP denomination in Mexico.

Secondly, missionary Minnie Alexander notes that Mary's book, *Life and Letters*, would inspire Minnie herself to take the Gospel to what is today Pakistan and would establish there a third denomination.

Thirdly, her courage to work in one of the most difficult evangelistic environments motivates us to consider that the work in Africa is not done. From her letters, "Fanatical devotion to Mohammedanism is rare except among the poor. But Christianity is not taking its place. There is a great spectre stalking through Egypt, and that is infidelity … the religion of Jesus is nonetheless abhorred."[50] Almost 150 years later we see that, if anything, the work among Muslim peoples has more needs than ever, especially in Africa.

Mary Galloway Giffen's life inspired a denomination to embark on a multigenerational mission to rescue those perishing in darkness, especially in Africa. The ARP denomination agrees with Prof E. L. Patton in the 1880s who said, "I do not hesitate to say that if the Due West Female College had sent forth from her walls only one such woman as Miss Mary E. Galloway, this institution would have been entitled to the lasting gratitude of the ARP church, of which she was the pioneer missionary."[51]

---

49 Galloway, *Mary Galloway*, 35.
50 Galloway, *Mary Galloway*, 127.
51 Galloway, *Mary Galloway*, 292.

Inset

The Resignation of Hope Waddell Hogg

Sherif A. Fahim

Introduction

"Did God actually say?", this is how the Scripture records the first attack on the word of God in the garden of Eden, when Satan tempted Eve and questioned the veracity of the word of God. It is a pattern that has not stopped! Satan utilises the same strategy against God's people throughout the ages to oppose God's kingdom and hinder God's work. Sometimes the attack may come from those who are outside, and the American mission in Egypt has faced many oppositions from Muslims and the Copts from the beginning of its work in Egypt in the midst of the 19th century. However, by God's grace, the word of God has flourished, more people have come to faith, and the church has grown. But then, we see an attack on God's work that came from within the church, even among one of the missionaries who were supposed to lead and teach this newly born church the way of truth, Rev. Hope Hogg.

Godly Missions Family

The Rev. Hope Waddell Hogg (1863–1912) served with the American mission from 1887 until 1894.[52] He was the son of one of the most faithful and influential missionaries in the United Presbyterian mission in Egypt, the late Dr John Hogg (1833–1886) and was named after his uncle, the noted Irish missionary in Jamaica and Nigeria, Hope Waddell of whom his mother saw as her "adoptive father" and to her children "adoptive grandfather" (see the chapter on Nigeria in this book and Hope Waddell the missionary there). The impact and the fruit of John Hogg's labours from 1854 to 1886 can never be denied! He was an outstanding pioneer missionary in Egypt.[53] Many of John Hogg's children followed the footsteps of their parents and became involved in the American mission in Egypt. "Miss Jessie Hogg served as a member of the mission in Asyut from 1886 until 1902; so also, was Miss Rena Hogg who served as a missionary in Asyut from 1899

---

52 Andrew Watson, *The American Mission in Egypt* (Pittsburgh: United Presbyterian Board of Publication, 1898), 368, 387.
53 For a quick overview of his work, I recommend reading "The Life and Impact of Dr John Hogg as a Missionary in Egypt," Milton Lipa, *Haddington House Journal*, 18, (2016).

until 1937 when she retired. Their youngest sister, Miss May Hogg, was for some years a nurse in the mission hospital at Asyut."[54]

Promising Qualifications

The records about Hope Hogg's academic and personal qualifications were outstanding. He completed his academic studies at the University of Edinburgh.[55] Then, he joined the American mission in Egypt on December 29, 1887, he located at Asyut in the American college,[56] and later became the vice-principal of the college. Rev. Hogg was born in the mission field in 1863; therefore, he learned from his earliest years to speak the language as a native.[57] This knowledge of the Arabic language was even enhanced as "he continued his special study of Arabic under sheikhs from the "Azhar" University."[58] This enabled him to teach, lecture and write examinations for his students in Arabic, which he used as his mother tongue.[59] Andrew Watson who was a coworker with Hope's father, John Hogg, and who had known Hope Hogg from his childhood, testified about Hope's mastery of the Arabic language and his academic training by saying, "From his critical knowledge of the language and his familiarity with Western methods of teaching, it was thought that he was better qualified for instructing the advanced students in the College in their own language than the native professors."[60]

In addition to all this upbringing and training, Rev. Hogg was a diligent worker and the Lord had granted him natural gifts in teaching. Rev. J. R. Alexander, who was the principal of the American College at Asyut and who worked closely with Hogg in the college, gave this very positive testimony about his colleague's personal and teaching skills

> Mr Hogg is a born teacher, more than any man I know. He is prompt and ready, painstaking and careful. His teaching is not only accurate and logical in statement, and clear in

---

54 Earl Edgar Elder, *Vindicating a Vision, the Story of the American Mission in Egypt, 1854–1954* (Philadelphia: The United Presbyterian Board of Foreign Missions, 1958), 27.
55 Andrew Watson, *Testimonials in Favour of Mr Hope W. Hogg, M.A. Formerly Vice-Principal of the American College at Assiout, Egypt, Now a Member of the Editorial Staff of the "Encyclopaedia Biblica"* (Place of publication cannot be determined, 1900), XVII. He was a contributor to the 1911 *Encyclopaedia Britannica*.
56 Watson, *The American Mission*, 368.
57 Watson, *Testimonials*, XVII.
58 Watson, *Testimonials*, XVII.
59 J. R. Alexander, *Testimonials*, XVI.
60 Watson, *Testimonials*, XVII.

exposition, but it is also characterized by a signal skill and fertility of resource in the resolving of difficulties, a felicity in the presentation of facts in such a way as to make them easily remembered, and a richness of illustration drawn from a fund of knowledge and learning, which is very extensive and is continually growing. He has power not only of holding the attention but also of creating an enthusiasm for the subject which he teaches. A diligent worker, and a patient and thorough investigator himself, he is successful in imparting his own habits and methods to his pupils; they become accurate scholars, thoroughly grounded in facts and principles.[61]

What a great testimony this was! When we think of all that has been said about Hope Hogg, we might have said with confidence that this person was the perfect fit to teach the word of God and that he was a perfectly suitable vessel in many ways whom the Lord could use in the land of Egypt and the Middle East. Surprisingly, Rev. Hope resigned on September 23, 1893, and left the mission at the end of May 1894.[62]

A Sudden Resignation

Against all expectations humanly speaking, Rev. Hogg resigned from the mission in Egypt, and then became a professor at Oxford and Manchester in England.[63] One might think that Rev. Hogg had just decided to move from one place to another or from one ministry to another! Interestingly, Andrew Watson did not give any details behind the reasons for this resignation in his major work on the American mission in Egypt. However, as we read one of the reports of the Board of Foreign Missions of the United Presbyterian Church in 1894, we understand the reason behind this resignation.

Obviously, Rev. Hope Hogg had taken a theological stance that "would have been unthinkable to his parents during their evangelistic efforts in Egypt."[64] Influenced by the higher Biblical criticism movements that had spread throughout Europe and New England in the 18th and 19th centuries, and what had now grown into what was emerging as the Modernist-Fundamentalist Controversy, Hogg followed these footsteps and started to question the

---

61 J. R. Alexander, *Testimonials*, XVI.
62 Watson, *The American Mission*, 387.
63 Elder, *Vindicating a Vision*, 27. He held the title of Professor of Semitic Languages & Literature at Manchester (1903–1912).
64 Jeffrey C. Burke, "The Establishment of the American Presbyterian Mission in Egypt, 1854–1940: An Overview," (Unpublished PhD thesis, McGill, 2000), 126.

inerrancy and infallibility of Scripture. The following minutes from the 1894 UP General Assembly Minutes gives a clearer picture of the whole situation:

> On the 23rd of September, much to the surprise and regret of the Board, Rev. Hope W. Hogg forwarded his resignation as a missionary in Egypt. Gradually he had come to a change of views, not only in relation to the distinctive principles of our Church, but also in regard to her creed with respect to the inerrancy and inspiration of the Scriptures and other matters. He had honorably refrained from teaching or preaching his peculiar views; but did not feel that he could conscientiously continue to do so. The resignation was laid on the table for a time in the hope that Mr Hogg might be led, on review of the matter, to change his views and so remain in the mission. There being no hope of this, the Board after most careful consideration of the case, saw no way open to them but to accept the resignation, and this was accordingly done on the 15th of January. Mr Hogg was, however, requested to remain in the mission until the close of the school year, provided he could do so without propagating his peculiar views. It is proper to add that all the correspondence in relation to this case was of the most friendly character, and Mr Hogg's whole course in relation to it was candid and honorable. The Board loved the father, and they regarded the son as one of their most scholarly and useful missionaries. That the resignation was accepted with regret need not be said.[65]

Conclusion

It is sad to see the way that the efforts of such a gifted, well-educated missionary were wasted and how he lost his position and his ministry in God's field in the MENA region. It is important to commend the Board's position though, that they insisted that Hogg not teach these views in the mission field. The Mission Board

---

65 *Minutes of the General Assembly of the United Presbyterian Church of North America* (Appendix) 8 (Pittsburgh: United Presbyterian Board of Publication, May 23rd to 30th, 1894), 505. One of the prominent members of the Foreign Missions Board from 1889, for 33 years was Melvin Grove Kyle, the UPCNA champion on the fundamentalist side in the Modernist-Fundamentalist Controversy and a close friend of J. Gresham Machen. Kyle was a leading evangelical scholar and Biblical archaeologist and UPCNA minister. See, Jeffrey S. McDonald, "Advancing the Evangelical Mind: Melvin Grove Kyle, J. Gresham Machen, and the League of Evangelical Students", *Religions*, 12:498 (2021). https://doi.org/10.3390/rel12070498

offered no compromise on the ground that Hope Hogg was a gifted scholar or a great teacher, or because of the legacy of his father in the mission field. This decision is often overlooked but reveals a remarkable early story in the emerging Modernist-Fundamentalist Controversy, one which merits much more research for full context and worthy of a major thesis study of the 1890s. The UPCNA has been overshadowed on the subject for this decade because the attention focuses upon the PCUSA but the Hogg resignation issue raises many more trajectories for exploration in another Presbyterian tradition, the UP. The Board understood that the health of the church was at stake if they would have become tolerant and buried their heads in the sand. This is a great lesson for us today in our churches, ministries and missions. We cannot tolerate abandoning of essential doctrines such as the inerrancy and infallibility of Scripture for pragmatic reasons. Hope Hogg was a missionary with great qualifications, but what would be the gain if such a talented person withheld the veracity of the word of God?! When the word of God was questioned in Eden the Fall took place; and whenever a church falls into the same satanic trap, its fall is inevitable!

Chapter 24

The History of Early Presbyterianism in Sudan, c.1890s to c.1950 (Part One)

Andrew Okuch Ojullo

Chapter Outline
1. Introduction
2. Context & Early Contact
3. Expansion of a Presbyterian Mission into Upper Nile Region
4. How Presbyterians reached out to the Anyuak People
5. Rev. McClure, the Main Missionary behind the Mission Work among the Anyuak People
6. Mission Work in Akobo and the Surrounding Region
7. North Sudan Mission Efforts
8. Conclusion

1. Introduction

This chapter provides a survey of the history of Presbyterian missions and churches in Anglo-Egyptian Sudan from c.1890s to about 1950 and will concentrate on this beginning period and provide context for this early mission period. This chapter will be continued in volume two, which will deal with the period following 1950. The chapter in volume two will be inclusive of the division of the two Sudans in 2011 and the development of other Presbyterian missions and churches in the two Sudans (Sudan and South Sudan) through to c.2022. That chapter will end with the diaspora Sudanese

▲ Map of Sudan showing Nile River that provided transport for the missionaries from Khartoum to Doleib Hill

Presbyterians as a dispersed people in other African countries and will also provide a glance at the Sudanese diaspora churches globally.

2. Context and Early Contact

Presbyterian missions first began in Egypt in 1854[1] when the Associate Reformed Church (USA) sent its first missionaries to do work there among the Jewish, Muslim, and Coptic peoples at the time when Sudan was unreachable due to the strict control of the Arabs in the region. The Nubian Kingdom, which was a Christian kingdom, had fallen into the hands of the Arabs who spread the Islamic faith far and wide in the region, especially the northern part of Sudan. Muhammad Ali (1769–1849), also referred to as Mehmed Ali, was the pasha of Egypt and Sudan,[2] within the Ottoman Empire. He was the Ottoman commander who was controlling the entire north of Sudan and was not a friend to Christians. Hence, it was very difficult for Christian missionaries to enter the region of Sudan. Attempts were made, but all were in vain. As a result, many missionaries remained in Egypt doing gospel work there as they waited for God's timing.

Sudan experienced worldwide attention following the defeat of General Gordon in 1885 by the Mahdists. In many ways that became an inspiration and motivating factor to evangelicals to do mission work in Sudan, much like Livingstone's death was inspirational for mission work in the interior of Africa a decade earlier.[3] Yet it would be another thirteen years before the rule of Egypt and Sudan was broken by Muhammad Ahmad bin Abdullah (1844–1885), a self-proclaimed Mahdist. In 1885 the Mahdists had moved their capital to Omdurman. They remained in power basically until 1898 when they were defeated by the Anglo-Egyptian army. It was this political victory which proved to open the way

---

1. In 1854 the first Associate Reformed Missionaries from the USA went to Cairo. In 1856 Dr John Hogg went to Egypt with the Scottish Society for the Conversion of Israel. He subsequently became part of the 1858 newly formed United Presbyterian Church of North America mission work in Egypt. See chapter 23 in this book about Egypt.
2. Who was Muhammad Ali? He was born in Kavala, Ottoman Macedonia to a family of Albanian origin. He was a military commander in an Ottoman force and was sent by the Ottomans to Egypt to recover Egypt from French occupation under Napoleon and he emerged as a leader whose regime was welcomed by the European powers who supported the secular-minded Turkish soldiers who came to govern Egypt. Egypt at this time was governed by the ruling Turkish-speaking Ottoman elite. After consolidating his power in Egypt, he turned his attention to Sudan because he wanted to build an Empire and to secure the source of the Nile by conquering Sudan. He would build a strong army by recruiting Sudanese slaves and accumulated wealth by exploiting Sudanese's gold mines. Ahmed, 19–20.
3. For a brief context see, Charles Partee, *The Story of Don McClure*, 24.

for Protestant Christian missions to Sudan. Sudan was reopened for the free entrance of the missionaries and their activities. In other words, Muhammad's fall saw Sudan getting into contact with the outside world again – especially Europe for the first time in its history. In time, missionaries in large numbers came to explore and to work with the unreached people of the Sudan. Many Western missionaries also died in Sudan in their endeavours to plant what Ahmed called "European Christianity" amongst the Sudanese people.[4]

It was in the 1890s when the Presbyterian missionaries, especially those from the United Presbyterian Church of North America, planned to enter Sudan via Egypt. As was mentioned earlier, the American United Presbyterian Mission had been doing mission work in Egypt since the 1850s – long before they were able to enter Sudan.[5] These American missionaries focused on evangelism among the Coptic community of Egypt; by the year 1895, more than five thousand Coptic converts were baptized and about seventy-five converts from Muslim families were baptised in Egypt.[6] Even when the missionaries moved down to Sudan, the work in northern Sudan was still connected with the Coptic Evangelical Church of Egypt as they concentrated on education and health alongside a small church composed mostly of Egyptian expatriates. However, later this church in northern Sudan became known as the Sudan Presbyterian Evangelical Church (SPEC).[7]

When Sudan was opened up for missions, the British governor in Egypt limited the number of missionaries who could enter Sudan, and there were some terms and conditions attached to this restriction as well. They were ordered not to be involved in direct evangelism, but the British government in the Sudan allowed them to do educational and medical work (like in Egypt) as long as no attempt to spread the Christian faith was made. Giffen recalled in his book when he wrote:

> We were informed that no Christian mission work would be allowed among the Moslem population in the Sudan. At the same time, it was pointed out to us that we might go beyond, to the black tribes of the White Nile, with liberty to open as many stations as we wished and with freedom to teach the people the Gospel as we pleased.[8]

---

4 Ahmed, 20.
5 Jean Jacques Bauswein & Lukas Vischer, 1999, 466–467.
6 Ahmed, 47–48.
7 Jean Jacques Bauswein & Lukas Vischer, 1999, 467.
8 Giffen, 1905, 63.

Sir Reginald Wingate, who was the deputy Governor General of the Anglo-Egyptian Sudan, was a devout Christian, and he encouraged the missionaries to go to south of Sudan and begin preaching there, for the south until then was unexplored. Wingate wanted to see Christianity come into this southern region because the entire north of Sudan was by then occupied by Arabs who penetrated into the region very early setting up their centres.[9] However, at the time when Christianity moved to the south, there were still missionaries who remained in the north, especially in the city of Omdurman where the missionaries first set their feet. The American United Presbyterian Mission both in the north and south concentrated on educational work, as mentioned above. Hence, they began a girls' boarding school in Khartoum North in 1908 and Bible work in the homes where they gave lessons in reading and writing, with the Bible as the main textbook, to Sudanese women. Their Bible class for Muslims at Omdurman was considered in the first decade of the twentieth century to be the biggest in all of North Africa because there were 120 students admitted who were taught Christianity by a converted Muslim.[10]

While in the north amongst the Muslims, there were strategies put in place. Education was used as a tool of change while modernisation was also used as a tool to attain a reformed Islam in the north. All these strategies were drafted to be carried out by both the government and the Christian mission according to Hassan, although there was to be no direct evangelism allowed in the northern part of Sudan amongst these Muslims.[11]

Omdurman

When Rev. J. Kelly Giffen (1853–1932), who was an American United Presbyterian missionary, heard that the town of Omdurman in Sudan was captured by the British and Egyptian troops from Muhammed Ahmed,[12] who led the Mahdists rebels, Giffen could not wait to see the American Mission enter Sudan and start work there. Giffen and Andrew Watson made a reconnaissance tour into Egyptian Sudan in 1899. Then they reported to the American Mission back in

---

9   Wheeler, 1982, 31.
10 Ahmed, 48.
11 Ahmed, 39.
12 Mohammad Ahmed was born in Dongola, Sudan a self-proclaimed prophet who considered himself to be the long looked for or expected Islamic leader who's coming was prophesied in the Koran and is anxiously awaited in the whole Mohammedan world. Ahmed claimed to be the religious leader who as a pious man armed against the corrupt regime in Sudan, winning victory over Egyptian soldiers in Sudan on 4 November 1883 at the town of Shekan near El-Obeid thus controlling the entire Sudan after he set up his headquarters at the west bank of the White Nile which later became known as Omdurman city.

Egypt recommending commencement of a mission in Egyptian Sudan. This recommendation was agreed to and the American Mission set aside Rev. and Mrs Kelly Giffen together with Dr Hugh T. McLaughlin, who was a physician, and his wife to start work in Sudan immediately.[13] These two couples arrived in Omdurman in December 1900 but wanted to press further. They had to wait until permission was granted for the opening up of the Upper Nile to the Presbyterian Mission and so in 1901 this was granted which opened up the region when they visited the Upper Nile region (southern Sudan is divided into three regions, Upper Nile, Bahr-el-Ghazal, and Equatoria Regions). The three regions of the south were divided up among three mission societies with Bahr-el-Ghazal under the Episcopal Church, Equatoria under the Roman Catholic Church, and Upper Nile was given to the Presbyterian missionaries.[14]

Doleib Hill

While they were in the Upper Nile region, they chose to set up their mission station at Doleib Hill near the junction of the Sobat and the White Nile Rivers, which is to the north-west of Pochalla town. There at Doleib Hills, they stationed the mission headquarters, and this was not officially opened until 17 February 1902 because of the delay that was caused by the British government in Sudan who were reluctant to give permission to the American missionaries.[15]

The first few months after the missionary families arrived at Doleib Hill were spent in putting up houses for the missionaries with the help from a few Shilluks who were the host community. The larger community of Shilluks did not want to help the missionaries in their work. Thus, Giffen came up with a plan for missionary work; he called it "The Dignity of Labour." This plan was based on two ideas. First, only by labour could improvements be made in the country. Secondly, working

▲ Map of South Sudan showing the three regions

---

13 Charles Watson, "Christian Missions in Egyptian Sudan," in *The Shilluk People: Their Language and Folklore* (Philadelphia: BFMUPCNA, 1912), lx–lxiii; Wheeler, 1982, 32.
14 Jean Jacques Bauswein & Lukas Vischer, 1999, 467.
15 Wheeler, 1982, 42.

▲ Book Cover on the Shilluk People

is a way to cure the sin of idleness. Giffen later recorded this when he said, "Without labour – productive, useful labour – there could be no development of character. We must teach people to do something before we can expect them to be anything."[16] It seems Giffen saw that it was laziness that made the Shilluk uninterested in any kind of work, or they saw work as a curse and did not want to have anything to do with it. The other reason could be that the Shilluk, having experienced forced labour from the Arabs, saw these missionary works as just another form of the same. Besides giving them the gospel, the missionaries taught the local Shilluk people many useful skills; such as carpentry, brick-making, new building methods and skills in agriculture.[17]

In 1906, the mission association, in their yearly meetings and spiritual assembly of the mission, was concerned about the potential for the spread of Islam along with the Arabic language that was used to evangelise the Shilluk people since the missionaries had not learned the Shilluk language. They ordered that missionaries should stop using Arabic and instead learn Shilluk language. It was imperative that they must learn and master Shilluk language. This decision brought in one missionary by the name of Rev. McCreery, a skilled linguist, who translated the first four chapters of the Gospel of John into Shilluk, completing the whole Gospel in 1911.[18]

3. Expansion of Presbyterian Mission in Upper Nile Region[19]

The missionaries were facing one problem in Doleib Hill. They had not yet learnt to speak in the Shilluk language; thus, they could not preach the gospel as there were no English translators. However, since they had spent some time in Egypt, they spoke Arabic to some extent and there were some Shilluk people also who

---

16 Giffen, 1905, 107.
17 Wheeler, 1982, 43.
18 Wheeler, 1982, 184.
19 In Upper Nile Region, the missionaries concentrated their mission works on 5 communities: the Shilluk, Nuer, Anyuak, Dinka, and the Murle community. By the time they were expelled in 1962, the New Testament Bible was partially or completely translated into these 5 languages.

spoke Arabic – especially a man called Muhammad whose father was an Arab and whose mother was a Shilluk woman. This Muhammad became a great help to the missionaries especially in translation as the missionaries began with him as their main translator. They went around villages preaching the gospel in Arabic with Muhammad as the interpreter.

At this Mission Headquarters, the missionaries set up a small building for worship on 15 May 1903 where fourteen people were recorded in attendance in the first service. The missionaries were encouraged, and the first baptism was carried out in 1913 when a man by the name of Nyidak was baptised. In 1919 two more Shilluks, a man called Deng and a woman by the name of Dak, were baptised.

The work began to grow although it was slow. By 1923 about 200 people had been baptised and there were five elders from the local people who helped the missionaries in the work. This development encouraged the missionaries to open a school in the area to train the Shilluk people, because the missionaries believed that the preaching of the gospel went together with practical service to the local people. The missionaries also believed that education could change the minds of the Shilluk people and cause them to understand the gospel easily. They also saw this as one way to empower development amongst the Shilluk people. Hence, the first school was opened in September 1903 which began in English with only two students. The first student was Nyidak, who was also the first convert. Nyidak learned to read and write and later became of great help to the missionaries in teaching the children.

However, the schoolwork was not well received by the Shilluk people as the missionaries had expected. Several reasons were outlined. One, the Shilluk people were not interested in education because they were ignorant of the importance of education. Second, it was a new thing they had never seen before. Education was not something of their ancestors and it was completely unknown to them, so it took convincing for them to understand and embrace education since the entire community was untutored at this point of time. Thirdly, there was not any object lesson from among their own people to which appeal could be made and the lack of trained helpers (Nyidak was not fluent in English) from them to assist the missionaries to make education appealing. For these reasons, and many others, the Shilluk people did not embrace education quickly.[20] The UP Mission was also involved with producing linguistic aids for teaching purposes with the Shilluk people. The mission was faced with establishing a written form of the language. Early missionaries such as Carson and McCreery worked at this and then the German linguist Diedrich Westermann was able to greatly advance

---

20 *Triennial Report on the Foreign Missions of the United Presbyterian Church of North America, 1917, 1918, 1919* (Philadelphia: Patteson, 1919), 201.

this work after Thomas Lambie first helped him learn the language. The first short grammar was published by the UP Mission, followed by a dictionary and a longer grammar and an ethnographic study all in 1912.[21]

After one year, the number increased to 16 students in 1904. Missionaries were encouraged again and opened a boarding section for the school which began operating in March 1924. This school gave birth to many other "bush schools" as they were called.[22]

Apart from preaching of the gospel and education, the missionaries were also involved in medical work amongst the Shilluk people with the help of Dr Hugh T. McLaughlin and Dr C. E. Wilkerson who later remained to be the only missionary at the station. The missionaries saw medical care as one way to show the love of Christ to the local people. When a man called Abbas[23] who helped Dr Wilkerson as a translator took his own life, Dr Wilkerson was so discouraged that he could not continue with the work. His own health failed; hence he was compelled to return to America in 1917.

The medical work was left in the hands of a Shilluk man whom Wilkerson had trained until the arrival of Dr P. E. Gilmor in early 1918. This was another interesting area that was witnessed by the missionaries. The Shilluk people did not really trust the mission medics but their own witch doctors. The Shilluk, like any other African communities, still held onto their traditional beliefs and practices; hence syncretism was still widely practiced at this time. It was reported that there was not a single Shilluk patient who went to the clinic who had not seen a witch doctor first. It was after their witch doctors had failed that they would run to the mission clinic and most of the time, they arrived at the mission clinic when the patients were too weak or their sickness had become chronic.[24]

---

21 Diedrich Westermann, *A Short Grammar of the Shilluk Language* (Philadelphia: BFMUPCNA, 1912). Westermann faced the issue of developing "points" for a language where words change meaning by pitch. See also, Diedrich Westermann, *The Shilluk People: Their Language and Folklore* (Philadelphia: BFMUPCNA, 1912). This is a book of 312 pages and also contains the first dictionary of the Shilluk language.

22 Wheeler, 1982, 44.

23 Abbas was a Fur who was picked by the missionaries trying to make a living along with two other boys and became a servant at the mission station. Abbas had lost his father and mother during the last days of the Mahdi's resignation at Khartoum while his brother was taken into slavery and his little sister lost. At the mission station, Abbas was converted to Christianity and learned to read and write in English. He became fluent in English and Shilluk language. Later, he was able to redeem his brother from slavery paying $100, the money he earned from working for the missionary. He married a Shilluk woman however, he took his own life later leaving a wife and children. It was reported that before his death, his wife had nothing to do with the church but after his death, she gave her life to Christ and became a committed Christian.

24 *Triennial Report … 1918*, 203–204.

Nasir Station

The missionaries expanded this medical work to the nearby villages and since the only possible way to travel around the region was by boat, the missionaries bought a boat from the local people in 1907 to take medicine to the Nuer people's villages along the Sobat River. This medical work saw tremendous success in the area. Even the Nuer people, who mistrusted the missionaries in the first place, were drawn to them because of the medical work. Hence when the missionaries finally decided to expand the mission work among the Nuer people, they decided to start with the medical work. Rev. Elbert L. McCreery[25] (1877–1955), who was a linguist, and Dr Thomas A. Lambie (1885–1954) were posted among the Nuer at Nasir[26] where they arrived on 4 June 1912. They recorded that the Nuer were more receptive to the gospel than the Shilluk. In 1923, the first hospital was built at Nasir with the help of a Christian from America who gave money to the missionaries for the project. Therefore, at Nasir, schools and one hospital were built as the gospel was being preached to the local Nuer people.[27]

These missionaries persevered through the various difficulties they went through, especially sickness in the area. However, in 1946, the congregation founded by the American mission in the Upper Nile region decided to form their own presbytery. The request was tendered in the same year and was granted in 1948. Hence, the Upper Nile Presbytery came into existence with its headquarter at Malakal town, which became the capital of the Upper Nile Region. This church in the south was merged with the Presbyterians in northern Sudan and was formed under one name, Presbyterian Church of Sudan (PCOS).[28] This presbytery was separated from the Evangelical Presbyterian Churches of Sudan (EPCS) and the Coptic Evangelical Church of Egypt (CECE) but still held fellowship with them.

Thereafter, the Dutch Reformed Church in America sent some missionaries to Sudan who were not part of the United Presbyterian Church in America, but they wanted to see the church in Upper Nile become more African and less tied to the United Presbyterian Church in America. Hence, there was a plan to form a fully independent church in the Upper Nile Region, though the plan still

---

25 McCreery later taught at Moody, Bible Institute of Los Angeles (B.I.O.L.A.), and Westmount. He authored, "An Exposition of the 18th Chapter of Isaiah," *The King's Business (monthly publication of BIOLA)* 22:6 (June 1931), 249–251,263. McCreery translated the Gospel of John into Shulla and also reduced both Shulla and Nuer into a written form.

26 Nasir had been conquered and settled by Nuer in the 19th century. The majority of the people by this time were Anyuak who were being absorbed into the Nuer. Most of the first early believers at Nasir were Anyuak. See, Werner, Anderson & Wheeler, 2000, 235.

27 Wheeler, 1982, 45.

28 Jean Jacques Bauswein & Lukas Vischer, 1999, 467.

linked the Upper Nile Presbytery with the Evangelical Presbyterian Churches in Sudan and Egypt in some ways. This Presbytery would remain independent of their control which was realised in 1948 and later the Upper Nile Presbytery became fully independent from all other Churches, especially the Evangelical Presbyterian Church of Sudan and Egypt, and was less tied to Presbyterian churches in America but enjoyed fellowship with them as mentioned above.[29]

4. How Presbyterians reached out to the Anyuak People

As noted above, the first United Presbyterian missionaries who moved to the south settled in Doleib Hill amongst the Shilluk people in 1902. The work soon expanded to adjacent neighbourhoods; the missionaries expanded their mission works to Nasir amongst the Nuer people, where they arrived on 4 June 1912 and established another post there. Around Nasir were Anyuak[30] people who were easily reachable by the missionaries. In addition to Nuer boys, the Nasir School also received Anyuak and Murle boys (from Akobo and Pibor respectively) sent by government administration who gained school confidence. The Nasir school system had some village schools and planted an out-school in Akobo among the Anyuak under the direction of Joel Gilo. Some girls' education started in 1935 in the greater Upper Nile region, but it did not show much progress until the 1940s.[31] Before this period, we see a picture of an out-school of Nasir, inspected by Rev. Will Adier (with Mun Omot from Torbar) who commended the amount of commitment put forth in the work done there right from the beginning by the missionaries. The first Anyuak to be baptized in 1923 was Bakat, who died the same year.[32]

The missionaries proceeded from Nasir to Akado (on the Ethiopian side) still amongst the Anyuak people, which became known as Pokwow. They succeeded in winning some souls who later became evangelists. They continued and penetrated to the Gilo region in the heart of the Anyuak land and established their base in Pinyudo, where they opened a clinic and lower primary school just like they did in Akobo and Akado. Although they established churches that have survived more or less up to today, they did not go to all the regions of Anyuak. Adingora commented that there was a task left for the Anyuak converts to carry out and win more souls to Christ.[33]

---

29 Wheeler, 1982, 83.
30 The Anyuak people are found in two towns in South Sudan: Akobo and Pochalla.
31 Adingora, 2019.
32 Werner, Anderson & Wheeler, 2000, 309.
33 Adingora, 2019.

5. Rev. McClure, the Main Missionary behind the Mission Work among the Anyuak People

At first, the American missionaries were very slow to extend their mission to the Anyuak people because of the fact that the missionaries had a shortage of funds for the mission. United Presbyterians in the USA annually reduced expenditure from 1926–1936, while at the same time they had already projects in the north of Sudan that hampered them from beginning new missions. They aimed to keep their work alive and not to extend it. This is one of the biggest barriers that kept the Anyuak out of the missionaries' dream.

Following his graduation from Westminster College, PA, Don McClure (who was later given the name of Odan by the Anyuak) had a burning heart to go to Africa (and specifically Sudan amongst the Shilluk people) and do the work of evangelism. He and his wife Lyda, having prayed for this great task, agreed to go for the Lord. McClure and his wife proceeded to southern Sudan and landed in Doleib Hill,[34] which was the American Mission Headquarter in the Upper Nile Region. His primary call was to preach the gospel to the unreached people in the region. Seeing that there had never been evangelism done amongst the Anyuak people, McClure planned to go to Akobo and he landed in Akobo in 1938 where he started a mission and served for most of the years of his service as a missionary in Africa. He opened mission stations at Akobo, Akado, Gilo, Shuma area near Dimma in the southern Gambella region of Ethiopia and went all the way to the Somalia region of Ethiopia serving the Lord Jesus Christ.

McClure's mission was supported by Emperor Haile Selassie of Ethiopia who told him, "You must hurry, if you don't reach them quickly for Christ, others will, then your case will be set back decades, perhaps centuries, time is short".[35] The Ethiopian emperor Haile Selassie spoke these words to Don McClure who dedicated his life to work with the Anyuak in both Ethiopia and Sudan. The words were truer than anyone could realize at the time. He was a very close friend to the Ethiopian emperor Haile Selassie which enabled him to organize assistance for the Upper Nile from Addis Ababa, Ethiopia. He continued to work in Ethiopia until the fall of and the death of the Emperor. After retirement, McClure continued as a volunteer at Gode, Ethiopia, until he was shot to death by a guerrilla movement in Ethiopia (called Ogaden) where he lost his dear life on 27 March 1977.[36]

---

34 McClure was at the Doleib Hill station from 1934 to 1938 before commencing work at Akobo.
35 Werner, Anderson & Wheeler, 2000.
36 Werner, Anderson & Wheeler, 2000.

6. Mission Work in Akobo and the Surrounding Region

Joel Gilo started work in Akobo as a teacher and evangelist under mission supervision in 1935; this was in the same year that McClure questioned why he was "working there in Doleib Hill. The oldest mission saw a need to move to a new place."[37] From then McClure concentrated his mission on the Anyuak people. McClure was motivated by the Anyuak traders who would go to Doleib Hill almost yearly to trade their canoes and tobacco for cows. McClure insisted on going to start a work at Akobo, and the mission insisted that unless there were houses, doctors and a lorry first in Akobo he would not be allowed to go. Despite all these terms and conditions, he declared to go by himself and build his own tukuls,[38] and he then hired a lorry, driving it to Akobo in 1937. It was in this year that McClure got clearance from the British authorities and finally launched an Anyuak mission at Akobo.

A vision to reach the Anyuak helped to rescue the sleeping American Mission in southern Sudan. Don McClure could not get back to southern Sudan on time when he went back to America because of the civil war that closed the way until 1943. When he finally came back, there was a famine in the area so he brought in dura,[39] which he used to help the local people as they worked for the mission – what he called "food for work"- clearing the mission land and building schools for food as wages so that the mission work could resume. In Akobo, McClure witnessed that the Anyuak people showed openness to education and to the gospel more than the Shilluk and the Nuer people of Doleib Hill and Nasir. An interesting account to that effect was given by Dale Ralph Davis in his commentary on the book of 2 Kings. He recounted,

> When Don McClure was serving as a missionary to the Anuaks in Sudan, one of the Anuak believers brought his son to McClure for medical attention. The lad had been fishing and he had been bitten by a very poisonous puff adder. The father was calm and told the missionary, 'if the medicine will not help him, then our prayers will. And if he dies, our lives are in God's hands.' McClure teased the father by saying, 'why didn't you kill a sheep and pour the blood on your son as you would have done three years ago?' the father lifted his hands above his head in horror: 'that was in other days. Now we believe only in the blood of Jesus.'[40]

---

37 Werner, Anderson & Wheeler, 2000, 309.
38 Thatch-grass houses with mudded walls.
39 Dura is the local name for sorghum.
40 Davis, *2 Kings: The Power and the Fury* (Fearn, Ross-shire: Christian Focus, 2005), 51.

That is how serious McClure was with his evangelism. The local Anyuak people embraced the gospel so well that if only McClure's plan wasn't cut short a great harvest would have been realised among these people.

He then widened his vision amongst the Anyuak people concentrating on agriculture (teaching the local farmers to improve their agricultural methods), but his request was turned down by the British government in Khartoum when he appealed for some help. The missionaries later transferred this plan and their agriculturalists to Ethiopia over the border.[41]

Anyuak Plan

In 1944 McClure proposed what he called the *Anyuak Plan* which called for 15 missionaries to be available amongst the Anyuak people to do a thorough work for 15 years evangelising, healing through the medical work, educating, leadership training, working in agricultural, doing Bible translation and then leaving the Anyuak people to carry on the work by themselves. It was a brilliant vision. Sadly, the Second World War interrupted the plan and prevented McClure from remaining in Akobo. However, his plan received some support from some of his friends in the mission, including J. Lowrie Anderson, the mission secretary in southern Sudan and the mission secretary of the board of USA, Glen Reed, who worked with him in Doleib Hill. McClure then went all over the USA stirring churches to back his Anyuak vision.[42] The United Presbyterian Church was seeking to join the Reformed Church in America at that time, and McClure visited some of the Reformed Churches (RCA) and they decided to support the Anyuak Plan. On his return to Akobo amongst the Anyuak, McClure went to Egypt with Evangelist Adwok Mayom and the Evangelical Church in Egypt decided to participate in southern Sudan, commencing in 1954.

Harvey Hoekstra (1920–2018)

While McClure was traveling around the USA stirring churches to support his Anyuak Plan, he went to Western Theological Seminary in Holland, Michigan to give a talk on his plan. At the seminary, there was a student by the name of Harvey Hoekstra who became very interested, especially when Rev. McClure mentioned that he wanted 15 missionaries to work among the Anyuak people for 15 years in the fields of education, medicine, and agriculture. McClure added that he also wanted to translate the Bible into the Anyuak language as a priority and that he needed a translator to do the work. Hoekstra talked to Rev. McClure afterward. Later, in 1948, Hoekstra and his dear wife, Lavina, arrived

---

41 Werner, Anderson, & Wheeler, 2000.
42 Werner, Anderson, & Wheeler, 2000, 347.

in Sudan and commenced the work of translation in Akobo town among the Anyuak. Rev. Hoekstra learned Dha-Anyua (Anyuak) and was given the name of Odola by the Anyuak people. When he learned the language, with the help of some Anyuak men such as Jok Deng, James Buya, Ezekiel Ochalla Lero, and Othow War-Adier, they poured their souls into the work of translating the New Testament in Dha-Anyua.

Then came that fateful day when the Government of Sudan announced that all missionaries should leave Sudan. Rev. Hoekstra was so worried because it was a time of trouble for all the missionaries in the Sudan, yet he wanted to have the New Testament Bible complete in Dha-Anyua sooner. He had a friend in the US who had given him a gift to enable him to print the first 1,000 copies, but they had not arrived. Rev. Hoekstra and his wife were at the airstrip in January 1962 waiting for the Mission Aviation Fellowship (MAF) plane to take them out of Akobo. When the plane arrived, the pilot handed him a package and asked him to open it saying there could be something of interest to him. He couldn't stop thanking God when he opened the package; it contained five copies of the complete Anyuak New Testament. Rev. Hoekstra notes that the Anyuak man standing next to him told him, "We don't know why our government is sending you, missionaries out of our country, but I want you to know that you are leaving behind God's best gift, you have given us his Word in our language."[43] There were 1,000 copies waiting in Khartoum at the time. Although Rev. Harvey Hoekstra and other missionaries were expelled from Sudan, they left when the New Testament was completed.[44]

Rev. McClure was not happy since his plan of 15 missionaries to work for 15 years among the Anyuak people was cut short. He refused to go back to the USA but crossed the border to Ethiopia where he opened a mission at Pokwow and Gilo River.

The first Presbyterian church among the Murle people

By 1947 a missionary by the name of Rev. Will Adair who served at Nasir station paid a visit to Jebel Boma, south of Pochalla town. Jebel Boma had been cut off from any mission fields in the country. However, Rev. Will found a church there with almost a hundred worshipers. These worshipers were almost all from Equatoria and their hymns and liturgy were all in Southern Arabic. This church had been planted by Dick Lyth who had been a CMS missionary in Yambio for a short time.

---

43 *Harvey Hoekstra's Message to the Anuak People* (2016). https://www.youtube.com/watch?v=dkxOReYvYKM.
44 The entire Bible in Dha-Anyua was completed (both New and Old) in 2013 when the first New Testament translation was also revised. The Anyuak now has the entire Bible printed and also in audio form.

How Lyth ended up in Jebel Boma

When civil war broke out, Lyth volunteered for the Sudan Defence Force. He became an officer in charge of 300 men, based at Boma and responsible for the long border with Ethiopia. He started a small church using hymns and readings that he translated into Juba Arabic. He required all believers to attend the church. By 1941, he was moved to Akobo and Pibor and made the District Commissioner. Lyth planted what were termed Markaz churches at Akobo, Pibor and Pochalla— as well as the one he left at Boma. Due to his keenness in spiritual matters, his fellow British called him the "Commissionary."[45]

7. North Sudan Mission Efforts

Khartum Station and Out-stations

Although direct evangelism was not allowed among the Muslims in northern Sudan, missionaries believed that they could still show the love of Christ to Sudanese people, and that they still could preach Christ through deeds. The missionaries directed their work amongst the Muslim Sudanese in the north. Immediately once Egyptian Sudan opened up for missionaries the APCM and the Evangelical Church of Egypt Mission came down in 1900. A station was opened in Omdurman that year. This expanded into a tri-station of Khartoum and Khartoum North in 1903, then out-stations developed at Port Sudan, Wad Medani, Atbara, Halfa, El Obeid, and Gedaref. All these stations were opened before and after the missionaries had moved into southern Sudan.

The missionaries in northern Sudan, like they had been doing in Egypt, centred their work on education and medicine, with evangelism sandwiching the two. As a result, a boys' school was established in 1905 in the north. This led to a girls' school that was opened 1909 which later became the first girls' secondary school in Sudan. At first, Sudanese families were reluctant to send their sons to missions' schools, but when the nationalist movement began to gain strength in the 1930s, they saw the advantage of Western education and sent their sons. However, from the beginning many Muslim girls were sent to these Christians schools because of the useful domestic skills they were taught there.[46]

The Church in northern Sudan began with Rev. Jabra Hanna who planted an Evangelical Church in 1900. Hanna was born in 1876 in Egypt and was schooled in the prestigious secondary school of the American Mission. After his graduation from the seminary in 1900, he was appointed to move to Sudan.

---

45 Werner, Anderson & Wheeler, 2000, 267.
46 *Triennial Report … 1918*, 204–215.

Rev. J. Kelly Giffen had purchased a property in Omdurman previously, which became the first Evangelical meeting place.

The first Omdurman service was attended by 20 people including some missionaries. Hanna soon made contact with new arrivals from Egypt and with Syrian Christians. He was ordained as a pastor in 1901 and in 1903 he pastored three struggling congregations in the Three Towns (Khartoum, Khartoum North, and Omdurman) with an average of 35 men and 6 women attending church services each week. By 1904, the number increased to 70 people attending each week and a new church was planted at Haifa with 15 members attending services at this new church plant. Rev. Hanna returned to Egypt in 1909 after he had successfully founded the Evangelical Church in northern Sudan. This church remained part of the Egypt-based Synod of the Nile until 1912 and 1913 when the Synod Assembly made it an independent presbytery.[47]

Projects done in Northern Sudan

Schools

By 1904, the Evangelicals had established schools alongside their four small congregations with a total enrolment of 247 students. The purpose of these schools was first, to attract Coptic children, and secondly, to provide an entrance for the Christian message to Muslim families.

Medical work

At first, Dr McLaughlin and his dear wife were sent to start medical work at Doleib Hill, but due to his wife's illness, the two left Doleib Hill in 1904. They opened a clinic in Khartoum North. However, by 1910, Mrs McLaughlin was too sick to remain, and the couple retired. Later, Dr Hugh Magill who worked at Doleib Hill also had fallen sick at the station and left for Khartoum where he picked up the work from Dr McLaughlin. This clinic was closed in 1915 due to lack of staff.[48]

8. Conclusion

The commencement of Presbyterian Mission work in Sudan began with the United Presbyterians of North America and the Evangelical Church of Egypt entering Sudan as a mission field at the end of the 1890s and establishing stations during the first decade of the twentieth century. It is a complex history in part due to the complexity of the political situation and also the complexity of the

---

47 Werner, Anderson & Wheeler, 2000, 180.
48 Werner, Anderson & Wheeler, 2000, 181.

ethnic and tribal divisions and groups in Sudan from the 1890s through to and after independence in the 1950s. The advance of the mission was with much sacrifice, and yet we also see certain indigenous "men of peace" emerging who were of great assistance. There were many strategies which the mission used to advance its work of God's kingdom in Sudan and also a long list of missionaries and indigenous church leaders, both Egyptian and Sudanese. Theologically the work in this period was evangelical in nature, and yet there may be some questions which need further exploration (for example, to dig deeper and to ask about syncretism) which at present are beyond the scope of this introductory paper. Of lasting value has been the Bible translation work which the UPC was involved in for the Shilluk and Anyuak tribes.

▼ Timeline of the UP Mission in Egyptian Sudan

1854	AUPM Missionaries working in Egypt.
4 Nov. 1883	Mohammad Ahmed won victory over Egyptian soldiers at Shekan town near El-Obeid in Sudan.
1895	More than 5,000 Copts convert and about 75 converts from Muslim families were baptised in Egypt.
1898	Pastor Llwellyn Henry Gwynne was waiting in Egypt for permission to enter Sudan.
1899/1900	Rev. J. Kelly Giffen visited Omdurman town with Dr Andrew Watson. Omdurman mission station begins 1900
1901	Rev. Giffen and Dr Hugh T. McLaughlin visited the Upper Nile Region in southern Sudan.
17 Feb. 1902	Presbyterian mission under AUPM was officially opened in Doleib Hills.
15 May 1903	A small building was set up for worship at Doleib Hills where 15 people attended the first service.
September 1903	The first school in Upper Nile was opened by the missionaries and 2 students reported in the first year but the number increased to 16 the following year.
1907	Missionaries bought a boat to take medicines to Nuer villages along Sobat River.
4 June 1912	Rev. McCreery and Dr T. A. Lambie were posted among Nuer people at Nasir.
1913	The first baptism took place when Nyidak was baptised at Doleib Hills.
1919	Second baptism service took place when a man called Deng and a woman called Dak were baptised.

1923	About 200 people had been baptised with 5 local ordained elders.
	The first hospital was built at Nasir among the Nuer people.
	The first Anyuak man called Bakat was baptised who died the same year.
March 1924	A boarding school was opened at Doleib Hills.
1935	Girl's education started in the Upper Nile Region.
	Joel Gilo started work in Akobo as a teacher and evangelist under mission supervision.
1938	Rev. Don McClure went to do mission work at Akobo among the Anyuak people.
1944	Rev. McClure proposed the Anyuak Plan, calling for 15 missionaries to work among the Anyuak for 15 years and then leave the work to the Anyuak thereafter.
1946	The church at Doleib Hills decided to form a presbytery
1948	Upper Nile Presbytery was formally formed

The Egyptian Sudan UPCNA Missionaries 1919[49]

Khartum	Rev. R. L. Edie
	Rev. J. Kelly Giffin
	Rev. R. F. Shields
	Miss Una Coie
	Miss Sara I. Dight
	Miss Elsie E. Grove
	Miss Emma M. McKeown
	Miss Kathryn MacKenzie
Doleib Hill/ Sobat River	Mr. C. B. Guthrie
	Rev. D. S. Oyler
Nasser/Sobat River	Rev. Dr T. A. Lambie
	Rev. P. S. Smith
Furlough	Rev. G. A. Sowash

---

[49] Adapted from *The 1919 Handbook on Foreign Missions of the United Presbyterian Church of North America*, 95.

Egyptian Sudan Statistics, December 31, 1917[50]

WORKERS	
AMERICAN	
Ordained Missionaries	4
Married Women Missionaries	6
Unmarried Women Missionaries	2
Industrial Missionaries	1
Medical Missionaries (men)	1*
Total Number of Missionaries on the Field	**14**
EGYPTIAN & NATIVE	
Licensed preachers	2
Evangelists (half year)	2
Teachers	20
Total Number of Egyptian and Native Workers	**24**
Total Number (American, Egyptian, and Native Workers on field in 1917	**38**

*Left the field in April because of a breakdown of health.

---

50 Adapted from, *The 1919 Handbook on Foreign Missions of the United Presbyterian Church of North America*, 102.

CHURCH	
Regular Preaching Stations	6
Out Stations	6
Organized Congregations	1
Total Membership	235
Net Increase	30
SABBATH SCHOOLS	
Sabbath Schools	5
Scholars	579

SCHOOLS			
Theological Seminaries	1	Students	33
Boarding Schools	2	Students	110
Day Schools	4	Students	742
Total Number of Schools	6	**Total Number of Students**	852

MEDICAL WORK	
Dispensaries	2
FINANCIAL SUMMARY 1917	
Congregational	$1,268.59
Educational	$2,058.10
TOTAL	**$3,326.69**

Questions for study (fact type):
1. Name the first two American Presbyterian missionary couples who were stationed in the Egyptian Sudan.
2. What year was the mission station at Nasir established and what people group were being reached here?
3. Name the man who established the written form of the Shilluk language. Who was the missionary who established a mission amongst the Anyuak people?
4. Briefly outline the ministry of Rev. Jabra Hanna in northern Sudan. Use the information questions—who, what, when, where, why, and how—to provide facts.

A Survey of Presbyterian Mission History in Africa

Questions for study (reflection type):
1. Look at the chart entitled "Egyptian Sudan Statistics, December 31, 1917
2. Workers." By 1917 there were 14 missionaries and 24 Egyptian and Native workers labouring in Sudan. Read Philippians 1:1–6. Explain the biblical concept of "partnership" in Christian missions and why it is important.
3. "Direct evangelism was not allowed among the Muslim in Northern Sudan." Missionaries believed that they could still show the love of Christ through deeds. Read Romans 10:1–15. Considering the scriptures, evaluate the effectiveness of this approach in North Sudan.

Select Bibliography

Adingora, J. Presbyterian mission work among the Anyuak people. A. Okuch, Interviewer, (16 November 2019).

Ahmed, H. M. *Sudan: The Christian Design; A Study of the Missionary Factor in Sudan's Cultural and Political Integration, 1843–1986.* Leicester: Islamic Foundation,1989.

Anderson, William B. "Thomas Lambie: Missionary Pioneer in Sudan and Ethiopia, 1907–1942." In *Gateway to the Heart of Africa*, eds., Francesco Pierli, Maria Teresa Ratti, & Andrew C. Wheeler. Nairobi: Paulines Publications, 1998, 126–145.

Balisky, E. Paul. *Thomas A. Lambie: Missionary Doctor and Entrepreneur*. Eugene, OR: Wipf & Stock, 2020.

Bauswein, Jean Jacques and Lukas Vischer. *The Reformed Family; Worldwide: A Survey of Reformed Churches, Theological Schools, and International Organizations*. Grand Rapids: William B. Eerdmans, 1999.

Freedom4Anyuak (Director). (2016). Harvey Hoekstra's Message to the Anuak People [Motion Picture].

Giffen, J. K. *The Egyptian Sudan*. New York: Fleming H. Rev.ell Company, 1905.

Lambie, Thomas A. *Boot and Saddle in Africa*. New York: Blakiston/Rev.ell, 1943.

Lambie, Thomas A. *A Doctor Carries on*. Original. New York, 1942. Reprint edition with new title, *A Doctor's Great Commission*. Wheaton, IL: Van Kampen Press, 1954.

Lambie, Thomas A. *A Doctor Without A Country*. New York: Fleming Rev.ell, 1939.

McCreery, Elbert L. "An Exposition of the 18th Chapter of Isaiah." *The King's Business* (monthly publication of BIOLA) 22:6 (June 1931): 249–251, 263.

The 1919 Handbook on Foreign Missions of the United Presbyterian Church of North America. Philadelphia: UPCNA, 1919. Sudan. sections: 79–91, 95, 102. https://babel.hathitrust.org/cgi/pt?id=wu.89077180644&view=1up&seq=7

Partee, Charles. *The Story of Don McClure: Adventure in Africa From Khartoum to Addis Abada*. Original 1990. Lanham, MD: University of America Press, 2004.

Triennial Report of the Board of Foreign Missions of the United Presbyterian Church of North America. Philadelphia: Pattison Printing House, 1919. Retrieved from Study Lib: https://studylib.net/doc/18463205/f-oreign-m-issions-united-presbyterian-church

Werner, Ronald, William Anderson, & Andrew Wheel. *The Day of Devastation, the Day of Contentment, the history of Sudanese across 2000 years.* Nairobi: Paulines Publications, 2000.

Wheeler, A. *The Church in Sudanese History*. Khartoum: Bishop Gwynne College, 1982.

Chapter 25

Ethiopia and the United Presbyterian Mission c.1918–c.1950s

J. C. Whytock

Chapter Outline
1. Introduction
2. The Flu and the Beginning of a Mission
3. The First Station: Sayo
4. More Mission Stations: Gorei & Addis Ababa
5. A War & Presbytery Affiliations of a Unique Kind
6. Postscript
7. Summary Conclusion
Bio Inset: Thomas Lambie
Bio Inset: Gidada Solan

1. Introduction

There is a fascinating chain to follow along the "Nile corridor" in the development of American Presbyterian mission work (UPCNA), which began in the 1850s first in Egypt, then c.1900 into Sudan, then finally c.1918 into the land of Abyssinia or Ethiopia. This short survey will tell this story of the American United Presbyterian Mission to Abyssinia/Ethiopia from c.1918 to c.1950s.[1] This mission begins in a most unique way and will expand amidst much controversy and difficulty. This chapter also includes two important biographical studies on Thomas Lambie, a key pioneer missionary, and Gidada Solan, a significant early indigenous Christian leader.

2. The Flu and the Beginning of a Mission

Protestant missions to the ancient lands of Ethiopia can be traced back to the Church Missionary Society efforts and then to work by Lutheran missionaries

---

1 Technically when the mission began the country was referred to as Abyssinia and after 1941 it was known as Ethiopia.

from Sweden, Germany, and Norway – all in the nineteenth century. Yet large areas of Abyssinia were without Protestant missions.

In the summer of 1918, Thomas Lambie had done a short exploratory visit from Sudan into Abyssinia. On that 1918-visit, he had spoken with the British major at Gambella about his desire to enter Abyssinia for mission work. The seed was planted and a few months later providentially the worldwide pandemic would bring this about.

By late 1918, the western Ethiopian highlands were experiencing a terrible epidemic resulting in a large number of deaths. This was what has been popularly called the *Spanish Flu* or influenza. An appeal was made through the governor of the Sayo region in Ethiopia to the British District Commissioner for help. This request was relayed to Dr Lambie of the UP Mission in Nasir, Sudan. Lambie was eager to accept this opening and permission was granted by the BFM for such an investigative visit and also by government officials in Sudan. Thus, the Lambies, together with the Giffens in Khartoum, and Ralph McGill in Cairo, all UP missionaries, proceeded to Gambella in Abyssinia. The families were left at Gambella and in 1919 the men then went separately up the plateau to Sayo spying out the land like in the Old Testament. The governor of Sayo region was pleased and requested Lambie to open a mission station in Sayo and provided a tract of land in Sayo for this.

Initially in 1919 this was just an extension of the Sudan field but in 1922 the UPCNA declared Abyssinia its own separate field. This first station (1919) was called Dembi Dollo and was in western Abyssinia in Sayo. This mission was at first to chiefly reach the Oromo peoples (formerly known as Galla). Thus, "the foot" of the American Presbyterian Mission was now "in the door" into ancient Abyssinia through a most unusual set of circumstances.[2] In 1893 the UP Mission had tried to enter back into Abyssinia but had been refused. Even earlier, in 1869, permission had been given for a mission into Abyssinia, when the UPCNA, GA granted permission through the BFM for those missionaries labouring in Egypt to extend their mission work into Abyssinia.[3] However, it would be fifty years before such was possible.

3. The First Station: Sayo

From this initial medical emergency response and investigation, a mission station developed at Dembi Dollo with a clinic, a school, and a church. One of the earliest converts of this mission in Sayo was Gidada Solon (see attached inset with this chapter). The BFM of the UPCNA sent more missionaries (Rev.

---

2 Cogswell, *No Turning Back*, 44–45.
3 *Triennial Mission Report of the BFM of the UPCNA, 1919–1921*, 4, quoted in Galloway, 80.

and Mrs Fred Russell and the nurse Ruth Beatty) to Dembi Dolo in 1922. Fred Russell discipled Gidada in his new faith as did another UP missionary who came, Rev. John Buchanan, and Gidada went on to be a wonderful evangelist in the province.[4]

Integrated mission work was done at Dembi Dolo, Sayo and the evangelistic work was blessed amongst the construction labourers, clinic patients, and school children. In 1932 the medical work at Dembi Dolo coalesced into a hospital which formally opened in 1933 as the Jean Orr Memorial Hospital with 25 beds. In 1945, 15,000 patients passed through this small hospital and 20,000 would have heard the Gospel there.[5]

The UPCNA mission into Abyssinia had two agendas:

> The evangelistic task of the missionary in Ethiopia is two-fold. The first is the quickening of the ancient Ethiopic Church, and second, the reaching of the millions who are not in that church.[6]

This introduces us to the delicate balance by which the UP mission had to engage in its work in Abyssinia. It had to tread carefully so as to not incur the wrath of the Ethiopic Church. Medical mission work helped with that bridge to the ancient church, as did schooling where eventually training in the Geez language was also provided for boys preparing for ministry in the Ethiopic Church. Secondly, the indigenous new believers took much initiative upon themselves to go out in Gospel teams of two to outlying villages and share the faith and establish small churches and schools. Bergsma commends the Oromo converts for their aggressive evangelistic work in the outstations. The main station in 1934 saw congregations on Sunday of between 400 and 550 people and during five years from 1929 to 1934 saw 128 people converted. These appear to be chiefly Oromo who were animists and bound in witchcraft and sacrifices to placate rivers or trees or things in nature. Opposition to the Gospel also came from these Oromo witchdoctors whose livelihood was being impacted by these evangelical missions as in Acts. The result was that many witch doctors moved further away from the mission stations to ply their trade.

It was really uncertain how this "church" would emerge structurally in Abyssinia in the 1920s and into the 1930s, but by 1931 it was becoming clear that a separate evangelical church was emerging in Sayo region. By 1928–30 there

---

4   Balisky, *Thomas A. Lambie*, 24.
5   Bergsma, "Ethiopia as a Mission Field," 18.
6   *BFM Annual Report of 1931*, 131 as quoted in Galloway, "The Formation of the Evangelical Church in Ethiopia," 89.

was an average attendance of over 200 at the church and Sabbath School at the main station and five outstations' schools/churches were emerging.

4. More Mission Stations: Gorei[7] and Addis Ababa

Gorei

Two more mission stations emerged, once again through an unusual method. The Lambie's were leaving for furlough in 1922. They decided to leave by crossing via Ethiopia rather than through Sudan. They stopped at Gorei, which is about fifty miles southeast of Demi Dollo. Here the governor encouraged Lambie to begin a medical clinic at Gorei and so Lambie bought a house and land for a future mission station work. The Lambies then proceeded onto Addis Ababa. Here they were well received by the Regent Haile Selassie who was pleased with the mission's work at Dembi Dollo and asked the mission to commence a hospital in Addis Ababa. Thomas Lambie was most zealous to commence such a hospital work and to extend the work of the American Presbyterian Mission thus across Ethiopia. The BFM, though desirous to see such expansion, saw financial restraint as the order of the day and would not finally support such an undertaking. As Cogswell writes, "Undaunted, Lambie went directly to the Church with his appeal. A generous layman, Mr W. S. George of Palestine, Ohio, donated the large sum needed to build the hospital in Addis Ababa. Thus, came into being the renowned George Hospital in Addis Ababa."[8]

The station at Gorei was to develop and missionaries (Rev. and Mrs Shields and Mrs Ruth Lobaugh Walker) were assigned there in 1924 for evangelistic work and to develop this station and a German medical missionary joined them (Dr Naglesbach). Medical mission work included treating leprosy and gunshot wounds, along with the normal routine of illnesses common to the area. The clinic did evangelism with all its patients. On the compound, a boys' school was first established and then also a girls' school. Regular Sunday services were held and in four years these were averaging over 200 in attendance plus another Sunday service for lepers.

Starting in 1927, mission outreach teams (mainly consisting of the schoolboys) went into outlying villages. The use of indigenous workers was critical for the spread of the Gospel outside of Gorei. This mission station faced much transience of population as it was a major trading location. Also, the station experienced opposition from the Ethiopic Church. When converts of the mission needed to be baptised, they had to pay money to the local Ethiopic priests to be baptised.

---

7   Original spelling was Gorei then it was switched to Gore.
8   Cogswell, *No Turning Back*, 45.

Rev. Shields was transferred to the new station at Addis Ababa, thus leaving no ordained minister. Then in 1934 an ordained minister was finally sent, Rev. C. F. Kenniweg, but the next year due to the Italo-Ethiopian war was forced to leave.[9] It was then up to the native evangelists and teachers to carry-on the station – and they did – amidst very trying days of war.

Addis Ababa

The George Hospital was begun in 1923 and Dr Lambie was in charge until 1927. A division of sorts arose in the UP Mission in Ethiopia in 1927. Dr Lambie challenged the UPC to continue to press forward into southern Ethiopia and the BFM of the UPC would not due to chiefly financial reasons. The result was that Lambie organised a new mission – the Abyssinia Frontiers Mission (AFM) in April 1927. The stress here was on the key word "frontiers" or reaching out to many of the unreached areas of Ethiopia. In September of 1927 the AFM was folded into the Sudan Interior Mission (SIM) at Rowland Bingham's urging. The result was that Lambie became involved with SIM, a more established faith mission which would go on to plant the largest number of evangelical churches in Ethiopia, out surpassing the UPC work in time.[10] The merged SIM established a leprosarium in Addis Ababa under Dr Lambie's oversight.

What then became of the Hospital in Addis Ababa after Lambie left in 1927? The Hospital, also known popularly as the American Mission Hospital, in Addis Ababa continued to attract much interest. In 1928 it came under the leadership of Dr Stuart Bergsma (1900–1986) from the Christian Reformed Church who was appointed superintendent of the hospital by the BFM of the UPCNA. He remained in this position through to 1934 and under his leadership the Hospital was serving 10,000 outpatients per year and 1,400 in patient residents. The UP Hospital became the largest hospital in Ethiopia during the 1930s with 100 beds. It had an X-ray department, a modern laboratory, and surgery. Bergsma authored a book *Rainbow Empire: Ethiopia Stretches out Her Hands*, which helps describe mission work at this hospital in Addis Ababa. Adjacent to the hospital was the UP Girls School in Addis Ababa, the first of its kind in that city. A church also met in the chapel of the Hospital.[11]

---

9   Galloway, "The Formation of the Evangelical Church in Ethiopia," 93–96.
10 Tucker, *From Jerusalem to Irian Jaya*, 341–346.
11 Bergsma, "Ethiopia as a Mission Field," 17.

5. A War and Presbytery Affiliations of a Unique Kind

The Second Italo-Abyssinian/Ethiopian War occurred between 1935–1936 when the Italians under the fascist dictator Mussolini's direction invaded Abyssinia. Abyssinia was subjugated to Italy and this Italian occupation lasted through to 1941 when Haile Selassie returned to power. These were very difficult years for the UP mission in Ethiopia, which will be described below.

In November 1936, the UP missionaries at the two stations of Sayo and Gorie had to be evacuated. Some went to open-up new unreached areas in Sudan in the UP mission there, some were transferred to India. The missions' properties in both Sayo and Gorie were then occupied by the invading Italian army. The hospital in Addis Ababa was allowed to carry on its work at that time.[12] Then in August 1939, the Italian army occupied the George Memorial Hospital in Addis Ababa. The remaining UP missionaries (Dr Cremer and his wife and three nurses) left after that occupation in Addis Ababa. Rev and Mrs Duncan Henry elected to remain but were forced then to leave the mission compound. They were taken in by the kindness of an African American who had been living in Addis Ababa for some time, Mr Daniel Alexander, and he provided accommodation for them to remain in the city. Rev. Henry carried on negotiations with the Italian Army for compensation for taking the properties in Sayo and Gorie; he eventually received some compensation for the mission but in Italian currency.

Rev. Henry communicated with the believers at Sayo realising that indigenous leadership was now critical to carry on the mission work. He asked believers there to recommend two men who were evangelists amongst them whom they thought best for leadership and might be considered for ordination as ministers. These men, Mamo Chorqa and Gidada Solan (both from Dembi Dolo, Sayo), were sent separately to join him in Addis Ababa. Rev. Henry then conducted a short period of intense training and examination of two months for each man in this most extraordinary situation the mission faced due to the occupation by the Italians. Mamo Chorqa was ordained first, and it was not long before 500 converts were baptised and added to the church around Sayo. Ruling elders were also added to the church there and in Addis Ababa. Then Gidada Solan was ordained for Sayo likely in 1939. Both men were enrolled under the UPCNA Allegheny Presbytery since this was Rev. Henry's home presbytery. The actual ordination for both Chorqa and Gidada by the laying on of hands was by Henry who organised "an ad hoc presbytery" to do this. This consisted of Rev. Henry of the UP Church, a former Ethiopian Orthodox priest now a Lutheran minister, and a Waldensian Italian Calvinist chaplain.[13] The Presbytery of Alleghany then

---

12 *Seventy-ninth Annual Report of the BFM, 1938* [UPCNA], 4.
13 Anderson, "Africa," 235.

memorialised the general assembly of the UPCNA to create the Presbytery of Ethiopia for the indigenous church called Evangelical Bethel Church.[14] In 1940/41 the three ministers (Chorqa, Solan, and Henry) were transferred to the new independent Presbytery of Ethiopia of an independent self-governing church, Evangelical Bethel.[15] Rev. Henry was imprisoned on two occasions by the Italian authorities during these years, and his son was also imprisoned on one occasion.

As stated above, in 1941, the Italian occupation came to an end, and, in January 1942, Emperor Haile Selassie was restored to full sovereignty in Ethiopia. Rev. and Mrs Henry were then invited by the new minister of education to serve as headmaster and headmistress of large government schools in Addis Ababa. The BFM decided not to reopen the George Memorial Hospital but instead handed it over to the government to operate. UP missionary Dr Dougherty made an investigative trip to Sayo area (likely late 1941 or early 1942 from Sudan) to see what remained of the mission there and reported the following:

> Instead of one organized congregation and the few preaching places which we had five years ago, the native evangelical Church now has seven organized congregations and some twenty-five other preaching points.[16]

The BFM also began the process in 1942 to try sending medical missionaries back again to Sayo. There was a general voice of thanksgiving that the indigenous church was thriving and moving forward in western Ethiopia despite years of challenge and persecution. Technically this indigenous Church emerged out of the UP Mission but was not directly accountable to it. Therefore, it was really a self-governing church from the beginning during the critical Italo-Ethiopian war years.

6. Postscript

Following the Second World War, post-1945, the Evangelical Bethel Church continued to expand its outreach as an independent native Church maintaining sister relations with the UPCNA. More stations were opened in 1948 and 1951 by the UPCNA, which became part of the indigenous church. Union discussions often took place between the Evangelical Bethel Church and the Lutheran missions of Ethiopia; the latter often received Bethel pastors to minister for them, and thus a polity emerged with elders also in this other mission. The two

---

14 *Eighty-first Annual Report of the BFM 1940* [UPCNA], 9–10.
15 *Eighty-second Annual Report of the BFM 1941* [UPCNA], 11.
16 *Eighty-third Annual Report of the BFM 1942* [UPCNA], 12.

groups finally united together with Bethel having its own synod and eventually growing to be four Bethel Synods within the unified *Mekane Yesus* Church.

7. Summary Conclusion

This historic survey highlights the intricate relationship of the UP Mission work from Egypt to Sudan and to Ethiopia. This string of mission stations is best seen when taken as a whole (see the chart in chapter 24). Yet in saying this, there are many unique features which did arise in this Abyssinian/Ethiopian field:

- the visionary spirit of Thomas Lambie must be clearly recognised here;
- it was the first time to reach the Oromo peoples;
- the sensitivities and challenges in developing a mission field in the context here of the ancient Ethiopian Orthodox Church have parallels also to Egypt;
- the Italo-Ethiopian war was clearly a defining period in the development of this field;
- the leadership by indigenous evangelists and then ministers is a very important aspect of this mission's development;
- the stories of great sacrifice once again are witnessed throughout the pages of this brief survey and must be acknowledged;
- and finally, the development of an indigenous church structure at times will call for ingenious flexibility of spirit and a willingness to work in some extraordinary ways.

Questions for study (fact type):
1. a) What world event of 1918 did God use to "open the door" for UP Missionaries to enter Ethiopia? b) Who was the key leader of these first missionaries?
2. Where was the first UP Mission Station established?
3. a) What other two mission stations developed before 1936?
   b) Why did these stations have to be evacuated in 1936?
4. Name the first two indigenous presbyterian ministers to be ordained.
5. Name the hospital in Addis Ababa that was built by the UP Mission. Who took over the governance of this hospital in 1942?

Questions for study (reflection type):
1. "This introduces us to the delicate balance by which the UP mission had to engage in its work in Abyssinia. It had to tread carefully so as not to incur the wrath of the Ethiopic Church."
 What is the Ethiopic Church? Describe this "delicate balance". Consider the medical work of the UP Mission. How does this follow the example of Christ during His earthly ministry?
2. "Rev. Henry communicated with the believers at Sayo realising that indigenous leadership was now critical to carry on the mission work."
 The Italo-Ethiopian war forced the foreign missionaries to leave Ethiopia or imprisoned them. Consider the rapid development of indigenous leadership. Discuss God's providential leading in this regard. Consider Paul's missionary methods from the Book of Acts in your answer.

Select Bibliography

Anderson, William. "Africa." In *A History of Presbyterian Missions 1944–2007.* eds. Scott W. Sunquist and Caroline N. Becker. Louisville, KY: Geneva Press, 2008, 234–255.

Balisky, Paul E. *Thomas A. Lambie: Missionary Doctor and Entrepreneur.* Eugene, OR: Wipf & Stock, 2020.

Bergsma, Stuart. "Ethiopia as a Mission Field," *The Missionary Review of the World.* 59.1 (January 1936): 14–19.

Bergsma, Stuart. *Rainbow Empire*: *Ethiopia Stretches Out Her Hands.* Grand Rapids: Eerdmans, 1932.

Cogswell, James A. *No Turning Back: A History of American Presbyterian Involvement in Sub-Saharan Africa, 18332000.* Philadelphia: Xlibris, 2007.

Galloway, Ralph K. "The Formation of the Evangelical Church in Ethiopia with Special Reference to the Work of the United Presbyterian Church." BST thesis, The Biblical Seminary in New York, 1949.

Kissling, Carl J. *May We Introduce Ethiopia.* Philadelphia: BFM, UPCNA, [1958]. 39 pages as an overview on the UPC mission to Ethiopia from the beginning to 1958.

Parker, Michael. "Lambie, Thomas Alexander." In *Encyclopedia of Christianity in the United States,* eds. George Thomas Kurian and Mark A. Lamport. Lanham, MD: Rowman & Littlefield, 2016, 1309–1310.

Tucker, Ruth A. *From Jerusalem to Irian Jaya: A Biographical History of Christian Missions.* Second Edition. Grand Rapids: Zondervan, 2004.

BFM Reports

The Triennial Report of the Board of Foreign Missions, 1919, 1920 and 1921.United Presbyterian Board of Foreign Missions of the United Presbyterian Church in North America. Philadelphia: Joseph Brennian Company, 1922.

Seventy-ninth Annual Report of the Board of Foreign Missions [UPCNA], 1938.

Eighty-first Annual Report of the Board of Foreign Missions [UPCNA], 1940.

Eighty-second Annual Report of the Board of Foreign Missions [UPCNA], 1941.

Eighty-third Annual Report of the Board of Foreign Missions [UPCNA], 1942.

Bio Inset

Thomas A. Lambie: Missionary-Entrepreneur[17]

E. Paul Balisky

Dr Thomas A. Lambie launched his missionary career in 1907 with the Foreign Missions Board of the United Presbyterian Church of North America (FMBUPC) in the Anglo-Egyptian, Sudan and this noted career ended in April 1954 when he died suddenly while in Jerusalem. Lambie pioneered the modern missionary movement in Sudan, Abyssinia, and Palestine through combining the Great Commission with the Great Commandment.[18]

Early years in USA and medical missionary service begins in Sudan

Lambie was born in 1885 in Pittsburgh, PA, one of nine children, and was raised under the tutelage of godly parents. During Lambie's medical training at Western Pennsylvania Medical College (1901–6), he attended various missionary conventions. In 1907, at the age of twenty-two, Lambie was accepted by the FMBUPC to serve in Sudan.

▲ Lambie as a young man

Lambie was initially stationed with two other single men at Doleib Hill, located on the Sobat River, a small Abyssinian tributary that flows into the White Nile. On one of Lambie's vacations in Alexandria, he spotted Charlotte Claney, a young Presbyterian missionary teacher who had recently arrived from America. In 1909 Thomas and Charlotte were married in Alexandria. Two children were eventually born to them: Wallace in 1910 and Betty in 1911.

In 1912 the Lambie family was assigned to Doleib Hill to serve among the Shilluk. Then in early 1917 they were asked to pioneer a new outreach based

---

17 This inset is an extensively edited revision and update from an earlier work done by the author.
18 Tibebe Eshete, *The Evangelical Movement in Ethiopia* (Waco, TX: Baylor Univ. Press, 2009), 77.

at Nasir, further east on the Sobat River among the Nuer people group. Lambie, much involved in building a home for his family and doing medical work, found little time to evangelise. He questioned whether he was accomplishing much. "Often I failed; but stumbling and falling, staggered by adverse circumstances, and weakened by malaria and dysentery and hard climate ... we struggled on."[19]

Abyssinia and the development of a hospital in Addis Ababa

The Abyssinian governor Dejazmatch Birru Wolde Gabriel, situated at his government post at Sayo some thirty miles north of Gambeila (Gambella), was entreating the British officials in Sudan to place medical personnel in that area, as an influenza epidemic was devastating the Abyssinian population (1919).[20] Lambie was soon involved in medical work there, which opened doors for him to share the good news with the local Oromo population. An early convert was blind Gidada Solan, who himself became an enthusiastic evangelist.[21]

In 1922 the Lambie family was due a furlough, and so they made their way by mule to Addis Ababa in preparation to take the train to Djibouti, from where they would sail to America. During their time in Addis Ababa, by God's providence, Dr Lambie was introduced to the regent, Ras Tafari Makonnen (who later took the name Haile Selassie), and negotiations were made that allowed the American Presbyterian Mission to build a hospital in Addis Ababa.[22]

The completed hospital (built 1923–1926) made a significant contribution to the medical needs of those in and around Addis Ababa, but Lambie was disheartened in that there was no advance being made by the United Presbyterian Mission Board to preach the gospel to the unreached in southern Abyssinia. Another factor that disheartened Lambie was an irreparable breach between him and another UPCNA surgeon.[23] The Lambies resigned from the FMBUPC in 1927, thus forfeiting the future possibility of scholarships for the education of their two children, medical assistance, and a generous pension in their retirement.[24]

---

19 Eshete, 101.
20 Richard Pankhurst, "The 1-lidar Beshita of 1918," *Journal of Ethiopian Studies* 13. 2 (1975): 103–13.
21 See inset on Gidada Solan in this chapter. Also, see autobiography by Gidada Solon, *The Other Side of Darkness* (New York: Friendship Press, 1972).
22 F. Peter Cotterell, "Dr. T. A. Lambie: Some Biographical Notes," Journal of Ethiopian Studies 10.1 (1972): 45.
23 Lambie, telegram to Mr W. Anderson, secretary of the FMBUPC, January 27, 1925, Margaret Hall Special Collection, SIM International Archives, Fort Mill, SC (henceforth SIM-IA).
24 Lambie, *A Doctor without a Country*, 164.

The formation of the Abyssinia Frontiers Mission and union with the SIM

Alfred Buxton of Great Britain, a former missionary to the Congo, read with great interest one of Lambie's magazine articles, "The Importance of Abyssinia," which appeared in the periodical *World Dominion*.[25] Buxton sailed to America to meet with Lambie and George Rhoad, a former missionary with the Africa Inland Mission in Kenya, with the idea of prayerfully and jointly developing a mission structure to evangelise the East African country of Abyssinia. On 4 April 1927, the Abyssinia Frontiers Mission (AFM) was established in New York. Lambie, with nearly ten years' experience in Abyssinia, drafted a twelve-page document setting out the purpose of this fledgling mission agency. The main goal of this new venture was to bring the gospel to the unreached populations – primal religionists and Muslims of southern Ethiopia – not to renew the historic Orthodox Church.[26] By September 1927 the AFM was invited by Rowland Bingham to join the SIM.

By 1936, sixteen mission stations were providing education and medical assistance in various localities in both southern and northern Abyssinia. Two functioning indigenous churches were active among two different people groups, and portions of Scripture were made available for the believers in three local languages – Sidama, Kambatta, and Wolaitta. The Abu Rumi Amharic translation of the Bible distributed by the Orthodox Church was already available to some Amharic speakers, among whom the SIM missionaries were located.[27] The ltalo-Ethiopian War was basically over when the defeated Emperor Haile Selassie and his entourage of high-ranking officials fled Addis Ababa by train for Djibouti and beyond on 2 May 1936. After the departure of Abyssinian officialdom, chaos erupted in Addis Ababa and eventually throughout the countryside. Eventually on May 5 the Italian military entered Addis Ababa, and calm ensued.[28] Lambie was asked by the Italian general Graziani to report on the ERC activities (Ethiopian Red Cross – Lambie was appointed the executive director to care for the wounded during the Italo-Ethiopian War 1935–37) as well as the location of the sixteen SIM stations. Lambie assumed that the Fascists might allow SIM to continue their missionary activity within the country. Lambie submitted his report in writing to the Italian regime, as he interpreted Romans 13:1, "Be subject to the higher powers."[29] Later, he regretted this action, for it alienated him from

---

25 Lambie, "The Importance of Abyssinia," *World Dominion*, September 1926, 193–98.
26 Thomas A. Lambie, "A New Mission to Abyssinia's Unknown Frontiers," 1927, EA-1, Box 82, File 13, SIM-IA.
27 Lambie, *A Doctor without a Country*, 191, 217. 19.
28 Thomas A. Lambie, "Record of Disaster," 1936, a fifteen-page report in EA-1, Box 82, File I, SIM-IA.
29 Lambie, *A Doctor without a Country*, 250. See also Cotterell, "Dr. T. A. Lambie," 50.

his former friend and benefactor now in exile, Emperor Haile Selassie. In 1942, with sincere sorrow, Lambie wrote to Rowland Bingham, "I should not have written as I did. The Italians, I heard, made quite a lot of this letter, and gave it wide publicity."[30]

This error in judgment by Lambie barred him from future ministry within Ethiopia, which, since 1941, was now once again ruled by Emperor Haile Selassie. But during the eight years that Lambie and his SIM colleagues ministered in former Abyssinia, they made every effort to establish a flourishing indigenous church. This modest beginning was the foundation for what is today the Ethiopian Kale Heywet Church, the largest evangelical denomination in Ethiopia.

Back in Sudan to face many challenges

After a twenty-year hiatus, the Lambies found themselves returning to Sudan in 1939, now to serve as the director of SIM Sudan. Lambie's foremost goal was evangelism in several new localities, in addition to the ongoing medical and primary educational ministries at six existing SIM stations. In all of this, however, Lambie's primary thrust was evangelism, which tended to rankle British government officials.

On 23 August 1940, the Italian air force bombed the Doro SIM station, killing Dr Robert and Mrs Claire Grieve, who was pregnant, and critically wounding Mrs Blanche Oglesby. This tragedy caused great anguish throughout the mission world. Lambie wrote to Rowland Bingham, general director of SIM, asking that "wisdom would be given [to us] as hard decisions need to be made."[31] Should SIM remain in view of a potential Italian incursion into Sudan?

▲ Book cover for Lambie's *A Doctor without a Country*

And then, as if these burdens laid on Lambie were not enough, he was being accused by his colleagues of being incompetent as a mission leader. Malcolm Forsberg expressed the mood of the SIM Sudan missionaries in a lengthy letter to Rowland Bingham: "Opposition to Dr Lambie's leadership is nothing new. I think you could discover that in Ethiopia there was considerable lack of confidence in him. We are

---

30 Lambie, letter to Rowland Bingham, March 16, 1942, as found in A. G. Roke, *They Went Forth* (Auckland: AlfRoke, 2003), 212.
31 Lambie, confidential letter to Bingham, September 2, 1940, KB-I, Box 121, File 4, SIM-IA.

unanimous in feeling we could no longer continue working under Dr Lambie's leadership. I suggest that Dr Lambie's recall be effected at once."[32] Bingham responded to Malcolm Forsberg in a kindly manner, "I cannot appoint a perfect man, because I know of none."[33] On 9 July 1942, exhausted and in need of medical attention, the Lambies left Sudan.

Medical missionary service in Palestine

While the Lambies were on their extended leave of absence (1942–45), Lambie heard that the Independent Board of Presbyterian Foreign Missions was investigating the possibility of expanding their medical ministry in Palestine. Thomas and Charlotte Lambie joined the mission in December 1945, then set sail for the Holy Land. This journey was met with tragedy for Charlotte. She died on 25 January 1946, in Port Said, Egypt, of cerebral haemorrhage and was buried there in the Anglican cemetery.[34] With deep grief, Lambie continued his journey to Palestine to eventually launch a seventy-five-bed TB sanatorium just south of Bethlehem.

In 1947, Thomas married former Abyssinia missionary nurse, Inna Schneck (who had more recently been serving in Nigeria under SIM), in a grand setting at the Jerusalem home of Mr and Mrs Alfred P. S. Clark of the Barclay Bank of the United Kingdom. Shortly after the wedding, the Lambies began fund-raising in the United States for the TB sanatorium.

When the Lambies returned to Palestine in late 1947, regardless of many setbacks, construction moved ahead on the TB sanatorium, located in Ain Arroub, just south of Bethlehem. This grand project was completed in 1953 and subsequently put into service. One year later, on 14 April 1954, Dr Thomas Lambie died suddenly at the Garden Tomb in Jerusalem while preparing a sermon for the Easter sunrise service four days hence. His body was interred in the Bible Presbyterian Church yard in Bethlehem.

A colleague's kind appraisal of Dr Lambie's missionary career

Clarence Duff, an SIM missionary colleague of Lambie in Abyssinia, wrote: "I regard Dr Lambie one of the best and greatest men it has been my privilege to know. If sometimes his judgment or his actions proved to be unwise, he rose above his faults, outlived them and the criticism incurred, and went on to fresh achievement."[35]

---

32 Forsberg, letter to Bingham, January 16, 1942, Malcolm and Enid Forsberg, Box 09, File 4, SIM-IA.
33 Bingham, letter to Forsberg and Alfred Roke, February 18, 1942, Malcolm and Enid Forsberg, Box 09, File 4, SIM-IA.
34 Lambie, letter to supporters, June 30, 1946, Margaret Hall Special Collection, SIM-IA.
35 Clarence W. Duff, *Cords of Love: A Pioneer Mission to Ethiopia* (Phillipsburg, NJ: Presbyterian & Reformed Publishing, 1980), 334.

Select Bibliography

Writings by Thomas A. Lambie in chronological order:

1935 *Abayte! Ethiopia's Plea*. Edinburgh: Turnbull & Spears.

1939 *A Doctor without a Country*. New York: Fleming Revell.

1942 *A Doctor Carries On*. Philadelphia: Blakiston Company.

1943 *Boot and Saddle in Africa*. Philadelphia: Blakiston Company.

1952 *A Bruised Reed: Light from Bible Lands on Bible Illustrations*. New York: Loizeaux Brothers.

1954 *A Doctor's Great Commission*. Wheaton, IL: Van Kampen Press.

1957 *A Bride for His Son*. New York: Loizeaux Brothers.

Writings about Thomas A. Lambie:

Anderson, William B. "Thomas A. Lambie: Missionary Pioneer in Sudan and Ethiopia, 1907–1942." In *Gateway to the Heart of Africa: Missionary Pioneers in Sudan,* eds. Francesco Pierli, Maria Teresa Ratti, and Andrew C. Wheeler. Nairobi: Paulines Publications Africa, 1998, 126–45.

Balisky, E. Paul. "Dr. Thomas A. Lambie: Pioneer Medical Missionary in East Africa." In *Transforming Africa's Religious Landscapes: The Sudan Interior Mission (SIM), Past and Present*, eds. Barbara M. Cooper, Gary R. Corwin, Tibebe Eshete, Musa A.B. Gaiya, Tim Geysbeek, and Shobana Shankar. Trenton, NJ: Africa World Press, 2018, 261–85.

Balisky, E. Paul. *Thomas Lambie: Missionary Doctor and Entrepreneur*. Eugene, OR: Wipf & Stock, 2020.

Donham, Donald L. "The Dialectic of Modernity in a North American Christian Mission" (chapter four), in *Marxist Modern: An Ethnographic History of the Ethiopian Revolution*. Los Angeles: University of California Press, 1999, 82–121.

Bio Inset

Gidada Solan 1899–1977[36]

E. Paul Balisky

This is a story of a blind man who faithfully served God. Whether as a beggar, student, evangelist, teacher, prisoner, minister, or elder church statesman, Gidada did everything with humility and confidence in God.

Gidada was born in a small village of Aleqa Sotelow, near Dembi Dolo, to Oromo parents in the mountain highlands of western Ethiopia. His parents named him Gidada, meaning, "The one who weeps for people." At the age of five he was left blind by a devastating smallpox epidemic that spread through western Ethiopia, wiping out a large segment of population, including seven of Gidada's siblings. His parents applied various potions to his blind eyes as recommended by the local traditional medicine man. Nothing helped restore his sight. Gidada became a beggar.

In 1919 Dr Thomas Lambie arrived in Sayo village to provide medical assistance for hundreds who were dying of influenza. In 1920 blind Gidada was the first convert of the American medical missionary.

Soon after Gidada's conversion, he evidenced a keen desire to learn. He also learned English at the American UP Mission compound. Then in 1924 Gidada was introduced to Braille. He learned to read in Amharic, Oromifa, and English. This opened up an entire world for him. He could now read for himself and the Bible, both the Old and New Testaments, became a living book to him. He now had a burning zeal to share with others his new life in Christ and what he read from Scripture.

In 1924 he married Dinse Sholi. Their first two children died soon after birth. To this sad couple Rahel was born in 1927. Later two sons Solomon (1935) and Negaso (1941) were born. Both these men made significant contributions to Ethiopia serving in public office. Dr Solomon served as Ethiopian ambassador to London from 1992 to 1998 and Dr Negaso was voted in as President of Ethiopia from 1996 to 2000.

By 1930, Gidada began evangelistic ministry throughout the Sayo district. He would personally visit *qallichas* (cult practitioners) and from his Braille Bible read

---

36 This is an edited and slightly revised version from what the author had formerly done for the DACB. We have used the spelling, *Solan*. Both spellings *Solon* and *Solan* are used in source materials.

some verses about the power of Jesus who died and rose again from the dead. By 1940 there were ten Evangelical Churches Bethel established. And from 1955 to 1965 Gidada and his wife and younger children transferred to Mizan Teferi to assist the American Mission in evangelising the traditional religionist Bench ethnic group. As he trekked on mule-back through dense forest from one Bench village to another, hundreds heard the gospel and responded.

In 1940 Gidada and several Sayo colleagues in Christian ministry were arrested by the Italians on charges of spying. As a result, they were tied up and loaded onto the back of an Italian truck as criminals. After several weeks of traveling over very muddy roads, they finally arrived at the Addis Ababa prison. After eight days in the crowded Addis Ababa prison, they were sent back to Jimma for further interrogation. Gidada's two colleagues were cruelly beaten, almost to death, for three consecutive days. Then it was Gidada's turn to face the interrogators and the beatings. When asked why he became an enemy of the Italians, he responded, "As you see I am a blind man. I told you I am a Christian and an evangelist for the Lord's work. Because I serve the Lord, am I an enemy of the government?" Gidada was sent back to his cell without a beating. When the British army liberated southwest Ethiopia in 1941, Gidada and his friends walked out of the Jimma prison and joyfully returned to their ministry in Sayo.

The persecution from 1951 to 1955 which faced the Sayo congregations within the Evangelical Church Bethel, came from an unexpected source – the Ethiopian Orthodox Church (EOC). When the American Mission entered Ethiopia in 1919 their goal was to work closely with the Ethiopian state church and not to establish independent congregations that would be in competition with the EOC. But during the Italian occupation of southwestern Ethiopia from 1936 to 1941, the EOC of Qellem Region was weakened. By 1951 the number of local Evangelical Church Bethel congregations had grown to twenty and elementary schools were established in most of these. Because the EOC looked upon this upstart evangelical movement as a competing church, they began to systematically close each church and arrest the leaders. Gidada was thrown into prison again – not by the foreign colonialists, but by Ethiopian Christians. Following his release, Gidada and other evangelical church leaders made their way to Addis Ababa to appeal their case to Emperor Haile Sellassie. The emperor heard their case and after a lengthy delay, ten of the twenty churches were reopened.

When the American Mission personnel in Ethiopia were in the process of being evicted by the Italians from Ethiopia, they realized that there were no ordained Ethiopian pastors

▲ Rev. and Mrs Gidada Solan

to carry on the official church ministry in the Sayo area. Dr Henry advised the church in Dembi Dollo to select someone from the congregation to travel to Addis Ababa and take a short course in preparation for ordination. It was decided that Mamo Chorqa and Gidada Solan should be ordained. In July 1938 the congregation selected Mamo Chorqa to be the first to come to Addis Ababa in 1939, Gidada Solan being the second choice. Mamo Chorqa's ordination to the Presbyterian ministry, after a brief four-week instruction by D. C. Henry was performed under rather unusual circumstances. In September 1938, Dr Henry asked Gidada Solan to come to Addis Ababa for ordination. This took place on 24 February 1939. Because D. C. Henry was ordained under the Allegheny Presbytery of New York (UPCNA), this Presbytery agreed that they would validate the ordination of both Mamo Chorqa and Gidada Solan. These ordained Ethiopian pastors were then enrolled as members of the Allegheny Presbytery "under extraordinary circumstances." Both men retained this relationship with the Allegheny Presbytery until 1947, when the Evangelical Church Bethel, now with some 150 congregations, became an independent Ethiopian church under national leadership, retaining the United Presbyterian Church polity and doctrine.

The crowning experience for Gidada, the elder Christian statesman, was to represent the Evangelical Church Bethel, accompanied by his son Solomon, at the General Assembly of the United Presbyterian Church which was convened in Pittsburgh in 1957. With the following words he addressed the large assembly, gathered from all continents, "Praise the Lord who made heaven and earth, who by His power has brought all of us together. He has made us one by the blood of His Son, Jesus Christ." At the final communion service of the assembly, the night before Gidada and his son Solomon left the U.S.A. for Ethiopia, Gidada, the "one who weeps for people" wept for joy. Sightless though he was, he experienced the fellowship of the worldwide church as they joined hands and hearts together.

Select Bibliography

Arén, Gustav. *Envoys of the Gospel in Ethiopia: In the Steps of the Evangelical Pioneers 1898–1936*. Stockholm: FS förlaget, 1999.

Birri, Debela. "History of the Evangelical Church Bethel." DTh thesis, Lutheran School of Theology at Chicago, 1995.

Solon, Gidada. *The Other Side of Darkness*, ed. Marion Fairman. New York: Friendship Press, 1972.

Lambie, Thomas A. *A Doctor Without a Country*. New York, London, Edinburgh: Fleming Revell, 1939.

Negasso, Gidada, "The Impact of Christianity on Qelem Awraja, Western Wallaga 1886 to 1941." BA thesis, Haile Selassie I University, 1971.

Part Four: *Themes*

▲ Dr Robert Kerr, missionary to Morocco

Chapter 26

Scots Presbyterians and the NGK/DRC of South Africa

Retief Müller

Chapter Outline
1. Introduction: The Background Context
2. First Scots Pastors in the DRC
3. Scots pastors, the British Empire and the Dutch settlers' discontent
4. The Scots' role in trans-Atlantic revivalism and evangelism
5. Scots Presbyterians in the DRC and their cooperation with Scots Presbyterians in Nyasaland/Malawi
6. Conclusion

1. Introduction: The Background Context

One of the most influential historical trajectories involving Scots Presbyterians in Southern Africa, occurred, in a sense, indirectly. That is to say that in this case it occurred via the vehicle of the Dutch Reformed Church of South Africa [*Nederduitse Gereformeerde Kerk van Suid-Afrika*] rather than directly through Presbyterianism.

The DRC arrived in the mid-17th century in what is today the Western Cape of South Africa, at the time named *Cabo da Boa Esperança*, and later more commonly known as the Cape Colony, especially after the final British annexation of the region in 1806. The original Dutch settlement was something of an informal arrival rather than a missionary outreach, coinciding with the opening up of travel routes and supply stations of the Dutch East India Company.

For the next century and a half, the DRC established itself as the nominal church of Dutch colonial officials and settlers in the Cape Colony. After the British takeover of the territory in the early 19th century, the new colonial authority also acquired oversight over church structures, including those of the DRC. Lord Charles Somerset, an early and influential governor of the Cape Colony, recognized the strategic importance of the DRC as one of the most prominent cultural institutions in the territory. From his point of view, representing the interests of the British Empire, it made sense to seek to anglicise institutions that were not naturally British leaning. The DRC was such an institution. It so happened that on an expanding colonial frontier, the DRC had numerous vacant pulpits, especially among the rural, frontier congregations on the eastern border of the colony. Coincidentally, there was some dissatisfaction among some members of the DRC regarding the liberal theological views many of their pastors had brought with them from the Netherlands. At the time all DRC pastors were Dutch trained, and the majority had studied at the University of Leiden, which was increasingly seen as a hotbed of liberalism or Dutch rationalism to name that intellectual tradition more specifically.

2. First Scots pastors in the DRC

Combined, these factors helped to create an environment where it became possible for Scots Presbyterian clergy to be eligible for serving in the DRC. Scots Presbyterians were understood to be Reformed and moreover, they were believed to be more orthodox than some of the Dutch ministers. Administrative disorganisation in the London Missionary Society's ranks at the Cape also played a contributing role in all of this. George Thom (1789–1842), a Scots Presbyterian, became the first LMS missionary to resign and join the DRC ranks in 1818.[1] This provided the catalyst for further recruitment drives occurring with the assistance of Lord Charles Somerset. Thom, while on furlough in Scotland in 1821, was tasked by Somerset to find able and willing ministerial candidates, as well as school teachers, to consider moving to South Africa. His efforts paid off in that he was able to recruit several candidates expressing themselves willing to serve in South Africa. Among them were Andrew Murray [senior] (1794–1866) from Clatt in Aberdeenshire, and William Robertson (1805–1879). Both Robertson and Murray (Church of Scotland) would over time become influential ministers in the Dutch Reformed Church in South Africa. Initially, Robertson was recruited as a teacher, and he was assigned to the district of Graaff Reinet where Murray was appointed to what would become his life-long parish. During this initial period Robertson resided in the parish with Murray.

After five years as a teacher in South Africa, Robertson found himself called to the ministry. He underwent the required theological training in Scotland, Dutch language training in the Netherlands, and after receiving ordination he was duly admitted as a minister in the DRC. He served in different congregations during his career, but his most important role in this regard was played during his tenure at Swellendam, during which time he served on two occasions as

---

1 See, Chapter two in this book for Thom's role in Cape Town to help with the first Presbyterian congregation there before he joined the DRC and his involvement in urging the Scottish Societies to commence mission work again in Africa, this time in what is now the Eastern Cape.

moderator of the DRC. Robertson became involved in many important ventures of the DRC, as did Andrew Murray. This included advocacy for the founding of a local seminary for the training of DRC ministerial candidates. Robertson would also at a later stage, in 1860, become directly involved in recruitment of Scots Presbyterian ministers to the DRC when he went to the Netherlands and Scotland in the role of lead recruiter, playing a similar role as George Thom had done in the original recruitment venture a few decades earlier. In the Netherlands Robertson could find no suitable candidates but in Scotland he successfully recruited eight prospective ministers or licentiates of the Free Church of Scotland. They were A. MacKidd, W. Cormack, D. MacMillan, J. McCarter, T. McCarter, T. M. Gray, A. McGregor, and R. D. Ross.

3. Scots pastors, the British Empire and the Dutch settlers' discontent

The name of William Robertson should also be noted in reference to an important 19th-century episode in DRC history. This concerned what had been named in subsequent Afrikaner history as the Great Trek. During the 1830s a wave of enthusiasm for migration beyond the borders of the Cape Colony swept up within the context of rural Dutch communities. The reasons for this enthusiasm were diverse, and Robertson outlined some of these in an 1836 letter he wrote on the subject to the journalist, John Fairbairn. However, the most important push factor had to do with the fact that many of these migrating Boers, as they would steadily become known, had objections against the abolitionary policies that were increasingly instituted in the Colony. Since many of them were slave owners, they felt financially challenged by these new measures, and so the migration occurred as a protest by colonists in search of independence from the rules of the Empire.

▲ Andrew Murray, senior

Robertson, Murray, and other Scots ministers tried in vain to convince their emigration-interested congregants to reconsider their plans. They warned that the migrants would find themselves effectively in rebellion against the divinely instituted secular authority. They argued that the migrants might be barred from the sacraments and other benefits of the church's ministry. As mentioned above, the Scots in the DRC were primarily placed in communities along the eastern frontier of the colony, and it is from these communities where the greatest proportion of eventual migrants originated. However, once it became clear that the migration could not be halted or reversed, the DRC changed its approach somewhat. A number of Scots, including Murray, Robertson, and John Taylor, who was minister in the hamlet of Cradock, at various points obtained permission from their church authorities to pay visits to the migrants beyond the boundaries of the colony to deliver evangelisation and in some cases even to administer sacraments.

In this way these Scots Presbyterian ministers helped to maintain a crucial link between the DRC and the migrating Boers, thereby ensuring that the Boers never became as independent of imperial influence as they might have hoped to be. Moreover, the Empire would literally follow on the migrants' heels as British interests in Africa increased and more and more territories started to be incorporated. An example of this was the establishment under British rule of the Orange River Sovereignty.

Andrew Murray married a Dutch woman by name of Maria Susanna Stegmann not long after arriving in South Africa. Together they had eleven children, many of whom proceeded to play influential roles in the DRC and related religious and educational organisations. The two oldest sons, John Murray (1826–1882) and Andrew Murray Jr (1828–1917) were especially prominent. John would be called in 1857 as the first professor at the newly established Stellenbosch Theological Seminary and Andrew Jr would become a world-renowned figure in the international Holiness movement, a writer of evangelical literature as well as an influential leader in missionary and ecumenical circles. In the 1850s he served as a young minister in the rural outpost of Bloemfontein in the Orange River Sovereignty. In this capacity he styled himself as a kind of missionary minister to the northern Boers, especially those who had settled beyond the borders of the Sovereignty, across the Vaal River, in nominally independent territory, temporarily outside of the shifting boundaries of the Empire. Young Andrew undertook four long evangelistic tours to that area, in one instance accompanied by his brother John. Towards the end of his tenure in Bloemfontein, Murray became involved in a somewhat controversial and ultimately unsuccessful effort to try and dissuade imperial authorities from their plan to relinquish the Orange River Sovereignty to the control of the resident Boers. Like many

▲ Andrew Murray, junior

mission interested people in 19th-century South Africa, the Murrays tended to view the rulership of the British Empire more favourably compared to any of the alternatives available. The Boer attitudes towards the indigenous population were particularly worrisome given their legacy of slaveholding, which had inspired their original migration out of the Cape Colony, as mentioned above. Hence the prospect of a Boer government in what would become the Orange Free State was looked upon as a regression of sorts by people like Andrew Murray.

4. The Scots' role in trans-Atlantic revivalism and evangelism

Despite a last-ditch effort by the imperial party in Bloemfontein to prevent the British withdrawal by sending a delegation to London comprising two prominent members, one of whom was Andrew Murray, all the protest was fruitless. Britain duly relinquished the Orange River Sovereignty in 1854. For the Murray family and the other Scots Presbyterians in the DRC, a new chapter awaited which had less to do with their political role within the British Empire and more with the religious life within the church in their adopted country. From the early 1860s onwards an international wave of awakenings and revivals within Protestant evangelicalism started to make an impact on the local scene in South Africa. Scots Presbyterians both within and outside of the DRC were heavily involved in generating this local wave of religious enthusiasm. Andrew Murray Jr had recently accepted a call to Worcester in the Cape Colony, and so it was fitting that he would play a formative role in a movement that effectively launched in South Africa with an ecumenical conference held at Worcester in 1860, the parish where he was to be installed as minister in the same time period. His father, Andrew Murray of Graaff Reinet was one of the leading proponents of revivalism within the DRC, and so he played a defining role at the conference, as did other Scots, including William Robertson, Robert Shand of Tulbagh, and several others. One reason why Scots were key players in the movement had to do with the fact that they were connected to a wider trans-Atlantic, mainly English-speaking evangelical movement that communicated internationally through publications and the relatively free movement of its advocates across oceans and borders. Hence when awakenings and revivals erupted in North America, Wales and elsewhere the news of what transpired travelled throughout the evangelical world, often with accompanying advice on how to foster similar developments locally. Such was the case with the Worcester conference where, for example, prominence of place was given on the programme to speakers like a certain Dr Adamson, formerly a minister at the Scotch Presbyterian Church in Cape Town who had just returned from North America where he had experienced the Second Great Awakening. Now he and others could share testimony about international revivals and their benefits to the church in South Africa.

The period of revivalism in the DRC was apparently wildly successful in inspiring the church membership with spiritual fervour. It served to institute a mission consciousness within a church that had been predominantly inward looking during its first couple of centuries on African soil. There were also indications that, at least for a time, it managed to repress the otherwise omnipresent race consciousness among rural Boers. There were testimonies of mixed-race revival meetings where in some cases leadership roles were taken up by so-called 'coloured' members including women. Although the crossing of racial boundaries during such events would be temporary, and in fact such boundaries would harden over time, the budding mission movement within the DRC proved to be more of an enduring legacy. In this the Scots Presbyterians and their descendants would be prominent, particularly within the context of the broader Murray family.

Andrew Murray Jr became a key figure in establishing further international links, including with Presbyterians in Scotland and beyond. However, his activities in this regard also extended to parachurch Christian organisations and Christian educational institutes. Regarding the latter, he established firm connections with the Mount Holyoke Female Seminary in Massachusetts during the late 19th century, and this transcontinental relationship resulted in a very fruitful and enduring partnership whereby American educationalists from Mount Holyoke would collaborate with Murray in the founding of several schools in South Africa based on the Mount Holyoke model. Andrew's wife, Emma, and several of their daughters became deeply involved in the local variations of this educational enterprise, which provided Christian education to young women, and which fostered a strong mission-interested piety. The most famous of these local Mount Holyoke modelled schools in South Africa was the Huguenot Seminary in Wellington, which was also where Andrew Murray had his parish as a DRC minister during the late-19th to early-20th century. The Huguenot Seminary produced several women missionaries who ended up doing invaluable work in the field in areas such as education and nursing. A number of these pioneer missionaries worked in areas to the north of present-day South Africa, like Mochudi in what is now Botswana and even as far afield as Nyasaland (currently Malawi). Several were Murray descendants themselves.

5. Scots Presbyterians in the DRC and their cooperation with Scots Presbyterians in Nyasaland/Malawi

This brings me to discuss a renewed engagement from a different direction between the DRC and Scots Presbyterians, and this concerns the context of Nyasaland which was a mission interest for both parties. To briefly tell this story we may begin with the way in which the DRC became involved in that area in the first place.[2] As with so many of the new initiatives within the DRC in the late 19th century, Andrew Murray Jr was also in this venture the catalyst in chief. Along with other mission enthused ministers who eventually organised themselves in the *Predikante Sendingvereniging* (Ministers' Mission Union), Murray started to explore possible locales to launch a 'foreign' missionary project for the DRC, which was a long-cherished dream of his. This eventually led to correspondences with representatives of the Free Church of Scotland's Livingstonia mission in Nyasaland. Initial discussions between Murray and Livingstonia's Dr James Stewart, best known for his role as principal of Lovedale College in South Africa, focused on the question of whether and how DRC missionaries might come to the aid of the Livingstonia mission, which had committed itself to a large area in central Africa, but without enough personnel to conduct all the work involved in evangelising that area. Murray and Stewart were able to come to an agreement to the effect that DRC missionaries would take over work in some of the areas to the South of Livingstonia. The first missionary from the DRC to avail himself for the project was Andrew Charles (A. C.) Murray, a nephew of Andrew Murray Jr. and a grandson of the original Andrew Murray of Graaff Reinet, who was the first Scots Presbyterian minister to be recruited from Scotland to serve in the DRC, as mentioned above. A. C. Murray would proceed to have his own conversations with representatives of the Free Church of Scotland in preparation of his ministry. Much of these initial conversations occurred in Scotland where A. C. Murray went to obtain, among other things, a basic course in medicine, which was a standard requirement for missionaries going to the tropics at the time.

Back in South Africa, Murray prepared to embark on a voyage up along the east coast that would eventually take him to the Zambezi River and from there to Nyasaland. Having arrived, Murray spent a considerable period of time with the Free Church of Scotland missionaries, much of it in the residence of Dr Robert Laws, the head of Livingstonia mission. Much of what Murray and many of the subsequent DRC missionaries knew about mission had been learned from the Scots. In fact, as far as the Livingstonia mission was concerned, the budding DRC enterprise to their South was simply an offshoot of their own mission, and in fact A. C. Murray and other early DRC missionaries remained part of the Livingstonia council for more than a decade. Initially the above-mentioned Ministers' Mission Union (MMU) acted as the effective sending agency for these missionaries, paying their salaries, and generally overseeing their activities. Oddly it was only in the early 20th century, that the DRC synod in the Cape

---

2 See chapters 14, 15, & 16 in this book for context and development on Livingstonia, Blantyre, and Nkhoma.

accepted the full responsibility for these missionaries from their church in central Africa, and officially took over the role formerly played by the MMU.

After the Nyasaland mission that had to a large extent been initiated as a Murray family enterprise officially became part of the DRC's mission, there still remained a remarkable degree of collaboration and eventually also ecumenical unity with the Scots Presbyterians. In addition to the Free Church of Scotland's mission in Livingstonia, the Church of Scotland also had a mission in the country, which was headquartered in Blantyre, to the South. The DRC mission thus ended up sandwiched in between these two Scots Presbyterian missions. Missionaries from the DRC, which eventually founded their headquarters in Nkhoma, collaborated with the Scots in Blantyre especially on the topic of scriptural translation. The DRC's William H. Murray and Blantyre mission's Alexander Heatherwick worked closely together on translation projects over several years.

At the same time, contact and collaboration with Livingstonia also continued apace. When the two Scottish missions started negotiations about the formation of a joint indigenous church in Nyasaland, the DRC was also brought into the discussions. The DRC mission at Nkhoma unfortunately had to deal with a home church in South Africa, which during the early 20th century was increasingly turning anti-ecumenical, nationalistic, and to a degree even anti-missionary. This meant that their participation in this venture was somewhat problematised even though the missionaries and the Malawians who had joined their churches were strongly in favour of greater church unity. Hence, when what would be the Church of Central Africa Presbyterian [CCAP] came into preliminary formation, this was initially only a union between the two Scottish missions and their local churches. However, after much negotiation and tension over the apartheid measures which the DRC

▲ Bambo Isake Mchochma Mlaliki, one of the early evangelists in the Nkhoma Mission – he took the name Andrew Murray.

representatives from South Africa insisted upon, the Nkhoma mission was finally able to join up with the CCAP after a conference representing all parties occurred in 1924. In this way the Nkhoma synod joined the already existing synods of Blantyre and Livingstonia in what would effectively be the first indigenous presbyterian church in central Africa. To say that this was an easily achieved or secure union would be contrary to the evidence. However, the mere fact that it was achieved at all might be said to be something of a miracle given the way things would develop for the DRC of South Africa in the 20th century.

6. Conclusion

The above narrative would serve as a basic introduction to connections between Scots Presbyterians and the DRC of South Africa, including in their communal central African mission fields in the 19th and 20th centuries. Much more could be said about this story and indeed more have been written about it elsewhere, including by this author. For further information about this topic, the sources listed at the end of this chapter might be suggested as points of departure.

Questions for study (fact type):

1. The Dutch arrived in Cape Colony in the mid-17th century. Give the full name of the denomination they brought with them. Where were their ministers trained for the first 150 years of their existence in South Africa?
2. As liberalism crept into the DRC, to which country did the denomination turn to recruit ministers?
3. Name the famous minister recruited from Aberdeenshire, Scotland to minister in the DRC. What year did he arrive in South Africa?
4. Who was the key ministerial leader in the revival of the 1860s in and around Worcester?
5. Name the missions that were established through the cooperation of the DRC, The Church of Scotland and The Free Church of Scotland.

Questions for study (reflection type):

1. "The period of revivalism in the DRC was apparently wildly successful in inspiring the church membership with spiritual fervour ... There were also indications that, at least for a time, it managed to repress the otherwise omnipresent race consciousness among rural Boers." Read Galatians 3:27–29 and 1 Peter 2:9, 10. Explain how Christ through the Holy Spirit unifies people from various cultural backgrounds.
2. As noted in question #5 above, the DRC partnered with The Church of Scotland and The Free Church of Scotland to evangelise and disciple. Read Philippians 1:3–5. In one paragraph, provide three reasons why the concept of partnership is essential in gospel work.

Chart of Church of Scotland and Free Church of Scotland ministers, licentiates, and students who served in the DRCSA as ministers and/or teachers in schools in SA in the 19th Century[3]

Key: When a name is in *italic* it means that individual transferred into the DRC while already labouring in South Africa with another body

Name	Status upon Arrival (Ord.[4], Lic., Stu.)	Arrival, Date into SA
Thom, George	Ord. 23 April 1812, CoS	LMS, then to DRCSA 1818
Taylor, John	Ord. 6 March 1816, CoS	LMS, then to DRCSA 1818
Murray, Andrew Sr	Ord. 14 March 1821, CoS	1822 Graaff-Reinet
Smith, Alexander	Ord. 10 January 1822, CoS	1822 Uitenhage
Sutherland, Henry	Ord. 1 October 1823, CoS	1824 Worcester
MacKenzie, Colin Fraser	Ord. 12 July 1824, CoS	1825 Beaufort West
Morgan, George	Ord. 8 September 1824, CoS	1826 Somerset East (DRC); then to Scots Presbyterian Church, Cape Town
Edgar, James	Ord. 28 March 1827, CoS	1828 Durbanville; Somerset West
Cassie, John	Ord. 15 March 1827, CoS	1828 Caledon, back to Scotland in 1850

---

3   The following charts were compiled by the Editor of the present volume. Five helpful sources to this chart have been Frederick Sass, "The Influence of the Church of Scotland on the Dutch Reformed Church of South Africa" (unpublished PhD thesis, University of Edinburgh, 1956), 72–75; Craig Thom, "Part 1: A Biography of George Thom—Missionary," in THOM [2014], 109–118; CoS *Fasti* volumes; *Free Church Annals*, 2 volumes; and John MacKenzie with Nigel Dalziel, *The Scots in South Africa* (Manchester, MUP, 2007), especially chapter six. On occasion I have verified or cross-checked with other sources.
4   Ordination unless stated otherwise is assumed as UK, same for licensing.

Pears, John	Ord. 20 December 1825, CoS	1829 Glen Lynden Presbyterian, then DRC; college instructor; Albany; Somerset East
Thomson, W. Ritchie	Ord. 21 March 1821, CoS	1821 GMS missionary; 1830 DRC Stockenström
Robertson, William	Ord. 22 June 1831, CoS	1831 Clanwilliam; Swellendam; Cape Town
Welsh, Alexander	Ord. 1 June 1832, CoS	1833 Glen Lynden
Shand, Robert	Ord. 19 June 1833, CoS	1834 Tulbagh
Reid, Thomas	Ord. 13 October 1835, CoS	1836 Colesberg
Bennie, John	Valedictory Service to set apart 23 January 1821	1821 GMS missionary; 1855 Middelberg DRC; Ord. 1831 by Presbytery of Kaffraria (independent)
MacKidd, Alexander	Lic. 5 September 1849, FCS[5]	1861 Zoutpansberg Ord. 29 August 1861, DRC, Cape Town
Cormack, William	Lic. 4 March 1857, FCS	1862 Burgersdorp Ord. 10 August 1862, DRC
McCarter, John	Lic. 11 August 1859, FCS	1862 Weenan; Ladysmith; back to Scotland 1875 Ord. 31 August 1862, DRC
McGregor, Andrew	Lic. 5 August 1858, FCS	1862 Robertson Ord. 11 September 1862, DRC
MacMillan, Dugald	Lic. 11 August 1859, FCS	1862 Harrismith; back to Scotland 1874 Ord. 17 September 1862, DRC
Gray, Thomas Menzies	Lic. 25 July 1860, FCS	1862 Aberdeen; back to Scotland 1886 Ord. 20 September 1862, DRC
McCarter, Thomas	Lic. 6 December 1854, FCS	1863 Calvinia; back to Scotland 1882 Ord. 24 January 1863, DRC
Ross, David	Lic. 30 July 1862, FCS	1863 Lady Grey Ord. 30 August 1863, DRC

---

5   Denotes a FCS presbytery *in* Scotland. The only exception was Cachet who was FCS Presbytery of Kaffraria, Cape Colony.

Craig, Richard	Ord. 9 December 1862, FCS	1863 Victoria West Presbyterian Church 1867 Weenan DRC
Turnbull, James	Ord. 5 July 1859, FCS	1860 Beaufort West Presbyterian Church 1867 Greytown DRC
Cachet, Frans Lion[6]	Ord. 25 Oct. 1860, FC Presbytery of Kaffraria	1862 Ladysmith DRC;1867 Utrecht DRC; 1876 Villiersdorp DRC; back to Netherlands 1880
Brebner, John	Lic FCS Ord. FCS	1861 Albert Academy, Burgersdorp; taught at Gill College, Somerset East 1869; Inspector 1874–1891 Orange Free State; Superintendent of Education OFS 1891–1899. Preached & served as an elder for DRC Bloemfontein.

Teacher Recruits[7] from Scotland:

Name	Year to SA	Places of Teaching
Innes, James Ross	1822	Uitenhage; South African College, Superintendent of Education Cape Colony
Brown, Archibald	1822	Stellenbosch
Robertson, William	1822	Graaff-Reinet teacher; Then became a minister, see list above.
Dawson, William	1822	Aberdeen; George; educational missionary
Rattrey, James	1822	Tulbagh
Blair, Robert	1822	Caledon
Arnold, E	1823	Swellendam

---

6   Cachet has the distinction of perhaps being the only person trained at the Free Church of Scotland Seminary in Amsterdam and was licensed there also. There is some confusion as to his licensure, was it a Presbytery of Europe for the FCS somehow overseeing the Amsterdam Seminary students?

7   I am aware that more names likely need to be added to this section. One of the challenges here is the word "recruitment." Many Scottish teachers came but technically not all had relationships with the DRC churches.

Reed, Joseph	1823/24?	Paarl
Whitten, James Reid	1878	DRC Normal School, Cape Town
Others as argued by Craig Thom who were recruited by James Rose Innes include:		
Paterson, John		Eastern Cape
McNaughton, John		
Black, Patrick		
Brebner, John Rev.	1860/1	Burgersdorp
Brebner, George Alan		
Comer, George		

Select Bibliography

Anonymous. "George Thom (1789–1842): Scottish Pioneer in South Africa." *The Banner of Truth* (1990) (https://www.christianstudylibrary.org/article/george-thom-1789-1842-scottish-pioneer-south-africa).

Duff, S. E. "The Dutch Reformed Church and the Protestant Atlantic: Revivalism and Evangelicalism in the Nineteenth-Century Cape Colony." *South African Historical Journal* 70.2 (2018): 324–347, DOI: 10.1080/02582473.2018.1468810

Du Plessis, Johannes. *The life of Andrew Murray of South Africa*. London: Marshall Brothers, 1919.

MacKenzie, J. M. & Dalziel, N. *The Scots in South Africa ethnicity, identity, gender and race, 1772–1914*. Manchester: Manchester University Press, 2007.

Müller, R. *The Scots Afrikaners: Identity Politics and Intertwined Religious Cultures in Southern and Central Africa*. Edinburgh: Edinburgh University Press, 2021.

Neethling, M. *Unto children's children: lives and letters of the parents of the home at Graaff Reinet, with short sketches of the life of each of the children, and a register*. London: Printed by T. H. Hopkins, 1909.

Pauw C. M. "Mission and Church in Malawi: The History of the Nkhoma Synod of the Church of Central Africa, Presbyterian, 1889–1962." DTh thesis, Stellenbosch University, 1980.

Pauw, Martin [C. M.]. "The role and influence of Andrew Murray Jr in missions within the Dutch Reformed Church and in wider context." *Stellenbosch Theological Journal*, 8.3 (2022): 75–101. https://dx.doi.org/10.17570/stj.2022.v8n3.a4

Parsons, J. W. "Scots and Afrikaners in Central Africa: Andrew Charles Murray and the Dutch Reformed Church Mission in Malawi." *The Society of Malawi Journal* 51.1 (1998): 21–40.

Robert D. L. "Mount Holyoke Women and the Dutch Reformed Missionary Movement, 1874–1904." *Missionalia* 21.2 (1993): 103–123.

Ross, R. J. "Abolitionism, the Batavian Republic, the British and the Cape Colony." Ed. Gert Oostindied. *Fifty years later: Antislavery, capitalism and modernity in the Dutch orbit.* Pittsburgh, Pa: University of Pittsburgh Press, 1995, 179–192.

Sass, F. W. "The Influence of the Church of Scotland on the Dutch Reformed Church of South Africa." PhD thesis, University of Edinburgh, 1956.

Sturgis, J. "Anglicisation at the Cape of Good Hope in the early nineteenth century." *The Journal of Imperial and Commonwealth History* 11.1 (1982): 5–32, DOI: 10.1080/03086538208582629.

Chapter 27

African Presbyterian Sung Praise – Principles, Early Psalters and Hymnals

Nancy J. Whytock

> Chapter Outline
> 1. Introduction
> 2. A brief overview of Presbyterian sung praise principles – lyrics and tunes
> 3. Definition of "African hymns"
> 4. Early Psalters – examples
> 5. Early Hymnals – case study examples
> 6. A Chart of Early Psalters and Hymnals
> 7. Conclusion
> Bio Inset: John Knox Bokwe – (15 March 1855 –22 February 1922)
> Bio Inset: Ephraim Amu – (13 September 1899 –2 January 1995)

1. Introduction

Augustine of Hippo (354–430 AD), that great Christian leader of Roman North Africa, wrote:

> Do you know what a hymn is? It is singing with the praise of God. If you praise God and do not sing, you utter no hymn. If you sing, and praise not God, you utter no hymn. If you praise anything which does not pertain to the praise of God, though in singing you praise, you utter no hymn.[1]

In this chapter we will look at African Presbyterian sung praise – examining the influence of Presbyterian missionaries in the 19th and early 20th centuries as they shared not only the gospel but also their praise principles and traditions. The development of indigenous African hymns will be highlighted, primarily through case study insets of John Knox Bokwe and Ephraim Amu along with

---

1 Julian, John, Ed. *A Dictionary of Hymnology*. (London: John Murray, 1892), 207.

reference to other African hymn writers whose names are found in early African Presbyterian psalters and hymnals.

2. A Brief Overview of Sung Praise Principles – lyrics and tunes

Psalm 100: A psalm for giving grateful praise

> [1] Shout for joy to the Lord, all the earth.
> [2] Worship the Lord with gladness;
>   come before him with joyful songs.
>
> [3] Know that the Lord is God.
>   It is he who made us, and we are his;
>   we are his people, the sheep of his pasture.
> [4] Enter his gates with thanksgiving
>   and his courts with praise;
>   give thanks to him and praise his name.
>
> [5] For the Lord is good and his love endures forever;
>   his faithfulness continues through all generations. [NIV]

Throughout all generations, songs of praise and worship have been offered to God. The ancient psalms and songs of praise of the Old Testament, the hymns and hymn fragments of the New Testament,[2] and the hymns composed by Christians on every inhabited continent of the world bear testimony to offering thanksgiving and praise to the triune God in song (Psalm 100:4).

Lyrics

The Regulative Principle

When considering Biblical guidelines for worship, including the lyrics of our sung praises, Presbyterians refer to "The Regulative Principle of Worship." Theologians debate the exact origins, development and fine-tuning of this principle which emerged as part of the 16th-century Reformation in Europe and was expressed by the Puritan formulation contained in the documents of the Westminster Assembly. It unpacks the second commandment along with other scriptures and directs:

> But the acceptable way of worshipping the true God is instituted by himself, and so limited to his own revealed will,

---

2 See Gordley, *New Testament Christological Hymns*, and Olds, *Worship*, 44–46.

that he may not be worshipped according to the imaginations and devices of men, or the suggestions of Satan, under any visible representations or any other way not prescribed in the Holy Scripture.[3]

We are only to worship God in the way He has commanded or what can be deduced from his Word by "good and necessary inference."[4] However, not all Presbyterians have interpreted this regulative principle in the same manner. The contrast in interpretations can be compared as follows:

	Interpretation A	Interpretation B
General Principle	Conformity to the Word of God	Conformity to the Word of God
Means of evaluating God's Word for worship principles	Whatever is *consistent* with Scripture	Whatever is *commanded* by Scripture
Means of understanding God's commands	By precept, principle, and example	Quest for explicit commands

R. J. Gore, Jr., a Presbyterian scholar, has written,

> For Calvin, then the requirement could be described quite simply as "whatever is consistent with Scripture." That is not the same as the Puritan "whatever is commanded by Scripture."[5]

And,

> The Reformers realized that God's commands are found in Scripture in 'precept, principle, and example. Their heirs tended to exchange this holistic openness to the Word of God for a quest for 'explicit commands.'[6]

This issue of exactly how to interpret and then apply the regulative principle has caused a great deal of tension and division amongst Presbyterians and others. For example, some interpret the regulative principle to mean only psalms

---

3 *Westminster Confession*, Chapter 21, paragraph 1. Besides the second commandment, see also Deut. 12:32; Matt. 15:9; Acts 17:25; Matt. 4:9; and Col. 2:23.
4 This phrase has been variously interpreted and has led to a great deal of debate concerning using hymns and psalms for worship versus using psalms exclusively.
5 Gore, *Covenantal Worship*, 89.
6 Gore, *Covenantal Worship*, 89.

can be sung in worship and others interpret it to mean that hymns faithful to the Word of God are also acceptable. This particular conflict in *applying* the regulative principle when it comes to what can be sung in worship has affected Presbyterians across Africa. In fact, it was a matter that was debated amongst the first Presbyterians who set sail for Sierra Leone in the late 18th century.[7]

In his book *Worship*, Hughes Oliphant Old says of one famous hymn writer, "The hymnody springs from the psalmody; it is inspired by the psalmody."[8] Old then concludes:

> The church has not always through its long history kept a balance between psalmody and hymnody. Pendulum-like the Christian devotion tradition has regularly swung from one extreme to another. For a while we seem to rely on psalms alone and then for a while "hymns of human composure" seem to monopolize our liturgical life. It is when there is a dynamic relation between the two that Christian doxology is best served.[9]

Cultural and Linguistic Influences

Yet beyond this issue of the Biblical integrity of the lyrics of our praises, there is also the matter of cultural and linguistic influences that must be analysed. Michael Gordley[10] explains that Christian hymns and psalms were sung by the New Testament Christians – both Jew and Gentile. Some of these hymns are recorded for us in the New Testament, as noted earlier. For example, John 1:1–17, Philippians 2:6–11 and Colossians 1:15–20 are believed by many scholars to be just some of the earliest Christian hymns,[11] and aspects of both Jewish and Greek cultural traditions are evident – in terms of idioms and metaphors.[12] While a study of these hymns is beyond the scope of this chapter, the integration of unique cultural and linguistic expressions in our hymns (and indeed in our paraphrasing of psalms and other portions of Scripture) continues to be displayed amongst the various people groups of the world. An illustration of this can be taken from what Jonathan Hehn notes, "The psalms sung in Calvinist churches were metrical paraphrases. Though Christians have always sung Psalms in

---

7 See chapter 1, of this work to note that the controversy over different psalm paraphrases was raging as Christian missionaries sailed for Africa in the late 18th century. This controversy continues to divide Presbyterians.
8 Old, *Worship*, 55.
9 Old, *Worship*, 55.
10 Gordley, *New Testament Christological Hymns*.
11 Gordley, *New Testament Christological Hymns*, 178.
12 Old, *Worship*, 44–45.

Christian worship, metrical psalmody in the sixteenth century was an altogether new way of singing them."[13]

The early psalters and hymnals in this study reveal some of the cultural and linguistic influences of the missionaries on both hymn singing and psalm singing as well as noting some names of early indigenous hymn writers.

Tunes

As we move from the lyrics of our praises to the tunes used to sing them, we should turn our attention to a theme already introduced: the relationship between God's revealed truth and culture. Music, like language, comes from deep within an individual – the mother tongue concept is also "the mother song" concept.[14] While this is a complex subject, certain questions need to be considered in the analysis of tunes:

1. Is any hymn/psalm tune capable of being true or untrue in and of itself – or is it only a means of expressing truth when accompanied by words?
2. Can a tune that was previously attached to unholy lyrics and practices be offensive to Christian converts who formerly associated it with ideas and practices clearly opposed to Christianity? And, likewise, is it possible that one Christian may in good conscience apply a tune to Christian lyrics while another finds this same tune offensive, perhaps dishonouring to the Lord?
3. Does this tune that I am now applying to these words give proper amplification to the words expressed?
4. Is this tune suitable for the language that is being sung so that it allows for proper pronunciation of that language? For example, if you take a tune such as "Amazing Grace" (common metre) and try to sing a common metre verse from Swahili or Xhosa or Igbo, you may soon find that the words of the hymn have to be mispronounced (using the wrong accent or stress, for example) in order to make them fit. Furthermore, the natural cadence of a language is bypassed so that the flow of language and therefore

---

13 Hehn, "Hymnody and Liturgy," in *The Oxford Handbook of Presbyterianism*, 494. See the present chapter, Section 4, "Early Psalters" for a brief discussion on the ancient practice of chanting.
14 In recent years a term for this concept has been adopted – "ethnodoxology." For more information on this growing field of study and influence, see https://worship.calvin.edu/resources/resource-library/ethnodoxology-calling-all-peoples-to-worship-in-their-heart-language/

meaning is removed. This is precisely what happened when many foreign missionaries arrived in Africa, brought their hymns, and then worked very hard to translate them into local African languages. They "fit" in terms of syllables and metre, but, in many instances, they caused singers to be forced to mispronounce words or change tone in order to hold onto the tune (and in tonal languages, a change of tone is a change of meaning).[15] Consider this quote regarding the singing of hymns and psalms, "… if music is based on words, and words have different rhythmic properties in the languages under study, then it would be no surprise if musical rhythm reflected linguistic rhythm."[16] Further,

5. Does this tune somehow relate to the musical experience and expression of those singing it?[17] For example, the same missionaries who translated hymns and psalms into local African languages brought their tunes from their homeland. The sound of those tunes was "foreign" in Africa. One could easily argue that they were inappropriate for Africa. However, many of the first converts amongst many tribes in Africa found those tunes to be true melodies to their hearts.[18] Why? Because those tunes came to them by the very people who brought them the good news of Jesus Christ. The tunes became lasting expressions of affection and gratitude to God for brothers and sisters who had left their homeland for Jesus' sake. However, what happened in subsequent generations? While these "foreign" tunes remained, there may have been less allegiance to them and an increased longing for "African" tunes – tunes that come from the hearts of Africans, tunes that allow for the proper pronunciation and expression of the local language.

---

15 For more on this subject, see June Dickie, "Singing the Psalms: Applying Principles of African Music to Bible Translation," *Scriptura* 116 (2017:1), 1–16. Felix Konotey-Ahulu wrote, "Because our Mother Tongue is Tonal, I devised a method of writing it to clarify the pronunciation of the written words the missionaries produced when translating the Bible and writing great hymns" – sent by private email to N. J. Whytock, 13 September 2022.
16 Aniruddh D. Patel and Joseph R. Daniele, "An Empirical comparison of rhythm in language and music," *Cognition* 87 (2003), B42. For more on this subject see, W. Menninghaus, V. Wagner, C. A. Knoop, & M. Scharinger, "Poetic speech melody: A crucial link between music and language," (2018). PLoS ONE 13(11): e0205980. https://doi.org/10.1371/journal.pone.0205980
17 Many Western hymns tunes are based on the heptatonic scale with its pattern of tones and semitones. This is a contrast to many ancient cultures, including traditional African music, which is based on the pentatonic scale and its use of whole tones.
18 John Knox Bokwe, *Amaculo Ase Lovedale* (Lovedale, SA: Lovedale Press, 1922, 5th edition), iii.

Some missionaries attempted to incorporate African music into Christian liturgy. The earliest of these were Scottish Presbyterians, who around the beginning of the twentieth century started to set Christian words to traditional African melodies. Generally such innovations did not take hold until Africans themselves began to express the Christian message in their own melodies.[19]

As we ask these five important questions related to tunes, we may acknowledge that the musical expression of one *culture* and *generation* can positively influence the musical expression of another, *so long as the influence takes place willingly rather than under compulsion.*[20]

3. Definition of "African Hymns"

Considering the above discussion and attempt to define biblical and musical principles for lyrics and tunes, the questions may logically be asked – what is an *African* hymn? Here the definition is complex, but it can basically be summarized into 7 categories, as outlined by noted musician and hymnologist C. Michael Hawn:[21]

1. Western hymns directly from European or North American hymnals in a colonial language accompanied on organ or piano; (this doesn't seem African but is a form of hymn singing still widely practised in Africa – "adopted African hymns"). Two of the most famous in this category are "What a Friend we Have in Jesus" and "What Can Wash Away My Sins?"[22]
2. Western hymns translated into a vernacular African language, often with some melodic and/or rhythmic alterations to accommodate the African vernacular (the two examples in #1 are also often found in this category in various African languages);

---

19 Tim Dowley, *Christian Music: A Global History* (Oxford: Lion, 2011), 188.
20 One powerful example of this type of willing influence is found in William Edgar, *A Supreme Love* (Downers Grove, IL: IVP Academic, 2022), 74–75. It is related to European Psalm singing and African American sung praise.
21 C. Michael Hawn, *The Canterbury Dictionary of Hymnology*. https://hymnology.hymnsam.co.uk/a/african-hymnody?q=african%20hymn
22 This was the era of prolific hymn writing in the west. It is estimated that in Britain alone over 400.000 hymns were written between 1837 and 1901. See, Ian Bradley, *Abide with me: the world of Victorian hymns* (London: SCM Press, 1997), xii.

3. Western hymns sung with African oral tradition performance techniques such as leader-response and use of percussion;
4. Blending of Western hymns with traditional compositional techniques including improvised harmonies, parallel harmonic progressions, and, in some areas multipart improvisatory vocal singing, as well as increased use of percussion and dance, further disguising the Western origins of the hymn;
5. African melodies with texts written by Western missionaries;
6. Congregational song compositions by Africans in Western or blended idioms;
7. Congregational songs composed by Africans in thoroughly traditional African musical styles.[23]

The "African" value of some of these categories may be questioned. However, hopefully the hymnals noted in this chapter will illustrate the matter of musical influences from one people group or person to another involving a spectrum with imitation at one end and originality at the other. The degree to which either is at work in a hymn/psalm composition may be attributed to a wide variety of factors, including leadership styles and influences. Also, it will be hard to establish the criteria for categories 3, 4, and 5 above, but hopefully students will use these categories to effectively evaluate their own "sung praise" traditions.

4. Early Psalters – examples[24]

While many Presbyterian mission stations were following the patterns above in terms of translating English hymns into local African languages/dialects, the

---

23 Vita Chenoweth (in reference specifically to the Anyuak people of Ethiopia) has said that Christian missionaries find that nationals respond enthusiastically to music written in their own musical traditions. That when a people develops its own hymns with both vernacular words and music, it is good evidence that Christianity has taken root. See, https://www.anuaklegacy.com/hymns [accessed 13 March 2023. Also sample recordings from the 1970s can be accessed at this same link.

24 Other full psalters have been produced but are really going beyond this historic period of missions for volume one. The Ndebele metrical psalter started in 1963 with Aaaron Ndelebe, Petros Mzamo and James Tallach as a committee. A metrical 1973 edition in the new Ndelebe orthography was printed by TBS. Likewise a full metrical Shona Psalter has been produced by the FPCS. The FPCS is also in process (2013ff) of translation work in Ekegusii (Kenya) for the metrical version of Psalms.

tradition of metrical[25] psalm singing (that was popularized at the time of the Reformation in Europe) was also brought to Africa. One author refers to the psalms as the "antecedents" of hymns.[26] Two examples of metrical psalters are noted here.

Egyptian Metrical Psalter

In the 1865 Annual Report of the Board of Missions of the United Presbyterian Church of North America,[27] it is noted that their missionaries in Egypt were engaged in preparing the entire Book of Psalms in a metrical version in the Arabic language. This project was given funding by the Board and in 1867, the first Arabic metrical Psalter was published in Beirut by The American Mission Press. Though it is a full psalter, the 150 metrical psalms are then followed by a section of hymns and then a section of spiritual songs for children. The section for children contains illustrations.

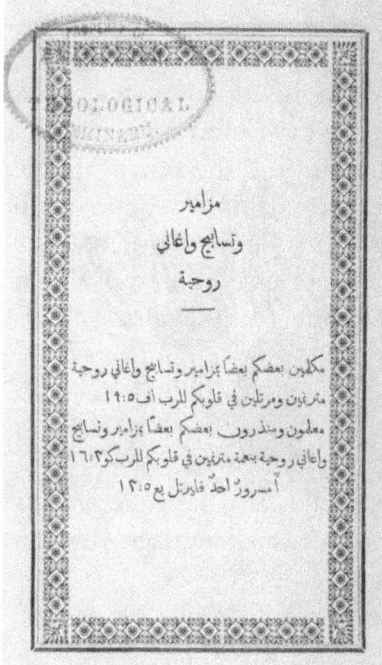

▲ 1867 Complete Arabic Psalter with hymns and spiritual songs

▲ 1920 Tune Book for Arabic Psalter

---

25 The term "metrical" indicates a psalm paraphrase that is written to conform to a set pattern of syllables in each line so that it can be sung to a tune that supports that pattern of syllables. For example, Common metre (CM) is a pattern of 4 lines for each stanza. The CM pattern is: 8 syllables, 6 syllables, 8 syllables, 6 syllables.

26 Brian Castle, *Sing A New Song to the Lord: The Power and Potential of Hymns* (London: Darton, Longman & Todd, 1994), 5.

27 *Sixth Annual report of The Board of Foreign Missions of The United Presbyterian Church of North America*. (Philadelphia: Christian Instructor Office, May 1865), 8.

It would appear the driving force behind this translation project was Rev. Dr Gulian Lansing. Ordained as a pastor in the Associate Reformed Presbytery in 1850, he served six years in Syria, and then from 1857 (to his death in 1896) he laboured in Egypt, first in Alexandria and then in Cairo. From 1858, he was under the auspices of the United Presbyterian Church of North America. Lansing wrote about his work and travels in his book *Egypt's Princes: A Narrative of Missionary Labor in the Valley of the Nile* (1864, 1865). In this book, he describes the beautiful and ancient practice of chanting the psalms as observed amongst the Coptic church:

> There were several poets present, and sometimes one of these, forming the people into a large circle, would take his place in the centre, and then giving them a chorus, like that in the 136th Psalm, he would each time improvise a sentence, and then they in full orchestra would break in with the chorus which he had given them. How magnificent it would sound to have that Psalm thus sung in our churches.[28]

Despite Lansing's glowing affirmation of the beauty of this ancient practice of chanting the Psalms, a 1920 tunes only book published by the United Presbyterian Mission in Egypt shows that Western tunes were being used to sing this UP Arabic metrical version of the psalms (as do the tune suggestions in the original 1867 edition). This 1867 psalter (together with the accompanying 1920 tune book) make it the earliest known complete metrical psalter on the continent of Africa.

Xhosa Metrical Psalter

The second complete (all 150 psalms) metrical psalter is the Xhosa Psalter[29] completed in 1922 at Lovedale in South Africa by John Knox Bokwe and William Kobo Ntsikana, assisted by John Boyana Radasi (Fingo – missionary) and Principal James Henderson of Lovedale in South Africa. It is important to note D. D. T. Jabavu's comments on the close connection between Hebrew and Xhosa linguistics:

> The Xhosa Bible, according to B. J. Ross is truer to the Hebrew than the English versions because the Xhosa tongue possesses close linguistic affinities and identity of religious customs, while the Hebrew poetry passages have been turned into

---

28 Gulian Lansing, *Egypt's Princes. A Narrative of Missionary Labor in the Valley of the Nile* (Philadelphia: UP Board of Publication, 1864), 249–250.

29 Some of the common psalms (eg. 1, 23, 100, 121) were translated prior to this, but not a complete metrical psalter.

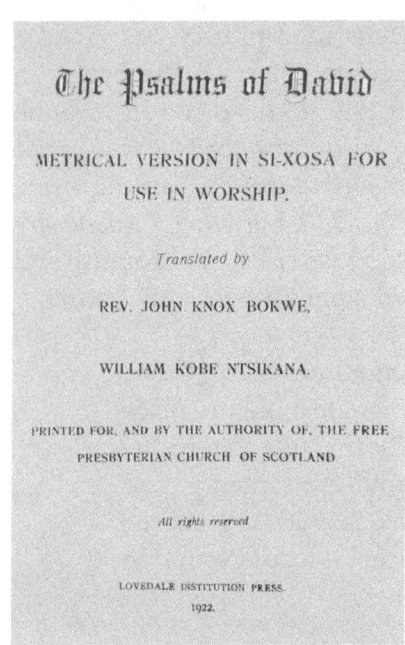

Xhosa poetry which retains the beauty of the original that is lost in the English prose.³⁰

Were Bokwe and Radasi able to retain this close linguistic affinity between Xhosa and Hebrew while adopting the metrical style of psalm singing? This would be a good subject for future in-depth analysis, particularly in light of the fact that the metrical version of this Xhosa psalter was designed to conform to Western tune patterns – similar to the Arabic Psalter above. The majority of psalms are in common metre; some are long metre – as in the 1650 Scottish Psalter.³¹

◀ The 1922 Xhosa Psalter

5. Early Hymnals ³² – case study examples

Chumie, South Africa³³ – Amaculo

In 1823, Rev. & Mrs John Ross arrived at Chumie (Tyumie) with a printing press. John Bennie had arrived two years earlier and had already made significant progress in learning to read and write Xhosa. He was ready and eager to begin printing Xhosa materials now that a local press was available. The first hymnal produced, *Amaculo*, contained 29 hymns – translations of English hymns – with Western metres. One of these hymns (in common metre), Kugqityiwe (It is Finished), was included in John Knox Bokwe's *Amaculo Ase Lovedale*, with music by John Knox Bokwe.³⁴ Hymnals continued to be refined and developed. For example, Tiyo Soga's personal 1849 copy *Incwadi Yamaculo Okivunywa Ezikolweni*

---

30 D. D. T. Jabavu, *The Influence of English on Bantu Literature* (Alice, SA: Lovedale Press, 1943), 21.
31 As already noted concerning Egypt, the ancient practice of chanting the psalms (and other portions of scripture) was practiced amongst the Xhosa people. See #16 and #21 on the chart in this chapter for examples of presbyterian hymn books that contain a section of scripture selections to be chanted.
32 Burnett makes the important point that the zeal to produce hymnals was not only for sung praise in worship but for teaching and learning Christians doctrine. Burnett, "Music and Mission: A Case Study of the Anglican-Xhosa Missions of the Eastern Cape, 1854–1880," 177–178, 185.
33 See Chapter 2 of this work, "Beginnings, Part Two: The Cape, c.1800–c.1840s, Taking Root."
34 See chart in this chapter . Bokwe, John Knox, ed. *Amaculo Ase Lovedale*, (Lovedale, SA: Lovedale Press, 1922), 100.

ZikaKristu Ezisemoxoseni shows his significant involvement in the development of Xhosa Presbyterian sung praise and his involvement in correcting and refining translated hymns and psalms.

Corisco, Equatorial West Africa[35] – Lembo La Benga

In the forward to *Lembo La Benga* (1873, published for the Corisco Mission, West Africa), R. H. Nassau explains the desire to produce a native hymnal. The initial work toward this vision involved translating English hymns into the Benga language. "Some are compositions, either original, or themes wrought from thoughts avowedly taken from existing hymns."[36] One of the early converts to Christianity in that region, Bojowa, worked alongside the missionaries (especially Rev. W. H. Clarke) in the translation work to ensure that both the language and tone were acceptable to the Benga-speaking people. All selections in this hymnal are in Benga. All selections are in metres and most have a suggested tune (not African tunes) noted to the right of each title.

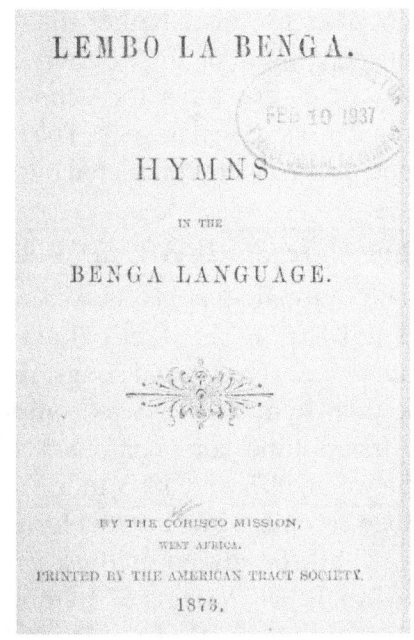

▲ Benga hymnal

Bojowa – translator

The translation of about one half of the 197 hymns/psalms is attributed to Bojowa (as noted above, he worked closely with Rev. W. H. Clarke, but Clarke insisted that Bojowa receive full credit for the work).[37] Bojowa was one of the early Benga converts to Christianity. Having been redeemed from a life of "vice and superstition,"[38] he went on to become particularly useful in this matter of translation. Bojowa travelled to America and this short trip (less than one year) had a profound effect upon his spiritual development. During this time, it was reported that "in the last year of his life, a strong and beautiful Christian character developed." It was the last year of his life, because, tragically, he drowned on his way back to Corisco.

---

35 See chapter 10 of this work, "Equatorial West Africa and American Presbyterian Missions: Gaboon, Corisco."
36 *Lembo La Benga* (West Africa: Corisco Mission, 1873), 7.
37 *Lembo La Benga* (West Africa: Corisco Mission, 1873), 6.
38 *Lembo La Benga* (West Africa: Corisco Mission, 1873), 6.

Mrs Mary Nassau – hymn translator

About one quarter of the remaining hymns in the Benga Hymnal are translations by Mrs Mary Nassau, who died in 1870 before the completion of this hymnal. Her husband, Robert Hamill Nassau,[39] wrote in his Preface to *Lembo La Benga*, "Mrs Nassau explained that, 'If I can make a pretty good Benga hymn, it does not matter to me whether the translation is close or otherwise.'"[40] This at least opened the door for original compositions, but no original compositions by Bojowe or any other indigenous Christians were published (or existed) at this point as far as can be seen. The remaining one quarter of these translated hymns and psalms were completed by "other missionaries and a few native members."[41]

Lovedale, South Africa[42] *– Amaculo Ase Lovedale*

This hymnal, *Amaculo Ase Lovedale*[43] was published in 1885 at the Lovedale Press, South Africa. This first edition was in the form of a small booklet containing about a dozen original songs, set in sol-fa notation to Xhosa words. It is the first known hymnal that was compiled by a black African and contains original African tune compositions.[44] These songs had been published individually between 1875 and 1885 in a Xhosa publication *Isigidimi Sama-Xosa*[45] and were then compiled into booklet form due to popular demand.

The fifth edition of *Amaculo Ase Lovedale*, published in 1922, is a 163-page hymnal that contains 87 hymns (psalms & paraphrases included). Each of the African hymn categories (above) are well represented. This hymnal is divided into four categories: Part 1 – "Selection of Melodies that introduced our fathers into Christian worship." These include four hymns by Ntsikana[46] (with their traditional Xhosa tunes, as written down and arranged by John Knox Bokwe –

---

39 See inset in chapter 10 of this work, "Equatorial West Africa and American Presbyterian Missions: Gaboon, Corisco."
40 *Lembo La Benga*, 7.
41 *Lembo La Benga*, 6.
42 See chapter 8 of this work, "'The Lovedale Method', Context, Development, and Transmission."
43 John Knox Bokwe, *Amaculo Ase Lovedale* (Lovedale, SA: Lovedale Press, 1922, 5th edition), iii.
44 See inset in this chapter on John Knox Bokwe.
45 Bokwe, John Knox, ed. *Amaculo Ase Lovedale*, Lovedale, SA: Lovedale Press, 1885, iii.
46 "Ntsikana, who later became a counsellor of chief Ngqika, heard the missionary Dr Van der Kemp of the London Missionary Society preach in about 1799–1800, but only underwent a conversion experience some 15 years later, in the absence of any white person. He began to preach among his people and won a number of converts. He conducted services for his converts, taught them what he had learned about Christianity (in an African way), and composed songs for their services … On his death-bed he sent his followers to join the new mission at Tyhume, which later moved to Lovedale in Alice." David Dargie, *Xhosa Music: Its techniques and instruments, with a collection of songs*. (Cape Town: David Philip, 1988), 4–5.

see inset in this chapter); Part 2 – English lyrics with tunes composed by John Knox Bokwe; Part 3 – A selection of Xhosa devotional hymns and songs for school children with lyrics composed by Africans and others, music primarily composed by John Knox Bokwe; Part 4 – School Songs with lyrics composed by Bokwe and others – both African and British – music arranged primarily by Bokwe.

Besides Bokwe, another key indigenous hymn writer in *Amaculo Ase Lovedale* is Ntsikana (noted above), one of the first converts to Christianity in what is today known as the Eastern Cape, South Africa.

> The way in which Ntsikana conveyed his teaching was infinitely winsome. He was probably illiterate, his congregation most definitely so and there were no books. But Ntsikana had something else: a message. He conveyed his message in the classic Africa way of communication: in song. He composed four hymns; or perhaps it would be more correct to say that four hymns 'entered' him. They became the central part of his order of worship. As he led a service, he wore his prestigious cloak of leopard skin, and in due course this garment acquired mystical association.[47]

Ntsikana's "Great Hymn" is in the traditional style of the praise poem (*isibongo*). It is an example of taking an old form of worship to false gods and then applying that form to the worship of God. The music is in pure Xhosa style. John Knox Bokwe wrote that this hymn with its traditional Xhosa music deeply affected Xhosa Christians in subsequent generations.

> In Ntsikana and his hymns, the early Xhosa image of God is drawn in strong colours. He obviously identified the Creator-God with the God of his fathers and was touched by the Suffering Hero whose blood was shed for the Xhosa. He expressed this faith with an immediacy of feeling and identification that did not appear again for a hundred years, until Isaiah Shembe, the Zulu, produced his *Izihlabelelo* – Book of Songs.[48]

---

[47] Sundkler and Steed, *A History of the Church in Africa*, 347.
See also, Janet Hodgson, *Ntsikana's great hymn: a Xhosa expression of Christianity in the early nineteenth century eastern Cape* (Cape Town, 1980).
[48] Sundkler and Steed, *A History of the Church in Africa*, 349.

Livingstonia, Nyasaland[49] – The Ngoni Hymn Book

A fourth example is *The Ngoni Hymn Book* [50] (revised 1937). Here we find 65 hymns and within them at the very least categories 2, 6 and 7 are represented. Selections are also included from *Amagama Okuhlabelela – Zulu Hymnal*.[51] Many indigenous writers, including well-known hymn writers – Malwera Thembo and Peter Thole[52] contributed Ngoni compositions for African-style music. A number of hymns are translations of Western hymns and record the Western hymn tune to be used. Improvisation into a more African style of singing would have been natural and continues up to the present. "The musically gifted Ngoni adapted their African songs to Christian hymns, producing as many as fifty with a characteristic African rhythm and flavour. In the first years, many were danced to as well as sung."[53] They were strongly encouraged in this enterprise by Rev. Donald Fraser who appears to have been ahead of his time in aggressively fostering freedom of musical expression and creativity during his missionary service.[54]

Congo Mission[55] – Musambu Ws Nzambi

A final example of the range of African hymns (as defined in the seven categories above) is the hymnal compiled by Lucy Sheppard in the Buluba (now known

---

49 See chapter 14 of the present work, "The Livingstonia Mission and Subsequent Synod."
50 *The Ngoni Hymn Book* (Blantyre: Livingstonia Mission, revised 1937).
51 *Amagama Okuhlabelela, Zulu Hymnal* (Boston, MA: The American Board of Commissioners for Foreign Missions, 1887).
52 For an in depth analysis of some of the early Northern Malawi hymn writers see, Augustine Chingwala Musopole, *Singing and Dancing for God: A Theological Reflection on Indigenous Hymns from Northern Malawi* (Luwinga, Mzuzu: Mzuni Press, 2022).
53 Sundkler and Steed, *A History of the Church in Africa*, 474. The Blantyre Mission experienced a similar blessing in encouraging indigenous music through the work of David Clement Scott: "Another of Scott's ideas was very far from typical of the Victorian mission station, this was moonlight dancing. On the nights when the moon was full and there was no cloud, Scott had the boarders gather on the bwalo (a large open space in front of a house or in the centre of a village) to dance and play games and sing as they would have done at home in the villages on such a night. He presided and saw that no unseemly songs were sung or dances danced. This must be contrasted with the fact that African dancing, often dancing of any kind, was frowned on by most missionaries working in Central Africa at the time. Blantyre's nearest neighbour, the Zambezi Industrial Mission founded in 1892, banned dancing and then went on to ban drumming also as evil." Andrew C. Ross, *Blantyre Mission and The Making of Modern Malawi* (Malawi: Luviri Press, 1996), 75. Note: a second edition was published in 2018.
54 Bengt and Steed, *A History of the Church in Africa*, 475–476. See also, Chapter 14 of this volume.
55 See Chapter 19 of the present work – "A History of the American Presbyterian Congo Mission (c.1891–c.1945)."

as Tshiluba) language in Central Africa[56] (DRC today) in 1898, *Musambu Ws Nzambi (Song of God)*.[57] Sheppard and her husband, William, were American Presbyterian missionaries. The hymnal contains "translations from Snyder, Morrison and Ibanche Station personnel."[58] Category 2 African Hymns are evident: translated hymns from popular English hymnody with accompanying European hymn-tune suggestions. "By 1902 it became clear that a new edition was already needed. During the intervening years a number of new hymns had been *translated*"[59] [emphasis mine]. Thus, in this early hymnal, there are no indigenous compositions – either lyrics or words.

6. A Chart of Some Early Psalters and Hymnals[60] – with brief analysis[61]

Name of Hymnal/ Psalter	Language	Publisher and/ or Place of Publication	Year	Related Chapter in this Volume
1. *Amaculo*	Xhosa	Glasgow Missionary Society, Chumie	Before 1830 two editions	Contains 26 & 29 entries Hymn translations, Western metres Chapter 2
2. *Choix de Cantiques Chrétiens, avec Des Cantiques à L'usage des enfans[sic] Francais et Anglais*	French & English	E. Baker [LMS], Mauritius	1838	106 French hymns & 14 hymns for children (in both French and English) and 4 doxologies Western metres and Western suggested hymn tunes Chapter 18

---

56 Benedetto, "Presbyterian Mission Press in Central Africa, 1890–1922," 56.
57 Benedetto, "Presbyterian Mission Press in Central Africa, 1890–1922," 59.
58 Benedetto, "Presbyterian Mission Press in Central Africa, 1890–1922," 65.
59 Benedetto, "Presbyterian Mission Press in Central Africa, 1890–1922," 60.
60 The author acknowledges the fact that many indigenous hymns and choruses were sung but not written down. For a fascinating account of indigenous music in The Cape Colony, see Chapters 2 & 3 of, Burnett, "Music and Mission: A Case Study of the Anglican-Xhosa Missions of the Eastern Cape, 1854–1880," 47–131. information.bris.ac.uk/ws/portalfiles/portal/220362551/Final_Copy_2020_01_23_Burnett_P_T_PhD.pdf
61 The author of this chapter welcomes correspondence from any readers with any information concerning other African Presbyterian hymnals. Please email: haddingtonhouse@eastlink.ca

3.	*Incwadana Inamaculo gokwamaxosa*	Xhosa	Printed by Aldum & Harvey, Grahamstown, ed., John Bennie, Lovedale	1st edition, 1839	Chapter 2 contains 56 entries including a words only version of Ntsikana's Great Hymn
			Printed by Jaffray & Rowles, Grahamstown, ed., John Bennie, Lovedale	2nd edition 1841	contains 97 entries
4.	*Hymns in Gaboon*	Mpongwe	American Board of Commissioners for Foreign Missions	1845	Hymns and catechism 48 pages Chapter 10
5.	*Incwadi Yamaculo Okivunywa Ezikolweni ZikaKristu Ezisemoxoseni*	Xhosa	Teachers' Press, Eqonci[sic] [King William's Town] – copy at Cory Library, Rhodes University was owned by Tiyo Soga and in it he has hand-written extensive revisions and corrections.	1849	130 hymns – various metres, Words only, no tune suggestions at least 5 hymns by Tiyo Soga 3 doxologies, 4 additional songs, for grace at meal times, Subject index and alphabetical index see same title 1900, in this chart
6.	*Arabic Psalter Mazāmīr wa-tasābīh wa-aghāni rūḥīyah*	Arabic	American Mission Press, Beirut, Syria [for UPCNA Mission Egypt]	1867	Metrical Psalms in Western metre with Western hymn tunes suggested, also contains a section of hymns and then spiritual songs for children with illustrations Chapter 23[62]

---

62 This psalter was eventually also used by the United Presbyterian Mission (UPCNA) in Sudan. See, *Triennial Report on The Foreign Missions of the United Presbyterian Church Of North America, 1916, 1917, 1918* (Philadelphia: The Board of Foreign Missions, 1919), 100.

7.	*Lembo La Benga*[63]	Benga	Corisco Mission, West Africa, American Tract Society	1873	197 hymn/psalm translations by mission personnel (including Mrs. Mary Nassau) and Bojowe with suggested Western tunes Chapter 10
8.	*Blantyre Mission Hymnbook*	Nyanja (Chinyanja/ Chewa)	Blantyre Mission	1882	8-page booklet, contents mainly translated hymns by Clement Scott Includes "Lord, A Little Band and Lowly" still sung today
9.	*Atwifo Kristofo Asore Nè Dwom [Liturgy and Hymns for the use of the Christian Churches on the Gold Coast speaking the Asante and Fante Language called Tshi Chwee, Twi)] [Tshi Hymnbook]*	Twi	Basel: Basel German Evangelical Missionary Society	1883 Second Edition	460 hymns – words only, plus 2 hymns by black slaves freed in America 1866, plus 13 hymns by indigenous hymn writers, pp. 290 mentions a Ewe hymnbook of 1867 Chapter 12 & Chapter 27 inset on Ephraim Amu
10.	*Izihlabelo Zogu Boña umLimo*	Ndebele	Cape Town: Saul Solomon & Co.	1884	52 hymns – all written in Western metre and verse except #52 looks African Chapter 2
11.	*Amaculo Ase Lovedale*	Xhosa and English (in 5th edition)	Lovedale, SA: Lovedale Press, compiled by John Knox Bokwe (1st known hymnal compiled by an African)	1st published 1885, about one dozen hymns with solfa notation several editions	4th edition, 1915 5th edition, 1922, -contains 87 hymns/songs/psalms in total, all with solfa Chapter 8
12.	*Chinyanja Hymns*	Chinyanja (Chewa)	Aberdeen: G & W Fraser, for The Livingstonia Mission	1891	97 hymns, 4 prayers, 4 psalms (23,24,100,121) Chapter 14

---

63 To view this hymnal online, see https://archive.org/details/lembolab00cori/page/n11/mode/2up

13.	*Dihela Tsa Tihèlō Ea Modimo*	Tswana (Sechwana) Includes Psalm 23, Psalm 67 and National Anthem	London Missionary Society	1894	Contains translations by David Livingstone & Robert Moffat 414 hymns – translations – suggested tunes– Western – many Sankey tunes
14.	*Musambu Ws Nzambi*	Tshiluba/ Tshikete	Richmond, Virginia, Curtiss Printing Company, for The American Presbyterian Mission	1898	46 hymn translations from English by mission personnel Compiled by Mrs. Lucy G. Sheppard, contains The Apostles' Creed, The Lord's Prayer, and Doxology See Chapter 19
15.	*Incwadi Yamaculo Yase*	Xhosa	London Society for Promoting Christian Knowledge	1900	Contains work by John Knox Bokwe. See inset Chapter 27, also John Bennie, Ntsikana, and Tiyo Soga Some Xhosa translators listed, Western tunes suggested 335 hymns translated, then #336 is a series of five hymns on the story of the crucifixion
16.	*Incwadi Yamaculo: okuvunywa Zilolo Zika Kristu; Ezisemoxoseni* (*a hymnbook for children- approved for use in the Christian schools*)	Xhosa	Lovedale, Printed by the Teachers' Press	1900	219 hymns, First hymn a version of Ntsikana's Great Hymn in 12s, all other hymns in Western metres with suggested Western tunes, P.M., C.M. or L.M. at least 26 hymns by Tiyo Soga and many other Xhosa contributors Also contains 30 songs for chanting from psalms and other scripture passages including Micah 6:8 – not paraphrases – taken from Xhosa Bible
17.	*Izihlabelo Zogu Boña UmLimo*	Zulu	The Gresham Press for London Missionary Society	1902	May contain translations from Lindley. See Chapter 6

18.	*Mukanda wa Misambu*	Buka-Lulua	Luebo, Congo: American Presbyterian Mission	1902	60 hymn translations from English 2nd edition – (one with words and music) A revision and enlargement of *Musambu Ws Nzambi* Chapter 19
19.	*Akwukwo Ukwe N'Asusu Ibo*	Ibo (Igbo) Divided into two sections: hymns for the morning and hymns for the evening	London: Society for the Promoting of Christian Knowledge	1904	All hymns translated from English, hymn tunes Western English and Igbo Index Chapter 9
20.	*Gwaba li no mba (Sekalaña Hymnbook)*	seKalaña	London Missionary Society	1904	96 hymns predominately hymn translations and Western tunes but some native compositions and native tunes – includes Psalm 23, section of Christmas hymns, same as 1920 edition with no additional native compositions by 1920
21.	*Incwadi Yama-Culo Ase-Rabe*	Xhosa	Lovedale Mission Press *1929 edition published for BPC, Congreg. Church, & missions of the UFCS	1910 Many editions: 1914, 1929, 1941, 1943, 1961	1914 edition contains over 220 hymns, 27 hymns by Tiyo Soga and includes many other Xhosa contributors. Over 50 hymns by Rev. John Bennie. Various metres – C.M., L.M. & P.M. Chapters 2, 8, 27 15 psalms and 17 other portions of scripture for chanting – not paraphrases – taken directly from Xhosa Bible.
22.	*Nyĩmbo cia Kũinĩra Ngai* [A Book of Hymns in the Kikuyu Language][64]	Kikuyu	London: Society for the Propagation of Christian Knowledge	1911 Later editions can be found for 1955 and 1956	69 pages, index of titles and first lines, blank pages for adding in other hymns. Chapter 20

---

64 There is some confusion about this hymnal and who the compilers and actual translators were. It seems that Arthur Barlow of the CSM was one.

23.	*IzihLabelo Zogudumisa Umlimu*	Ndebele	Vryburg, Cape Province, SA: The South African District Committee of the L.M.S. by John Whiteside	1915	189 hymns Translated Western hymns and Western tunes Includes isiXhosa hymns – a few translated from Lovedale Amaculo Ase Lovedale – has solfa for all selections, Lowell Mason selections also included
24.	*Zolembedwa M'Chinyanja Ndi M'Chiyad*	Chewa (Nyanja)	London	1916 *1910 Mvera Conference of Nyasaland Missions agreed to produce a combined hymnbook for the Nyanja-speaking churches. 2 or 3 hymns with native music included - one tune a native canoe song sung on the Zambezi River[65]	400 hymns Mostly European translations, some African hymn writers (less than 10), pg. 287 has an African hymn both words and music, solfa included for all selections, Includes some psalms. Chapter 15
25.	*Ñwed Iquö ke Efik*	Efik	Exeter, England: James Townsend & Sons	1920	all 245 hymns (including a few psalms), plus doxology, translations from English Influenced by UP Mission – Mary Slessor, etc. Chapter 9
26.	*Tune Book for Arabic Metrical Psalter*	Arabic	The Board of Foreign Missions of The United Presbyterian Church, Philadelphia	1920	predominantly Western tunes, at least one "Coptic" tune and one "Eastern" tune Chapter 23

---

65 Alexander Hetherwick, *The Romance of Blantyre: How Livingstone's Dream Came True* (London: James Clarke, n.d.), 204–205.

27.	*Gwaba Li No Mba a no boka Mlimo nge lulimo gwe Kalaña*	Kalaña	London Missionary Society	1920	96 hymns – predominantly Western metre and hymn translations, some native compositions and tunes Apostles' Creed & Magnificat included
28.	Indumiso Zika Davide 1922 Xhosa Psalter	Xhosa	Lovedale, South Africa "printed for, and by the authority of, The Free Presbyterian Church of Scotland"[66]	1922	Full psalter with C.M. and some L.M. Translated by Rev. John Knox Bokwe and William Kobe Ntsikana[67] Chapters 8 & 27
29.	Inyimbo Sha Bwinakristu	Bemba	Printed at Lovedale Press for Livingstonia Mission, Lubwa, N. Rhodesia	Abridgement of hymnbook published in 1929 by The Religious Tract Society of London	Approx. 160 hymns 9 written with "native air", all others Western metre with Western tune selections, mainly from *Christian Hymns* words only- many handwritten corrections
30.	Amagama Okuhlabelela	Zulu	Boston: The American Board of Commissioners for Foreign Missions	Original (words only) 1887 – 3rd edition 1932	Contains material from The United Free Church of Scotland – see Chapter 27
31.	Kitabu Cha Tuni za Nyimbo Za Dini	Swahili	London: Society for Promoting Christian Knowledge	1st edition? 2nd edition, 1937	Evidence of adapting to African tunes suitable for Bantu rhythms
32.	Izingoma zo Bukristu	Ngoni	Mission Press, Blantyre, Nyasaland	1st edition? Revised ed. 1937	Chapters 15 & 27
33.	Incwadi Yeendumiso	Xhosa	Free Church of Scotland, Lovedale Press	1964 (worked on for well over a decade)	Full psalter with Lord's Prayer and Apostles' Creed Various metres, including 12s and 13s no tune suggestions

---

66 *Indumiso Zika Davide* (Lovedale, 1922), title page.
67 Grandson of first Xhosa convert, Ntsikana.

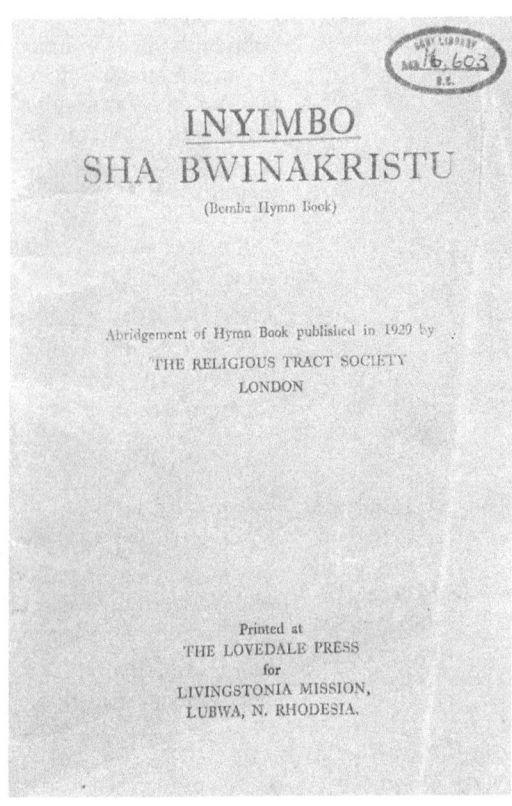

▲ Bemba hymnal

Analysis

In the thirty-three examples cited, the vast majority of hymns are translations of Western hymns – mainly from English but also some from German. The recommended tunes are from Western hymnals. The psalter metres and tunes are also Western. Throughout the examples cited, there are hints of indigenous involvement – some African translators, some African composers, and some African hymn writers (lyrics). Thus, the seven categories by Hawn – in Section 3 of this chapter – are all represented but categories 1 and 2 are by far the majority categories. Category 7 is the rarest, yet obviously the most "African" in terms of indigenous creative expression.

7. Conclusion

Presbyterian missions across Africa significantly contributed to the sung praises of Christians on the continent and even beyond. African Presbyterian composers, such as Peter Thole (Malawi), Ephraim Amu (Ghana), John Knox Bokwe and Tiyo Soga (South Africa), composed hymns that continue to be sung to this day – and not just in Africa.[68] Likewise, there has been a tremendous influence on African Presbyterian sung praise from Western tunes, metrical psalms, and translated Western hymns that also continues to this day. Tinyiko Maluleke writes concerning the modern profile of a representative South African Christian: "The choruses that sustain her and fellow members of her Charismatic or African Initiated Church are excerpts from old hymns written or translated by the first generation of missionaries from the hymnals of their European home churches."[69] The entwined impact is undeniable.

---

68 Music by Amu, Soga, and Bokwe can be heard on YouTube. Three of Peter Thole's songs and tunes are available on https://hymnary.org/
69 Ross, Asamoah-Gyadu, and Johnson, *Christianity in Sub-Saharan Africa*, 53.

Yet the debate also continues: are these "Western" songs authentic expressions of sung praise from African brothers and sisters? This debate has centred around the matters discussed in the opening sections of this chapter – the distinction between biblical principles for sung praise versus the unique linguistic challenges, cultural settings, and local traditions of any people group.

We will never know how different the history of African Presbyterian sung praise may have been if converts, indwelt by the Holy Spirit, had simply been given the Scriptures and from that their own psalmody, hymnody and melodies would have developed. What we do know is that the combined efforts of Presbyterian missionaries and indigenous believers have been immense. As iron sharpens iron, so many have sharpened each other in a sincere effort to encourage and enable thousands upon thousands to sing the praises of God across the continent of Africa.

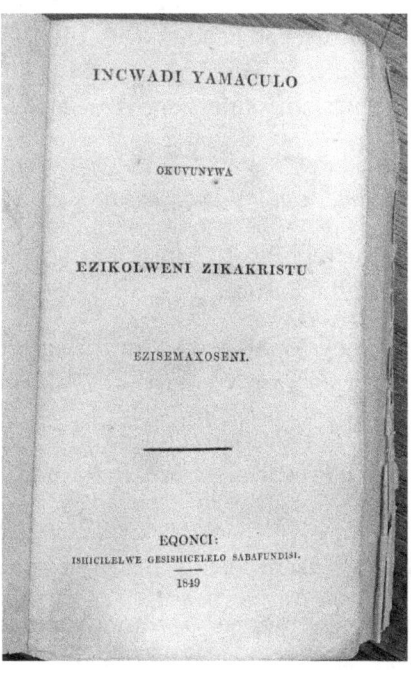

▲ Title page of Tiyo Soga's copy of the 1849 *Incwadi Yamaculo*

Questions for study (fact type):

1. What is the name of the principle that Presbyterians and others use to guide them in what is or is not acceptable for the sung praise of God?
2. Name the first *complete* psalter that was produced by Presbyterians on the continent of Africa. Name the second complete psalter. For each of these, list the year each was published, the language, and the place. This information can be found in the text and in the chart.
3. Name two of the most famous African Presbyterian hymn writers and beside each name record their home country, the year of their birth, and the year of their death.
4. Make note of an African language that is not represented on the chart. Explain how you might be able to find out more information about any early hymns produced in this language.

Questions for study (reflection type):

1. In this chapter, five questions have been offered concerning the tunes used for singing psalms and hymns. Look up the term *"adiaphora."* How does this term apply to the use of tunes in worship? How might the principle of 1 Corinthians 10:23-33 apply to tunes?
2. Write one paragraph of biographical information on Lucy Sheppard (compiled hymnbook listed on chart #14). See also Chapter 19.

Select Bibliography

Avery, Tom. "Music of the Heart: The Power of Indigenous Worship in Reaching Unreached Peoples With the Gospel." *Mission Frontiers: The Bulletin of the U.S. Center for World Mission* (May–August 1996). Accessed May 6, 2022: http://www.missionfrontiers.org/issue/article/music-of-the-heart

Benedetto, Robert. "The Presbyterian Mission Press in Central Africa, 1890–1922." *American Presbyterians* 68.1 (Spring 1990), 56.

Burnett, Philip T. "Music and Mission: A Case Study of the Anglican-Xhosa Missions of the Eastern Cape, 1854–1880." PhD thesis, University of Bristol, 2020.

Gordley, Matthew E. *New Testament Christological Hymns: Exploring Texts, Contexts, and Significance*. Wheaton, IL: IVP Academic, 2018.

Gore, R. J. *Covenantal Worship: Reconsidering the Puritan Regulative Principle*. Philipsburg, NJ: Presbyterian and Reformed, 2002.

Hawn, C. Michael. *The Canterbury Dictionary of Hymnology*. https://hymnology.hymnsam.co.uk/a/african-hymnody?q=african%20hymn

Hehn, Johnathan, "Hymnody and Liturgy." In *The Oxford Handbook of Presbyterianism*, eds., Gary Scott Smith and P. C. Kemeny. Oxford: OUP, 2019.

Olds, Hughes Oliphant. *Worship*, eds. John H. Leith and John W. Kuykendall, Guides to the Reformed Tradition. Louisville, KY: Westminster John Knox Press, 1996.

Patel, Aniruddh D. and Joseph R. Daniele. "An empirical comparison of rhythm in language and music." *Cognition* 87 (2003) B35–B45.

Pieters, Vivienne. "Music and Presbyterianism at the Lovedale Missionary Institute, 1841–1955." Unpublished thesis, University of South Africa, 2021.

Ross, Kenneth R., ed. *Christianity in Malawi—A Source Book*. Gweru, Zimbabwe: Mambo Press, 1996.

Ross, Kenneth R., J. Kwabena Asamoah-Gyadu and Todd Johnson, eds. *Christianity in Sub-Saharan Africa*. Edinburgh: Edinburgh University Press, 2017.

Sundkler, Bengt and Christopher Steed. *A History of the Church in Africa*. Cambridge: Cambridge University Press. 2000.

Bio Inset

John Knox Bokwe
(15 March 1855–22 February 1922)

Nancy J. Whytock

One of the most noteworthy African Presbyterian hymn writers must certainly be John Knox Bokwe of the eastern part of what was known in his lifetime as the Cape Colony, South Africa. Bokwe was born in Ntselamanzi, near Lovedale, in what is now called the Eastern Cape Province, South Africa. His father, Cholwephi, was one of the first students to be enrolled at the Lovedale Mission school. His mother, Lena Bokwe, was the daughter of Nxe. Nxe was converted to Christianity through Ntsikana, the first known Christian convert amongst the Xhosa. Ntsikana is regarded as one of the first Christians who tried to express Christianity through African culture.

John Knox Bokwe was taught by William Kobe Ntsikana, a grandson of Ntsikana. In 1867, Bokwe (age 12 years) met the Rev. James Stewart family and was employed by them, primarily as a messenger. That was the same year that Rev. James Stewart became the principal at Lovedale. Rev. Stewart, like Ntsikana, was committed to adapting Christianity to African culture. One such adaptation would surely involve music. Bokwe showed both musical interest and ability, and it was in Rev. Stewart's house that he learnt to play the organ and the piano. Bokwe himself describes his knowledge of music as "self-acquired."[70] In 1866 Bokwe was admitted to the preparatory classes at the Lovedale Institution. He then entered the college in 1869 and finished his schooling in 1873.

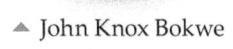
▲ John Knox Bokwe

---

70 John Knox Bokwe, *Amaculo Ase Lovedale* (Lovedale, SA: Lovedale Press, 1922, 5th edition), iii. See chart in this chapter for more bibliographical information on Bokwe and his work.

▲ Amaculo ase Lovedale, 5th edition

Bokwe's writing skill, combined with his developing musical abilities (he became conductor of the Lovedale Mission's brass band), made him a natural talent as a hymn writer. In 1875, Bokwe started to compose hymns. These hymns were shared in local magazines. One of Bokwe's chief motivations was to prepare tunes that would allow the Xhosa language to be sung with the proper accents. The hymns that the first Xhosa converts had learned to sing were translated hymns by the missionaries – primarily Rev. John Bennie. Such hymns "butchered" the Xhosa pronunciation, even though the words fit metrically. Bokwe's hymns were immediately, and naturally, well received. His collected compositions were produced in book form in 1885.

Interestingly, this collection includes "African hymns" in all the forms identified by Hawn.[71] It is a tribute to his esteem for the work of the early missionaries that the first part of the book includes a section of tunes that the missionaries taught the first converts to sing. These were "[t]he Church praises which helped to win the fathers to acceptance of the Gospel."[72] In other words, though the Xhosa language must be mispronounced to sing these hymns, yet as a mark of affection and thanksgiving, they were included. He was truly a man of intercultural, inter linguistic ability, yet thoroughly African and devoted to the development of Xhosa Christian praise. Unlike Ntisikana's "pure Xhosa rhythm and sound," Bokwe's work shows evidence of European influence and as such Bokwe was a pioneer of "makwaya" (meaning "my choir"),[73] which is a combination of Africa group singing style along with the European choral style.

---

71 ee footnote 11 of this work.
72 See footnote 11 of this work.
73 C. Michael Hawn, *The Canterbury Dictionary of Hymnology*. https://hymnology.hymnsam.co.uk/m/makwaya

Creative tension was evident in his attempt to remain faithful to his traditional context and to adopt a style fitting to the recent Western Victorian evangelical musical tradition. Bokwe incorporated traditional African musical forms into his compositions as can be seen from his work on Ntsikana's music.[74]

Two of his most famous compositions are:

1. Thou Saviour of Sinners – *Msindisi Waboni* (music by Bokwe)
2. A Plea from Africa – *Umtandazo Nge-Africa* (music by Bokwe)[75]

In 1900, Bokwe became an evangelist at Ugie and later a probationer minister. In 1906 he was ordained as a minister of the United Free Church. Bokwe was well trained at Lovedale and was committed to Stewart's ideals of education. There was no school at Ugie, so he opened a school for children in the town. Eventually, he also went out into the outlying areas, opening schools and churches. His Lovedale Hymnal includes many songs for children.

By 1920, Bokwe's health had deteriorated to the point that he was forced to retire. It is not surprising that he chose to return to the Lovedale area where his own life had been so profoundly influenced. Dr Stewart was gone and Bokwe befriended his successor, Dr Henderson. Their association was primarily marked by their mutual desire to translate the Scottish metrical psalms into Xhosa. One can understand that given Bokwe's talents in both language and music, his contribution to these efforts was immense. As already noted in this chapter, the Xhosa Bible, according to B. J. Ross, is truer to the Hebrew than the English versions because the Xhosa tongue possesses close linguistic affinities and identity of religious custom with the original Hebrew text and context.[76]

This is an illustration of the complexity of interlinguistic praise influences.[77] It also illustrates the necessity of allowing the mother tongue and culture to

---

74 Graham Duncan, "John Knox Bokwe (1855–1922): A model of creative tension in the late 19th and early 20th-century South Africa." *HTS Teologiese Studies / Theological Studies* [Online], 78.4 (2022): 10 pages. Web. 24 Feb. 2023. This is an excellent article on the life of John Knox Bokwe to commemorate the centenary of his death.
75 Both compositions in *Amaculo Ase Lovedale*, 5th edition.
76 D. D. T. Jabavu, *The Influence of English on Bantu Literature* (Alice, SA: Lovedale Press, 1943), 21.
77 For more discussion on this topic, see "Poeticizing The Psalter in an African Language," Ernst Wentland, article in *Open Theology* (2016); 2: 165–178.

express truth by the power of the Holy Spirit at work in believers from every tribe, tongue, and nation. Psalm 119:11–16.

Bokwe died at his home at Ntselamanzi, near Lovedale, on 22 February 1922. He was buried in the Gaga Cemetery, alongside other missionaries associated with Lovedale.

Bokwe produced the first known notated composition by a black South African (*Msindisiwaboni* – Saviour of Sinners, Xhosa words by Rev. J. A. Chalmers[78]); went on to produce 40-odd original compositions; and was the first black African to have compositions published by what was to become Africa's largest mission institution, Lovedale (see Chapter 8). Aside from this catalogue of firsts, the story of Bokwe's first published tune, and others like it, speaks to us today about intercultural musical influences. Bokwe was an African Christian who embraced his identity in Christ and expressed this identity through his beloved Xhosa culture. His willingness to engage in other cultural influences is an example of one who had a deep appreciation for the "every tribe and every language" nature of the Church universal. Not surprisingly, many of his hymns are still being sung today.

> *And they sang a new song, saying:*
> *"You are worthy to take the scroll*
> *and to open its seals,*
> *because you were slain,*
> *and with your blood you purchased for God*
> *persons from every tribe and language and people and nation."*
> (Rev. 5:9) NIV

---

78 *Amaculo Ase Lovedale*, 5th Edition, 51, 84.

Bio Inset

Ephraim Amu
(13 September 1899–2 January 1995)

Nancy J. Whytock

Ephraim Amu, born at the very end of the 19th century, is another fine example of an African hymn writer. However, his pursuit of African expression was not without controversy or personal cost.

Amu was born in Peki-Avetile in the Volta Region of Ghana, the youngest of eight children[79] born to Stefano Amu Yaw and Sarah Akoram Amma. His father was a farmer. He was also a singer (cantor) and drummer and Ephraim seems to have received his musical gifts from that side of the family.[80]

In 1906, Ephraim began his formal schooling in his home village at the Breman Mission School. In 1847, the Bremen Mission, in close cooperation with the Basel Mission, began working with the Ewe people in the east part of present-day Ghana. The link between the Bremen Mission and the United Free Presbyterians in Scotland[81] is the link that influenced Amu's personal journey into Presbyterian church membership, Presbyterian church service, and career opportunities.

Following his primary education, Amu began middle school at Peki-Blengo in 1912. It was here that he was formally introduced to music and the harmonium, primarily through one of his teachers, Theodore Ntem. He also began to study music theory under the tutelage of Rev. Allotey-Pappoe[82] of the Wesleyan Methodist Church.

After four years, Amu enrolled in the Basel Mission Seminary at Abetifi with the intention of training as a catechist and a teacher. It was while studying at the seminary that Amu learned the Twi language. Twi is more widely spoken and

---

79 Alexander A. Agordoh, *The Music of Amu and Nayo* (Accra, Ghana: Royal Gold Publishers Ltd., 2004), 15.
80 Adolphus R. Turkson, "A Voice in the African Process of Crossing from the Traditional to Modernity: The Music of Ephraim Amu" in *Ultimate Reality and Meaning*, March 1987, Vol. 10, No. 1, 39–53.
81 https://www.oikoumene.org/member-churches/evangelical-presbyterian-church-ghana accessed 23 April, 2021
82 Alexander A. Agordoh, *The Music of Amu and Nayo* (Accra, Ghana: Royal Gold Publishers Ltd., 2004), 15.

though Amu's first language was Ewe, Twi was to be the language of his best-known songs.

In 1920, following completion of his seminary course, Amu returned to his home town of Peki-Blengo and began teaching at the Blengo middle boarding school. For the next six years, he composed choral music, practised the harmonium, and taught music. He tried out his compositions with the students to see what appealed to them and what worked. This gave him instant feedback and gave his work a quality of freshness as he refined his compositions to satisfy the youth in his charge.

Given his growing abilities, it is not surprising that in 1926 Amu was invited to Akropong to join the staff of the Scottish Mission Seminary there. This seminary was established in 1827 by Basel missionaries but was later "adopted" into Presbyterianism by the United Free Presbyterians of Scotland.

▲ Ephraim Amu

It was during this period of Amu's life that he produced some of his best-known works that were published while serving at The Scottish Mission Seminary. He was particularly inspired by Rev. Wm. Ferguson to produce "authentic" African music. This inspiration, together with his determination and skill as a composer, led to his first published work – *Twenty-five African Songs* (London, 1932).[83]

What made his music *African*? Amu studied the sound and structure of the Twi language. He also studied the traditional philosophical knowledge (proverbs, wise sayings, myths, etc.) of his people. Further, he studied the rhythms of the drum language. This study inevitably led to a crisis point in Amu's life: Is there a contradiction between being African and being Christian? How can these two be reconciled? Or can they be reconciled? Atiemo writes:

---

83 Only three known published works:
   Amu, Ephraim, *Twenty-five African Songs in the Twi Language. Music and words by E. Amu*. (Sheldon Press, 1932).
   Amu, Ephraim, *Amu choral works*. (Waterville Publishing House, 1993).
   Amu, Ephraim, "How to Study African Rhythm." *The Teachers' Journal* (Accra) 6.2 (1933): 33–34.

By 1927 Ephraim Amu had introduced a new African music, 'which blended the effect of African and European aspects in composed songs'. The publication of his *25 African Songs* in 1932 had a tremendous impact on the evolution of African Christian music in Ghana. Although some African composers had produced works that had laid the foundation for the revolution that occurred with the launch of Amu's works, the latter came up at a time when the assimilation of the Christian message by the ordinary people seemed to have become more in-depth and widespread. Many 'literate and semi-literate' composers followed the pattern he set such as, Otto Boateng, R. O. Danso, J. H. Nketiah, Asante Akuffo, T. Kwami, Kwesi Baiden, Z. Nayo, and Onwona Osafo. In 1930 Dr Otto Boateng, a contemporary and a colleague of Ephraim Amu started a Singing Band in the Presbyterian Church in Akuapem Larteh. This movement quickly spread in Presbyterian Churches throughout Ghana. The new 'African music' introduced by Amu became the main musical form performed by these bands. The many composers inspired by the works of Amu and Otto Boateng became itinerant music masters, moving from place to place, teaching their own compositions and also those of Amu and Boateng.[84]

Amu began to see the place of culture in his own life and responded not only by continuing to compose Christian music for his people, but also in terms of his dress.

As a catechist Amu was obliged to preach in European attire – woollen jacket, long-sleeved white shirt, tie, trousers and black shoes, all this in tropical weather. What seemed to bother Amu was not so much the physical discomfort of dressing in this was as the symbolic violence it perpetrated. The message was that African dress was inappropriate for anyone entering the Presbyterian pulpit. In spite of his deep-seated Christian convictions, Amu could not abide by this prohibition. But the matter of dress was the final straw that forced the Presbyterian Church Synod to sack Amu.[85]

---

84 Abamfo Ofori Atiemo, "'Singing with understanding:' the story of gospel music in Ghana." *Studies in world Christianity* 12.2 (2006), 148.
85 Kofi Agawu, *The Amu Legacy*. Africa 66 (2), 1996, 275.

Agawa goes on to point out: "Amu's critics were not uniformly 'European' or 'white' or 'Christian' or 'missionary'; he had advocates among each group."[86] Almost immediately, Amu was offered a position at the former Prince of Wales College now – Achimota Secondary School. He accepted this offer and served there from 1934–1936.

Amu's complex relationship with European musical influences was further developed between 1937 and 1941 as these were the years he spent in London, England at the Royal College of Music. Here he achieved his ARCM diploma and here he was particularly influenced by his studies in counterpoint as he began to integrate these principles into Ghanaian music.

> His early works (c.1923–27) are mostly choral and are characterized by homophonic textures and functional harmonies. In works from his middle period (c.1928–40), such as 25 *African Songs* (1932), he favoured complex rhythmic and contrapuntal treatments, emphasizing cross-rhythms, triplets and speech-tone contours.[87]

Upon his return to Ghana, Amu returned to Achimota School but now took on a teaching role at the training college where he was to have tremendous influence on the student music teachers. In 1959, the school at Achimota was transferred to Kumasi and Amu moved along with it. This was like moving home for Amu and in 1960, he retired and moved to his hometown – Avetile.

Amu's "retirement" was short-lived as in 1961 he was called upon to assist in establishing The Institute of African Studies at Legon. He was made a senior fellow of the new institute and served in this capacity for the final ten years of his career. On 27 March 1965, The University of Ghana conferred an honorary Doctor of Music degree on this noted Ghanaian musician and composer.

During this period of his life, he also paid particular attention to making bamboo flutes (atenteben) and has become particularly known for composing music especially for this instrument.

Amu retired again in 1971 and returned to his hometown. It is regrettable that to date no complete works of his compositions have been published. However, his lasting legacy as a Christian who courageously sought to point the way to sung praise through Ghanaian culture and music remains an example for current hymn writers in this West African country and beyond. The influences of other cultures were not ignored but were *willingly* integrated into a style that

---

86 Kofi Agawu, *The Amu Legacy*. Africa 66 (2), 1996, 276.
87 Stanley Sadie, Ed. *The New Grove Dictionary of Music and Musicians* (London: Macmillan Publishers Limited, 2001), 521.

allows one to experience the blending of the tribes in worship before the throne of God.

> He was a staunch Presbyterian and served the Evangelical Presbyterian Church, Ghana with all his heart. He single-handedly made the advance at incorporating indigenous music in church worship in the Presbyterian denominations especially in the E.P. Church and the Presbyterian Church of Ghana.[88]

Select Bibliography

Agawu, V. K. "The Impact of Language on Musical Composition in Ghana: An Introduction to the Musical Style of Ephraim Amu." *EtnM*, xxviii (1984): 37–73.

Agawu, V. K. "Conversation with Ephraim Amu: the Making of a Composer." *The Black Perspective in Music* 15.1 (Spring 1987): 50–63.

Agyemang, F. M. *Amu the African: a Study in Vision and Courage*. Accra, 1988.

Atiemo, Abamfo Ofori. "'Singing with understanding:' the story of gospel music in Ghana." *Studies in World Christianity* 12.2 (2006): 142–163.

Agordoh, Alexander A. *The Music of Amu and Nayo*. Accra, Ghana: Royal Gold Publishers Ltd., 2004.

Avorgbedor, Daniel, "Amu, Ephraim." In *The New Grove Dictionary of Music and Musicians*, ed. Stanley Sadie, second edition. London: Macmillan Publishers Limited, 2001.

Laryea, Philip T. *Ephraim Amu : nationalist, poet and theologian (1899–1995)*. Akropong-Akuapem, Ghana: Regnum Africa Publications, 2012.

---

88 Alexander A. Agordoh, *The Music of Amu and Nayo* (Accra, Ghana: Royal Gold Publishers Ltd., 2004), 18.

Chapter 28

Presbyterian Ethiopianism in South Africa and Malawi

Rhodian Munyenyembe

Chapter Outline
1. Introduction – Working Definition
2. Historical Background
3. Presbyterian Missions in South Africa and Malawi
4. Ethiopianism as a Movement
5. Presbyterian Ethiopianism in South Africa
6. Presbyterian Ethiopianism in Malawi
7. The Ethiopian Movement in Retrospect
8. Conclusion

1. Introduction – Working Definition

This chapter discusses the birth and development of the African Independent Churches (AICs) that broke away from Presbyterian missions in South Africa and Malawi. In the typology of African Independent Churches, also known as African Instituted Churches, African Indigenous Churches, or African Initiated Churches, one category of AICs is the Ethiopian type.[1] This type has been described as comprising those churches that broke away from missionary Christianity led by the African elites who felt oppressed under white missionary supervision. These churches are different from other AICs in that they are very similar to their parent denominations in terms of theology, polity, and liturgy. Their characteristic features are the absence of a white missionaries in the church's administrative structure and an attempt to contextualise the Christian faith within the African cultural milieu.

2. Historical Background

For a working definition of Presbyterianism, see the introductory chapter in this book. In brief, here a recap as follows: Presbyterianism is a form of Christianity

---

1 For a thorough treatment of the typology of AICs see Sundkler, *Bantu Prophets in South Africa*.

that emerged from the pastoral and theological endeavours of the Genevan reformer John Calvin, who in the 16th century established the Geneva Academy, which propagated and transmitted this branch of Christianity known today as Reformed Theology. Many Protestant churches that embraced Reformed Theology also embraced a government of the church by the elders (*presbuteroi* in Greek), hence Presbyterian. The Presbyterian system of church government is based on the authority of the teaching and ruling elders who form the various administrative courts of the church from the session, which is the lowest court, to the Synod or General Synod/Assembly. This system found its way into the Netherlands and eventually South Africa through the Dutch Reformed Church, even though the Dutch Reformed Church never used the word Presbyterian in its name. It also found its way into 16th century Scotland through the ministry of John Knox, who was one of the international students of John Calvin. From Scotland, the Presbyterian branch of Christianity found its way into South Africa and Malawi besides going to many other places in the world.

3. Presbyterian Missions in South Africa and Malawi

South Africa

Presbyterianism came to South Africa, c.1800–c.1840s as detailed in chapter two of this book through soldiers and a minister, mission societies, settlers, and latterly through ecclesial missions.[2] Our concern in this chapter is to look at churches that broke away from Presbyterian missions to form African Independent Churches categorised as Ethiopian.

Malawi

Presbyterian missions came to Malawi as a consequence of the influence of Dr David Livingstone, a Scottish missionary explorer, who visited the area in the second half of the 19th century and recommended the establishment of Christianity, commerce, and civilization in the vicinity of Lake Malawi.[3] (For detailed studies see chapters 14, 15, & 16 in this book).

The first Presbyterian mission in Malawi was that of the Livingstonia Mission of the Free Church of Scotland, which was established in the country in 1875. This mission was initially established in the southern part of the country at a place known as Cape Maclear. However, due to the prevalence of malaria and generally unsuitable conditions for a Scottish settlement, the mission headquarters moved up north to Bandawe in 1881. It then moved further north to Khondowe in 1894

---

2   See the Select Bibliography for Chapter Two for sources.
3   McCracken, *A History of Malawi 1859–1966*, 2–7.

among the Phoka-Tumbuka people. From Khondowe, the Livingstonia Mission was destined to have influence not only in Malawi but in the rest of Southern Africa through its Overtoun Institution.[4]

The second Presbyterian mission in Malawi was the Blantyre Mission of the (established) Church of Scotland in 1876. The scout for Blantyre Mission, Henry Henderson, accompanied the missionary party of the Livingstonia Mission in 1875, but he was eventually joined by the first missionary party of Blantyre in 1876. The Blantyre Mission station had a terrible beginning with a scandal bordering on human rights abuses of natives due to the mission's attempt to exercise civil jurisdiction within its vicinity. The first leaders of the mission were dismissed after a damning inquiry report, and a new leadership team was put in place, thereby re-founding Blantyre Mission in 1881.[5] The success of the Blantyre Mission is evidenced by the presence of an iconic church building known as St. Michael's and All Angels', which was opened in 1891, and the fact that the City of Blantyre, which is Malawi's commercial capital, is named after the mission itself is because it grew from the initial mission and mission-related settlements and enterprises in the area.[6]

The third Presbyterian Mission in Malawi was the Dutch Reformed Church Mission of South Africa. This mission was established in the central region of Malawi in 1889. It is credited with the evangelisation of the Central Region of Malawi with a characteristically conservative Reformed Presbyterian culture which is more pronounced than that of its Scottish sisters.[7]

The three Presbyterian missions discussed above merged in 1924/1926 to form the Church of Central Africa Presbyterian (CCAP), while the former mission churches became autonomous synods in a General Assembly. The Livingstonia Mission became the Synod of Livingstonia while the Blantyre Mission became the Blantyre Synod, and the Dutch Reformed Church Mission became the Nkhoma Synod. The Nkhoma Synod gave birth to the Harare Synod of the CCAP in Zimbabwe in 1965, while the Synod of Livingstonia gave birth to the Synod of Zambia in 1984.[8] This chapter is primarily concerned with the churches that broke away from these mission churches, especially those categorised as Ethiopian type of AICs.

---

4   McCracken, *Politics and Christianity in Malawi 1875–1940: The Impact of the Livingstonia Mission in the Northern Province*, 179–196.
5   Ross, *Blantyre Mission and the Making of Modern Malawi*, 63.
6   Ross, *Blantyre Mission and the Making of Modern Malawi*, 63.
7   Pauw, "Mission and Church in Malawi: The History of Nkhoma Synod of the Church of Central Africa Presbyterian, 1889–1962."
8   Munyenyembe, *Pursuing an Elusive Unity: A History of the Church of Central Africa Presbyterian as a Federative Denomination (1924–2018)*, 78–82, 86–87.

4. Ethiopianism as a Movement

The term Ethiopianism is a bit confusing because it has nothing to do with the present-day country of Ethiopia, despite the similarity. The name has religious and political connotations, though its source is overtly religious. The Bible in Psalm 68:31 says: "Ethiopia shall soon stretch out her hands to God" (KJV). During the Atlantic Slave Trade, many Africans who had converted to the Christian faith understood this verse as a kind of prophecy about their own time of redemption from white rule and oppression to a time of freedom and prosperity illustrated by their uninhibited worship of God whether in America or back in their original continent of Africa. The word Ethiopia in this context referred to the black race in general, and so the black Americans[9] appropriated it to their circumstances. Religiously it meant that the time had come for Africans to relate to God directly without the help or leadership of white missionaries.[10] This thinking found expression in the establishment of African Independent Churches, which though not theologically different from their missionary parent churches, emphasised the sociological difference of the absence of a white person in whatever capacity in church administration and spirituality matters. Outside of the sphere of religion, Ethiopianism meant Africans were reclaiming their independence from Western domination by taking their land from Westerners. This desire was concretized in the slogan: "Africa for the African," and many felt it was time Africans threw off the shackles of European colonialism. Such ideas led to uprisings on the continent as Africans started agitating for freedom from European control.

On the part of Europeans, they were generally very much afraid of the Ethiopian Movement, with many exaggerated rumours of how Africans were planning to kill all Europeans in Africa and to take over control of missions, government, and everything on which Europeans were exerting their power.[11] The suspicion about what Africans were going to do was fuelled by their association with black Americans, where black Americans were considered a bad influence on Africans on the African continent, whether through travel to America or through correspondence.[12] It is such connections of black people across continents united in their desire for freedom from white domination that has led some scholars to associate the Ethiopian Movement with Pan-Africanism.[13]

---

9   Historically the word used in context, and today, generally, *African American*.
10 Lahouel, "Ethiopianism and African Nationalism in South Africa before 1937 (Éthiopianisme et nationalisme africain en Afrique du Sud avant 1937)," 681–688.
11 Thompson, "Prester John, John Chilembwe and the European Fear of Ethiopianism," 18–30.
12 Shepperson, "Ethiopianism and African Nationalism," 9–18.
13 Graham, "Ethiopianism in Pan-African Perspective, 1880–1920."

The first independent church to be known with the name Ethiopian was Mangena Maake Mokone's Ethiopian Church, founded in 1892 as a reaction against the attitude of white Wesleyan ministers towards African ministers in South Africa.[14] Many breakaways of a similar nature were to take place in subsequent years. A detailed description of all that transpired in the Ethiopian Movement is beyond the scope of this chapter. Our interest, however, is to survey those AICs that broke away from Presbyterian missionary churches in a way that can be interpreted as being influenced by the Ethiopian Movement. We will start with developments in South Africa then move over to Malawi.

5. Presbyterian Ethiopianism in South Africa

The South African situation presents a fascinating case. Some of the Presbyterian breakaway churches occurred as early as the 1890s. They eventually influenced the direction that the Presbyterian missionaries were to take vis-à-vis the aspirations of the black South Africans: to have a say in the affairs of the church and to run their own congregations independent of white missionary control.

Independent Native Presbyterian Church Open for Reunion

In 1896, Rev. Edward Tsewu formed a separate church from the Free Church of Scotland in Johannesburg. However, he claimed that it was not a secessionist church but a temporary separation while there were differences with the mission church. He named his church Independent Native Presbyterian Church Open for Reunion in the hope that there could be some earnest discussions to resolve the issues.[15] Nevertheless, the Free Church of Scotland deposed him and replaced him with a white minister in the name of Rev C. B. Hamilton. This gesture might have made Tsewu realise that there would be no reunion with the Free Church of Scotland. He consequently joined the African Methodist Episcopal Church despite his preference for the Presbyterian system.[16]

The Presbyterian Church of Africa

The Presbyterian Church of Africa (PCA) was founded in 1898 by Pambani Mzimba, an ordained Presbyterian minister of the FCS in South Africa. Some

---

14 Khoapa, "Mokone, Mangena Maake," *DACB*, accessed on 12.01.2022 from https://dacb.org/stories/southafrica/mokone-mangena2/.
15 Millard, "A Study of the Perceived Causes of Schism in Some Ethiopian-Type Churches in the Cape and Transvaal, 1884–1925," 208–209.
16 See, Graham, "'Pull up a good tree and push it outside'? The Rev. Edward Tsewu's dispute with the Free Church of Scotland Mission."

scholars argue that Rev. Tsewu influenced Mzimba's secession.[17] Mzimba was ordained in 1875, and he served the Free Church of Scotland with dedication until 1898, when he felt he could no longer continue to serve under the supervision of white missionaries. Like other AICs, PCA was born out of the frustrations of an African in areas of power, resources, and race relations at the hands of the white missionaries who had brought the Christian faith but were unwilling to treat their black brothers with equality. The attitude of many white missionaries was that of paternalism even when dealing with highly educated and gifted African leaders in the church. The formation of the Presbyterian Church of Africa was, therefore, a protest against the treatment of natives.[18] According to Switzer, "the ordained African clergy wanted to become equal partners with the missionaries in the church's ongoing life. When they were denied this role, they felt they had no choice but to separate."[19]

▲ Pambani J. Mzimba

Pambani Mzimba married Martha Kwatsha, who was from the famous Soga family, and together they had six children (four girls and two boys).[20] Pambani Mzimba's life, education, and ministry was one of the success stories of the missionary activities of the Free Church of Scotland in South Africa, especially at Lovedale. Mzimba served the Free Church for 22 years after his ordination before severing ties with the Scottish

---

17 Graham, "Scottish Presbyterian Church Mission Policy in South Africa 1898–1923," 82–84.
18 Graham, "'African Churches Willing to Pay their Own Bills': The Role of Money in the Formation of Ethiopian-type Churches with Particular Reference to the Mzimba Secession," 52–79, (53).
19 Switzer, *Power and Resistance in an African Society: The Ciskei Xhosa and the Making of South Africa*, 187. It is worth noting that Pambani Mzimba's church also experienced a breakaway or rather a split-off in **1908 when Rev E. J. Marumo** established the **African Presbyterian Bafolisi Church**. This church, established on the 12th of September 1908, was specifically established to promote the faith-healing ministry, which Rev Marumo could not exercise freely while under Pambani Mzimba. While this church came into existence when the Ethiopian Movement was prominent, it is difficult to classify it as an Ethiopian AIC because its formation was not a reaction against white missionary Christianity but against a fellow black man's leadership, which means that the reasons for its formation were neither racial nor social. The African Presbyterian Bafolisi Church of Southern Africa has experienced numerous breakaways in its history, primarily due to succession wrangles. See, Monareng, "An Investigation of Schisms within the African Presbyterian Bafolisi Church of Southern Africa," 5.
20 Millard, "Mzimba, Pambani Jeremiah," *DACB*, https://dacb.org/stories/southafrica/mzimba-pambani/, accessed 10.04.22.

missionaries.[21] At first the understanding of many of the Christians who had followed Mzimba was that they were going to continue owning the property of the Free Church. Some even thought they would inherit Lovedale Institute after James Stewart's death.[22] When it was realised that as a break away church, they did not have the right to possess Free Church property, the Mzimbites, as they were known in missionary circles, faced the reality of developing their church without overseas support.[23] The PCA experienced slow growth during Pambani Mzimba's time, but by the time of his death in 1911, the foundation of the denomination had been solidly laid down. By 1911 the church had four ordained ministers and two presbyteries. Pambani Mzimba was succeeded by his son Livingstone Ntibane Mzimba, who is his only well-known child.

The new leadership was able to send 15 student ministers to study in the USA and later they were able to train in South Africa. As an Ethiopian church, the PCA focussed on evangelising fellow black people from its establishment until 1973 when its general synod rejected the idea of being an exclusively black church for lack of scriptural backing, thereby making the denomination open to other races. This clearly shows that even though Ethiopian churches started as a reaction against white domination, they still hankered for the catholicity of the Church.[24] The PCA is today found not only in South Africa but also in Zimbabwe, Zambia and Malawi where new congregations are still opening.[25] It currently has an overall total membership of 3,381,000 with 175 ordained clergy and 242 congregations.[26] It has been a member of the World Council of Churches since 1981, and it is a founding member of the Association of African Independent Churches.

---

21 PCA, "Our History," https://web.archive.org/web/20151116063313/http://presbyterianchurchofafrica.co.za/history.php, accessed 20.04.22.

22 PCA, "Our History," https://web.archive.org/web/20151116063313/http://presbyterianchurchofafrica.co.za/history.php, accessed 20.04.22.

23 PCA, "Our History," https://web.archive.org/web/20151116063313/http://presbyterianchurchofafrica.co.za/history.php, accessed 20.04.22.

24 Similarly in Malawi, the Blackman's Church changed its name to the Church of Africa Presbyterian without the adjective black even though some people still call it the Blackman's Church up to this day because of its historical roots.

25 WCC, "Presbyterian Church of Africa," https://www.oikoumene.org/member-churches/presbyterian-church-of-africa, accessed 10.04.22.

26 WCC, "Presbyterian Church of Africa," https://www.oikoumene.org/member-churches/presbyterian-church-of-africa, accessed 10.04.22.

The Bantu Presbyterian Church of South Africa: Complexity of classification

The Bantu Presbyterian Church of South Africa was established in 1923 as a specifically Black Presbyterian church alongside the Presbyterian Church of South Africa (PCSA), the Church of white settlers. This Church does not suit the definition of an Ethiopian AIC because it was not a break away from missionary Christianity. However, it is worth noting that this Church was established to give leeway to African initiatives in the Church. Consequently, BPCSA was from the beginning recognized as a church of Black Africans though supported by white missionaries because it had not rebelled against white mission Christianity as was the case with other Ethiopian AICs. It is interesting to note that while the sending Church in Scotland wanted the mission churches to mature quickly and become autonomous, the missionaries in the field were reluctant to let go of their organisations, fearing that the time was not yet ready for such a development. Therefore, the formation of BPCSA was an experiment on how African Christians would run their affairs in the Church after the end of missionary control so that the Church could get rooted in the African soil. Many believe that Pambani Mzimba's Presbyterian Church of Africa accelerated power transfer to African leaders in the Presbyterian missions for fear of further breakaways. Unlike in pure AICs, the sending Church through its Mission Council and missionaries continued to dominate the affairs of BPCSA. As Duncan argued, "independence could therefore only be obtained by establishing an independent church."[27] I have observed elsewhere that this is still the case with the Malawian synods of CCAP, which fail to fully unite as one denomination because the synods are autonomous and still influenced by the mother churches that established their missions.[28]

Due to ecumenical endeavours, there were attempts to unite the Bantu Presbyterian Church of South Africa with other denominations between 1940 and 1999. In 1979 the BPCSA changed its name to Reformed Presbyterian Church of Southern Africa and continued discussions with other churches under the new name. Due to racism and institutionalised apartheid that engulfed South Africa from the 1940s to the early 1990s, it was not easy for the RPCSA to join hands with the PCSA and other churches of European origin. However, after the release of Nelson Mandela from prison and the transition period to a multiracial South Africa (culminating in the 1994 general elections), churches of various racial backgrounds could come together again to negotiate unity as equal partners. Consequently, the Reformed Presbyterian Church of Southern Africa (formerly

---

27 Graham, "From Mission to Church: The Formation of the Bantu Presbyterian Church of South Africa," 329–360.
28 See, Munyenyembe, *Pursuing an Elusive Unity: A History of the Church of Central Africa Presbyterian as a Federative Denomination (1924–2018)*.

Bantu Presbyterian Church in South Africa) and the Presbyterian Church of Southern Africa (formerly Presbyterian Church of South Africa) of mainly white settler communities came together to form the Uniting Presbyterian Church in Southern Africa in 1999. This development shows that changes in the wider socio-political sphere could influence Presbyterian churches of diverse racial backgrounds in South Africa to consider unity.

6. Presbyterian Ethiopianism in Malawi

In Malawi, the phenomenon of AICs was quite prominent during the missionary era. However, our emphasis on Presbyterian Ethiopianism finds fertile ground in the Livingstonia Mission of the Church of Central Africa Presbyterian in the northern part of the country.

The African National Church

The African National Church (known locally as *Nashonale*) is considered the first breakaway church from the Livingstonia Mission in 1929. Unlike subsequent breakaway churches, the leadership of this church is not easily recognisable and, therefore, not readily identified with one person. However, credit for founding this church is generally given to Paddy Nyasulu and Isaac Kondowe. Paddy Nyasulu had served as a teacher at Livingstonia, where he had received his education before entering government service as a clerk. At the formation of the church, Isaac Kondowe was still serving as a teacher.[29] The first Malawian ethnic group to be attracted to this church in large numbers was the Henga. The ANC attracted many educated people of the time from the catchment area of the Livingstonia Mission, especially those that were disgruntled with the mission's way of practising the Christian faith. They readily allowed beer drinking and polygamy, which attracted many older African people who could not abandon these traditional cultural elements. Their legal and liturgical documents were impeccable, testifying the quality education that the Scottish missionaries had introduced. Nyasulu himself had been suspended from the Livingstonia Mission for marrying a second wife, but he later went on and married two more wives when he was in his early fifties in the 1930s.

The ANC had started as a church of the Livingstonia Mission's former "educated" members, but it did not continue with that character as time went on. As one of the classical AICs in Malawi, the ANC is not very prominent but still registers its presence in some urban and rural areas of Malawi, especially in the northern region of the country.

---

29 MacDonald, "Religious Independency as a Means of Social Advance in Northern Nyasaland in the 1930s," 106–129.

The Last Church of God and His Christ

The Last Church of God and His Christ is one of the churches that started in the northern region of Malawi as a reaction against Western Christianity as represented by the Livingstonia Mission.[30] Though this church also originated from the catchment area of the Livingstonia Mission, its formation is not that of a breakaway church or split off because its founders were not clergy or prominent leaders in the Livingstonia Mission. The founding of the Last Church of God and His Christ is credited to Jordan Msumba of Usisya in Nkhata-Bay District. Jordan Msumba was educated in the Livingstonia Mission schools, and he was baptised as a Livingstonia Christian in the early 1900s.[31] Between 1907 and 1909, he joined the Watchtower Movement of Elliot Kamwana, which became a rival of the Livingstonia Mission among the Tonga people of Nkhata-Bay.[32] Due to chieftaincy quarrels with his relatives, Msumba left Usisya for South Africa in 1917. While in South Africa, he joined the Seventh Day Baptist Church because of Joseph Booth's influence.[33] He later abandoned the Seventh Day Baptists and re-joined the Watch Tower Movement. In 1920, Msumba was deported from South Africa because of suspected lunacy. Msumba established the Last Church of God with its focus on polygamy. He did not reject the rest of the Christian doctrines but felt that not allowing polygamy among Africans was difficult for many African Christians. Interestingly, the things for which the Last Church was initially known (i.e., polygamy and communal beer drinking) are now repudiated by the contemporary leadership of the church. This shows that the Last Church of God wants to remain relevant to its context. Having emphasised polygamy and beer drinking in the early years of its history, the church has now realised that those are not the things that matter in contemporary Africa, hence taking on the characteristics of a mainline denomination to attract more members.[34]

The Church of Africa Presbyterian (CAP)

The Church of Africa Presbyterian started in 1933 with the name the Blackman's Church that is in Tongaland.[35] Its founder is the famous Yesaya Zerenji Mwasi, who was one of the first three Africans to be ordained ministers in the Livingstonia

---

30 See, Gondwe, *A History of the Last Church of God and His Christ*.
31 Kalinga, "Jordan Msumba, Ben Ngemela and the Last Church of God and His Christ, 1924–1935," 207–218.
32 Donati, "'A Very Antagonistic Spirit': Elliot Kamwana: Christianity and the World in Nyasaland," 13–33 (17).
33 See, Langworthy, *"Africa for the African": The Life of Joseph Booth*.
34 Gondwe, *A History of the Last Church of God and His Christ*, 199–204.
35 Parratt, "Y. Z. Mwasi and the Origins of the Blackman's Church," *Journal of Religion in Africa*, 193–206.

Mission in 1914.[36] Mwasi rose through the Livingstonia Mission's ranks to the Presbytery Moderator position and later on Presbytery Clerk temporarily. He was one of the most brilliant and articulate products of the Livingstonia Mission's Overtoun Institution. His frustrations with the Scottish missionaries led to his resignation from the Livingstonia Mission, and he expressed his ideas in a letter to the mission, which is now published as a booklet titled *Essential and Paramount Reasons for Working Independently*.[37] In this write-up, Mwasi explains his motive for leaving the Livingstonia Mission in a way that shows that he was far ahead of his time in articulating what has now come to be termed African Christian Theology. Mwasi wanted to establish a church where Africans would worship God freely as Africans in their African way:

> I wish to *naturalize* and *nationalize* God, Christ, faith – in short Christianity. There is no saying that Object and Goal of the missionary enterprise is to naturalize Christianity – to grow out of its own soil, having its own customs and traditions purified by the Gospel of Christ. An exotic Christianity will never take vital root in the life of the natives.[38]

Apart from founding this church, Mwasi was also involved in proto-nationalist movements known as native associations that mushroomed in Malawi before nationalist political parties.[39] In this regard, he was instrumental in the founding of the West Nyasa Native Association for which he was its secretary.[40] His influence was such that the district commissioner in Nkhata Bay felt the whole association was a one-man organisation.[41]

In its history, the Church of Africa Presbyterian has not significantly impacted education. Yet, Mwasi had grand plans for educating the black people in Malawi. He made grand proposals for raising funds and pioneering the work of education among Africans. Still, the colonial government did not create a conducive atmosphere for the success of his plans. Besides, fellow black people within the catchment area of his church could not passionately embrace his vision of education. Many of Mwasi's ideas appeared to be too advanced for his time and

---

36 McCracken, *Politics and Christianity in Malawi 1875–1940: The Impact of the Livingstonia Mission in the Northern Province*, 240.
37 See, Mwasi, *Essential and Paramount Reasons for Working Independently*.
38 Mwasi, *Essential and Paramount Reasons for Working Independently*, 17.
39 See J. Van Velsen, "Some Early Pressure Groups in Malawi," in *The Zambesian Past: Studies in Central African History*, 367. Also, Robert I. Rotberg, *The Rise of Nationalism in Central Africa: The Making of Malawi and Zambia, 1873–1964*.
40 McCracken, *Politics and Christianity in Malawi 1875–1940: The Impact of the Livingstonia Mission in the Northern Province*, 238.
41 McCracken, *Politics and Christianity in Malawi 1875–1940: The Impact of the Livingstonia Mission in the Northern Province*, 238.

generation, but he has been vindicated as a great visionary with the advantage of hindsight. It is worth noting that the Synod of Livingstonia of the CCAP has of late reconciled with the Church of Africa Presbyterian because the contemporary Malawian leaders of the Synod realise that they are now enjoying the fruits of what Mwasi stood for in a generation that did not understand him. As Paratt observed:

> Here is no visionary claiming a special divine revelation, nor black Messiah claiming semi-divine status: Mwasi's is a reasoned, impassioned plea for indigenous Christianity. Orthodoxy is not in question; the reality and relevance of a church of 'the African soil' is.[42]

It is interesting to note that when Yesaya Zerenji Mwasi died in 1955, his funeral ceremony was conducted by two pastors of the Church of Central Africa Presbyterian (Rev. Bright Mhone and Rev. Henry B. Makwakwa), his former denomination. It was revealed that this was his wish which has made some scholars to assume that Mwasi had only seceded administratively but deep down in his heart he still considered himself a member of the Livingstonia Synod of the CCAP.[43]

The CAP is one of the prominent African Independent Churches in Malawi with a membership that goes beyond the boundaries of Malawi to South Africa, Zambia, Zimbabwe and Tanzania.[44] In 1964 it established its women's guild known as Union Women's Guild.[45] In 1983 CAP established its synod known as Ching'oma Synod named after the church's headquarters in the Nkhata-Bay district in Malawi.[46] The church is ecumenically connected through its membership in organisations such as the Malawi Council of Churches and the Evangelical Association of Malawi. Of late, the church has become quite popular in Malawi because of one of its contemporary Gospel music groups known as the Great Angels Choir.[47] As of 2022, the church claims to have the following statistics:[48]

---

42 Parratt, "Y.Z. Mwasi and the Origins of the Blackman's Church," *Journal of Religion in Africa*, 193–206 (206).
43 Oswald Jimmy Banda, "African Indigenous yet Presbyterian: A History and Life of the Church of Africa Presbyterian from 1933 to 2013," (Unpublished PhD thesis, Mzuzu University, 2022), 41.
44 Oswald Jimmy Banda, "African Indigenous yet Presbyterian," 143.
45 Oswald Jimmy Banda, "African Indigenous yet Presbyterian," 58.
46 Oswald Jimmy Banda, "African Indigenous yet Presbyterian," 58.
47 Oswald Jimmy Banda, "African Indigenous yet Presbyterian," 156.
48 Source: Rev. A. C. Banda, Official correspondence with the author, 17.05.2022. These statistics appear reasonable because in a study done in the northern area of Malawi between 2019 and 2021 the total population of the church was around 8600. See Oswald Jimmy Banda, "A Study of Some African Independent Churches in Northern Malawi," (Unpublished PhD Research Module paper, Mzuzu University, 2021), 6–8.

Male membership in Malawi: 11,000
Female membership in Malawi: 16,000
Male membership outside Malawi: 2,000
Female membership outside Malawi: 3,000
Number of presbyteries: 12
Number of congregations: 55
Number of serving ministers: 51

The statistics above show that CAP is not a very big church. Still, it is well established in Malawi, and its presence in Tanzania, Zambia, Zimbabwe, and South Africa testify to its resilience amidst the challenges that many AICs face.

The African Reformed Presbyterian Church (ARPC)

The African Reformed Presbyterian Church was formed by Rev. Yafet Mkandawire of Deep Bay in Karonga District of northern Malawi in 1932.[49] Mkandawire was one of the Livingstonia Mission's early ministers ordained after a prolonged period of serving the mission. The ARPC was initially very successful in its operation of schools besides evangelisation. However, like the rest of AICs, it could not soon forge ahead with education matters due to inadequate funding.[50]

Eklezia Lanangwa (The Free Church)

This church was founded by Rev. Charles Chidongo Chinula, born in 1885 and died in 1970. In 1934, the Rev. Charles Chidongo Chinula applied to the government to register a new denomination out of the Livingstonia Mission known as "Eklezia Lanangwa" in the Chitumbuka language which can be translated as the Free Church or the Christianity of Freedom. Chinula had been defrocked from the Livingstonia Mission on the grounds of immorality. Still, he had a lot of grievances against the mission, including its failure to re-admit penitent offenders and flouting its procedure in dealing with suspended church members. Chinula felt the only solution was to come out of the Livingstonia Mission and start his church where freedom and brotherly love would be promoted.[51]

It is interesting to note that in 1935 Yafet Mkandawire's African Reformed

---

49 MacDonald, "Religious Independency as a Means of Social Advance in Northern Nyasaland in the 1930s," 106–129 (114).
50 MacDonald, "Religious Independency as a Means of Social Advance in Northern Nyasaland in the 1930s," 106–129 (114).
51 Phiri, *Chidongo Chinula*. See also Ndekha, "Chinula, Charles Chidongo 1885–1970." Interestingly, Chinula, not long before he died personally returned to the CCAP, but without the CAP following his example.

Presbyterian Church and Charles Chidongo Chinula's Eklezia Lanangwa joined forces with Yesaya Zerenji Mwasi's Blackman's Church that is in Tongaland to form the Church of Blackmen of Africa (*Mpingo wa Ŵafipa wa mu Afrika*). It is this Church of Blackmen of Africa that later on became the Church of Africa Presbyterian (CAP) while recognizing Yesaya Zerenji Mwasi as its sole founder.[52]

7. The Ethiopian Movement in Retrospect

The independent Presbyterian churches were not the first or last African Independent Churches to emerge. However, many of them seem to have been greatly influenced by the Ethiopian Movement, whose goal was to unite Africans and free them from a white-dominated life, whether in the realm of politics or church life.

The education brought in by Western missionaries accorded many Africans the opportunity to advance beyond the life that many of their people, who had not gone to school, were living at the time. However, the missionaries, who were Christian brothers from the white stock of humanity, lacked the wisdom to recognize the status thus attained by the African elites. This made many African church leaders experience frustration at the hands of the missionaries. Besides, the monopoly of real ecclesiastical power and monetary resources made the African leaders of the church feel oppressed without any remedy within the mission churches at the time. The founders of Ethiopian AICs' maintenance of the mission churches' doctrine, liturgy, polity, and dress shows that they were not against the mission churches but only their oppressive tendencies towards the indigenous peoples. One can argue that this was inevitable because of the 19th and 20th century missionary endeavours' connection with colonialism and Western imperialism in general.

The Ethiopian Movement registered a real milestone in ensuring that Africans became the shapers of their destiny in church matters. The missionaries were able to see new churches mushrooming up, which were not under their supervision but carried on with the message they had brought even if their emphases were being downplayed in favour of African emphases. Similarly, the question of race was also tackled. However, it was going to take some time before the political aspirations of the movement were to find fulfilment in the independence of African nations in general and the attainment of multiracial political pluralism in South Africa in particular.

Interestingly, the Ethiopian Movement, especially among the Presbyterians, was fuelled by the high level of education that the Scottish missionaries accorded indigenous church leaders through their highly acclaimed institutions in both

---

52 Banda, "African Indigenous yet Presbyterian: A History and Life of the Church of Africa Presbyterian from 1933 to 2013," 1.

South Africa and Malawi. The institution responsible for the high education standards for the blacks in South Africa was the Lovedale Institute of the Free Church of Scotland. At the same time, in Malawi, it was also a Free Church institution known as the Overtoun Institution in the Livingstonia Mission. The influence of the Overtoun Institution reverberated in the whole of Southern Africa in the first half of the 20th century. The current University of Livingstonia is a successor of the Overtoun Institution.

While the classical AICs were very successful in many respects, elsewhere I have argued that they have not been very successful in contributing towards social transformation after independence, possibly due to their lack of adequate finances, sustainable structures, and passionate successors to the founding fathers, when compared to the now African-led, post-mission churches.[53] Nevertheless, that some of these churches are still in operation today is a clear testimony to the authenticity of their Christian expression, which was born out of oppression and antagonism of the very harbingers of the good news they continue to spread. I argue that the legacy of Ethiopianism continues in the current African Christian Theology debates.

8. Conclusion

While some independent Presbyterian churches that emerged due to the influence of the Ethiopian movement have continued to exist into the 21st century, others died along the way or were absorbed by more prominent denominations. Still, in some instances, the founders of independent presbyterian churches returned to their mother presbyterian churches. Irrespective of the fate of some of these churches in history, their emergence and protest during missionary Christianity in Africa was a testimony to the importance of relating the Christian message to the culture of the people who receive it. The Gospel of Jesus Christ is unique, and so are the various cultures of the world that embrace it following missionary endeavours. Presbyterian Ethiopianism represented the reaction of one group of a theological tradition to the propagation of the Christian faith that neglected the importance of peoples and their cultures. The Presbyterian missionaries were only children of their time, so they treated Africans in a generally accepted way among westerners at the time. Therefore, it is essential to remember today that people of all cultures deserve respect and that the Gospel of Jesus Christ does not come to kill and condemn everything from a people's culture. The Gospel will only thrive in an authentic cultural expression.

---

53 Munyenyembe, *Christianity and Socio-cultural Issues: The Charismatic Movement and Contextualization in Malawi*, 26–27.

Questions for study (fact type):
1 Paraphrase in your own words a working definition of the term "Ethiopianism."
2 What particular verse in the Psalms has become closely associated with Ethiopianism?
3 Name the first church to break away and use the name "Ethiopian" in South Africa.
4 Name the two first clearly defined Ethiopian Churches within the Presbyterian fold in South Africa.
5 Name four Ethiopian-type Presbyterian churches in Malawi.

Questions for study (reflection type):
1 Discuss how education provided by mission entities was actually a contributing factor to the development of Ethiopianism. Provide examples.
2 Write a short reflective paper (one to two pages) of your assessment of Ethiopian Presbyterianism with both positive and negative reflections.

Select Bibliography

Banda, Oswald Jimmy. "A Study of Some African Independent Churches in Northern Malawi." PhD Research Module paper, Mzuzu University, 2021.

Banda, Oswald Jimmy. "African Indigenous yet Presbyterian: A History and Life of the Church of Africa Presbyterian from 1933 to 2013." PhD thesis, Mzuzu University, 2022.

Donati, Henry. "'A Very Antagonistic Spirit': Elliot Kamwana: Christianity and the World in Nyasaland." *The Society of Malawi Journal* 64.1 (2011): 13–33.

Duncan, Graham A. "'Pull up a good tree and push it outside'? The Rev Edward Tsewu's dispute with the Free Church of Scotland Mission." *Nederduitse Gereformeerde Teologiese Tydskrif* 53 (2012): 20–61. https://repository.up.ac.za/bitstream/handle/2263/20326/Duncan_Pull%282012%29.pdf?sequence=1&isAllowed=y

Duncan, Graham A. "Ethiopianism in Pan-African Perspective, 1880–1920." *Studia Historiae Ecclesiasticae* 41.2 (2015): 198–218. DOI: http://dx.doi.org/10.17159/2412-4265/2015/85.

Duncan, Graham A. "From Mission to Church: The Formation of the Bantu Presbyterian Church of South Africa." *The International Journal of African Historical Studies* 49.3 (2016): 329–360. Published by Boston University African Studies Center Stable URL: https://www.jstor.org/stable/44723412.

Duncan, Graham A. "Scottish Presbyterian Church Mission Policy in South Africa 1898–1923." MTh thesis, University of South Africa, 1997.

Duncan, Graham A. "The Origins and Early Development of Scottish Presbyterian Mission in South Africa (1824–1865)." *Studia Historiae Ecclesiasticae* 39.1 (2013), [online]. Available from <http://www.scielo.org.za/scielo.php?script=sci_arttext&pid=S1017-04992013000100006&lng=en&nrm=iso>. access on 17 Mar. 2022.

Duncan, Graham. A. "'African Churches Willing to Pay their Own Bills': The Role of Money in the Formation of Ethiopian-type Churches with Particular Reference to the Mzimba Secession." *African Historical Review* 45:2 (2013): 52–79. 10.1080/17532523.2013.857092.

Gondwe, Wezi Makuni. *A History of the Last Church of God and His Christ*. Mzuzu: MZUNI Press, 2018.

Kalinga, Owen J. M. "Jordan Msumba, Ben Ngemela and the Last Church of God and His Christ, 1924–1935." *Journal of Religion in Africa* 13.3 (1982): 207–218. Stable URL: http://www.jstor.org/stable/1581437.

Khoapa, Bennie A. "Mokone, Mangena Maake." DACB, accessed on 12.01.2022 from https://dacb.org/stories/southafrica/mokone-mangena2/.

Lahouel, Badra. "Ethiopianism and African Nationalism in South Africa before 1937" (Éthiopianisme et nationalisme africain en Afrique du Sud avant 1937). *Cahiers d'Études Africaines* 26.104 (1986): 681–688. https://www.jstor.org/stable/4392069.

Langworthy, Harry. *"Africa for the African": The Life of Joseph Booth*. Blantyre: CLAIM-Kachere, 1996.

MacDonald, Roderick J. "Religious Independency as a Means of Social Advance in Northern Nyasaland in the 1930s." *Journal of Religion in Africa* 13, Fasc. 1 (1970): 106–129. Accessed on 10.1.2022 from https://www.jstor.org/stable/1594819.

McCracken, John. *A History of Malawi 1859–1966*. Suffolk: James Currey, 2012.

McCracken, John. *Politics and Christianity in Malawi 1875–1940: The Impact of the Livingstonia Mission in the Northern Province*. Second Edition. Blantyre: CLAIM-Kachere, 2000.

Millard, Joan Anne. "A Study of the Perceived Causes of Schism in Some Ethiopian-Type Churches in the Cape and Transvaal, 1884–1925." DTh thesis, University of South Africa, 1995.

Monareng, Leqeku Amos. "An Investigation of Schisms within the African Presbyterian Bafolisi Church of Southern Africa." MTh thesis, University of the Free State, 2017.

Munyenyembe, Rhodian. *Christianity and Socio-cultural Issues: The Charismatic Movement and Contextualization in Malawi*. Mzuzu: MZUNI Press, 2011.

Munyenyembe, Rhodian. *Pursuing an Elusive Unity: A History of the Church of Central Africa Presbyterian as a Federative Denomination (1924–2018)*. Carlisle: Langham Monographs, 2019.

Mwasi, Yesaya Zerenji. *Essential and Paramount Reasons for Working Independently.* Blantyre: CLAIM-Kachere, 1999.

Ndekha, Louis W. "Chinula, Charles Chidongo 1885–1970." DACB, https://dacb.org/stories/malawi/chinula-charles/

Parratt, John. "Y.Z. Mwasi and the Origins of the Blackman's Church." *Journal of Religion in Africa* 9.3 (1978): 193–206. https://www.jstor.org/stable/1581164.

Pauw, Christof Martin. "Mission and Church in Malawi: The History of Nkhoma Synod of the Church of Central Africa Presbyterian, 1889–1962." DTh thesis, University of Stellenbosch, 1980.

PCA. "Our History," https://web.archive.org/web/20151116063313/http://presbyterianchurchofafrica.co.za/history.php, accessed 10.04.22.

Phiri, D.D. *Chidongo Chinula.* London: Longman, 1975.

Ross, Andrew C. *Blantyre Mission and the Making of Modern Malawi.* Blantyre: CLAIM-Kachere, 1996.

Rotberg, Robert I. *The Rise of Nationalism in Central Africa: The Making of Malawi and Zambia, 1873–1964.* Cambridge MA.: Harvard University Press, 1965.

Shepperson, George. "Ethiopianism and African Nationalism." *Phylon* (1940–1956), 14.1 (1953): 9–18. Clark Atlanta University, https://www.jstor.org/stable/272419.

Sundkler, B.G. *Bantu Prophets in South Africa.* London: Oxford University Press, 1961.

Switzer, L. *Power and Resistance in an African Society: The Ciskei Xhosa and the Making of South Africa.* Pietermaritzburg: University of Natal Press, 1983.

Thompson, T. Jack. "Prester John, John Chilembwe and the European Fear of Ethiopianism." *The Society of Malawi Journal* 68.2 (2015): 18–30. Society of Malawi – Historical and Scientific Stable, https://www.jstor.org/stable/43694112.

Van Velsen, J. "Some Early Pressure Groups in Malawi." In *The Zambesian Past: Studies in Central African History*, eds. Eric Stokes and Richard Brown. Manchester: Manchester University Press, 1966.

WCC. "Presbyterian Church of Africa," https://www.oikoumene.org/member-churches/presbyterian-church-of-africa, accessed 10.04.22.

Chapter 29

Old Princeton Seminary & the Missionary Imperative

James M. Garretson

Chapter Outline
1. Introduction: Old Princeton Seminary
2. Background: The Missionary Movement, Context
3. Princeton and Missions
4. Student Mission Involvement
5. Domestic and Foreign Missions with attention to Africa
Inset: Old Princeton Seminary & the Missionary Imperat ive

Princeton Theological Seminary, in the historic period of Presbyterian missions in Africa, was the seminary which had from what is known the most alumni involvement in Africa amongst the American presbyterian-related theological seminaries. The contribution via Old Princeton was found in what are now various West African countries (Liberia, Equatorial Guinea, Gabon, Cameroon); in North Africa (Egypt, Algeria, Sudan, Ethiopia) and was through both the PCUSA and the UPCNA; and in Southern Africa (South Africa, Zambia, Zimbabwe); and there may be other countries as well.[1]

This chapter provides context to the rise of Princeton Seminary; background to the rise of the mission movement; missions and Princeton in general; and then specifically student involvements culminating in key names of Princeton alumni who served in Africa. From its founding in 1812 to c.1930, 70 non-African born Princeton Seminary alumni served in Africa and 38 African-born alumni.[2] This total is inclusive and represents those who served other missions, other than

---

1 Robert Speer, sees only Oberlin as a challenger here in general for foreign missions alumni, but Oberlin Institute/College was more a preparatory level institution and distinct from Princeton in other ways. Oberlin had much foreign mission involvement, yet Princeton was distinctive in many regards as a seminary level institution and also theologically. "Princeton on the Mission Field," 419–420, or was Speer meaning Lane Seminary? It is unclear.
2 It could be argued that the two numbers could be added together making the Princeton and Africa connection of alumni actually 107/108. Wallace and Noll, "The Students of Princeton Seminary, 1813–1929," 209, 211. See chart at end of this chapter.

Presbyterian, but it makes the point as to Princeton's role. A chart is included in this chapter which is an attempt to begin to show the alumni who served in Presbyterian and other missions in Africa. No doubt this chart will be expanded as research continues.

1. Introduction: Old Princeton Seminary

Founded in 1812 by the Presbyterian Church in the United States of America (PCUSA), Princeton Theological Seminary, New Jersey was intended for the preparation of future pastors, theologians, and missionaries. As "a nursery of vital piety" and "sound theological learning," the founders envisaged an institution that would both supplement and offset curriculum taught at Princeton College in the early nineteenth century.[3]

The seminary's founders were all committed churchmen and experienced pastors; accordingly, the curriculum reflected interest in subject matter that would both inform the mind and stimulate the heart. Ideal graduates would be men competent in theological knowledge but also men equally familiar with the "life of God in the soul of man." Understanding of the religious affections and the means of grace were essential for ministering to the whole man in formation of Christian character through expression of love toward God and neighbour.

▲ Princeton Theological Seminary, Alexander Hall

---

3   For a brief history see Seldon, *Princeton Theological Seminary: A Narrative History 1812–1992*; for an institutional history see Moorhead, *Princeton Seminary in American Religion and Culture*; for a comprehensive account of the spiritual life and history of the seminary from its founding through its reorganisation in 1929 see Calhoun, *Princeton Seminary, Vol. 1: Faith and Learning, 1812–1868* and Calhoun, *Princeton Seminary, Vol. 2: The Majestic Testimony, 1869–1929*; for a related and briefer study see Steward, *Princeton Seminary (1812–1929): Its Leaders' Lives and Works*.

Several of the seminary's founders were among its first professors. Both Archibald Alexander (1772–1851) and Samuel Miller (1769–1850)[4] were seasoned ministers and accomplished scholars when appointed to their respective roles in 1812 and 1813. In background and temperament, the two men were vastly different, but they shared a common commitment to experimental Calvinism and the Westminster standards.

Charles Hodge (1797–1878) was added to the seminary faculty in 1820; like his predecessors, he would shape generations of students through his lectures and publications. As a student, Hodge embraced his mentors' examples; as a professor, he embodied his predecessors' approach to ministerial instruction and served as a bridge between the founding instructors and later generations of faculty.[5]

The seminary grew in popularity and became a destination school for students from various denominational backgrounds. Faculty such as A. A. Hodge (1823–1886), W. H. Green (1825–1900), B. B. Warfield (1851–1921), and J. Gresham Machen (1881–1937), would achieve international recognition. The combination of intellectual rigour and "experimental" Calvinistic spirituality established the seminary's reputation as a bastion of confessional integrity during its first century of operation.[6]

Concurrent with the school's growth during the late nineteenth century was development of Protestant Modernism and accompanying influence of Higher Criticism. By the early twentieth century, internal conflicts within American Presbyterianism regarding denominational polity and the role of creeds and confessions in defending orthodoxy also came to fruition after years of debate and acrimony in ways that divided the seminary board, administration, and faculty. The older confessional theology of American Presbyterianism was being rewritten or abandoned; modernistic tenets were prevalent. For those who valued the vision of its founders and institutional heritage, the distinctives of "Old Princeton" were essential to preserve if the blessing of God were to remain on the seminary.

---

4   For biographies, see James W. Alexander, *The Life of Archibald Alexander* (New York: Charles Scribner, 1854; repr., Harrisonburg: Sprinkle Publications, 1991). Likewise, Samuel Miller Jr., *The Life of Samuel Miller, D.D., LL.D., Second Professor in the Theological Seminary of the Presbyterian Church, at Princeton, New Jersey* (1869; repr., Stoke-on-Trent, Staffordshire, UK: Tentmaker, 2002).

5   For Hodge, Archibald Alexander Hodge, *The Life of Charles Hodge, D.D., LL. D., Professor in the Theological Seminary, Princeton, N.J.* (New York: Charles Scribner's Sons, 1880; repr. Edinburgh: Banner of Truth, 2010); for contemporary biographies see Paul Gutjahr, *Charles Hodge: Guardian of American Orthodoxy* (New York: Oxford University Press, 2011); Andrew A. Hoeffecker, *Charles Hodge: The Pride of Princeton* (Phillipsburg: P & R, 2011).

6   For a collection of memorial and biographical addresses beginning with the founding faculty to B. B. Warfield's death in 1921 see James M. Garretson, *Pastor-Teachers of Old Princeton: Memorial Addresses for the Faculty of Princeton Theological Seminary 1812–1921* (Edinburgh: Banner of Truth, 2012).

The future proved otherwise as faculty transitioned and the board reconfigured. Machen believed the institutional identity that characterised the school for its first century ended with the death of Warfield in 1921. By 1929, the seminary was reorganised in accord with the interests of modernistic theology, precipitating schism in the school and exodus of key faculty. Westminster Theological Seminary was founded in response to the institutional changes at Princeton.

Although "Old Princeton" is often remembered for its approach to apologetics and theology, the school was also committed to instruction in pastoral theology and missions.[7] By personal example, classroom instruction, and the "Sabbath Afternoon Conferences," students received counsel on how to prepare and serve as gospel ministers. Emphasis was placed upon the formation of "eminent" piety for effectiveness in pulpit and pastoral ministry. Piety was viewed essential for individual growth as a Christian, and eminent piety for effectiveness in ministry. The faculty believed that piety infuses and enlivens ministerial labour with unction – ministry exercised in power and demonstration of the Spirit. Power in the pulpit and pastoral care of congregations would be enhanced by the minister's commitment to personal godliness. Students learned that spiritual work demands spiritual men, the absence of which may result in barrenness in one's labours.[8]

While formal training enlarges the mind and piety ennobles the heart, empowerment for ministry, the Princetonians emphasised, is especially rooted in deepening love for Christ. Just as preaching is to be Christ-centred, so too are the affections of the minister to be centred upon Christ. To know one's identity in Christ is to cultivate a transformed heart in a believer's service as disciple and ministerial servant. As students learned, love to Christ also meant acting in his interests and on behalf of his love. Shepherding the sheep for whom he died was to be accompanied by active love to the lost through evangelistic preaching, personal and public witness, and support of the missionary imperative in both domestic and foreign missions.[9]

As a ministry of the Presbyterian Church, the seminary was beneficiary to

---

7 For a collection of sermons, lectures, articles, and essays on the theology of ministry students received during the school's first century see Garretson, *Princeton and the Work of the Christian Ministry*, 2 vols.

8 For a study on Alexander's theology of preaching see James M. Garretson, *Princeton and Preaching: Archibald Alexander and the Christian Ministry* (Edinburgh: Banner of Truth, 2005); for a related study on Samuel Miller's instruction on preaching and pastoral ministry see James M. Garretson, *An Able and Faithful Ministry: Samuel Miller and the Pastoral Office* (Grand Rapids: Reformation Heritage Books, 2014).

9 Calhoun's unpublished doctoral dissertation remains the most thorough treatment of Princeton's early mission emphases. Calhoun, "The Last Command: Princeton Theological Seminary and Missions (1812–1862)."

the missionary-mindedness of its denomination. In 1789, the new denomination formed its first General Assembly. A year later, the Assembly appointed a missions committee; in 1816 a board of missions was formed tasked with the missionary imperative.

The new era in Presbyterian missionary involvement paralleled emerging national and international interest in Christian missions. Often viewed as "the great century" in missionary expansion, nineteenth-century Christianity witnessed unprecedented advances in missionary fervour. While missionary activity occurred throughout the history of the Church, various factors gave rise to transatlantic missionary enthusiasm.

2. Background: The Missionary Movement, Context

British and European Christianity were both heir to Reformation doctrine and its expression in later years through Puritan and Pietist practice. Protestant convictions on the gospel message and calling of the Christian church as witness and messenger would raise new awareness of the mission mandate. At times hampered by circumstances or narrow in focus, generational awareness of mission outreach matured in practice. The renewal of spiritual life that occurred during the Evangelical Awakening in the British Isles and related developments on the European continent would also lead to vibrant missionary activism.

In the early eighteenth century, Pietism spawned Moravian missions. Originating in Europe, Moravian witness during a transatlantic voyage to Georgia proved instrumental in the subsequent conversion of John Wesley. In America, Jonathan Edwards's writings on revival, prayer, and the history of redemption stirred interest in advance of God's kingdom. Among the most enduring of Edwards's publications is *The Life and Diary of David Brainerd*, missionary to the Delaware Indians. Brainerd's uncompromising devotion, deep piety, selfless sacrifice, and premature death became a model of missionary commitment for generations. Scottish and American support for monthly "concerts of prayer" likewise provided decades long enthusiasm for the spread of God's kingdom throughout the earth.[10]

Rooted in developments during the mid-eighteenth century, the ebb and flow of prayerful interest in the glory of God and salvation of the lost would break forth in a tidal wave of missional engagement toward the end of the century, its full flowering unfolding in the coming years. Fuelled in part by a

---

10 Miller's forgotten but still valuable work on the monthly concerts of prayer remains a useful study. See Samuel Miller, *Letters on the Observance of the Monthly Concert in Prayer: Addressed to the Members of the Presbyterian Church in the United States* (Philadelphia: Presbyterian Board of Publication, 1845).

millennial eschatology popular at the time, the church looked forward with fresh exuberance at the successful – and worldwide – advance of God's kingdom. Optimistic in outlook, postmillennialism provided grist for colonial Christianity in its hopes for a new society organised under Christ's Lordship – at least in its New England version – as well as the eschatological backdrop for the founders of Princeton Theological Seminary.

The conversion of William Carey in 1779 was a watershed moment in birthing a new missionary consciousness. The English shoe cobbler would become one of the most famous figures in global missions. A Calvinistic Baptist minister and friend of Andrew Fuller, Carey's burden for the gospel's global outreach can be found in his seminal work, *An Enquiry into the Obligation of Christians to Use Means for the Conversion of Heathen*. First published in 1792, Carey and his colleagues' love for the lost led to the formation of the Baptist Missionary Society a few months later. Soon afterwards, Carey and his wife left for India, where he would spend the remainder of his days.

Carey's labours in Serampore encouraged growing missionary enthusiasm for the entire world. What was once considered "an unnecessary and hopeless undertaking" was replaced by a prayerful and passionate burden for the lost. Interdenominational and intercontinental in outreach, Protestant global effort extended to Burma (Adoniram Judson), China (Robert Morrison), India (Alexander Duff), South Africa (Robert Moffat), the South Seas (John Williams), and Tierra del Fuego (Allen Gardiner). Judson and his wife would make missionary history in 1812 as the first American couple sent together as overseas missionaries. Judson's life, like Carey's, became a model for missionary voluntarism.

American Christianity was also heir to Reformation doctrine through Puritan immigration to North American colonies. The impact of the Great Awakening and Second Great Awakening was likewise a catalyst for evangelistic enthusiasm. Both awakenings alerted American Christians to the need for domestic and foreign missions. Individuals and congregations were affected, as were denominations.

The Second Great Awakening benefitted from developments in American denominational life that aligned intersecting evangelical convictions in cooperative outreach to their communities and expanding frontier. Missionary and voluntary organisations multiplied during the early years of the nineteenth century,[11] a time of activism historians refer to as "The Evangelical Empire."

---

11 Among the new organisations devoted to missions, bible distribution, and Christian literature were the American Board of Commissioners for Foreign Missions (1810), the American Education Society (1816), the American Bible Society (1816), the American Tract Society (1825), and the American Home Missionary Society (1826). Additional organisations include the American Colonization Society (1817), the American Sunday School Union (1824), the American Temperance Society (1826), and the American Anti-Slavery Society (1833). Numerous state and local organisations existed alongside more well-known national entities.

Interest in salvation of the lost was paralleled by care for the destitute and ministry to growing urban populations spawned by industrialisation. Social ills were addressed through temperance movements, a focus on public morals, Sabbath observance, and engagement with the deepening divide in American society over slavery. Bible and tract distribution organisations were popular as publication of Christian literature flourished.

As organised religion became detached from government sponsorship and voluntarist in nature, inter-denominational and para-church organisations gained influence in directing the missionary emphases of nineteenth-century American Christianity. Core Christian values seemed adequate for cooperative ventures at first but would be stretched in a few decades as theological differences emerged from the democratisation of American Christianity and diminution of Reformed doctrinal conviction. Denominational identities became more pronounced as church leaders moved to consolidate confessional convictions through strengthening of denominational literature and boards.

3. Princeton and Missions

Understood in its historical context, the founding of Princeton Theological Seminary occurred during a period of expanding missionary consciousness. As society benefited from the salutary effects of revival, the seminary in turn would advance the record of God's bounty in their approach to pastoral theology and emphasis upon domestic and foreign missions.

▲ Archibald Alexander

The Seminary Plan, which Alexander and Miller helped produce, listed as one of its objectives a statement on missionary preparation: "It is to found a nursery for missionaries to the heathen, and such as are destitute of the stated preaching of the gospel; in which youth may receive that appropriate training which may lay a foundation for their ultimately becoming eminently qualified for missionary work."[12]

Alexander and Miller embodied the mission ethos of the Seminary Plan. As a young man, Alexander had served as a missionary on the colonial "frontier." Miller learned the challenges of urban ministry in one of the nation's fastest growing cities. Both men

---

12 Cited in Calhoun, *Princeton Seminary* 1:139-40.

addressed the missionary task in their sermons and publications before and during their work as professors at the seminary.[13]

For the founding faculty, missions were a matter of personal conviction and public interest. Mission lay at the heart of gospel proclamation; implicit to the calling of ministerial office, is obligation to the missional task. Whether in its more formal expression as a ministry of a denomination, or more narrowly in individual involvement, missionary outlook belonged to the essence of ministerial service and training students received at the seminary.

Alexander and Miller initially celebrated the cooperative ventures in domestic and foreign missions. A shared commitment to "experimental" Christianity marked the era's burgeoning Christian enthusiasm for rescuing "heathen" and Christianisation of cultures.[14] Both were active in a variety of denominational and para-church missionary organisations.

Like many of his contemporaries, Alexander supported return of freed slaves to Liberia as a transplanted Christian colony beneficiary to the introduction of Christianity through experience of institutional slavery in its American context.[15] Popularised by the American Colonization Society, the practicalities and cost soon eroded confidence in the project, even as American society in the South became increasingly dependent on slave labour for commercial interests.

By the 1830s, denominational division over divided doctrinal loyalties would result in Alexander and Miller's reconsideration of interdenominational

---

13 For Alexander's observations see Archibald Alexander, *A Missionary Sermon, Preached in the First Presbyterian Church in Philadelphia, on the Twenty-third of May, 1814* (Philadelphia: William Fry, 1814) also found in Garretson, *Princeton and the Work of the Christian Ministry* 1: 288–307. For Miller's thoughts see Samuel Miller, *A Sermon, Delivered in the Middle Church, New Haven Connecticut, Sept. 12, 1822, at the ordination of the Rev. Messrs. William Goodell, William Richards, and Artemas Bishop, as Evangelists and Missionaries to the Heathen* (Boston: Crocker and Brewster, 1822) also found in Garretson, *Princeton and the Work of the Christian Ministry*, 1:422-45. See also Samuel Miller "The Earth Filled with the Glory of the Lord," *The American National Preacher* 10, no. 7 (December 1835): 289–304. For Hodge's views see Charles Hodge, *The Teaching Office of the Church: A Sermon by the Rev. Charles Hodge, D.D., Preached in the church on University Place, New York, on Sabbath evening, May 7, 1848, at the request of the Executive Committee of the Board of Foreign Missions of the Presbyterian Church* (New York: Board of Foreign Missions, 1882) also found in Garretson, *Princeton and the Work of the Christian Ministry* 2: 185–201.
14 For observations related to gospel proclamation and elevation of pagan cultures see James W. Alexander, "Foreign Missions," *Biblical Repertory and Princeton Review* (hereafter BRPR) 15 (July 1843): 349–369.
15 For Alexander's thoughts on Liberia and the question of colonisation see Alexander, "History of the American Colony in Liberia," *BRPR* 12 (April 1840): 206–225., idem., Archibald Alexander, "Mr. Kennedy's Report on African Colonization," *BRPR* 16 (January 1844): 57–86. For the still standard book length treatment see Archibald Alexander, *History of Colonization on the Western Coast of Africa*.

alignments which put at risk the Presbyterian heritage and confessional theology taught at the seminary.[16] Cooperative unity, with all its initial promise, undermined foundational doctrines whose dilution would compromise the work of Christian missions some would argue.

4. Student Mission Involvement

The interest in Christian missions that marked the beginning of the nineteenth century in England and America was reflected in widespread student enthusiasm for involvement in missionary activities. Missionary fervour generated formation of numerous mission and Bible distribution "societies" on college and seminary campuses.[17] By 1857, seventy student-initiated campus societies had been founded.

Students at Williams College in Massachusetts were instrumental in modern mission enthusiasm. Student involvement in the "haystack prayer meeting" precipitated pledges to foreign mission service and subsequent founding of the "Society of the Brethren," an informal but now organised student effort to advance interest in missionary labour.

Several of the Williams' graduates became students at the newly founded Andover Seminary (1808). A similar society to the Williams' "Brethren" was formed, student enthusiasm grew, and missionary interest expanded. By 1811 the "Society of Inquiry on the Subject of Missions" was organised. Andover Seminary became a model of missionary activism for Princeton Theological Seminary students. By 1820, students at Princeton had organised a corresponding Brotherhood society "for the purposes of prayer and conference on the subject of missions."[18]

The society was kept secret at first, eager to influence campus conviction on the importance of missions through example and testimony. Meetings were held for prayer and discussion among the dozen or more students who showed interest in the gatherings. Members actively spoke with fellow students about the importance of missions, and an inner group who had committed to missionary service met privately with Dr Alexander for counsel and encouragement.

An earlier and more well-known society was organised among Princeton students in 1814. The "Society of Inquiry on Missions and the General State of Religion" aimed to gather "important information respecting domestic and

---

16 For observations on Presbyterian missions see Archibald Alexander, "Presbyterian Missions," *BRPR* 10 (October 1838): 535–542. See also T. M. Moore, "The Missionary Bearing of Calvinism," *BRPR* 17 (April 1844): 184–199.
17 Founded in 1813, the Bible Society of Nassau Hall at Princeton was the first college bible society in the United States.
18 Cited in Calhoun, *Princeton Seminary* 1: 142.

foreign missions, with a view of ascertaining our personal duty as to engaging in them."[19] The Society met on the first day of each month during which meetings reports were read, correspondence received, mission-themed messages were presented, and conversation held on topics of practical interest for missional outlook. Annual public addresses were delivered by the Society at the local Presbyterian church. Student interest led to the formation of a small library of mission related material, collection of artifacts (including small idols), and reading room for study and reflection.

The Society corresponded with fellow students at colleges and seminaries throughout the United States. Minutes and correspondence were preserved, record to the extensive student missional involvement during the early decades of the nineteenth century.[20]

Several factors were critical to student missionary enthusiasm. Student testimony bears witness to the influence of the original faculty in furthering the cause of Christian mission in the lives of students. Through sermons, lectures, publications, personal counsel, and participation in student gatherings, the Princeton faculty elevated awareness of missionary obligation. Guest speakers, missionary correspondence, and the reading of Christian biography stirred missionary aspiration. The monthly Concert for Prayer was also instrumental in reinforcing the work of the Brotherhood and Society meetings. Missional interest was systemic to the campus atmosphere.

In 1836, the Rev. Dr John Breckinridge was appointed Professor of Pastoral Theology and Missionary Instruction. Breckinridge served at the seminary for two years before leaving to assume a position with the Presbyterian Board of Foreign Missions.[21] While his appointment had its detractors with respect to the separation of mission subject matter from the rest of the curriculum, all were agreed on the need for additional organisations and faculty to properly address enlarging missionary awareness. Although a faculty proposed missionary institution never came to fruition and development of a missiological curriculum would lie well beyond nineteenth century efforts, Princeton was the one American school in the first half of the nineteenth century that had a missions course listed in its curriculum. Most often, however, mission topics were interwoven throughout general course content while modelled in faculty interest.

---

19 Cited in Calhoun, *Princeton Seminary* 1: 144.
20 The Society "passed out of existence" in 1859. Student mission enthusiasm waned during the turbulence of the 1860s but returned in the following decades with expansion of global mission initiatives.
21 For Breckinridge's thought on missions see John Breckinridge, "The Claims of Foreign Missions," *Biblical Repertory and Theological Review* 2 (October 1830): 587–600. Also, *The Spruce Street Lectures* (Philadelphia: Russel and Martien, 1833), 255–297.

5. Domestic and Foreign Missions with attention to Africa

It is estimated that one out of four Princeton students entered domestic missions in the first fifty years of the seminary's history. While only 42% of students between 1812–1862 completed the prescribed three-year course between 1812–1862, 50% of students who served as foreign missionaries in the same period completed the full course of studies.

Calhoun reports that of the 2300 students who trained at the seminary during the first forty years, 600 went to destitute places in the United States; 37 to the American Indians; 17 to the slave population; and 117 to foreign mission fields. Foreign mission service included work in Afghanistan, Africa, Armenia, Burma, Greece, Hawaii, India, Japan, Palestine, Persia, Siam, and South America.

Missionary service in the nineteenth century was often accompanied by illness, opposition, and hazardous travel. Few would return to family and friends from the foreign mission field. Mission work made for lonely but highly dedicated lives.

Africa, the "white man's grave," was a point of missionary destination for Princeton students. In many parts of Africa, however, climate and disease proved a challenge for adaptation and survival. Students sometimes died shortly after arrival. Wives who accompanied their husbands also died prematurely through illness or martyrdom. While "a land as beautiful as our own," the challenges for African missions often seemed insurmountable.[22] In a public address given in 1872, Charles Hodge bore testimony to the challenge:

> What I have done is as nothing compared with what is done by a man who goes to Africa, and labors among a heathen tribe, and reduces their language to writing. I am not worthy to stoop down and unloose the shoes of such a man. [23]

Students viewed themselves as "co-workers with God" in gospel outreach. Faculty and students believed that human beings shared a common humanity and depravity and were therefore in equal need of the gospel remedy. Colour of one's skin or place of birth made no difference to the students.

Men of high attainments were desired for the mission field. Correspondence to Princeton students from the London Missionary Society urged the importance of an educated ministry for service in Africa. After reporting that "the poor

---

22 Breckinridge once remarked "Africa has been made by *Christian* America and *Christian* Europe into a field of blood, a market, where men are bought and sold." Cited in Calhoun, "The Last Command," 233.
23 Cited in Calhoun, "The Last Command," 193.

Hottentots were greatly rejoiced at the accounts you have given us of the success of the Gospel in America," John Philips wrote:

> I know of no situation upon earth that requires a greater knowledge of this world, and more of the philosophy of religion and human nature, than are required in the mind of the man who has to begin and conduct the affairs of an African mission.[24]

Missionary work during the nineteenth century often trailed national and imperialist interests. Imperial expansion provided pathways upon which missionary presence followed. And yet for all the challenges it presented to the purity of gospel motives, missionary labour in the early decades of "Old Princeton" never lost sight of gospel priorities in expectation of the millennial hope toward which they laboured in service to the Christ they loved.[25]

Old Princeton and missionaries in Africa

John Pinney, James L. Mackey, and George Simpson were among early Princetonian missionaries to Africa. David A. Wilson served in Liberia. A request for missionaries among the towns on the Muni River in Western Africa was answered with the arrival of George McQueen, William Clemens, and Edwin T. Williams in Corisco. Robert H. Nassau earned an additional degree in medicine from the University of Pennsylvania to equip him for his service at the Lambarene mission station, later made famous by the work of Albert Schweitzer. Andrew Watson served for over five decades in Egypt with the UPCNA. Calhoun succinctly summarises student missionary service in Africa:

> Africa especially was a challenge and a sorrow to the Princeton students. Joseph Barr had died in 1832 before he could sail for the 'dark continent.' David White and his wife died within days of reaching Cape Palmas in 1837. Still the students could not believe that Africa was to 'be given up.' Oren Canfield and Jonathan Alward went in 1841. Alward lived only a few days after his arrival and was buried next to the grave of the Whites. Canfield died of malaria a year later. Robert Sawyer

---

24 Cited in Calhoun, "The Last Command," 108; 227–228.
25 Walter Lowrie's remarks are representative: "The country is populous … their superstitions are old, foolish, and feeble. They have a reverence for white men and would probably be willing to receive instruction. There is a glorious promise that 'Ethiopia will soon stretch forth her hands unto God.'" Cited in Calhoun, "The Last Command," 432.

arrived at Monrovia in December 1841. He managed to preach and begin Christian schools before he died, after just two years in Africa. A small beginning, however, had been made in fulfilling Philip Milledoler's charge in 1812 that the students from Princeton plant 'the standard of the cross on the remotest shores of heathen lands.'[26]

While missiological understanding would advance in relation to ethnic, cultural, social, and political dynamics, the early Princetonians recognized the transnational and transcultural nature of the gospel message and thereby placed emphasis on eternal gospel verities whose relevance is not restricted by temporal factors.

To understand the dedication of Princeton Seminary students to missions in Africa and other countries is to grasp the theology of pastoral ministry first taught by the original faculty and fostered generationally into the early twentieth century. Although details of respective missionary labours vary and may be hard to reconstruct, the theology of missionary identity taught at "Old Princeton" remains relevant for those eager to see the advance of God's kingdom in the twenty-first century in a manner faithful to the gospel message and the Church's calling.[27]

▲ Clarence W. Duff

▲ Robert H. Nassau

---

26 Calhoun, *Princeton Seminary* 1:209–210. From, Milledoler, *The Sermon delivered at the Inauguration of Archibald Alexander ... .and the Charge ... to the Students ...* (New York: Whiting & Watson, 1812), 118.

27 See the chapters on Liberia (chapter three), Corisco and Gabon (chapter ten), and Egypt (chapter 23) in this volume to find Princetonians and their respective mission work in Africa in the 19th-century.

Questions for study (fact type):
1 Briefly explain the origins of Princeton Seminary by answering these information questions: *who* were the key founders, *what* was the purpose, *when* was it founded, *where* was it located, *why* was this seminary needed, *how* were the founders qualified to train others for ministry?
2 The nineteenth century has been called "the greatest century of missions." Make a list of five of the most famous missionaries from this century. Beside each name, put both their country of origin and the country where they served as missionaries.
3 Identify three ways that Princeton professors *Archibald Alexander* (1772–1851) and *Samuel Miller* (1769–1850) emphasised the vital importance of missions to their students.

Questions for study (reflection type):
1 "By 1820, students at Princeton had organised a corresponding Brotherhood society 'for the purposes of prayer and conference on the subject of missions.' The society was kept secret at first, eager to influence campus conviction on the importance of missions through example and testimony." Read Matthew 7:15–19. Why did the members of this Brotherhood at Princeton keep their society secret at first?
2 "While missiological understanding would advance in relation to ethnic, cultural, social, and political dynamics, the early Princetonians recognized the transnational and transcultural nature of the gospel message and thereby placed emphasis on eternal gospel verities whose relevance is not restricted by temporal factors." Explain what it means to place emphasis on eternal verities when ministering to people of any culture.
3 Examine the chart below (Appendix) of Princeton graduates who went on to serve as missionaries in Africa. Choose one graduate of interest to you and research them on the internet. Write one paragraph about them—concentrate on facts—dates, places, significant achievements, death.

Select Bibliography

Alexander, Archibald. "History of the American Colony in Liberia." *Biblical Repertory and Princeton Review* [BRPR] 12 (April 1840): 206–225.

Alexander, Archibald. *History of Colonization on the Western Coast of Africa*. Philadelphia: William S. Martien, 1846.

Alexander, Archibald. "Presbyterian Missions." *BRPR* 10 (October 1838): 535–542.

Calhoun, David B. "The Last Command: Princeton Theological Seminary and Missions (1812–1862)." PhD thesis, Princeton Theological Seminary, 1983.

Calhoun, David B. *Princeton Seminary, Vol. 1: Faith and Learning, 1812–1868* and *Princeton Seminary, Vol. 2: The Majestic Testimony, 1869–1929*. Edinburgh: Banner of Truth, 1994 & 1996.

Garretson, James M. *Princeton and the Work of the Christian Ministry*, 2 vols. Edinburgh: Banner of Truth, 2012.

Moorhead, James. *Princeton Seminary in American Religion and Culture*. Grand Rapids: Eerdmans, 2012.

Roberts, Edward H. Compiler, *Biographical Catalogue of the Princeton Theological Seminary, 1815–1932*. Princeton: Trustees of the Theological Seminary of the Presbyterian Church, 1933.

Seldon, William K. *Princeton Theological Seminary: A Narrative History 1812–1992*. Princeton: Princeton University Press, 1992.

Speer, Robert. "Princeton on the Mission Field." In *The Centennial Celebration of the Theological Seminary of the Presbyterian Church in the United States of America at Princeton, New Jersey*, eds B.B. Warfield, W. B. Armstrong, H. Mc. Robinson. Princeton: Trustees of the Princeton Theological Seminary, 1912, 418–436. [Speer includes Pinney, Mackey, Nassau, Watson, and McClenahan concerning missions in Africa.]

Steward, Gary. *Princeton Seminary (1812–1929): Its Leaders' Lives and Works*. Phillipsburg: P & R Publishing, 2014.

Wallace, Peter and Mark Noll, "The Students of Princeton Seminary, 1812–1929: A Research Note." *American Presbyterians* 72.3 (1994), 203–215.

Inset

Princeton Theological Seminary Alumni who served in Africa, 1812–c.1930

J. C. Whytock, compiler [28]

PART 1: General Africa[29]

Name	Class Year	Agency/Denominational Affiliation	Mission Location
Barr, Joseph Welsh[30]	1832[31]	agent Amer. Colon. Society; WFMS, PCUSA	to have gone to Liberia
Pinney, John Brooke	1832	agent Amer. Colon. Society; WFMS, PCUSA	Liberia
Laird, Matthew	1833	agent Amer. Colon. Society; PCUSA	Monrovia, Liberia
Venable, Henry Isaac	1834	ABCFM/PCUSA	Zululand, SA
White, David	1835	Berkshire Congreg. Assoc.	Cape Palmas, Liberia
Canfield, Oren Kasson	1838	ABCFM?/PCUSA	Liberia

---

28 Based largely upon the official Catalogue of PTS 1815–1932 but also numerous other cross checks. Edward H. Roberts, compiler, *Biographical Catalogue of the Princeton Theological Seminary, 1815–1932* (Princeton: Trustees of the Theological Seminary of the Presbyterian Church, 1933).

29 Note for Part 1: According to Wallace and Noll, there should be 70 but I only found 65 with certainty. I did not include #66 & 67, William Ramsey & Stephen Rose Wynkoop. But 65 in the general list do all seem correct and verifiable. There appear to be three missing. Forty-four of the sixty-five alumni in Part One were born in the USA.

30 Barr was ordained on 12 October 1832 by Presbytery of Philadelphia and died 28 October 1832 before his ship set sail for Liberia.

31 Class years are the exit year but inconsistent in the *Catalogue*. Barr is listed for class 1833 but died 1832 but perhaps this means he did not complete a full course yet was still ordained by decision of the ordaining body. So, I have tried when glaring on occasion to correct the class year to be reflective of actual exit year left PTS.

Alward, Jonathan Pennington	1840	PCUSA	Cape Palmas, Liberia
Sawyer, Robert Wood	1841	PCUSA	Settra Kroo, Liberia
Simpson, George W.	1849	PCUSA	Corisco
Mackey, James Love	1849	PCUSA	Corisco
McQueen, George	1852	PCUSA	Corisco
Clemens, William	1853	PCUSA	Corisco
Williams, Edwin Theodore	1853	PCUSA	Monrovia, Liberia; Corisco
Ogden, Thomas Spencer	1857	PCUSA	Corisco
Nassau, Robert Hammill	1859	PCUSA	Corisco, Gabon, EG, Cameroon
Wood, Francis Marion	1861	PCUSA	Mission Institution, Wellington, SA
Watson, Andrew[32]	1861	UPCNA	Alexandria, Mousouria, Cairo (Egypt)
Menaul, John[33]	1868	PCUSA	Corisco
Gillespie, Samuel Lovejoy	1871	PCUSA	Gabon, Evangasimba, W. Africa
Marling, Arthur Wodehouse[34]	1881	PCUSA	Gaboon, W. Africa, Angow, W. Africa
Stewart, Thomas McCants	1881	AME(?)	Liberia

---

32 Born in Oliverburn, Scotland in 1834.
33 Born in County Tyrone, Ireland, 1834.
34 Born in Newmarket, Canada, 1855,

Princeton Theological Seminary Alumni who served in Africa, 1812–c.1930

Bannerman, William Sullivan[35]	1890	PCUSA	Gaboon, W. Africa, Ogowe River
Jackson, Frederick Wolcott, Jr	1891	PCUSA	Egypt
Milligan, Robert Henry[36]	1891	PCUSA	Kamerun, W. Africa
McClatchey, Thomas[37]	1894	?	South Africa but unknown what he did
Hickman, Frank Des Passos	1895	PCUSA	Cameroun, W. Africa
McCleary, Charles Warner	1895	PCUSA	Elat (Ebolewoe), Cameroun
Melkonian, Samuel Melkon[38]	1897	PCUSA	Armenian Evangelical Church, Alexandria, Egypt
Wood, Clinton Tyler	1897	PCUSA/RCA/DRCSA	Miss. Institution Wellington, SA
Boppell, Charles Jacob	1898	PCUSA	Gaboon, W. Africa
Devor, Henry Harry	1898	PCUSA	Batanga, Lolodorf, W. Africa
McClenahan, William Lorimer	1898	UPCNA	Alexandria, Mansura, Maadi (Egypt)
Scott, Joseph Landor[39]	1898	PCI	Stellenbosch, Transval (SA)

35 Born in Chatsworth, Canada, 1856.
36 Born Listowel, Canada, 1868.
37 Born Drumrainey, County Down, Ireland, 1857.
38 Born in Tarsus, Turkey, 1871.
39 Born in Dungannon, Ireland, 1873.

Watson, Charles Roger[40]	1899	UPCNA	Amer. Univ. Cairo, Egypt
Giffen, Bruce Johnston[41]	1902	UPCNA	Egypt
Mitchell, David Russell[42]	1902	PCI/CoS	St. Andrew's Church, Alexandria, Egypt
Mackintosh, Finlay Grant[43]	1905	PCC	(Presbyt. College) Egypt
McCoy, William[44]	1905	PCUSA/PCSA ?	Krugersdorp, SA
Angus, Samuel[45]	1906	UFCS ?	Scotch Church, Algiers[46]
Smith, Frederick[47]	1913	PCE/PCI ?	Gold Coast, W. Africa
Robinson, Ralph Jay	1913	ARP/UPCNA	Assuit College, Egypt
Elder, Earl Edgar	1914	UPCNA	Egypt
MacKay, Callum Nicholson Miller[48]	1914	PCUSA/PCSA	Pretoria, Johannesburg, Boksburg
McNeill, Joseph	1917	PCUSA	Cameroun; Rio Benito, Guinea Espanola W. Africa
Davis, Roy Lee	1917	ARP	Egypt

---

40 Born in Cairo, Egypt of UP missionaries, in 1873.
41 Born in Ramle, Egypt of UP missionaries, in 1878.
42 Born in Belfast, Ireland, 1872.
43 Born in Pictou County, Canada, 1877.
44 Born in Belfast, Ireland 1875.
45 Born in Craigs, County Antrim, Ireland, 1881.
46 He was licensed and sent as a chaplain to the Algiers Scotch Church. He served there, 1911–1912 and he was a known specialist in North African Latin Christianity and Greek inscriptions. He became noted later for his theological divergencies.
47 Born in Bangor, County Down, Ireland, 1888.
48 Born in Torbreck, Scotland, 1878 and started his training at BTI, Glasgow.

Neely, Harry Campbell	1919	PCUSA	Lolodorf, Cameroun, West Africa
Hunt, James Galloway	1919	UPCNA	Cairo, Egypt
Neale, James Ralph	1920	UPCNA	Assuit, Egypt
May, Philip Jonathan	1922	PCUSA	Lolodorf, Cameroun
Moore, Leopold Paul Jr.	1923	PCUSA	Metet, Edea, Sakbayeme, Cameroun
Reed, Glenn Patterson	1923	UPCNA	Anglo-Egyptian Sudan
McClellan, Harvey Hutcheson	1924	UPCNA	Sudan
Newhouse, William Darst	1925	PCUSA	Lolodorf, Bafia, Metet, Cameroun
Grissett, Finley McCorvey	1925	PCUSA	Kribi, Cameroun
Reed, Arthur Grove[49]	1925	UPCNA	Alexandria, Egypt
Anderson, Llewellyn Kennedy[50]	1926	PCUSA	Bafia, Cameroun
Purdy, Ray Foote	1926	PCUSA/PCSA	Pretoria, SA
Armstrong, Klair Long	1927	PCUSA	American University, Cairo, Egypt
Duff, Clarence Walker	1927	PCUSA	Hosanna, Kambata, Southern Ethiopia
Woodbridge, Charles Jahleel[51]	1927	PCUSA	French Cameroun, W. Africa

---

49 Born in Fauoun, Egypt, 1904.
50 Born in Beauharnois, Quebec, Canada, 1900.
51 Born in Chinkiang, China, 1902.

Imrie, John Mark[52]	1927	PCUSA	Edea, Cameroun, W. Africa
Underhill, Irwin Winfield Jr.	1928	PCUSA	Sangamalina, Cameroun, W. Africa
Whittier, Chester Eugene	1928	PCUSA	Lolodorf Cameroun, W. Africa
Koning, John Willard	1930	PCUSA	Cameroun, W. Africa
Krug, Adolph Nicholas[53]	1929	PCUSA	Batenga, Efulen, Elat, W. Africa, Benito, Spanish Guinea; Foulassi, Cameroun

PART 2: DRCSA Students[54]

Name	Class Year	Degree	Location
Albertyn, Johannes Rudolph	1904	BD	Willowmore, Kimberley, SA
Rust, Hendrik Jacobus	1904	BD	Graaff-Reinet, Moorreesburg, SA
Malan, Daniël Gerhardus	1905	BD	Wellington, Cape Town, Paarl, prof. StellTS

---

52 Born Toronto, Canada, 1888. He studied at PTS from 1926–27, was ordained and went to Cameroun for three years then returned to PTS, exiting the second time in 1931.
53 Born Homberg, Germany, 1873.
54 Note for Part 2: South African born and returned to South Africa DRCSA (37 but 38 by including one wife who may have been an audit student but is officially listed in the *Catalogue*). Note by way of comparison: approximately 50 to 55 DRCSA students also went from South Africa to Scotland to train in theology between 1830 and 1931. They studied at Aberdeen University; University of Edinburgh; New College, Edinburgh (FCS then UFCS); and at St. Andrew's University. A special arrangement also allowed four students to obtain the St. Andrew's University BD in the early 1890s by taking it at Stellenbosch. The largest concentration of these students (38) studied at New College (FCS then UFCS), Edinburgh. This latter statistic is very comparable if not exact to the number of DRCSA students who went to Princeton Theological Seminary to study.

Perold, Jan Gabriel	1905	BD	Paarl, Victoria West, Lichtenburg, Mooirivier
Cillié, David Petrus	1906	BD	Worcester, Laingsburg, Blandfort, Johannesburg, Ventersburg
Kriel, Laurens Mathys	1906	BD	Cape Town, Vredenburg, Utrecht (SA)
Lategan, Daniel	1906	BD	Phillipstown, Miss. Instit. Wellington, Nu Bethesda, prof. StellenboschTS
Naudé, Willem Johannes	1906	BD	Kroonstad, Aliwal North
Malan, David Johannes	1908	BD	Queenstown, Darling
Retief, Jacobus Arnoldus	1908	BD	Mvera, Nyasaland, Nkhoma
Keet, Barend Bartholomeus[55]	1911		Paarl, Graaff-Reint, Prof. StellTS
van der Merwe, Jacobus Alwyn	1911	BD	Laingsburg, Calvinia
Barnard, Daniel Francois	1912	BD	Cape Town
Blignault, Jan Hendrik	1912		Smithfield
Fourie, Louis Johannes	1912		Jeppestown, Middleburg
Joubert, Daniel Stephanus Burger	1912	BD	Worcester, Potchefstroom
Nicol, William	1912	BD	SCA Cape Town, Johannesburg, Pretoria.

---

55 Continued his studies at Free University Amsterdam and obtained the ThD.

Roos, Johannes Daniel	1912		Zwartequs
Shaw, Petrus Johannes Bekker	1912		Kakamas
van Rooyen, Gert Cornelius	1912		Pretoria, Machadodorp, Durban
Hitchcock, Pieter Cornelius	1914		Barberton
Kriel, Jacobus Petrus	1914	BD	Kuilsriver
Steyn, Hendrik Pieter Marthinus	1916		Steytlerville, BFBS Cape Town
de Villiers, William Robertson	1916	BD	Stellenbosch, Tulbach, Bloemfontein
de Klerk, Peter William Abraham	1917		Mosselbaai
de Villiers, Dirk Christian	1917		Maitland
Rossouw, Servaas Hofmeyr	1917		Senekaly, Albertina, Swellendam
Snyman, Dwight Randolph	1921	BD	Woodstock, Stellenbosch
Weich, Stefanus Francois	1921	ThB, ThM	Kenhardt, Ottosdal
de Wet, Hendrik Adrian	1921		Boksburg, Pietermaritzburg, Rossville, Christina, SA; Lusaka, Northern Rhodesia & Southern Congo
de Wet, Hendrick Christoff	1922	ThM	Northern Rhodesia; Bloemfontein, SA
Greyling, Eben-Haëzer	1926	ThM	Tulbagh, SA
Greyling, Elizabeth Hermina	1926[56]		Andover (?), SA

---

56 The entry should be *studied at PTS 1925 and 1926*, hence class of 1926 but in the *Catalogue*, Elizabeth is listed as class of 1928.

Latsky, Peter Sterrenberg	1929	ThM	Cape Town
Louw, Daniel Johannes	1929	ThM	Citrusdal
Retief, Malcolm Wilhelm	1929	ThM	Madzi, Wayo, Northern Rhodesia
Botha, Louis Laurie Nel	1931	ThM	Middleburg, Ladysmith
Meiring, Arnoldus Mauritius	1931	ThM	Rondebosch

▲ Mission Institute, Wellington, South Africa.

Chapter 30

Jewish and Muslim Missions in Northern Africa

J. C. Whytock

Chapter Outline
1. Introduction
2. Scottish Presbyterians & Jewish Missions North Africa
3. The Scottish Society for the Conversion of Israel & the United Presbyterians: Algiers & Alexandria
4. Church of Scotland Jewish Missions: Ethiopia & Alexandria
5. Robert Kerr, The Federal Mission and the Central Morocco Mission
6. The North Africa Mission
7. The Southern Morocco Mission
8. Summary Conclusion

Inset: The Scotch Church, Algiers c.1880s to 1935

1. Introduction

North African missions are complex all on their own. First, what really is North Africa, a debated term today? Many see it as the modern five countries of Morocco, Algiers, Tunisia, Libya, and Egypt, and others may also include Sudan and Mauritania and on occasion some will also include Ethiopia. For our purposes, Ethiopia will be included here as we will be examining a very specific type of mission which will broaden out this chapter on North Africa.[1]

Mission work across North Africa was not straightforward with a single mission entity being involved within this large loosely defined region in the historic period of Presbyterian mission history. Part of the complexity of this, is that there have been various societies and faith missions involved, with churches also added into the mix. The other significant factor is that this has been a very closed area for regular mission activity and church planting. This chapter will concentrate on the involvement of Presbyterians through societies, churches, and faith missions in North Africa in a thematic line distinct from the chapters

---

1   An inclusion will be made to Ethiopia in section one as it pertains to Jewish evangelism.

which focused upon Egypt and Ethiopia and church missions of the American United Presbyterians. The predominant theme here gives attention to mission work to reach the Jewish and Muslim peoples of North Africa – an often-untold missions history from the historic period.

2. Scottish Presbyterians & Jewish Mission in North Africa

Introduction

The earliest Presbyterian mission concern for this region, as defined above as North Africa, was related to Jewish missions. We can trace this back to the Church of Scotland mission of inquiry in 1839.[2] The Scottish Presbyterian Church (CofS) was desirous to establish a mission to the Jews, so they sent forth a delegation (Robert Murray M'Cheyne, Andrew Bonar, Alexander Keith and Alexander Black) to survey the situation of the scattered Jewish communities and to create a full documentary report of their findings. In their *Narrative*, mention is made about the Jewish communities in Alexandria and in Cairo. The delegation also attended a synagogue in Alexandria and interviewed those in attendance. Of this visit nothing directly came as a mission result to North Africa in the immediate years which followed the *Narrative*. However, the seeds were planted, and interest awakened in evangelical Presbyterian Scotland and beyond. This *Narrative* was a catalyst for Jewish mission endeavour across the spectrum of Scottish Presbyterian branches. Presbyterians historically had an interest in Jewish evangelism. The Westminster Larger Catechism expressed this in the answer concerning the extension of the Kingdom in the Lord's Prayer and likewise in the Westminster *Directory of Public Worship*.[3] Further, North Africa in the 19th century still had large centres of Jewish population. Alexandria's Jewish diaspora was historically significant as it was a place associated with the Septuagint translation (the LXX for short). Numerically, there were significant numbers of Jews spread throughout North Africa and in Ethiopia in the 19th century. It is very difficult to get accurate numbers, but in many locations, it could be a few thousand in a city and in the Atlas Mountains, there were many

---

2 Andrew A. Bonar and Robert Murray M'Cheyne, *Narrative of a Mission of Inquiry to the Jews from the Church of Scotland in 1839*. Second Edition. (Edinburgh: William Whyte, 1842), 62ff. The latest print edition of this work has been edited by Allan Harman as *Mission of Discovery: The Beginnings of Modern Jewish Evangelism, the Journal of Bonar and McCheyne's Mission of Inquiry* (Fearn, UK: Christian Focus, 1966). Note, this work was also published by the Presbyterian Board of Publications in Philadelphia. It garnered great interest amongst various streams of Presbyterians..

3 Larger Catechism Q and A 191. Some have noted parallels between Scottish Presbyterians and Judaism: interest in the Psalms, the covenants, and Sabbath-keeping.

villages of Berber-speaking Jewish peoples and in other areas Arab-speaking Jews. The oldest grouping of Jews was generally referred to as the Maghrebi Jews and then came the Sephardic Jews from Spain/Portugal from the 14th century to the 16th. The two groups mixed so that by the mid-19th century in North Africa they were really intermingled in many locations. In Ethiopia during the 1860s numbers ranged between 50,000 to 200,000 of Falasha Jews, a distinct group from those in the Maghreb and Egypt. This contrasts with today where many of these Jews have dispersed out of North Africa and Ethiopia. For example, Morocco perhaps had as many as 250,000 Jews or more in the 19th century yet in the 21st century has perhaps 2,000.

At Pentecost there were Jews from modern Libya present and the man who carried the cross of Jesus was from Libya. He may have been a Jew from that diaspora community. Mark 15:21: *"And they compelled a passerby, Simon of Cyrene, who was coming in from the country, the father of Alexander and Rufus, to carry his cross"* and Acts 2:8, 10 *"And how is it that we hear, each of us in his own native language … Egypt and the parts of Libya belonging to Cyrene …"*. These two scripture texts give linkage to Jews in North Africa and set an attitude of historical perspective as we delve into our subject. In the mid-19th century, in Scotland and many other countries in the West, much interest developed about the conversion of the Jews and the second coming of Christ. This was an undercurrent for many to become involved with Jewish missions, although that is not the only reason. A broader perspective was that this was an unreached people group who needed to hear the gospel and be reached. Thus, there are various undertones giving the rationale for missions to the Jews but one constant was to see Jews come to faith in Jesus Christ the Messiah.[4]

3. The Scottish Society for the Conversion of Israel & the United Presbyterians: Algiers & Alexandria

We begin the story of Scottish Presbyterian Mission stations in North Africa with the establishment of a new society who was the first chronologically to establish a station in this region. In 1845 a Scottish Society that formed, originally called the Glasgow Christian Society on Behalf of the Jews. The name was changed in 1848 to the Scottish Society for the Conversion of Israel as a more encompassing society name. The mission statement of this Society was clearly stated in its name, which may sound blunt today: it was to see Jewish peoples

---

4 Many Scottish Presbyterians who supported and promoted Jewish missions were in the category of premillennialists. This would be more in the category of *historic premillennialist* than the modern understanding of dispensational premillennialists. Eschatology and prophecy were an uncurrent for some at this time but not all.

converted to faith in Jesus Christ the Messiah. Although it could be considered a nondenominational society, this Society was heavily supported and intertwined with the United Presbyterians in Scotland with only occasional congregational or individual member support from the Free Church, Reformed Presbyterian Church, and Congregational Churches.[5] The established Church of Scotland had its own mission to the Jews, as did also the Free Church of Scotland but not with stations at this time in North Africa.

In 1850 the Scottish Society for the Conversion of Israel established a mission station in Algiers with Rev. Dr Herman Philip[6] as its pioneer missionary ordained by the United Presbyterian Church for service with this Society. Two years later, in 1852, Philip pioneered a second mission station for the Society and was transferred to Alexandria, Egypt where he and Rev. R. G. Brown established a school in June 1854.[7] Rev. Benjamin Weiss[8] became the missionary of the Algiers station in 1852, replacing Philip, and Weiss would remain there until the early 1860s. While under Weiss, the mission in Algiers had for several years the assistance of a former Roman Catholic Italian priest J. B. Campazzi, and of colporteurs to distribute materials in different languages. Weiss would periodically go on tours inland to the Atlas Mountains (presumably in modern-day Morocco) visiting villages where he could find Jewish people and speak and distribute literature.[9] One report stated that two rabbis were baptised in Algiers by Weiss. There seems to have been much confusion and tension between Weiss and the United Presbyterian Church about this mission in its latter years. The Scottish United Presbyterians took over the Society in 1856/57 yet the American United Presbyterians would also assume some of the Societies' former work in Egypt a couple years later, also to make matters a little more confusing!

Likewise, the Scottish United Presbyterian Church who had taken over the Society's stations in Algiers decided to hand-over this mission station to the

---

5 Two prominent names in the Free Church who seem periodically connected to this Society were Professor "Rabbi" John Duncan and Rev. Andrew Bonar by speaking and attending annual meetings on occasion.
6 Dr Philip was the son of a German Rabbi. He was converted and worked with the Church of Scotland in Jassy, modern Iaşi, Romania, 1841, before associating with the Society for the Conversion of Israel in 1850. Catherine Edwards, *Missionary Life Among the Jews in Moldavia, Galicia and Silesia: Memoir and Letters.* (London: Hamilton, Adams & Co., 1867), 52. Philip was ordained on 7 August 1850 in Edinburgh, *United Presbyterian Magazine*, (Sept 1850), 426.
7 He would have one colleague sent out by the Society for three years, Rev. R. Grant Brown, 1853–56. *The Friends of Israel*, 52.
8 Weiss wrote two commentaries while in Algiers, one on Ecclesiastes and the other on Psalms, the latter which one finds reference to in Spurgeon's *Treasury of David*. B. Weiss, *Psalms ...* (Edinburgh: Oliphants, 1858).
9 *The Friends of Israel*, 299.

Union of Evangelical Churches in France. This French Church appointed Rev. M. Ribard as the pastor of the congregation in Algiers and in charge of the mission station and its Bible colportage work, school, and village missions. The United Presbyterians continued to send an annual grant for the Algiers station but did not directly appoint any personnel to this station and left that with the French Church.

In Alexandria, Egypt, the mission was both educational missions for Jewish children and others *and* medical missions for Jews and others. There was also Jewish literature distribution to those travelling from across North Africa who were Jewish passing through Alexandria. Likewise, Jews were fleeing Crimea because of war at this time and were settling in Alexandria and Rev. Philip was also involved with reaching out and ministering to these Jews from Crimea. The Scottish Society for the Conversion of Israel had also established a Girls School in Alexandria in 1856 focussing upon Jewish children. Miss Pringle from Elgin, Scotland was sent by the Society to establish this school and was funded by the Ladies Association in Paisley. This Girls' school for Jewish girls was transferred over to the newly organised American United Presbyterian Mission in 1858/9 and Rev. Gulian Lansing and Miss Sarah Dales of that mission. This school also had John Hogg of Scotland serve at it while he had started a Boys' School in Alexandria at the same time which again would be taken over by the American UPs in 1858/9.[10]

In 1856 there was a proposal to establish The Protestant College of Alexandria under the auspices of the Scottish Society for the Conversion of Israel in addition to the Girls' School in Alexandria. John Hogg, a member of the Scottish United Presbyterian Church was recruited by the Society to become the teacher and went later that year.[11] Hogg's connection to this Society was actually short-lived as the Society handed-over its four stations to the Scottish United Presbyterian Church in 1857/58 and the Scottish United Presbyterian Church decided to consolidate the inherited Society work all to Algiers.[12] Hogg was realigned with the American United Presbyterian Church and its mission in Egypt. The story is worth thinking over as it shows a common reality in missions, often they are begun by a Society and supported by churches who in the end may inherit the

---

10 Jeffrey C. Burke, "The Establishment of the American Presbyterian Mission in Egypt, 1854–1940: an Overview" (unpublished PhD thesis, McGill University, Montreal, 2000), 103–105.
11 Rena L. Hogg, *A Master-Builder on the Nile: Being a Record of the Life and Aims of John Hogg, DD.* (New York: Revell, 1914), 67. John Hogg's wife's uncle was Hope Waddell of the Jamaican Mission and also of the Calabar Mission. Hogg ended up serving in the Girls' School also and the proposed College never came into fruition.
12 The Scottish Society for the Conversion of Israel's four mission stations were: Hamburg, Glasgow, Algiers, and Alexandria.

Society's work. Hogg's initial involvement in Egypt is often ignored or forgotten, so it is good to see it first in its overall context.

The United Presbyterian Church of Scotland did not abandon its Jewish mission in North Africa completely after withdrawing its own personnel in Algiers and Alexandria. It continued to help with finances for the Algiers station and expressed a desire to open a new station in the early 1880s. This latter vision was to become the Federal Mission in Morocco and we will follow this as a separate point in this chapter. Statistically it is very difficult to ascertain how many Jewish people became Christians through this Society's and the Scottish UP's direct work in Algiers or Egypt over the decade of the 1850s.

4. The Church of Scotland Jewish Missions: Ethiopia & Alexandria

Another often untold story, was for about six years in the 1860s there was a Scottish Presbyterian mission undertaken by the Church of Scotland to the Falasha Jews in Ethiopia.[13] The chief missionaries or "agents" as it reads in official reports, were Wilhelm Staiger[14] and Brandeis who endured together with others incredible deprivations and imprisonment under Emperor Theodore.[15] After they were released at the instigation of the British Army this mission field was abandoned in 1868.

Briefly the Church of Scotland undertook itinerating Jewish missions also in Tunis. The chief station however for the CofS mission to Jews was in Alexandria which began in 1858 centred upon schools and reached a high of 400 Jewish children in their Alexandrian mission schools. Again, the Scottish mission kept to the double-pronged strategy of education and evangelism.[16] One of their

---

13 There are various theories about the origins of the Falasha Jews often referred now as Beta Israel. See David Kessler, *The Falasha: A Short History of the Ethiopian Jews*. Third Revised Edition (London: Frank Cass, 1996). The Falasha Jewish community numbers about 180,000 today in Israel. "Falasha Jews Demand a City of Their Own in Israel" July 29, 2020, *Asharq Al-awsat*, accessed 19 March 2021. https://english.aawsat.com/home/article/2418436/falasha-jews-demand-city-their-own-israel

14 Staiger was "lent" from the Basler Pilgermission to this new CofS mission to Ethiopia. By "lent" it means the CofS provided the funding. After Ethiopia, Staiger went to serve in the CofS Jewish mission in Alexandria for three years and then to Beirut in the CofS mission there for 33 years.

15 Yaron Perry, "German Mission in Abyssinia: Wilhelm Staiger from Baden, 1835–1904," *Aethiopica: International Journal of Ethiopian and Eritrean Studies* 11 (2008), 48–60.

16 There are no mention of these Church of Scotland Jewish mission works in Africa in Hewat, *Vision and Achievement,* nor that of the United Presbyterian Church and its work to Jews in North Africa. This is the forgotten story of African Presbyterian mission work.

missionaries there for 22 years was Rev. James Yule originally from Ireland. At least twelve ordained ministers served this Jewish mission in Alexandria, many staying two to three years, some up to ten years. Several taught in the schools as part of their mission work or also served at either St. Andrew's Church of Scotland in Alexandria or at St. Andrew's Church of Scotland, Cairo.[17] This mission continued through to the early 1900s.

Summary to points 1-4

From 1850 into the 1860s the Scottish Society for the Conversion of Israel and latterly directly the United Presbyterian Church in Scotland had conducted mission work focusing upon Jewish peoples in the areas of Algiers and Alexandria. It was a multifaceted mission in each location with various methods employed. The difficulty was that to be limited to Jewish peoples was too narrow and the reality was the mission in each station became much broader in focus ministering also to Arab and Berber Muslims, Europeans, and Coptic Christians.

John M'Kerrow wrote about the United Presbyterian Church and its mission to the Jews:

> The mission to the Jews, undertaken by the United Presbyterian Synod, has hitherto proved, in a great measure, unsuccessful. There is great difficulty in missionaries getting access to the Jews; and when they do get access to them, they have more than ordinary prejudice and bigotry to contend with. Those who have the courage to become converts, are persecuted with the bitterest hostility by their friends and acquaintances. In very many instances they lose their means of subsistence, and they are obliged to change their place of residence, and to seek for a livelihood among strangers.[18]

The story of mission work to the Jewish peoples has been one of hard labour and few rewards. Such was the case it seems also in the 19th century in Algiers and Alexandria and also in Tunis and Ethiopia. It is not generally viewed as the

---

17 *Fasti Ecclesiae Scoticanae*, volume seven, the section on C of S Jewish missions, 713–717 and also for the two St. Andrew's congregations, 557. I have found twelve as having served in Alexandria for the Jewish work, in addition to Steiger as above, all ordained while serving except one (Duncan): George Brown, William Charteris, Peter Donaldson, Hugh Duncan, David Fenwick, William Kean, George Munro Mackie, William Frank Scott, Daniel Scrimgeour, William M. Tait, Malcolm T. Shiell, and James W. Yule. It is harder to find lists of the female teachers – one was Miss Calder.

18 M'Kerrow, *United Presbyterian Missions*, 497.

star of mission success and has often been forgotten in the history of Christian missions. The Society for the Conversion of Israel and the United Presbyterian Church and its mission in Algiers and Alexandria has been overshadowed by the Scottish mission work of the CofS and of the FC in Budapest and Jaffa in the 1840s which became the prominent story in Jewish missions so the work of the Society for the Conversion of Israel and the UP Church in North Africa were greatly eclipsed. Although CofS Jewish mission work in Tunis and Alexandria has also often been overshadowed as well in light of Hungary, yet in terms of personnel the list of involvement in Alexandria is very long and spans over thirty years. Likewise, the story of the CofS Mission to the Falasha in Ethiopia is virtually forgotten.

5. Robert Kerr, the Federal Mission and the Central Morocco Mission

i) A Federal Mission to Morocco

We have already seen that the Scottish United Presbyterian Church had desires for a new mission station for Jewish missions in the 1880s. This became a reality in the Federal Mission between the Scottish UP Church and the Presbyterian Church of England.[19] (The Presbyterian Church of England, or a branch of it before the 1876 union, had established its own Jewish Missions Committee and was active in Jewish missions work particularly in London.[20])

A Scottish UP medical doctor was selected for this new Jewish Federal Mission station in Rabat, Morocco. Dr.

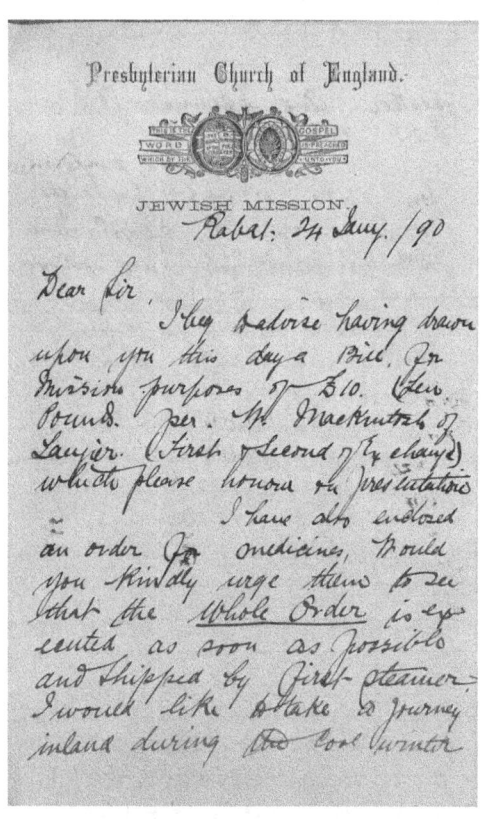

▲ Letter of Robert Kerr on PCE Jewish Mission Letterhead

---

19 For more details about the Federal Mission concept see, Whytock, "Robert Kerr & Morocco," (forthcoming).
20 The English Presbyterian Church was aiding in Tangiers with donations to work there through NAM before it opened its station in Rabat. The English Presbyterian Church supported its own missionaries to the Jews in London. Prominent missionaries there were Dr Schwartz and Rev. Theodore Meyer. *The Messenger & Missionary Record of the Presbyterian Church of England*, (London: James Nisbet, 1871), 17, 154.

Robert Kerr (1855–1918) had been serving in Glasgow with the Glasgow City Mission for almost five years doing evangelistic work and medical work. Kerr was chosen to be the pioneer medical missionary for the new Federal Mission to both Jews and Muslims in Morocco in 1886. The Scottish UPC provided a grant to the PCE for this Federal Mission work in Morocco and the CFM of the Scottish UPC gave their blessing to sending out their son under the PCE Jewish Committee banner. It appears that the grant was for seven years from the UPCS to the PCE Committee for Jewish Missions.[21] Kerr was commissioned (or a valedictory service as they were then called) twice, first in Glasgow by the UPs and then at a special service held at Highbury Park Presbyterian Church, London on 17 February 1886 by the PCE for this pioneering mission to Morocco. Kerr arrived at Rabat, Morocco on 2 March 1886.[22]

Kerr entered central Morocco in 1886 shortly after the new North Africa Mission (NAM) faith mission had begun their work further north in Morocco. He was a close associate of many in NAM and often joined them when able for joint prayer gatherings and fellowship times and assisted in their work throughout the years. When he first arrived his first task was to locate a house and a building for a clinic in Rabat. This was not easy to do as he was Christian and there was much opposition for Muslims to lease buildings to a Christian in Rabat. There were separate quarters of the city where Muslims lived and Jews must live and the Europeans or others.

▲ Gateway to Rabat, Morocco

Kerr had a gift as a writer and communicator. He authored two books, *Pioneering in Morocco*, and *Morocco After Twenty-Five Years*[23] which give us a real glimpse into his character, mission work, and the peoples with whom he ministered. He was also a popular speaker whenever back in Britain speaking in many Presbyterian churches – UP, Free, then United Free, and PCE and also for conventions such as for the Mildmay Missions to the Jews.

In the first book, *Pioneering in Morocco*, we find the theme of spiritual darkness a prominent element, in keeping with so many scriptures which speak of the

---

21 Kerr, *Morocco After Twenty-Five Years*, 222–224.
22 Kerr, *Morocco After Twenty-Five Years*, 224.
23 Robert Kerr, *Pioneering in Morocco: A Record of Seven Years' Medical Mission Work in the Palace and the Hut* (London: Allenson, 1894) and *Morocco After Twenty-Five Years* (London: Murray & Evendon, 1912).

darkness of this world without the light of the gospel.[24] For example, he recorded with exacting detail two very strange religious groups that he encountered in Rabat, the *Aissau-i-as*, popularly known as "the sheep-eaters" since they devour live sheep, and the other the *Hamaja* who would cut their heads and spill blood and drink it from each other, hence popularly known as "the head cutters."[25] It seems these were both some type of off-shoots from Islam developed by individual, self-appointed leaders and developed as a type of folk religion. He was not trying to be a sensationalist in his writing, rather recording what he witnessed and then compared it to what the Bible said about such practices as signs of spiritual darkness. His goal in writing *Pioneering* was to lead "many to take an interest in Dark Morocco" and to help them see that here the "Missionary enterprise in Morocco must always be twofold, as we have to combat with Mohammedanism [in all its forms and off-shoots] and Judaism." He showed that medical missions were a way to gain access to some homes and hearts, but the opposition was immense.[26] An interesting story he relates was about vaccinating against small-pox as there was a terrible epidemic but the resistance was strong by many Jews and Muslims. Many held to "a superstitious belief that if all their children are vaccinated by a Christian he will insert a small quantity of blood, and sooner or later they are sure to become Christians."[27]

Kerr spoke openly how he saw Islam, "The Koran is at variance with every fundamental truth in the gospel, and Islam can only be called a vindictive and licentious religion ..." He expanded with examples of the nature of this vindictive religion (as he calls it) which encourages licentious living which Kerr likened to the ancient Epicureans.[28] He likewise made a study of the Jewish faith as practised in Rabat and concluded:

> Regarding God's ancient people, in many respects (with all their faults) they are unique, and a standing monument to the *truth* of God ... The purity of their lives, compared with their Moslem neighbours', an unprejudiced observer cannot fail to see ... One often wonders how the Jews should fail to see, from Daniel ix and Isaiah liii, that the Messiah has come, and that He must needs die – a Sacrifice for sin once for all ... (2 Cor. 3:14).[29]

---

24 Such as Ephesians 5: 7–14.
25 Kerr, *Pioneering*, 38–40.
26 Kerr, *Pioneering*, 5,9.
27 Kerr, *Pioneering*, 86.
28 Kerr, *Pioneering*, 6–7.
29 Kerr, *Pioneering*, 7–8.

ii) A Faith Mission: The Central Morocco Mission

Kerr was supported by the Federal Mission for eight years (1886–1894), primarily through the grant from the Scottish UP Church. He was ordained by the PCE as a ruling elder after serving five years as a medical missionary in Morocco. Then after eight years Kerr resigned from the Federal Mission and tendered his notice to the Jewish Mission Committee of the PCE, who was the overseeing body for this Federal Mission. In essence Kerr believed that the Committee did not have proper respect for himself and the work. It also seemed that there was not universal sympathy within the PCE for this mission field in Morocco, and in the end, basically handed over the mission to the Kerrs inclusive of the lease for the mission compound in Rabat to be assumed by the continuing mission.[30] Dr Kerr and his wife saw the great need for mission work in central Morocco as did others and thus the mission took on a new name and became a *faith mission of sorts*[31] but still primarily funded by the Scottish UPs. It was known after May 1894 as the Central Morocco Mission.[32] It focused primarily upon Rabat, Salee, and Casablanca, and also Meqinez radiating out from these centres and with its centre of operations remaining the Medical Mission House in Rabat. The mission averaged about four or five workers and at its height had eight associated as missionary workers with it. Today, we would call Kerr's approach holistic missions, but a holistic mission which was boldly to speak verbally about Jesus Christ and the scriptures, never divorced from deeds of compassion and love.[33] Another way to see this mission is to see it in terms of the David Bebbington formulation of evangelicalism. It was clearly evangelistic in approach, focused upon discipleship and preaching, the extensive use of literature, schooling in an informal manner, and medical missions. The stated objective of the CMM was:

---

30 See, Whytock, "Robert Kerr & Morocco," (forthcoming) for a more detailed chronology of his resignation from the Federal Mission.
31 The fullest work on faith missions is, Klaus Fiedler, *The Story of Faith Missions: From Hudson Taylor to Present day Africa*. (Oxford: Regnum,1994). A faith mission is usually defined by an approach to financial support as trusting in the Lord and is generally interdenominational. It is not always an adequate term to use as also some societies operated much along that same principle at times as denominational missions. There is a need for some allowance of nuance of thinking here.
32 It is often stated that the CMM mission was founded in 1886 which was the year the Kerr's went to Morocco. It would appear that the central mission office for the UK from 1894 and for several years was at 18 Dunard Street, Glasgow and the secretary was James Easton.
33 Thorsten Prill "Evangelical Mission Organisations, Postmodern Controversies, and the New Heartbeat of Mission" *Foundations* 61.2 (2011), 7. Prill sees this type of approach in contrast with much of modern missions talk on holistic mission which diminishes the verbal proclamation of the Gospel.

> To carry the Gospel to the Jews, Moors, Arabs, and Berbers in Central Morocco; to supply the sick with medical advice and medicine, and to teach and circulate the Scriptures and religious literature.[34]

Statistically this mission did an impressive medical work and helped open doors between cultures in the name of Christ. Often Kerr saw well over 5,000 patients annually, sometimes closer to 9,000 plus in addition his numerous house visits to Jewish homes to see the sick, his Bible and Christian literature work, that also of his wife's work at the medical mission house and hospital, Sunday services and Bible studies, it was an incredible ministry of being spent in the service of the Master. The medical missionary couple (both were physicians), the Darmonds, were associated with CMM and served in Casablanca. Israel Darmond was a converted Moroccan Jew who before his medical training had been an assistant with a missionary friend of Dr Kerr.[35] The Darmonds focused very much upon Jewish work in Casablanca.

Kerr also is a bridge between the Presbyterian denominational church missions to Jews and Muslims in Morocco and the faith missions which also emerged at this same period. Kerr did mission work for both a denominational body and also for a faith mission but he also was linked to two other faith missions operative in Morocco, namely the North Africa Mission and the Southern Morocco Mission. There are many lines of overlap and interplay between all three of these bodies. For example, David Muir came out as a Scottish Missionary to work with the Southern Morocco Mission but did six-months training first with Dr Robert Kerr in Rabat. Kerr knew John Anderson of Ardrossan the founder of the Southern Morocco Mission before Morocco as both were Scots and travelled in much the same evangelical circles in West Scotland. Likewise, female missionaries of the North Africa Mission would stay and help at the Medical Mission of Kerr in Rabat. Thus, these three missions laboured alongside each other as brothers and sisters in Christ sharing the same evangelical passion for mission and the conversion of souls.

▲ Dr Kerr setting out to Sallee on visitation when it was all barricaded, and all other Europeans afraid to go in for fear of their lives

---

34 Beach & Burton, *World Statistics*, 36.
35 Whytock, "Robert Kerr & Morocco," (forthcoming).

The Central Morocco Mission annual reports virtually read like a UP and then United Free Church mission society and also some from the PCE as a sponsored mission society.[36] Technically it would be placed in the category of faith missions but in reality, operated more like an UP and then United Free voluntary missionary society. This does raise a question about the widespread popular image of a faith mission. It also does show that in North Africa denominational missions did not generally result in church establishment and thus more independent missions often arose.

Robert Kerr died in Morocco in 1918. The hope had been that his son William would return and be in charge of the CMM. However, with the war and the son's role in the Royal Army Medical Corps it seems that the mission merged or was unable to be sustained. It has been very difficult to locate the archives of the CMM thus there are some unanswered questions about what exactly happened to this mission after Kerr's death in 1918. Nevertheless, the total years of this Federal and then CMM mission was at least 32 years.[37]

6. The North Africa Mission

The North Africa Mission (NAM) had its origins as the *Mission to the Kabyles and Other Berber Races* in 1881 when the first team of four missionaries went to Algeria: George Pearse, Henri Mayor, Edward Glenny and Selim Zeytoun. The Pearses had previously been in Algiers ministering to French troops but had met the Kaybles. They were burdened for them and shared this with Henry Grattan Guinness and from this came the formalised mission of 1881. Glenny would be the driving force behind this mission for several years and helped expand and develop it. He was open Brethren in orientation in the spirit and ethos of George Mueller and Hudson Taylor. The mission name was changed in 1888 to the North Africa Mission (NAM) which again reflected the realities of mission in a complex context where singling out one grouping was often not wise. In 19 years, this mission grew to 115 missionaries ministering in Morocco, Algeria, Tunisia, Libya and Egypt.[38] It attracted workers from the open Brethren, Baptist churches in the UK and Southern States, a variety of different Presbyterians, Anglicans and others. Typically, faith missions are interdenominational and labour together for evangelistic work, colportage work, skills development, and medical purposes.

---

36 *Central Morocco Mission, Annual Report, 1915–16*. (Glasgow: Pickering & Inglis, 1916). One of the annual subscribers was Sir J. P. Maclay who also supported the SMM and Lovedale. The directors tended to be UP/UF ministers and lay business or medical leaders.
37 Whytock, "Robert Kerr & Morocco," (forthcoming).
38 See Francis R. Steele, *Not in Vain: The Story of the North Africa Mission* (Pasadena, CA: William Carey Library, 1981), chapter 2, 13–39 on the beginnings of the NAM.

One of the early workers serving a variety of tasks was Hughina Tulloch (1845–1886) who went with NAM to Tangiers, Morocco to help with the children of a missionary family and do medical mission work there. She contracted typhoid and died in December 1886 having served but two years. She was the first NAM missionary to die on the field of which there were many. A hospital was established in Tangiers and named in her memory, the Tulloch Memorial Hospital, a pioneering endeavour in that region. Hughina Tulloch's father was a Free Church of Scotland minister at Eddrachillis in Sutherland-shire.[39] It is uncertain if she went out as a lay Free Church member or not to the mission. The faith missions also like the societies gave room for the laity to serve in their ranks and thus they attracted a wide-range of denominational evangelical workers. It is difficult to conclusively say how many Presbyterians served with NAM as denominational labels are seldom used in official literature of the faith missions. Also, since the workers were outside of denominational structures, they were not always recorded as missionaries of that denomination. This was often before secondment agreements or recognition as serving with another agency, as is often the case today by many denominations.

One family name associated with NAM that is Presbyterian is the name of Steele. Francis Rue Steele (1915-2004)[40] was a teaching elder (ordained 15 December 1958) first in the Evangelical Presbyterian Church, then into the merged denomination of the Reformed Presbyterian Church, Evangelical Synod, and then was received into the Presbyterian Church in America through joining and receiving.[41] He had a tremendous impact on recruiting and helping many find their way into mission work to Muslims. He was a missionary statesman in his own right and spoke much about mission work to Muslims and travelled extensively in the Muslim world. Steele included selections from their 1957 diary of speaking ministry across North Africa in his book, *Not In Vain*.[42] He served first on the council of NAM its American branch for three years (1949–1953), and then as director and minister-at-large for NAM for 37 years, for a total of 40 years with NAM, and also authored its history. He had been associate professor of Assyriology at the University of Pennsylvania and the assistant curator of the Babylonian Section of the University

---

39 Rev. George Tulloch, 1793–1880.
40 https://thisday.pcahistory.org/2017/09/september-7-francis-rue-steele-1915-2004/
41 Francis R. Steele served on the committee on translation in 1966 for the NIV. The other Presbyterians on that committee were R. Laird Harris and Edmund Clowney. His father, Edward A. Steele was also involved with NAM and served on the North America Council of NAM. Note the Evangelical Presbyterian Church had come out of the Bible Presbyterian Church. Prominent names in the EPC were Francis Schaeffer and Robert Reymond. This denomination is not to be confused with a latter denomination of that same name in the United States.
42 Steele, *Not In Vain*, 91–106.

Museum. He served with NAM during Dr Ian Malcolm Tait's time on the British Council of NAM and also while Tait taught for six years at Covenant College and Covenant Seminary in the USA. Thus, the NAM connections run in various directions in America in Presbyterian interest and support.

7. The Southern Morocco Mission

The Southern Morocco Mission's origins are with John Anderson (c.1842–1926) who was in Morocco in 1887 for health-recovery purposes. Anderson was a prominent Scottish layman, Bible teacher, evangelist, mission organiser, Bible school educator, and editor of the periodical *The Reaper* and in latter years a Presbyterian preacher at St. Andrew's Presbyterian Church, East London, South Africa. He helped establish the Ayrshire Christian Union and worked as a shipping agent at Ardrossan. During his Morocco trip he met Dr Robert Kerr who aided his recovery and together they discussed the need for a new mission in the south. Likewise, Anderson met with Edward Glenny of the newly established NAM and discussed sending workers from Scotland from the evangelistic work there to Morocco to serve. Glenny also suggested the needs in southern Morocco were vast and encouraged Anderson to launch a new mission focusing upon the south. Thus, in a gracious way a new mission was formed with a specific unreached geographic area. The Southern Morocco Mission was born in 1888 with the advisement of Kerr of the Federal Mission and Glenny of NAM and the support initially of the Ayrshire Christian Union. Recruits followed from the west of Scotland who would join this mission – names like Cuthbert Nairn, Jessie Nairn, James Haldane, David Muir, and Hugh Paton. The brother and sister Nairns would be the first missionaries to serve in this new field. Following language studies, they took up the work and opened a new mission station in Marrakesh as the earliest Protestant missionaries to reside there.[43]

One SMM missionary, Hugh Paton, a Free Church student at the Bible Training Institute (BTI), was one of the top students there and was recruited by Anderson for the SMM. Paton served three years in Morocco with SMM, returning to Scotland at the end of 1899. When back in Scotland Paton was a noted speaker for the SMM, sharing the platform with Alexander Whyte and spoke to large audiences raising the profile of this mission field. Paton concluded his ministry as an ordained Presbyterian minister and evangelist in Australia.[44]

---

43 Geoffrey Grogan, "Bible Training Institute to Glasgow Bible College," in *Traditions of Theology in Glasgow 1450–1990: A Miscellany*, ed. William Ian P. Hazlett (Edinburgh: Scottish Academic Press, 1993), 75–78; Steele, *Not in Vain*, 126–135.

44 Susan E Emilson, "Hugh Paton," *Australian Dictionary of Evangelical Biography*, accessed on 24 March 2021, https://sites.google.com/view/australian-dictionary-of-evang/home

Paton was born in Largs, Ayrshire. Ayrshire was a good base of the SMM as also for the CMM.

Anderson became the principal at the Bible Training Institute in Glasgow in 1892 and remained in that post through to 1913.[45] The Southern Morocco Mission and the BTI were very intertwined during these years as once a home council was formed for the SMM the office was at the BTI and most of the recruits to the mission attended the BTI. A member of the General Council for many years of SMM was Sir Joseph Paton MacLay, the noted shipping magnate of the time and committed evangelical Presbyterian Christian. He was also the supporter of the Lovedale Bible School in South Africa and of the Kerr's Central Morocco Mission (CMM). MacLay also visited the mission fields in Morocco several times. The SMM also had a very active Ladies Auxiliary which was vital to the financial needs of the mission.

SMM was interdenominational or as some might prefer to call it nondenominational or trans denominational and comes out of the context of the revivals which had taken place in West Scotland and also the evangelistic ministry of different evangelists in Ayrshire and Glasgow. Thus, the connections to the Ayrshire Christian Union, the Glasgow United Evangelistic Association, and also the Glasgow Medical and City Missions are all very strong and the common linkage. It was the atmosphere of encouraging laity to do evangelistic work or other types of Christian ministry and service. With the Bible Training Institute in Glasgow being developed there was a training centre for both foreign missions and home missions work then for laity – the "gap" men and women – through this bible school, which was all part of a growing network of such bible schools that were developing in the 19th and early 20th centuries. The largest denominational group of students at the BTI in the first 40 years came from Free Church, and the United Presbyterians, a close second, and then as the merged United Free.[46] These students along with others had been impacted by revivals and evangelistic ministries and a desire to serve the Lord but did not have university education. The SMM was the logical overseas mission for them to join and hence we find a strong link to Free and United Free personnel and support.

---

45 Frank Waddleton, "The Bible Training Institute, Glasgow." (Unpublished Diploma in Adult Education, University of Glasgow, 1979).

46 Graham Jonathan Cheesman, "Training for Service: An Examination of Change and Development in the Bible College Movement in the UK, 1873–2002" (unpublished PhD thesis, Queen's University, Belfast, 2004), 57.

> ***Southern Morocco Mission***[47]
> ***Origin*** – Founded in 1888 under circumstances which conveyed a clear and imperative call to take up work in a needy and **unoccupied** part of the Mission Field.
> ***Object*** – To carry the Gospel to the Moors, Jews, Arabs, and Berber tribes of South Morocco, and the regions beyond.
> ***Methods*** – Preaching the Gospel; Medical Work in Hospitals, Dispensaries, and in the People's Homes; Female Missions to the Women; Children's Homes and Classes; Itineration; and Scripture Distribution.
> ***Support*** – The Mission is supported entirely by the free-will offerings of the Lord's people. Its needs are laid before God in prayer, and information regarding the work is given in the Organ of the Mission, or otherwise.

The SMM established four mission stations in southern Morocco and then worked out from those: Marrakesh, Mogador, Mazagan, and Saffi. These were unreached areas and also the villages beyond each. Several mission schools were established first for girls and then also for boys. These were consistent with the model of the two-fold Scottish ideal of evangelism and education being handmaids. Local Moroccans also in time were trained and involved in these mission schools. From the very beginning SMM was involved in medical mission work. This was the primary avenue of mission which Cuthbert Nairn and his wife focused upon. This work grew so that up to 50,000 patients visited this medical mission and the other dispensaries annually. Cuthbert Nairn died a martyr's death in 1944 at the medical mission in Marrakesh having served there for 56 years. A daily register kept for 45 years by the SMM dispensaries recorded 1,200,000 people availed themselves of the services of the medical mission work. At the medical mission and at the dispensaries enquirers classes for converts and enquirers were conducted, and Bible classes were also held along with literature work. A night Shelter was also run by the SMM, averaging about 60 men each night. This was one of the mission works of James Haldane (1886–1973)[48] and his wife for many years. James Haldane was a noted Arabic linguist and itinerant preacher across

---

47 *Southern Morocco Mission: A Review of the Work, 1914.* (Glasgow: Pickering & Inglis, 1914), 13. This printed synopsis as given here remained basically constant from the beginning of the mission until it amalgamated with NAM officially in 1961.
48 See, Gordon Fyles, "The Life of James Haldane: A North African Investment in Mission," *The Banner of Truth,* Issues 191–92 (1979), 12–28. Haldane also wrote three works: *Missionary Romance in Morocco, Morocco in Mufti,* and *Trekking Among Moroccan Tribes.* Haldane served 39 years in Morocco and became the field superintendent of the SMM in 1935, retiring in 1951.

over 1,000 villages in southern Morocco. The women missionaries, single and married, of SMM were actively engaged in addition to teaching in the mission schools or assisting in the medical work with extensive visitation to Muslim women in their homes. For 25 years David Muir engaged in Jewish mission work for SMM in the Jewish quarters (Millahs) in the southern cities and towns and into the villages in the Atlas Mountains. "The command to preach the Gospel to every creature embraces these persecuted Israelites, and one of our missionaries, Mr. David Muir felt called to devote himself for their evangelisation."[49]

The SMM, laboured closely with NAM and CMM. All three missions also were supportive of the Mildmay Mission to the Jews when it did itinerant work in Morocco amongst the Jews. In the late 1950s SMM became affiliated with NAM and then formally in 1961, SMM joined NAM basically in a joining and receiving arrangement. The Scottish central office for SMM/NAM remained in Glasgow.

8. Summary Conclusion

The missionaries of this chapter saw themselves as committed to what the Apostle Paul was called to do. They laboured amidst many trials and misunderstandings seeing this as the cost they were called to bear for the Lord. From the first mission work of the Society for the Conversion of Israel working in Algiers and Alexandria, *to* the labours of the Church of Scotland in Ethiopia, *to* that of the Federal Mission of the Scottish UPC and the Presbyterian Church of England Jewish Committee and Robert Kerr in central Morocco and what became the Central Morocco Mission, *to* the work of the North Africa Mission, and *to* the Southern Morocco Mission, there was an abiding commitment to evangelism and conversion and the bringing of Gospel light to all peoples. It is one of the forgotten chapters of mission history in Africa. There is need for more research and discussion about these denominational and faith missions and their relationship to Scottish, English, and American Presbyterian Churches. In popular missions' history there is virtually no mention of Presbyterians working in Morocco etc. and it is usually perceived as a Brethren or an early Pentecostal field yet the above shows that it is all much more complex than that popular image and that in particular this was the domain of lay Presbyterian missionaries as well.

In reviewing this chapter, one is immediately struck by the radical shift from these historic missions and the emphasis on evangelism and conversion to the post-modern, pluralistic or postmodern age of today where such goals are

---

49 *Southern Morocco Mission: A Review of the Work, 1921.* (Glasgow: Pickering & Inglis, 1921), 9.

muted or often not seen as primary. To many it will all sound very antiquarian and difficult to fathom that the essence of missions expressed here must centre upon the aim of conversion.

Questions for study (fact type):
1 Who were the Falasha Jews? Who were the Sephardic Jews? Who were the Berber Jews?
2 Describe the 1839 Scottish Mission of Inquiry visit to Egypt. Who was in the delegation?
3 Where was the first mission station in Africa established by the Scottish Society for the Conversion of Israel? Describe those who laboured at this mission.
4 What was the Federal Mission to Morocco?
5 Identify these three faith missions: CMM, NAM, and SMM.

Questions for study (reflective type):
1 Discuss if in this chapter there are illustrations supportive or not of the Bebbington quadrilateral definition of evangelical.
2 Discuss how you see mission work to the Jewish people today from scripture. In your answer consider the following amongst other matters: Is there a mandate for evangelism today? Is this to be a matter of intercessory prayer? Where do the Jews live today?

Select Bibliography

Beginnings with Jewish Missions

Bonar, Andrew A. and Robert Murray M'Cheyne, *Narrative of a Mission of Inquiry to the Jews from the Church of Scotland in 1839*. Second Edition. Edinburgh: William Whyte, 1842.

Fasti Ecclesiae Scoticanae, ed. Hew Scott. Volume 7. New Edition. Edinburgh: Oliver and Boyd, 1928.

M'Kerrow, John. "Missions to the Jews." In *History of Foreign Missions of the Secession and United Presbyterian Church*. Edinburgh: Andrew Elliot, 1867, 496–504.

The Friend of Israel 3 (Jan. 1855–Feb. 1857), Glasgow: Thomas Murray, 1857. *Full accounts of the work of the Society for the Conversion of Israel.*

Thompson, A. E. *A Century of Jewish Missions*. London: Revell, 1902.

Robert Kerr and Morocco

Bench, Harlan P. & Burton St. John eds. *World Statistics of Christian Missions: Containing a Directory of Missionary Societies …* New York: Committee of Reference & Counsel FMCNA, 1916.

Kerr, Robert. *Pioneering in Morocco: A Record of Seven Years' Medical Mission Work in the Palace and the Hut*. London: Allenson, 1894.

Kerr, Robert. *Morocco After Twenty-Five Years*. London: Murray & Evendon, 1912.

Meyer, Louis. *Directory of Protestant Jewish Missionary Societies and Centers Throughout the World*. Chicago: Chicago Hebrew Mission, 1912.

Ngo, May. *Between Humanitarianism and Evangelism in Faith-based Organisations: A Case from the African Immigration Route*. New York/London: Routledge, 2018.

Rutherfurd, J. & Edward H. Glenny, *The Gospel in North Africa*. London: Percy Lund, Humphries & Co./North Africa Mission, 1900.

Whytock, Jack C. "Robert Kerr & Morocco: A Forgotten Chapter in Presbyterian Mission History." *Haddington House Journal* 25 (forthcoming 2023). This article is based upon archival materials held with the archives of The United Reformed History Society, Westminster College, Cambridge and at SOAS, London.

North Africa Mission

Steele, Francis R. *Not in Vain: The Story of the North Africa Mission*. Pasadena, CA: William Carey Library, 1981.

Southern Morocco Mission

Southern Morocco Mission: A Review of the Work, 1914. Glasgow: Pickering & Inglis, 1914.

Southern Morocco Mission: A Review of the Work, 1921. Glasgow: Pickering & Inglis, 1921.

"Widow of a Missionary Martyr: The Home Call of Mrs. Mary Nairn." *North Africa* 35 (Nov/Dec 1960): 99–100.

Inset

The Scotch Church, Algiers c.1880s to 1935

J. C. Whytock

There is a little-known story today about what was once the Scotch Church (*Eglise Ecossaise*) of Algiers, later called St. Andrew's. Its roots go back to tourists, expat residents, locals, and migratory individuals and families of north Africa who lived or stayed in Mustapha, Algiers. The area was a popular destination for British, American, and French expats to come and especially winter between the years c.1850 and 1939. The United Presbyterian Church in Scotland had an interest in Algiers particularly in Jewish missions since 1850 through the Scottish Society for the Conversion of Israel and their first station in Algiers in 1850 (see section 1 in this chapter). Thus, the Scottish UPs had a long interest in Algiers.

A winter congregation for the English-speaking community was formed in the 1880s. A church building was built and opened in 1886/7 in Mustapha at 119 ter rue Didouche Mourad as a welcoming evangelical Presbyterian church connected and owned by the Scottish UP Synod. The church building was provided by the generous donation of Sir Peter Coats of Paisley, Scotland who gave the building to

▲ The Scotch Church/*Église Ecossaise*, Mustapha/Algiers

the UPC. The design was modelled after one that he provided as Memorial Church of Minishant, Ayrshire, Scotland in 1877. (Coats died in Algiers in 1890). The Scottish UPs provided annually for up to six months a preacher to come and preach and care for the needs of the community there. Occasionally some stayed for a year or more. The Scotch Church provided a home for a variety of evangelical Presbyterians and others to worship. It also had a reading room/library attached to it. It seems that attendance varied and could be between 60 to 80. As a church it went through the permutations of the mergers in Scotland, UP through to 1900, then UFCS, then finally CoS. A complete list of ministers who served it is not available, but some names are Revs. Boyd, Whyte, and Wilson and perhaps the most noted was Rev. Samuel Angus who served in 1911–12 before going onto Australia where he was for years involved with the PCA GA over his theological views.

The church was also involved locally and connected with other missions. The French McCall Mission of Paris and its agent in Algiers was in good relations with the congregation as were agents doing Jewish missions in Algiers and also the BFBS. In April 1890 the church was the scene for one of its largest gatherings in its earliest years and that was the baptism of Dr Abdel Kader Ould Bouzian formerly of Morocco and who had been converted from Islam and was being baptised at the Church. The service was shared between Rev. Boyd the UP minister and Rev. Lowitz a Jewish convert and missionary. This baptism story was recorded in the *Glasgow Herald*. Bouzian was serving as the surgeon at the civil hospital in Mustapha.[50]

By the mid-1930s there was a decline in English residents and the church was closed as an English language congregation. There is a lack of clarity as to what happened to the building during the Second World War and if another congregation used it.

Select Bibliography

"Baptism of a Mohammedan in a Presbyterian Church." *Glasgow Herald* (3 May 1890).

Missionary Record of the United Presbyterian Church. New Series. 9.4 (2 April 1888), 97.

Perkins, Kenneth J. "So Near and Yet So Far: British Tourism in Algiers, 1860–1914."
In *The British Abroad Since the Eighteenth Century, Volume 1: Travellers and Tourists* eds. Martin Farrand & Xavier Guégan. Basingstoke, UK: Palgrave MacMillan, 2013, 217–235.

Ross, Christopher. "American Embassy Properties in Algiers: Their Origins and History" (1991).

---

50 It appears that on 29 July 1890 Dr Bouzain married a Scottish woman, Jane Agnew Tulloch, in Algiers performed by a French Reformed minister.

Chapter 31

The Legacies of the African American Missionaries at the American Presbyterian Congo Mission

Kimberly D. Hill

Chapter Outline
1. Introduction: Origins
2. Historical Context
3. The Founding of the American Presbyterian Congo Mission
4. Professionalization and Human Rights
5. Conclusion: Major Trends and Legacies

1. Introduction: Origins

In several ways, the history of the American Presbyterian Congo Mission (APCM) met and surpassed its denomination's goals for successful outreach on the African continent. It became well-known as part of an international coalition seeking human rights reform during the first decade of the twentieth century. The APCM also became a rare and early site of interracial collaboration performed by ministers from the American South. The motivations behind these accomplishments can be traced back to over a century before the APCM was founded. Since 1826, the American Board of Commissioners for Foreign Missions (ABCFM) corresponded with the American Colonization Society to plan a new mission station in Liberia.[1] Samuel Hopkins, one of the ABCFM co-founders may have inspired this collaboration with his comments in the 1770s; he endorsed the appointment of African Americans to lead Christian ministries on the African continent.[2] The Colonization Society brought that vision closer

---

1 Emily Louise Conroy-Krutz, "The Conversion of the World in the Early Republic: Race, Gender, and Imperialism in the Early American Foreign Mission Movement," (Unpublished PhD dissertation, Harvard, 2012), 197.
2 David Killingray, "The Black Atlantic Missionary Movement and Africa, 1780s–1920s," *Journal of Religion in Africa*, 33, Fasc. 1 (Feb. 2003): 8.

to fruition by sponsoring formerly enslaved people and African American expatriates as settlers abroad.

American Presbyterians partnered with the ABCFM during the 1820s and commissioned missionaries to the African continent in 1833. In that year, John B. Pinney and John Leighton Wilson accepted appointments in Liberia. Pinney became an interim governor of the Liberian settler communities.[3] Wilson focused more on evangelising local Africans yet also became involved in political affairs through disputes over the leadership of his new community.[4] Both men confronted controversies about slavery as part of their missionary roles and worked with African Americans as fellow ministers, community leaders, or neigbours. The intersections between religious activism and politics in the careers of Pinney and Wilson indicated how reactions to the slave trade would continue to influence Presbyterian interventions on the continent. The varying roles that African Americans played as travelers and as missionaries for the denomination included church leadership, diplomacy, teaching, publication, and agriculture. The question of how much authority accompanied these responsibilities had political ramifications in the historical contexts of American Jim Crow and Belgian colonialism.

2. Historical Context

Racial Segregation in the southern states following the American Civil War

The term "Jim Crow" referred to patterns of legal and informal racial segregation that proliferated in the United States after 1877. These patterns of segregation were most prominent in the southern states that seceded as the Confederacy during the American Civil War. The federal government's decision to stop enforcing the civil rights of African Americans about twelve years after the war left the reconstruction of the former Confederacy incomplete. Southern state governments and some private citizens responded by using financial burdens, criminal statutes, and extralegal violence to enforce racial hierarchies of citizenship well into the twentieth century. Many of these statutes made it difficult for African Americans to negotiate or break labour contracts, which was an advantage for landowners in this agricultural economy. The continued necessity of working on southern cotton plantations trapped the descendants

---

3 For Liberia see chapter 3 in this present volume. Also, Robert E. Speer, *Presbyterian Foreign Missions* (Philadelphia: Presbyterian Board of Publication, 1901), 21–22.

4 Eugene S. VanSickle, "The Missionary Presence and Influences in Maryland in Liberia, 1834–1842," (Unpublished MA thesis, West Virginia University, 2000): 34–37.

of formerly enslaved people in peonage while they also faced diminishing opportunities for voting, political leadership, and education.

Race Relations within the PCUS after Emancipation

These shifts in race relations also influenced the Southern Presbyterians (also formally known as the Presbyterian Church in the United States or PCUS). The denomination affiliated with the Confederate States and included several members who were former slave owners. After emancipation and Reconstruction, Southern Presbyterian reactions to increasing levels of black leadership appeared ambivalent. The PCUS helped to promote African American leadership by establishing a segregated seminary in 1877 and encouraging the founding of new black Presbyterian churches. But the Stillman seminary administrators struggled to attract financial support from other church members. The PCUS also encouraged the formation of an independent Afro-American Presbyterian denomination in 1898, which lasted only about two decades. Like the students at Stillman, most African American Presbyterian ministers also had to perform agricultural and vocational work that left little time for church-related responsibilities. The goal of sustaining black Southern Presbyterian churches became more challenging as thousands of African Americans fled the exploitative cotton sharecropping system and joined what became the Great Migration into the northern and western states. The denomination's pattern of creating limited venues for African American ministries clashed with the continuing paucity of resources for those ministries. And that pattern set a precedent for managerial practices at the American Presbyterian Congo Mission.

Race relations in Congo Free State

The creation and governance of the Congo Free State also influenced the development of the Congo Mission. King Leopold II of Belgium claimed private ownership of Congo in 1885 with the stated goal of welcoming humanitarian initiatives in Central Africa. An African American journalist named George Washington Williams was one of the first observers to document the oppressive conditions that were being enforced by colonial officials and rubber traders in actuality. He made this argument denying the king's professed positive influence over the country:

> Against the deceit, fraud, robberies, arson, murder, slave-raiding, and general policy of cruelty of your Majesty's Government to the natives, stands their record of unexampled

patience, long-suffering and forgiving spirit, which put the boasted civilisation and professed religion of your Majesty's Government to the blush.[5]

Though Williams passed away a year after publishing most of his warnings about the Congo Free State, his criticisms sparked international scrutiny. The empathy Williams expressed towards the perspectives of Africans in Congo also led King Leopold II to be wary of African American travelers in the region. Belgian officials developed a more specific exclusionary process in the 1920s and 1930s as a precaution against African nationalist sentiments. The popularity of Marcus Garvey and the Universal Negro Improvement Association spread the message of "Africa for the Africans" beyond the organization's home bases in Jamaica and New York. African leaders who inspired mass movements or protests within colonised Congo were sometimes accused of supporting Garveyite principles. For similar reasons, European colonialists monitored and often discouraged international travel by African American leaders during the early twentieth century. The accomplishments of some of the American Presbyterian Congo missionaries were complicated due to this type of surveillance within Belgian Congo.

Even before any personnel arrived at the Congo Mission, colonial interests shaped its future by influencing the Presbyterians' destination. One of the early initiatives of the Congo Free State government was to invite settlement by western traders and Christian organizations. British Protestant missionaries established two early mission stations near the coast, and Catholic missions were being founded further inland. King Leopold II met with one of the APCM co-founders and suggested the Kasai region as a mission station location. His strategy helped to ensure that this part of central Congo would attract a growing presence of westerners relying on communication, commerce, and transportation. The increased demand for access to the Kasai region hastened the construction of nearby roads and a railway while strengthening colonial authority over the region's residents. These residents included subjects of the Kuba kingdom, which was one of the last remaining Congolese societies to resist European and American intervention. The accomplishments of several African American Presbyterian missionaries grew from the tension between expanding western influence around the mission stations and the efforts to retain the autonomy and cultures of Kuba people.

---

5 "George Washington Williams's Open Letter to King Leopold on the Congo." 18 July 1890. BlackPast.org. Accessed 2 February 2022. https://www.blackpast.org/global-african-history/primary-documents-global-african-history/george-washington-williams-open-letter-king-leopold-congo-1890/

3. The Founding of the American Presbyterian Congo Mission

Vision for the Mission

Church historians tend to depict the APCM as a project that extended from the Southern Presbyterian denomination's historic affiliation with American slavery. Stanley Shaloff introduces the mission as part of John Leighton Wilson's vision for the communities he served in Liberia and Gabon before becoming an administrator of PCUS overseas missions. Shaloff argued that Wilson expected a future African missions station "in some measure to test the capacity of the American Negro to elevate his brothers in Africa."[6] Shaloff interprets the founding of the Stillman seminary (originally called Tuscaloosa Institute) as another stage in missions preparation because it provided higher education and networking opportunities for five of the African American men who joined the APCM staff before 1940. Robert Benedetto added further details about Wilson's interest in evangelising the Central African interior by taking advantage of its plentiful rivers and by translating local languages. He also emphasizes that Wilson expected success in this venture because "Providence had endowed the South with a culture and society in which whites and blacks shared a common, if unequal, existence."[7]

William Henry Sheppard

The timing and objectives of the APCM developed in reaction to staffing changes more than as the result of administrative planning. A Stillman seminary alumnus named William Henry Sheppard was the first PCUS member to apply for service as a missionary to the African continent. Sheppard started requesting an appointment to overseas ministry about three years before the Congo mission station came to fruition. His application languished with the Executive Committee on Foreign Missions until a white minister named Samuel Lapsley offered to travel with Sheppard.[8] The team arrived in the Congo Free State in 1891. After they chose a base of operations, the team expected to focus on evangelism and church founding. But Lapsley's death from a tropical illness in 1892 left Sheppard as the de facto APCM leader for almost a year. He adjusted to the loss by seeking alliances through the ruling family of the largest African society in the region. And nine more African American missionaries joined Sheppard in the following decade as he sought to link the future of the Congo Mission with the interests of the Kuba kingdom.

---

6   Stanley Shaloff, *Reform in Leopold's Congo* (Richmond, VA: John Knox Press, 1970), 15.
7   Benedetto, "Introduction," in *Presbyterian Reformers in Central Africa*, 6.
8   See chapter 19 in this present volume and the inset on Sheppard within that chapter. Also, Phipps, *William Henry Sheppard: Congo's African American Livingstone*, 10–11.

Six white Presbyterians affiliated with the APCM between 1892 and 1893 as reinforcements, and they oversaw the slow but lasting expansion of its first mission station.⁹ This Luebo station grew through the migration of Luba people who had been displaced by the internal slave trade. Their need for provisions and stability made the Luba more likely to consider working with the American Presbyterians as church members, students, and maintenance staff. But this method of growth also clashed with some of the strategies that William Henry Sheppard hoped to continue as mission policy. Sheppard established a second mission station called Ibaanj closer to the Kuba kingdom in 1898, and he encouraged his colleagues to conduct ministry and diplomacy that took Kuba interests into account. The ensuing competition to determine which regional ethnic groups would become the focus of APCM outreach helped to characterize the Presbyterians' legacies in Congo.

▲ William Sheppard with Congolese men

4. Professionalization and Human Rights

Post-emancipation "freedom' in religious and socio-economic terms

Scholarship focused on Sheppard and other African American APCM staff tends to emphasise their interests in Pan-Africanist sentiment and African American professionalisation as motives for the ministry.¹⁰ Before earning a degree

---

9   The next six missionaries who joined the APCM after Sheppard and Lapsley were George Adamson, Margaret Adamson, Arthur Rowbotham, Margaret Rowbotham, Dewitt Clinton Snyder, and Matie Snyder. Benedetto, "Introduction," in *Presbyterian Reformers in Central Africa*, 7.

10 For examples, see James Campbell, *Middle Passages: African American Journeys to Africa* (New York: Penguin Press, 2006); Ira Dworkin, *Congo Love Song: African American Culture and the Crisis of the Colonial State* (Chapel Hill: University of North Carolina Press, 2017); Kimberly Hill, "Anti-Slavery Work of the American Women of the Presbyterian Congo Mission," in *Faith and Slavery in the Presbyterian Diaspora*; Kimberly Hill, "Maria Fearing: Domestic Adventurer," in *Alabama Women: Their Lives and Times*; Kimberly D. Hill, *A Higher Mission: The Careers of Alonzo and Althea Brown Edmiston in Central Africa*; Sylvia Jacobs, "Their 'Special Mission:' Afro-American Women as Missionaries in the Congo, 1894–1937," in *Black Americans and the Missionary Movement in Africa*; Pagan Kennedy, *Black Livingstone: A True Tale of Adventure in the Nineteenth-Century Congo*; Phipps, *William Henry Sheppard: Congo's African American Livingstone*; James A. Quirin, "'Her Sons and Daughters Are Ever on the Altar': Fisk University and Missionaries to Africa, 1866–1937," *Tennessee Historical Quarterly* 60.1 (2011): 16–37; Walter L. Williams, *Black Americans and the Evangelization of Africa* (Madison: University of Wisconsin Press, 1982).

▲ Hampton Institute

from Stillman, Sheppard enrolled at Hampton Institute in his home state of Virginia. Hampton became known as the inspiration for Booker T. Washington's Tuskegee Institute and its focus on industrial education. But Sheppard and his colleagues acted as part of a broader intellectual tradition that developed before Washington became a famous leader. They represented a post-emancipation generation seeking to define "freedom" in religious and socioeconomic terms. That type of freedom entailed a wider range of work options for black employees and entrepreneurs as well as opportunities for public service. Historically black colleges and universities (HBCUs) proved significant for the goal of defining freedom because they provided credentials, professional skills, and a nurturing environment for students likely to be segregated from other institutions. And HBCUs became crucial recruiting grounds during the first decade of Southern Presbyterian missions to the Congo Free State.

African American Women in the APCM

Sylvia M. Jacobs notes that each of the African American women who joined the APCM before 1910 received training and connections to the mission through a historically black college or university. Lucy Gantt, Lilian Thomas, and Maria Fearing met at Talladega College in Alabama. As one of the premier liberal arts HBCU institutions, Talladega prepared these future missionaries for language study, translation work, and teaching roles abroad. Lucy Gantt married William Henry Sheppard before venturing to the Congo Free State with him and her two Talladega associates in 1894. Althea Brown brought to her APCM career a musical background similar to that of Lucy Gantt, a classics degree, and valedictorian status at Fisk University. She met and married Alonzo Edmiston after about two years of service as a teacher and foster mother. Annie Katherine Taylor graduated from Scotia College in North Carolina before applying for Southern Presbyterian missions service. Taylor also married a fellow missionary (Adolphus A. Rochester) and taught home economics to African girls.[11]

---

11 Sylvia Jacobs, "Their 'Special Mission:' Afro-American Women as Missionaries in the Congo, 1894–1937," 156–170.

Influence of Stillman Seminary on the work in Congo

Rochester was one of two APCM staff members with roots in the Caribbean rather than the American South. He migrated from Jamaica to attend Stillman, and Joseph Phipps applied to the APCM after growing up in St. Kitts. Phipps also had Congolese ancestry.[12] Though he did not attend a historically black institution, Phipps found his initial connection to the APCM by traveling and working with a Stillman professor named Samuel Verner. That professor's ongoing business interests in the Congo Free State also became the catalyst for Alonzo Edmiston to enter the mission field in 1904. Edmiston, Rochester, Henry Hawkins, and Lucius DeYampert followed William Henry Sheppard's example by seeking appointments to the APCM after receiving seminary training at Stillman Institute. Two of these men (Sheppard and DeYampert) had prior experience as pastors, but all of them anticipated that their missions duties would involve more tasks than church founding and direct evangelism. Their work in Congo included construction, farming, political mediation, shipment coordination, nursing, teaching, and invention. They needed the skills to maintain mission stations that provided resources and shelter in the midst of an oppressive colonial context.

Southern Presbyterians and Human Rights in Congo and America

World-building was part of the ideology of African American professionals during the late nineteenth century. These professionals laid the foundation for later black educators, lawyers, medical professionals, and ministers to thrive in communities where such services had been unavailable or denied in the past. Laying that foundation during the rise of American Jim Crow required imagination and determination to surpass the few service vocations that African Americans were expected to fill at the time. It also required flexibility about the locations where African American professionals would complete their accomplishments. Sheppard envisioned the status of his Ibaanj mission station as reflecting the enhanced status of the African American missionaries who managed it. He described the station as "a very attractive one" with landscaping and architecture that "caused more than one passing trader or State officer to say that this is the prettiest station in the Kassai."[13] It attracted professional recognition while facilitating ministry in a region experiencing increasing instability. The APCM was celebrated by American supporters in part because the missionaries were helping African communities withstand political and economic challenges while overcoming challenges to their own livelihoods.

The Southern Presbyterians got involved in a growing human rights campaign

---

12 Phipps, *William Sheppard: Congo's African American Livingstone*, 121.
13 William Henry Sheppard quoted in Phipps, *William Sheppard*, 119.

against the governance of the Congo Free State after the arrival of William M. Morrison. Morrison served as the APCM supervisor from 1897 through his death in 1918. He observed how villages around the mission – and even the mission buildings themselves – were being disrupted by armed representatives of the State who gathered tax payments or drafted local people into forced labour. Robert Benedetto's edited volume *Presbyterian Reformers in Central Africa* includes the large body of correspondence that Morrison produced and received while encouraging other leaders to condemn the regional rubber company and its Belgian managers.[14] William Henry Sheppard played a major role in this process by gathering primary evidence of regional atrocities, publishing his account, and describing the violence during his American speaking tour. The Congo Free State government retaliated by charging Sheppard and Morrison with libel, leading to a highly publicized trial in 1909.

It was noteworthy how the interests of the African American missionaries intersected with those of their African neighbours during the years leading up to the libel trial. Sheppard showed empathy at great personal risk by taking photographs and notes of the ways that local Africans were killed or threatened into raising revenue for the Free State government. He later postponed describing these problems in the United States out of concern that white audiences would condemn him for criticizing a European government.[15] In the meantime, a small team of his black colleagues managed the Ibaanj mission station that Sheppard designed to enable outreach to the Kuba kingdom. They specialized in studying and translating the Bushoong language of the Kuba even though the APCM supervisor preferred to focus linguistic pursuits on the language groups more common near the Luebo station. Althea Brown Edmiston linked her professional status to ongoing Presbyterian interest in Kuba culture through her eventual publication of the first Bushoong dictionary and grammar book. That level of commitment was evident in Brown Edmiston's choice to focus on colonial abuses as the reasons for the 1904 Kuba uprising that destroyed the APCM Ibaanj station.

The ruler of the Kuba kingdom (known as "Lukenga" in Bushoong) called for rebellion against the Congo Free State government and all westerners after authorities imprisoned him during a tax negotiation. His subjects responded by attacking and burning European and American outposts in that part of Central Congo, including Ibaanj. Though Brown Edmiston lost her house and most of her possessions after fleeing from the violence, she still argued that the government inspired more concern among the APCM staff and the Kuba people alike. In a 1906 article for the Presbyterian *Missionary* magazine, she observed that

---

14 Benedetto, *Presbyterian Reformers in Central Africa*.
15 Pagan Kennedy, *Black Livingstone: A True Tale of Adventure in the Nineteenth-Century Congo* (Santa Fe: Santa Fe Writers Project, 2013), Kindle edition, location 2706-2712.

"[t]he smallest rumour of State officials coming in our midst fills the Bakuba with terror" and she worried that "[t]he 'State' seems bitterly opposed to our being here."[16] Brown Edmiston continued Sheppard's example of prioritizing the perspectives of local African people in the interests of sustaining the mission work.

Tangible signs that African Americans earned professional recognition through the APCM included the pay scale, education benefits, awards, and titles. William Henry Sheppard, Alonzo Edmiston, and Althea Brown Edmiston received honours from the Royal Geographic Society and the Belgian government respectively for their discoveries and contributions. The missionaries were referred to as "Mr.," "Miss," or "Mrs." in denominational publications even though that courtesy was not customary in the American South. The PCUS also avoided race discrimination in the compensation for mission staff.[17] The Executive Committee on Foreign Missions supplemented this compensation with funding for missionaries' older children to attend boarding schools and universities in the United States if the children did not remain abroad. The Edmistons' sons used this benefit to attend Fisk University and North Carolina A&T University. The U.S. government also acknowledged the professional status of African American missionaries in 1905 when Sheppard was invited to meet President Teddy Roosevelt at the White House and in 1909 when the American Consul-General attended the libel trial of Sheppard and Morrison.[18] The implication that a Belgian accusation against a black American posed a national security issue rested on an interpretation of citizenship rights that was unique and notable at the time.

▲ Alonzo & Althea Edmiston with their eldest son, Sheman Kueta Edmiston

5. Conclusion: Major Trends and Legacies

African Americans phased out of APCM

The conclusion of the libel trial preceded a significant policy shift for the APCM. Its initial phase developed slowly on two mission stations and with notable

---

16 Althea Brown Edmiston, "Six Months at Ibanj," *Missionary* (June 1906): 256.
17 Benedetto, "Introduction," in *Presbyterian Reformers in Central Africa*, 34.
18 Phipps, *William Sheppard*, 156, 169.

setbacks. Its priorities were based partly on the interests of local African people and partly on the skills of those missionaries who proved capable of remaining in the Congo Free State for several years. Starting in 1910, the Executive Committee on Foreign Missions exercised more authority over the types of ministers who would reinforce the APCM and the preferred standards for their productivity. The denomination sought more white recruits with experience in industry, agriculture, and management. It also adopted an unannounced policy to appoint no additional African Americans to the APCM.[19] Most of the black missionaries were dismissed or denied permission to return to Congo in the following years. Alonzo Edmiston left in 1908 after facing accusations that he and Althea Brown lacked adequate preparation for ministry. William Henry and Lucy Gantt Sheppard were advised to resign in 1910. Joseph Phipps, Henry Hawkins, and Lilian Thomas DeYampert were furloughed in the following decade. In the meantime, Maria Fearing was forced into retirement and Lucius DeYampert's request to return with Fearing and his wife remained unfulfilled. The four African American missionaries who were allowed to work at the APCM between 1915 and 1941 did so by blending into the Southern Presbyterians' calls for efficiency and standardization.

Educational Legacy

The Edmistons were reappointed quietly between 1911 and 1912 to reinforce the mission's expansion goals. Alonzo Edmiston managed African workers at the rebuilt Ibaanj station as they grew and gathered produce for the larger Luebo station. For about two years, he also lived at the Luebo station as an assistant on the farm that was intended to become an APCM cotton plantation. From 1918 to 1937, Althea Brown Edmiston devoted most of her time to teaching local children who enrolled in a Presbyterian school and were expected to complete much of the agricultural labour. She also travelled between the newer stations, using her nursing training to help establish Presbyterian hospitals. This work kept Brown Edmiston distanced from the Kuba territory. Though the APCM adopted Luba instead of Bushoong as its official local language, she still raised enough funds to publish her dictionary about Kuba language and culture in 1932.[20] Likewise, Adolphus Rochester was assigned to a station far from the Kuba kingdom where he focused on teaching, evangelism, and nursing. He remarried after the sudden death of Annie Katherine Taylor Rochester in 1914. Edna Rochester, his second wife, shared teaching responsibilities with Brown Edmiston while they were all assigned to the Mutoto mission station. Each missionary's duties helped to create institutions at the APCM while making the maintenance of those institutions more sustainable or profitable.

---

19 Dworkin, *Congo Love Song*, 136.
20 Benedetto, "The Presbyterian Mission Press in Central Africa, 1890–1922," *American Presbyterians* 68. 1 (1990): 55–69.

APCM Goals Toward Three-Self Principle

Before the founding of the APCM, the Southern Presbyterian denomination was sponsoring overseas missions in Asia and Latin America. Both mission fields became known for contributing to the "three-selfs" principle of governance and financial support.[21] The Southern Presbyterian push for efficiency was an extension of ecumenical interest in self-supporting missions during the early twentieth century. For example, the Presbyterian Lavras industrial school in Brazil was celebrated as a model of vocational education by 1910.

Industrial Training

Industrial training also became part of the APCM legacy through the contributions of missionaries including Alonzo Edmiston and William Henry Sheppard. Sheppard graduated from one of the most influential industrial schools in the United States (Hampton Institute). Though he did not start industrial training at the Congo Mission, his academic background helped to solidify expectations that African Americans could apply this pedagogy abroad. The Belgian government and the American National Geographic Society commended Edmiston in the 1920s because he conducted successful experiments to make the mission farms and produce-based businesses more productive. The trend toward industrial education was not evident at its founding, but it became a significant feature of the Congo Mission.

Lasting Contribution of African American Presbyterian Missionaries in the USA

Legacies from the work of African American Presbyterian missionaries were also evident stateside. Several of them contributed to educational programs and community development even after they were dismissed from the APCM. By leading a church in Louisville, Kentucky, William Henry and Lucy Gantt Sheppard popularised and strengthened the local Presbyterian community centre for black youth.[22] The community centre became the place where Cassius Clay (Muhammad Ali) and other successful boxers started to train. Lucy Gantt Sheppard also worked with Maria Fearing and Lilian Thomas DeYampert to lead sessions for the PCUS Woman's Auxiliary conferences at Stillman Institute.

---

21 William L. Sachs, "'Self-Support': The Episcopal Mission and Nationalism in Japan," *Church History* 58.4 (1989): 489–501; C. Peter Williams, *The Ideal of the Self-Governing Church: A Study in Victorian Missionary Strategy* (New York: E. J. Brill, 1990); Henry F. Williams, *In South America: The Brazil Missions of the Presbyterian Church in the United States* (Richmond, VA.: Presbyterian Board of Publications, 1910).

22 Phipps, *William Sheppard*, 184–185.

Their presence as colleagues and noted leaders may have influenced Hallie Paxson Winsborough, the PCUS Secretary of Woman's Work, to participate in the Commission on Interracial Cooperation and the Association of Southern Women for the Prevention of Lynching during the 1930s.[23] And the Edmistons devoted part of their sabbatical time to networking with pastors, intellectuals, civil rights activists, and labour leaders in Selma, Alabama. Some of these neighbours and acquaintances (particularly Amelia Boynton Robinson) drew national attention during the protests for the 1965 Voting Rights Act.[24]

Current American Presbyterians continue the memory of APCM service through naming tributes such as the Sheppard database at the Presbyterian Historical Society (Philadelphia) and the Reformed Theological Seminary (Atlanta) Edmiston Centre for the Study of the Bible and Ethnicity.

APCM sets the standard for recognizing the interests and initiatives of local Africans

Though the APCM closed when the nation transitioned into the Democratic Republic of the Congo, Presbyterian involvement in the nation's church activities revived through new outlets. One of the best reflections of African American missionaries' legacies shows through the ways that Congolese Presbyterians still set the terms and direction for ministries and community service in the region where the APCM was based. In these twenty-first century partnerships, it is standard practice for American Presbyterian ministers and volunteers to recognize the interests and initiatives of local Africans.

Questions for study (fact type):
1 Name the Belgian king who was very influential in the Belgian Congo and was highly controversial.
2 What denomination of American Presbyterians established the American Presbyterian Congo Mission? Name this particular denomination by its formal name and also name it by its common popular name.
3 Create a list of several African American Presbyterian missionaries who served in the Belgian Congo.
4 Write one paragraph on *one* of the three historic colleges–Hampton Institute, Fisk University, *or* Talladega College.

---

23 Julie Durway, "'The Field is Endless:' Hallie Paxson Winsborough and Interracial Work in the PCUS Woman's Auxiliary, 1912–1940," *Journal of Presbyterian History* 78. 3 (Fall 2000): 207–219.
24 Hill, *A Higher Mission*, 150–152.

Questions for study (reflection type):
1 William Morrison and William Sheppard worked closely together to expose the atrocities of the Belgian government against the local people. Sheppard took great risks in photographing and journaling examples of these cruelties. Morrison and Sheppard took a stand against the injustice they encountered, even though it frequently put them in harm's way. Read Micah 6:8. Explain why it was critical for these American missionaries to stand up for justice.
2 "*Each missionary's duties helped to create institutions at the APCM while making the maintenance of those institutions more sustainable or profitable.*" One of the "three-self" principles is "self-support." Consider this quote and discuss any practical measures that you would take to make sure that an institution is sustainable and/or profitable for the future.

Select Bibliography

Benedetto, Robert. "Introduction." In *Presbyterian Reformers in Central Africa: A Documentary Account of the American Presbyterian Congo Mission and the Human Rights Struggle in the Congo, 1890–1918*. New York: Brill, 1996.

Benedetto, Robert. "The Presbyterian Mission Press in Central Africa, 1890–1922." *American Presbyterians* 68.1 (1990): 55–69.

Durway, Julie. "'The Field is Endless:' Hallie Paxson Winsborough and Interracial Work in the PCUS Woman's Auxiliary, 1912–1940." *Journal of Presbyterian History* 78.3 (Fall 2000): 207–219.

"George Washington Williams's Open Letter to King Leopold on the Congo." 18 July 1890. BlackPast.org. Accessed 2 February 2022. https://www.blackpast.org/global-african-history/primary-documents-global-african-history/george-washington-williams-open-letter-king-leopold-congo-1890/

Hill, Kimberly D. "Anti-Slavery Work of the American Women of the Presbyterian Congo Mission." In *Faith and Slavery in the Presbyterian Diaspora*, ed. by Peter C. Messer and William Harrison Taylor, 205–230. Bethlehem, PA.: Lehigh University Press, 2016.

Hill, Kimberly D. "Maria Fearing: Domestic Adventurer." In *Alabama Women: Their Lives and Times*, ed. by Susan Youngblood Ashmore and Lisa Lindquist Dorr. Athens, GA: University of Georgia Press, 2017, 90–107.

Hill, Kimberly D. *A Higher Mission: The Careers of Alonzo and Althea Brown Edmiston in Central Africa*. Lexington: University of Kentucky Press, 2020.

Jacobs, Sylvia. "Their 'Special Mission:' Afro-American Women as Missionaries in the Congo, 1894–1937." In *Black Americans and the Missionary Movement in Africa*, ed. Sylvia M. Jacobs, 155–176. Westport, CT: Greenwood Press, 1982.

Kennedy, Pagan. *Black Livingstone: A True Tale of Adventure in the Nineteenth-Century. Congo* Santa Fe: Santa Fe Writers Project, 2013.

Phipps, William E. *William Henry Sheppard: Congo's African American Livingstone*. Louisville, KY: Geneva Press, 2002.

Quirin, James A. "'Her Sons and Daughters Are Ever on the Altar': Fisk University and Missionaries to Africa, 1866–1937." *Tennessee Historical Quarterly* 60.1 (2011): 16–37.

Stanley Shaloff, *Reform in Leopold's Congo*. Richmond, VA: John Knox Press, 1970.

Chapter 32

Revival and Exile: The Madeirans, A Story of Influence on the Fringe[1]

Nancy J. Whytock

Chapter Outline
1. Introduction
2. Dr Robert Kalley – planting the seed of God's Word
3. The Bible Readers
4. Rev. William Hewitson – the seed takes root
5. Driven into Exile – August 1846
6. New Life in Trinidad & Rev. Da Silva
7. Relocating to the USA
8. Rev. Antonio De Mattos
9. Conclusion

1. Introduction

The island of Madeira, though Portuguese, lies within the geographic bounds of Africa, not far off the coast of Morocco. In this chapter, we will follow the story of the work of the gospel from 1838–1850, as well as the exile of many Christians from Madeira to Trinidad and eventually Illinois, USA.

2. Dr Robert Kalley – planting the seed of God's Word

Robert R. Kally (1809–1888) was a Scottish physician who felt called to go to China as a missionary and came under the care of the London Missionary Society. In 1838, he and his wife, Margaret Crawford,[2] left Scotland on a ship bound for China. While on board, Mrs Kalley became seriously ill and it was thought she could not survive the entire journey, so the decision was made to come ashore in Madeira.

---

1 This chapter follows the story of revival and expulsion as told by Blackburn in his work, *Exiles of Madeira*. Other sources have been used to supplement this account.
2 They were a newly married couple. Margaret died in 1851 and Kalley remarried – see footnote 29.

This small island in the north Atlantic was predominantly Roman Catholic and Dr Kalley quickly discerned that the spiritual state of the people was desperate.

> He looked about on the people and pitied their ignorance and blindness, just as Paul did in Athens. For centuries they had been denied the use of the Bible. The Romish priests may have had a few Bibles, but they would not let the people have them. It was a sin for any one to search the Scriptures for himself. Many of the islanders had never seen a Bible, nor known there was such a book.[3]

Dr Kalley accepted the providence of the Lord in taking him to Madeira and set out to learn Portuguese as a first step in preparing for his new field. In 1839, Kalley obtained a Portuguese medical qualification. He also returned briefly to London to be ordained by the Congregationalists as a minister.

With these necessary credentials in place, Dr Kalley set to work sharing the Word of God and also using his medical training to establish a hospital. The ministry of body and soul was always offered together – Kalley consistently made the point that sickness of soul was of far greater concern than physical ailments.

Schools were established with the chief desire to teach people to read in order that they could study the scriptures for themselves. Kalley paid the teachers with his own money. Eight hundred men and women were soon attending these schools (generally the evening classes) as well as children. Some schools met in private homes. Between 1839 and 1845, the number taught to read the Bible was over 1000.[4] As many as 2500 attended these evening schools during the same time period.

Church meetings were held as early as 1842 and hundreds came to hear the Word of God. Some walked for 10–12 hours to attend meetings, climbing over mountains 3000 feet high. Many of the meetings were held on a mountainside and for months not less than 1000, but at times up to 5000, attended these meetings.

3. The Bible Readers and Persecution

The study of the Bible began to show people that there were serious errors in Roman Catholic doctrine.[5] Thus began the opposition to the "Bible readers" (as

---

3   Blackburn, *Exiles of Madeira*, 20.
4   Baillie, *Memoir*, 154.
5   Blackburn, *Exiles of Madeira*, 28.

they became known) which was to lead from anger to violence and eventually exile.

The Roman Catholic Bishop, after scrutinising the Bible Kalley was distributing, pronounced a curse on it even though it was shown by careful comparison to be the same Bible that was also in the bishop's possession. Kalley was warned not to teach from it on threat of arrest and imprisonment.

In 1843, severe persecution broke out against the Bible readers. Many were beaten and 22 were imprisoned in the Funchal jail.[6] They were very poorly treated there. In fact, they would have starved to death if English friends resident on the island had not visited them. Bible readers were denied their homes and land, their businesses, and any form of justice, yet they remained faithful.

After two years, the 22 prisoners were released but their enemies were furious and vowed to murder them. Open violence broke out and the murder of Dr Kalley was planned. Many Bible readers fled to the caves and woods. Some died in their attempts to escape.

▲ Robert Kalley

The government formed an idea to massacre the Christians and they were told that if they persisted in reading The Word of God, they would be burned. The Christians would not relent.

Friends in Scotland encouraged Dr Kalley to flee. He wrote home in response:

> You reminded me of the order given, when persecuted in one city to flee into another; but you will also remember that it is said of the hireling that he fleeth, because he is an hireling, and the wolf comes, and catches the sheep. Were I to flee, I believe the poor sheep of Christ's fold would feel deeply discouraged, and the wolf would catch them. The Lord can deliver out of the paw of the lion, and of the bear. He would deliver them though I were away; but it is necessary for us always to examine well, and seek to know the will of God, for it is not for us to run whenever the lion growls. Let those who have no hope, or confidence in the Eternal, fear men that shall die, but let not us fear earth or hell.[7]

---

6   Blackburn, *Exiles of Madeira*, 37. Funchal is the capital city of Madeira.
7   Blackburn, *Exiles of Madeira*, 47.

Kalley himself was under the protection of the 1386 Treaty of Windsor between England and Portugal, but the government found a law from the Inquisition of 1603 and imprisoned him for 5 months.

During this time, hundreds of people visited Kalley for spiritual instruction and encouragement (3 allowed at a time). No singing or Bible reading was allowed. Threats were made to his visitors that their names would be recorded and serious repercussions ensue, but this did not deter them.

Dr Kalley was released from prison in 1844 (ahead of the 22), but a new Portuguese governor took office and made it his primary objective to see that Kalley was driven from the island and his work stamped out. Beatings and murder of Bible readers was openly encouraged. It is understandable that at the time of release of the other 22 prisoners, anger had already turned to violence. Those who became martyrs of the faith were not allowed a grave except in the highway.

4. Rev. William Hewitson – the seed takes root

Kalley yearned for help so that he could remain on the island but be less visible in his ministry with the hope that such violent opposition would quiet down. Help came in the person of William Hepburn Hewitson[8] from Ayrshire, Scotland (1812–1850). Hewitson had been converted in 1840 under the ministry of Robert Murray McCheyne. On 7 November 1844, he was ordained by the Presbytery of Edinburgh (Free Church of Scotland) and headed first to Lisbon, Portugal. Dr Kalley met Rev. Hewitson in Lisbon with much rejoicing – the man who was to take the front place in Madeira as the under-shepherd of the new converts. The newly ordained minister headed to Madeira in January 1845.[9]

▲ W. H. Hewitson

As very few converts had officially renounced Rome, the young minister set up a church in the house of Rev. J. J. Wood, a minister from England, where Hewitson was also given

---

8   Baillie, *Memoir of The Rev. W. H. Hewitson,* 1851; *Annals,* vol.1, 185, which gives 1852 as the death date but this is highly unlikely given that the *Remains* were first published in 1851.
9   The first Church of Scotland minister to the English Presbyterians at Funchal, Madeira seems to have been Rev. John Morrison Whitelaw, 21 June 1842 who had a short ministry on the island. *Fasti Ecclesiae Scoticanae,* vol. 7, 558. Madeira became of interest to the post-Disruption FCS and subsequently the UFCS.

lodging.[10] He began with just 25–30 attending, but the church quickly began to grow.

When Mr Wood's house became too small, the church was moved to another home (with a large garden) that Hewitson rented. One day converts were waiting at Hewitson's home for him to return. Police surrounded the home and waited to beat the Bible readers, destroy their properties, and arrest and imprison them at the first sign of interaction with this Scottish missionary. Hewitson approached his home on a pony and sensed the danger he was about to put his congregants in, so he simply rode by in order to spare them the serious consequences of being in fellowship with him.

In 1845, Hewittson began to prepare elders for ordination. He saw this as an urgent matter as he was aware that the persecution could soon escalate and he would almost certainly be exiled or killed. Three or four men were identified, but the most promising of them all was soon after imprisoned for four months, having first been severely beaten for his outspoken renunciation of Rome. At this time Hewitson's health began to break down and he was taken away from Funchal to recuperate. The house meeting had to be stopped for a time as Kalley was away in Scotland.

From this period of sickness and recovery, Hewitson determined to employ a new method:

> The converts should hold meetings from house to house, and those best instructed should conduct them. It was a happy plan. He organized a class, who should study the gospel, in order to be qualified to teach others. Some came eighteen miles to attend it. One person, just released from jail, was asked to lead in prayer, but feeling his need of learning and good language, he said, "Excuse me, for I can only pray as I have been taught by the Holy Ghost!" Would that all Christians could thus learn from the Spirit of God![11]

Opposition increased. Kalley returned to the island but was forbidden to teach or preach. English merchants were instructed not to host any meetings of Portuguese Bible readers in their homes. Hewitson continued to teach and prepare those who could lead meetings. "There were hundreds – yes thousands – ready to listen to the word of God, but the hoof of oppression kept them down."[12]

---

10 Blackburn, *Exiles of Madeira*, 62.
11 Blackburn, *Exiles of Madeira*, 62.
12 Blackburn, *Exiles of Madeira*, 62.

5. Driven into Exile – August 1846

Lawlessness and violence against the Bible readers continued into 1846. Two spinster sisters from England, both Miss Rutherford – one an invalid, had a summer residence in Funchal. They were Christians and friends of the Bible readers. They had often allowed some of the female Portuguese Bible readers to come to their home to hear the Bible read. On the morning of 2 August 1846, a group of 30–40 worshippers, male and female, gathered in their home for worship. Rev. Hewitson was in Scotland and had sent a letter – which was really a written sermon – that was read on this occasion. The leader of the meeting was Mr Da Silva, a man who had left everything to follow Christ.[13]

A Jesuit priest, Canon Telles, aware of the meeting, came with a crowd to intimidate the worshippers and stop the gathering. Other priests were with him. As the worshippers began to leave the meeting, they were both physically and verbally abused to the point that most of them had to retreat indoors again to protect themselves. The house remained under siege for the afternoon, and late that afternoon Dr Kalley, unaware of the trouble, arrived because he was making a call to check on the invalid sister. He barely escaped on his horse while many were chanting calls for his murder.

The priests would not relent and continued to stir up the mob (using money and liquor as reward) to intimidate those held hostage in the house. The police were there and would not intervene. Eventually the police left, but the priests and their supporters did not. By late evening, Miss Rutherford was on the balcony courageously and earnestly pleading with the mob to retreat and control themselves for the sake of her invalid sister and also their own sakes as lawbreakers that were subject to punishment by British law. The mob replied that they were not subject to British law and would enter the house and murder all Portuguese found within its walls.

Shortly thereafter, the mob advanced and smashed in windows and doors to gain unlawful access. After much searching in this spacious home, the hiding victims were located and the first was severely beaten with the intent of murder when the police reappeared with some soldiers. The two men found in the act of murder were taken into custody and this caused the others to retreat at last for fear of imprisonment, knowing full well that they were committing such acts in the home of British citizens. However, they need not have feared as neither the British consul nor the Portuguese authorities made any efforts to prevent these circumstances from being repeated. The leaders of the mob well understood the disposition of the authorities and were encouraged in their work.[14]

---

13 For a full account of the conversion and sufferings of Da Silva, see Blackburn, *Exiles of Madeira*, Chapter XI.
14 Blackburn, *Exiles of Madeira*, 91.

This lack of consequences for violent behaviour toward the Bible readers emboldened their enemies; Dr Kalley was by far the most hated as it was through his pioneering efforts that the Word of God had been offered to the people of Madeira. Threats increased throughout the following week and by August 8th, Kalley was actively fortifying his own home having come to the realization that neither British nor Portuguese authorities had any interest in protecting him as plots for his murder were revealed. His own guard even betrayed him to his enemies, and by late that evening, Kallay was forced to disguise himself as a peasant in an effort to escape. He reached The Quinta dos Pinheiros (Bachelors' Hall) – a British-owned residence – by 3 am. His family also fled through the night in various directions, as did his faithful servants.

Later that day, Sunday, August 9th, the bloodthirsty mob descended on Kalley's residence. They were angry not to find him there and set about destroying his home and his extensive and valuable library – especially the scriptures, which they burned. Kalley was high up in the city overlooking this event and realised that his only hope of survival was to get to a British vessel that was anchored offshore. Disguised as a woman and escorted in a hammock (this was a common mode of transportation for any who were sick or infirm), he was carried to the shore and his identity discovered only minutes before he was successfully transferred to a small boat that took him out to the British ship. The captain, once he had discovered who it was, welcomed Kalley. Amazingly, Kalleys' family also made it to the ship.[15]

The following day many other English residents were forced to leave their homes.

> The sick were treated without mercy. Eleven such families were insulted and threatened. One English gentleman, who helped his friends to get safely away on ships, was threatened with murder and obliged to flee. It would not do to help any one to remain safe on the island, nor to help any one to flee away! One British lady died after reaching a vessel in the harbour, from the violence to which she, in her sickness, was exposed; others came near losing life through fatigue and alarm.[16]

The native Bible readers were now severely persecuted. Their houses were broken into and plundered, their steps were watched by spies, and they were driven by the hundreds into the mountains and hunted down. Every copy of

---

15 Blackburn, *Exiles of Madeira*, 112.
16 Blackburn, *Exiles of Madeira*, 114–115.

▲ Harbour, Funchal, Madeira, 1840

the Word of God on which the priests could lay their hands was immediately committed to the flames. But thanks be to God, the Bibles were not all destroyed. Some enclosed their Bibles in small boxes and buried them in the earth. Others opened a place in the stone wall of the house, put in the Bible, and then plastered over it. And others wrapped them in cloth and hung them in trees of very thick foliage. In such ways at least fifty Bibles and three hundred New Testaments were preserved.[17] Over the years, some of these Bibles (that were buried during the violence of the persecution) have been uncovered.

The only human escape for the Bible readers was to seek refuge on English ships that came into the harbour at Funchal.[18] The *William of Glasgow* anchored in the harbour and waited to take on board as many as possible. Twelve English refugees were already on board and wrote to Mr Hewitson (still back in Scotland):

> This ship is to take away two hundred of your flock to Trinidad. Seventy are already on board. The sound of the hymns is very sweet, as it rises from the hold. It is a great privilege to be near them in this time of need, and to see that their faith does not fail. They never speak against their persecutors – they only mention them with pity. Sometimes I overhear them in prayer, praying for their enemies, and for those who have turned back again to the houses of idolatry. They have all been in hidings on the mountains, and many of them have nothing left but the clothes they wear.[19]

---

17 Blackburn, *Exiles of Madeira*, 117–118.
18 "The British government eventually obliged the Portuguese authorities in Lisbon to pay Dr Kalley damages for the heavy losses he had sustained, but the rank and file of the Madeirans received no compensation whatever for the material losses they had sustained." W. B. Forsyth, *The Wolf from Scotland: The Story of Robert Reid Kalley*, 77.
19 Blackburn, *Exiles of Madeira*, 118–119.

By Sunday, 23 August 1846, the *William Of Glasgow* had 200 refugees on board; it was full to capacity and set sail for Trinidad. Soon after this the Lord Seaton vessel also took about the same number.

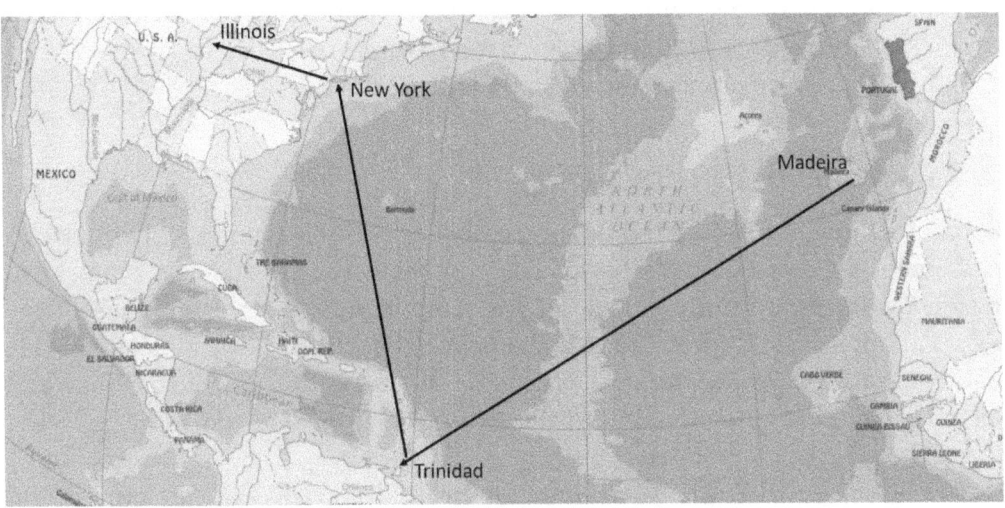

▲ Map of The North Atlantic Ocean showing the route of the Madeiran Refugees

6. Trinidad and Rev. Da Silva

In January of the following year, 1847, Rev. Hewitson set sail from Scotland for Trinidad to bring encouragement to the newly arrived refugees from Madeira. On route, he visited Funchal and quietly met with some of the remaining believers in that city before reboarding his ship and landing in Trinidad on February 4. There were now about 450 exiles in Trinidad, most of whom were numbered with the converts to Christ, but not all as some Roman Catholic families had also decided to leave Madeira. 85 members of the church were there.[20] Three of the seven elders, and four of the nine deacons had come from Madeira.[21] About thirty persons soon applied for membership in the church.[22]

Hewitson resided in Port of Spain, as did many of his congregation. A Sunday school was started, a school was established, and his discipleship class recommenced. Exiles from Madeira continued to arrive. The organization of the church was completed in April 1847, about two months after the arrival of Mr

---

20 This number appears low as many who had come to Christ had not yet formally renounced Roman Catholicism and joined the Presbyterian Church. Hewitson began organizing everyone and preparing them for church membership now that they were free of persecution.
21 This means that some elders and deacons were also still in Madeira to lead the Bible readers there.
22 Blackburn, *Exiles of Madeira*, 152–153.

Hewitson. He made plans to leave in May.²³ Therefore, it was important to find a leader. Mr Da Silva, from Madeira, was named the successor.²⁴ He had studied theology in Scotland and The Free Church of Scotland named him as their missionary.²⁵ Following a unanimous call by the congregation, he was ordained and installed over his first and only charge, at Port-of-Spain, in April 1847. By this time, there were approximately 600 in his flock.²⁶

7. Relocating to the USA

Soon after this, the young exiled church began to look for somewhere else to call home as the working conditions and climate were not suitable for long term residency. In response to their pleas, The American Protestant society sent the Rev. G. Gonsalves to Trinidad. Mr Gonsalves had been born at Madeira. He had been a Romanist. After his conversion, he came to the United States and laboured for several years among the five or six thousand Portuguese living along the New England coast.

In December 1848, De Silva, in poor health, left Trinidad for New York, ultimately in search of good land for his congregation. His health did not permit him to remain with his congregation until they were safely settled in the USA; he died 10 January 1849 in his 49th year. This Christian leader had suffered much, having lost his family wealth and having been deprived of his wife and children – all consequences of coming to Christ.

The exiled Portuguese Christians of Madeira continued to be scattered. Some landed in Demerara (today part of Guyana), others at St. Vincent and others at St. Kitts (both in the Caribbean). How many fled from Madeira is not known. Some little groups may have perished, with no one left to tell the story. Some were heard of in British Guyana. Many were separated from family members and had no way of finding where they were or if they were even alive. For those left behind in Madeira, the persecution continued.

Through the tireless work of Gonsalves and The American Protestant Society, friends in England and the USA became financially and practically involved in finding a suitable place for the refugees to gather and settle in America. They were willing to go anywhere. They were now mostly farmers and mechanics. They wished to be in a colony by themselves in a new land. The American Protestant Society paid for their immigration to the USA.

News traveled to the various groups of refugees that were scattered and

---

23 Hewitson returned to Scotland in 1847 and died there in August 1850.
24 For an account of Da Silva's conversion, see Chapter XI, Blackburn, *Exiles of Madeira*, 136.
25 Blackburn, *Exiles of Madeira*, 161.
26 Blackburn, *Exiles of Madeira*, 161.

they began to make their way to New York. Through an arrangement with the American Hemp Company, they were to settle in Island Grove, Illinois, between Springfield and Jacksonville. Unfortunately, the company reneged on its promise, leaving hundreds of Portuguese refugees stranded in New York.

On 15 September 1849, a representative of the American and Foreign Christian Union wrote to Erastus Wright of Springfield asking if that city might be willing to take in any of the exiles. The response was positive, and the citizens of Springfield rose to the occasion.

> The first group arrived in Springfield November 13, 1849, and numbered 280 persons. A smaller group came to Jacksonville a short time afterward. At their arrival a general call was made upon the people for food, clothing and housing for the weary exiles, and those who could give them work to do.[27]

Most of them settled as a group on the north side of town, along Miller and Carpenter streets between Ninth and Tenth, in an area that became known as "Madeira." In the next few years, hundreds more exiles followed.[28]

8. Rev. Antonio De Mattos

The need of a pastor to replace Rev. Da Silva was met in Mr Antonio De Mattos (1822-1891),[29] one of the converts from Madeira. He had fled to Scotland in 1846 (after being driven out of his family home), where he became qualified for preaching the gospel. He was ordained in Scotland by the Free Church of

---

27 "Exiles of Madeira' Settled In Springfield 75 Years Ago," *The Daily Illini* (Thursday, Dec. 24, 1925), 5. Illinois Digital Newspaper Collections https://idnc.library.illinois Accessed 2 February 2023.

28 Erika Holst, "When Springfield took in Portuguese refugees," *Illinois Times* (24 September 2015). https://www.illinoistimes.com/springfield/when-springfield-took-in-portuguese-refugees/ Accessed January 31, 2023.

29 Portuguese Christian, Antonio, from Madeira Island, settled in Jacksonville, IL with wife Isabella, and organized the Portuguese Presbyterian Church there in 1849. He continued as pastor there until 1869. Antonio had been banished from his father's home in Madeira and gone to Scotland where he studied, was licensed and ordained under the Free Church of Scotland, then to Illinois. Isabella was the daughter of James Paterson, who emigrated from Scotland to Saint John, New Brunswick, Canada. https://langumfoundation.org/travel-to-collections/de-mattos-family-papers/ Accessed 2 Feb. 2023.

Scotland[30] and sent to the USA to take the place of Mr Da Silva[31] as the pastor of this gathering group of exiles. On route to America, he stopped in Madeira and Trinidad to encourage the Portuguese Christians. Mr De Mattos then took up his duties as the minister of the Portuguese Presbyterian churches in Springfield and Jacksonville, Illinois. By 1853, there were about one thousand Portuguese exiles in the two places where he preached.[32]

▲ First Presbyterian, Portuguese, Springfield

The same year, Kalley and his second wife, Sarah, visited the settlements in Jacksonville and neighboring Springfield.[33] During the early 1850s, Dr Robert Kalley stayed with the Corneau family while serving as the minister for the Springfield exiles.[34] Dr & Mrs Kalley went on to serve in Brazil from 1854-1876. In the providence of God, this young doctor who had set sail for China was greatly used amongst the Portuguese speaking people not only of Madeira but later in the USA and Brazil.

Thirty years after the arrival of the first refugees from Madeira to Illinois, the Illinois State Register noted:

> As a rule they came here poor in purse but rich in determination. They all managed as soon as possible to acquire a piece of ground, no matter how small, which they can call their own, and they cultivate this with all the care and diligence they

---

30 https://langumfoundation.org/travel-to-collections/de-mattos-family-papers/ Accessed 6 Feb. 2023.
31 Blackburn, *Exiles of Madeira*, 211.
32 Special note should be taken of one young exile – Emanuel Nathaniel Pires (1838–1896) He was born in Madeira, attended Princeton Theological Seminary, 1863–1866; ordained as an evangelist by the Presbytery of Sangamon in 1866 and served as a missionary to Brazil from 1866–1869 before returning to serve in the various Portuguese Presbyterian churches in the Springfield and Jacksonville areas of Illinois until his death. See, Edward Howell Roberts, Compiler. *Biographical Catalogue of the PTS, 1815–1932*. (Princeton: Trustees of the Theological Seminary of the Presbyterian Church, 1933), 257.
33 Kalley and his second wife (married in England in 1852), Sarah P. Wilson, went to Illinois in 1853 to visit the refugees. His first wife had died in Beirut in 1851.
34 https://storymaps.arcgis.com/stories/7412509a969c462399f9f986b9c802f4

formerly bestowed upon the little patches of earth between the rocks and hills of their rugged native isle. As a class they are industrious, frugal, upright, peaceful, law-abiding citizens.[35]

9. Conclusion

The story of the development of the Presbyterian Church in Madeira, and its developments as a diaspora church, shows the inter-continental influence of gospel work. From Scotland to Madeira to Trinidad and the USA, a network of congregations was used to minister to one another in the face of persecution and displacement. The significant leadership of Kalley, Hewitson, Da Silva, and De Mattos is worthy of further study. Some planted, some watered, but God gave the increase.[36]

Questions for study (fact type):
1 Name the missionary who served in Madeira and recovered the Bible there for the Madeirans. Give brief biographical details about him – birth date, death date, nationality, special training, etc.
2 Who were "the Bible Readers"? Explain.
3 Name the missionary that was sent to support Kalley's work. What years did he serve in Madeira? What year did he visit Trinidad?
4 Who was the minister of the Madeiran refugees while in Trinidad? Give birth and death dates along with place of birth and place of death.
5 Who was the first minister of the Portuguese Presbyterian Church in Illinois?

Questions for study (reflection type):
1 The Roman Catholic leaders in Madeira strongly opposed the distribution of Scriptures in Portuguese. Why were they so angry about this? Consider Psalm 119:105–112 and use this passage to assist you with your answer.
2 Consider the following two quotations:
"In 1845, Hewitson began to prepare elders for ordination. He saw this as an urgent matter as he was aware that the persecution could soon escalate, and he would almost certainly be exiled or killed."
and,
"Hewitson resided in Port of Spain [Trinidad], as did many of his congregation. A Sunday school was started, a school was established, and his discipleship class recommenced."
How was Hewitson's strategy like the Apostle Paul's? Support your answer using 1 Timothy 3.

---

35 Erika Holst, "When Springfield took in Portuguese refugees." Accessed 31 January 2023.
36 1 Corinthians 3:6–7.

Select Bibliography

Baillie, John. *Memoir of The Rev. W. H. Hewitson*. New York: Robert Carter and Brothers, 1851.

Blackburn, William M. *The Exiles of Madeira*. Philadelphia: Presbyterian Board of Publication, 1860.

Forsyth, William B. *The Wolf From Scotland: The Story of Robert Reid Kalley – Pioneer Missionary*. Welwyn: Evangelical Press, 1988.

Epilogue

An Epilogue on Historic Beginnings and Developments

J. C. Whytock

There are four *key* summations to review this survey volume of the historic period of Presbyterian mission in Africa: geographic expansion, multifaceted mission approaches, multiple tributaries, and changes afoot. The two charts included are meant to illustrate and support these summations.

Geographic Expansion

The nineteenth century, popularly known as the great century of missions, was a century characterised by extensive mission expansion. This volume has viewed the century through the lens of *the long* century, c.1790s through to c.1930s. In 1789, there were no Presbyterian mission works on the continent of Africa; by the eve of the Second World War, this same continent was abundantly spotted with such mission works. If we try to describe this African geographic mission expansion, it would be between 45 and 48% of the modern African countries having been impacted at some level by a Presbyterian mission's presence over *the long* century. The list of modern countries includes Morocco, Algeria, Tunisia, Libya, Egypt, Sudan, South Sudan, Ethiopia, Kenya, Tanzania, Zambia, Malawi, Zimbabwe, Mauritius, South Africa, Botswana, Gabon, Equatorial Guinea, Cameroon, Democratic Republic of the Congo, Nigeria, Togo, Ghana, Liberia, and Sierra Leone. In addition, there were islands, viewed as geographically African yet politically mixed or otherwise. Clearly Africa was a key region for Presbyterian missionary endeavour in the long century; a very quick review of the contents of this volume makes this abundantly clear.

What is less easy to summarise here is the influence of the bisecting theme of imperialist expansion. Both were rapidly occurring in this long century – the imperialist and the missionary. Sometimes they overlapped and intertwined; sometimes they clearly worked against each other, which made, and continues to make, the stories complex.

As has been seen in this volume, this geographic expansion was diverse, not just because of its intersection with imperialist expansion, but also because of linguistic and tribal diversities. A common theme in this survey has been that of language, translation, and transmission. Presbyterians played a key role in reducing many tribal languages to written form and then engaged in Bible translation efforts. Sometimes these were solo efforts, sometimes team efforts of the mission and indigenous leaders, or sometimes they crossed mission lines and formed translation alliances. Full charting of these endeavours alone would certainly be a worthy research project. A good start has been made in many chapters to begin to identify key works, but much more will need to be done on this subject. One also wonders just how many times *Pilgrim's Progress* was translated and published across Africa by Presbyterian-related missions in this long century. A cursory review indicates many times and across diverse languages and tribes. Another chart is needed.

> "Never before in a period of equal length had Christianity or any religion penetrated for the first time as large an area as it had in the nineteenth century."
>
> "Never before had any religion been planted over so large a portion of the earth's surface."
>
> "Never before had Christianity, or any religion, been introduced to so many different peoples and cultures."
>
> "Never before had so many hundreds of thousands contributed voluntarily of their means to assist the spread of Christianity or any other religion."
>
> "Never before ... had Christians come so near the goal of reaching all men with their message."
>
> "Never had it exerted so wide an influence upon the human race."
>
> "Measured by geographic extent and the effect upon mankind as a whole, the nineteenth century was the greatest thus far in the history of Christianity."
>
> – Kenneth Scott Latourette

Multifaceted Missions

Mission strategy in this historic period clearly emphasised evangelism – bringing the light of the Gospel to all peoples across Africa. Yet this single emphasis is often stated with three, four, or five prongs of strategy and activity: evangelism, discipleship, education, medical mission, and industrial mission. Again, a cursory review shows almost all missions at some point undertaking most of these activities.

We have seen in this volume that sometimes a missionary evangelist and an indigenous evangelist were the key leaders in a mission, but sometimes God used an evangelist who was also a medical person. The priority of evangelism used all strategies, whether medical or educational, for Gospel evangelism, witness, and testimony. Likewise, the use of industrial training was coupled with the plea of commerce but was not (for the majority) ever far removed from the evangelistic thrust. One would be hard pressed to find a large-scale social gospel agenda in this long century. The Gospel work did have its diversities, yet it also very much had a missional centre which was rooted in the call of conversion and new life in Jesus Christ – the hallmark of evangelicalism. As this long century ended, change was coming, as will be seen in Volume Two.

What is also very clear is that the undertaking of missions in Africa by Presbyterians can never be defined as the reserve of the ordained missionary; the number of lay Christian missionaries and workers, male and female, is astounding. The long lists of missionaries in many fields speak to us today of an incredible movement of people for a Gospel undertaking, with much sacrifice, and the raising up of a large personnel force to carry this out. Many leaders are enshrined as key to certain fields or crossing between fields, but the wider missionary force must also be acknowledged together with the indigenous workers, evangelists, Bible women, and ordained office bearers.

This volume has tried to also highlight the story of some of these early indigenous leaders across different mission fields in Africa. Below is a chart that helps to remind us of some of the names of the earliest ordinands. It is hoped that we can continue to expand this chart and add any that have been missed. A second chart follows, namely a listing of the first presbyteries in various mission fields in the historic period. Of course, the creation of presbyteries is a logical development of Presbyterian church-planting efforts. A chart can only say so much. However, it helps to show the scope and the basic facts of name and year. Separate histories of these presbyteries would be valuable for tracing their twists and turns, strengths and weaknesses as a body, their achievements and sometimes yes, their demise as well. There is so much more that needs to be written and studied; here is but another example of the need to continue the narrative of finding, recording, writing, and reaching for analysis.

Multiple Tributaries

Presbyterianism, like many Protestant, denominational groupings, contains within itself a multitude of distinct separate denominations often based on national boundaries, but sometimes based on distinctive theological positions, even within a country where there are two or more national Presbyterian bodies. Even within a denomination, there may be various parties or factions. Some of these latter parties may form alliances across denominational lines of different Presbyterians and/or even go outside their own denominational group to a close cousin, such as a Congregational grouping. In this historic survey from the c.1790s to the eve of the Second World War, we have found many different tributaries of Presbyterian entities labouring in missions across Africa.

At least ten different tributaries organizationally can be identified. They are: nationally defined denominational single entities, nationally distinctive theological positioned denominations which have emerged from a mother body, alliances in the form of voluntary societies crossing Presbyterian and/or other closely related denominations, colonising societies, independent Presbyterians, Presbyterian women's society missions, faith missions of Presbyterians, faith missions which include Presbyterians but also a wider multitude of denominations, inter-denominational Presbyterian or ecumenical Presbyterian attempts to do mission work, and business oriented lay-Presbyterian missions. Then to these ten different organisational mission structures we can add the many national cultural backgrounds of these bodies to increase the diversity of the tributaries even more.

This volume has tried to survey the whole rather than just a particular Presbyterian mission tributary stream. By seeing the wider picture, we begin to realise the magnitude of the undertaking in Presbyterian mission history and are also in a better position to see common themes emerging from one mission to another.

Change Afoot

Transition rarely occurs neatly in one single year to make dating simple and clear-cut in mission work. This is the case here where this volume ends, circa the Second World War. Transition and agitation had started for indigenisation in some missions before the eve of the Second World War and several will see such after the Second World War. There are other changes, such as theological shifts that were emerging, that were more global but would also have their impact within Presbyterianism in Africa in time.

As we close the door of this volume and look to volume two, we will see new themes emerge: as already noted, indigenisation, which paralleled independence and nationalist movements across Africa; the employment of new language for partnerships in mission and the development of sister church relations; the emergence of congregation-based (local church) partnerships in missions and presbytery-based partnerships in missions; the rise of the phenomenon of short-term missions (STM); and, an increase in parachurch mission activities amongst Presbyterians. Thus, volume one ends with pointers of change coming. Despite these changing themes, there will be themes and matters of continuity explored – part of a continuous line of Presbyterian mission endeavour in Africa. The words of Hebrews speak to us as we survey Presbyterian Mission history in Africa:

> since we are surrounded by so great a cloud of witnesses, let

us also lay aside every weight and the sin that clings so closely, and let us run with perseverance the race that is set before us, looking to Jesus the pioneer and perfecter of our faith.
Hebrews 12:1-2

List of First Ordinations Historic Period[1]			
Region or Mission Field	**Sponsoring Body**	**Name of Ordinand**	**Date**
1. South Africa[2] (Eastern Cape)	UPCS FCS FCS	1. Tiyo Soga (ordained in Glasgow, Scotland UPCS) 2. Mpambani Mzimba 3. Elijah Makiwane	1856 1875 1875
2. West Africa (Liberia)	PCUSA	Edward Blyden (Born in the Virgin Islands, Caribbean)	1858
3. Equatorial West Africa (Corisco)	PCUSA	Ibia J'Ikenge	1870
4. Egypt (North Africa)	UPCNA	Tadros Yusif	1871
5. Nigeria (West Africa)	UPCS	Esien Esien (Essien) Ukpabio	1872
6. Gold Coast (Ghana) (West Africa)	Basel Mission, then received by UFCS	1. David Asante (ordained in Basel, Switzerland) 2. Peter Hall 3. N. Asare 4. E. Obeng 5. Jerimiah Anoba	1862 1882 1882 1882 1882
7. Central & East Africa (Blantyre)	CoS	1. Harry Kambwiri Matecheta 2. Stephen Kundecha	1911
8. Central & East Africa (Livingstonia)	UFCS	1. Yesaga Zenenje Mwase 2. Hezekiah Tweya 3. Jonathan Chirwa	1914

1 *First* here is sometimes a multiple listing of the first ordinations of ministers occurring within a few days of each other as it was deemed less than fair to not include many of these who were all trained and ordained basically together. Also, two or three were ordained in Europe but were ordained to serve in Africa and are included by denominations in their own lists of firsts, hence they are included as proper to this list of first ordinands.
2 The first ordination of a minister by a presbytery in Africa, was the ordination of John Bennie by the Presbytery of Kaffraria in 1831. Bennie was a missionary of the GMS.

9. Belgian Congo (Central Africa)	PCUS	1. Kubeya Lukenyu 2. Musonguela 3. Kachunga		1916
10. Central & East Africa (Nkhoma)	DRCSA	1. Andreya Namkumba 2. Namoni Katengeza 3. Lamek Kasuzi Manda		1925
11. Kenya (East Africa)	CoS	1. Musa Gitau 2. Benjamin Githieya 3. Joshua Matenjwa 4. Simeon Karechu 5. Joshua Riunga 6. Paulo Kahuho 7. Jeremiah Waita 8. Solomon Ndambi		1926
12. Abyssinia/ Ethiopia	UPCNA (Allegheny Presbytery)	1. Mamo Chorqa 2. Gidada Solan		1939

The First Historic Presbyteries in Africa c.1790s to c.1940		
Date	Presbytery Name	Superior Body if any
1824	**Presbytery of Kaffraria**	GMS, Independent
1844	**Presbytery of Kaffraria** FCS	FCS/Synod of Kaffraria
1847	**Presbytery of Kaffraria** UPCS	UPCS
1889	**United Presbyterian Presbytery of Adelaide** UPCS (Formed by dividing the Presbytery of Kaffraria UPCS into two presbyteries)	UPCS
1848	**Presbytery of West Africa** [Liberia]	Synod of Philadelphia PCUSA
1852	**Presbytery of Natal** (by ministers Revs. Campbell, Lindley, and Posselt to ordain Charles Scott who then joined this new presbytery)	Independent when established[3]
1858	**Presbytery of Biafra**	UPC/SMS
1860	**Presbytery of Corisco**	Synod of New Jersey PCUSA
1860	**Presbytery of Egypt**	UPCNA
1889	**Presbytery of Transkei** (Formed out of the Presbytery of Kaffraria FCS)	FCS/Synod of Kaffraria

---

3   Dalziel, "The Origin and Growth of Presbyterian Ordinances," 685. This Presbytery received aid and ministers from various Presbyterian bodies, FCS, CoS, UPCS, PCC, PCUSA, and PCI over the years.

1890	**Presbytery of Transvaal**[4] (Formed out of the Presbytery of Natal)	Independent when established
1893	**Presbytery of Cape Town** or **Cape Presbytery**	Independent when established
1898	**Presbyterian Church of Africa** [5][True Free Church]	Independent
1899	**Presbytery of Livingstonia**	FCS
1899	**Presbytery of Orange River** (Formed out of the Presbytery of Natal)	PCSA
1899	**Presbytery of Thebes, Presbytery of Assiut, Presbytery of Middle Egypt, Presbytery of Delta**	Synod of Nile (URCNA)
1900	**Presbytery of Kaffraria** UFCS	UFCS
1903	**Council of Congregations** [Nkhoma]	DRCSA
1904	**Presbytery of Blantyre**	CoS
1906	**Presbytery of Kaffraria** (reconstituted FCS)	FCS [post-1900 remnant]
1918	**Synod of the Gold Coast Presbyterian Church**	UFCS
1920 1936	**Presbytery of Kenya Colony** **Overseas Presbytery (CoS) [East Africa]**	CSM CoS
1936	**Presbytery of Corisco**[6] **Presbytery of Metet** **Presbytery of Sanaga**	
1940/41	**Presbytery of Ethiopia**[7]	Independent

---

4 Dalziel, "The Origin and Growth of Presbyterian Ordinances," 619. It had been hoped that a Synod could be formed of the two Presbyteries of Natal and Transvaal, but this did not happen in 1890, in part, due to the union discussions for a *united* Presbyterian Church in South Africa with a GA and synods.

5 Constituted first presbytery in 1898 and shortly thereafter a synod and then a general assembly. See, Malinge McLaren Njeza, "'Subversive Subservience:' A Study of the Response of Tiyo Soga and Mpambani Mzimba to the Scottish Missionary Enterprise," (Unpublished PhD thesis, University of Cape Town, 2000), 200.

6 The historic 1860 Presbytery of Corisco had expanded its boundaries considerably from its original Island location. It was divided into three presbyteries in 1936 and the new boundary of the Presbytery of Corisco was defined in 1936 as the "southernmost section of Cameroun from Elat westward, as well as in Corisco and Spanish Guinea." Cogswell, *No Turning Back*, 30.

7 Three ministers transferred to make this new independent presbytery for the Evangelical Bethel Church. The two indigenous ministers briefly were on the role of the Allegheny Presbytery UPCNA (functioned more like sister relations rather than a superior court relationship).

Index

A

Abyssinia 491, 604ff, 614ff
Adamson, James 64ff, 106ff, 628
Adamson, George 457ff, 741
Addis Ababa 568, 592, 604, 607ff, 615ff
African Academy 56f
African American(s) missionaries 100, 232, 235, 239ff, 252, 324, 453, 455ff, 468, 472, 741ff, 239, 740ff, 736ff
African American Women 235, 477ff, 736ff, 746
African Initiated/Independent Churches 660, 672, 686
African (Black, Indigenous) Leadership 116, 118ff, 123, 178, 250, 260ff, 302, 338, 372ff, 391ff, 396ff, 399, 411, 420ff, 433, 469, 493, 546, 563f, 594, 609, 611, 629, 680f
African National Church 680ff
African National Congress 121, 126, 142
African Presbyterian Bafolisi Church 677
African Reformed Presbyterian Church 684
African Traditional Religion 127, 130, 136, 214, 229, 364, 542, 616, 621, 701
Agriculture (Training) 170, 184, 306, 311ff, 362, 382, 386, 413ff, 464, 478, 587, 594, 737, 764
Akropong 274ff, 279, 283ff, 292ff, 317ff
Akropong Seminary 317ff
Alexander, Archibald 696ff
Alexandria 552ff, 558ff, 576, 614, 647, 706ff, 714ff,
Algiers 714ff
American Board of Commissioners for Foreign Missions 86ff, 108, 146ff, 153ff, 160ff, 231ff, 652ff, 695, 736ff

American Colonization Society 83–100, 250, 254, 266, 695ff, 736
American Presbyterian Congo Mission 453ff, 456, 469, 473, 652, 736ff, 747ff,
American Revolutionary War / Independence War 51
American Civil War 95, 737
Amu, E. 320, 638, 655, 660, 667ff
Anderson, Samuel 448f, 451
Anglican Church 45, 52, 134, 138, 198, 201, 205ff, 217, 222, 224, 357ff, 380, 392, 396f, 446f, 500, 540, 571, 618, 648, 653, 726
Anyuak People 582ff, 591ff
Apartheid 105, 112, 116ff, 133, 139f, 193, 500, 631, 679
Asante, David 285ff, 292ff, 308, 319, 769
Ashanti 279, 284, 288, 294, 297ff, 304ff
Associate Reformed Presbyterian Church 33, 86, 93, 552, 555ff, 561, 583, 647

B

Baker, Edward 442f, 450f
Bantu Presbyterian Church of South Africa 103, 116ff, 679ff
Baptism 75, 76, 80, 141, 146, 182, 211, 213, 221, 285, 299, 304, 331, 362, 369, 435, 458, 463, 492, 504, 505, 506, 521, 563, 588, 598, 735
Baptist (Church) 31, 52ff, 59, 63, 86, 198, 217, 333, 454, 456ff, 503ff, 681, 695, 726
Balu Apostles 333
Baluba 457ff, 466
Barnett, James 552ff
Basel Mission 271ff, 276–315, 317–322, 339, 342, 655, 667ff, 769

772

Index

Batanga 324
Beaton, Patrick 446, 448, 451
Belgian Congo 476–479, 770
Belgian Society of Protestant Missions 539, 545, 547
Bennie, John 74ff, 182
Bethel (Church) Mission 136, 361, 443, 538–547, 610f, 621ff, 771
Bible Readers 752–759
Bible Women 198f, 233, 235f, 255, 370, 767
Black Loyalists 51f, 55
Blantyre (Scotland) 355
Blantyre (Mission) Synod 188, 195, 354, 368, 370–426, 482, 769, 771
Blyden, Edward W. 93, 94ff, 769
Blythswood 188, 201, 482
Boers of South Africa 108ff, 151–163, 626ff, 629, 632,
Bokwe, John K. 195, 197, 638, 643, 647–660, 663–666
Bremen Mission 271f, 276ff, 294–315, 667
British & Foreign Bible Society 289, 446, 447, 465
Brunton, Henry 55–59
Burnshill Missionary Station 76, 129, 169, 172–176
Burnside, Janet 134

C

Cairo 37, 415, 420, 552, 557–559, 561–563, 566, 567–569, 571ff, 576, 605, 647, 706–709, 715, 720
Calabar 190ff, 196, 201, 205–214, 217–219, 223, 227–229, 277, 312, 320, 490, 718
Calvinist Society 62, 105f, 231
Cameroon 240ff, 244ff, 323–342, 346ff, 477, 690, 706, 765
Cape (Cape Colony) 50, 61–80, 102–108, 122, 129ff, 132ff, 138, 150–157, 179, 187, 624ff, 419, 441, 444, 517–519, 624–630, 658, 663

Cape Maclear 195, 361–366, 372, 381–382, 425, 673
Cape Palmas 84, 89, 91, 148, 232, 701, 705
Cape Town 61–80, 102–112, 149, 360, 373, 408ff, 415, 419, 518, 635–636, 710–713, 771
Carey, W. 270, 288, 695
Central Africa 354–360, 364, 366, 370f, 380–381, 394, 414–416, 422, 426, 428, 435–436, 455, 462, 466, 469, 473, 476, 630ff, 653, 738, 740–746
Central Morocco Mission 198, 724–731
Children's home 534ff, 730
Christaller, J. G. 273ff, 288ff, 319
Church Missionary Society 58, 487, 604
Church of Africa Presbyterian 681ff
Church of Central Africa Presbyterian 364, 371, 379ff, 395, 407ff, 419–422, 428, 431, 631, 674, 679, 680, 683
Church of England 41, 59, 63, 111, 358, 721,
Church of Scotland (Presbyterian) 80ff 118, 320, 358–360, 366, 371, 374, 376, 379–387, 394–400, 408, 418, 428, 430, 439, 444–450, 468, 482, 488ff, 495, 508, 512, 515, 517–518, 531, 625, 631, 633, 659, 674, 676, 714–717, 719ff, 731, 754
Ciskei 119, 179, 180ff, 199, 677
Clapham Academy (African Academy) 57–58
Clapham Sect 52–53, 56–57
Clarke, John 53ff, 56, 58
Clerk, Alexander W. 275, 292
Colonisation/colonialism/colonists 83, 84ff, 94, 97, 105, 697, 736
Comprehensive Approach 186, 195–201, 412, 482, 540, 542
Congregational Church 64, 72, 98, 106, 108, 109, 121, 134, 159, 163, 187, 233, 238, 441, 449, 717, 752, 767,
Congo 453–469, 471–474, 533, 539–545, 582, 616, 652, 736–748, 765
Coptic Church 552–566, 571–574, 583–484, 590, 647, 720
Corisco 231ff, 249ff, 326

773

Index

D

Da Silva, 759
Danish Mission Society 272ff, 282ff, 306
Deacons 63, 389, 391, 396, 405, 430, 459, 526, 542f, 759
De Mattos, Antonio 761ff
Dewar, Alexander 167–179, 369
Diaspora 45, 51, 59, 72, 221, 230, 275, 278, 299, 444, 450, 582f, 715, 716, 741, 763
Dimbaza 178, 199
Discipline (Church) 119, 182, 217, 262, 286, 308, 362, 388, 391, 392, 410, 421, 501, 563
Disruption 67f, 184, 355, 754
Doleib Hill 568, 582–594, 597ff, 614
Dougall, James 43, 191
Dutch East India Company 624
Dutch Reformed Church in South Africa 63, 65ff, 106ff, 108, 155, 159, 193, 363f, 367f, 403–406, 428ff, 624ff, 633, 673f
Duff, Clarence W. 182f, 186, 618, 695, 702, 709

E

East Africa Scottish Mission 196, 481ff, 490, 511ff
East(ern) Africa 191, 195–198, 353ff, 481–489, 490–508, 769–770
Eastern Cape 69, 73ff, 78ff, 103–110, 127, 142, 182ff, 198, 358, 362ff, 380, 382, 390, 625, 636, 648, 651, 653, 663, 769
Economic 55, 80, 84, 103, 107, 120, 123, 182, 197, 209, 218, 225, 230, 280, 289, 364, 371, 374, 380, 385f, 396, 399, 409, 412ff, 446, 514, 553, 741ff
Edinburgh Missionary Society 54
Edmiston, Alonzo and Althea Brown Edmiston 459, 466, 741f, 744–749
Education 78, 80, 88, 94–97, 107, 110, 120, 128f, 134, 139, 147f, 162f, 181–201, 214f, **221–223**, 230, 235, 239, 241, 249f, 252, 261f, 275, 280, 286f, 291f, 299, 306f, 311, 317ff, 323, 328, 334, 342, 360, 362, 368f, 370, 374, 381–388, 395, 405–407, 412f, 414, 418, 421, 428–437, 440, 444f, 448, 466, 468, 471, 482, 487, 491–502, 506ff, 511–516, 524ff, 533, 541, 542, 553, 560–566, 584–589, 593f, 596, 601, 610, 615–617, 627–629, 635, 665, 667, 677, 680, 682–686, 718, 729f, 740–747
Egypt 420, 552–568, 571–573, 575–576, 577–581, 582–591–601, 604–611, 614, 618, 646–648, 690, 701, 706–709, 714–719, 726
Elders 41, 63, 88, 110, 112, 115, 171, 236, 296, 311, 324, 374, 393f, 396, 405, 419, 421, 459, 466, 496ff, 510, 526, 532, 573f, 588, 609f, 673, 755, 759
Ellis, Harrison W. 94
Equatorial West Africa 231–241, 469f, 769
Ethiopia 146, 194, 566, 568, 582, 591ff, 604–618, 620–622, 709, 714–721, 731, 765, 770f
Ethiopianism 672–687
Evangelical Presbyterian (Church) 30, 44, 54, 69, 98, 208, 464, 715, 727, 729, 734f
Evangelical Presbyterian Church South Africa 121,
Evangelical Presbyterian Church, Ghana 303, 667, 671
Evangelical Presbyterian Church in Rwanda 455, 545
Evangelical Presbyterian Churches of Sudan 590–591
Evangelical Revivals/Awakening 225, 354, 628, 694, 729, 751

F

Falasha Jews 716, 719, 721, 723
Famine 135, 185, 309, 487, 593
Fearing, Maria 458f, 472, 478, 741f, 746f
Federal Mission (to Morocco) 719, 721–724, 728, 731
Female genital circumcision/mutilation 495, 501f, 514f
Fetichism/Festishism 240, 244, 246

Index

First Presbyterian Portuguese, Springfield 762, 766
First World War 191, 272, 273, 278, 294, 295, 300, 307, 309, 338, 370, 391, 395, 539, 543f
Frank James Industrial School 336f
Free Church in South Africa 116, 167–179
Free Church of Scotland 66–68, 109f, 116, 126, 167–169, 175–179, 184, 186, 188, 194f, 199, 208, 354–359, 375–380, 403, 428, 457, 469, 485, 518, 626–636, 673–678, 686, 717, 727, 754, 760f
Free Church of Scotland (United), 79, 104, 118, 120, 128, 170, 184, 188, 190f, 208, 272, 277, 302, 311f, 320, 374, 371ff, 408, 468, 482
Free Presbyterian Church of Scotland 517ff, 659
Freetown 52, 58
Frontier Settler Church of the Cape 69ff

G

Gaba, Burnet & Ntsikana 174
Gaboon 231ff, 349
Ghana (Gold Coast) 115, 270–288, 291, 292, 293, 295, 298–314, 317–322, 660, 667–671, 765, 769
Genadendal Mission Station 75
Geographic (expansion) 37, 42, 43, 102, 103, 214, 279, 375, 472, 566, 728, 745, 747, 751, 765, 766
Giffen, Mary G. 575ff
Glasgow 128–134, 137, 141, 169, 176, 358, 398, 461, 494, 514, 518, 527, 560, 716, 718, 722, 724, 726, 728, 729, 731, 735, 758, 759, 769
Glasgow (African) Missionary Society 54, 73–80, 127, 183, 184, 201, 653
Good, Adolphus C and Lydia Walker Good 97, 239, 326f, 346ff
Gorei 607ff
Gospel Missionary Society 499, 502–506
Govan, William 184
Greig, Peter 55, 57, 60
Griqualand East 119, 172ff
Guinea (Equatorial, Spanish) 50ff, 231, 234, 236, 241, 244, 246, 690, 708–710, 765, 771

H

Hampton Institute 742
Hanna, Jabra 596, 601
Harrison, Jellorum 56–60
Heatherwick, Alexander 390ff
Henderson, Henry 382
Hewitson, William 754ff
Hoekstra, Harvey 594
Holy Communion (Lord's Supper) 63, 75, 80, 136, 160, 170, 233, 236, 252, 331, 563, 458, 496, 521, 532, 553, 622, 696
Hope Waddell Training Institute 196, 220, 222
Hospital 187, 190, 199ff, 215, 219ff, 234, 238, 532, 245, 373ff, 394, 397f, 416, 464, 472, 494f, 501, 505, 514, 531ff, 547, 563, 578, 590, 599, 606ff, 615, 725ff, 730, 735, 746, 752
Hospitality 13, 254, 263, 265
Hogg, Hope W. 577ff
Hogg, John 563
Human rights 674, 736, 741ff
Hymns/Psalms and Hymnals/Psalters 71, 76, 78, 126, 130, 138, 142, 143, 212, 237, 245, 252, 287, 288, 293, 318f, 372, 390, 395, 412, 443, 459, 460, 465f. 469, 477ff, 499, 521, 595f, 638–661, 663–666, 667–670

I

Ibiam, Francis 217, 220
Ilala 367, 382
Inanda 157
Independence 42, 51, 91, 93, 99, 105, 114, 119, 120, 178, 205–225, 265, 277, 286, 288, 313, 535, 598, 626, 675, 679, 685, 686, 768

Index

Industrial 45, 55, 170, 186ff, 191, 193, 195, 196, 198, 200, 223, 234, 236, 241, 253, 288, 290, 318, 336, 342, 358, 360, 362, 366, 374, 381, 386, 400, 405, 413–414, 435, 461, 464, 471, 482, 496, 500, 524, 600, 652, 696, 742, 747, 766, 767

Ingwenya 530

Islam/Muslims 9, 56, 66, 225, 278, 280, 340, 361, 363, 420f, 542, 552–554, 560, 564–565, 571, 576, 583, 585, 587, 714ff, 723, 735

J

Jamaica 52f, 55, 84, 205, 208ff, 212, 275, 312, 317, 468, 577, 718, 739, 743

Jewish missions 714ff, 719ff, 724, 734ff

J'Ikenge, Ibia, 248ff, 324

Johannsen, Ernst 542ff

Jolobe, James J. R. 115, 117, 197

K

Kaffraria 76ff, 110, 130

Kalley, Robert 751ff

Kenya 115, 181, 189, 191, 194–196, 200, 201, 320, 390, 482ff, 490–508, 511–516, 535, 540, 582, 616, 645, 770f

Kerr, Robert 721ff

Khoisan 75, 134

Kibwezi 196, 481, 483–486, 511

Kikuyu 196, 390, 485–488, 491–508, 511–516, 657

King Leopold II – see Leopold II, King

Kingsley, Mary. H 262

Knapp, William & Myrtle 505

Knox, John 10, 32, 115

Koran 585, 723

L

Lambie, Thomas A. 614ff

Language (indigenous, learn, use, vernacular) 56, 57, 71, 89, 90, 94, 112, 139, 148, 149, 150, 152, 158, 159, 171, 186, 190, 197, 198, 200, 212, 217, 232, 233, 237, 245, 247, 252, 256, 277, 280, 282, 287, 288–301, 315, 318, 319f, 324, 326, 328, 330, 332, 336, 339, 356, 365, 390, 393, 417f, 432, 440, 444, 446, 447, 450, 457, 459, 465f, 469, 476, 478, 498, 499f, 518, 521, 543, 556f, 573, 578, 586–589, 594, 595, 606, 616, 642–646, 649, 653, 657, 664–666, 667–668, 684, 700, 716, 717, 728, 735, 740–746, 755, 765ff

Lansing, Gulian 558ff

Lapsley, Samuel N. 455

Last Church of God and His Christ 681

Latourette, Kenneth S. 42, 766

Laws, Robert 168, 187, 195, 196, 201, 358, 360–371, 381, 383, 390–395, 404, 408, 412, 426, 429, 431, 433, 630

Le Brun, Jean 440ff

Leopold II, King 453, 456, 461, 462, 473, 742ff, 738–740

Liberia 83–99, 231–235, 241, 697, 705f, 736–741, 765, 769f

Lindley, Daniel 108ff, 146ff

Literacy 56, 58, 152, 159, 211, 221, 417, 450, 459, 498f, 534

Literature/Linguistic work 336, 417, 459

Livingstone, D. 113, 185, 195, 228, 270, 345, 359, 411, 471, 482, 583, 656, 673

Livingstonia 175, 181, 188, 354ff, 426, 652

London 12, 31, 51ff, 56ff, 62, 72, 74, 130, 435, 456, 471f, 499, 526, 532, 620, 628, 670, 721f

London Missionary Society 43f, 54, 64, 105, 127, 131, 134, 136, 147ff, 183, 355, 370, 415, 439ff, 519, 525, 625, 650, 652, 656ff, 700, 751, 752

Lovedale 111, 117, 128–139, 173, 181–202, 320, 358–363, 425, 464, 482, 630, 647, 650–659, 663–666, 678

Luebo Mission Statian 457ff

Lutheran Church/Mission 65ff, 107, 604

M

Macaulay, Zachary 52ff

MacDonald, Duff 386f, 391

Madeira 751–764

Makiwane, Cecilia 187f
Malawi 170, 194ff, 354–376, 379–400, 403–422, 428–437, 672ff
Mansfield, Lord 51
Marriage (practices) 54, 89, 107, 134, 142, 233, 149, 248–251, 254, 257, 264, 265, 295, 308, 338, 347, 444, 472, 488, 507, 511, 514, 521
Martyr 57, 58, 59, 700, 730, 754
Matecheta, Harry K. 391ff, 428ff
Mauritius 439–450
McCague, Thomas 556ff
McClure, Don 592
McCulloch, J.D. 168
McKnown, Martha 565
Medical mission/work 107, 152, 187f, 218–220, 244, 284, 327f, 339, 355ff, 360ff, 415ff, 460, 494f, 522, 589ff, 597, 607, 614–618, 620, 724–726, 730, 766
Methodist Church 9, 52, 59, 86, 92, 138, 201, 224, 404f, 496, 667
Mgwali 135ff
Miller, Samuel 692–694, 696ff
Ministers' Mission Union 630
Mission of Inquiry 715, 732
Missionary Societies 50, 54–58, 79, 272–273, 455, 547, 768
Mission Strategy 58, 68, 315, 376, 404, 469, 508, 766ff
Missionary deaths 13, 87, 170, 187, 195, 196, 200, 229, 234, 236, 245, 246, 249, 257, 285, 297, 299, 312, 327, 330–332, 336–337, 340–350, 357, 361, 362, 383, 390, 406, 426, 449, 454, 457, 465, 468, 472, 484, 486, 488, 490, 492, 494, 521, 558, 576, 584, 591, 599, 614, 618, 620, 650, 686, 700–701, 726, 727, 735
Moffat, Robert 150f, 196, 356, 482, 519, 695
Morgan, George 67, 107
Morocco 198, 721–732
Motherkirk 62, 68
Mozambique 403, 419
Multifaceted mission 770
Multiple tributaries 771

Murray Andrew Jnr 188, 627–629, 630
Murray, Andrew Sr 64, 68, 625ff
Murray, Andrew C. 404–416, 431, 630ff
Murray Andrew G. 419
Murray, William H. 406, 418, 432, 631
Mve, Oban 328
Mvera Church 404
Mwasi, Yesaya Zerenji 368, 372, 433, 438, 681ff, 685, 689
Mzamo, Petros 529
Mzimba, Pambani, J. 677ff

N
Namalambe, Albert 408
Nassau, I. 234ff, 326
Nassau Robert H. 244ff, 251, 324, 477, 702
Natal 109, 152ff
Nigeria 205–225, 227–230, 577,
Nile Corridor 43, 551ff
Nkhoma Mission 403ff 631f, 674, 354, 363, 371, 403–426, 431ff
North Africa 718ff

O
Oldham, J. H. 277
Ordain (First African Ministers) 126ff, 134, 162, 169, 174, 213, 216, 224f, 230, 236, 253f, 302, 319, 332, 338, 368–370, 392, 397, 428, 433f, 467, 474, 502f, 506, 518, 532, 571–574, 609, 622, 665, 676ff, 748
Oromo 605–606, 611, 615, 620
Oromo Slaves 193–203
Overtoun 170, 190, 196, 368–370, 393, 407, 427, 429, 431, 433, 674, 682, 686

P
Paedobaptist 66, 86, 237, 315
Palestine 607, 614, 617–618, 700
Paris Evangelical Missionary Society 239, 326, 348
Partnerships in mission 772, 748, 768
Pears, John 71

Index

Pentecostal/Charismatic Churches 504, 547, 731,
Persecution 262, 533, 562, 610, 621, 752–763
Philip, Hermann 559f, 717f
Philip, John 64, 106ff, 146–149, 441, 701
Phipps, Joseph E. 476ff
Pilgrim's Progress 770
Pinney, John B. 86
Polygamy 162, 217, 250–257, 262, 300, 389, 520, 680f
Port Louis 441ff
Presbyterian Church in Mauritius 450
Presbyterian Church in Rwanda 545ff
Presbyterian Church in the United States 232ff, 248ff, 455, 471, 738
Presbyterian Church in the United States of America 86, 99ff, 147, 159, 231–246, 249–269, 324–351, 690–710
Presbyterian Church of Africa 676ff
Presbyterian Church of East Africa 481ff
Presbyterian Church of England 111, 721, 731
Presbyterian Church of Ghana 277
Presbyterian Church of Liberia 98
Presbyterian Church of Nigeria 205ff
Presbyterian Church of Southern Africa 104f, 109f, 113f, 124, 680
Presbytery of Kaffraria 76–79, 82, 169, 634f, 769, 770
Priest, James M. 92ff
Pringle, Thomas 70ff
Printing press 75, 152, 194, 197, 200, 233, 340, 415, 417, 443, 466, 648
Princeton Theological Seminary 11, 83, 86ff, 95, 147, 244, 553, 690–703, 705–713

R

Race relations 55, 95, 110–117, 133f, 138, 140, 143, 151, 156, 184, 188, 190–193, 246, 258, 282, 389, 518, 629, 675, 677, 678, 685, 726, 742, 736, 738, 745, 766
Radasi, John B. 517ff
Repatriation/Resettle 52, 83, 84ff, 527

Riis, Andreas 283ff, 317
Roman Catholic 183, 327, 368, 397, 419, 428, 468, 539, 540, 554, 586, 717, 752f, 759, 763
Ross, John 76ff, 126, 171, 182
Rwanda 538–547

S

Sanneh, Lamin 206
Scandal 383ff
Schism 95, 258ff, 693
School (Mission School) 55, 66ff, 74–76, 89f, 94–97, 107f, 112, 117, 128, 155, 162, 169ff, 176–178, 182–188, 191–193, 196, 200, 221ff, 233–236, 240, 249–254, 286–291, 300, 317–322, 327ff, 334–336, 346, 361–365, 465, 523, 557, 572, 597, 665, 667–670, 684, 702, 718, 730, 747, 752
School (Bible) 178, 191, 194, 198f, 729
School (Sunday/Catechism) 53, 108, 152, 213, 254
Scotch Church, Algiers 738ff
Scotch Presbyterian 624ff
Scott, David C.R. 491ff
Scott, Henry E. 493
Scottish Highlanders 62f, 105
Scottish Missionary Society 54, 56, 208, 770
Scottish Society for the Conversion of Israel 720ff
Schweitzer, Albert 244
Second World War 42, 271, 306ff, 391, 417, 493, 508, 594, 610, 735, 765ff
Selassie, Haile 609
Settler 53, 69–72, 90f, 97, 108ff, 113, 136, 271, 385, 389, 432, 492f, 500f, 513, 642, 626, 676, 680, 737
Shangani 527ff
Shepherd, R. H. W. 74, 128, 145, 186–189, 191–193, 198, 203, 362
Sheppard, W.H. and Lucy Sheppard 455, 460, 465,
471ff, 652f, 661, 744, 748, 740
Sierra Leone 50–59, 84f, 208, 317, 641

Sister church relations 772

Slavery/slave trade 51, 58, 64, 85, 95, 106, 151, 170, 194, 206ff, 210–211, 228, 284, 296, 356, 357, 359, 363, 380, 382, 384, 385, 406, 411, 675, 737, 741

Slessor, Mary 215, 227ff

Soga, Tiyo 126–143, 185, 197, 648, 654ff, 660f, 677, 769

Solan, Gidada 620ff

Southern Morocco Mission 732ff

South Africa 61–80, 102–123, 126ff, 167ff, 624ff, 672ff

St. Andrew's Scottish Church 65ff, 106ff

St. Michael's and All Angels' Church 388f, 392, 394, 674

Steele, Francis R. 731

Steward, James 111, 185ff, 358ff, 373, 482, 526, 678

Stillman Seminary 747

Sudan 582ff, 614

Susa/Susaland 56–58

Sutherland Highlanders 62

T

Tallach, John 521–535

Taylor, Hudson 724, 726

Theology (convictions, views) 44, 171, 185, 240, 277, 288, 373, 376, 413, 448, 504, 579, 598, 625, 673, 675, 686, 691, 696, 735

Theological Institution 11, 12, 86, 92, 94, 132, 143, 147, 162, 178, 183, 184, 224, 244, 337, 397,455, 471, 553, 556, 563, 571, 572, 594, 748, 762, 601, 627, 690–702, 704–713, 742, 747, 762

Theological education/study/training/ 115, 120, 133, 134, 163, 199, 214, 224, 251, 259, 317, 318, 328, 337f, 343, 357, 395, 415, 420, 433–436, 503, 625

Thom, George 62ff, 106, 633, 636,

Thomson, William. R. 74ff

Three–Self Principle 258, 398, 399, 401, 747, 749

Togo 190f, 270–285, 294, 300–305, 360, 307–313,

Trade/traders 52, 55, 57, 184, 195, 209, 215, 218, 234, 248, 253, 263, 271, 280, 284, 290, 296, 318, 332, 339, 356ff, 372, 386, 414, 457, 476, 481, 530, 593, 606, 738, 739, 743

Transkei 33, 110, 119ff, 126 172ff

Translation 51, 56, 76, 137–139, 142f, 152, 171, 182, 197f, 233, 237, 244, 271–273, 288f, 297, 299f, 315, 321, 330, 362, 393, 390, 393, 395, 412, 417–418, 423, 426, 440–444, 460, 465f, 469, 498f, 505, 521, 588, 594, 595, 598, 616, 631, 643, 645, 647, 648–660, 715, 727, 765f

Trinidad 751, 758–763

Tulloch, Hughina 727, 731

Tutura 140–142

U

Ukpabio, Essien E. 213f, 224

United Free Church of Scotland 118, 118, 120, 126, 168, 170, 184, 190f, 277, 302, 311, 320, 355, 371, 408, 468

United Presbyterian Church of North America 552, 558, 584, 604, 614, 646f

United Presbyterian Church of Scotland 104, 116,167, 205–214, 227f, 312, 355, 560f, 719, 722, 769f

Uniting Presbyterian Church of Southern Africa 102ff, 120

Union Chapel 64f, 69

Union Nyanja Bible 417f, 427

Uniondale 130f

Universities' Mission to Central Africa 357, 359, 366, 426

V

Vaccinating 723, 727

Van der Kemp, Johannes 74, 127, 650

Vlok, Theunis. C. B. 404–406, 419, 420, 431

Von Bodelschwingh, Friedrich 540ff

W

Waddel, Hope M. 209ff, 577

Walls, Andrew F. 60, 182, 213, 221

Index

Watson, Andrew 553, 561f, 578f, 585, 701
Watson, Minnie C. 511–516
Watson, Thomas 196, 482, 484f, 486ff, 500, 511f
Watson–Scott Memorial Church 498
Watts, Isaac 53, 56, 440f, 443f
Weiss, Benjamin 717
West(ern) Africa 50ff, 61, 83, 85, 89, 95, 97, 190f, 201f, 205, 223, 231, 234, 239, 244ff, 248f, 317, 326, 337, 341, 454, 649, 670, 690
West Indies Missionaries 274
Westminster Catechism/Confession/Documents 40–41, 53, 63, 77, 76, 80, 155, 157, 111, 212, 213, 395, 408, 440, 464, 490, 518, 547, 640, 692, 715
Wilkie, Arthur W. 189ff, 229, 278, 288, 302f, 311ff, 316
William Dager Theological Seminary 337
Wilson, David A. 701
Wilson, George 482ff
Wilson, Jane 89f, 150f
Wilson, John L. 86, 88ff, 182, 232f, 454, 460, 465ff, 737, 740
Wilson, Matthew 485ff
Wilson, William 233
World Council of Churches 220, 547, 677f

Women 31, 55, 75, 131, 150, 177f, 198f, 218f, 221f, 227, 229f, 233ff, 241, 249f, 252, 254ff, 260, 262ff, 274, 283, 293, 306, 314, 324f, 327, 329, 334, 337f, 342, 347, 350, 355, 370, 372f, 379, 392, 396f, 412, 414, 416f, 435, 442, 463, 464, 474, 478, 495, 501f, 514ff, 525, 547, 585, 597, 600, 629, 683, 729ff, 742, 748, 752, 767f

X

Xhosa(s) 33, 74f, 78ff, 108, 128–143, 178, 182, 195, 197, 202, 362, 365, 375, 381, 426, 521, 642, 647ff, 663ff
Xhosa Missionaries 362

Y

Yusif, Tadros 571ff, 769

Z

Zambia 102ff, 109ff, 112ff, 168f, 170, 174, 201, 356f 361, 363, 366, 368ff, 395, 415, 417ff, 422, 674, 678, 683f, 690, 765
Zimbabwe 102ff, 109ff, 112ff, 168, 201, 395, 419f, 517ff, 530, 535f, 674, 678, 683f, 690, 765
Zimmermann J. 273, 280, 288ff, 318f, 318
Zulu(s) 108, 148f, 152–165, 356, 518f, 651f, 656, 705

www.ingramcontent.com/pod-product-compliance
Lightning Source LLC
Chambersburg PA
CBHW080401300426
44113CB00015B/2373